SERIES V   CYCLE B

LECTIONARY PREACHING WORKBOOK
Revised

For All Users
Of The Revised Common,
The Roman Catholic, And
The Episcopal Lectionaries

Russell F. Anderson

CSS Publishing Company, Inc.
Lima, Ohio

LECTIONARY PREACHING WORKBOOK, SERIES V, CYCLE B
REVISED EDITION

This book is dedicated to Marian Lucille Anderson, my mother, whose witness, prayers, and teachings have been the primary influence in my spiritual formation. The light of her faith continues to shine in the hearts and lives of those who were touched by her and through them thousands of other people are being blessed.

Scripture quotations are from the *New Revised Standard Version of the Bible*, copyright 1989 by the Division of Christian Education of the National Council of the Churches of Christ in the USA. Used by permission.

Scripture quotations are from the Holy Bible, New International Version. Copyright (c) 1973, 1978, 1984 International Bible Society. Used by permission of Zondervan Bible Publishers. All rights reserved.

Scripture quotations are from the Revised Standard Version of the Bible, copyrighted 1946, 1952 (c), 1971, 1973, by the Division of Christian Education of the National Council of the Churches of Christ in the USA. Used by permission.

Revised and reprinted from *Lectionary Preaching Workbook*, Series V, Cycle B, ISBN: 0-7880-0821-8, printed in 1996 by CSS Publishing Company, Inc.

For more information about CSS Publishing Company resources, visit our website at www.csspub.com or email us at csr@csspub.com or call (800) 241-4056.

ISSN: 1938-5552

Cover design by Barbara Spencer

ISBN-13: 978-0-7880-2574-7
ISBN-10: 0-7880-2574-0

PRINTED IN USA

Table Of Contents

Preface

Since his seminary days, preaching has been the author's first love. He discovered that God had given him the ability to see the texts in fresh ways and to communicate the gospel in a thoughtful, yet passionate, manner. This book will stimulate your creative juices and enable you to view the lectionary texts from various angles or perspectives. Numerous sermon approaches are presented in each chapter, described in a single paragraph. These paragraphs are preceded by suggested sermon titles that catch the attention of the worshipers, even before the preaching commences. Many of these "Sermon Angles," as they are called, are further developed by sentence outlines, providing a framework onto which you can construct your own creative sermon. This author has expanded the scope of the *Lectionary Preaching Workbook* to include two to four illustrative stories in each chapter, which are fresh and penetrating revelations of the gospel at work in the modern world, not golden homiletical oldies that have been circulating since the middle ages. Another plus is that the various seasons in the first half of the church year, beginning with Advent, include suggestions as to how you can develop the appointed texts into a thematic sermon series for the season, if you choose. In addition, each chapter contains a specially written Prayer Of The Day, which captures the theme of the day in crisp, contemporary language.

May the Holy Spirit guide you in the central task of proclaiming the gospel of our Lord and Savior, Jesus Christ.

— Russell Anderson

Editor's Note Regarding The Lectionary

During the past four decades, there has been a movement in the direction toward a uniform lectionary among various Christian denominations.

Striving toward the goal of increased Christian unity, the Revised Common Lectionary was developed. This created a three-year cycle of scripture lessons to help unite Christians of many faiths. It is believed that if we are reading the same scriptures together, our goal of being strengthened and more united would come to fruition.

CSS Publishing Company has embraced this goal of uniformity and unity. We recognize, however, that some churches are using variations of the Revised Common Lectionary. We are currently using the semi-continuous version of the lectionary.

— Rebecca Allen, Managing Editor

Sermon Planner/Builder

Date: _____ Cycle / Season: _____ Sunday: _____

Cycle/Season/Sunday theological clue: _____

_____

Psalm/central thought: _____

_____

Collect/prayer concern/focus: _____

_____

Sermon text(s): _____

_____

Summary of sermon text(s): _____

_____

_____

_____

_____

_____

_____

_____

Pastoral perspective: _____

_____

_____

_____

_____

Stories/illustrations: _____

_____

_____

_____

_____

Type of sermon: _____

Sermon plan/sketch: _____

_____

_____

_____

_____

_____

Introduction

A Word About The Structure Of This Book

As one might expect from the title, the chapters in this book follow the liturgical calendar. A brief introduction precedes each season in the church year. Each chapter, in turn, divides into three major sections.

The first section, **Brief Commentary On The Lessons**, concisely reveals the content and context of the lection. The exegesis is far from exhaustive, since there are ample resources to aid you in this task. The intent is to capsulize and summarize the meaning of the text as it was originally spoken. Before we can deduce theological principles applicable to our day, we need to probe the original purpose and setting of the text. The preacher should also consult commentaries and other exegetical resources, when he or she decides on a text.

The second section of each chapter, **Theological Reflection On The Lessons**, probes the lections for theological themes. We need to ask, "What message about the nature of God relates to the needs of the people? What universal theological principles might we deduce from the lessons?" This provides the bridge from the original context to the contemporary context.

A third section, **Sermon Approaches With Illustrations**, builds on the previous two parts. At this stage, we find a compelling twist for one of the theological themes. In some cases, I further develop the theological themes in the previous section but in many instances I present an entirely new angle. We begin with a sermon title that grabs the imagination and sparks interest in the sermon. The *Sermon Angle* briefly explicates the theological theme. The scripture texts are like jewels with many facets. When pondered from various angles, we see differing aspects of the same reality. The outlines, usually stated in sentence form, further develop the central idea.

Methodology

I don't believe that there is only one right way to preach. Some preachers were taught to develop a three-point sermon. Others contend that the sermon should be a development of one major point. Still others insist that expository preaching is the only way to go. Some homilists plan out their sermons months in advance, while many others compose their sermons the week prior to delivery. Laying out sermon themes months in advance is recommended and particular planning should be given to the preaching task in the first half of the church year, where the shorter liturgical seasons lend themselves to sermon series. Planning well ahead also enables you to coordinate your worship services with the musical program of your congregation. Nevertheless, we are not all linear thinkers and planners. Those who begin their preparations for preaching at the beginning of the week can still preach a highly effective sermon if they give adequate time for study, prayer, meditation, and incubation.

To sum up the matter, multiple styles of preaching can be highly effective when the preacher knows and loves his or her congregation, knows and loves the Lord, is a person of prayer, a keen observer of human affairs and a student of the scriptures, who works hard at his or her calling. Most of my pastoral career, I preached from an extended outline, thoroughly thinking through the introduction, conclusion, and major transition points. This served me quite well but when I purchased a computer and started writing my sermons out in manuscript form, I felt that my preaching improved because the whole effort was thoroughly thought out. In so doing, I was kept from redundancy and was able to make the language of the sermon more vivid and visual. A word of warning: Though it is good to write out your sermons, a preacher should never read a sermon. I find that I must thoroughly familiarize myself with my sermon, so that I can interact with my people during its delivery.

Every sermon should be packed with similes, metaphors, and images that make speech pictorial. One or two short stories or illustrative anecdotes are a must. These accounts must carry out the point that the preacher is trying to make and be woven closely into the fabric of the sermon. The preacher must resist the temptation of employing a story merely because it is funny or cute. In addition, the story or illustration must not usurp attention away from the overall plan of the sermon. This means that it must be more than superficially related to the point that one is trying to make. Contemporary observations from newspapers, magazines, movies, books, and everyday life work best. Interpreting events that have happened in the community can create rapport with your listeners. For instance, in my community, a police officer was murdered and this event touched the entire city. I was able to weave this event into the theme of the day. Many source books for illustrations and stories appear superficial and artificial. A good preacher is a keen observer of life, who is able to discern the hand of God in human history. There are only a few instances in this book when I suggest that the preacher might tie together two or more readings for the same sermon. While it may be relevant to show how the gospel theme is also found in the Old Testament, for instance, it is best to concentrate on one text and probe deeper therein.

Martin Luther always contended that every sermon should contain law and gospel. The law makes us despair in our human goodness so that we might be more ready to embrace the gospel of new life in Christ. This principle remains relevant but I believe that we need to use the law judiciously and the gospel freely. Many of the people in our pews are already racked with guilt. They come to church for some hope, some good news. Don't interpret this to mean that we should be loose with the truth. The Word of God takes some stands that are not popular in our culture. We must hold to God's standards and not ignore or compromise the same just to be in sync with the spirit of the time. The good news goes beyond the wonderful truth that we are saved by grace through faith to embrace the deeper truth that our lives can be changed, transformed through the gospel. Through the power of the Spirit, we can gain victory over our failures, compulsions, addictions, and especially our sins. However, the power of the gospel to transform must not end with us; Christ would have us challenge the church to let the Spirit use us as agents of renewal and redemption.

Much preaching falls on deaf ears because we are still assuming that Christendom is alive. That is, our proclamation is based on the assumption that our culture is Christian. That's a big mistake! We live in a secular culture that does not know, let alone appreciate, our Christian beliefs and culture. A majority of the younger generations, acculturated by the mass media, are biblically illiterate. Even those who do know the Christian ethic are not living by it, in many cases. This means that we must get back to the basics of the Christian faith and interpret it for an alien culture, our western culture.

Every time we preach, we need to ask the same question we put forth when we prepare for a meeting. What do I want, by the grace of God, to happen? Do I merely intend to instruct, inform, or inspire? Or, do I want my people to respond in some specific way? I believe that most sermons should give the listeners some indications as to how they can respond to the gospel message. For example, on the Second Sunday of Advent one year, I passed out invitations to the Christmas Eve Services and asked the congregation to respond by inviting their friends to worship on Christmas Eve.

Why Lectionary Preaching?

There are many good reasons for lectionary preaching. Here are a few of them.

1. It keeps us in continuity with a tradition of the church that dates back centuries.
2. It prevents the preacher from getting on his or her hobbyhorse and serves to enable him or her to plumb all the mysteries of faith.
3. We are united with sister churches by meditating on essentially the same scriptures.
4. The liturgical calendar, from which the lectionary derives, helps us remember that all time is sacred and that life is a journey from birth through death to resurrection.
5. We are forced to grow as we struggle with difficult passages.
6. It helps us see how the gospel grows out of the Old Testament tradition and gives us a greater appreciation of our Jewish roots. The first lesson and the gospel usually correlate, while the second lesson, which takes the form of semi-continuous reading from a book of the Bible, often stands alone.

The Church Year Calendar

The Christmas Cycle

Advent	**Color**
Advent 1	purple or blue
Advent 2	purple or blue
Advent 3	purple or blue
Advent 4	purple or blue

Christmas	
Christmas Eve	white
Christmas Day	white
Christmas 1	white
Christmas 2	white

Epiphany	
The Epiphany Of Our Lord	white
The Baptism Of Our Lord/Epiphany 1/Ordinary Time 1	white
Epiphany 2/Ordinary Time 2	green
Epiphany 3/Ordinary Time 3	green
Epiphany 4/Ordinary Time 4	green
Epiphany 5/Ordinary Time 5	green
Epiphany 6/Ordinary Time 6	green
Epiphany 7/Ordinary Time 7	green
Epiphany 8/Ordinary Time 8	green
The Transfiguration Of Our Lord (Last Sunday After Epiphany)	white

The Easter Cycle

Lent	
Ash Wednesday	black or purple
Lent 1	purple
Lent 2	purple
Lent 3	purple
Lent 4	purple
Lent 5	purple
Passion/Palm Sunday	scarlet or purple
Maundy Thursday	scarlet or white
Good Friday	black or no paraments
Holy Saturday	white

Easter	
Easter Vigil	white or gold
Easter Day	white or gold
Easter 2	white
Easter 3	white

Easter 4			white
Easter 5			white
Easter 6			white
The Ascension Of Our Lord			white
Easter 7			white
The Day Of Pentecost			red

The Pentecost Cycle

The Season After Pentecost

Revised Common / Episcopal	Lutheran (Other than ELCA)	Roman Catholic	Color
The Holy Trinity	The Holy Trinity	The Holy Trinity	white
		Corpus Christi	green
Proper 4	Pentecost 2	Ordinary Time 9	green
Proper 5	Pentecost 3	Ordinary Time 10	green
Proper 6	Pentecost 4	Ordinary Time 11	green
Proper 7	Pentecost 5	Ordinary Time 12	green
Proper 8	Pentecost 6	Ordinary Time 13	green
Proper 9	Pentecost 7	Ordinary Time 14	green
Proper 10	Pentecost 8	Ordinary Time 15	green
Proper 11	Pentecost 9	Ordinary Time 16	green
Proper 12	Pentecost 10	Ordinary Time 17	green
Proper 13	Pentecost 11	Ordinary Time 18	green
Proper 14	Pentecost 12	Ordinary Time 19	green
Proper 15	Pentecost 13	Ordinary Time 20	green
Proper 16	Pentecost 14	Ordinary Time 21	green
Proper 17	Pentecost 15	Ordinary Time 22	green
Proper 18	Pentecost 16	Ordinary Time 23	green
Proper 19	Pentecost 17	Ordinary Time 24	green
Proper 20	Pentecost 18	Ordinary Time 25	green
Proper 21	Pentecost 19	Ordinary Time 26	green
Proper 22	Pentecost 20	Ordinary Time 27	green
Proper 23	Pentecost 21	Ordinary Time 28	green
Proper 24	Pentecost 22	Ordinary Time 29	green
Proper 25	Pentecost 23	Ordinary Time 30	green
Proper 26	Pentecost 24	Ordinary Time 31	green
Proper 27	Pentecost 25	Ordinary Time 32	green
Proper 28	Pentecost 26	Ordinary Time 33	green
	Pentecost 27		green
	Reformation Sunday		red
All Saints	All Saints	All Saints	white
Christ The King	Christ The King	Christ The King	white
Thanksgiving Day, USA			white

Preaching From The Gospel Of Mark

About The Author

The gospel for Cycle B of the lectionary is based on Mark. Mark was a second-generation Christian, whose home in Jerusalem was a center of church life. Mark was the nephew of Barnabas, the apostle Paul's companion on his first missionary journey. For some reason, Mark went back home while the journey was still in progress. When the second missionary journey came about, Barnabas wanted Mark to come along but Paul felt differently. This caused Paul and Barnabas to go their separate ways. Yet, when Paul wrote to the Colossians while being imprisoned in Rome, he indicated that Mark was with him. Mark had redeemed himself and remained steadfastly with the apostle at the very end of his life.

About The Date And Setting Of The Book

Most scholars agree that Mark was written between 64-68 AD, during the time of Nero's persecution of the church. The gospel was probably written in Rome and it definitely was penned for a Gentile audience. It contains several words translated from the Latin; "taking **counsel**" (3:6); **Legion** (5:9); **tribute** (12:14).

About The Gospel

The vast majority of New Testament scholars agree that Mark is the oldest extant gospel. Others may have been crafted but Mark is the oldest of those which survived. When one studies the gospels, it takes no genius to observe that the first three gospels have a great number of verses in common. Since Mark was first, the others must have used Mark as a source. Some posit that there was a common written source from which they all borrowed. Of the verses in Mark, only a small fraction of them do not appear in Matthew or Luke. Over half of the verses that Matthew and Luke have in common with Mark are copied almost verbatim.

Where did Mark get his material? The preaching of Peter was the probable source. Papias, a second century writer and bishop of Hieropolis in Asia Minor, was the first to assert that Mark employed Peter as his main source, though he adds that Mark sometimes changes Peter's sequence of events. What reinforces this assertion is the fact that Mark has the ring of an eyewitness. He reveals touches that could only be known by someone who had been there. For instance, in the story where Jesus blesses the children and is rebuked by his disciples for doing the same, only Mark mentions that Jesus took children in his arms (Mark 10:13-16). Another example, in the feeding of the 5,000, only Mark adds that he had them seated in groups of fifty. These little touches make the narratives come alive and lend authenticity.

Mark's gospel, from its very beginning, presents Jesus as the "Son of God." Witnesses are amazed at Jesus' authority and power. Yet, in this gospel we see the Lord's humanity most clearly. He relates that Jesus was a carpenter (6:3), while Matthew apparently found it too bold to suggest that the Son of God was a workingman and makes Jesus the carpenter's Son, which of course, was also true (Matthew 13:55). Jesus clearly displays human emotions — he was angry (3:5), hungry and moved with compassion (6:34). He was brought up short by their unbelief (6:6).

Mark tells his story simply and keeps his narrative moving along at a good clip. He is fond of using the words "straightway" or "immediately." He portrays Jesus as a man with a mission, a man of action. He conveys a sense of immediacy by employing the present tense, which is often changed in translation. In keeping with the active mode of the gospel, it deletes much of the teaching ministry of Jesus, such as the Sermon on the Mount.

Mark concludes as abruptly as it begins, with the announcement of the Lord's resurrection. The original ending to the gospel has been lost. Verses 9-20 of chapter 16 are not in the most ancient manuscripts.

About Mark's Portrayal Of Jesus

Mark reveals a Jesus who is the Son of God, filled with power and authority. He is a man of action, with a passion to reveal the kingdom of God by word and, especially, in deed.

At the same time, Mark probably does the best job of any of the gospels in showing forth the humanity of Jesus. He was tempted, he hungered, he felt anger, and on the cross experienced a sense of abandonment.

The greatest attribute of Mark's Jesus is his zeal to save sinners. About one-third of the gospel is devoted to the suffering and death of the Lord.

The Structure Of Mark

The gospel can be roughly divided into two parts. The first part of the gospel deals mostly with his Galilean ministry (1-9) and the second part of the book focuses on Jerusalem and Judea, where he will offer up his life for the sins of the world. Mark's gospel reaches its climax in Peter's confession (8:27-30). From that time on, Jesus concentrates on his sacrificial death in Jerusalem. John Brokhoff refers to Mark's gospel as a passion story with a very long introduction.

The outline of the book can be broken down as follows:

1. Preparation and presentation of Jesus (1:1—2:12)
2. Initial opposition to Jesus (2:13—8:26)
3. Teachings of Jesus (8:27—10:52)
4. Rejection and suffering of Jesus (11:1—15:47)
5. The resurrection of Jesus (16:1-20)*

* Note — The earliest manuscripts end with verse 8.

About The Use Of Mark In Series B

Mark's gospel turns up a total of 31 times during the "B" cycle. Those occurrences break down according to season as follows:

Advent — Two Sundays (Advent 1 and 2)
Christmas — None
Epiphany — Eight Sundays
Lent — Three Sundays (Lent 1, 2, and 6)
Easter — Easter Sunday
Pentecost — Eight Sundays (Pentecost 2-9 and Pentecost 15-27)

John is employed nineteen times and Luke is used four times, basically to fill in the gaps, except Pentecost 10-14, which deal with Christ as the Bread of Life (John 6).

The Advent Season

Background Of The Season

The roots of this season of preparation stem back to fourth-century France. Originally it extended over a period of seven weeks, but in the sixth century the Bishop of Rome condensed it to four. In the childhood of the church, Advent was strictly observed, with daily fasting and worship. The word advent means literally "to come to." This refers to God's incarnation into our world in the person of Jesus.

The Message Of Advent

The message of Advent can be summed up in three phrases. Jesus has come. Jesus is come. Jesus will come again as Lord of all. Most churches seem to focus on the first statement. The Lord has come. The emphasis is placed on what God accomplished through the birth of Jesus some 2,000 years ago. This gives the Christian faith a historical grounding. The Lord of the church is not a figment of someone's imagination; his existence in place and time is firmly established. Luke contributes historical details to the setting in which Jesus was born (Luke 2:1-2).

The second statement, the Lord is come, informs us that the incarnation, God taking on human form, is something we can experience in the present. Jesus is still with us through the power of the Spirit. If the incarnation is merely a past or a future event, it cannot profoundly impact our lives. Yet, before he returned to the Father, Jesus communicated to the church the promise of his presence (Matthew 28:20). The Christ comes to us through other people, vessels into which his Spirit is poured. Like the blessed Virgin Mary, we are servants of the Lord, receptacles and dispensers of God's grace. During this season a major thrust would have us extend our antennas so that we might receive signals of divine presence that bounce all around us.

The third phrase of Christ's coming tells us that Jesus *will come* again as Lord of all. This is the future tense of Advent. This introduces the penitential aspect of Advent. When Jesus comes again it will not be as the infant lowly but as the judge of the living and the dead, the Lord of all creation. Numerous parables of Jesus warn us not to be caught off guard or unprepared. He will return suddenly, at a time we do not expect. Except for some groups of enthusiasts, this aspect of Advent remains relatively neglected. Such notions can be discomforting and anxiety provoking because we are aware of our sin and imperfection.

Theological Themes In Advent

Anticipation

The Lord is coming both within the context of history and at the end of time. We can, we must, live in a state of anticipation. It's the kind of anticipation and longing found amongst lovers who have been parted. They can hardly wait to be united with the loved one.

Fulfillment

The Advent pericopes attempt to demonstrate how Jesus fulfills the messianic expectations of the Old Testament prophecies. Of course, the church awaits the ultimate fulfillment of Christ's kingdom in the *parousia.*

Preparation

Active preparations are needed before the reunion of the church with its Lord. The repentance that John the Baptist heralded registers at the top of this "to do" list. Faith goes along with repentance, if our lamps are to be in readiness for Christ, the Bridegroom. That faith will find expression in acts of love toward those in need. Of course, nobody can be ready for Christ's coming without a working knowledge of how to employ scripture and prayer in the journey of life.

Submission

The blessed Virgin Mary and Joseph are perfect signs of submission to the will of God. The kingdom of God, as the name implies, informs us that God remains the absolute ruler. Christ reigns as king of all creation and potentate of his body, the church. The kingdom can never be a democracy. The Lord will never force our submission but we cannot enter the kingdom without its being rendered.

Celebration

The season of Advent has a penitential aspect to it, of course, but there is cause for celebration, because "the Lord is at hand." This should not be a no-holds-barred season of revelry but a period of quiet rejoicing.

Peacemaking

The Messiah, expected by the Hebrews, was to be a peacemaker who would reign in righteousness and peace. When the Christ completes his reconciling work at the *parousia*, all forces opposed to goodness will be abolished and God's peace will reign supreme.

Justice

John the Baptist is a prominent figure in the Advent pericopes, who employed Isaiah's image of leveling in preparation for the Lord's coming. We live in a world of injustice and inequality but the kingdom of God promises justice for the poor and the downtrodden. Justice and peace are closely wedded concepts, as the psalmist states so poetically: "Steadfast love and faithfulness will meet; righteousness and peace will kiss each other" (Psalm 85:10).

Unifying Theme For Advent

The Advent Season presents a great opportunity to develop a preaching theme that carries through the season. From the Old Testament lessons I have pulled several concepts of God and organized them under the banner "Advent Images Of God."
This theme might be developed like this:

Advent 1
Text: Isaiah 64:8
Theme: God is the potter and we are the clay. This text emphasizes both the fragility of human existence and our worth in God's estimation. Though we are flawed pots, God will renew us.

Advent 2

Text: Isaiah 40:1-11

Theme: God is the shepherd and we are the sheep for whom he lovingly cares.

Advent 3

Text: Isaiah 61:1-3

Theme: The Lord is a liberator, freeing us from our captivity to sin and death.

Advent 4

Text: 2 Samuel 7:15b-16

Theme: The Lord is a house builder, constructing an eternal house in which we can dwell.

Advent 1

Revised Common	Isaiah 64:1-9	1 Corinthians 1:3-9	Mark 13:24-37
Roman Catholic	Isaiah 63:16b-17; 64:1, 3b-8	1 Corinthians 1:3-9	Mark 13:33-37
Episcopal	Isaiah 64:1-9a	1 Corinthians 1:1-9	Mark 13:(24-32) 33-37

Advent Theme: Advent Images Of God
God Is The Potter And We Are The Clay

Theme For The Day: The return of the Lord. In Isaiah 64:1 the writer earnestly hopes that God will rend or tear the heavens and come down to restore his people and subdue their foes. In Paul's introduction to 1 Corinthians he prays that the Lord would sustain them until the revealing of the Lord Jesus. The gospel has Jesus warning his disciples to watch closely for his return.

BRIEF COMMENTARY ON THE LESSONS

Lesson 1: Isaiah 64:1-9 (C, E); Isaiah 63:16b-17; 64:1, 3b-8 (RC)

As the Israelites returned from exile in Babylon, they had high hopes for a bright future but the reality of post-exilic life soon dampened their spirits. The devastation of the city and the temple was overwhelming and the task that confronted them was daunting. Alternately, the writer seems to blame God (63:17) or their own sinfulness (64:5-7) for their dire situation. Yet he continues to trust in the Lord and pray with great passion that the Lord would rend the heavens and come down in a dramatic demonstration of redeeming power (64:1), like the acts of wonder and might God showed when the people of Israel made their way through the wilderness to the promised land. The passage ends on a note of pessimism tempered with hope. Using the image of the potter and the clay, the prophet derives comfort from the fact that though the Hebrews had been shattered by the ordeal of exile, they still retain great value as God's special creation.

Lesson 2: 1 Corinthians 1:3-9 (C, RC); 1 Corinthians 1:1-9 (E)

This introduction to 1 Corinthians contains Paul's usual greeting and prayer of thanksgiving. This lection is probably included here for its reference to the *parousia*. He expresses faith that God had equipped them with all the gifts necessary to sustain them until the return of Christ. Yet this confidence does not stem from the sufficiency of their own gifts but their faithful God, who would maintain them to the end (v. 9).

Gospel: Mark 13:24-37 (C); Mark 13:33-37 (RC); Mark 13:(24-32) 33-37 (E)

This entire thirteenth chapter contains eschatological material. Jesus confesses to his disciples that he cannot reveal when the end will occur (v. 33). This contains a clear warning against setting eschatological timetables. The key word in this passage is "watch," employed four times. Like a faithful steward, the follower of Christ discharges his duties so well that he continues in constant readiness for his Master's return.

Psalm Of The Day

Psalm 80:1-7, 17-19 (C); Psalm 80 (E) — "Restore us, O God; make your face shine upon us, that we may be saved" (v. 3).

Psalm 84:8 (RC)

Prayer Of The Day

O Lord, our God, you are our potter and we are the clay. We confess that we have become cracked and disfigured through sin. Graciously forgive and reform us into vessels fit for your habitation. In the name of Jesus. Amen.

THEOLOGICAL REFLECTION ON THE LESSONS

Lesson 1: Isaiah 64:1-9

The blame game. The prophet blames the Lord for his nation's sorry condition (63:17). The Jews felt that God had hardened their hearts, just as he was accused of hardening the heart of the Pharaoh prior to the Exodus. Of course, the Hebrews attributed most everything to the hand of the Lord, the curse of tragedy as well as the blessing of salvation. We must recognize that God is not the cause of all that happens; he may permit things but that is not the same as causation. We live in an era when blaming others for our problems and misfortunes is wildly popular. Playing the blame game may be a way to cope with frustration but not a good way.

He prayed for a power play. The prophet prays that God would rip the heavens apart and make his power felt on earth, giving hope to his own and instilling fear in his foes (64:1). How often we get impatient with God's apparent passivity. We wonder why he doesn't act more aggressively to punish evildoers and come to the aid of his people. When Jesus was born, God did break open the heavens and come down but only a few were aware of this gentle theophany.

The universality of sin. Verses 5b through 7 contain a confession of sins. Note the word all. "We have all become like one who is unclean" (v. 6a). We are *all* sinners and all deserve God's righteous judgment. Advent has a definite penitential aspect to it and so it behooves us ALL to confess to God the pollution of our heart.

The image of God as the potter (v. 8). What is the prophet trying to convey through this image of God as the potter and we as the clay? He could be asserting God's right to do with us as he pleases, since he is the potter-creator. He could also be lifting up our human vulnerability and the transience of earthly existence. Both ideas probably underlie our passage. Yet I believe that this statement holds high our unique relationship with the almighty. God is our Father and we are his masterpiece. Underlying this relationship is this assumption: since we are the Lord's special handiwork, he will not utterly cast us aside. Just as the potter sometimes has to rework and reform the clay to get it into the proper shape and form, so the Lord will lovingly remake us into a vessel fit for his Spirit.

Lesson 2: 1 Corinthians 1:3-9

Waiting — active and passive. It seems that we're always waiting for something: waiting in line at the grocery store, waiting to speak on the phone, or waiting for the weekend. Waiting can be active or passive. To illustrate, yesterday my wife and I went to the health club. She left early and we agreed to meet at a certain time upstairs. I got up there by the appointed time but she was not to be seen. I sat down in the lounge and passively waited for her to come in and find me.

Fifteen minutes went by and she still wasn't there. I was about to get up when she bounded though the door. "Where were you?" she exclaimed. "I've been waiting out in the parking lot. I thought you'd be looking for me through the window." We had both missed the time of our meeting because we assumed a passive rather than an active waiting stance.

Paul speaks of waiting for the appearance of Christ as Lord and king (v. 7). It is plain that he was referring to an active kind of waiting because he speaks of the gifts with which they were equipped for the wait (v. 7). These spiritual gifts were not to be guarded but used in the service of Christ. Only active waiting will prepare us for the time of Christ's visitation.

Crossing the finish line. The apostle assures the Corinthians that the God who had begun a good work in them would bring it to completion by the time of Christ's return. The Lord would keep them strong to the end, so that they could indeed cross the finish line of faith. Note that the emphasis was not their own strength but Christ's faithfulness (v. 9).

Gospel: Mark 13:24-37

Cosmic homecoming? In the eschatological scenario, the victorious Christ sends his angels to gather the elect from the "ends of the earth to the ends of heaven" (v. 27). This is a highly speculative thought, but could it be that when Christ gathers the elect, they will not be limited to earthlings? Perhaps the universe harbors other races whom he has reached out to save. The *parousia* would thereby become a cosmic homecoming of grand proportions!

This generation will not pass away until all has taken place (v. 30). The preceding verses detail various signs of the end times. Some assert that Jesus was wrong in his assertion that his generation would not pass away until all this had taken place. Not so, most of the signs have to do with the destruction of Jerusalem and the temple. Some who were alive when Jesus uttered these words saw the destruction of the holy city.

Pass away. In verses 30-31, the phrase "pass away" occurs three times. Even the universe is on a time clock, with a beginning and ending. Only God's word remains eternal, a sobering thought indeed. Yet through water and the word we partake of the eternal.

Unknown date and time. Jesus asserts that nobody knows the date or time of his second coming, not the angels or the Son himself (v. 32). If only those who set up elaborate timetables of Christ's second coming would let this fact sink in!

Watch! Our neighborhood is protected by "Neighborhood Watch." The community is organized to watch for and report events and persons that look suspicious. The program heightens the vigilance of residents and makes would-be thieves uncomfortable at the prospect of being watched. A householder must be watchful at all times for the possible coming of a thief. Christians must be ready at all times to receive the Lord Jesus. Therefore, "Watch!"

What time is it? The word for time in verse 34 is *kairos*, referring to time as a special event, the qualitative dimension of time. We live in a culture that zeros in on chronological time. If the worship service goes ten minutes over the hour, numbers of worshipers experience apoplexy. They have allotted one hour to God and no more. Because of their focus on chronological time, they are apt to miss the time of Christ's visitation, as he comes to us in worship. Certainly we cannot escape the reality of chronological time but must put it in perspective. The *kairos* happenings are what define our life. What time are you focused on?

SERMON APPROACHES WITH ILLUSTRATIONS

Lesson 1: Isaiah 64:1-9

   Sermon Title: Advent Images: Thou Art The Potter, We Are The Clay
   Sermon Angle: See "Theological Reflections On The Lessons"
   Outline:
   1. God is the potter.
      — Our creator.
      — God has the right to fashion and recreate us.
   2. We are the clay.
      — We are creatures of the earth and temporal.
      — We are not ordinary clay but the workmanship of God.
      — Sin makes us cracked pots but our creator can refashion us.
   3. We can entrust our lives to the potter.

* * * * *

Parenting is probably the closest thing in our society to being a potter, except that parents are not dealing with an inert object but a living being, created in the image of God. What an awesome task to ply loving and gentle hands to our progeny, as they turn time and again on the potter's wheel of life! Sometimes we hold too tightly, trying to force them into a particular shape or form and they crack from the pressure. Other times we become preoccupied with other things and let our precious clay turn unattended and it becomes distorted by those who would turn the clay to their own selfish purpose. Our God-given task is not to shape this precious genetic clay in our own image but to help uncover the perfect form hidden within.

* * * * *

The awesomeness of the parenting task weighs heavier than it ever has because of the mobility of our society and the breakdown of the family, among other factors. Parents no longer have models of child-rearing formerly provided by the extended family. Consequently they are turning to so-called outside experts. More neophyte moms and dads have looked to Dr. Benjamin Spock for advice than to anyone else. Since his book *Baby And Child Care* was first published in 1946, he has sold 40 million copies of the various editions of the book. Recently Dr. Spock has become alarmed about the kind of kids that are turning out these days, rude, aggressive, noisy, and disrespectful. He feels that parents are neglecting their parenting task of shaping and molding the personality and character of their children. The good doctor accuses many parents of being more vitally concerned about their careers than their families.

* * * * *

Sermon Title: A Call To Action
Sermon Angle: Isaiah calls on God to rend the heavens and come down (v. 1). The city and temple have become decimated. All that the Israelites held sacred and dear has been trampled into the dust. Now the people earnestly pray that the Lord would rouse himself and demonstrate his power. We can identify with that cry for divine intervention when we see the forces of evil

arrogantly trample over the rights of the weak. In the seasons of our weakness and humiliation, we have cried out to God for aid, but sometimes the Lord seems far removed. This sense of being distant from God happens even to the choicest of God's saints. The problem is not that God removes himself from us but that our sin separates us from the Lord. We don't need the Lord to rend the heavens, we need to rend our hearts.

Outline:
1. The Israelites, returning home from captivity, were discouraged at their sorry plight. It seemed that God had removed himself.
2. In the face of evil, it is natural to question God's presence and power.
3. It is sin that places a barrier between ourselves and the Lord.
4. If we would ask God to rend our hearts, God would also rend the heavens and come to us.

Sermon Title: How Can We Be Saved?

Sermon Angle: The prophet bemoans the proclivity of God's people to continue in sin. In light of the extreme seriousness of sin, he questions how they can ever be saved (64:5). Even their righteous acts have become polluted with sin (v. 6). Like clay, God's people are earthly and subject to decay. Though we cannot change ourselves, God can refashion us. He is the potter and we are the clay (v. 8).

Lesson 2: 1 Corinthians 1:3-9

Sermon Title: Active Waiting

Sermon Angle: Paul notes that the Corinthians were not lacking in spiritual gifts as they eagerly waited for the Lord to return. Those gifts were to be employed in ministry. Therefore, theirs was not a passive but an active waiting. Advent is a time of active waiting, as we share the gifts of God with the world. Indeed, our entire Christian existence is one of actively and eagerly waiting for the revealing of the glory of Christ.

Outline:
1. Nothing is more depressing than to witness passive waiting (many in nursing homes).
2. Passive waiting immobilizes a person.
3. Active waiting is what the New Testament calls for.
   — It elicits anticipation.
   — It calls for preparation.
   — It involves ministry (using our spiritual gifts).

Sermon Title: Finishing The Race

Sermon Angle: Life resembles a race. Sometimes it seems like a 100-yard dash. Other times it seems more like a marathon, requiring endurance and stamina. So, too, our Christian faith calls for spiritual endurance if we are to complete successfully the journey begun in baptism. In this passage we receive assurance that the Lord will give us the strength to complete the race and win the prize.

Gospel: Mark 13:24-37

Sermon Title: Keeping Watch

Sermon Angle: Jesus instructs his followers to keep watch for the coming of the kingdom. Recall that, according to Luke 2, the shepherds were out in their fields keeping watch over their flocks by night when the angels announced the nativity of our Lord. In contrast, the disciples were not able to keep watch with Jesus in the Garden of Gethsemane. They fell asleep and the Enemy caught them off guard. Jesus kept alert through the power of prayer and warns his disciples to keep watch so as not to be caught off guard.

Outline:
1. Keeping watch is one of the main themes of the season.
   — The shepherds kept watch over their flocks when the angelic messengers heralded the nativity.
   — The magi were watching the heavens and followed the star.
   — In the gospel Jesus warns us to keep watch for the kingdom.
2. Watching is not passive but active and involves ...
   — openness to the *kairos* [the special moment] (v. 33).
   — being a good steward (v. 34).
   — a heightened spiritual consciousness.
3. Keep your watch for the coming of Christ.

* * * * *

What do we do as we hope for Jesus' coming? For those of us who believe that Jesus is coming, there are two responses, one passive and one active. The passive response can be called WAITING, the active response, WATCHING. To understand the difference between the two, picture the people in a nursing home. Some are waiting: waiting for someone to stop by, waiting for someone to break the loneliness of their existence, to bring joy and love into their lives. But nobody comes, or only infrequently does a visitor appear. The waiter becomes passive.

Then there are the watchers. They know that someone is coming to see them. They may not know exactly when, but they know someone will come because he has come before and he can be relied upon. They are looking forward to the visit with great anticipation. They are anxious to fix themselves up and make their rooms presentable. They rehearse what they might discuss. They make sure nothing else intrudes into the visitation. Then they watch, listening to the footsteps they have come to recognize and to love. And because their lives have a forward view, they have a joy they communicate to those about them. Rather than retreat to a shell, they reach out to others and tell them about the one who is coming. Jesus enjoins us not to merely wait for his coming but to watch for it.

* * * * *

Sermon Title: Doorkeepers
Sermon Angle: Jesus compares the kingdom to the man who goes away, having put his servants in charge. The doorkeeper is especially assigned the duty of keeping watch for the Master's return (v. 34). We are all doorkeepers for the Lord. We are the means through which Christ comes into our world and through which others come into the presence of Christ. Are we falling asleep on the job?

Advent 2

Revised Common	Isaiah 40:1-11	2 Peter 3:8-15a	Mark 1:1-8
Roman Catholic	Isaiah 40:1-5, 9-11	2 Peter 3:8-14	Mark 1:1-8
Episcopal	Isaiah 40:1-11	2 Peter 3:8-15a, 18	Mark 1:1-8

Advent Theme: Advent Images Of God
                          The Shepherd King

Theme For The Day: Christ as our shepherd king. Isaiah 40 has the Lord coming to save and comfort his dispossessed people. He comes as a mighty king who will rule his people in justice. At the same time, he is a loving shepherd, caring for his wounded sheep. The Old Testament held up the ideal of the king of Israel as a shepherd. In so doing the emphasis shifts from the desires of the king to the needs of the people. The gospel lesson from Mark 1 has John the Baptist pointing to this ruler who was mightier than himself.

BRIEF COMMENTARY ON THE LESSONS

Lesson 1: Isaiah 40:1-11 (C, E); Isaiah 40:1-5, 9-11 (RC)

This passage commences the second major division of the book of Isaiah, addressed to the exiles in Babylon. They are words of comfort and hope. The time of punishment has passed; now the Lord will prepare a level path for the captives to return to Jerusalem. Through his acts of liberation the Lord's glory will be revealed, which is contrasted with the temporal state of humankind (vv. 6-9). The inhabitants of Jerusalem are to herald to the surrounding region the salvation of the Lord, who comes in kingly might, yet gently cares for his own like a shepherd.

Lesson 2: 2 Peter 3:8-15a (C); 2 Peter 3:8-14 (RC); 2 Peter 3:8-15a, 18 (E)

The epistle of 2 Peter was penned at a later time from that of 1 Peter. Some scholars believe that it was authored by someone other than Peter. The author addresses a concern that took a number of years to develop, namely, the *parousia*. They are reminded that God counts time differently than humans. His delay reflects his earnest desire that all people repent and come to the knowledge of the truth. God will destroy the earth and the heavens with fervent heat and create a new heaven and earth. Believers are to prepare for this new state of being by living lives of holiness.

Gospel: Mark 1:1-8 (C, RC, E)

Mark starts his gospel with a simple but bold statement of the underlying premise of his book: Jesus, the Christ, is the Son of God. He opens with the prophecy of the messenger (John the Baptist) who was to prepare the way for the Christ, as he quotes from Malachi 3:1 and Isaiah 40:3. Mark notes that great throngs of people went out to John in the wilderness to be baptized as a sign of repentance. Through moral and spiritual cleansing, the prophet sets out to make Israel ready for the "Anointed One," who was greater than the forerunner because he would baptize with the Holy Spirit.

Psalm Of The Day

Psalm 85:1-2, 8-13 (C); Psalm 85 (E) — "Righteousness goes before him and prepares the way for his steps."

Psalm 84:9-14 (RC)

Prayer Of The Day

Lord Christ, through repentance and faith make us truly a people prepared for the advent of your kingdom, when you fully establish your mighty yet gentle rule eternally. In Jesus' name. Amen.

THEOLOGICAL REFLECTION ON THE LESSONS

Lesson 1: Isaiah 40:1-11

Comfort the afflicted. The true role of the prophet remains to comfort the afflicted and afflict the comfortable. The latter task had been accomplished; the Israelites had paid double for their sin (v. 2). Now God was going to provide comfort for his hurting children. The gospel of John picks up on the comforting theme with the idea of the Holy Spirit as *Paraclete*. The Greek word means both to be called to one's side and to speak words of comfort and encouragement. God comforts us through his presence and through his word, which he speaks through his people. The one who comforts, in God's name, provides not only sympathy but strength.

The desert experience. "In the desert prepare the way of the Lord" (v. 3). Why in the desert? The desert was the haunt of demons, the locale of aridity, sin, and alienation. Our journey back to the Lord begins in the desert, when we confront our demons in Christ's name. When we realize our captivity and cry out to God, the Lord levels the path for us to march back into his gracious presence.

Where have all the flowers gone? "Where have all the flowers gone, long time passing? Where have all the flowers gone, long time ago?" hauntingly sang Peter, Paul, and Mary in a song popularized in the '60s. While this song protests the futility of war, it also reminds us of our human mortality. This is the same thought lifted up by Isaiah in verses 6-8. Like flowers and grass we fade and die. Even so, the Creator raises the flowers and the grass to newness of life. Will he not do the same for all who turn to him in hope?

The shepherd king. Disney tells the story of the *Lion King* and the Bible proclaims the truth of the shepherd king (vv. 10-11). He is the sovereign Lord who comes in demonstration of power (v. 10). Yet this mighty king is also the gentle and compassionate shepherd who lovingly gathers his sheep in his arms (v. 11).

Lesson 2: 2 Peter 3:8-15a

Slaves of time (vv. 8-9). The believers whom Peter addresses were concerned that the Lord was not returning as quickly as they had imagined. Peter counsels that God is not subject to time, that with God 1,000 years is like one day to us. We Westerners are slaves of time, shackled to the clock. Even our appointment with the eternal God at worship does not escape the constraints of time. Church members are geared to sixty-minute services and God forbid that the sermon go more than fifteen minutes. One of the greatest benefits of heaven will be a total release from our slavery to time.

God is long-spirited. The epistle puts a positive construction on Christ's tarrying. It has to do with his character. God is patient and merciful, not wanting any to perish but that all might come to the knowledge of the truth. The word interpreted as "patient" or "long-suffering" (*makrothumeo*) means literally "long-spirited." God is long on the spirit of patience, compassion, and mercy. How long-spirited are we?

The day of the Lord will come. Peter assures that, though he delay, the day of the Lord will indeed come and at an unexpected moment. The thief in the night imagery means to convey the suddenness and surprise of this event (v. 10).

Holocaust (v. 10). Peter envisions the entire earth consumed in a holocaust. The earth itself is temporal and passing. It will be replaced by a new heaven and a new earth where only righteousness dwells. Like space travelers who travel to an entirely new solar system, God will transport us into a universe (heaven) permeated with righteousness.

Therefore. This passage contains two conditional clauses. In verse 11, Peter asks the rhetorical question: Since the world was going thus to melt away, what kind of lives should the believer live? In verse 14 he adds that since we wait for a new heaven and earth, we should strive to live pure and holy lives and be ready for the advent of Christ. Knowing the end of existence as we now experience it should motivate us to live faithful lives.

Gospel: Mark 1:1-8

The beginning of the gospel. Mark begins the gospel of Jesus Christ with the ministry of John the Baptist. John preached repentance and that didn't seem like good news. Actually repentance was just the needed condition in order to receive the good news. The gospel was of the coming Messiah. Thus the baptist's preaching was the beginning of the gospel of Jesus Christ. Yet gospel and grace existed even before the advent of Jesus, the Christ. The Old Testament and the New Testament are shot through with the good news of grace and forgiveness. The ministry of John heralds the beginning of a watershed new beginning of the grace of God in Jesus.

A voice crying in the wilderness (v. 3). John was literally a voice crying in the wilderness. He had forsaken the holy city and the temple, probably because of their corruption. He was probably influenced by the Essenes, whose desert commune was an attempt to flee the contaminating effects of society. Yet prophets of every era have been those crying out in the wilderness. They have been shoved to the periphery of existence, mocked, ignored, and feared. Many Christians feel that way at the present time, as news media and government officials sometimes ridicule our values. Some of those in the so-called religious right endeavor to seize power as an avenue of publicly proclaiming the values they hold dear. Yet such power can make those who claim it callous to the needs of those who differ from them and imperious to the Spirit of God. Then God will send other prophets who will make their haunting cry echo from the wilderness.

We wish to see Jesus. Some Greeks came to Philip and said: "Sir, we wish to see Jesus" (John 12:21). One pastor has this phrase printed on a card and affixed inside his pulpit. This reminds him that his role is not to magnify himself but the Lord Jesus Christ. John the Baptist did an exemplary job of maintaining a low profile so that people might see Jesus. He proclaimed: "After me will come one more powerful than I ..." (v. 7).

SERMON APPROACHES WITH ILLUSTRATIONS

Lesson 1: Isaiah 40:1-11

Sermon Title: The Shepherd King

Sermon Angle: Many kings have boasted of their might and power, which they have attempted to illustrate through acts of war or by making grand monuments to their own glory. To maintain authority a ruler has to demonstrate strength and determination. However, few kings have prided themselves on their mercy and compassion. The Old Testament writers held out for the kings of Israel the ideals of strength and mercy, when they envisioned them as shepherds of the people. Few of the kings realized that ideal. Isaiah envisions the Lord as a shepherd king. He is coming to rule in might (v. 10). Yet he employs that strength to comfort, protect, and guide (v. 11). Our king exercises his power not for his own enjoyment but for the benefit of the sheep.

Outline:
1. The Israelites experienced the powerlessness and humiliation of defeat and captivity.
2. God responded to their plight with the promise of being their shepherd king.
   — As king, he had power (v. 10).
   — As shepherd, he had compassion and tenderness (v. 11).
3. As our shepherd king, the Lord mixes power with compassion.

Sermon Title: Shout It Out!

Sermon Angle: Isaiah envisions a herald crying (shouting) out the good news of national salvation. The first shout of the messenger was to prepare the way for the Lord God, to make his paths straight (v. 3). God was coming to save his people. A second cry: "All flesh is grass ..." (v. 6). To see God, we must confess our dependence on his power. The third cry or shout: "Here is your God!" (v. 9). In Christ, God has come close to his human children. These three shouts can be used as a basis for the sermon.

Lesson 2: 2 Peter 3:8-15a

Sermon Title: Moving Beyond Time

Sermon Angle: Peter addresses the concern about the tardiness of the Lord's return. He consoles that "with the Lord one day is like a thousand years and a thousand years are like a day" (v. 8). He is attempting to express the truth that God lives beyond time; he is not governed by the earthly dictates of times and seasons. We are such slaves of time; we live by the clock! Eternal life, which for believers begins in this life, moves us into an existence beyond time and space. Yet we continue to be enslaved to time and agendas. This clouds our vision of the timeless, the eternal. In this world we cannot escape the clutches of time and space, but we can at least be cognizant of the eternal and attempt to experience it through contemplation, worship and prayer.

Outline:
1. The church that Peter addressed was governed by time (vv. 8-9).
   — They thought God should operate within their time frame.
2. Our society is even more engrossed in time concerns. (Give examples.)
3. God, who entered into time in Jesus, remains outside time and space.
4. We live in time, yet must also begin to dwell in the realm of the eternal. (Give examples.)

*   *   *   *   *

We need constant reminders that the eternal God stands outside the realm of time and that if we are to approach him, we must enter that realm of the eternal. Unfortunately, our preoccupation with chronological time fuels our impatience and causes us to miss God's in-breaking into our lives.

The church that Peter addresses had become impatient waiting for Christ to return in kingdom power. Like them, we may have grown tired of waiting. What a delight it is when that which we have earnestly hoped for really happens! I know all about waiting, hoping, and praying for the kingdom to come. You see, I live in Nebraska. Like almost everybody in the state, I am an avid Nebraska Cornhusker football fan. Every year we are one of the top-rated and most successful teams. Yet the gold crown of number oneness had eluded us for years and we had lost several bowl games. Tom Osborne remains one of the most winning coaches in college football. But on New Year's Day, 1995, the miracle happened! We overcame the Miami Hurricanes in the last quarter to lay claim to the grand prize. What we hoped for really happened!

Rabbi Mendel Katzman, a member of the ultra-orthodox Lubavitcher Jewish sect, during those years, experienced something of an epiphany after the victory. This group passionately looks for the Messiah. Their leader, whom many of the sect thought might be the Messiah, died toward the end of 1994. Katzman explained in the *Omaha World Herald* that it was difficult to maintain hope in the face of centuries of disappointments. Nebraska football fans' unwavering faith in their team was an inspiration, he reported. Their faith was finally rewarded, which renewed his hope that his faith in the coming of the Messiah would also be rewarded. It would be all the more sweet for having had to wait so long.

*   *   *   *   *

Sermon Title: The Late Great Planet Earth

Sermon Angle: I do not identify with the apocalyptic prognosticating of the likes of Hal Lindsay. Nevertheless, the end of the world and the birth of a new cosmos is not only biblical but seems perfectly logical. If God's judgment doesn't put an end to earthly existence, entropy will certainly overcome us. The intimations of mortality, which grow in intensity as the years pile on, make us aware of the fleeting nature of all creation. Peter reveals that the end of existence ought to inform our present manner of living (vv. 11-14). Holy and godly lives, not despair, should be the result. God has something wonderfully new in store!

Outline:
1. Earthly existence will melt away when the Lord returns (v. 10).
2. Knowledge of the end prompts us to holy and purposeful lives (v. 11).
3. Those who live godly lives will see a new heaven and earth (v. 13).

Gospel: Mark 1:1-8

Sermon Title: The Beginning Of The Gospel

Sermon Angle: Mark begins his gospel recounting the ministry of John the Baptist. John's message was one of preparing the way of the Lord through repentance. Repentance is the beginning of the gospel. The good news of John has it that we can change and become new creatures. Repentance remains the necessary first step for entering into the gospel and the kingdom of God in Christ.

Outline:
1. We prepare for Christ's advent through repentance.
2. Repentance is the beginning of the gospel.
   — The good news is that God can change us.
3. The good news is fulfilled in the One to whom John pointed (v. 7).

*   *   *   *   *

The message that John preached didn't seem like very good news. John was telling the people that they had to change; that's what repentance is, radical change. The good news of Jesus is that we can change through the power of the gospel; we can start all over again.

A gifted homiletics professor told of his first day in algebra class. It was his second year of the subject, but he just couldn't seem to get it. He was paralyzed with fear and his stomach seemed as if it were bouncing up and down on a trampoline. A new teacher walked in. She looked a lot like the old teacher. She was holding a book that looked a lot like last year's book. Before the class began, he thought he'd go up to the teacher and explain to her what a dunce he was with algebra. So he confessed his troubles, but she wasn't interested. "Oh yes, that may be true, but that was before you had me as your teacher. You are going to find that I do things differently. I don't like to get students who have done well in algebra before they have me. Too many prejudices. I prefer getting people who don't know a lot about algebra so I can teach them from scratch." The student went back to his seat and breathed a sigh of relief. It was a new beginning and he could change with the help of his teacher.

That, my friends, is the good news of Jesus Christ. We can change; we can become new, loving, hopeful, joyful human beings, through the transforming power of Jesus Christ.

*   *   *   *   *

Sermon Title: Back To The Basics

Sermon Angle: In the last several years a movement has gotten underway to simplify our Christmas celebrations and get back to the basic meaning of Christmas. We have obscured the reason for the season with a plethora of shopping and partying that leaves us exhausted. John the Baptist was a back-to-basics individual. Simple apparel (camel's skin clothing). Simple diet (locusts and wild honey). Down-to-earth housing (the wilderness). John's was a simple message: repent! Get right with God! Live new lives! In our day of wrapping religion in the latest psychological or entertainment fad, isn't it about time we got back to basics?

Outline:

Introduction: Do you feel that life has become too complicated? Do you look back longingly to a simpler era? Are you preparing more for Christmas and enjoying it less? Then get back to the ABCs of Christmas.
1. John lived a very fundamental lifestyle.
2. John proclaimed a very simple message:
   — repent
   — follow Jesus
   — receive the Holy Spirit.
3. Let's get back to the basics of Christianity and Christmas.

Advent 3

Revised Common	Isaiah 61:1-4, 8-11	1 Thessalonians 5:16-24	John 1:6-8, 19-28
Roman Catholic	Isaiah 61:1-2, 10-11	1 Thessalonians 5:16-24	John 1:6-8, 19-28
Episcopal	Isaiah 65:17-25	1 Thessalonians 5:(12-15) 16-28	John 1:6-8, 19-28 or John 3:23-30

Advent Theme: Advent Images Of God
The Lord Is Our Liberator

Theme For The Day: Joy and anticipation concerning what God was about to do. Isaiah promises the oil of gladness (Isaiah 61:3) as God brings the captives of Israel back to their homeland. In Thessalonians, Paul charges the church always to rejoice (v. 16). In the gospel, John delineates his message as pointing to the one who was to follow him: The one who would be much greater than he. All of these messengers were filled with a sense of joyful expectancy.

The third Sunday in Advent has in some traditions been known as "Rejoice Sunday," with the rose candle in the Advent wreath representing the believers' attitude of joy as we watch for Christ's coming. The theme of rejoicing comes clearly through the first two lessons.

In the medieval church this third Sunday in Advent was known as "Minister's Sunday" and was utilized as an occasion for ordination. This presents another viable approach. The first lesson heralds the anointing of the prophet and the gospel highlights the ministry of John the Baptist who, in turn, announces the ministry of the Messiah.

BRIEF COMMENTARY ON THE LESSONS

Lesson 1: Isaiah 61:1-4, 8-11 (C); Isaiah 61:1-2, 10-11 (RC)

This passage springs from an inspired sixth century BC prophet, who proclaimed a brilliant message of hope for the returning Babylonian captives, although they would find their land in ruins. The Lord's liberation would confer a spirit of joy. The people respond to this good news with an affirmation of praise (vv. 10-11). Verses 1-2a were the basis for our Lord's first sermon to the hometown crowd (Luke 4). Jesus aims to free the oppressed.

Lesson 1: Isaiah 65:17-25 (E)

Lesson 2: 1 Thessalonians 5:16-24 (C, RC); 1 Thessalonians 5:(12-15) 16-28 (E)

This lection, from one of Paul's earliest epistles, deals with the questions that believers had concerning the *parousia*. Namely, what will happen to those who die before the *parousia* and when will it take place? Today's text contains ethical admonitions that flow from steadfast confidence in the second coming of Christ in glory. Christ will keep them faithful, ready for his coming. Therefore, they should rejoice and give thanks.

Gospel: John 1:6-8, 19-28 (C, RC, E)

John the Baptist is presented as the one who gives witness to the light and truth. John's ministry caused quite a stir and raised questions as to his identity. The religious leaders in

Jerusalem sent representatives to ascertain John's identity. "Who are you?" they asked. "Are you the Christ?" "No." "Are you Elijah?" (He was expected to precede the Messiah.) "No." Jesus sees the answer differently because he clearly identifies John as the Elijah figure (Matthew 11:14; Mark 9:13). Evidently John is unconscious of his crucial role. "Are you the Messiah?" "No." "Are you a prophet?" "I am not!" John defines himself more in terms of who he is not rather than who he is. When he does identify himself, it comes across more in terms of function rather than title: the preparer of the way. Clearly John sees his role as being part of the supporting cast rather than as that of the star. He is not even worthy to unloose the sandals of the Messiah (the servant's role).

Psalm Of The Day
Psalm 126 (C, E) — "The Lord has done great things for us" (v. 3).

Prayer Of The Day
Liberating Lord, when we have become captive to the powers of sin and death, you break the bars of our oppression with your mighty forgiveness and grace. We thank and praise you for freeing us through the redemption that comes through your Son, Jesus, our Lord. Amen.

THEOLOGICAL REFLECTION ON THE LESSONS

Lesson 1: Isaiah 61:1-4, 8-11
Liberation theology. In recent decades liberation theology has caught hold in places like Mexico and South America. The liberationists maintain that God holds a preferential regard for the poor and oppressed. This has made them bold to challenge power structures and politics as usual. Though liberationists have sometimes become mired in Marxist thinking, they have a point. God does come to the rescue of the poor and oppressed. Like the prophet of Isaiah 61, God has ordained his church to proclaim "liberty to the captives." However, this liberation does not come about because of political education but through the Spirit of the Lord.

Anointed and appointed. The prophet announces that he has been both anointed with the Spirit of God and appointed to preach the good news to the poor and oppressed. God gave his prophet a mission that could only be accomplished through divine empowerment. God never gives us a task without the power to complete it, the power of his Spirit.

Clothed for salvation. The prophet uses the image of clothing several times in this passage (vv. 2, 10). God has clothed his people with the garment of salvation and the robe of righteousness (God's action) and the garment of praise (our response to God's salvation). He pictures a wedding feast where the bride and groom are decked out in their festive robes. God would marry his sinful people once more and there will be much rejoicing.

Lesson 2: 1 Thessalonians 5:16-24
Keepers of the flame. These words of admonition instruct the believers how they might keep the flame of faith alive in a hostile world, a world where it seems that God is withholding his saving presence. Prayer and thanksgiving are the chief tools. Then Paul warns them not to put out the Spirit's fire (v. 19). Our congregation has embarked on a course to train people to reach out to those who have ceased being active in the church. One of the assumptions of the course has it that the inactive person remains a part of the church until he or she decides

otherwise. The flame of faith may be burning dimly but it's still alive. The church must gently fan the spark into full flame.

Fire was a crucial commodity in ancient societies. Since it took a great deal of effort to start a fire, great care was taken to keep the flame alive. Certain people were appointed keepers of the fire, guardians to protect the sacred flames from going out. The fire of the Spirit came down upon the church at Pentecost and it is the function of the church to keep that fire from blowing out.

Faith that's more than skin deep. Paul prays that God might sanctify the believers "through and through." He prays that they might be wholly Christ's in spirit, soul, and body (v. 23). Real faith does not rest on the surface but penetrates to the marrow of our being.

Gospel: John 1:6-8, 19-28

Willing witness. The writer of the gospel seems to indicate that God sent John the Baptist into the world for one major purpose — to bear witness to the light, the truth, the Christ (vv. 6-8). Some people resist becoming witnesses because they don't want to get involved in some-body else's life. They would rather draw attention to themselves than to people or truths outside themselves. By nature, the witness registers as less important than that to which he witnesses. John had no such scruples but was always willing to witness to the truth, no matter what the consequences. We, too, are called through our baptism to be willing witnesses to the light of Christ.

The first cheerleader. John stands as one of the most powerful figures in the biblical record, yet remains one of the most self-effacing. John didn't care about being number one. He didn't seek to bask in the spotlight or, to use football terminology, be the quarterback. John repeatedly refused the top spot, content to stand on the sidelines and be the cheerleader. Rah, Rah, Rah! Go Jesus!

Boxes. The religious authorities in Jerusalem were anxious about this hermit prophet. They were the masters of religious categories (boxes) and John didn't fit into any of them. He was the son of a priest but certainly wasn't acting in a priestly fashion. Could he be the Christ? The great Elijah who would prelude the Messiah? No, he claimed neither title. He was merely a voice crying in the wilderness: "Prepare the way of the Lord." He didn't fit any of their boxes. Conse-quently, the religious leadership likely rejected or, at best, turned a deaf ear to this haunting desert voice. Through the centuries the church has all too often rejected those figures who did not fit the established boxes.

Authority. What the priests and Levites were looking for was a sense of authority. They had been authorized by the Sanhedrin (probably) to find out John's authority (v. 22). Yet John's authority came directly from God. The deputation that paid John a visit submitted to the author-ity of their ecclesiastical superiors while John found his source of authority in the God who had called him.

SERMON APPROACHES WITH ILLUSTRATIONS

Lesson 1: Isaiah 61:1-4, 8-11
Sermon Title: The Spirit Makes The Difference
Sermon Angle: Every year we observe the Martin Luther King holiday, dedicated to the memory of a man whose mission was to free people. He didn't employ tanks or guns but the power of the word. Through his biblically inspired oratory he enabled people of all races to

shake off the shackles that enslaved them. On television, his son, a handsome young man with a deeply resonant voice like his father's, spoke. He obviously had many of the gifts his father possessed but his life has had little impact on the world. What makes the difference? The answer can be found in Isaiah 61:1-3. Martin Luther King was clothed with the Spirit of God. The Spirit makes all the difference in the world.

Sermon Title: There's Power In The Word
Sermon Angle: Back in the '60s there were those in churchly circles pronouncing the death knell to the sermon. They had lost faith in the power of the spoken word. They were wrong. When a preacher allows the Spirit to proclaim the good news of God's liberation and freedom, people will listen and respond. Dr. Martin Luther King is an outstanding example of this principle. The word also has the power to free us from other kinds of bondage — selfishness, addiction, and fear. We must continue lifting up the Lord's liberating good news and grace.

Sermon Title: The Lord Is My Liberator
Sermon Angle: The prophet announced that the Lord would free his exiled people from their bondage and bring them home. This freedom would become manifest in different ways. First, as a word of liberation (to proclaim liberty to the captives). Second, as a word of comfort (v. 20). Third, as a word of favor (grace). These three points can be the outline for your sermon.

* * * * *

The Lord still liberates people from bondage. Take the case of Allen Underwood, a drug addict and dealer who spent years of his youth running on the wild side. In 1985 he landed in prison for his drug activities, where he and his wife came to the sober realization that they must radically transform their lives or it was curtains for them. They both became disciples of Christ, who transformed their lives. When Allen got out of prison, he began to speak about his former life in schools, jails, and wherever people would listen, and how he intended, with the Lord's help, to turn it around. One of the officers who arrested Allen testified to the authenticity of Allen's faith. "He's probably ministered to more people than most Christians do in a lifetime," the police officer from Grand Island, Nebraska, stated. It would be nice to leave the story on this happy note but it seems that, though God can liberate us from our bondage, we still have to live with the consequences of our actions. Allen was diagnosed HIV positive in 1992 and died toward the end of 1994. Of course, in death God performs his greatest act of liberation.

* * * * *

Lesson 2: 1 Thessalonians 5:16-24
Sermon Title: Wholly Holy
Sermon Angle: Some years back I bought a book called *Wholly Holy*. Those two words summarize what Paul communicates through verse 23, where he prays that God might sanctify the believers wholly — body, soul, and spirit. In the modern world we experience fragmentation of our being. True spirituality aims to integrate our being and make us whole. Through a life of holiness (one that is grounded in Christ) we come to experience wholeness. This sermon could be devoted to discussing how such a life might be lived.

33

Outline:
1. Discuss the fragmentation of our lives.
2. Establish that God wants us to be whole. (Discuss holiness.)
3. Put forth some strategies for wholeness (prayer, worship, recreation, and so on).
4. God will make us holy if we let him (v. 24).

Sermon Title: Jubilation!

Sermon Angle: The third Sunday in Advent has been dubbed "Rejoice Sunday." Some churches feature a rose candle in the Advent wreath to put across this theme of joy. Our lesson begins: "Rejoice always" (v. 16). This injunction seems unrealistic and out of touch with reality. Sickness, death, and tragedy sometimes steal into our lives without warning, smashing to pieces that which we hold dear. Yet joy is possible in all circumstances if we do not confuse joy with happiness. Happiness comes from the root word "hap," which means chance. Happiness depends on things going our way. Joy, on the other hand, comes from the certain knowledge of our Lord's abiding presence in all circumstances and of our coming victory through the power of the Spirit.

*   *   *   *   *

(Before sermon, write the word "joy" on sticky notes. Stick them on several worshipers.)
Good morning! This is the season of giving, so I want to share with you some serendipity. *(Pass out the stick-ons to four or five people.)* What do I mean by serendipity and what makes these stick-ons serendipitous? It seems that somebody at the 3M Company developed an adhesive but it didn't adhere very well; you could easily pull it apart. This guy thought he had failed! Then the idea came to him or to one of his coworkers. Wait a minute! We could put this adhesive on note pads and post messages where they could be seen. Voila! A serendipity! These notes have to be a huge moneymaker. A serendipity is a happy discovery we make while doing something else or seeking something else. Serendipities are never intentional. They just happen, when we have the eyes to see them. Serendipities happen to all of us, but we are not always attuned to receive them.

Now, those of you who received a note this morning have probably noticed that the word "Joy" is inscribed on the note. That's because JOY is SERENDIPITOUS. If you set out to be happy or joyous, you will probably fail. Joy comes as a by-product of seeking something greater. Our lesson informs us that joy comes as a result of loving and serving Jesus, as we watch for his return.

*   *   *   *   *

Gospel: John 1:6-8, 19-28

Sermon Title: A Life Of Witness

Sermon Angle: This passage tells us that God sent John the Baptist for the express purpose of bearing testimony to Christ; he was sent as a witness to the anointed one. John's whole life was one of witness. As followers of Christ, we too are sent to bear witness to Christ. Our job is to point the way to the one who takes away the sins of the world. This Advent season, with its emphasis on the Baptist, provides a great opportunity to encourage one another to offer our whole life to the Lord in witness to his saving grace.

Outline:
1. John's whole life was one of witness.
2. John pointed away from himself to Christ, to the light.
3. Some Christians give only a fraction of their life to Christ.
4. If we give our whole life to God, our whole life will be a witness.

Sermon Title: Know Thyself

Sermon Angle: The deputation from Jerusalem really hit John up with a barrage of personal questions. Who are you? What are you doing? Why are you doing it? John responded out of a clear sense of self and of mission. He knew himself as a servant, sent to prepare the way for the Messiah. John knew himself in relationship to the Lord. Without such knowledge, nobody can know himself. The preacher's task is to challenge the worshipers to know themselves in Christ.

Outline:
1. This text confronts us with the question of identity.
2. John was able to make a powerful witness because he knew himself.
3. Such people cause others to take notice (v. 19).
4. John did not attempt to become what he was not (vv. 19-21).
5. He defined himself through his mission (v. 23).
6. Knowing ourselves entails knowing Christ and his will for our lives.

Sermon Title: Witnesses To The Light

Sermon Angle: This lection opens with the statement that John was not *the* light but came to bear witness to the light (vv. 7-8). Witnesses in court are called upon to witness to the works of darkness and sin. A person can't go through a day without hearing testimony concerning the works of darkness. Our obsession with trials involving famous people, such as the O. J. Simpson trial, exposes our keen fascination with the realm of darkness, regardless of whether the famous person is innocent or guilty. If only we gave half as much attention to those who have committed outstanding acts of goodness, love, and grace. Like John, we have been called to bear witness to the light which is Christ.

Outline:
1. The O. J. Simpson trial and others demonstrated our fascination with evil.
2. Why do we find the realm of spiritual darkness more compelling than the realm of light?
3. The chief function of John was to point to the light.
4. It is our calling also to witness to the light.

Advent 4

Revised Common	2 Samuel 7:1-11, 16	Romans 16:25-27	Luke 1:26-38
Roman Catholic	2 Samuel 7:1-5, 8-12, 14, 16	Romans 16:25-27	Luke 1:26-38
Episcopal	2 Samuel 7:4, 8-16	Romans 16:25-27	Luke 1:26-38

Advent Theme:　　Advent Images Of God
　　　　　　　　　　The Lord Is Our House Builder

Theme For The Day: Both Old Testament and gospel portray the theme of God building a house, a kingdom, or a people. In the Old Testament text, King David desires to build a temple for God but finds out that God is going to be the one building a house (dynasty) of David's descendents. In the gospel, the angel Gabriel informs the Virgin Mary that God is going to build up his kingdom through the son she was to conceive through the Holy Spirit.

BRIEF COMMENTARY ON THE LESSONS

Lesson 1: 2 Samuel 7:1-11, 16 (C); 2 Samuel 7:1-5, 8-12, 14, 16 (RC); 2 Samuel 7:4, 8-16 (E)

David wants to build in Jerusalem a temple for the Lord but Nathan, the prophet, forbids it in the name of the Lord. The drift of the message is that the Lord doesn't need such a house. From the time of the wilderness wandering, his special abode has been the tabernacle. Some scholars regard much of this passage as a later attack on temple worship inserted in the original material, though their arguments are not completely convincing. The text is a wordplay on the word "house" (Hebrew — *bayrith*). David desires to construct for the Lord a physical house but is told that God would himself make of David (his family) a house, defined as family or dynasty (v. 15). The Lord would carve out for his people a place of safety and security (v. 10). David's throne would endure forever. Of course, David's dynasty came to an end in 587 BC and so the prophecy was not fulfilled in the intended manner. The Christian church interprets this passage messianically and regards Jesus as the Son of David who ushers in the eternal kingdom, not just for Israel but for all believers.

Lesson 2: Romans 16:25-27 (C, RC, E)

This doxology provides a fitting conclusion for Paul's epistle to the Romans because it lifts up the gospel of Christ as the revelation of the mystery of salvation. Through the gospel God hopes to bring all people into the family of God. The prophetic promises, fulfilled in Christ, are received through faith.

Gospel: Luke 1:26-38 (C, RC, E)

The angel Gabriel announces to the Virgin Mary that she is to bear the Messiah. Mary quakes in the presence of the heavenly messenger but still has the courage to ask how this might come to pass. She is told that it would be the work of God's Holy Spirit in fulfillment of the prophecies of the old covenant. As a sign, the angel relates that the Lord had already brought about a miraculous pregnancy in the life of her older kinswoman, Elizabeth (vv. 36-37). Mary receives the glorious announcement in humble submission to the will of God. In this passage we view continuity and novelty. God would fulfill his promise to his people in a wonderful and vastly more inclusive manner.

Psalm Of The Day

Psalm 89:1-4, 19-28 (C) — "I will appoint my firstborn, the most exalted of all the kings of the earth" (v. 27).

Psalm 132 (E)

Psalm 88 (RC)

Prayer Of The Day

Creator God, on the foundation of Israel you have built a house where there is room for all, where Jesus Christ lives as the true cornerstone. Unite us with him and all the saints in a living structure that will never crumble. Through Jesus Christ, our Lord. Amen.

THEOLOGICAL REFLECTION ON THE LESSONS

Lesson 1: 2 Samuel 7:1-11, 16

God doesn't need a house. That was the basic message that Nathan delivered to David. However, the Lord does desire a home. Houses are made of wood, stone, brick, and mortar. Homes are made of family members who love and care for us. Houses are inanimate; homes are living, breathing organisms. God tells David that he will build the house for him, not the other way around, a house not made of wood and stone but flesh and blood. Is there a home in your house for the Lord to dwell in?

How to build a secure house. In verse 16 God promises David that his house and kingdom would remain secure forever. That promise only has reality through the kingdom of Christ. We inhabit an age where crime and the fear of crime have led to a siege mentality. Americans are buying guns and security systems as never before. Women crowd into courses teaching self-defense. In the Middle Ages castles were constructed for maximum security, with moats, walls, and watchtowers. In the long run, they provided little security and were soon obsolete. In the modern era we have tried to make our national house safe through sophisticated weaponry. What makes a house secure? God does!

God on the move. God reminds David that in the wilderness wandering period his name was worshiped in a tent. Such is the way of a nomadic people whose god travels with his people. Our God is not planted in one place but travels about with us. The God revealed in the Old and New Testaments is on the move.

From pasture to palace (v. 8). God reminds David that he called him from being a shepherd to being a king. The Lord had highly exalted his servant. David was sent to establish the reign of God over his people in the land of Israel. Though God could not be planted in a particular place, he certainly strove to establish his people, the Jews, in a certain locale (v. 10). To belong to a place gives one a sense of security, of belonging. Home and family come to be associated with a particular place. Millions have given their lives to protect their home turf. Nevertheless, history shows any homeland to be fleeting and uncertain. The Hebrews had to learn that their only security was their relationship with Yahweh, not their anchor hold to the promised land.

Lesson 2: Romans 16:25-27

Personal gospel. Paul refers to "my gospel" (v. 1). This expression seems rather arrogant. After all, it isn't Paul's gospel but the gospel of Christ. Yet there remains a truth here. The Christian gospel must become a part of us, it needs to be personalized and integrated into our being.

Personal, not private. The gospel must be personalized but not privatized. As Paul explains, this gospel was a secret for a long time but now is being made known to all nations by the command of the eternal God. We have an obligation to make known the mystery of God.

Standing firm. Paul commends his hearers to the God who is able to make them stand firm. If they did not keep their focus, it would be easy to be swept away by the forces of paganism. In our era we, too, need to remember to stand firm against the forces that deny God or those who would keep faith and life in separate compartments.

Gospel: Luke 1:26-38

Voice messaging. One can hardly live through a day without encountering a voice messaging system. If you want new products, hit #1 on your phone. If you want to talk to so and so, punch #2. The impersonality of such systems can be deeply frustrating. When God wants to convey a message of great import, he sends his personal messengers. Some of them are called prophets and teachers but the Lord also has otherworldly messengers known as angels. The word *angelos* means both angel and messenger. God sent not just any angel but a special angel by the name of Gabriel. God has a better way of doing voice messaging.

Greetings, favored one (v. 28). That was the message with which the angel greeted Virgin Mary. Mary certainly was favored beyond all other mortals. Was she favored because of her moral purity? That was an issue but that alone doesn't explain it. Did the Lord sense that Mary would be receptive to his grace and so he favored her? Mary certainly was that sort of person but this still doesn't cut to the heart of the matter. The prime reason for Mary's favored status was the sovereign grace of God. The Lord doesn't favor people because of any quality within them. It's God's nature to bestow his favor, even on the sinful, the weak, and the undeserving. God grants his favor to all who freely let the gospel conceive new life in their hearts.

Holy fear. When Mary encountered the angel, her first impulse was fear, even though the message was one of grace (v. 29). Such a response is quite natural, as we can see from numerous accounts in scripture. When we sinners stand in the presence of the one who is eternal and holy, we are overwhelmed with a sense of our imperfection. However, for those who are open to his grace, God moves quickly to allay our fears with his favor.

Beyond limits. After the angel announced that Elizabeth was also pregnant, he pronounced that nothing was impossible with God (v. 37). God remains beyond limits even though we humans try to establish the borders across which even the almighty cannot pass. For instance, some might say that God only works through medical technology but that he doesn't heal instantaneously through the power of prayer. Or we claim that the Lord works though one ecclesiastical structure but not another. Or we exclaim, "God will never be able to get through to that person!" Isn't it time we freed God from our rationalistic constraints?

SERMON APPROACHES WITH ILLUSTRATIONS

Lesson 1: 2 Samuel 7:1-11, 16

Sermon Title: The Lord Has Built A House For You

Sermon Angle: David wanted to build the Lord a house to dwell in but was told through prophecy that the Lord was going to construct a house for David. David intended a building but the Lord was not thinking of *house* in human terms. He would make of David a great people, a nation. Through Christ, we are brought into God's household.

Outline:

1. David wanted to construct a house for God.
2. God didn't want a house to dwell in.
3. The Lord wanted to make a nation (house) of David's descendents.
4. Through Mary's Son, God built a house for all people (gospel lesson).
5. We inhabit this house through faith.

* * * * *

At the time of this writing (January 1995) a devastating earthquake has struck Kobe, Japan, toppling thousands of buildings, even those termed "quake proof," crushing hundreds under the debris. The scenes I viewed on CNN of blazing fires, smoldering rubble, and scores of dazed victims seeking shelter seemed like scenes from some apocalyptic novel. The anchorman asked the on-the-scene reporter how the people were reacting to this tragedy. He stated that the course of events seems to have had an equalizing effect on the populace. The old social distinctions lost their relevance. One could not tell if the person waiting in line for assistance was a doctor or a laborer. The earthquake merged the homeless sufferers into a family of the dispossessed where each had equal standing.

Before the quake, when each had a place to live, most of the dispossessed would not have been eager to extend hospitality and warmth to those they encountered on the streets. Ironically, after their dwellings were destroyed, these same folks were willing to share whatever habitation they had with their nameless neighbor. It takes more than a house to make a home.

* * * * *

Sermon Title: How To Build God's House

Sermon Angle: What kind of house does God require? Down through millennia, humankind has built its temples as a place to worship its gods. They thought of the deity or deities in territorial terms, the god of this place or that place. The God of the Old Testament dwelt in a tent leading his people on a pilgrimage. Yahweh didn't require a fixed structure. He preferred to live within the community. It seems that the temple was something of a concession to the wants of the people. Through the womb of the Virgin Mary God has come to dwell evermore intimately with his people. He resides in our hearts and relationships. Was that not the gracious message the angel conveyed to Mary?

* * * * *

39

It's ironic that building programs can sometimes destroy rather than build up the church. I know of an architect turned pastor whose prime aim upon arriving at a certain congregation was to build a new church building. The board was hesitant. "Pastor, we can't afford the kind of structure you envision." One key leader added, "No self-respecting bank would even give us the loan we need." "Tell you what," said the pastor. "If I obtain the loan, will you go along with it?" The leader agreed, thinking that there was no way. To cut to the quick, the pastor obtained a loan. Not a good one, a five- to seven-year balloon loan. The whole principal came due in a relatively short period of time. The congregation began to sink under this tidal wave of debt, which caused the congregation to assume a survival mentality. All energies were consumed by the debt. Only through hard work and the grace of God did these people of God keep their head above the surface. This story illustrates what happens when pastors and congregations become focused on building structures and monuments rather than the people of God and the mission of Christ.

* * * * *

Lesson 2: Romans 16:25-27
Sermon Title: The Power Of Good News
Sermon Angle: Paul's benediction states that God is able to strengthen believers through the gospel. Good news certainly has an uplifting effect, just as bad news can make our knees buckle. God empowers us through the good news of Christ and we are called to witness to the gospel and spread good news. God strengthens us through such proclamation. Preaching still has power, God's power.

Gospel: Luke 1:26-38
Sermon Title: Angel Messaging
Sermon Angle: Modern technology has come up with voice messaging in order to connect people to those with whom they need to communicate. Sometimes you encounter several dead ends before you reach someone who has the right word for you. God has angel messaging for those really important events. He sent the angel Gabriel to Mary to announce the joyous news of Jesus' birth. All of us have had angels bear a message of hope or help at various times. No, not many of us have encountered visitors from heaven, but we have received human messengers (angels) who were heaven-sent. Such messengers have communicated God's grace to us. We also are called to be such messengers.
Outline:
1. God sent Gabriel to Mary as his heavenly messenger.
2. The angel allayed Mary's fears and imparted direction.
3. At what points in your life has God sent you a messenger of grace?
4. To whom is God sending you as his messenger of the gospel?

* * * * *

Angels have become a hot topic in the past few years. Several books have gained immense popularity, such as Sophy Burnham's *A Book Of Angels*, which recounts her experience with angels as well as the encounters of other people. It seems that rationalism has not proven satisfying. Millions are seeking to connect with the transcendent, the supernatural. While some of these attempts to connect with the supernatural are misguided, this openness to the things of the spirit can be an asset. Many of us in the mainline churches have spent most of our energies in merely talking about God rather than actually enabling people to connect personally and experientially with God.

*   *   *   *   *

Sermon Title: Christ Bearers

Sermon Angle: Mary was given the glorious news that she was going to bear the Christ, the Son of God. She quite naturally questioned how this might be since she had no husband and was told it was through the power of the Spirit. While we honor Mary, is it not true that every Christian is a Christ bearer? When we yield our lives to God, as did Mary, the power of the Spirit comes upon us. The difference is that Mary conceived in her womb and we conceive Christ in our hearts and minds through faith.

Sermon Title: Possibilities Unlimited

Sermon Angle: Nothing is too great for God. As the angel told Mary, "For nothing is impossible for God" (v. 37). Some have questioned whether the virgin birth was possible. Following the same logic, you'd have to question the miracles of Christ and the greatest miracle of all, the resurrection. All things remain possible for God. Taking that thought a step further, all things are possible for us through the power of God. As Paul stated: "I can do all things through Christ, who strengthens me." This sermon could challenge listeners to overcome their fears through acting out in faith.

Outline:

1. God gave new life to Mary and Elizabeth when it seemed impossible.
2. New life comes when we permit God's Spirit to take control.
3. What hurdle are you facing that seems impossible?
4. Yield yourself to God, like Mary did (v. 38).

Christmas Eve/Christmas Day

Revised Common	Isaiah 9:2-7	Titus 2:11-14	Luke 2:1-20
Roman Catholic	Isaiah 9:1-7	Titus 2:11-14	Luke 2:1-14
Episcopal	Isaiah 9:2-4, 6-7	Titus 2:11-14	Luke 2:1-14 (15-20)

Theme For The Day: God has come among us in the person of his Son. Let us rejoice!

BRIEF COMMENTARY ON THE LESSONS

Lesson 1: Isaiah 9:2-7 (C); Isaiah 9:1-7 (RC); Isaiah 9:2-4, 6-7 (E)

This lovely poem was composed at a time of historical darkness. The Assyrians had defeated Zebulon and Naphtali, taking them captive in 734 BC. The threat of national annihilation was very real. Nevertheless, Isaiah holds high the light of hope, anchored not in humans but in God's deliverance. The Messiah, the ideal king and servant of God, becomes the object of that hope. Through this "Anointed One" God will usher in permanent peace with righteousness. Christians have long maintained that Jesus, the Christ, fulfills that hope.

Lesson 2: Titus 2:11-14 (C, RC, E)

The book of Titus lays out the responsibilities of the various groups within the church, starting with the bishops and elders. This passage follows a section on the responsibility of slaves to their masters. Rather than change the social systems of this world, believers are instructed to discharge their duties with utmost fidelity. It is expected that Christ will change everything at his expected imminent return. What matters is that the grace of God has appeared for the salvation of all people (v. 11). Therefore, believers are to await their blessed hope by assuming a life of godliness and goodness.

Gospel: Luke 2:1-20 (C, E); Luke 2:1-14 (RC)

Luke's poetic account of our Lord's Nativity never fails to capture our attention and fill our souls with rapture. The juxtaposition of the heavenly and miraculous (angelic choirs and virgin birth) alongside earthly elements (a humble virgin, lowly shepherds, and a birth in a stable) grabs our attention. Heaven has invaded the earth. Note the prominence of songs of praise. Christmas remains more a song to be sung than merely a story to be told.

Psalm Of The Day
Psalm 96 (C, E) — "O sing to the Lord a new song; sing to the Lord, all the earth" (v. 1).
Psalm 95:1-3, 11-13 (RC)

Prayer Of The Day
O Lord, our king, you have invaded the night of our sin and suffering with the glorious news of a newborn Savior and king. When the carols fade, empower us to sing your praises and proclaim the good news of Christ's coming. In Jesus' name. Amen.

THEOLOGICAL REFLECTION ON THE LESSONS

Lesson 1: Isaiah 9:2-7

Old but ever new. Isaiah exalts, "Unto us a child is born." Yet this child is to bear the weight of the government on his shoulders. Oddly, he is dubbed "everlasting Father" (v. 6). This newborn king comes from the same substance as the Ancient of Days. As the Nicene Creed states: "He [Christ] is very God of very God."

Wonderful counselor. We consider a counselor to be a personal guide but Isaiah refers here to the governance of the nation. Our ruler has the wisdom to lead us out of the darkness of human greed and bondage. When will the nations of the world seek his rule?

Everlasting Father. The *U.S. News and World Report* cover for February 27, 1995, featured a picture of a father holding his child, with the caption "Why Fathers Count." Two of every five children do not live with their fathers. Who can deny that fatherlessness looms as one of our most disturbing trends? The image of father may be tarnished but this does not diminish his importance. How wonderful to know that God will always be there for us as our "Everlasting Father"!

Lesson 2: Titus 2:11-14

Grace for all. Picture a mother dog who has given birth to a large litter of puppies who are scrambling to find an available nipple to feed on. What often happens is that the weaker and more docile pups have to be satisfied with what is left. Consequently, they don't become as strong and are known as the "runts of the litter." When it comes to receiving the milk of God's grace we all have equal access. "The grace and loving kindness of God appeared for the salvation of all people" (v. 11).

A glory concealed and revealed. The glory of God remained largely concealed in the person of Jesus. This glory could only be seen through the eyes of faith. Titus speaks of waiting for the "glory of our great God and Savior, Jesus Christ" (v. 13). The glory of Christ will be fully revealed to all when he comes in kingdom power.

Moral revolution. Christians are not only saved from the penalty of sin to await Christ's coming in power but are being transformed morally and ethically in the interim between the Lord's two comings. This involves two things: renouncing godless ways and worldly ambitions on the one hand, and devoting ourselves to a life of good works on the other. Christ's salvation brought about a spiritual revolution in our way of relating to God but a moral revolution in our way of relating to others.

Gospel: Luke 2:1-14 (15-20)

To be delivered (v. 6). Note the passive voice here. Luke doesn't state that the time came for the Virgin to deliver (active voice) but that she was delivered (passive voice). Mary is not the actor in this drama, God is; she merely allowed herself to be acted upon. Redemption occurs when we permit God's Spirit to act upon us and through us.

Unwrapped? (v. 7). After the Virgin Mary gave birth, she wrapped her baby in swaddling clothes, according to the custom of the day. Such wrapping quiets the infant by providing a snug and secure environment similar to the womb. God's Christmas present came wrapped in a tiny package. Have we unwrapped the gift of Christ through faith and drawn him close to our bosom?

How great our joy (v. 10). The Christmas proclamation contains news of unbounded joy, so the angels announced to the shepherds. The promise of the Messiah had been fulfilled in the birth of the Bethlehem babe. Their joy was heightened by the realization that the Messiah was a personal gift to them, lowly though they be. "For to you is born this day in the city of David a Savior" (v. 11).

See for yourself. After the angels announced the birth of the Christ Child, the shepherds responded: "Let us go now to Bethlehem and see this thing which the Lord has made known to us" (v. 15). The gospel invites us to see and experience for ourselves. We see this concept in the call of Jesus' first disciples, according to the gospel of John. They said, "Rabbi, where are you staying?" "Come," he replied, "and you will see" (John 1:38b-39a). To be real, the story of Christ must be revealed in a first person form. Christian faith begins as a story we've been told but needs to move to a story we have come to experience.

SERMON APPROACHES WITH ILLUSTRATIONS

A Preaching Theme Drawn From ALL The Lessons
Sermon Title: This Christ Is For YOU!
Sermon Angle: All three lessons point out that the gift of the Messiah-Savior is very personal and all-inclusive.
Outline:
1. Lesson 1: Isaiah 9:6 — "For to us is born a Savior...."
2. Lesson 2: Titus 2:11 — "The grace of God has appeared for the salvation of all humanity."
3. Gospel: Luke 2:11 — "For to you is born this day ... a Savior."
4. Have you received God's gift to you?

Lesson 1: Isaiah 9:2-7
Sermon Title: Light In Our Present Darkness
Sermon Angle: Isaiah offered hope for those facing the very real possibility of national annihilation. Those who walked in darkness would see a great light. Perhaps this hope was occasioned by the birth of one from David's lineage. At any rate, Isaiah was confident God would supply light in their present darkness. We, too, experience the darkness all around in the form of a deteriorating social structure, where only about half of the children in our country live with both parents, and where violence is a constant threat. Only the light of Christ can save us.
Outline:
1. Discuss the darkness that Isaiah's countrymen faced.
2. Christmas occurs during the darkest time of the year.
   — We acknowledge the darkness of human sin. (Give examples.)
3. Christmas celebrates the light of Christ in our present darkness.

Sermon Title: The Perfect Government
Sermon Angle: "And the government will be upon his shoulder" (v. 6). The hope of Israel's prophets focused on the righteous rule of God through his anointed one. Unfortunately, no human being or political system was capable of such governance, as the history of Israel bears out so graphically. Only God can bring in the reign of everlasting peace and righteousness. That hope will only be fulfilled when the kingdom has fully come in the person of Jesus, the Christ.

Outline:
1. Since the glory days of King David, the Jews longed for the perfect king.
2. Since the enlightenment, people have sought other types of perfect government.
3. Imperfect people cannot usher in a perfect government.
4. Christians seek God's perfect reign in the kingdom of Christ.

Lesson 2: Titus 2:11-14
Sermon Title: Grace For All
Sermon Angle: The grace of God is not stingy or exclusive but generous and abounding. "The grace of God has appeared for the salvation of all people" (v. 11).
Outline:
1. Humans tend to bestow their gifts on their own clan or kin.
2. We also bestow gifts on those we deem deserving.
3. God's gift of grace and love overflow to all who will claim it.

Sermon Title: The Passion Of Christmas
Sermon Angle: Christians normally associate the word "passion" with the account of our Lord's suffering and death. At Christmas we also celebrate the passion of our God to save sinners and make us holy. Titus teaches that receiving God's grace causes us to renounce worldly passions and become zealous (passionate) for good works. Has the passion of God ignited in your heart?
Outline:
1. God's passion is to save all (v. 11).
2. The gospel turns our human passion upside down (v. 12).
3. God's passion centers on perfecting a people who are passionate for goodness.

Gospel: Luke 2:1-14 (15-20)
Sermon Title: The Questions And Answers Of Christmas
Sermon Angle: A good news story will answer the questions — who, what, where, why, so what? Luke's account provides some concrete answers.
Outline:
1. Who is born? A Savior, Christ the Lord (v. 11).
2. Where? In a Bethlehem stable. Is he also born in our hearts? (v. 11).
3. Why? To save us and rule us (v. 11).
4. So what? This Christ is for us (v. 11) that we might live for others.

Sermon Title: Where To Look For God
Sermon Angle: Yuri Gagarin, the first Russian astronaut, made the flippant observation that he didn't see God in outer space. His problem was that he was looking in the wrong place; he wasn't looking low enough. The Christmas gospel finds Christ in the lowliest of places (a manger), accompanied by the humblest of people (shepherds, Mary, and Joseph).
Outline:
1. Are you having trouble locating God in your life?
2. Perhaps you are looking in the wrong places.
3. Christ was born in the humblest of circumstances.
4. Look low to find Christ: in your pain, your sin, and your weakness.

*   *   *   *   *

Gagarin thought that if God exists the deity could be viewed in the far reaches of outer space. The gospel tells us that we have already closely encountered the king of the universe in this world in the person of Jesus. After all, that's the meaning of Immanuel: God with us. The movies *Close Encounters Of The Third Kind* and *E.T.* lend themselves to the Christmas story.

A couple of years ago, when I was teaching a confirmation class, we were discussing the story of our Lord's Nativity and I challenged them to find the extraterrestrial creatures contained in the Christmas story. Their first response was, "You're putting me on!" Finally, one of the students questioningly replied: "Angels?" "Right on!" I said. Angels are big right now. Even non-traditional believers accept angels. If angels aren't extraterrestrials, I don't know who are.

In Stephen Spielberg's smash movie, *E.T.*, a little boy first encounters an extraterrestrial alien stranded on earth. The name of the extraterrestrial is E.T., and it is a little wizened creature with a wrinkly appearance and long fingers. When the boy and E.T. first meet each other, they are both frightened but soon become friends. This close encounter of the extraterrestrial kind caused alarm and defensive measures among the officials because of the fear that the presence of an alien signaled an attempt to invade and conquer the earth. However, E.T. was a friendly, peaceful creature who posed no threat at all.

Christmas is also a story of close encounters between heaven and earth. As we have already mentioned, it is a story of numerous encounters between angels and humans. An angel announced the birth of John the Baptist to his father Zechariah, as he ministered in the temple. An angel announced to the blessed Virgin Mary that she would become pregnant with the Messiah and then told Joseph not to be afraid to take Mary as his wife, even though she was pregnant. When Jesus was actually born, an angel announced the good news to shepherds, according to Luke, who were soon joined by a chorus of the heavenly host, singing praises to God. In Matthew's version of the nativity, an angel warns Joseph to take Mary and the child and flee to Egypt, to escape the wrath of King Herod. After the king died, an angel told Joseph that it was safe to return home.

Yes, Christmas is a story of close encounters with extraterrestrials, angels, who serve out their role as messengers, but they are not the main characters. They are only the supporting cast. The main close encounter comes in the form of the baby Jesus, who would save all people from their sins. The Christmas story is like the movie *E.T.* in that the main characters are children or child-like. Both E.T. and Jesus appear on this earth weak, vulnerable, and at the mercy of others. However, the Christmas story differs in that Jesus is no alien. He is born into the world as one of us. Jesus fulfills the prophecy of Isaiah that Jesus will be called Immanuel, God with us. God came so close in Jesus, yet most people did not realize it.

*   *   *   *   *

Sermon Title: Joy To The World

Sermon Angle: Christmas is supposed to be a time of great joy and happiness. Sadly, the pains and pressures of life can steal our joy. This season finds many people crying on the inside and laughing on the outside. Joy remains far from universal, even in the most celebrative season. The angel announced to the shepherds that their news of great joy would reach all people (v. 10).

Outline:
1. How well has your joy held up this Christmas season?
2. What's the formula for joy? Don't focus on what you have to do but what God has already done for us.
3. We must be sensitive to the needs of the sad and sorrowing.
4. Hold high God's promise that his good news will bring joy to all the world.

* * * * *

The angels informed the shepherds of a sign: a babe wrapped in swaddling cloths and lying in a manger. Believers have long looked for signs or omens to substantiate their faith, and the Bible provides several examples where God provides a sign. One Native American legend tells of a "white buffalo woman" who visited a starving tribe, giving them spiritual knowledge that allowed them successfully to hunt the buffalo throughout the Great Plains. A highly revered medicine man named Floyd Hand contends that the buffalo woman has returned and will bring about a wonderful human reconciliation.

Thousands of Native Americans saw the birth of a white buffalo, named Miracle, as a sign pointing to the fulfillment of this prophecy. According to a past article in *U.S. News*, some 32,000 people made the sacred pilgrimage to Janesville, Wisconsin, to view the sign. Some of the believers wept; offerings of sage, tobacco, and small pieces of netting called "dream catchers" were tied to the fence. Miracle's owner refused to charge admission, observing that "folks walk out of there like they have looked upon Christ."

This story points to the need for signs of hope. Nevertheless, for us Christians, only the sign of the infant in swaddling cloths provides hope for a future reconciliation of all creation.

Christmas 1

Revised Common	Isaiah 61:10—62:3	Galatians 4:4-7	Luke 2:22-40
Roman Catholic	Sirach 3:2-6, 12-14	Colossians 3:12-21	Luke 2:22-40
Episcopal	Isaiah 61:10—62:3	Galatians 3:23-25; 4:4-7	John 1:1-18

Theme For The Day: Hope for the future. Simeon and Anna viewed Jesus as the fulfillment of their people's hopes and dreams. In a similar manner we see our hopes being fulfilled in our children and youth. We can be advanced in years and still live in hope.

BRIEF COMMENTARY ON THE LESSONS

Lesson 1: Isaiah 61:10—62:3 (C, E)

The prophet of the third portion of Isaiah (circa 530 BC) holds up a brilliant hope for the discouraged Israelites returning from exile to their own land. He thanks God for clothing him in the Lord's robe of righteousness. He compares God's salvation to a new planting (v. 11). It doesn't look like much now but it will grow. In another metaphor he compares the relationship between the Lord and his people to that of a new bride and groom (vv. 3-5).

Lesson 1: Sirach 3:2-6, 12-14 (RC)

The blessings of honoring one's mother and father.

Lesson 2: Galatians 4:4-7 (C); Galatians 3:23-25; 4:4-7 (E)

When the time was right, God sent his Son, fully human, to redeem sinful humanity and make us God's children. God has given his Spirit to those who are his own and through his Spirit we cry out to God as our dear Father. We are no longer slaves to sin but children of God.

Lesson 2: Colossians 3:12-21 (RC)

Chapter 3 begins with the proposition that if we have been raised with Christ, then seek the things that are above. In the same vein, believers are to put to death what is sinful (vv. 5-9). Continuing with the thought with which the chapter begins, Paul urges the believers to put on Christ's garment of righteousness. This garment will be made visible in such things as compassion, kindness, humility, and so forth.

Gospel: Luke 2:22-40 (C, RC)

Mary and Joseph, being a devout couple, brought Jesus to the temple. Two ceremonies took place. First the "Redemption of the Firstborn." Every male, man, or beast, was regarded as belonging to the Lord. To fulfill this duty, an offering of five shekels was mandated. The other ceremony was for Mary's purification. For thirty days after childbirth, women were considered ritually unclean. A lamb and a pigeon were called for, but since that was beyond the means of many poor women, the law admitted that two pigeons would suffice. The fact that Mary offered the lesser offering indicates the modest economic means of the holy family.

While discharging these duties, an old man, Simeon, and an old woman, Anna, who were looking and longing for the Lord's Messiah, spied Jesus and spoke of him as the fulfillment of

Israel's spiritual longings. Simeon was now ready to die because he had seen the dawning of the fulfillment of God's deliverance.

Gospel: John 1:1-18 (E)
See Christmas 2.

Psalm Of The Day
Psalm 148 (C); Psalm 147 (E) — "Praise the Lord!" (Psalm 148:1a).
Psalm 127:1-5 (RC)

Prayer Of The Day
God of hope, you fulfilled your promise of a Savior to the children of Israel through Jesus, your Son. Help us to persevere in hope as did Simeon and Anna, especially during times of discouragement and trial, that we might rejoice as our redemption draws near. In Jesus' name. Amen.

THEOLOGICAL REFLECTIONS ON THE LESSONS

Lesson 1: Isaiah 61:10—62:3
The joy of the wedding (61:10). The joy of God's redeemed is like the joy of the bride and the groom. Isaiah predicted that the returning exiles would know that kind of joy. We now know, through Christ, that this kind of joy will only be a constant reality in the kingdom of heaven. Normally the greatest joy for a new bride and groom is to be in the beloved's presence. Unfortunately sin dulls that joy. However, in the kingdom, our joy of being in the bridegroom's presence will not grow dim.

The robe of righteousness. It was and is expected that both participant and guest of a wedding wear appropriate attire. In our western culture, the bride wears a white dress, symbolic of purity. Isaiah exalts that God has clothed his people with the robe of righteousness. That is certainly true for those of us who have put on Christ.

God marries his people. The imagery of marriage turns up frequently in the Bible to illustrate the relationship of God to his people and is the primary image of this passage. God loves us, delights in us, and has pledged himself to us (covenanted with us). Such a love calls for faithfulness on our part.

Lesson 2: Galatians 4:4-7
The time was ripe. Paul maintains that God sent Christ in the fullness (completeness) of time. The word for time (*kairos*) denotes quality of time, not quantity. Not only was the time right, it was ripe. When a fruit reaches its zenith of sweetness, firmness, and tastiness, we say that it is ripe. God never rushes things but waits until the time is ripe or right, as when he sent his Son. We also must be ready to pick the fruit of God when it is ripe.

A familial spirit. Paul argues that followers of Christ are no longer slaves of sin, held captive under the law, but have been granted the gift of being God's children. As God's children, we have been gifted with the Spirit of his Son, which is also the Spirit of the Father. The Holy Spirit comes as a familial Spirit and is shared by all who belong to Christ's family.

Lesson 2: Colossians 3:12-21

Therefore. "Put on then ..." (v. 12). All of the admonitions in this chapter are based on a prior action or decision. Verse 12 harks back to verse 10, which refers to our having put on Christ's new nature. If we have put on the new nature, we must also put on the behavior that flows from that new state of being. Our life of faith remains the consequence of God's prior action. Doing flows from being and must be consistent with it.

Love is above (v. 14). Love is higher and more important than all the other things we are asked to put on. Not only is love above in importance but in origin. We figuratively speak of God and goodness as coming from above. Certainly love emanates from above, from God. Is love above all other realities in our lives?

The incarnate word and Word. The apostle urges his hearers to let the word of God dwell in them richly (RSV). He refers to the scriptures, psalms, and hymns. The Word (Christ) becomes incarnate in us as we permit God's word to be absorbed into the center of our being as we dwell in it and on it.

Gospel: Luke 2:22-40

Worship in the Spirit. The words "Spirit" or "Holy Spirit" are employed three times in verses 25-27. Because Simeon was filled with the Spirit he was able to recognize the Messiah. Also it was through the Holy Spirit that he worshiped and praised God as he held the Christ in his arms. True worship only occurs when we open our spirit to God's Spirit.

From the particular to the universal. God's revelation moves from the universal to the particular, that he might lift us from our particularity to his universality. The Lord appeared to a particular people at a particular time, that he might unite all people in his love. Simeon acknowledges this truth in his song (vv. 31-32).

Free at last. Simeon prayed that the Lord would let him depart in peace. He was now ready to die, since he had seen the fulfillment of God's promise. This figure of speech derives from the manumission of slaves. What was Simeon asking to be freed from? The power of sin? The dominance of the law? Perhaps. Most likely, he is praying that the Lord would free him from the constraints of the body. For those who love the Lord, death is not eternal imprisonment in a grave but freedom from the bonds of earthly existence.

The power of persistent prayer. Simeon and Anna present us with images of hoary holiness. Their faith was phenomenal! For decades they persisted in praying for the redemption of their people, the fulfillment of God's promises. Anna, it seems, spent most of her time in the temple praying. Their experience holds out the promise that God will reveal himself to those who continue to seek him. The case of Simeon and Anna also presents us with an interesting question. Would God have revealed his salvation in Christ without the earnest, persistent prayers of people like them?

December meets January. Simeon and Anna represent December. In December we're moving toward the close of the year. We strive to complete our mission in life and look forward to the time when we can celebrate its completion. For some people December has arrived. The baby Jesus represents January. The promise of a whole new wonderful life and mission was wrapped in his being. Yet there would be deep pain and suffering (vv. 34-35). Jesus symbolizes the promise of life and salvation. Simeon and Anna represent promise fulfilled. January offers us the promise of the race of life. In December the goal line of that race is just ahead. Whether we live in January or December, the Lord's faithful have great cause to rejoice.

SERMON APPROACHES WITH ILLUSTRATIONS

Lesson 1: Isaiah 61:10 — 62:3

Sermon Title: Dressing For Salvation

Sermon Angle: In verse 10 the prophet exalts that God has clothed him with the garments of salvation. We don't pick out the wardrobe. God has already done so. We are saved not by our efforts but God's grace. By the light of the gospel, we see that faith in God's Son is the robe of righteousness. The world teaches us to dress for success but the Bible instructs us how to be clothed for salvation.

Outline:
1. The importance of being dressed properly for the occasion.
2. The world teaches how to dress to get yourself noticed.
3. The Bible teaches the importance of being clothed with faith, love, and so forth.
4. Rejoice! God has clothed us with the garment of salvation (v. 10).

Lesson 2: Galatians 4:4-7

Sermon Title: Under The Law

Sermon Angle: Paul takes pains to point out that God's Son was born *under* the law so that he might redeem those who were also under the sway of God's laws. The gospel lesson makes a similar point when it states that Mary and Joseph brought Jesus to the temple so that they might fulfill the requirements of the law. Jesus always lived under the laws of God (not necessarily of man) so that he might fulfill them in our stead. Many people now think that they are above the law or beyond the law. Not so! By putting on Christ through faith we meet the just demands of God's law.

Outline:
1. Jesus was born under the law (v. 4) and subject to all human obligations.
2. Some people act as if they were above the law. (Give examples.)
3. Jesus fulfilled the law of God in our place.
4. Through faith we earn the right to be called God's children (vv. 5-7).

Gospel: Luke 2:22-40

Sermon Title: The Christmas Spirit

Sermon Angle: We sometimes refer to the celebrative attitude visible in the Christmas season as the "Christmas spirit." That assessment is not necessarily correct because the "Christmas spirit" is much more than a jolly ho-ho demeanor. The Christmas spirit is embodied in the words and deeds of Simeon and Anna. It comes as a spirit of joy, hope, expectancy, and worship. Luke goes to lengths to point out that Simeon was filled with the Holy Spirit, which made it possible for him to recognize and celebrate the Christ Child.

Outline:
1. Now that the Lord's birthday party is ended, has your Christmas spirit gotten up and gone?
2. What does it mean to have the Christmas spirit and what is its origin?
3. Simeon and Anna incarnate the Christmas spirit — they lived hopeful, prayerful, worshipful, and vigilant lives — pointing the way (v. 38) to others.
4. Their lives point to how we can have the Christmas spirit all year long.

*   *   *   *   *

The good news of Christmas proclaims that God comes to us in the midst of the mess, right where we are. God came to Wendy, a mother and also professor of spirituality at a Catholic university, in the midst of the meat department of a supermarket. The overheated store brought beads of sweat to her brow and the smell of liver made her vaguely nauseous in her pregnant state. Striving to keep her toddlers at bay and struggling to complete preparations for the holiday, all joy faded from her countenance. At this nadir of Christmas spirit, her ears were captured by the familiar carol.

Joy to the world, the Lord is come! The words bore a hole in her soul as they paraded across the eyes of her mind.

Let earth receive her king! She stood transfixed, with tomato paste in her hand.

Let every heart prepare him room. She reported: "The floodgates of my heart were flung open and a vast and spacious wonderment filled me." (gleaned from an article in the *Omaha World-Herald*, "The Christmas Promise" by Julia McCord)

*   *   *   *   *

Sermon Title: Lifting Up The Christ

Sermon Angle: Simeon took the baby Jesus up in his arms and blessed God (v. 28). He not only embraced this little one as his Messiah but he lifted him up to God in worship and to the world in witness, as did Anna. To be a Christian involves the same steps. Embracing Jesus in faith; then lifting him in thanksgiving to God for the gift of salvation and lifting him in witness to others as the fulfillment of our hopes.

Outline:
1. To be a Christian means to lift up Jesus Christ in faith, as did Simeon.
2. Lift Christ up in worship (v. 28).
3. Lift him up in witness (vv. 29-32).

*   *   *   *   *

The last point in the above outline is borne out by this story. Joy Thompson of the *Press Telegram* was bemoaning to a friend the ruthlessness of business practices in this era of downsizing, takeovers, and layoffs. The friend sent her to a meeting of the "Fellowship of Christ International." This group of CEs views such matters from a very different perspective. The president of the group stated that people, not profits, are the most important and valuable asset. "People are forever" was the subject of the morning's focus, with the discussion centering around how employers could and should treat their employees with respect and decency. The discussion leader asked the participants whether they prayed for their employees and if they knew their people well enough to know what to pray for. Lifting up Christ begins with Sunday worship but must be completed in the places where we live and work.

*   *   *   *   *

52

Sermon Title: Growing In Grace

Sermon Angle: Growth is such a wonderful gift! Do you recall the excitement of growing up when you were a child? Do you recall measuring your growth and comparing it to that of your friends? Maybe you were one of those children who didn't grow very fast for a long period. You were probably very anxious about your lack of growth. Too bad adults lose their excitement for growth. I'm not speaking of physical growth but in other ways, especially spiritually. Jesus grew physically, intellectually, and spiritually (v. 39). He grew so well that even death couldn't stop his development. Are you looking to Jesus for the grace of growth and for growth in grace?

Christmas 2

Revised Common	Jeremiah 31:7-14	Ephesians 1:3-14	John 1:1-18
Roman Catholic	Sirach 24:1-2, 8-12	Ephesians 1:3-6, 15-18	John 1:1-18
Episcopal	Jeremiah 31:7-14	Ephesians 1:3-6, 15-19a	Luke 2:41-51 or Matthew 2:1-12

Theme For The Day: God's immeasurable grace. The Lord's restorative grace is promised in the first lesson. In the second lesson, that grace has been restored to the community. The gospel eloquently asserts that grace upon grace has been bestowed through the *Logos*, Jesus Christ, the Word made flesh.

BRIEF COMMENTARY ON THE LESSONS

Lesson 1: Jeremiah 31:7-14 (C, E)

This passage derives from the "book of consolation" portion of Jeremiah, compiled by Baruch, and covers the 622 BC to 609 BC period. God promises to redeem the remnant from captivity. They will return with tears of joy welling in their eyes. The earth will participate in the restoration by bountifully yielding her produce; it will be a well-watered garden (v. 12). All inhabitants will rejoice.

Lesson 1: Sirach 24:1-2, 8-12 (RC)

Praise of wisdom.

Lesson 2: Ephesians 1:3-14 (C); Ephesians 1:3-6, 15-18 (RC); Ephesians 1:3-6, 15-19a (E)

A hymn of praise to God for spiritual blessings in "heavenly places." This expression is found only in this epistle, referring to a spiritual realm above and beyond the earthly. Because of his great love, God destined us to be his sons and daughters before the foundation of the world. Salvation takes on cosmic dimensions: "to unite heaven and earth in him" (v. 5).

In verses 15-19, the apostle gives thanks for their faith and love and prays that the Lord might fill their hearts with wisdom, knowledge, and revelation.

Gospel: John 1:1-18 (C, RC)

The prologue of John rings lyrical in praise of the divine *Logos* or Word. This *Logos* is the eternal creative and redemptive power of God himself. Instead of a nativity account, such as we find in Matthew and Luke, John takes us to the beginning of the created world. That dynamic Word not only created all things but became a human being in Jesus Christ, the foremost display of God's surpassing grace and truth. The life of God is revealed as light, which the darkness (evil) cannot snuff out. John the Baptist bears witness to the light, which reveals our sins and gives us the power to become the children of God.

Gospel: Luke 2:41-51 (E)

The only story of Jesus' adolescence in the gospels. Jesus goes up to the Passover in Jerusalem with his family, friends, and neighbors. His parents are nearly a day into their return journey before they realize that Jesus is not with their group of pilgrims. They return to Jerusalem and finally, after three days, find him asking questions of the scribes in the temple. All who hear the proceedings are impressed with his knowledge. Mary accuses her son of treating them poorly. The boy Jesus replies that they should have known where to find him, in his Father's house. Already Jesus exhibits a high degree of self-awareness through his reply. He returns obediently with his parents to Nazareth. The Lord displays obedience to both his heavenly Father and his earthly parents.

Psalm Of The Day
Psalm 147:12-20 (C, RC) — "Praise the Lord."
Psalm 84 (E) — "How lovely is your dwelling place" (v. 1).

Prayer Of The Day
God of grace and glory, we praise you for your Word made flesh in Jesus, our Lord. Empower us to bear witness to the light of your creative power and redeeming love, that all people might know the joy of being your beloved child. In Jesus' name. Amen.

THEOLOGICAL REFLECTION ON THE LESSONS

Lesson 1: Jeremiah 31:7-14
Songs of salvation. This passage comes as a song of praise in anticipation of God's salvation: "Sing aloud with gladness ..." (v. 7). The Lord would bring back the people from exile and they would again worship the Lord freely in their own land. Songs of praise and thanksgiving to God for the gift of salvation should roll naturally from the lips of the redeemed of the Lord.

The God of consolation. Verse 9 states that the captives will return with weeping; with consolation, the Lord will lead them back to their homeland. The burial service found in the *Lutheran Book of Worship* opens by referring to the "God of all consolation." Our God does not prevent pain and sorrow from striking us but he does share in the pathos of our existence. The second of our Lord's Beatitudes states: "Blessed are those who mourn for they shall be comforted" (Matthew 5:4). We weep but our weeping is not inconsolable. We mourn but are comforted with the knowledge of God's saving presence. Our God comforts us in our sorrows that we might also comfort others in their sorrows.

Paradise regained. Jeremiah promises that the lives of the Israelites will be like a "well watered garden" (v. 12). That is the basic definition of the word "Paradise." When a person's life throbs with purpose and joy, he experiences his life as a paradise. However, when a person feels depressed, he is likely to describe his or her life as parched and arid. Jeremiah may have been referring not only to an external reality but also an internal state. When God restored them to favor, it would seem like paradise regained. We can all experience our lives as a "well-watered garden" when we live in harmony with God's Spirit.

Lesson 2: Ephesians 1:3-14
Destined in love (v. 5). How wonderful to know that we were conceived in love. How tragic, on the other hand, to conclude that you were not conceived in love, with purpose. Such a realization can cause a person to lash out against self or the world. The gospel states that the Lord destines all people to live as his beloved children. No matter what our origin, we are destined in love to be God's precious children. Unfortunately not all people will realize or accept that destiny which comes through faith.

Praise Father, Son, and Holy Spirit. Our duty and delight is to live to the praise of God's glory. All three persons of the Trinity are lifted up as objects of praise: the Father (v. 6), the Son (v. 12), and the Holy Spirit (vv. 13-14). The Father sends the Son and the Son sends the Spirit, a three-tiered waterfall of divine grace and love. A life of praise and thanksgiving is the only fitting response.

The cosmic Christ. In Ephesians, God's plan of salvation becomes explicitly cosmic, to unite all things through Christ in heaven and earth (v. 10). As I write this, the people of Oklahoma City are struggling with the pain of the devastating bombing of their federal building. Hundreds of Rwandans in refugee camps are murdered in cold blood. Talk show hosts stir up hate. How desperately we need to catch the vision of the cosmic Christ, whose passion and goal is to unite all things in heaven and earth.

Gospel: John 1:1-18

In the big inning. You've probably heard this one. "Did you know that God is a big baseball fan?" "What are you talking about?" "Genesis opens with the statement, 'In the big inning God created the heavens and the earth.'" Well, if you believe that one, I have another one for you. In the big inning was the Word. But the Word didn't shout "You're out!" Rather, the Word gave a message filled with grace that proclaims, "You're in! You are accepted!" That was the word from the beginning.

Incognito. The Word came into the world through the incarnate Jesus, yet the world did not recognize him (v. 10). He came to his own special people and they did not acknowledge him (v. 11). God sneaked into the world incognito, unrecognized by all but a few. The Lord of existence comes to us under the guise of frail human flesh, not in heavenly power and glory.

Perceive, believe, conceive. Because the Word does come into the world incognito, we need to have the eyes of our souls opened that we might *perceive* the Christ. The next step would have us believe in the Word and accept the message he brought (v. 12). Finally God would have us conceive the Word. Faith moves us beyond intellectual consent to giving birth to the Spirit of Jesus within our hearts.

No grace without truth (v. 14). The concepts of grace and truth are wedded in John's theology. Some churches attempt to dispense God's grace without his truth. They would preach that God is love without the corollary truth that the Lord is also holy. Through the grace of Christ we are able squarely to face the truth of our sinful human state and our spiritual impotence. This grace enables us to face the truth and become new people in Christ.

SERMON APPROACHES WITH ILLUSTRATIONS

Lesson 1: Jeremiah 31:7-14

Sermon Title: Proclaim Salvation

Sermon Angle: Jeremiah, sometimes called the weeping prophet, commands his people to praise the Lord with songs and shouts and proclaim his salvation (v. 7). We are so timid. Some claim that their faith is so personal that they couldn't possibly share it with others. Hogwash! Scripture makes clear that which we believe in our hearts will naturally be expressed with our lips.

Outline:
1. These words of hope came to a captive people.
2. They were called to proclaim a national salvation that was yet to come, based on a belief in God's promises and God's faithfulness.
3. God is acting in Christ to free us from the captivity of sin and death.
4. As we proclaim this salvation, God works to bring it to fruition.

Sermon Title: The Homecoming

Sermon Angle: Jeremiah paints a picture of God's scattered children returning home to their land and to their Father's house. Does anything pull at our heartstrings more than being united with those we love? Can anything bring greater joy? Homecoming is one of the major themes of the Christmas season. God made his home with us in Christ that we might come home to God and God's people.

Outline:
1. Jeremiah proclaims Israel's homecoming (v. 9 ff).
    — It will be a time of feeding and fulfillment (v. 12).
    — Also a time of rejoicing (v. 13).
2. Think of a special homecoming you've experienced.
3. Christ came into our world so that we might come home to God.
4. Have you experienced the joy of coming home to God?

Lesson 2: Ephesians 1:3-14

Sermon Title: The Original Big Spender

Sermon Angle: Some people get carried away with their Christmas shopping, even to the extent of spending lavishly. I suppose that's all right if they can afford it and they are doing it out of love. God is the original big spender. He freely bestowed upon us his grace through Christ (v. 6) or, as verse 8 expresses it, "lavished upon us" (RSV). God gave himself to us, even yielding up the life of his Son at the hands of sinful humans. The only proper response on our part is to give ourselves to the Lord and to others.

Outline:
1. God is the original big spender.
    — He gave us his Son.
    — His Son gave up his life for us.
2. What has been your response to this lavish grace?
    — Do you just parcel out little pieces of yourself to God and others?
    — Or, do you give your all?
3. The Christmas season calls us to give ourselves away.

Gospel: John 1:1-18

Sermon Title: Christ And Culture

Sermon Angle: Jesus was a Jew and Christianity arose in the context of Judaism. As the church reached out to the Gentile world, this presented a problem. The Jewish ideas, such as that of Messiah, would not have a great deal of appeal in the non-Jewish world. John must have searched for symbols that spoke to his Greek-educated audience but which also had a point of contact with Christianity's Jewish roots. The tool that he chose was the concept of *Logos*. This concept was employed in Jewish intertestamental books and was an integral part of Greek thinking. John realized that Christianity had to be packaged into familiar cultural concepts. This process of interpretation continues not only as Christianity strives to reach new cultures but as the culture in which we live also transforms. The content of the gospel is immutable but the cradle in which it is placed changes. The preacher must raise the question: "How well is the gospel being communicated to the culture in which we live?"

Outline:
1. Why doesn't John have a Nativity story?
   Answer: He is trying to relate to a non-Jewish audience.
2. Explain the *Logos* (Word, wisdom) concept.
   — Christ is the *Logos* and was present before the created world.
   — The grace of Jesus is inherent in creation itself.
   — In Christ, the *Logos*, we see the wisdom and knowledge of God.
3. John places Christ in a different cradle.
4. In what kind of cradle must we place Christ, so that he speaks effectively to the cultures of which we are a part?

* * * * *

The concept of the *Logos* apparently originated in the city of Ephesus, the same city from which John wrote his gospel. Heraclitus, an Ephesian philosopher, maintained that everything was in a state of flux. His most popular illustration of this principle was the river. He said that a person could step into a river, then step out of the river, only to return a few moments later. He contended that the river the person stepped back into was not the same river as before. Everything was in the process of flux. A person might assume that such a world would soon degenerate into chaos. Not so, says Heraclitus, there is a principle of order, purpose, and design. He dubbed it the *Logos*.

In the bullet pace of modern existence we can more easily than Heraclitus' contemporaries comprehend the process of flux and fluidity. More than ever, we can derive comfort from the concept of the *Logos* because it tells us that there is purpose in existence; even the madness we see around us will be made to conform to the grace and love we see in Jesus, the Word become flesh.

* * * * *

Sermon Title: Was God Always A Christian?
Sermon Angle: "In the beginning was the Word ... and the Word became flesh...." This assertion tell us that the grace and love of God we see in Jesus Christ always existed. Some people have gotten the wrong idea from reading the Bible. It might seem that the God in the Old Testament is harsh, even violent, but that the God we see in Jesus shows a loving and forgiving face. William Barclay tells the story, in his commentary on the gospel of John, of one little girl's explanation for some of those places in the Old Testament where God was depicted with an angry face. She explained: "Oh, that's before God became a Christian." John is trying to tell us here that God has always been a Christian. That is, grace and love have been the chief defining characteristics of God from the beginning. Some of those vengeful images of God come from an incomplete understanding of the divine nature.

Outline:
1. Has God always been a Christian?
2. John replies a resounding, "Yes!"
3. When confronted with seeming pointless pain and sorrow, we might also ask, "Is God really a Christian?"
    — Remember, "the light shines in the darkness ..." (v. 4).
    — God's love comes through human flesh and lives with us (v. 14).
4. Do our lives proclaim that God is still a Christian?

*   *   *   *   *

The horror of the bombing of the federal building in Oklahoma City, in April of 1995, may have caused some people to question the presence of the Word in our midst. Yet consider this. Thousands of rescue workers gave freely of themselves and their time to rescue victims and minister to the throngs of hurting people. One nurse, married only a few months, when she heard of the disaster rushed to the scene of carnage to serve the needs of the wounded. Unfortunately, a wall fell on her and crushed her. Yet even in death she gave of herself by donating her organs. The Word continues to become flesh and live among us, full of grace and truth.

The Epiphany Season

Epiphany Through The Centuries

After Easter, Epiphany is the second oldest season in the church year and was celebrated on January 6 by churches in Asia Minor as early as the second century. Epiphany celebrated both the birth and baptism of our Lord. This date was picked because it was the festival of the sun god. Instead of celebrating the birth of the sun god, the church lifted up the birth of the Son of God. The pagan festival reveled in the lengthening light of the sun, physical light, while the Christian festival exalted in spiritual light, the light of revelation. The church took over a pagan festival and converted it to its own purposes, much in the same way that the world of commerce has taken over Christmas to promote its products. When that festival was later moved to December 25, the birth of Jesus came to be associated with that date, while January 6 was retained as the date to celebrate the Baptism of our Lord.

The Eastern church continued to celebrate the baptism of Christ on January 6, while the Western church associated Epiphany with the story of the magi. The church of the East lifted up the Lord's baptism, so as to combat Gnostic heresies that claimed that Jesus was adopted as the Son of God in baptism. The story of the magi was also appropriate because it proclaims that the light of Christ dispels the darkness for all people. Unfortunately, the average Christian associates the story of the magi with the birth of Christ. Matthew's account declares that the magi paid homage to the Christ Child at his home, not at the manger.

Since medieval times, Christmas has assumed increasing dominance over Epiphany. Since the latter festival falls on a weekday six years out of seven, most churches neglect even to celebrate the day of Epiphany. Some churches may make reference to it on the Sunday following the Epiphany, which is designated as The Baptism Of Our Lord. The problem here is that there is no opportunity to deal with the significance of the magi account.

The Meaning Of The Name

The Greek word for Epiphany can be translated "the manifestation" or "the appearing" or "the showing forth." The baptism of Jesus manifested who he was: God's Son. The account of the magi reveals that the light of salvation reaches into the darkest corners of the world, shedding its rays on all who would believe. The light which Epiphany witnesses to is more like a spotlight than a flood lamp. The light of Christ pierces the darkness of sin and death but a person must choose to step into the light. If not, he remains in the darkness.

Epiphany As A Season

Epiphany is much more than a festival. Rather, it is a season that comprises at least half of the Christmas cycle of the church year. The church year can be divided into three cycles: the Christmas cycle, made up of Advent, Christmas, and Epiphany; the Easter cycle, comprised of the seasons of Lent and Easter; and the life of the church cycle (Pentecost), which fills out the rest of the ecclesiastical calendar. The season of Epiphany runs from six to nine weeks, depending on the date of Easter. It is shorter if Easter comes early and longer if it occurs late.

Color conveys mood and meaning. Two colors are employed during the season of Epiphany. White is used for the Festival of Epiphany, The Baptism Of Our Lord (first Sunday after Epiphany), and The Transfiguration Of Our Lord, which is the last Sunday in the season. White conveys joy, celebration, and openness. White reflects the light and makes it possible to see that which is in its path. The light of Christ reveals not only the nature of God but also who we are and what we can become in Christ. Green paraments hold forth for the remainder of the season. It is the color of growth. Just as Jesus grew in wisdom and understanding, so too must we grow in our knowledge of the truth of God and in our ability to reflect the light of Christ.

Epiphany Today

Not very many Christians understand the significance of Epiphany. Is it any wonder that they don't get excited about something that doesn't seem to touch them where they live? The biblical stories of the magi and our Lord's baptism need to impact our daily lives. Epiphany presents a golden opportunity to lift up the universal mission of the church as a whole.

Why not use this opportunity to enable our members to define their individual missions? The light and love of God has penetrated their lives. In what ways are they reflecting the light of Christ? Why not have a mid-week meal and then break down into small groups to study the church's mission from a biblical perspective? Have groups define their congregation's mission in concrete terms. Some congregations have mission statements that could serve as a starting point. If not, a congregational mission statement could come out of these groups. Then ask them to define on paper their own personal mission as a follower of Christ. What people are in their field of mission? How are they currently showing the light of Christ? How do they intend to do so in the near future? In the following weeks ask them to share their own personal mission stories.

A weeklong or weekend Mission Festival featuring missions and missionary speakers could also get the spiritual juices flowing. Their stories of Christ's light penetrating the darkness of sin can lift us out of our post-Christmas doldrums. Different groups in the church could be involved. This would take a good deal of planning months in advance of the festival.

Possible Homiletic Series For The Epiphany Season

Sometimes a unifying theme for a season can give your people a concrete interpretive handle. The theme that I have chosen is "Mission Mandates." We have already discussed how Epiphany is a good time to focus on our Christian mission. Each Sunday we will pull from the texts a different aspect of the church's mission. Advent and Christmas are a time to reflect and wonder at the mystery of the incarnation, but Epiphany presents us with the need to take action and launch forth with our mission of spreading the revelatory light of Christ. If you are not comfortable with this unified approach to Epiphany, many other homiletic options are suggested.

The Epiphany Of Our Lord

Sermon Title: Mission Mandate: Follow The Light!

Sermon Text: Matthew 2:1-12

Sermon Theme: The magi followed the star in hopes of finding the promised king. They didn't have much light and they didn't know where it would lead them, but they followed what light they had. The star led them to the King of kings.

The Baptism Of Our Lord — Epiphany 1

Sermon Title: Mission Mandate: Live As A Covenant People!

Sermon Text: Isaiah 42:6 and Mark 1:10-11

Sermon Theme: We are the servants of God because of the covenant God made with us in baptism, just as Israel was called to be his covenant people. Our mission is to bring to the world the light of God's redeeming love and favor, the same favor Jesus experienced in his baptism.

Epiphany 2

Sermon Title: Mission Mandate: Witness To The Christ!

Sermon Text: John 1:43-51

Sermon Theme: Christ calls Philip to follow him, who immediately finds his brother and invites him to encounter Christ, the light of the world. "Come and see" remains the invitation that we must issue to a skeptical world.

Epiphany 3

Sermon Title: Mission Mandate: Proclaim Repentance!

Sermon Text: Jonah 3:1-5, 10 and Mark 1:14-20

Sermon Angle: Jonah reluctantly preached a message of repentance to the people of Nineveh. God desires all people to repent and be saved. Our mission is to proclaim repentance to a sinful world and to rejoice when it happens.

Epiphany 4

Sermon Title: Mission Mandate: Minister With Christ's Authority!

Sermon Text: Mark 1:21-28

Sermon Angle: Jesus preached, taught, and healed with amazing authority, not someone else's authority but his own. Though the mandate cannot be found in this text, Christ later gives his followers his authority to carry out his mandate for mission.

Epiphany 5

Sermon Title: Mission Mandate: Pray Up, Then Move Out!

Sermon Text: Mark 1:35-39

Sermon Angle: Jesus was besieged by needy people. To recharge his spiritual batteries he engaged in regular prayer with the Father. However, he resisted the temptation to become the personal physician of one set of people. The claims of the kingdom needed to be heard in other places. The church must follow our Lord's example: Pray up and then move out.

Epiphany 6

Sermon Title: Mission Mandate: Offer Spiritual Cleansing!

Sermon Text: Mark 1:40-45

Sermon Angle: The first lesson features the cleansing of Namaan the leper by Elisha. The gospel tells of Jesus healing a leper who spread abroad the good news of his healing. Our Christian mission impels us to cleanse and heal those who want to be made whole.

Epiphany 7

Sermon Title: Mission Mandate: Share Christ's Forgiveness!

Sermon Text: Mark 2:1-12

Sermon Angle: Jesus healed the paralytic by freeing him from his sins. The authority with which he forgave sins caused great scandal in the religious community. Sin still paralyzes, but we have the authority of Jesus to free people from their sins.

Epiphany 8

Sermon Title: Mission Mandate: Announce The Marriage!

Sermon Text: Hosea 2:19-20 and Mark 2:18-22

Sermon Angle: Hosea foresees a time when the Lord and his people will be united in a loving marriage of eternal duration. In the gospel, Jesus metaphorically refers to himself as the bridegroom. How can his disciples be expected to fast when the bridegroom is at hand? The relationship of the believer and the Lord is like a marriage that moves toward the goal of perfect union. Our mission compels us to make known the Lord's invitation to the marriage feast that has no end.

The Transfiguration Of Our Lord

Sermon Title: Mission Mandate: Become Transformed By His Glory!

Sermon Text: 2 Corinthians 3:18 and Mark 9:2-9

Sermon Angle: All three texts make reference to scenes of divine glory. To witness such a scene is transforming. We are called to invite others to witness with us the glory of the risen Christ and be transformed thereby.

The Epiphany Of Our Lord

Revised Common	**Isaiah 60:1-6**	**Ephesians 3:1-12**	**Matthew 2:1-12**
Roman Catholic	**Isaiah 60:1-6**	**Ephesians 3:2-3a, 5-6**	**Matthew 2:1-12**
Episcopal	**Isaiah 60:1-6, 9**	**Ephesians 3:1-12**	**Matthew 2:1-12**

Theme For The Day: The light of the Lord's saving presence is announced in the Old Testament and revealed in the New. The Gentiles, as well as the Jews, are led by God's revelatory light to pay homage to God's anointed one.

BRIEF COMMENTARY ON THE LESSONS

Lesson 1: Isaiah 60:1-6 (C, RC); Isaiah 60:1-6, 9 (E)

The light of God's glory has been shed on the chosen nation and all the people who live in darkness will be drawn to the light, together with Israel's scattered citizens. Their neighboring realms will pour their wealth into Israel — gold and frankincense.

Lesson 2: Ephesians 3:1-12 (C, E); Ephesians 3:2-3a, 5-6 (RC)

The mystery of the gospel, withheld from former generations, has now been revealed in Christ to all people, including the Gentiles. All believers are members of the household of faith and have direct access to God.

Gospel: Matthew 2:1-12 (C, RC, E)

The visitation of the magi.

Psalm Of The Day

Psalm 72:1-7, 10-14 (C); Psalm 72 (E) — A prayer for the reign of God's righteous king.
Psalm 71 (RC)

Prayer Of The Day

O light of the world, lead us through the darkness of our ignorance and sin into the light of your love and grace. There let us bow at your feet and present to you the gifts that you deserve. In Jesus' name. Amen.

THEOLOGICAL REFLECTION ON THE LESSONS

Lesson 1: Isaiah 60:1-6

Arise and shine. The city of Jerusalem had been raped and pillaged by her enemies but is ordered to "rise and shine." The light of God's presence will cause her to sparkle again. Those who destroyed her will also restore her glory and luster. The Lord is the source of her glory and was about to make his presence known in his land.

The new Jerusalem. The old Jerusalem had been destroyed by enemies in punishment for apostasy. God had removed his glorious presence and the nation was led captive. The Lord was now re-establishing his presence in the holy city. It would not be the same city as before; the Lord was establishing something new. Unfortunately, the new Jerusalem would fall victim to the same old problems. The Revelation of John picks up on the concept of the new Jerusalem but portrays it as an eschatological event. The new Jerusalem becomes a symbol of the kingdom of heaven.

Lesson 2: Ephesians 3:1-12

Proclaiming the mystery. The word "mysterion" can be interpreted "secret." Paul relates that Christ called him to reveal the mystery of the gospel. The content of that mystery is that salvation through Christ is offered to the Gentiles as well as the Jews. That intention of God had not previously been known. The secret is out that God offers salvation to all.

Mystery religions. Mystery religions pervaded the ancient Near East. Their life centered around secret religious rites and ceremonies that told the myth story of the god or goddess. Only those initiated into the cult could participate in the rites, called mysteries. Many such religions had initiatory rites employing water or blood and sacred meals, by which the worshiper communed with the god or goddess. Mystery religions pried religion free from its traditional association at that time with state and family and made it a matter of personal choice. Christianity shares in many of the characteristics of a mystery religion but there are profound differences. The central story (myth) is based on historical reality, on the life, death, and resurrection of Jesus of Nazareth. Secondly, Christianity has no secret rites or ceremonies. The mystery has been revealed concerning how God redeems sinners and grants them eternal life (Ephesians 3:3-5).

Made a minister (v. 7). Paul was made a minister or servant of the gospel by the grace of God. He hadn't earned it (v. 8). All Christians are made ministers in our baptism. What does it take to make a minister? The grace of God and a willingness to serve in his name.

Gospel: Matthew 2:1-12

Magi. The magi, meaning astrologer, has traditionally been rendered "wise men." It is believed that they came from Babylonia, Persia, or Arabia. They were probably of a priestly cast and were familiar with the Hebrew prophecies of a redeemer-king. The appearance of the heavenly luminary was taken as a sign of the fulfillment of the prophecies.

A sign positive and negative. When Simeon spoke to Jesus' parents in the temple, he referred to the baby as a sign that would be "spoken against" (Matthew 2:34). For the magi, the sign of the star was a positive sign. They came to worship the new king (v. 2). Herod and other central figures in Jerusalem viewed this birth with fear and suspicion (v. 3). The birth of Christ continues to be a mixed sign; some see it as the promise of the righteous reign of God, while others view it as an acute threat to their own plans and schemes.

Faith journey. The magi traveled on a faith journey. When they embarked from their homeland, they didn't know exactly where the star would lead them. They had no certainty that they would find the newborn king but they took the risk and their faith was rewarded. Contemporary faith trekkers have an advantage over the wise men; we know the identity of our king. The object of our journey is not to find our king but to follow our king into uncharted territory. Our faith journeys still entail risk and uncertainty.

The joy of journey's end. When the magi found the object of their search, their hearts exploded with rapturous joy expressed in worship (vv. 10-11). Envision the unutterable joy that will flood our hearts when we complete our earthly faith journey and gaze into the face of our Lord and king.

They opened their treasures (v. 11). No act of worship is complete without opening our treasures and laying them at the feet of the one we call Savior and Lord.

SERMON APPROACHES WITH ILLUSTRATIONS

Lesson 1: Isaiah 60:1-6
Sermon Title: Arise And Shine!

Sermon Angle: The captives are ordered to arise, like the sun, and shine. How could they when the darkness of death clung to their souls like a wet garment? The glory of the Lord shone upon them. God was the source of their light and, after a long night of sorrow, was about to dawn upon them. The people of God do not have to manufacture the light, merely reflect it.

Outline:
1. After a long night of captivity, the day of favor had dawned.
2. The Jews were to reflect the Lord's redemptive light.
3. The light of salvation is revealed in Christ.
4. Arise from spiritual slumber, turn your face to Jesus, and shine for all to see.

Lesson 2: Ephesians 3:1-12
Sermon Title: The Gospel: An Open Secret

Sermon Angle: The word for "mystery" interprets in English as secret. Paul discusses the mystery that was revealed to him (v. 3). Possessing a secret can be exciting. Such knowledge makes a person feel important and possibly a little smug. The real joy comes not from possessing the secret but in sharing it. It was Paul's privilege to share the secret of salvation for all people. For many the grace of God remains a mystery (secret). The mission of the church compels us to share the mystery of the gospel with all who will hear. It's an open secret.

Outline:
1. Explain the meaning of the word "mystery."
2. We have an important mission — life and death information to share.
3. Share the secret of salvation — share the joy!

Gospel: Matthew 2:1-12
Sermon Title: The Quest For The King

Sermon Angle: The wise men journeyed to find the one born king of the Jews. They reasoned that such a one could be found in the palace of a king. So they visited King Herod. The wise men of Herod's court informed them of the scriptural prophecies that this king was to be born in Bethlehem. Most people are searching for their king, for a person, or a cause to which they can gives themselves. They have given their hearts to a political ideal or party, to a guru, or teacher or some other authority figure. Such obeisance has often led to destruction and death. We have found a king that we can believe in and follow implicitly.

Outline:
1. The magi were on a king quest.
2. Their quest was successful.
3. Most people embark on such a search for ultimate meaning and authority.
4. In Christ we find a king to whom we can give ourselves joyously and find authority for our lives.

Sermon Title: Look Up And Down

Sermon Angle: The wise men were astrologers whose business it was to look up to the heavens. It was their belief that there were heavenly powers that controlled earthly events. They held that there was a power or powers greater than those on earth and a basic interconnection between stellar and earthly events. In other words, they viewed reality through a wide-angled lens. Yet their eyes weren't so filled with stardust that they couldn't recognize transcendent reality in a very lowly and earthly shape and form. They fell down at the feet of a peasant child, not yet weaned from his mother's breasts, and paid him kingly homage.

Outline:
1. The wise men continually looked up to the stars.
2. Their transcendent vision set them on an earthly quest for meaning and authority.
3. Christians look up to the Word of God for light; we look down on the earth and find him.
4. In Christ we see the light of God's presence and fall down to worship our king.

*   *   *   *   *

Star Dust

Did you know that precious metals, such as silver, platinum, and gold, are literally made from star dust? These elements were not formed within the earth but are the products of dying stars. At least that's the information I gleaned from "The Learning Channel." Apparently, the core of these stars became so dense that gravity caused them to collapse in upon themselves in a cataclysmic explosion that sent tons of star dust to other places. Gravity pulled these clouds of star dust together in a process that leads to the birth of a new star or planet. Think of it! That band of gold around your finger is the stuff of stars. Indeed, the elements of which our bodies are made is also the stuff of stars. In some mysterious sense we are star children, both physically and spiritually. When the wise men laid before the Christ Child their treasure of gold, they were giving him star dust, the substance of another world that had been reborn. It made a fitting gift for the One who had come from the eternal God and would one day return to the eternal God, who was himself the light of God's presence.

*   *   *   *   *

Sermon Title: Mission Mandate: Follow The Light!

Sermon Angle: The magi followed the star in hopes of finding the promised king. They didn't have much light and they didn't know where it would lead them but they followed the light provided them and it led them to the King of kings.

Outline:
1. The wise men were not God's covenant people, yet they saw the star and followed the light.
2. All people have some of the light of God's truth but they don't all follow the light (not even some who have seen the light of Christ).
3. Have we embarked on a spiritual pilgrimage to follow the light and worship the one who is the light of the world?

The Baptism Of Our Lord/Epiphany 1/Ordinary Time 1

Revised Common	Genesis 1:1-5	Acts 19:1-7	Mark 1:4-11
Roman Catholic	Isaiah 42:1-4, 6-7	Acts 10:34-38	Mark 1:7-11
Episcopal	Isaiah 42:1-9	Acts 10:34-38	Mark 1:7-11

Theme For The Day: The baptism of Jesus and baptism of the Spirit. In Isaiah the Spirit is given to God's servant (generally regarded as the nation of Israel). In Acts Peter proclaims that the Spirit comes to everyone who fears God and does what is right. The gospel tells of the descent of the Spirit of God on Jesus following his baptism by John.

BRIEF COMMENTARY ON THE LESSONS

Lesson 1: Genesis 1:1-5 (C)

The text describes creation in its earliest stages; the earth was a formless, watery void. The Spirit of God acted on the waters and created life. This text was selected for The Baptism Of Our Lord because of the association of the Spirit of God with water. Light issued as the first act of God's creation.

Lesson 1: Isaiah 42:1-4, 6-7 (RC); Isaiah 42:1-9 (E)

This is the first servant song. Opinions vary as to the identity of the Servant. Many identify the Servant as the nation of Israel, others identify it as some individual, while still others claim that it refers to both. God has favored his Servant with his Spirit, that he might patiently bring forth justice and righteousness to the earth. The God of creation, who created light and life, has commissioned his Servant to share the light of the knowledge of God with the nations.

Lesson 2: Acts 19:1-7 (C)

In Ephesus, Paul found a small band of Christians. He inquired as to how they had received the Holy Spirit when they came to faith. They replied that they had never even heard of the Holy Spirit. Paul then inquired concerning the nature of their baptism. They responded that it was the baptism of John the Baptist. After the apostle more carefully explained the Christian faith, they were baptized in the name of Jesus. Then Paul laid his hand on them, conveying the Spirit, which came upon them in the form of tongues and prophecy. (See also Acts 8:14-18.)

Lesson 2: Acts 10:34-38 (RC, E)

Peter witnesses to Cornelius and his household about Jesus in response to visions that both men received. Peter comes to understand that God intends the gospel not only for the Jews but also the Gentiles. Peter relates how God anointed Jesus with the Holy Spirit, which gave him the power to heal, deliver from the devil, and do such great good.

Gospel: Mark 1:4-11 (C); Mark 1:7-11 (RC, E)

Mark's gospel commences with the ministry of John the Baptist. John describes his baptism as being preparatory in character. His baptism was one of repentance and forgiveness. The Messiah, the one who was coming after him, would baptize with the Holy Spirit. The bestowal of the Spirit would bring people into spiritual communion with God. Jesus is baptized by John with the accompanying voice from heaven proclaiming that Jesus was his beloved Son.

Psalm Of The Day
   Psalm 29 (C) — "The voice of the Lord is upon the waters ..." (v. 3).
   Psalm 89:1-29 (E) — "I will make him the firstborn, the highest of the kings of the earth" (v. 27).
   Psalm 28 (RC)

Prayer Of The Day
   God of favor, you acclaimed Jesus your beloved Son in his baptism by John in the Jordan River and gifted him mightily with your Spirit. As you have also shone your favor upon us through our baptism, so fill us with the fullness of your Spirit that we might accomplish the tasks you have given us to do. In the holy name of Jesus. Amen.

THELOGICAL REFLECTION ON THE LESSONS

Lesson 1: Genesis 1:1-5
Spirit on the move. God's Spirit is dynamic, ever on the move. Genesis describes the Spirit of the Lord as moving over the waters. Spirit and wind come from the same root word, so if we think about the characteristics of wind we come to comprehend some basic truths about the Spirit. We can't see the wind, we can only observe the movement of objects acted on by the wind. Likewise, we cannot see the Spirit but only observe the Spirit's movement in the world, in the church, and in our own hearts.
   The deep. The writer of Genesis teaches that the world we live in was founded on a watery chaos (the deep). We have here an interesting correlation with science, which teaches that all earthly life emanates from the depths of the sea. When we think of the Spirit, we have to think deep. Spirit comes wrapped in a thick shroud of mystery. As Paul reasoned, we can only begin to comprehend the things of the Spirit through the gift of the Spirit.
   Let there be light (v. 3). God spoke light into being before anything else, his greatest creative stroke. Not only is light necessary in creating and sustaining life but it is also the prime form of energy associated with God's being. When God makes himself known, the theophany is always accompanied by fire or light. In the prelude of the gospel of John the creative and redemptive Word is described as light that shines in the darkness. God creates light but it is our responsibility as his children to let the light shine. In other words, we must not block the light but let it shine through us.

Lesson 1: Isaiah 42:1-9
Behold my servant (v. 1). Isaiah proclaims, "Behold my servant, my chosen, in whom my soul delights...." The terms "servant" and "chosen one" don't seem to be parallel terms. Besides, attention is not generally given to servants; those who wait on others don't often find themselves in the spotlight. The prophet announces that the nations were soon going to notice God's servant, Israel, because he had placed his Spirit upon his people. In the gospel we hear the heavenly voice booming, "This is my beloved Son, listen to him." Behold my Son, my chosen! We are told to pay keen attention to the Beloved, and what made him noteworthy was

the fact that the Son shone forth as the preeminent servant. Behold the servant Son, the chosen, who gave his life as a sacrifice of service. Such servanthood needs lifting up.

Lesson 2: Acts 19:1-7

Did you receive the Holy Spirit? The group of twelve Christians had not heard the whole gospel. Paul asked, "Did you receive the Holy Spirit when you believed?" (v. 2). It was news to them. Paul more fully explained the gospel, baptized the twelve, and then laid his hands on them. Christianity is not just a matter of intellectual assent to theological propositions; more importantly, it is receiving the Spirit of Christ into our heart.

Legalistic Christians. The twelve disciples that Paul found might be termed legalistic Christians. They had received the baptism of John; they knew they needed to be better, to clean up their act. It doesn't appear that they had experienced the grace of Christ through his Spirit. They were attempting to earn God's grace through their own power. Through their encounter with Paul they experienced something extra, the grace of God.

Lesson 2: Acts 10:34-38

Good news of peace (v. 36). Peter characterizes the ministry of Jesus as the good news of peace. He is our peace with God. He frees us from our sins as he liberates us from the dominion of the devil.

The power cell for goodness (v. 38). Peter tells how God anointed Jesus with the Holy Spirit and power, then relates how he went about doing good. The Spirit of God is the power cell of goodness. In this century we have witnessed the awesome power of evil to wreak destruction. Years ago, thousands of allied soldiers witnessed the handiwork of the evil one as they liberated Nazi concentration camps. Yet, that horrible power could not sustain itself. The power of Christ's goodness continues to transform lives after 2,000 years.

Gospel: Mark 1:4-11

Opening act. Many highly touted musical groups have a less luminous group open for them. Their function is to get the crowd prepared for the main act. That was exactly what John the Baptist was doing, getting the people ready for the main attraction. Don't focus on me, he said. Just prepare for the one who is coming after me.

D-Day. Many years ago the allied troops landed on the beaches of Normandy. They launched during a brief window in a stormy pattern of weather. Once those tens of thousands of soldiers were underway in the boats that would bring them to the beaches, there was no turning back. "D" stands for "deployment," but the word "decision" would do as well. What an agonizing decision that must have been for General Eisenhower and the high command. When Jesus went to John to be baptized, that was Jesus' "D-Day." Then he was irrevocably committed to the battle with Satan's minions for the hearts and souls of humanity. Those who belong to denominations that practice adult baptism as the normative mode customarily emphasize the decision of discipleship that precedes baptism, while the liturgical churches emphasize God's prior act of grace conveyed through infant baptism. The latter then associates decision and deployment with confirmation.

B- and C-Day. The day that Jesus went to John for baptism could be referred to as B-Day, baptism day, and C-Day, confirmation day. Jesus' deployment as Messiah was initiated through his baptism. As Jesus came up out of the baptismal waters, B-Day also became C-Day, confirmation day, as he heard the voice from on high, "You are my beloved Son; with you I am well pleased." Though our baptism as Christians does not equate to that of our Lord's, our B-Day also becomes a C-Day, as God assures us that we are eternally the children of his love and favor.

SERMON APPROACHES WITH ILLUSTRATIONS

Lesson 1: Genesis 1:1-5
Sermon Title: By Water, Word, And The Spirit

Sermon Angle: The creation account in Genesis 1 says that in the beginning the Spirit of God moved over the waters. Then God spoke light into existence. There we have it, the three building blocks of creation — God's Spirit, water, and the word. Those are also the elements present when God recreates or redeems his human creation. God's Spirit and God's word combine with the waters of baptism to create new spiritual life. We can't explain it, only celebrate the mystery of new life.

Outline:
1. God's Spirit created the world through water and the word.
2. Jesus was enthroned as Messiah through water and the word (gospel).
3. We are adopted into God's family and empowered for ministry through water and the word.

Lesson 1: Isaiah 42:1-9
Sermon Title: Mission Mandate: Live As A Covenant People!

Sermon Angle: A word of hope came to God's oppressed people through Isaiah. God was giving his Spirit to them; they would be a covenantal sign of God's redemptive love (v. 6). They had a mission to be a light to the nations and free those who were oppressed (v. 7). This is the same mission Jesus took upon himself in his baptism and which comes to us in our baptism. How are we doing as the Lord's covenant people?

Outline:
1. God had made the Jews his covenant people in order to bring all people into God's family (v. 6).
2. God declared his covenant of love with his Son through his baptism (Mark 1:11).
3. The Lord established his covenant with us in our baptism.
4. Live out Christ's covenant of love, that all people might know his grace.

Lesson 2: Acts 10:34-38
Sermon Title: He Is Lord Of All!

Sermon Angle: This text presents a strong case for the universality of the church. The Spirit was leading Peter and the whole church from the particularity of God's revelation to the Jews to the universality of a gospel for all people. Peter had to acknowledge what we are often reluctant to admit, that God shows no partiality, Christ has no favorites. God accepts all who respond to him in faith and strive to do his will.

Outline:
1. Humans tend to make God in our image.
2. God created us all and is Lord of all (v. 36).
3. Peter came to see that God had spoken to Cornelius, a non-Jew and enemy of his people. Peter's understanding of God ballooned from a tribal deity to the universal God.
4. Is your faith narrow and tribal or global and catholic?

Gospel: Mark 1:4-11

Sermon Title: The ABCs Of Our Lord's Baptism

Sermon Angle: We can summarize the fundamentals of our Lord's baptism as follows:

A. Affirmation. In Jesus' baptism, the Father affirmed that he was dearly loved. This satisfied his need for identity.

B. Belonging. The Father affirmed that Jesus was his beloved Son. He belonged. This satisfied his need for social bonding in the family of God.

C. Continuation. The Father blessed the Son with his Spirit that he might continue to accomplish the will of God. This fulfilled his need for inspiration and strength.

Sermon Title: The ABCs Of The Holy Spirit

Sermon Angle: The Spirit of God comes wrapped in mystery. Yet our three lessons shed light on this mystery. The Genesis text reveals the creative nature of the Spirit. He gives form and purpose to void and chaos. The second lesson demonstrates that the Spirit shows no favorites based on human differences. The gospel shows that the Spirit is identified with the ministry of Jesus coming as an affirming, loving Spirit.

Sermon Title: Baptism: Personal And Communal

Sermon Angle: Mark's account of our Lord's baptism emphasizes the personal aspects of this awesome experience. The voice from heaven was not for the benefit of the onlookers but for Jesus himself. "You are my beloved Son...." Matthew has: "This is my beloved Son" (Matthew 3:17), an announcement to others. Jesus noticed the heavens open and the gentle Spirit descend like a dove. This was clearly a personal spiritual experience of affirmation for Jesus. Christian baptism is similar in this regard. It comes to us as a personal word of affirmation and acceptance. That's why we always use the personal name of the baptized when the waters of grace are poured. However, Christian baptism is clearly communal as well. We see this meaning also in the baptism of our Lord. He was baptized into the sinful human family through John's baptism of repentance. His baptism identified him with our sinful race. We, on the opposite pole, are baptized into the family of God, the kingdom of heaven.

Outline:

1. Jesus' baptism was personal and corporate. (Explain.)
2. Our baptism is personal (God personally forgives, accepts, and empowers us).
3. Our baptism is communal (the Christlife can only be realized in community).
4. Our baptism commissions us for lifelong mission in the kingdom.

* * * * *

This little story illustrates the second point above. A little boy was dying of cancer. His parents hadn't had time to become part of a faith community. Yet, as the life force began to ebb in their precious little one, they realized that they needed, and especially their son needed, spiritual guidance. A pastor came to see the little boy and taught him Psalm 23 but with a special technique. He taught him to take his hand and as he grasped his first finger say, "The," then take the next finger and utter, "Lord," and follow it with the third finger and say, "is," the fourth finger, "my," and finally, the fifth finger, "shepherd." The pastor instructed the boy to hold tightly to the fourth finger as a way of reminding him that he belonged to the Lord. "The

Lord is my shepherd." One morning, the parents entered their son's hospital room to find his hands clasped above his head. He had stopped breathing. Then they noticed. Their son was holding tightly the fourth finger. "The Lord is my shepherd." He had died with the reassurance that the Lord was "his" shepherd.

In the same way our baptism reminds us, especially when the devil tries to steal our assurance, that we belong to the Lord. He is our Savior, our Lord, our shepherd. When Martin Luther was tempted to doubt his salvation, he would cry out: "I am baptized, I am baptized."

Epiphany 2/Ordinary Time 2

Revised Common	1 Samuel 3:1-10 (11-20)	1 Corinthians 6:12-20	John 1:43-51
Roman Catholic	1 Samuel 3:3-10, 19	1 Corinthians 6:13-15, 17-20	John 1:35-42
Episcopal	1 Samuel 3:1-10 (11-20)	1 Corinthians 6:11b-20	John 1:43-51

Theme For The Day: The call of God. The boy Samuel had to be taught not only to hear the call of God but to recognize the call as coming from God and respond affirmatively. In the second lesson, the Corinthian Christians had to be made to realize that they must respond to Christ's call not only with their minds but also their bodies. In the gospel, Christ calls his first disciples.

BRIEF COMMENTARY ON THE LESSONS

Lesson 1: 1 Samuel 3:1-10 (11-20) (C, E); 1 Samuel 3:3-10, 19 (RC)

The young Samuel has been apprenticed to the elderly priest, Levi, and is sleeping near the place where the Ark of the Covenant is kept. Three times the lad hears his name called and, thinking it was Levi, goes to him. By the third time, Levi realizes that the Lord was calling to Samuel and instructs him to respond: "Speak, Lord, your servant is listening" the next time he hears the voice.

Lesson 2: 1 Corinthians 6:12-20 (C); 1 Corinthians 6:13-15, 17-20 (RC); 1 Corinthians 6:11b-20 (E)

The Corinthians lived in a culture of sexual impurity, not too different from that which we inhabit. It was no surprise that many of the new Christians engaged in pornographic activities. In fact, their twisting of the doctrine of grace gave them license to engage in adulterous activities. If God forgives us in Christ, why not sin? They also separated the things of the body from the things of the Spirit. They held that the body was of lesser importance, having no real eternal significance. Therefore, it didn't matter what a person did in his body. Paul preached a holistic theology of the human person; body and spirit are fused. He taught that the body of the believer becomes one with the Body of Christ in spiritual union. The new believers were taught the ethical implications of Christian discipleship.

Gospel: John 1:43-51 (C, E); John 1:35-42 (RC)

John the Baptist was conducting his ministry of baptismal cleansing when he observed Jesus and pointed to him exclaiming: "Look, the Lamb of God!" Two disciples followed Jesus to his home. One of the two was Andrew, who went to call his brother Peter the very next day (vv. 35-42). Then Jesus decided to go back to Galilee, where he called Philip. Philip hurried to his brother, Nathanael, with the claim to have found the Messiah. Nathanael was not impressed but went with his brother to meet Jesus. In that encounter Jesus commends Nathanael's honesty. Nathanael wonders how Jesus knows him. Jesus replies that he saw him under the fig tree before his brother called him. The call of Christ goes out through those who themselves have encountered Christ.

Psalm Of The Day

Psalm 139:1-6, 13-18 (C) — "I will praise you for I am fearfully and wonderfully made" (v. 14).

Psalm 63:1-8 (E) — "I will praise you as long as I live" (v. 4).

Psalm 39 (RC)

Prayer Of The Day

Lord of life, you have called us to follow like Andrew and Philip. Make the ears of our spirit sensitive to your voice that we might both hear and heed your call to discipleship. In the powerful name of Jesus we pray. Amen.

THEOLOGICAL REFLECTION ON THE LESSONS

Lesson 1: 1 Samuel 3:1-10

When God is silent. The passage relates that the word of God was very rare in Samuel's day (v. 1). Had God removed himself? No, the word of God was not heard because this was an age of spiritual impurity and darkness. The religious establishment, the mediator of God's presence, was corrupt. Eli's sons were employing their religious positions for selfish advantage and Eli didn't have the gumption to reign in these rebels. God had become nearly mute because of an oppressive spiritual atmosphere.

Lack of vision. God's lack of communication is linked with the dearth of spiritual visions. Spiritual visions were the customary means by which the prophets received messages from on high. There were not many visions in those days (v. 1). Also, Eli's physical sight had grown dim (v. 2). Here we see a pathetic figure of a religious leader who had lost most of his physical and spiritual vision. Lack of spiritual vision haunts every age. Jesus speaks of the folly of the blind leading the blind. The dangers of the world in which we live are heightened because so many of our leaders lack a worthy spiritual vision of where God is leading us.

The lamp of the Lord had not yet gone out (v. 3). The sanctuary lamp was supplied with just enough fuel to burn through the night. The verse suggests that the supply of oil was running low. Therefore, it was probably near dawn. Some ages of humankind are more spiritually enlightened than others, but even in the darkest of times the lamp of God's eternal presence has not gone out. Elijah had forgotten that when he complained to the Lord, during the time that Jezebel was chasing him, he thought he was the only one left who worshiped the Lord. God reminded him that there were thousands who were still reflecting the light of their faith. Or, as the prologue to John's gospel states, "The light shines in the darkness but the darkness has not overcome it" (v. 5).

Lesson 2: 1 Corinthians 6:12-20

Christian freedom. Paul attempts to address the problem of moral license that so plagued the Corinthian church. Some members of that church maintained that Christ freed them to do as they wished. Paul corrected them by teaching that Christian freedom means that we are no longer slaves of the tyranny of sin; we are free to do that which is good and loving.

A theology of the body. The Greeks thought that the body was of no importance. Paul teaches that our body belongs to the Lord (v. 13) and is a temple of God. Therefore, we should honor and respect it as a holy place. In his case against prostitution he teaches that our bodies are members of Christ's body, the church. Christianity elevates bodily existence.

75

Shun immorality (v. 18). Paul uses the word "immorality" in a narrow sense here, referring to sins committed with the body, sexual sins. He seems to regard them with special horror, probably because he witnessed the destructive hold that such sins could have on people. Shunning immorality in Corinth was a Herculean task. Temptations of the flesh abounded, a situation not too far different than we face in this land of freedom. Television, magazines, and movies make alluring the sins of the flesh. Sex marketing transpires not on the street corners but in our living rooms. It's harder and harder to shun immorality. Why is Paul so insistent on giving sexual immorality the cold shoulder? Because such sins seem so natural and innocent. We can walk away at any time, so we reason. A little titillation here, a little stimulation there won't hurt anyone. But then slowly, strand by gossamer strand, sexual sins weave their sensuous silk about us so that we are no longer free; we are prey.

Gospel: John 1:43-51

Jackpot. When Philip found Jesus he was really excited. He had hit the spiritual jackpot by finding the one who fulfilled the hopes of the Hebrew religious community. He was so enthusiastic that he ran to Nathanael to share the joy of his discovery.

Come and see. Nathanael's somewhat cynical response, "Can anything good come out of Nazareth?" did not dampen Philip's excitement at finding the Christ. Philip's response was super. He could have let this comment discourage him. He could have become argumentative and testy. But why? He didn't have to prove anything. "Come and see!" he urged. Philip knew that he didn't have to sell Jesus; Jesus would sell himself. All that any of us can do as witnesses of the gospel is extend a gracious invitation: come and see!

What you see is what you get. Jesus met Nathanael with a compliment. "Here is a true Israelite in whom there is nothing false" (v. 47). Nothing phony, nothing pretentious, nothing dishonest about Nathanael. What you see is what you get.

A passage to heaven. Last week's gospel of our Lord's baptism has Jesus coming out of the Jordan River as the heavens opened and the Spirit descended on him like a dove. In this week's gospel, Jesus announces to Nathanael, "I tell you the truth, you shall see heaven open and the angels of God ascending and descending on the Son of Man" (v. 50). The metaphor of the ladder draws on the story of Jacob's dream when he slept in Bethel as he fled the wrath of his brother (Genesis 28:10-17). Jesus is our passage to heaven, a doorway to the divine. We cannot climb up, but through faith we are transported into the nearer presence of God.

SERMON APPROACHES WITH ILLUSTRATIONS

Lesson 1: 1 Samuel 3:1-10

Sermon Title: Learning To Recognize God's Voice

Sermon Angle: The young Samuel was an apprentice minister and while he slept in the sanctuary, near the Ark of the Covenant, which symbolized God's presence, he heard God's voice. The problem was that he didn't recognize God's voice, thinking it was Levi. Levi, finally realizing that the Lord was trying to get the lad's attention, told him how to reply. Samuel learned to recognize the voice of the Lord and to listen.

Outline:
1. Samuel lived in God's house but didn't know the Lord or recognize his voice.
2. Levi helped Samuel recognize God's voice and respond.

3. Some of us have been brought up in God's house (the church) but have not come to recognize the Lord's voice.
4. We learn to hear God's voice from those who are spiritually mature and from worship and the practice of prayer.

Sermon Title: Sleeping In Church

Sermon Angle: Just about every preacher has had somebody fall asleep during his or her sermon. In my last parish, one farmer closed his eyes during every sermon I ever preached. Too bad I didn't have a Super Soaker water gun. But let's be honest, we have all slept in church on some occasions. Our eyes may have been open but our minds were on the golf course, the movie theater, or even the bedroom. The young Samuel slept in church not only physically but spiritually, until God finally woke him. The message that God gave Samuel (not in this pericope) was that religious leaders were spiritually asleep and were about to be rudely awakened by the Lord himself.

Outline:

Introduction: Have you ever slept in church? Take comfort because you are not the first. Remember Eutycus who fell asleep during the apostle Paul's late night sermon and then fell out of the second-story window? In this lesson we see that Samuel slept regularly in church.
1. Like Samuel, we can be in God's house, a part of his family, and not know his voice. Spiritually asleep.
2. Learn to recognize God's voice — through spiritual mentoring, study, prayer, and worship.
3. First give God your ear, and then your life, in humble obedience.

* * * * *

The United States was founded on a religious vision, a city set on a hill, a community where God is ruler. John Winthrop wrote in the prologue to the *Mayflower Compact* that those who signed the covenant to establish a colony in America were doing so to the "glory of God" and "the advancement of the Christian faith." He envisioned that if the citizens of this new land were faithful to God "the Lord will ... command a blessing upon us in all our ways." Much of the spiritual struggle in our land today is between those who still view America as a nation under God and those who hold to a secular vision of America as a place where we have the right to do our own thing.

* * * * *

Lesson 2: 1 Corinthians 6:12-20

Sermon Title: Body Language

Sermon Angle: We communicate who we are not only through our words but via our bodies. Our bodies communicate love, hate, boredom, worry, and a host of other messages. The Corinthians had disregarded body language as an expression of their true selves. Paul maintains that our bodies are temples of the Holy Spirit that communicate his true presence. We are to praise God through our bodies.

Outline:
1. Our bodies send messages.
2. Many Corinthian Christians communicated a body language that contradicted their faith in Christ.

3. Is your body glorifying God? Does your church body glorify Christ?
4. Make certain your body language glorifies the Lord!

Sermon Title: A Glorified Body

Sermon Angle: The New Testament speaks of the resurrected body as a glorified body. Yet, in this lection Paul urges the church "glorify God in your body." In other words, praise God in and through your body. The object is not to glorify our bodies but glorify God through our bodies. We glorify the Lord through our bodies by living lives of obedience and spiritual integrity. We glorify God in our bodies by using them as God intended, not perverting them into instruments of power or selfish self-satisfaction. To recap, we glorify God in our bodies by keeping them holy to the Lord. Every Christian should have a glorified body.

Outline:
1. Millions of people spend every spare moment in glorifying themselves through their bodies (bodybuilding, dieting, makeup, sports, and so forth).
2. The Corinthians worshiped their bodies through the pursuit of hedonistic pleasures.
3. The result was a degradation of their personal bodies and of Christ's body.
4. Glorify God in your body by taking care of it and using it in the service of Christ.

Gospel: John 1:43-51

Sermon Title: Mission Mandate: Witness To The Christ!

Sermon Angle: Jesus called Philip to be his disciple and Philip was so enthusiastic about his newfound Lord that he ran to Nathanael with the news that he had found the Messiah promised in the scriptures. Nathanael was skeptical but Philip persisted. "Come and see" (v. 46). To know Christ is to share Christ. The good news cannot be contained. Christians are not called to convert anyone; that's the Lord's job. Our call is merely to share what Christ means to us and to invite friends and neighbors to come and see for themselves.

Outline:
1. Our relationship with Christ cannot be bottled up.
2. The Spirit moves us to share him with others (like Philip).
3. We can witness to Christ most effectively with friends and neighbors.
4. Invite friends or neighbors this week to check Christ out for themselves.

Sermon Title: In Search Of An Authentic Faith

Sermon Angle: Nathanael was like Thomas; he wasn't willing to accept easy answers. He wasn't willing merely to borrow someone else's faith. He had to experience it for himself. When Jesus met him, he complimented Nathanael as a man of integrity. He wasn't willing to hide behind an unexamined and superficial faith-mask. He would accept nothing other than an honest-to-God faith, an authentic faith. What is an authentic faith? These elements need to be present: 1) A well-thought-out belief system, 2) a decision of the will to follow Christ in response to his gift of grace, and 3) an authentic experience of the Spirit of Christ through prayer, word, and worship, that shows itself in a life of obedience and service.

*   *   *   *   *

A majority of Americans hold that our land is gripped by a moral and spiritual malaise. Over 65% of Americans maintain that religion is losing its influence on American life. Interestingly, 62% of these same people hold that religion is gaining influence in their own lives.

Apparently, we don't see ourselves as part of the problem. Stephen Carter, author of *The Culture of Disbelief*, lays blame for our societal decay on the fencing out of religion from our public life. He maintains that we have insisted that the religiously faithful act as if their faith did not matter.

On the outside America is just as religious as ever. The vast majority of Americans believe in God. In fact, it could be argued that we are more religious than ever. The percentage of Americans who belong to a church is nearly four times what it was when we gained our independence over 200 years ago. So the debate is not whether or not it's all right to be religious but about the role of religion and spirituality in the public domain. Can any faith be deemed authentic if it does not inform who we are and how we conduct ourselves in the public domain?

Epiphany 3/Ordinary Time 3

Revised Common	Jonah 3:1-5, 10	1 Corinthians 7:29-31	Mark 1:14-20
Roman Catholic	Jonah 3:1-5, 10	1 Corinthians 7:29-31	Mark 1:14-20
Episcopal	Jeremiah 3:21—4:2	1 Corinthians 7:17-23	Mark 1:14-20

Theme For The Day: The right time. In the first lesson (Jonah 3) Jonah warned the inhabitants of Nineveh that it was time to repent. In the second lesson Paul thinks that the time of Christ's return is very near. The gospel begins with our Lord's call to repentance and faith.

BRIEF COMMENTARY ON THE LESSONS

Lesson 1: Jonah 3:1-5, 10 (C, RC)

After being vomited up by the great fish, Jonah reluctantly agrees to preach repentance to the citizens of Nineveh. The populous city readily repents and God retracts his decision to punish the sinful people. This story reveals to the Hebrews and to us that God's call to repentance and faith goes to all people, regardless of race or nationality.

Lesson 1: Jeremiah 3:21—4:2 (E)

The Lord pleads with his people to repent of their sins so that the nations will come to experience God's blessings.

Lesson 2: 1 Corinthians 7:29-31 (C, RC); 1 Corinthians 7:17-23 (E)

Everything that Paul says in this passage is colored by his expectation of the imminent second coming of Christ. In light of this hope, he counsels detachment from the world of ordinary human events — marriage, commerce, and so forth. These things are not ultimate. His attitude toward marriage especially must be understood in light of the *parousia*. In Ephesians he holds marriage in a much more favorable light.

Gospel: Mark 1:14-20 (C, RC, E)

Following the arrest of John the Baptist, Jesus launches his public ministry. Mark summarizes the soul of his message in verse 15: "The time has come ... The kingdom of God is near. Repent and believe the good news." The message was the same as John's but the understanding of those terms is different. It's hard to find the good news in John's teachings, except for his pointing to the One who was greater than he. The Lord's announcement of the kingdom is followed by the call of Andrew and Peter, James and John, by the Sea of Galilee. Jesus forms the redemptive community around himself.

Psalm Of The Day

Psalm 62:5-12 (C) — "For God alone my soul in silence waits" (v. 5).
Psalm 130 (E) — "Out of the depths I cry to you, O Lord!" (v. 1).
Psalm 24 (RC)

Prayer Of The Day

Great God, you sent your Son to announce your kingdom and to make us ready for your rule. By your Spirit, prepare our hearts through daily turning from our sins and toward the good news proclaimed through the life, death, and resurrection of your Son. In his name we pray. Amen.

THEOLOGICAL REFLECTION ON THE LESSONS

Lesson 1: Jonah 3:1-5

The hound of heaven. Jonah attempted to flee from the Lord but to no avail. He was swallowed by the fish and then spit out. Then God came to him again with the charge to go on a mission to Nineveh and proclaim his message. Jeremiah also tried to turn his back on the distasteful mission God gave to him. Yet the message burned in his heart so hotly he had to speak. If the hound of heaven wants us to carry his message, he has a way of being convincing.

Change of heart? It doesn't seem that Jonah really had a change of heart. Sure, he did what God wanted him to do but not from the heart, not willingly. God can make us do something but he has a much more difficult time changing our hearts. God, on the other hand, not only repented of his threatened judgment against Nineveh, he had a change of heart.

Lesson 2: 1 Corinthians 7:29-31

Coming up short on time (v. 29). It seems like the only occasions in which we have too much time is when we're at the dentist or when our bore of a cousin descends like a vulture for a week's visit. Oh yes, I almost forgot about those times conscientious church members inform you when the sermon is over twelve minutes and the service is over an hour. With these few exceptions, it seems that we're constantly coming up short on time. Paul's awareness of the shortness of time promoted him to give the advice in our text. The apostle felt that God was about to consummate the kingdom, which Jesus had commenced. He was wrong about that and we can see from his later writings that he altered his position. Nevertheless, it remains true that the kingdom could come at any time and the things we labor for so diligently will have little meaning. Paul's advice still hits the bull's-eye: don't get too attached to the things of this world, even the good things. Adopt the values of the coming kingdom that are eternal.

Gospel: Mark 1:14-20

The appointed time. The RSV version contains this phrase in the first verse of our second lesson, 1 Corinthians 7:29. I like that imagery because it speaks of a special time for a special event. When John the Baptist was arrested, Jesus realized that the appointed time for him had arrived. He was well aware that the appointed time arranged by the Father was soon to arrive. What had befallen John was a harbinger of his destiny. He had to make the most of each day and every opportunity.

What time is it? According to Jesus, it is time to repent, time to embrace the good news, time to follow him. Our minds are focused on earthly things. Maybe we're possessed with our job or preoccupied with that which gives us pleasure. It's time to embrace the good news of the kingdom. Once we repent we are prepared to accept the good news because we're open to God.

Fill 'er up. Before the days of self-serve gas, when you wanted to have your tank topped off you would wheel into the gas station and announce "Fill 'er up." Time can be equated to an empty gas tank. To run the engine of life, the tank needs to be filled with the proper fuel. A lady in my last parish learned how crucial the right fuel was when she filled the tank of her diesel car with unleaded. After snorting and sputtering for a few miles it died! Others simply neglect to fill their tank and seem to be constantly running on a nearly empty tank. Jesus realized, as he commenced his ministry, that his tank was nearly full; time was full — filled. Being filled with the Spirit, he called his first disciples and labored toward the fullness of the kingdom.

A matter of urgency. Following Jesus was a matter of urgency, the kingdom of God was a matter that required immediate attention. That's the point that Mark is attempting to put across. "And immediately he called them" (v. 20). Though these fishermen undoubtedly had encountered Jesus before, they too responded immediately to Jesus' call. James and John left their father and placed their fishing business in the hands of their hired servants. A person has to act with dispatch when opportunity knocks.

SERMON APPROACHES WITH ILLUSTRATIONS

Lesson 1: Jonah 3:1-5
Sermon Title: Prophet, Heed Your Own Message!
Sermon Angle: God called Jonah to preach repentance to the citizens of the city of Nineveh. Jonah saw these people as wicked, needing repentance and deserving judgment. The prophet didn't perceive his own sinfulness and his own need to repent. He didn't listen to his own message. Regardless of the response of the listeners, if the prophet or preacher doesn't include himself or herself in the audience, the preaching falls short of the mark. Furthermore, when the preacher doesn't have an earnest concern for the well-being of his congregation, in the words of Jesus, he is only a hireling. Jonah needed desperately to listen to the message God gave him to deliver.

Sermon Title: The ABCs Of Preaching Repentance
Sermon Angle: There is a right way and a wrong way to preach repentance.
Outline:
1. Preach repentance only when God lays it on your heart.
2. Preach to yourself as well as others. You also need to repent.
3. Rejoice when those to whom you preach turn to the Lord. Don't be like Jonah.

Lesson 2: 1 Corinthians 7:29-31
Sermon Title: Placing A Price Tag On Time
Sermon Angle: An economic principle has it that there is a direct relation between the amount of a commodity and the worth of that commodity. Gold and diamonds are relatively scarce and so they are relatively expensive. We term them "precious." The same rule relates to time. The less time we have, the more precious its value. It may be foolish to waste time in our youth but absolutely criminal to trash time when we are advanced in years. Paul counseled the Corinthians that they had precious little time (v. 29) so they had better invest it in that which was eternal.

Outline:
1. State the price principle — the more scarce, the more precious.
2. We look at time differently when young — supply seems infinite.
3. Age makes us cognizant of what was true all along — time was always precious.
4. God's prophets remind us that time is very short and very precious.
5. Response: (gospel lesson) Repent and believe the good news.

* * * * *

The Lord taught me yet another lesson concerning the preciousness of time. Our appointed time could come more quickly than we ever imagined. The message came home to me seventeen months ago when my father died after a rather long struggle with cancer. Just two months ago, I took my mother to see her physician. The doctor called me in and said, "I'm really worried about your mother. We need to do some tests." Two days later she was admitted to the hospital. Five days after that a biopsy was performed which confirmed the worst. "How much time does she have, doctor?" my sister asked with tremulous lips. "Two days to two weeks." The words nuked our airy hopes like a SAM missile. Mom's birthday was coming up in a couple of weeks. She requested that her children, grandchildren, and friends write her letters. It was hard. How does one distill a bucket of water into a single precious drop? We all did the best we knew how as we shared the ways that Mom had touched our lives, as we groped to grasp and transmit the impact that her life had upon our own. Through it all, Mom shared her concerns for us and her love for us and for the Lord she had endeavored to serve through the years. Our mutual acknowledgment of the preciousness of time enabled us to use it wisely. There was no time for pretending, for playing games. Only time for loving, caring, and sharing. The time we had was short but oh, so very precious. All of us would agree, no price tag could ever be placed on that brief time we had together.

* * * * *

Gospel: Mark 1:14-20
   Sermon Title: Mission Mandate: Proclaim Repentance!
   Sermon Angle: Jesus picked the haunting echoes of John the Baptist's call to repentance as he inaugurated his ministry in Galilee: "Repent and believe in the good news." That one phrase capsulizes our Lord's message. Christ commands his followers likewise to preach repentance. We embrace this task with the enthusiasm demonstrated by fishermen left with the odious task of cleaning fish. We see it as a completely negative task. Not so! Yes, repentance forces us to confront our sins but with the goal in mind of burying those dead fish so that we might go fishing for the really big one. Repentance *is* good news because it tells us there is something that we can turn to. We can turn to the gospel, to the kingdom of Christ, where we can know and love him forever.
   Outline:
1. Christ issued the call to repent of sins and believe the good news.
2. There is a budding awareness that our society needs to turn back to God.
3. Christ's mandate directs his followers to proclaim repentance.
4. Repentance prepares us to receive the good news of forgiveness and new life.

Sermon Title: What Time Is It?

Sermon Angle: Every now and then someone asks, "What time is it?" As you may know, the New Testament has two different concepts of time. *Chronos*, time as duration, and *kairos*, time pregnant with meaning. Jesus is aware of the shortness of *chronos* but majors on proclaiming time as *kairos*. What time is it?

Outline:
1. Time filled with meaning, purpose, and opportunity (v. 15).
2. Time to repent (v. 15).
3. Time to believe the good news (v. 15).
4. Time to follow him (v. 17).

Sermon Title: Reasons To Go Fishing

Sermon Angle: Most fishermen don't need much of a reason to go fishing. Any old excuse will do. However, there are certainly different reasons for going fishing. The men in the gospel fished for a living. Others fish to gain peace of mind, still others for the challenge of outsmarting the fish. Jesus called Andrew, Peter, James, and John to become fishers of men. The object was not to gain something for themselves but to give something (the gift of eternal life) to others.

Outline:
1. How many of you enjoy fishing? What are your reasons?
2. The apostles featured in today's gospel fished to gain a living.
3. Christ challenges them with a higher calling: fishing to bring others into the kingdom, so they might gain a life, eternal life.
4. Christ's commission is to go fishing — share the gospel of God in your family life, vocational life, recreational life, and church life.

* * * * *

Those who have followed in the footsteps of Peter, James, and John have also been fishermen and women. The Christian church is the world's largest fishing society. Our commission by Christ is to "Go Fishin'!" To bring men and women into the kingdom of God. Imagine this fishing club where the members merely sat around swapping fish stories about the big one they landed, the whopper that broke away, but they never stepped into a boat or cast their line in the water. What kind of a fishing club would it be whose members were content to admire the trophies on the wall but never to go out and actually go fishing? A lot of churches are like that. They sit around bragging about the days when their boat was full of fresh fish. They look nostalgically to the days when the main purpose of their church was to go fishing, to reach others for Christ. But they never actually go fishing, they merely talk about going fishing. That's not what we're about as a church.

What does it mean to go fishing with Jesus? First of all, you need to enjoy fishing. It isn't something that fills you with fear, frustration, or dread. It gives you joy to see lives changed by the power of God's love. But let's face it, we're not going to enjoy something until we try, then we land a few, share the joy of the catch with others, and then work on becoming a better fisherman.

Secondly, you go where the fish are. The reason many fishermen get skunked is they don't go where the fish are. What does that mean for us as a church? We find where the needs are and

84

then seek to meet them. We need to reach the youth and so give time, effort, and money into youth outreach. There are many divorced people who are hurting in the church and in the community. A group where these needs are addressed and God's grace is experienced would gather people who are open to the gospel. I could give many more examples but do you get the point? We can't just fish in the same old way and the same place we always have. Nor can we expect the fish to swim to us. We must seek to attract them with the gospel at the point of their need.

Thirdly, you have to use the right bait. I've found that if I'm fishing for crappies, I had better not use worms. I might catch one now and again on a worm but I've had much better luck with minnows. I know it sounds crass to talk about bait when it's people you're talking about. We're not trying to trick people, so that we can get them to the place where we can feed on them. We aren't trying to lure people to their death but to a life with God that is eternal.

Some churches use entertainment. Other churches promise prosperity and happiness. Others still appeal to social prestige. The only bait worthy of the gospel is love. Love that accepts people where they are. Love that is shown through actions. God has given each of us people that perhaps only we can reach with the gospel. Think about it. Who are they? Identify them. Write their names down. Then reflect on specific ways that you can share God's love with them. Maybe they need a friend. Perhaps they have kids and would appreciate a chance to get away by themselves. Offer to babysit. A parent has died. Send them a card of condolence. Call them up a week or two after the funeral. Yet get the idea. Now do it! Do it as a fisher of men and women. If we let God use us as his love connection, he will amaze us with the results. Of course we are not accountable for results. That's up to the Lord. All that God asks us to do is to be fishermen and fisherwomen for Christ.

Remember, our commission is to go fishin'!

Epiphany 4/Ordinary Time 4

Revised Common	Deuteronomy 18:15-20	1 Corinthians 8:1-13	Mark 1:21-28
Roman Catholic	Deuteronomy 18:15-20	1 Corinthians 7:32-35	Mark 1:21-28
Episcopal	Deuteronomy 18:15-20	1 Corinthians 8:1b-13	Mark 1:21-28

Theme For The Day: Divine authority. Deuteronomy has Moses predicting that God will send a prophet like him, who will rule with authority. The gospel features Jesus acting with authority by casting out demons. In the second lesson Paul reminds us that our actions must be governed by love's authority.

BRIEF COMMENTARY ON THE LESSONS

Lesson 1: Deuteronomy 18:15-20 (C, RC, E)

The book of Deuteronomy reinterprets the laws of Moses for a new generation. It comes in the form of addresses by Moses as the Israelites are about to enter the promised land. This is probably the book that was found during the reign of Josiah and served as the basis for religious reforms, namely, the centralization of the cult in Jerusalem. In this passage Moses promises that God will send a prophet like himself who will preach and act with authority. God will judge those who refuse to listen to his prophet.

Lesson 2: 1 Corinthians 8:1-13 (C); 1 Corinthians 8:1b-13 (E)

Eating meat offered to idols was a bone of contention for early Christians in the Roman empire. Some of the meat offered at the pagan temples was sold at the marketplace. Some Christians thought that it was all right to eat this meat, others did not. Here was another situation regarding this meat. All of the Christians had relatives and friends who might invite them to a banquet at one of the rooms in a pagan temple. The Christian might rightly reason that idols don't really exist and so it's all right to banquet socially at a pagan temple. Paul counsels that it might be all right to dine on this meat but not if it would cause a weaker believer to eat such meat and be conscience stricken. The situation described by Paul doesn't exist any longer but the underlying principle remains: all that we do should be governed by love for the neighbor.

Lesson 2: 1 Corinthians 7:32-35 (RC)

Gospel: Mark 1:21-28 (C, RC, E)

After calling four disciples, Jesus launches his ministry in the town of Capernaum, along the Sea of Galilee, by teaching in the synagogue. Jesus astounds his listeners by speaking with such authority; he taught as if he had a direct line from God, not quoting the noted rabbis. This sense of authority was doubly reinforced by his confrontation with a man possessed by a demon. Jesus immediately drove out the unclean spirit. This exorcism dramatically illustrates his mastery over the powers of evil.

Psalm Of The Day
   Psalm 111 (C, E) — "The fear of the Lord is the beginning of wisdom" (v. 10).
   Psalm 94 (RC)

Prayer Of The Day
   Great God, you have empowered your Son with your Holy Spirit and empowered him to preach, teach, and heal with authority. Strengthen our faith in him that we might speak and act as one who bears the stamp of your word and Spirit. In Jesus' powerful name we pray. Amen.

THEOLOGICAL REFLECTIONS ON THE LESSONS

Lesson 1: Deuteronomy 18:15-20

Mediators of the covenant. The Israelites shunned the immediate presence of God; it was too frightening (v. 16). They demanded someone to stand between them and God. Moses was the greatest of all the Old Testament mediators of God's covenant. In this passage Moses promises that the Lord will send another prophet of his stature to speak God's word. Actually, the Lord sent someone greater than Moses to mediate his presence and pronounce his word; he sent Jesus to stand between us and the white-hot holiness of the Lord.

Puppet or interpreter? The Lord promises to put his words in the mouth of his special prophet (v. 19), but how does he do so? Is the prophet merely a puppet and God the ventriloquist communicating his message word for word? Or does the prophet stand in the presence of God's holy ones and attempt to report what he has seen and heard but in his own language and thought form? I feel more comfortable with the latter analogy. I don't think God takes pleasure in making puppets.

Hear and heed. The responsibility of the prophet is to speak the Lord's message. The recipients of the prophet's message are required both to hear and heed the word of the Lord. Consider this interaction between father and son.

Father: Please cut the grass this afternoon.
Danny: *(silence)*
Father: Did you hear me?
Danny: Yes, father.
(Father comes home in the evening and the lawn hasn't been touched.)
Father: Didn't you hear me tell you to cut the lawn?
Danny: I did hear you but I never said I'd do it.

Lesson 2: 1 Corinthians 8:1-13

Knowledge in the service of love. "Knowledge puffs up, but love builds up" (v. 1). Some people spend their lives in the pursuit of knowledge; others devote themselves to the art of loving. Paul indicates that love looms larger than knowledge on God's scale of values. We ought not disparage knowledge and particularly the pursuit of truth. Yet knowledge is dangerous because it tends to puff up with pride. Love, on the other hand, concentrates on the other person and seeks to build him up. Knowledge is valuable but must be placed in the service of love.

God the Father, the destination; Jesus, the way. Paul maintains that there is one God and Father, from whom are all things and for whom we exist, and one Lord, Jesus Christ, through whom are all things and through whom we exist. God the Father is the destination; Jesus Christ is the means to this destination. Jesus said himself, "I am the way ..." and, according to the book of Acts, early Christians were known as the followers of the way.

Consideration for your neighbor's conscience. Paul argues that Christians need to gauge the appropriateness of their behavior not only by their conscience but by the conscience of other people. He seems particularly concerned that Christians not do anything to cause other believers spiritual harm. Paul invokes the principle of love; if my action harms another person, even though it may be all right in itself, love dictates that I desist. Eating meat offered to idols was a moral issue for the apostolic church. Gambling presents a contemporary issue that lifts up the same principle. It can be argued that for millions of people gambling is harmless fun. They know how much they are willing to lose and stop when they reach that limit. They have control over their gambling. But let's say that a church member sees a leader in the church gambling. He thinks, "Well, it's all right" and proceeds to roll the dice. This person, however, has little internal control over his gaming. In fact, he soon becomes addicted and plummets into financial ruin. Does not the principle of Christian love dictate that we, people of knowledge and control, desist from gambling for the sake of our weaker brothers and sisters?

Gospel: Mark 1:21-28

Immediately. Right after picking some of his disciples, Jesus wasted no time before engaging in ministry. It was the sabbath day and "immediately" he entered the synagogue and taught. Jesus didn't have to decide whether or not he was going to synagogue. It was his custom to worship with the community of believers and so he went immediately. Jesus was a man with a mission to bring in the kingdom of God. There was no time to lose! The logical place to begin was the religious community, immediately!

Taught with authority. Those worshipers were astonished by the authority with which Jesus taught. What are the components of such authority? 1) To speak and act in a way that leaves no doubt that you know your subject. Jesus didn't just know about his subject; he knew his subject (the kingdom of God) firsthand. 2) To have your actions and your life corroborate your words. Casting out the demon gave credence to Jesus' teachings. 3) There must be immediacy. Hearers must see how the teachings can make a difference in their lives right now. Jesus employed everyday images, symbols, and stories to make God's truth come alive.

Spiritual battle. The man who entered the synagogue was probably seeking wholeness though such a person was not supposed to enter a holy place. A community of unclean spirits had splintered his being. In the presence of Jesus the spirits felt threatened. "What do you want with us, Jesus of Nazareth? Have you come to destroy us?" (v. 24). Precisely! He was launching his initial attack against the forces of evil.

Know your enemy (v. 24). The unclean spirits knew Jesus' identity. It's interesting to note that they are the first to acknowledge his identity. Jesus likewise recognized what he was dealing with. The first rule of war is to know your enemy, because if you don't he will launch a surprise attack that could devastate you. Unfortunately, some churches seem to regard other churches that hold different ideas as the enemy. How the forces of evil must rejoice at such times! Let us join together in a united front against our common enemy, the prince of darkness.

SERMON APPROACHES WITH ILLUSTRATIONS

Lesson 1: Deuteronomy 18:15-20
Sermon Title: How To Distinguish A True Prophet

Sermon Angle: The people of Israel are promised a prophet like Moses. What are the characteristics of a real prophet? How will the people be able to know when he arrives? 1) He will not raise himself up, God will. 2) He will mediate between the Lord and the people. 3) God will put his words in the prophet's mouth. How can we tell if the message comes from the Lord? It will not conflict with what God has already revealed.

Sermon Title: Hear And Heed

Sermon Angle: God says that anyone who doesn't listen to his prophet will have to answer to the Lord himself. It isn't enough just to hear God's prophet, one must also heed his or her message. Sometimes we preachers wonder if anyone really listens to us. That is, does it alter their values, behavior, and so forth? I was pleasantly surprised when a member of the church I serve called and reported that my sermon had inspired him to give a goodly amount of money. He wanted to know what the needs were. Praise the Lord! Worshipers do hear and heed, some of them, the message the Lord gives us to preach.

Outline:
1. God puts his word into the mouth of his preachers.
2. God expects us to take his prophets seriously.
3. This involves not only hearing but heeding his or her message.

Lesson 2: 1 Corinthians 8:1-13
Sermon Title: The Biggest Fool Is A Knowledgeable Fool

Sermon Angle: You've heard the saying, "There's no fool like an educated fool." Knowledge and education can puff one up with pride. Paul states that the person who thinks he really knows something does not know as he ought (v. 2). Rather than seek knowledge for its own sake, the child of God should seek to know God as perfectly as he knows us. We come to know God, the fount of all knowledge and wisdom, not through our mind but through the power of love.

Outline:
1. The biggest fool is a knowledgeable fool.
2. Superior knowledge may make him feel superior in every way.
3. Love is the more excellent way (1 Corinthians 13), better than knowledge.
4. Knowledge puffs up, love builds up others in community.

Sermon Title: Christians Are In The Business Of Raising, Not Razing

Sermon Angle: The apostle makes a key point concerning the nature of love. "It builds up" other people; it builds up the church; it builds up society. Prejudice and hatred, on the flip side of the coin, raze (demolish) everything in sight. A sermon on this topic could encourage the members of your church to be constructive in all their words and actions. God gives us his love that we might build up both church and society.

Outline:
1. Knowledge or perceived knowledge causes some people to tear others down.
2. Love builds up the other by affirming them as inherently precious.

3. Are your words and deeds razing or raising (spell out both words) the lives of others?
4. God raised us up in Christ that we might raise up one another in love.

Sermon Title: The Burden Of Maturity

Sermon Angle: Paul makes a strong case that those who are spiritually knowledgeable (mature) have a responsibility to set an example for those whose faith is not as fully developed. In the case of eating meat offered to idols, he sees nothing inherently wrong with doing it. However, he cautions the Corinthians also to consider the effect their actions have on others. A less mature person might follow their example and engage in an activity that harms his conscience. The #1 ethical principle for the spiritually mature is the rule of love. Living by this principle might seem a burden but, in the end, will make everyone more free.

Outline:
1. Knowledge and maturity can be a burden. (Give examples.)
2. Part of the burden is determining what effect our actions have on others (the rule of love).
3. Paul uses the meat issue to illustrate the principle.
4. Where do we see the principle in a contemporary context? (Gambling?)
5. The love of Christ can make restrictions on our freedom seem no burden at all.

Gospel: Mark 1:21-28

Sermon Title: Mission Mandate: Minister With Christ's Authority!

Sermon Angle: All that Jesus did conveyed a sense of authority, which we see plainly in this lection. In the synagogue he taught with authority. He presented eternal truths in a fresh manner and in a way that touched people's lives. His words of authority were backed by authoritative actions. He demonstrated the power of God in the exorcism. He had power over the forces of darkness. Christ commissions the church to minister with his authority, the authority of divine truth.

Outline:
1. Today's text highlights Jesus' authority.
2. We live in a world almost devoid of accepted authority.
3. Even in the church we have lost touch with Christ's authority and have substituted the latest psychological, sociological, or political fad.
4. Relativism has also diluted Christ's authority.
5. Christ calls us to follow him as Lord and minister to the world with his authority.

Sermon Title: Jesus, The Exorcist

Sermon Angle: The ancients believed that demons were everywhere, a concept that most Westerners have difficulty accepting. Did Jesus believe in their existence or was he just utilizing the common conception? I choose to accept that Jesus did believe in the demonic and that the demonic is real. How can you not accept the reality of the demonic when you look around? Parents murder, rape, and abuse their children. Authority figures abuse their position. Teenagers murder innocent children. Jesus, the Lord, has the power to cast out the demons that we let into our lives.

Outline:
1. The realm of the evil and demonic are real.
2. We permit demonic forces to enter our lives — gossip, jealousy, rage, war.

3. Jesus has power and authority over the demonic (illustrated in our text).
4. He can free us from demonic forces if we give him access.

*   *   *   *   *

Years ago the movie *The Exorcist* was all the vogue. The story line had a raging demon take possession of a young girl, played by Linda Blair. Her parents seek help in the form of a priest exorcist who does battle with the demon in the name of God. The encounters between the exorcist and the possessed were so vivid that little kids who viewed the movie had nightmares for weeks. The possessed girl rolled her eyes into the sockets, out of her mouth gushed forth all manner of putrid fluid, and in a guttural voice, straight out of hell, she cursed the exorcist. The demon was finally dislodged only after a gigantic struggle and the death of the first exorcist.

It's not a great movie. I just want to make a couple of points. First, the demonic seldom exhibits itself through such theatrics. The devil prefers to operate incognito. Second, the demonic cannot take possession of us unless we open the door and permit entrance. However, once the demonic gets hold of us, there is no way to dislodge it except through the power of Christ. The movie agrees with the gospel account of Jesus' exorcism; demons will not leave willingly. Only superior spiritual force compels them to vacate, and then, kicking and screaming.

Epiphany 5/Ordinary Time 5

Revised Common	Isaiah 40:21-31	1 Corinthians 9:16-23	Mark 1:29-39
Roman Catholic	Job 7:1-4, 6-7	1 Corinthians 9:16-19, 22-23	Mark 1:29-39
Episcopal	2 Kings 4:(8-17) 18-21 (22-31) 32-37	1 Corinthians 9:16-23	Mark 1:29-39

Theme For The Day: The Lord's saving help for the downtrodden and the weak. We also see how Jesus' life of prayer energized him for ministry.

BRIEF COMMENTARY ON THE LESSONS

Lesson 1: Isaiah 40:21-31 (C)

This chapter begins the second major section in the book of Isaiah, the so-called Deutero-Isaiah. It was written during the Babylonian captivity period, approximately 540 BC, to give hope to the dejected captives. The prophet reminds the Hebrews that their God is creator of heaven and earth and nothing is impossible for him. In fact, this author employs the word "created" more than any other biblical writer (*The Oxford Bible*, p. 871). The people are warned against cynicism and pessimism, thinking that God has forgotten them. God does not grow weary or faint. He remains willing and able to save them. If they but wait patiently on the Lord, he will renew their strength.

Lesson 1: Job 7:1-4, 6-7 (RC)

Job expresses dire despair at his misery. He sees no hope and compares his life to a slave waiting for the evening shadows or a worker for his wages. Life is fleeting and, as Job sees it from the pit of his distress, without hope.

Lesson 1: 2 Kings 4:(8-17) 18-21 (22-31) 32-37 (E)

Lesson 2: 1 Corinthians 9:16-23 (C, E); 1 Corinthians 9:16-19, 22-23 (RC)

Paul asserts his right to preach the gospel free of charge. He certainly has the right to receive payment for sharing the gospel but chooses to waive this privilege. He does this that he might proclaim the gospel without strings or external influences. Paul earned his living as a tent maker. Paradoxically, though he is free, he has willingly become the slave of all people for the purpose of winning all possible people to the faith. His strategy of birthing Christians involves identifying with the people he hopes to reach. To the Jews he is a Jew; to the Gentiles he becomes a Gentile; to the weak, he also lacks strength. The apostle's aim of sharing the gospel dictates almost everything that he does.

Gospel: Mark 1:29-39 (C, RC, E)

This lection continues last Sunday's text. Jesus leaves the synagogue in Capernaum and enters the home of Peter and Andrew. The ministry begun in the synagogue continues in a home. Peter's mother lies ill with a fever. Jesus takes her by the hand and restores her not only to health but service; she commences to serve them dinner. After sundown, the end of the sabbath, crowds of people come to the home for healing. They could not come sooner because a request for healing would be considered work. Jesus mercifully heals them all and casts out demons. He orders the demons to silence, part of the messianic secret. Early in the morning, he arises and departs to a quiet spot for meditation and prayer. Such fellowship with God maintains his vision and strength for ministry. His disciples find him to report that crowds of people are looking for him. He retorts that they must depart for other towns in Galilee. Jesus' ministry moves forward by leaps and bounds.

Psalm Of The Day
    Psalm 147:1-11, 20c (C) — "He [the Lord] heals the brokenhearted and binds up their wounds" (v. 3).
    Psalm 142 (E) — "Give heed to my cry for I am brought very low" (v. 6).
    Psalm 146 (RC)

Prayer Of The Day
    Lord God, it is your delight to show mercy on the sick and to free the oppressed. Communicate your love and grace to us in this place of prayer, that we too might minister in your most holy name to those brought low by adversity or weakness. In the most powerful name of Jesus. Amen.

THEOLOGICAL REFLECTION ON THE LESSONS

Lesson 1: Isaiah 40:21-31
Abandoned by God? The defeated and humiliated people of Israel felt abandoned by their God. Even the very symbol of their religion, the temple, had been decimated. The people had profound doubts about God's care for them or his strength. The first sentiment is found in the phrase "My way is hid from the Lord ..." (v. 27). The sense that their God was powerless comes through Isaiah's comments as he responds to the duress of his people and is indicated by passages such as: "He does not faint or grow weary ..." (v. 28b). Can there be greater despair than to feel bereft of your God?

Strength for the journey. To complete an arduous journey requires rest. Strength comes through rest. Isaiah encourages his people to rest in the Lord, to wait on their God. He promises that those who do so will "renew their strength, they shall lift up with wings as an eagle, they shall run and not be weary ..." (v. 31).

Understanding the law of lift. In order to fly a person needs to understand the principles of aerodynamics, the laws of lift and of drag. Isaiah instructs his grounded kinsmen concerning the laws of spiritual aerodynamics. If they would have their faith take flight, they must understand that they must wait on the Lord in faith, trust in his grace and goodness. Then, only then, would their faith take flight. We dare not be ignorant of the law of spiritual lift and drag.

Lesson 1: Job 7:1-7
Life is hard! Several years ago we had an exchange student from Germany who would frequently repine, "Life is hard!" That's how Job felt, like his life was that of a slave. Not only was life difficult but devoid of meaning, he felt (v. 3). Just the other day a couple I know experienced the pain that life can sometimes afflict. Their daughter has cancer and only weeks to live. Life can indeed be hard but faith tells us that God's love for us has not waned.

Lesson 2: 1 Corinthians 9:16-23

The necessity of preaching the gospel (v. 16). Paul experienced not only a state of urgency but of necessity in proclaiming the gospel. The gospel was not something that he chose but that chose him. Christ had commissioned him, on the road to Damascus, to be his ambassador. So many Christians do not feel a sense of necessity in proclaiming the gospel; for most, it is strictly optional. Wouldn't you say that something seems to be lacking here?

Gospel freebies. Paul asserts that his only source of pride is that the gospel he preaches is free of charge. By that he meant to say that he did not make his living from the gospel but was self-supporting. Of course, in truth the gospel is always free. No one can afford to pay for it, no one can earn it. It comes gratis, a freebie. Our problem is that freebies are generally regarded as not being worth very much. That's why so many Christians still try to earn it. To try to pay God for his greatest gift is about as insulting to God as it would be for a wife whose husband offered to pay her for making love.

Gospel: Mark 1:29-39

Love-lift (v. 1). Peter's mother-in-law lay ill with a fever when Jesus and his disciples entered Simon's home. Immediately Jesus took her by the hand and lifted her to health. Right after that she began serving them. Did he heal her so that he might gain a servant? No, love motivated Jesus to lift her up. Service was the woman's response of gratitude. Who are the people whom you've encountered recently who need a love-lift?

House calls. Not many physicians are willing to make house calls anymore. The sick are required to come to the physician. Jesus made house calls from the very beginning of his ministry, as the healing of Simon's mother-in-law demonstrates. Jesus was always willing to take God's grace to the point of human need. He didn't show forth the attitude of one of my former parishioners: "They (inactive members) know where the church is. They can come whenever they want."

How to beat a path to your door. There is a maxim in advertising that if you provide what people want, they will beat a path to your door. That was certainly true with Jesus. To put it crassly, Jesus' actions in the synagogue advertised a product that many people wanted. They desired healing in body and spirit; they craved wholeness. Jesus dramatically demonstrated that he could fulfill their need. That's why the crowds beat a path to his door. They undoubtedly needed more than mere physical or mental healing, they needed reconciliation with God, but the obvious need was Jesus' point of contact. The church must employ the same strategy, fulfill an obvious need, so that we might eventually minister to the deeper needs of the spirit.

How to greet the day (v. 35). Mark tells us that Jesus rose a great while before the break of day and went to a secluded spot where he prayed. He had so much to do that he had to spend a great while in prayer. How do you greet the day? With a groan or sigh? A shower and shave? We'd be wise to follow our Lord's example and greet the day with prayer.

Message on the move (v. 38). When the disciples found Jesus at his place of prayer they reported that everyone was looking for him. Jesus replied that there were other places of need. He needed to go and preach to the other villages of Galilee. It was his purpose to disperse his message to as many people and places as possible. The gospel cannot be put in a bottle.

SERMON APPROACHES WITH ILLUSTRATIONS

Lesson 1: Isaiah 40:21-31

Sermon Title: Gain A Wider Perspective

Sermon Angle: The captive Jews existed in a trench of despair. The prophet encouraged the people to obtain a more expansive outlook. "Lift up your eyes and look to the heavens ..." (v. 26). He urges them to expand their outlook, not only in terms of space but of time: "The Lord is the everlasting God ..." (v. 28). Despair and depression narrows our perspective, which can lead to giving up. Faith gains us a wider perspective as we look up to the Lord.

Outline:
1. Despair caused the Jews to feel that God was unconcerned about their plight (v. 27).
2. Isaiah urges a wider faith perspective.
   — God is the creator of the universe (v. 26).
   — God is eternal (v. 28).
   — He gives strength to his weary people (v. 29).

Sermon Title: On Eagle's Wings

Sermon Angle: God gives strength to the weak and the weary. God himself is the source of strength. All who place their hope in him will soar, as on eagle's wings. The Lord becomes the wind beneath their wings.

Outline:
1. The lives of the captive Israelites had plummeted into hopelessness (v. 27).
2. God would raise up those who admitted their weakness and looked to the Lord for strength (v. 29).
3. As the eaglet soared on its mother's wings, so God would raise up his earthbound children (v. 31).

Lesson 2: 1 Corinthians 9:16-23

Sermon Title: Would You Like An Endless Line Of Credit?

Sermon Angle: Credit card companies are anxious to give everyone a line of credit. It may start small but grow bigger and bigger as you demonstrate that you are faithful in making the minimum payment. How would you like an endless line of credit and no minimum payment? Sounds too good to be true, doesn't it? Paul states that the gospel is free of charge (v. 18). God extends to us an endless line of credit because of credits that Christ earned for us on the cross.

Outline:
1. How would you react if someone mailed you a credit card with an endless line of credit and no minimum payment? (Share some possible scenarios.)
2. The gospel is such an endless line of credit (v. 18).
3. To receive it, we must really believe it! (John 3:16).

Sermon Title: Entering The Other Person's Story

Sermon Angle: Paul states that he had become all things to all people for the sake of the gospel (v. 22). To put it differently, Paul attempted to enter into the other person's story: his thoughts, feelings, and culture. To communicate effectively necessitates such a practice and this is certainly true of the gospel.

Outline:
1. To share the gospel necessitates entering the other person's story.
   — We must enter his world before the gospel can enter his life.
   — Jesus entered our story to save us; we must do the same for others.
2. To communicate Christ we need to cross cultural barriers.
3. Human distinctions (our stories) are not ultimate, the gospel (God's story) is.

Gospel: Mark 1:29-39

Sermon Title: Mission Mandate: Pray Up, Then Move Out!

Sermon Angle: Jesus was besieged by needy people. To recharge his spiritual batteries he engaged in regular prayer with the Father. However, he resisted the temptation to become the personal physician of one set of people. The claims of the kingdom needed to be heard in other places. The church must follow our Lord's example: Pray up and then move out.

Outline:

Introduction: It's important to begin the day properly. What does it take? Plenty of rest? A nutritious breakfast? A refreshing shower? A good, stout cup of coffee? Jesus has a better idea.
1. Pray up — He rose early to seek God's guidance and strength (v. 35).
2. Move out in mission and service (v. 38).
3. The mission of the church remains — seek God's will, then do God's will.

* * * * *

Jesus had a plan. One of the reasons that he spent so much time praying was that he needed the Father's inspiration to flesh out the details of the plan. Before you can arrive someplace, you need to envision it and have a road map for getting there. The plan needs to be concrete and visual. The book *Jesus, CEO*, by Laurie Beth Jones, makes the point that the plan needs to be conveyed through pictures. The author employs the analogy of civil rights, which she maintains is an intangible idea. It's difficult for most people to grasp such concepts. However, blacks being forced to sit in the back of the bus is an image we can all relate to. Jesus proclaimed the inbreaking of the kingdom of God, a theoretical construct. However, Jesus created hundreds of images of what the kingdom of God might look like through his parables and healings. An essential aspect of Jesus' mission was to concretize, first for himself and then for his hearers, the kingdom. His mission of mercy was a concrete expression of his prayer vision.

* * * * *

Sermon Title: Love Lifted Me

Sermon Angle: When Jesus healed Peter's mother-in-law, he reached out and lifted her up. Love reached out to this woman prostrate with fever and lifted her up. This scene reminds me of the episode on the Sea of Galilee, when the disciples were assailed by a storm and Jesus walked out on the water to aid them. Peter asked Jesus to bid him come on the water. Peter stepped in the water, but when he looked about him at the tempest he began to sink with fear. The Lord reached down to lift him up and get him back to the boat. It is that scene that prompted the gospel song "Love Lifted Me" (found in *The Hymnal For Worship & Celebration*, 505). Jesus in love reached down to save us. Can we do less than be extensions of his saving arms for others?

Outline:
1. Jesus reached out to lift Peter's mother-in-law from her sickbed.
2. The love of Jesus is expressed in more than words, but also loving actions.
3. Sometimes people need more than advice; they need a lift.
4. The love of God has lifted us up.
   — Christ reaches down to us through the gospel and through the actions of those who live out his love.
5. Reach out to others with Christ's lift of love.

Sermon Title: House Church

Sermon Angle: Simon's home became the very first Christian church; it was a house church. Even today you can witness the excavations of that very house in the village of Capernaum. It was a mere stone's throw from the synagogue and not very large. For the first three centuries of its existence the Christian church met in homes, in catacombs, and in the woods. No imposing ecclesiastical structures existed. Still, the faith prospered. We would do well to regard our homes as house churches, places of healing, worship, and service.

Outline:
1. Jesus ministered in the synagogue, the home, or wherever there was need.
2. In the early church the faith was centered in the homes.
3. In our day we have come to regard ecclesiastical sites and structures as the center of our Christian life, rather than the home or the marketplace.
   — Life is divided into the sacred (churchly) and the profane (worldly).
4. Do you proclaim the gospel in the places you inhabit?

Epiphany 6/Ordinary Time 6

Revised Common	2 Kings 5:1-14	1 Corinthians 9:24-27	Mark 1:40-45
Roman Catholic	Leviticus 13:1-2, 44-46	1 Corinthians 10:31—11:1	Mark 1:40-45
Episcopal	2 Kings 5:1-15	1 Corinthians 9:24-27	Mark 1:40-45

Theme For The Day: God's cleansing presence and power, with or without water. In the first lesson Elisha cleansed Namaan, the Syrian, by telling him to wash in the Jordan River. In the gospel Jesus cleansed a leper who requested healing by touching him.

BRIEF COMMENTARY ON THE LESSONS

Lesson 1: 2 Kings 5:1-14 (C); 2 Kings 5:1-15 (E)

Namaan, a general from the army of the Syrians, was sent to the king of Israel by his own king, asking that he be healed of his leprosy. An Israeli girl, absconded in war, informed her master of a prophet in Samaria who could do miracles. The king of Israel thinks this is a pretense for a quarrel. Elisha, a ninth-century prophet, hears of the situation and asks the king to send Namaan to him. When the general's chariot rolls up to Elisha's door, he is greeted by Elisha's servant, who relays the prophet's instructions to wash in the Jordan River. Namaan is insulted that the prophet doesn't give him VIP treatment and is going to storm off in a rage, but his servants encourage him to obey the prophet; he does and is healed. The story demonstrates the superiority of Israel's God but also his grace even to Gentiles.

Lesson 1: Leviticus 13:1-2, 44-46 (RC)

The chapter contains laws concerning the treatment of infectious skin diseases. Due to a lack of knowledge concerning the nature of disease, many skin disorders were referred to as leprosy. The afflicted person was required to be examined by a priest, who might isolate him or her for a period of seven days. If the disorder appeared to lessen, the afflicted one would be declared clean. If the person developed reddish-white patches in which the hair in the sore turned white, that person was pronounced unclean, made to wear tattered clothes and disheveled hair, forced to disassociate from society and cry "Unclean" anytime he or she approached other people. Such disease was considered a sign of sin and so society did not regard these poor souls with compassion.

Lesson 2: 1 Corinthians 9:24-27 (C, E)

Paul encourages spiritual self-discipline. He employs metaphors from two sports that he undoubtedly witnessed in the Greek games, running and boxing. He urges believers to run the race of the Christian life with vigor, straining for the prize, eternal life. In the boxing analogy he makes the point that he doesn't just swing wildly, beating the air; he makes every punch count.

Lesson 2: 1 Corinthians 10:31—11:1 (RC)

The believers are enjoined to make everything they do count for Christ and guard against actions, which would give offense and thus hinder the spread of the gospel. Paul encourages them to follow his lead.

Gospel: Mark 1:40-45 (C, RC, E)

A leper approaches Jesus, kneeling at his feet and begging for mercy. "If you want to, you can make me clean" (v. 40). Of course, being banished from society would not do wonders for one's self-image. The leper had some hope but was not sure Jesus would want to help. The Lord was moved with compassion, touched him, and pronounced him clean. Jesus' contact with the leper was a break from tradition, though he did instruct the man to go to a priest for the required cleansing rites, which would certify him as ready to re-enter normal society. Jesus strongly urges the man not to broadcast his healing because he knows that the publicity would not enable him to move about as freely. The man does so anyway, which forces Jesus to change his mission strategy. He can no longer enter the towns due to the crowds; the people must come to him in the country.

Psalm Of The Day

Psalm 30 (C) — "O Lord, I cried to you for help, and you have healed me" (v. 2).
Psalm 42 (E) — "Hope in God; for I shall again praise him ..." (v. 11b).
Psalm 31 (RC)

Prayer Of The Day

Merciful Lord, in desperation we flee from the uncleanness of our sins, fall at your feet, and plead for your cleansing. Thank you, Jesus, for your compassion and your healing grace. In your powerful and precious name we pray. Amen.

THEOLOGICAL INTERPRETATIONS OF THE LESSONS

Lesson 1: 2 Kings 5:1-15

Achilles' heel. Namaan was a successful general and courageous but he still had his Achilles' heel, his vulnerable spot. Was it his leprosy? No, it was his pride that almost prevented him from being healed of his disease. No matter what our station in life, we, too, have our Achilles' heel. Getting in touch with vulnerabilities keeps us humble enough for the Lord to use us to his glory.

God gives victory to our enemies? Verse 1 makes an interesting assertion, that it was the Lord who granted Namaan victory over Israel. Perhaps this is a warning not to take the Lord for granted. If we forget the Lord and do that which is unjust, we cannot expect victory in our lives, even if we are God's baptized children. Defeat by our enemies might be one way God gets our attention.

Listen to the little people. Namaan was an important man in his region of the world. Yet he had the wisdom to listen to his wife's servant, a prize of battle. He listened to one of the little people that God has made so many of. She was a vehicle that enabled him to pass from death to life. Then, when he was about to stomp away from Elisha's house in rage, other servants importuned him to do as the prophet directed. A wise leader listens to the rank and file.

Great expectations. Namaan had great expectations as he wheeled up to Elisha's house. The prophet would come out clad in his best robe, bow in deference to one more eminent than he, and then, wave his hand over the leprosy as he chanted some incantation. Instead Elisha gave word through his servant that Namaan should wash in the Jordan River. What an insult! Often God doesn't meet our need in the way we had envisioned. He asks us to trust him and obey him.

Lesson 2: 1 Corinthians 9:24-27

Self-discipline. Athletic training points to the vital role of self-discipline. The body needs to be brought under control in order to attain the goal. An athlete exercises self-control not only in sports but, as Paul states, "in all things" (v. 25). Giving in to bodily impulses dissipates energy. The follower of Christ must bring body and mind under the control of God's Spirit to win the heavenly prize.

Energy conservation. When Paul states that he does not box as one aimlessly beating the air (v. 26), he's talking about energy conservation. Back in the '70s, the Arab oil embargo shocked us into realizing that we could not continue being so profligate in our use of energy. The price of gas went up dramatically to cool demand; it was rationed in some cases. Autos started becoming more economical and much information was disseminated as to how we could make our buildings more energy efficient. We Christians waste enormous amounts of energy in worrying, chasing after material security, or in trying to pretend we are someone we are not. Churches waste energy in clinging to traditions that serve no useful purpose, in preserving personal power bases, and by not having a clear fix on our mission. In battling the forces of darkness, we must make every punch count.

Gospel: Mark 1:40-45

Sin and sickness. The leper had faith enough to believe that Jesus could heal him or make him "clean," as he put it. The term "clean" indicates the common belief that disease, especially this one, was a result of some spiritual uncleanness or sin. We know that sin did not cause this disease. Nevertheless, the man really was unclean. He may have had foul discharges from the sores on his body. He felt unclean, unacceptable to God or society, and the way that the world treated him reinforced his uncleanness. As he approached people, he had to yell out "Unclean! Unclean!" Jesus did not accept the common notion of sin and sickness, nor did he regard this leper as unclean.

God is always willing. The leper prefaced his petition with the phrase, "if you are willing" (v. 40). His hesitancy is understandable. However, faith shows us that Jesus is always willing to reach out his hand to help and heal. He may not do everything we ask in a manner that fulfills our expectations, but he is always willing to remove our uncleanness. There are many in the world who approach those who bear the name of Christ and ask: "If you are willing, you can make me clean." Are we willing to reach out Christ's hand of mercy to touch people and make them clean?

The One that gets used. The US West yellow pages advertises that their book is the one that gets used, yes, even abused. God is often the One who gets used. We have a problem, we turn to the Lord. The problem is solved, we soon forget about him. Jesus was concerned that people would want to use his wonder-working power without being converted or spiritually transformed. The healings by Christ were meant to draw attention to the claims of God's kingdom, so that people might turn to the Lord for renewal of their minds as well as their bodies. That explains why Jesus told the healed leper not to tell anyone about his deliverance. The Lord may not mind being used but he certainly does not desire to be abused.

Responding to the marketplace. Jesus' popularity flared up as a result of his healing ministry. At first he preached and taught from the village synagogues. When the crowds swelled he had to respond to the spiritual marketplace and let the people come to him in the country. The church should take a lesson in this; we cling too long to outmoded methodologies for mission.

SERMON APPROACHES WITH ILLUSTRATIONS

Lesson 1: 2 Kings 5:1-15

Sermon Title: Listen To The Children

Sermon Angle: My grandmother was fond of saying, "Children are meant to be seen, not heard." She apparently was not taught to value the thoughts and feelings of children. Children were supposed to act like adults. Namaan listened to his wife's maid when she told him about the prophet in Samaria. This girl had faith that Elisha would heal her master. Children have something to teach us about faith and love.

Outline:

Introduction: We often forget that this story would not have happened without this girl. Consider this extraordinary girl.

1. She was kidnapped and yet seemed to bear no animosity against her captors.
2. She was genuinely concerned about her master — this shows her love.
3. She offered a solution — this showed her wisdom (v. 3).
4. She believed that the prophet would heal her master (v. 3) — this showed her faith.
5. Listen to the children, they have much to teach us about faith and love.

Sermon Title: The King And The Kid

Sermon Angle: The reactions of the king of Israel and the maid girl to Namaan, the leper, are at opposite ends of the continuum. The girl believed that Elisha could and would heal her master, while the king of Israel threw up his hands in frustration (v. 7). He reacted with cynicism and frustration rather than faith. He interpreted that the king of Syria just wanted to pick a fight with him (v. 8). He viewed Elisha not as a resource for making peace but as an obstacle to his ambitions.

Sermon Title: There Is More Than One Way To Get Clean

Sermon Angle: This lesson and the gospel present two ways to get clean. Namaan was told to go wash in the Jordan River in order to get cleansed of his leprosy, something that he at first refused to do. Bathing in water is the usual way to get clean. Since water is such a great cleansing agent, it became also a perfect sign of spiritual cleansing through holy baptism. In the gospel, Jesus effects a dry cleansing of the leper through word and touch. Words have the capacity to make us feel dirty or clean. Words of acceptance and forgiveness are especially powerful cleansing agents. Christ also touches our hearts through holy communion and makes us feel clean inside and out.

Outline:

1. Discuss various ways of cleansing and the importance of feeling clean.
2. Elisha cleansed Namaan through Jordan River water.
3. In the gospel, Jesus cleansed this leper through word and touch.
4. In baptism we are washed of our sin and declared acceptable to God.
5. In communion Jesus touches us with cleansing grace and forgiveness.

Lesson 2: 1 Corinthians 9:24-27

Sermon Title: Why Do You Run?

Sermon Angle: Every day, as I take my daughter's basset hound for a walk, I encounter runners. One runner pants so loudly that I can clearly hear his gasping a half block away. Why are all these people running? To take off pounds? To improve their health? To drain off frustrations? To live longer? There are many good reasons to run, I suppose, but none powerful enough to prompt me to put on my Nikes. Some of us just aren't joggers but we are all runners in the race of life. Are we competing against all the other runners or against the clock? Are we running with Jesus or do we expect Jesus to run with us? There is a difference! Are we running because someone or something is chasing us or because we seek the glorious prize of eternal life with God? What about you? Why exactly are you running?

Outline:
1. Paul ran with purpose because he had his goal clearly focused (v. 26a).
2. Many people run for sport. For what purpose?
3. We are all runners in the race of life but why are we running? To what end?
4. Run with Jesus to obtain the imperishable prize.

*　*　*　*　*

The blockbuster movie, *Forrest Gump*, illustrates the question posed above. That is, why are we running? Where are we going? Forrest was a somewhat mentally deficient boy who started running to elude his persecutors. The doctor placed braces on his legs but one day when some bullies were chasing him down the road in their truck, he ran so fast that the braces just fell away. Forrest could run really fast. They put him on the college football squad and he ran around the ends and through the middle. He ran so fast that he scored touchdown upon touchdown. The problem was that he was so intent on his running that he didn't halt after reaching the goal line and so they placed a sign at the end of the field that read "Stop, Forrest!"

His girlfriend, his only friend, Jenny, went away and then his mother died. After a time, he started running. At first he was just going to run to town but when he got there he decided to run across the county, then the state, and then the country. He ran back and forth across the country three or four times. As he ran, people started running with him. They figured that he knew where he was going. They imagined that there was a cause or that he was going to momentarily utter some word of wisdom. Finally he got tired of running and went home.

I wonder how many of us are running merely because other people are running and we figure that they must know where they are going?

*　*　*　*　*

Gospel: Mark 1:40-45

Sermon Title: Mission Mandate: Offer Spiritual Cleansing!

Sermon Angle: The first lesson features the cleansing of Namaan the leper by Elisha. In our gospel Jesus heals a leper who spread abroad the good news of his healing. Our Christian mission impels us to cleanse and heal those who want to be made whole.

Outline:
1. The leper begged Jesus to cleanse him of his leprosy.
2. He wasn't sure Christ wanted to heal him (v. 40).

3. Jesus stood ready to cleanse him.
4. The pollution of our sins is great; the mission mandate for the church is for us to be cleansed by Christ, that we might clean up the world.

Sermon Title: What A Pity!

Sermon Angle: Jesus was moved with pity at the plight of leper; that pity moved him to action. What a pity! We use the phrase to mean "Isn't that too bad!" Jesus expressed his pity not through words but through actions of deliverance and mercy.

Outline:
1. What a pity! Jesus was moved to pity by the sight of the leper and his plea.
2. His pity led him to reach out his hand to cleanse and heal.
3. Our feelings may be moved by the plight of the unfortunate but that isn't enough.
4. Our pity must lead us to acts of compassion.

Epiphany 7/Ordinary Time 7

Revised Common	Isaiah 43:18-25	2 Corinthians 1:18-22	Mark 2:1-12
Roman Catholic	Isaiah 43:18-19, 21-22, 24b-25	2 Corinthians 1:18-22	Mark 2:1-12
Episcopal	Isaiah 43:18-25	2 Corinthians 1:18-22	Mark 2:1-12

Theme For The Day: Forgiveness of sins. In the first lesson God identifies himself as the one who "blots out your transgressions." In the gospel Jesus heals the paralytic by pronouncing the forgiveness of his sins.

BRIEF COMMENTARY ON THE LESSONS

Lesson 1: Isaiah 43:18-25 (C, E); Isaiah 43:18-19, 21-22, 24b-25 (RC)

The prophet announces that the Lord is about to accomplish a new thing: He will free Israel from captivity and restore them to a more idyllic existence. The image here is that of a new exodus, as God provides for his people, as he leads and guides them back home (vv. 19-20). God will be gracious, even though the worship of his people has been deficient. Using imagery from the law court, Yahweh promises to blot out his people's sins (v. 25).

Lesson 2: 2 Corinthians 1:18-22 (C, RC, E)

Paul's critics accuse him of being vacillating. He retorts by asserting the gospel, which he preached to them was not "Yes" and "No" but only "Yes." Jesus is the confirmation, the "Yes," to all the promises of God. God has given his Spirit as a guarantee of his covenant.

Gospel: Mark 2:1-12 (C, RC, E)

After a trip about Galilee, Jesus returns home. When his neighbors discover that he has returned, the Lord is besieged with needy people. Friends of a paralyzed man carry him to Jesus but cannot get near because of the crowds. They show their determination and resourcefulness by removing a section of the roof and lowering their friend to Jesus on a stretcher. Jesus was impressed by the faith of these people and pronounced forgiveness on the paralyzed person. The audacity of Jesus in pronouncing forgiveness scandalizes the religious leaders who are present. Jesus perceives the offense on the part of these scribes and justifies his action by asserting that he has the authority to forgive sins.

Psalm Of The Day
Psalm 41 (C) — "Heal me, for I have sinned" (v. 4).
Psalm 32 (E) — "When I kept silent, my bones wasted away" (v. 3).
Psalm 40:5 (RC)

Prayer Of The Day
Gracious Lord God, you take delight in showing mercy and releasing your children from the paralyzing power of sin. Free us also from sin's strong grip, that we might joyfully go forth singing your praises. In the name of Jesus, who makes us free. Amen.

THEOLOGICAL REFLECTION ON THE LESSONS

Lesson 1: Isaiah 43:18-25

Perceiving God's new thing (v. 19). God declares through his prophet that he is about to do a new thing: He is going to send his people home, release them from captivity in Babylon. God was about to act. The spiritually alert could perceive it. Every day God does new things. How quick are we to perceive the Lord's doing?

The new exodus (vv. 18-21). Second Isaiah employs the image of the exodus, God's greatest act of deliverance. That was the act that defined Israel as God's people. The new thing that the Lord was about to do was patterned after the exodus. Even new things tend to fall into patterns.

Weary of God? (v. 22). The Revised Standard Version of the Bible says: "but you have been weary of me." The New RSV interprets: "you have not wearied yourselves for me." The latter version is probably more accurate when you consider the context. Yahweh is sharing his disappointment at the people's lack of devotion for him in worship. However, they really boil down to the same thing. We get weary of the Lord and it is reflected in our devotional life. Worship constitutes the language of our relationship with God.

We have wearied God (v. 24). The prophet depicts a very human side of God, he gets tired of our sins and lack of devotion to him and to that which is good. Our sins burden God but, because he is gracious and forgiving, he blots out our sins and remembers them no more.

Lesson 2: 2 Corinthians 1:18-22

Yes! Often a person celebrates some triumph by shouting "Yes!" Yes, I have it! Yes, I've accomplished it! Yes, she will marry me! Unfortunately, many people experience religion as a great "No!" No, you can't do this or that! Paul exults that Jesus is God's great "Yes!" In Jesus we experience that God is not against us but for us. God does not aim to restrain us but free us. He is the affirmation of all the promises of God (v. 20).

Seal of approval. Years ago, certain products were advertised as having received the Good Housekeeping seal of approval. Also, appliances had the guarantee, UL approved (Underwriter's Laboratory). These seals tell consumers that these are tested products that they can depend upon. God has given his seal of approval to those who follow Christ. That seal is the Holy Spirit, which indicates that we belong to him and that all his promises will be fulfilled.

Amen! My Aunt Hildur told me some years ago of the gentleman who belonged to our small Swedish Lutheran church; he was dubbed "Baptist Johnson" because he would often yell out "Amens" during the sermon. Amens are appropriate whenever the gospel is proclaimed. It means, "Yea, truly, it is so!" Because of the grace revealed to us in Jesus and the Holy Spirit, we can shout "Amen!" to life and "Amen!" to the gospel (v. 20).

Gospel: Mark 2:1-12

Blocked entry (v. 2). So many people were gathered about Jesus, presumably in his house, that no one else could get in. It was this blocked entry that led to these resourceful men lowering their sick friend to Jesus through the roof. Nothing was going to prevent them from gaining Jesus' aid on behalf of their friend. I wonder how often hurting people find a blocked entry at the door of the local congregation. I don't mean to refer to a massive crowd but other barriers much less obvious. How often is the entry blocked by apathy, lack of interest in the community, or uncaring attitudes toward those of a different racial, social, or ethnic mix? Or perhaps the entry is blocked by lack of imagination, faith, and risk taking. Are there barriers in your congregation that prevent folks from gaining access to Jesus' healing touch?

Carried. The paralytic was carried by others into the presence of Jesus. Sometimes weakness, ignorance, or spiritual paralysis prevents us from obtaining access to God. All of us need to be carried into Christ's presence at one time or the other. Perhaps as an infant we were carried in the arms of our parents to the baptismal font to obtain Christ's saving grace. Our family carried us physically, emotionally, and spiritually for a long time until we were able to stand on our own two feet. During periods of duress, we continue to be carried along by the prayers and concern of our caregivers, who take pains to bring us into the very presence of the Lord.

A can-do faith. The men who carried their paralyzed friend had a faith that wouldn't stop! Theirs was a can-do faith. When they got to the house where Jesus was ministering and found the door jammed (forgive the pun), they might have given up and gone home. Not these guys! How often do we let obstacles stop us rather than work around them?

Faith is communal (v. 5). The paralyzed man was healed by the faith of his community of friends or neighbors. Their faith, not his own, brought healing. While faith has a personal dimension, it is basically communal. Our faith in Christ came to us through the church community and through this community it is nourished. Jesus took note of the faith of this small band of men and then healed their friend.

Some sickness comes from sin. We need to be careful here but some sickness is related to sin. Studies show that constant anger and an unforgiving spirit can eat away at the body and the spirit. The pious of Jesus' day attributed all sickness to sin. Thus, when Jesus healed the paralyzed man through the forgiveness of sins, he was challenging their beliefs. If the man's sickness resulted from sin and if the man was healed, as they could all see, then Jesus must have affected the forgiveness of sins. This conclusion would be unacceptable to the religious leaders but it left them in a quandary.

The power of acceptance (v. 5). The sick person was probably paralyzed by guilt and fear. He didn't feel acceptable. Jesus speaks kindly to him. "My son, your sins are forgiven." We can free people from sin's deadly hold by being channels of God's accepting love.

SERMON APPROACHES WITH ILLUSTRATIONS

Lesson 1: Isaiah 43:18-25
Sermon Title: Grounds For Divorce?

Sermon Angle: Divorce has grown far too prevalent in our culture. There are many reasons, some valid, many others not, why two people get divorced. One of the worst reasons is voiced all too frequently: "I'm just tired of him/her." Some have broken their pledge of fidelity because someone else comes around who seems more exciting. In this passage God's people have grown tired of God and God has grown tired of his people. They've reached a low point in the relationship. Does God divorce his people? No, he promises to restore, forgive, and do a new thing.

Outline:
1. Have you ever grown tired of God? Has your relationship with the almighty become stale? That's what happened with God and his people in today's text. Puny attempts at worship highlighted the problem.
2. We also become tired of one another when there is a breakdown of communication and love (the marriage relationship and friendships).

3. We often break off the relationship that becomes stale but God doesn't; he shows forgiveness and grace.
4. God has time and again done a new thing (v. 19) to restore his relationship with his people. What new thing does God want for you in your relationships?

* * * * *

The River Wild illustrates that new things are possible in our stale and ineffectual relationships. Gail, a former river rafting guide finds herself in a dysfunctional marriage. Her husband, Tom, doesn't seem to have time for his family. Tom has lost the respect of his son, Roark. The family has planned a rafting trip to the Snake River but Tom opts out at the last minute for work-related reasons. He later decides to join them, just as they are about ready to embark. Gail's parents live in that region and, before the trip, mother and daughter have a little *tête à tête* about Gail's marriage. Gail woefully informs her mom of her dire marital straits. Gail tells her mom that Tom continues to spend all his waking hours at work and she is sick of it. She complains: "It's hard!" Her mom doesn't reciprocate with sympathy. "You don't know what hard is," she retorts. "That's because you give yourself an out. In our generation, we had no outs. It was a pact of marriage."

This dialogue hits on something really significant. It you don't have an out, you are more likely to work on the relationship. If the Lord had given himself an out, where would we be? He would be justified in divorcing himself from us. Thank God that he hasn't given himself an out.

* * * * *

Sermon Title: A New Thing

Sermon Angle: Yahweh announces that he is about to do a new thing (v. 19). Some people project God as the immutable ultra-conservative of the universe. He never changes. Yet our God exhibits a boundless creative imagination and delights in that which is fresh and new. Every day comes fresh and new, never exactly the same as the one before. Isaiah refers to the new act of redemption that the Lord was going to accomplish. Let us be alert to the new things God is affecting around us and through us.

Outline:
1. God was about to do a new act of creation and redemption with his captive ones. The people were called to perceive this new thing even before it happened (v. 19).
2. Our redemption in Christ comes to us ever new and renewing.
3. Are we alert to the new things that God is doing in our lives?

Lesson 2: 2 Corinthians 1:18-22

Sermon Title: Affirmative Action

Sermon Angle: Paul affirms that all the promises of God find their "Yes" in him (v. 20). In Jesus we see God's affirmative action. He didn't just talk about saving us but sent his Son. All this was done because of his great love for us. We also see God's affirmative action in the giving of the Holy Spirit; he continues to act by way of comforting and guiding us.

Outline:
1. The gospel is not ambiguous, it is God's "Yes" for us.
2. God's promises are affirmed in the actions of Jesus (v. 20).
3. Christ commissions us to be agents of his affirmative action (v. 21).

Sermon Title: Shout Amen!

Sermon Angle: When someone prays at our family gatherings, my sister has a practice of saying "Yes, Lord!" This can be a little disconcerting if you're not used to it but it is her way of saying "Amen!" She is affirming what was just prayed. When something appeals to us as beautiful, true, and right, we need to shout "Amen!" The world has enough nay-sayers; we need more of God's people to shout "Amen" when something impresses us as good.

Outline:
1. Our world is awash in negativism.
2. Even our churches can catch a negative spirit.
3. Jesus is God's affirmation, God's amen!
4. Let us affirm Jesus and all that is good and true.

Gospel: Mark 2:1-12

Sermon Title: Is There A Door Jam At Your Church?

Sermon Angle: Because Jesus attracted such large crowds, the door to the house where he was ministering became jammed. The above title is a poor attempt at a pun on the word "jam." Seriously though, are there forces blocking the door to your church? A lack of friendliness or hospitality? Perhaps an unattractive building? A lack of vital programming or worship? It's time to make the door to your church accessible to all.

Outline:
1. The paralytic couldn't reach Jesus because the door was jammed with people.
2. This man had strong-willed friends who wouldn't take "No" for an answer and so they tore down the roof.
3. Are there obstacles that jam the door to your church? Discuss them.
4. People shouldn't have to commit acts of desperation to gain access to Jesus.

Sermon Title: Mission Mandate: Share Christ's Forgiveness!

Sermon Angle: Jesus healed the paralytic by freeing him from his sins. The authority with which he forgave sins caused great scandal in the religious community. Sin still paralyzes but we have the authority of Jesus to free people from their sins.

Outline:
1. The paralytic was frozen by his sins.
2. His friends realized his helpless state and carried him to Jesus.
3. Jesus freed him up by declaring that he was forgiven (v. 5).
4. Jesus has the power to convey God's forgiveness (vv. 9-10).
5. He entrusts his church with the power to free others from the paralysis of sin through Christ's forgiveness and grace.

Sermon Title: A Faith That Won't Quit

Sermon Angle: The faith of those who carried the paralyzed man comprises a compelling part of this story. They wouldn't take "No" for an answer; they wouldn't let any obstacle stop them. They had passion and determination! They must have really believed that Jesus could heal their friend. Jesus responded to their faith by healing and forgiving the man they cared about so very much. This exemplifies what the Lord was speaking of when he taught that faith can move mountains.

Outline:
1. The stretcher bearers had a faith that wouldn't quit.
2. Most of us let obstacles deter us or derail us.
3. We could all bring about miracles if we had that kind of faith and determination. (Give examples.)
4. Jesus can give us a faith that won't quit if we would exercise the faith that we have.
5. May God give us a faith that won't stop until we reach Jesus with our need.

Epiphany 8/Ordinary Time 8

Revised Common	Hosea 2:14-20	2 Corinthians 3:1-6	Mark 2:13-22
Roman Catholic	Hosea 2:16-17, 21-22	2 Corinthians 3:1-6	Mark 2:18-22
Episcopal	Hosea 2:14-23	2 Corinthians 3:(4-11) 17—4:2	Mark 2:18-22

Theme For The Day: The marriage covenant in both the first lesson and the gospel provides an image of the kind of intimacy that God seeks with his people. For Hosea this means going back to the honeymoon period (the exodus). In the gospel, Jesus suggests that he is the bridegroom and his disciples are the bride. It was a fitting time to celebrate the marriage.

BRIEF COMMENTS ON THE LESSONS

Lesson 1: Hosea 2:14-20 (C); Hosea 2:16-17, 21-22 (RC); Hosea 2:14-23 (E)

The prophet Hosea speaks the word of God to the eighth-century people of Israel (the northern kingdom). It was an age of great apostasy. The people had largely forsaken their God and taken part in sensuous fertility rites in worship of Baal. In the verses just prior to this text, Hosea declares God's anger and punishment. In verses 14 and following the prophet holds up a great hope that the Lord would woo his unfaithful people back to himself. The wilderness, the place where Israel was formed as a people, is the setting for this courtship. God entreats his fickle people to retreat to the wilderness where God would renew their covenant and restore their relationship. The relationship between the Lord and his people will be as intimate as that of a husband and wife who dearly love each other.

Lesson 2: 2 Corinthians 3:1-6 (C, RC); 2 Corinthians 3:(4-11) 17—4:2 (E)

Paul's credentials as an apostle of the gospel were challenged by Jewish-Christian missionaries who carried letters of recommendation written by influential Christians. Paul did not see the need of such letters. Rather, he asserts that his letters of recommendation are written on the human heart, not with pen and ink but by the finger of the living God. Transformed lives are his letter of recommendation, which are available to be read by all people. The Lord himself, not any human authentication, makes us competent to be ministers of the gospel.

Gospel: Mark 2:13-22 (C); Mark 2:18-22 (E, RC)

The foes of Jesus criticize him for not making his disciples fast, as did the followers of John the Baptist. Although obligatory fasting took place only one day a year, the day of atonement, pious Jews were in the habit of fasting two days a week, Monday and Thursday, from 6 a.m. to 6 p.m. Jesus responds that his disciples cannot fast now for it is the time of the wedding feast, but the day would come when he (the bridegroom) would no longer be with them physically; they would fast then. To understand Jesus' words it is good to know something of the Jewish wedding customs of that time. When a man and woman were married the community would celebrate in their home for a week. During that time people were released from ordinary obligations, even the religious rules of fasting. This was the time to celebrate the union that his disciples and he had consummated, replied Jesus. The marriage feast of discipleship marks the beginning of a new relationship of the spirit, rather than one of old ways and old rules.

Psalm Of The Day
    Psalm 103:1-13, 22 (C); Psalm 103 (E) — "The Lord is compassionate and gracious" (v. 8).
    Psalm 102 (RC)

Prayer Of The Day
    Gracious God, great is your faithfulness. We have gone after other loves, we have committed ourselves to those people and causes that are not worthy, yet you remain committed to us. Thank you, Lord, for your love and forgiveness, which makes it possible for us to live in a committed relationship with you and with others. In the name of Jesus. Amen.

THEOLOGICAL REFLECTION ON THE LESSONS

Lesson 1: Hosea 2:14-20
The language of courtship. This text clearly employs the language of courtship, not the language of the law court or of judgment. Yahweh is going to lure his beloved people, attract them to him out in the desert. This presents an image I'm not so sure we're comfortable with — God the suitor, God the lover. Imagine God stripping himself of his grandeur, of all pride, to make himself appealing to his unfaithful people. Hosea's relationship with his wife was a metaphor of the Lord's passionate love for his betrothed. We see that same passionate love lifted up on the cross.

Repristination. God invites his people to go back to the wilderness, the site of their original courting, that the relationship between God and his people might be repristinated. The word "pristine" connotes fresh, new, and pure. It doesn't take long for love's pristine fragrance and color to fade. Love can only be reborn when we are willing to continually renew our pledge of love to one another and to the Lord.

How to green your valleys. The renewal of God's covenant with his people is tied in to the renewal of the land as well. The wilderness or desert becomes the place where God will give his people a fertile vineyard. The valley of Achor, which means "valley of contention," becomes the door of hope (v. 15). God will transform the arid place of conflict into a green valley of hope and life. God can transform our valleys if we let him.

Lesson 2: 2 Corinthians 3:1-6
Letter of recommendation. Pastors often get requests to write letters of recommendation. In seeking a job, we may have sought to obtain letters of recommendation that would make us look good to the potential employer. Paul felt that such letters were unnecessary for himself. The lives transformed by the gospel he preached was his best recommendation. Christ would have our lives be a letter of recommendation for him. It's not that words are superfluous; they are merely insufficient, or even counterproductive, if not backed by a transformed life.

Competent ministers. Paul maintains that the source of his confidence and competence comes from the Spirit of God (vv. 4-6). Martin Luther was appalled by the level of ignorance and incompetence that he found in the churches he visited in Germany. The people and the priests didn't know the basic elements of the faith. This led to his *Large* and *Small Catechism*, which are still used today. All Christians are ordained in their baptism as ministers of the gospel. Yet most Christians feel incompetent to minister in Christ's name. How many church members have excused themselves with "I could never teach!" or "I could never share my faith in

Christ!" We need to remind one another that our competency does not originate from within us; God remains the source of our competence.

Gospel: Mark 2:13-22

Feasting and fasting. Jesus was questioned about why he and his disciples did not fast as pious Jews. He basically replied that there is a time for feasting and a time for fasting but currently it was feast time. Since he was with his disciples, it was a time of celebration, which Jesus compared to a marriage feast (v. 19). The time would come when he would soon be taken from them. Then it would be a time of fasting (v. 20).

New and old. Jesus' gospel was new and fresh. The old covenant faith had grown worn, empty, and inflexible. Jesus knew that a patch job would not do. You don't sew a new piece of cloth onto an old piece (v. 21). The new will pull away from the old. Nor do you put new wine in old skins (v. 22). The spirit of the new wine would explode its container. The old containers of religion cannot contain the expansive spirit of the new faith.

Reformation or revolution? In our attempt to domesticate Jesus we have turned him into a reformer rather than the revolutionary he is. His intent was not just to reformulate the old way of relating to God; he came to set a new course for a radical righteousness. That's what he indicated by parables of the old and new cloth and the old and new wineskins. Jesus' gospel was more revolutionary than evolutionary, which is not to say that Jesus totally disregarded the religious traditions he was taught.

SERMON APPROACHES WITH ILLUSTRATIONS

Lesson 1: Hosea 2:14-20

Sermon Title: Love, Sex, And God

Sermon Angle: Most of us are comfortable when the words "love" and "sex" are used together. We are also at ease when the words "love" and "God" are used in sync. However, if we associate the words "sex" and "God" we may get a little on edge, just as we become ill at ease in dealing with our parents' sexuality. In Hosea's day the Canaanite Baal worship made a close association of human sexuality and the worship of God. The sexual act was also an act of worship. Hosea also employed sexual imagery in discussing the relationship of the Lord with his people, particularly the imagery of courtship and marriage. Yahweh promised to lure his wayward lover (the people of Israel) (v. 14). The people were the bride and God the bridegroom.

Outline:
1. Are you uncomfortable associating the concepts of love, sex, and marriage?
2. The Canaanite Baal religion worshiped their gods through sex; many moderns worship sex as our god.
3. Hosea metaphorically uses the marriage relationship to illustrate Yahweh's relationship with his people.

Sermon Title: The Power Of Hope

Sermon Angle: At a time of national crisis, Hosea has hope in the Lord. He portrays God as a jilted lover who will never give up on his beloved. He foresees a day when God and his people will recapture the joy of the honeymoon period. The wilderness (v. 14) represents the period when the relationship was fresh and powerful. Hosea had hope that things would get better and he communicated that hope to his people because he knew that they needed it. The valley of Achor (meaning "valley of contention") will be transformed into a door of hope. God can enable us to wring hope from the driest times.

Outline:
1. The Israelites were facing national extinction (explain the historical situation).
2. Hosea gives hope that the relationship of God and his people will be restored through the Lord's everlasting love.
3. When God is with us no situation is hopeless.
4. Godly hope can free us from the prison of despair.

*   *   *   *   *

The Shawshank Redemption is a movie that holds high the banner of hope. Andy, a bank vice president, is wrongly convicted of killing his wife, who was found riddled with bullets in the arms of her lover. Andy is sent to Shawshank prison. Like most prisons it is a hellhole of hopelessness. This prison is particularly foul because it is run by a corrupt and brutal warden. Andy becomes a friend of Red, who is serving a life term for murder. Red sees little reason for optimism but Andy refuses to relinquish his hope. He obtains financing for a prison library, which helps liberate the prisoners through discovering new worlds of the mind and spirit where they are no longer bound. One day he locked himself in the prison's public address center and played a record of lovely music; his aim was to lift the spirits of the inmates. This infuriated the warden, who locked him in solitary confinement for two weeks. After coming out, fellow inmates asked him how it went. "Easiest time I've served," he replied. "I had my record player." "They let you have a phonograph?" "It's in here," he added, pointing to his heart. He explained that which we hold in our heart and mind cannot be touched by outside forces. Red didn't agree. He viewed hope as a "dangerous thing." I won't spoil the story by revealing the ending, except to say that both Andy and Red were led to a new life by the power of hope.

*   *   *   *   *

Sermon Title: Mission Mandate: Announce The Marriage!

Sermon Angle: God promises that he will be joined to his people forever in marriage (vv. 19-20). The relationship between the Lord and his people is like the marriage covenant, except for the fact that God alone initiates the relationship. Actually, the Lord had already covenanted with his people before that, beginning with Abraham. What we have here is kind of a renewal of the covenant, the marriage of God and his people. In the gospel lesson, Jesus takes up the marriage metaphor and refers to himself as the bridegroom (Mark 2:19). The church then becomes the bride and is referred to as such in the book of Revelation. It might be more accurate to refer to the relationship of God and his people as an engagement, with the consummation of the relationship and the marriage feast taking place in the kingdom of heaven. The mission of the church is to announce the marriage of Christ and his church.

Outline:
1. Hosea announces a renewal of the (marriage) covenant of God with Israel.
   — God will woo his people.
   — He will deal tenderly and lovingly with them.

113

2. In the gospel, Jesus calls himself the bridegroom.
3. Christ betroths himself to the church (the pledge of his love is seen on the cross).
4. In baptism and holy communion the covenant is made personal.
5. The wedding feast takes place in the kingdom of heaven for all who remain faithful.
6. Let us announce the wedding and busily extend invitations.

Lesson 2: 2 Corinthians 3:1-6

Sermon Title: Special Delivery

Sermon Angle: Apparently some folks in Corinth thought Paul needed letters of recommendation from apostolic leaders in the church. Paul retorts that the believers themselves are their letter of recommendation, written not in ink but with the finger of God's Spirit. All Christians are called to be letters from Christ, special delivery letters.

Outline:
1. Some members of the Corinthian church sought ecclesiastical credentials from Paul.
2. Paul insisted that changed lives of believers were authentication enough.
3. When God's love and grace are imprinted on us by God's Spirit, it proves that we are a letter from God, a special delivery letter.

Sermon Title: Confidence In The Lord's Competence

Sermon Angle: Paul was confident that the Lord wouldn't have given him the task of preaching the gospel without equipping him and making him competent. Yet the source of his competence was the Lord, not himself (vv. 5-6). More than ever, people are flocking to competent churches, churches that know their ministry role and make every effort, through the power of the Spirit, to do the job excellently. Competent churches really believe that the Spirit has given each believer gifts that he has empowered us to put into practice.

Outline:
1. Confidence and competence are needed for success.
2. The apostle Paul had both confidence and competence.
   — His confidence was based on the Lord's faithfulness (vv. 4-5).
   — His competence was a gift of God.
3. Overconfidence in ourselves leads to the sin of pride but to excuse ourselves from ministry for lack of competence indicates a lack of faith in God's Spirit.
4. The Lord imparts to each believer and to the whole church competence for ministry.
5. Let us confidently look to the Lord for competence as we minister in his name.

Gospel: Mark 2:13-22

Sermon Title: A Time For Fasting, A Time For Feasting

Sermon Angle: When Jesus was asked why he and his disciples were not fasting as others were, he responded that fasting was inappropriate as long as he (the bridegroom) was with them. They would fast when he was taken away from them. There are seasons of fasting and feasting. Soon Lent will be upon us, a traditional time of fasting. Easter season is the prime time of feasting. There are also personal times of separation from God which call for fasting, and times of intimacy with the Lord which indicate a time of feasting. We all look forward to heaven as the feast which has no end.

Outline:
1. Jesus was criticized for not fasting more. He celebrated life as a feast of God's grace.
2. Yet he knew that there would be a time of separation from his disciples when fasting would be in order.
3. In the church year we balance times of fasting and feasting.
4. Personally, sometimes life is a fast and sometimes a feast. We must know when each is appropriate.
5. Live in hope of the marriage feast that has no end.

Sermon Title: New Containers For New Wine

Sermon Angle: Jesus warns against placing new wine in old wineskins. The new wine will burst the dried-out old skins. He was speaking of the new wine of the gospel that could not be contained by the rigid religious structures of Judaism. This is not to say that he intended the destruction of the old. It is certain that he foresaw a radical new way that people would relate to God. The gospel of Jesus, filled with the Holy Spirit, is ever bursting the old containers in which we have poured it.

Outline:
1. Jesus warned that his new gospel could not be contained by the old wineskins of Judaism (v. 22).
2. When we see the faith as old wine for old wineskins, we are in mortal danger (traditionalism).
3. The gospel of Jesus is constantly renewed by the Spirit and must be poured into new containers.

* * * * *

George Barna, author of *The Frog In The Kettle*, asserts that Christians need to awaken to a spiritual crisis that will only intensify as the decade proceeds. He makes his point with the analogy of the frog. You place a frog in a pot of boiling water and it will sense immediately that it is a hostile environment and jump out. However, if you put a frog in a pot of cool water and then turn up the heat very gradually until it reaches boiling, it will not sense the change in the environment and take evasive action. Something like that is happening in our churches.

The Transfiguration Of Our Lord
(Last Sunday After Epiphany)

Revised Common	2 Kings 2:1-12	2 Corinthians 4:3-6	Mark 9:2-9
Roman Catholic	Daniel 7:9-10, 13-14	2 Peter 1:16-19	Mark 9:2-10
Episcopal	1 Kings 19:9-18	2 Peter 1:16-19 (20-21)	Mark 9:2-9

Theme For The Day: Seeing the vision of God's glory. This being The Transfiguration Of Our Lord, the last Sunday in the bright Epiphany season before the fast of Lent, we need to fix the vision of the glorious Christ in our hearts and minds. God's blessings are promised to those who have the faith to catch the vision.

BRIEF COMMENTARY ON THE LESSONS

Lesson 1: 2 Kings 2:1-12 (C)

It seems to be general knowledge among the prophetic school associated with Elijah that the prophet is going to be taken into heaven on a certain day. Elisha, the prophet's understudy, also becomes privy to this fact. Elijah tries to leave Elisha behind but the young man refuses to leave his mentor's side. Finally, Elijah asks what Elisha is seeking. He unabashedly requests a double portion of Elijah's prophetic spirit. Elijah promises that the wish would be granted if he could see him being taken away. As the chariot of fire and horses of fire gallop with Elijah into glory, Elisha exclaims: "My father, my father! The chariots of Israel and their horsemen" (v. 12). This is a type of transfiguration, a brief vision of the realm of light and glory. Recall that Elijah makes another appearance when Jesus is transfigured.

Lesson 1: Daniel 7:9-10, 13-14 (RC)

Lesson 1: 1 Kings 19:9-18 (E)

Lesson 2: 2 Corinthians 4:3-6 (C)

Accusations had been made against Paul that his gospel was veiled or obscure. He admits that the gospel is obscure for those who are perishing. It is veiled because the god of this world (Satan) has blinded them to the gospel. The God of creation has caused the light of Christ's glory to shine through the lives of those who live by the gospel. The transfigured Christ shines through those who proclaim Christ in word and action.

Lesson 2: 2 Peter 1:16-19 (20-21) (RC, E)

Gospel: Mark 9:2-9 (C, E); Mark 9:2-10 (RC)

Peter, James, and John view the transfigured glory of Christ Jesus on the mountain. Jesus was heading toward Jerusalem and the cross. Yet he had to check his course with his Father. He receives the confirmation he sought, as the divine Spirit transforms his whole body. Moses and Elijah appear with him. His course is also confirmed by the greatest lawgiver and the greatest prophet. Jesus stands as the fulfillment of the Old Testament faith. The disciples react with awe and fear as the divine voice identifies Jesus as God's beloved Son. They are to follow him. The Transfiguration stands as a prefigurement of Christ's resurrected glory. After the cross it will help confirm the disciples' faith.

Psalm Of The Day
Psalm 50:1-6 (C) — "God shines forth" (v. 2).
Psalm 27 (E) — "The Lord is my light and my salvation..." (v. 1).
Psalm 96 (RC)

Prayer Of The Day
God of glory, we have let the darkness of human sin cloud your luminous presence. Open our eyes that we might catch the vision of Christ in all his heavenly splendor. Then make our words and actions mirror his glory. In the name above all names, the glorious name of Jesus, we pray. Amen.

THEOLOGICAL REFLECTION ON THE LESSONS

Lesson 1: 2 Kings 2:1-12
Power of persistence. Elisha is a study of the power of persistence. Elijah could not shake him. Elisha would not leave his master because he knew that the Lord was going to take Elijah to glory that day and he wanted to obtain his blessing.

Bless me, father. Elisha considered the older man his spiritual father and wanted to follow in his footsteps. He sought his father's blessing above all else, so great was his love and respect for his spiritual father. Finally, Elijah asked Elisha what he desired. The younger man responded: "A double portion of your spirit." Wouldn't it be wonderful if every son and daughter respected their father so much that they sought to possess the spirit of his or her father? What better inheritance could fathers pass on than a spirit of faith, love, respect, and deep loyalty to the Lord? Fathers, bless your children by passing on to them the Spirit of Christ that gushes up from the wellspring of your very being.

Catch the vision. Elijah promised Elisha that he would receive a double portion of his spirit if he observed Elijah's ascent into heaven. This would require that he focus his spiritual sight and attune his powers of spiritual observation. Or, looking at it from another angle, if Elisha was able to see the chariots of fire (angelic messengers), it would indicate that the Lord had granted Elisha's wish. In other words, the ability to perceive the spiritual reality would prove that his petition was granted. In order for us to catch the vision, it must be our passionate prayer that the Lord open the eyes of our spirit.

Lesson 2: 2 Corinthians 4:3-6
What's the weather in your church? Paul was accused of preaching a gospel that was veiled, hidden, or obscured. Most people in our culture don't even know what a veil is. However, all of us understand the weather. Thus, we might equate veiled with cloudy, partly veiled with partly cloudy, and unveiled with clear skies. To really see the gospel means that nothing obscures the Son of God. Most Christians do cloud other people's vision of the good news. Perhaps our faith is superficial or inconsistent. We fail to walk our talk. Such behavior clouds the gospel. What's the weather like most of the time where you live and where you worship?

The god of this age. When Paul speaks of "the god of this age" he is speaking of Satan. His point? Satan has blinded unbelievers so they cannot perceive the light of the gospel. Yet the god of this age assumes many forms. What are some of the gods of this age? How about pernicious individualism, which unlooses the cords of community? How about materialism? Our obsession with personal rights? Hedonism? Those who serve the various manifestations of the god of this age cannot see the light of God in the transfigured face of Jesus.

Who does your life proclaim? (v. 5). How important it is to know who we are and whose we are! Paul had it straight. His mission was not to proclaim himself but Jesus Christ as Lord and Christians as Christ's servants. Unfortunately, in our culture we have been fed a steady diet of narcissism. Look out for number one, we are told. This philosophy has also invaded the church. Too many people seek out the church as a means promoting their own needs rather than worshiping Jesus Christ as Lord. When non-Christians look at us, do they see Jesus?

Gospel: Mark 9:2-9

No razzle-dazzle. In the movie, *Leap Of Faith*, the evangelist combined razzle-dazzle showmanship and psychology to milk the people's spiritual yearnings for his own gain. During the religious show he would put on a sequined jacket that shined like forty million dollars under the spotlight. He used the jacket to focus attention on himself and create an aura of divine glory. It was just a prop. When Jesus was transfigured, it was no razzle-dazzle, no show. If Jesus had intended it to draw attention to himself, he would have let it happen in a crowded place. No, this is purely an instance where God is glorifying his Son and confirming the direction of his life. It was primarily for Jesus' benefit. Peter, James, and John, for their part, would observe another aspect of Jesus that they would not fully comprehend until after Christ's resurrection.

Summit. When the leaders of the world get together to discuss mutual problems, we call it a summit because high-level officials are conferring. The transfiguration of our Lord was the ultimate in summit meetings. The foremost of the lawgivers and the foremost of the prophets conferred with the soon to be crucified and risen Son of God. Do you suppose that they were there to provide encouragement and advice? Jesus did not act alone.

Listen. The voice from the cloud of God's glory pronounced Jesus as the Father's beloved Son, instructing the disciples to listen to him. We can't blame Peter for babbling, under these circumstances, but you can't talk and listen at the same time. Jesus was heading toward the cross. The time of crisis would soon arrive. It was imperative for the disciples to listen to the Lord's parting instructions. We would probably see more transfigurations if we would listen more intently with the ears of our spirit.

SERMON APPROACHES WITH ILLUSTRATIONS

Lesson 1: 2 Kings 2:1-12
Sermon Title: Out Of School
Sermon Angle: Elisha was about to lose his teacher and mentor. Every place that he went with Elijah, the prophets would ask Elisha: "Do you know that today the Lord will take away your master from over you?" He replied, "Yes, I know it, be quiet." Elisha was about to graduate from Prophet University. He would be on his own. Did he look on this change of affairs positively? Did he celebrate his freedom or did he quake in fear at the prospect of being on his own? Did he grieve the expected loss of this vital relationship? Perhaps he felt a combination

of all these feelings and more. He must have realized that Elijah had thoroughly prepared him but he needed more. He needed the same Spirit of the Lord that his teacher had. He asked for a double portion of Elijah's spirit because that was the portion of the inheritance that a father would leave to his eldest son. Elisha was wise enough to know that though he would no longer have Elijah's physical presence, he would have the spiritual presence of his master and teacher within himself.

Outline:
1. Elisha realized that he was soon to take over Elijah's role on his own.
2. Wanting a double portion indicated his desire to be Elijah's spiritual son, the eldest son, the heir who would carry on in the father's name.
3. Elisha would succeed without his teacher; he had internalized the spirit of his teacher.
4. Who are your spiritual mentors and teachers? Have you internalized their teaching?
5. The Spirit helps us internalize the presence of the incarnate Christ.

Sermon Title: What Kind Of Inheritance Will You Leave?

Sermon Angle: Elijah was a father figure for Elisha. Elisha realized that soon he would be deprived of his father's physical presence. More than anything, he wanted to be the older man's legitimate heir. He didn't want land or money; he craved nothing more or less than the spirit of Elijah. He desired what his spiritual father had; he wanted to carry on the work that Elijah had begun. Elisha desired to be a godly man, like his father. Perhaps contemporary fathers should not feel as driven to leave a material legacy to their children and give far more attention to the spiritual legacy they are leaving their children. Wouldn't it be wonderful if our children wanted nothing more than a double portion of our spirit?

Outline:
1. Elijah mentored for Elisha the life of a godly man.
2. When Elijah was taken to heaven, he left Elisha a living faith, not material trinkets.
3. What kind of an inheritance are you leaving the world? Will others be energized by the fire of your faith?
4. Give yourself to setting in order your legacy of faith and love.

*　*　*　*　*

My oldest sister is probably the most spiritual of the children in my family. When Mom died, she didn't give a care about the material possessions left behind. The only thing she asked for was Mom's well-worn Bible. I suppose it's a link to the spiritual legacy that Mom imparted to her over the years.

*　*　*　*　*

Lesson 2: 2 Corinthians 4:3-6

Sermon Title: Removing Cataracts

Sermon Angle: Many people develop cataracts over their eyes if they live long enough. Because a thin film grows over the lens of the eye, vision gradually clouds. Because of the miracle of modern medical technology, cataracts can be removed and a new lens implanted. How wonderful it must be to see things as they really are. Paul claims that the god of this world (Satan) has blinded the minds of unbelievers so that they do not recognize spiritual truth (v. 4).

We might say that these folks have spiritual cataracts. Coming to faith in Christ removes the cataracts so that we might see spiritual reality that was formerly hidden from us.

Outline:
1. Some people accused Paul of preaching an obscure gospel (veiled).
2. Paul retorts that it is hidden because unbelievers let Satan blind them (cataracts).
3. Coming to faith equates to having the cataracts of our spiritual sight removed.
4. Let us be transformed by gazing into the face of the risen Christ (v. 6).

Sermon Title: Who Does Your Life Proclaim?

Sermon Angle: Paul denies that he has ever promoted himself. Rather, his party has proclaimed Jesus as Lord. He and the other missionaries were only servants of Jesus. We've all met people who are constantly promoting themselves. Even some ministers have fallen into the trap of drawing attention to themselves rather than the Lord they proclaim. For us Christians, the only fitting object of our proclamation is Jesus Christ. We are merely the messengers. Who does your life proclaim?

Gospel: Mark 9:2-9

Sermon Title: Mission Mandate: Become Transformed By His Glory!

Sermon Angle: All three texts make reference to being transformed by an encounter with spiritual reality. Talk of an unseen world of spiritual reality leaves many people skeptical in our Western world. We put credence only in that which we can experience through our senses. On the other hand, the new age movement, which readily embraces all sorts of spirituality, may be a response to our shallow materialism. The problem here is that spiritual reality is sought for its own sake and is often divorced from biblical revelation. The three texts for Transfiguration relate transforming encounters with God's Spirit. Elisha was transformed through his long relationship with Elijah, which ended in a blaze of glory. Peter, James, and John were certainly changed by their experience of the glorified Christ on the mountain. The second lesson tells how ordinary believers are transformed through their relationship with the Spirit of Christ.

Outline:
1. Christianity is not in the business of information about God but transformation by God.
2. Elisha was transformed by his association with Elijah.
3. The Transfiguration was a major piece in the transformation of Jesus' disciples.
4. Believers are transformed gradually by a faith relationship with the Spirit of Jesus (2 Corinthians 3:18).

Sermon Title: Peak Experience

Sermon Angle: Jesus took Peter, James, and John on top of the mountain so that they might renew their spirits and gain spiritual insight. I am writing this chapter in the Rocky Mountains, a marvelous place to gain perspective. Yet we don't need to be in the mountains to experience a peak experience. We can gain such perspective by retreating with Jesus to a place of prayer. His Spirit will lift our hearts and minds to new heights of communion and insight.

Outline:
1. The Transfiguration was a peak experience.
2. Jesus received confirmation from the Father.
3. The disciples received new insight about Jesus.
4. In focused prayer we can attain a peak experience of confirmation and transformation.

* * * * *

As I write, 70,000 men are gathered together at Mile High Stadium in Denver for Promise Keepers. The men are praying, singing, celebrating, clapping, and worshiping Jesus Christ as Lord and Savior. For most of these men, it is a peak spiritual experience. Yet the aim of this group is not merely to linger in the glow of Christ's glory but to be more faithful and loving husbands and fathers and to overcome the barriers of race and denomination. They will have to come down from the mountain peak but perhaps they will not be the same men as they were before; one hopes they will have an awareness of the reality of the risen Christ.

The Lenten Season

Historical Development

Lent is rooted in the historical practices of the first-century church. Originally Lent lasted only forty hours, representing the forty hours Jesus' body lay in the tomb. In the third century the church in Jerusalem extended the season to six days and dubbed it Holy Week. Each day of Holy Week, worship services would be conducted in the proper geographic location — Pilate's Hall, the Upper Room, and so forth. When the Western church celebrated Holy Week, they substituted the stations of the cross for the geographic locations. Special emphasis was accorded to the so-called tritium — Good Friday, Holy Saturday, and Easter.

Next, the six days of Holy Week were extended to 36 days, a tithe of the 365-day calendar. Charlemagne rounded this period off to forty days in 731 AD. The number "40" had biblical precedent. Jesus fasted for forty days in the wilderness at the onset of his public ministry. Moses communed with God for forty days atop Mount Sinai in order to receive the Ten Commandments. The Israelites wandered for forty years in the wilderness. Thus, forty is a nice round number indicating a long time.

Lent is actually 46, not forty, days since Sundays are not considered as a part of Lent. That's why we speak of Sundays "in" Lent, not Sundays "of" Lent. Nevertheless, observance of the season has spilled over into the Sunday observance. We see indications of this with the liturgical color of purple in the paraments and the absence of the "Alleluia" and the "Glory To God."

Determining The Date Of Lent

The beginning of Lent is based on the timing of Easter. The date of Easter derives from the Jewish lunar calendar. Easter occurs on the first Sunday following the first full moon in Spring. The starting date for Lent traces back 46 days from the Easter Feast. For the first millennium of the Christian church, the first day of Lent was called the "Beginning Of The Fast." In 1099, Pope Urban changed the name to "Ash Wednesday." Ashes are a traditional symbol of penitence and remorse. The practice of imposing ashes on the first day of Lent continues to this day in the church of Rome as well as in many Lutheran and Episcopalian quarters. As the ashes are imposed in the shape of a cross on the forehead of the worshiper, the priest or pastor intones "Remember that you are dust and to dust you shall return." This solemn reminder of our mortality spurs us to get right with God, who alone holds the key to eternal life. Many Protestant churches abandoned the imposition of ashes as being too Romanist or perhaps out of deference to the teachings of Jesus in Matthew 6:16-18, which state that when we fast we should not look dismal like the hypocrites.

The Significance Of Lent For The Believer

In the fourth century, Lent was a six-week period of catechesis for those who were preparing to become members of the church through Holy Baptism. It was an intense period of examination, prayer, repentance, and education to prepare the candidate for initiation into the mysteries of the faith, the sacraments. The candidate took on a new identity and became a new person in Christ. Those deemed ready to be admitted into the mysteries were baptized very early Easter morning to demonstrate that they were dying and rising with Christ. After Christianity became legalized in 325 AD, Lent gradually became a general period of penitence for all believers. It remains a time when the church holds high the sufferings of Christ and his death on the cross. This observance should not be a macabre attempt to inflict personal suffering on ourselves.

Rather, grasping the enormity of Christ's sacrifice and sufferings on our behalf, we are to respond with renewed repentance and faith.

Theological Themes Of Lent

Sacrifice — The first lesson for the first Sunday in Lent is the story of God's testing of Abraham by asking him to sacrifice his son Isaac. Of course, the sacrifice of Christ on the cross permeates every aspect of our Lenten observance.

Repentance — The church opens Lent with a call to repentance on Ash Wednesday. Joel 2:12 dramatically introduces this theme in these words: "Yet even now," says the Lord, "return to me with fasting, with weeping, and with mourning; and rend your hearts and not your garments."

Suffering and death — Lent addresses the most troubling issue of mankind since the fall: What is the meaning of suffering and death? No philosophical answers are forthcoming. Rather, the Lenten texts confront us with the bold assertion that God himself suffers with us, redeeming our suffering and death.

The disciplines of Lent — These are prayer, fasting, and almsgiving. These disciplines are held up for us in the Ash Wednesday gospel (Matthew 6). These are the tools with which we can draw closer to Christ and experience a renewal of our spiritual center. Jesus prayed and fasted for forty days in the wilderness at the beginning of his public ministry. When Lent draws to a close, we find Jesus praying passionately in the Garden of Gethsemane. Abundant opportunities and encouragements to pray should be offered during the Lenten season. Fasting remains a solidly biblical practice that is largely ignored by Protestants. The Roman church has also lessened the requirements for fasting. From the earliest times of the church, fasting was practiced on Fridays and on the Friday and Saturday of Holy Week. Fasting is a means of subordinating our physical needs to the spiritual. Also, fasting has been employed as a means of identifying with the sufferings of Christ. Unfortunately, self-denial has little appeal to the Western mind. Lent provides us with a wonderful rationale for engaging in the third discipline of Lent, almsgiving. God has given himself to us in Christ; we show our appreciation by giving to God and others. Many congregations have special projects to which they contribute during Lent and provide special offering envelopes, folders, and the like. Church members respond more favorably to giving more during Lent than they do to an appeal for increased prayer and fasting. It's easier to open our pocketbooks than it is to rend our hearts.

Worship Suggestions For Lenten Mid-Week Services And Holy Week

Many churches hold special services during the Lenten season that center around the passion of our Lord. Often these services are held on Wednesdays. These services should be knit together by a theme. Some churches prefer alternatives to preaching for the proclamation, employing drama, music, and so forth. This can be effective if it deals with passion themes because such productions can involve a number of people. To make these services more practical, why not ask different lay people to give short witness talks as to how their faith has enabled them to surmount various human struggles? For instance, "How My Faith Helped Me Cope With Cancer." Topical series are popular and there are many such on the market. However, if you buy one of these series, be sure to adapt it to your situation. Another possibility is to take the passion story that is featured on Passion/Palm Sunday, the sixth Sunday in Lent, and have a teaching series based on it. Ask people to bring their Bibles or have preprinted sheets for participants to fill in at various points. If it's a small group, give opportunity for discussion.

Some churches have services of devotion each day in Holy Week but they are not well attended. A majority of congregations focus on Maundy Thursday and Good Friday. Maundy Thursday seems to be the best attended. "Maundy" derives from the Latin word *mandatum*, meaning "command." This harks from the story where Jesus washes his disciples' feet (John 13) and gives his disciples a new commandment, "That you love one another as I have loved you" (v. 34). Some congregations hold symbolic foot washing ceremonies as a part of the liturgy, which dramatically illustrate Christ's call for us to be servants. This account is not featured in the "B" series of the lectionary. Rather, it is Mark's account of the institution of the Lord's Supper.

Good Friday is the most solemn of the Lenten services, as we remember our Lord's suffering and death on the cross. Many churches and communities hold services around the seven last words of Jesus from the cross, which are pulled from all four gospels. These services are not recommended because they are a rather artificial construct, which destroys the integrity of the individual gospel accounts. This year's lectionary series features the passion according to John. Why not read this account in a dramatic fashion, giving the various roles to different people in the congregation and reserving some parts for men, women, and the congregation as a whole? Lights and shadows, sights and sounds should be employed at strategic points for greater impact. Tenebrae, a service of shadows, comes in many creative forms and is still used in many churches.

Holy Week opens on Passion/Palm Sunday, formerly Palm Sunday, which features Mark's account of the passion. Since most of the members of the church probably did not attend the Good Friday service, it would be good to feature a dramatic reading of Mark's passion account, assigning roles to various people. Involve men, women, children, choirs, and so forth. Such accounts can be purchased at various ecclesiastical bookstores. The Palm Sunday portion of the Passion story can be featured at the very beginning of the liturgy. This liturgy should begin in a place large enough to accommodate the worshiping congregation but outside the worship center of the church. After the Palm Sunday reading, the congregation processes into the nave (worship area) of the church with palms raised. The subordination of the Palm Sunday emphasis to the Passion story was instituted through the Revised Common Lectionary. It was felt that the church needed to provide an opportunity for most Christians to hear the passion story as a whole. This is something of a concession to the reality of modern life, which recognizes that most members will not attend all of the special Lenten liturgies during the week.

Roman Catholic and a few Protestant churches observe the Easter vigil on Holy Saturday evening. This would be a good time to baptize adult converts to the faith. This liturgy harks back to the early centuries of the church but it is very difficult to attract very many to this service.

A Suggested Sermon Series For Sundays In Lent

With all the emphasis in contemporary society on physical fitness, why not emphasize Lent as a time for increased spiritual fitness? Our spirit as well as our body must be toned up and strengthened for the spiritual battles that lie ahead. Each chapter contains sermon outlines for the following themes and titles.

Series Title: "Forty Days To Spiritual Fitness"

Ash Wednesday
>*Sermon Title:* Three Exercises You Can Do In Private
>*Sermon Theme:* The right way to practice prayer, fasting, and almsgiving.
>*Sermon Text:* Matthew 6:1-6, 16-21

Lent 1
>*Sermon Title:* Repentance — Begin Your Spiritual Fitness Program With This Exercise
>*Sermon Theme:* The call to regular and ongoing repentance.
>*Sermon Text:* Mark 1:12-15

Lent 2
>*Sermon Title:* Cross Bearing — The Essential Exercise For Christian Discipleship
>*Sermon Theme:* Cross bearing. Suffering for the sake of the gospel.
>*Sermon Text:* Mark 8:31-38

Lent 3
>*Sermon Title:* Cleansing — An Exercise You Must Do At Church
>*Sermon Theme:* Root out the leaven of corruption in the church.
>*Sermon Text:* John 2:13-22

Lent 4
>*Sermon Title:* Lift Up Christ — An Exercise That Will Strengthen The Entire Body
>*Sermon Theme:* God lifted up Jesus on the cross. We must lift up Jesus through faith and witness.
>*Sermon Text:* John 3:14-21

Lent 5
>*Sermon Title:* Follow Christ — An Exercise That Leads Through Pain To Glory
>*Sermon Theme:* Following Christ all the way to the cross.
>*Sermon Text:* John 12:20-33

Passion/Palm Sunday
>*Sermon Title:* Be Loyal — Don't Give Up The Exercise Of Your Faith
>*Sermon Theme:* The women stayed by Jesus all the way to the end and were the first to see the risen Christ. Like them, we must follow Jesus even when things look the darkest.
>*Sermon Text:* Mark 15:40-47

Suggestion: Think about having a Lenten fitness program that combines both physical and spiritual exercises.

Ash Wednesday

Revised Common	Joel 2:1-2, 12-17	2 Corinthians 5:20b—6:10	Matthew 6:1-6, 16-21
Roman Catholic	Joel 2:12-18	2 Corinthians 5:20—6:2	Matthew 6:1-6, 16-18
Episcopal	Joel 2:1-2, 12-17	2 Corinthians 5:20b—6:10	Matthew 6:1-6, 16-21

Theme For The Day: A call to repentance and renewal. The people are called to return to the Lord with acts of worship, giving, and devotion that spring from the heart.

BRIEF COMMENTARY ON THE LESSONS

Lesson 1: Joel 2:1-2, 12-17 (C, E); Joel 2:12-18 (RC)

We know little about the writer of this book and there are no historical markers by which to judge the period in which it was composed. Many scholars believe that Joel lived in the Persian period (559-331 BC). We do know that he had a keen interest in the temple and can surmise that he hails from priestly origins. An invasion of locusts causes a call to repentance. The prophet sees this devouring army as the arm of God's judgment. God is trying to arrest his people's attention. Yet the Lord is merciful and kind (v. 13) and stands ready to bless his people when they return to him.

Lesson 2: 2 Corinthians 5:20b—6:10 (C, E); 2 Corinthians 5:20—6:2 (RC)

This lection is part of Paul's defense of his apostleship. As an ambassador of the gospel, Paul appeals to the Corinthians to be reconciled with God by accepting his forgiveness offered in Christ. The sinless Christ took on himself the burden of our sin (v. 21) in order to reconcile us with God. He urgently appeals for the Corinthians to accept God's gracious offer *now*. "*Now* is the acceptable time, *now* is the day of salvation" (v. 2).

Gospel: Matthew 6:1-6, 16-21 (C, E); Matthew 6:1-6, 16-18 (RC)

Jesus abhors the kind of piety expressed in blowing one's own horn (v. 2). To aim for the praise and admiration of humans is unworthy of a disciple of Christ. True religion springs from a heart that sincerely loves the Lord. Prayer and giving flow from the same spring, from a heart that loves God. Almsgiving must not be identified only with money. Alms consisted of any kind deed arising from a heart filled with mercy and compassion. The Septuagint translates certain Hebrew words for both righteousness and kindness as "alms." Frequently, the helping words "to do" are united with the word "alms"; this shows almsgiving as an action that arises from the believer's heart.

Psalm Of The Day

Psalm 51:1-17 (C) — "Have mercy on me, O God...."

Psalm 103 or 103:8-14 (E) — "Bless the Lord, O my soul, and do not forget his benefits — who forgives all your iniquity and heals all your diseases ..." (vv. 2-3).

Psalm 50 (RC)

Prayer Of The Day

Merciful and gracious God, our sins have turned that which is living into dust and ashes. Accept the ashes of our heartfelt repentance and breathe new life into our animated human dust, that we might stand eternally in your most holy presence. In the name of him who died and rose again, Jesus, our Lord. Amen.

THEOLOGICAL REFLECTION ON THE LESSONS

Lesson 1: Joel 2:1-2, 12-17

It ain't over 'til it's over. I believe that was one of Yogi Berra's colorful witticisms. The prophet Joel said just about the same thing: " 'Even now,' declares the Lord, 'return to me ...' " (v. 12). It wasn't too late to return to the Lord. There was time for amendment of life; there was opportunity to turn over a new leaf. Satan's mightiest weapon comes encapsulated in these words: "It's too late." "It ain't over 'til it's over."

Rend and return (v. 13). Pious Jews might tear (rend) their garments to show contrition or sorrow. Joel calls the people to rend their hearts (be broken-hearted) and return to the Lord, their God. There can be no returning without rending. A person cannot return to the Lord until he recognizes that he has turned away and feels in his gut the pain that his sin has caused our gracious God.

A time for trumpets? Verse 15 orders the sounding of the horn, the *shofar* or ram's horn. The purpose? To gather the people in solemn assembly. In contrast Jesus, in the gospel lesson, warns against sounding our individual horns prior to a religious act. To call attention to ourselves and our righteousness is always wrong, but gathering the community for repentance and renewal is what Lent is all about. Young and old, people and priests must respond to God's trumpet call.

Lesson 2: 2 Corinthians 5:20b—6:10

Beggars for Christ (v. 20). The apostle begs and pleads with the Corinthians to become God's friends through Christ. Being reconciled to God is not a matter of indifference. God's heart aches for his separated children. Does our heart also ache for all those estranged from the Lord?

We are God's goodness (v. 21). Paul presents an interesting dichotomy. The sinless Christ became the incarnation of sin on the cross so that through faith in Christ we might become the incarnation of God's righteousness. Both sinfulness and righteousness are not merely that which we do but that which we are.

The time is NOW! We humans have a tendency toward procrastination. Why do today what we can put off until tomorrow? Paul pleads: "See, *now* is the acceptable time, see, *now* is the day of salvation." In Luke 9:59-61, Jesus invites two men to follow him. Their reply? Later. One said: "Lord, first let me go and bury my father." Another man seemed ready to follow but added: "... but let me first go and say farewell to those at my home." Jesus wouldn't allow for hesitancy. "No one who puts a hand to the plow and looks back is worthy of the kingdom of God" (v. 62). The opportunities that God extends at the present time must be seized or forever lost.

Reconciliation. When William Tyndale was translating the Bible, he was looking for an English word to translate the Greek *katallage* as well as the Latin word *reconciliation*. He came up with the word "atonement" (at-one-ment), which he used in Romans 5:11. The King James

Version followed Tyndale's lead but later translations reverted to reconciliation, probably to avoid confusion with the various theories of the atonement. The concept of reconciliation for the Old Testament and the New start from opposite points. The Jews believed that all unintentional sins were absolved when a person took part in the rites associated with the day of atonement (*Yom Kippur*). This ritual centered around the prayers and sacrifices of the high priest (Leviticus 16:1-31; 23:26-32). All other sins could be absolved only through prayer and repentance. Later, the rabbis taught that good works could bring atonement. One problem consisted in knowing how many good works were sufficient to confer atonement. The other difficulty stems from the fact that this line of thinking makes God the object and humans the subject of atonement. Christianity teaches that God is the subject of atonement and humans are the object. God has taken the initiative in overcoming the estrangement brought on by our sins. "God was in Christ reconciling the world to himself" (2 Corinthians 5:19).

Gospel: Matthew 6:1-6, 16-21

Hypocrites. Three times Jesus warns not to do as the hypocrites. Originally the Greek word *hypocrisis* was not negative. A person known by this name would answer questions, recite poetry, and act, as in a play. In the New Testament and especially in the thinking of Jesus, *hypocrisis* is completely negative. It means to pretend to be one thing, while being something quite contrary. It has the connotation of staging a show that has the intent of fooling the audience into thinking that this was real life and not an act. For Jesus the chief exemplars of hypocrisy were the scribes and Pharisees, many of whom loved to make a public display of their religiosity.

Don't toot your own horn (v. 2). When the king would make a public appearance, the fanfares would majestically sound. When the president of the United States makes a special public appearance, the band plays "Here Comes The Chief." The tooting of the horn serves to draw attention to important people. However, those who would like to think that they are VIPs draw attention to themselves by tooting their own horn, so to speak. A child of God does not need to draw attention to himself or his virtue; what can be greater than being a child of the king?

Who's your audience? Jesus warns against the danger of performing religion in order to be noticed by other people. Do we go to church to look religious? Do we pray long and eloquent prayers to reap the praise of others? The only proper audience for our religious devotions is the Lord. What God thinks of our performance is all that matters.

Reflex religion. Jesus teaches that the outward expression of faith must become second nature. "But when you give alms, don't let your left hand know what your right hand is doing" (v. 3). I'm not talking about the lamentable practice of doing acts of worship and devotion with your mind in overdrive. Rather, I'm making a point that God's goodness and grace should become so much a part of who we are that expressions of faith and charity spring naturally, like a reflex.

SERMON APPROACHES WITH ILLUSTRATIONS

Lesson 1: Joel 2:1-2, 12-17

Sermon Title: Make A U-turn

Sermon Angle: Normally, U-turns are proscribed by law but God calls his people, through his prophet Joel, to do a U-turn. God orders his people to turn their lives away from their rebellion and back to his merciful presence. When he pleads for them to return to him with all their heart (v. 12), it's the same as asking them to do a U-turn. Only a complete turnaround, involving will, intellect, and actions, will do.

Outline:
1. The Jews were called to turn their lives completely around (a U-turn).
   — Paying lip service would not do.
   — Ritual turning alone wasn't enough.
   — God's grace and mercy encouraged such turning.
2. Our repentance is often only partial or superficial.
3. Only a complete U-turn will do.
4. Such a move is only possible through the power of Christ.

Sermon Title: It's Not Too Late

Sermon Angle: The situation was serious but there was still time. The nation of Israel faced a crisis; the anvil of judgment was raised above their heads but the action of the people might still avert its crushing force. It was not too late: "Yet, even now ... return to me ..." (v. 12). The saddest words are these: "It's too late." When it comes to our relationship to God, as long as there's life, there's hope. If we genuinely repent, our relationship with the Lord turns over a new leaf.

Outline:
1. The Israelites faced an imminent crisis.
2. Joel holds out hope for God's mercy (v. 12).
3. If the people turn back to God, God will turn away the hand of judgment.
4. Some of us may think it's too late for us or our nation (our sins are too serious).
5. It isn't too late to return to God with our whole being (with all our heart).

Sermon Title: A God Of Holy Passion

Sermon Angle: The phrase in verse 13 translated "slow to anger" is the Hebrew *aph*. This word makes reference to the nose or nostril and, by association, the face. It is also used for rapid breathing, such as in making love or showing anger. The usage here suggests that God's anger and holy passion does not flare up easily or suddenly. Our God is not a God of unbridled passion, always ready to strike out, but of holy passion, characterized by tenderness and forgiveness.

Sermon Title: When God Sighs

Sermon Angle: The Hebrew word translated "repent" (vv. 13-14), referring to God, is *nacham*. One of the meanings of this word is "sigh" or "breathe strongly." How our sins must make God sigh! A person usually sighs when bored, grieved, angered, or under pressure. A sigh serves as a pause that allows a person to get control of his emotions. Giving pause allows a person to alter or change his response in a more creative direction. God's sigh (repentance) breathes new life into our broken relationship with the ground of our being. What makes God sigh? Our sins. When we sigh (pause to reconsider and repent), God inspires us with his Spirit to turn our lives around.

Outline:
1. Explain the meaning of *nacham* (sigh, repent).
2. Our sins make God sigh rather than lash out in anger.

3. God takes a breath and considers how he might breathe new life into his relationship with his children.
4. If we sigh (truly repent) of our sins, the Spirit will breathe new life into our being.

*   *   *   *   *

Walter Wangarin Jr. relates a moving personal story involving his son, apparently an impulsive little boy who permitted his desires to dominate his conscience. One day, his father happened into his room and observed the boy on the bed with a pile of comic books. The father was perplexed. "Where did you get all those comic books?" He said, "I took them out of the library." "You mean that you took from the library? You stole them from the library, isn't that right?" demanded the father. "Yes." So the father called the library and told them what his son had done and that they would come in shortly to return them.

Some time later, after they had returned from vacation, Walter opened the drawer in his son's dresser and found another pile of comics. The boy confessed that he had stolen them. The father took him and the books into the living room and burned the comics in the fireplace, reinforcing to his son that what he had done was a sin. He had broken God's commandments.

A year later, the son committed the same sin. The father ruefully ordered the son into the next room, where he was going to be spanked. The boy did not shed a tear but the father, not wanting his son to see the tears in his own eyes, announced that he was leaving the room but would return in a few minutes. Out in the hallway, the father sobbed. Some years later, the family was driving home from the shopping center when the subject of the comic books came up. "What made you stop stealing?" asked the mother. "The spanking your father gave you?" "No," he responded, "it is because when he stepped out of the room I could hear him crying."

We may not be moved to repentance by our Father's punishments or threats, but knowing how our sins break our Father's heart and bring tears to his eyes, if I could be allowed these anthropomorphisms, might help change our course.

*   *   *   *   *

Lesson 2: 2 Corinthians 5:20b—6:10

Sermon Title: God's Beggars

Sermon Angle: Paul begs the Corinthians to become reconciled with God. The task of presenting the gospel is not a matter of indifference but of highest importance. How many of us really care for neighbors who are separated from God? If the Lord remains there for us when we need him, we don't worry too much about the neighbor's spiritual state. We're so geared into the concept of the church as a spiritual supermarket, where we can shop for the latest religious goodies, that we forget that the church is really a mission outpost for making God's plan for reconciling creation known to all nations. We are beggars, since everything we have and are comes from the Lord. Our task is to beg others to accept the reconciliation that comes through Christ.

Outline:
1. Paul sees his task as being a beggar for Christ (v. 20b).
2. Paul was passionate for the church's task of reconciliation through Christ.
3. We are all beggars, since salvation is a free gift.
4. We are commissioned to share Christ's reconciliation (one beggar offering another beggar the bread of life).

130

Gospel: Matthew 6:1-6, 16-21

Sermon Title: Three Exercises You Can Do In Private

Sermon Angle: If you choose to employ the suggested theme for a Lenten series "Forty Days To Spiritual Fitness," this sermon could launch it. There are all kinds of fitness programs and exercise regimens. However, the program that wins the prize for originality is the video, *Buns Of Steel.* Let me suggest three simple exercises that can strengthen, invigorate, and firm up the body of Christ. Jesus used them and taught them. They are giving to the poor and needy, prayer, and fasting. Like most exercises, there is a wrong way and a right way to perform these exercises. They must not be done for show or the benefit of other people. Rather, these exercises must be directed toward God alone. Like physical exercise, these exercises must be practiced daily to have a significant strengthening effect on our spirit.

Outline:

1. Ask how many have tried or are engaging in an exercise program.
2. Discuss the physical fitness craze.
3. Why do we exercise?
   — To appear good to others?
   — To heighten our self-esteem?
   — Christian stewardship of our bodies?
4. Christians should give as much attention to spiritual fitness.
5. Jesus talks of three exercises to firm up a flabby soul — giving to the needy, prayer, and fasting. Find a quiet spot and exercise regularly.

Lent 1

Revised Common	Genesis 9:8-17	1 Peter 3:18-22	Mark 1:9-15
Roman Catholic	Genesis 9:8-15	1 Peter 3:18-22	Mark 1:12-15
Episcopal	Genesis 9:8-17	1 Peter 3:18-22	Mark 1:9-13

Theme For The Day: God's good news. God shows his graciousness through the covenant he established through Noah. God would never again destroy the world through flood. In the gospel Jesus announces the kingdom of God. All we have to do is repent and believe the good news.

BRIEF COMMENTARY ON THE LESSONS

Lesson 1: Genesis 9:8-17 (C, E); Genesis 9:8-15 (RC)

Humans become so corrupt that Yahweh drowns them all in a great flood, except for Noah and his family. Noah, his family, and various animals are kept safe on the ark, which the Lord told Noah to construct. Yahweh promises never again to destroy all the world through flood. This is a universal covenant with all humankind and all the creatures of the world. The sign of the covenant comes in the form of a rainbow. The ancients thought of the rainbow as God's weapon, his bow, with which he shot lightning bolts. Putting his bow in the heavens where all could see it demonstrates that God's wrath has been put aside.

Lesson 2: 1 Peter 3:18-22 (C, RC, E)

Christ is our once-and-for-all time sacrifice for sin, offered to make us right with God. Verses 19-20 are unique in the New Testament by claiming that after his physical death, the Spirit of Jesus went to Sheol, the Jewish abode of the dead, and preached repentance to the spirits of those who were destroyed during the time of Noah. With the flood imagery in mind, Peter compares the flood to Christian baptism. The flood was an instrument of judgment for the unrepentant. In contrast, baptism into the death and resurrection of Christ saves us. Water, in the flood account, symbolizes death, but for Christians the water of baptism remains the prime symbol of life.

Gospel: Mark 1:9-15 (C); Mark 1:12-15 (RC); Mark 1:9-13 (E)

Mark sets the stage for Jesus' public ministry. John the Baptist has been preaching a baptism of repentance. Jesus comes to John for baptism, a type of ordination. Note there is no protest from John. The heavens open and the Spirit descends on Jesus like a dove. A voice from heaven proclaims Jesus God's beloved (chosen) Son. The same Spirit drives Jesus into the wilderness, where he is tested for forty days by Satan. No specifics of Jesus' temptation are revealed by Mark, in contrast to what we find in Matthew and Luke. These actions conclude the preparatory phases of Jesus' ministry. Now Jesus stands ready to launch his mission. Verse 15 summarizes the entire ministry of Jesus, as told by Mark. "The time is come ... The kingdom of heaven is near. Repent and believe the good news."

Psalm Of The Day
Psalm 25:1-10 (C); Psalm 25 (E) — "Make me to know your ways, O Lord" (v. 4).
Psalm 24 (RC)

Prayer Of The Day

O merciful Lord, your Son strove with Satan and won. By the power of your Spirit, give us the vision to see our sins and the strength to turn our back on the same, that we might know the joy of your kingdom. In the powerful name of Jesus. Amen.

THEOLOGICAL REFLECTION ON THE LESSONS

Lesson 1: Genesis 9:8-17

Never again. It almost seems like God regrets his having covered the earth with a flood. God promises to establish his covenant with all creatures on earth and never to destroy them again by flood (v. 11). This raises an interesting question. Has God ever regretted anything he has done? If so, why doesn't he undo it? Maybe God feels like parents do sometimes when they have to discipline their children. They regret having to take such drastic actions but do it anyway for the good of the entire family.

Celestial disarmament? The Lord promises to place his bow in the heavens as a sign of his covenant of peace. In the thinking of the ancients the rainbow was God's weapon, the instrument with which he shot his arrows (lightning bolts). God is putting his weapon on the table so all can see and be at ease. It's true that the covenant only mentions that God will never destroy creation with a flood, but I wonder if more isn't suggested here. Is God renouncing violence as the means of solving problems?

Lesson 2: 1 Peter 3:18-22

Final sacrifice. In the Noah story we have most of the world dying for the sins of humankind. In the story of Christ's sacrifice we have one sacrifice by God for the sins of the world. Christ's sacrifice was the final sacrifice, once and for all.

Second chance. This passage asserts that the spirit of Jesus went to the abode of the dead during the period that his body lay in the tomb for the purpose of preaching repentance to those who perished during the great flood. Perhaps this passage had a formative influence on the Roman Catholic doctrine of purgatory. It seems that Noah's contemporaries were given a second chance to repent. The Lord does indeed give us many chances to repent in this life, but will he give us another opportunity after death? I wouldn't count on it!

Water of life (v. 21). During the flood the waters brought death. In baptism the waters bring us from death into life.

Gospel: Mark 1:9-15

Spirit driven. Jesus was Spirit driven. Mark reports that immediately after Jesus' baptism and acclamation by the Father, the Spirit drove him into the wilderness. The earthly Jesus did not live by his own power but was propelled and energized by God's Spirit. The secret of the Christian life is being Spirit driven rather than being driven by self-serving ambitions.

Major and minor scale. Music has its major scales and its minor scales. The major scale is celebrative, happy, and outgoing music. Minor scale music is more moody, brooding, and introspective. Life itself has its major and minor scales. Most of us would rather play out our lives in the major scale; we would prefer that our lives would always be upbeat and buoyant. Yet if life were always on the major scale, it might prove to be superficial, even boring. Interesting music and fulfilling living have contrast, with changes of tempo, mood, and scale. The baptism of Jesus was definitely major key, life on the upbeat. He knew himself to be the beloved Son of

God. But right after this bright experience, the downbeat was unmistakably sounded. Jesus was driven into the wilderness, thought of as the abode of Satan and evil spirits, where he was tempted by Satan. His life became a struggle for clarity and strength. We need to remember that God is the conductor of the symphony of life, which includes both major and minor keys.

The wilderness experience. The wilderness of Israel is not the same as what we think of as wilderness. The lovely mountain wilderness, which now surrounds me, points to the greatness of our Creator at every turn. However, it was a desert wilderness that Jesus entered — harsh, hot, and inhospitable. Yet even in this barren and mysterious place Jesus was not alone. Mark notes that ministering angels were sent to him. Life sometimes assumes the nature of a hostile wilderness for us. The wild beasts of tragedy, sickness, and death threaten our life. Sometimes the Lord himself may drive us to the wilderness of testing. With the help of God's Spirit and through the power of prayer, we can come through these wilderness experiences with clarity of mind and strength of purpose.

Initiative and response. Jesus opened his ministry by proclaiming "... the kingdom of God has come near; repent, and believe the good news" (v. 15). God takes the initiative in establishing the kingdom. All we have to do is respond. Our response is first of all to believe the good news and then to repent by letting the Spirit turn our lives in a new direction.

SERMON APPROACHES WITH ILLUSTRATIONS

Lesson 1: Genesis 9:8-17
Sermon Title: You're In Good Hands

Sermon Angle: Most homeowners take out insurance against man-made or natural catastrophes. One prominent company advertises "You're in good hands with Allstate." After the flood, God covered the whole world and every creature with an insurance policy (maybe we should dub it an assurance policy) that guarantees that all creation will never again be inundated by floodwaters. This is more than flood insurance. I see it as a promise that God will never again make all creation suffer near-extinction as the divine punishment for the sins of humankind. Creation is in good and loving hands.

Outline:
1. The flood was divine punishment for human sinfulness.
2. Creation suffered near-extinction.
3. God made his covenant of peace with all creation after the flood, symbolized by the rainbow (flood assurance).
4. The world is in good hands with God.
5. Let us care for the earth as extensions of God's loving hands.

Lesson 2: 1 Peter 3:18-22
Sermon Title: The Final Solution

Sermon Angle: God had a huge problem to solve, human sinfulness. The flood solution didn't work too well. Sin still darkened the heart of those spared in the ark. God called the people of Israel to be his own people, to live by his laws, and to love him. They too fell far short of the mark. Finally God sent his Son to die for our sins, once for all (v. 18). Christ is God's final solution for the problem of sin, which leads to death. All who accept the Lord's solution are saved.

Outline:
1. Humans present God with a huge problem — sin!
2. God employed various remedies — the flood, the law, punishments — but they were only penultimate remedies.
3. God finally sent his Son to rob sin of its power to destroy — the final solution.
4. Have you embraced God's final solution for sin?

Sermon Title: How To Clear Your Conscience

Sermon Angle: We have all done things that weigh heavy on our conscience. Some are so deeply troubled that they seek professional help. Counselors can help us deal with problems but only God can free us from guilt and give us a clear conscience. Baptism is God's way of washing away the film of guilt that clouds our vision of ourselves, our God, and others. Peter goes so far as to say that baptism saves us not by removal of dirt from the body but from the heart, mind, and conscience (v. 21). The world tries to clear the conscience by eliminating sin, Christ does so by freeing us from guilt. Baptism clears our conscience through the application of a generous lather of God's grace, acceptance, and forgiveness.

Outline:
1. Tell of a time when you were plagued by a guilty conscience.
2. Tell what you and others have done in dealing with a cloudy conscience.
3. Reveal God's remedy for a troubled conscience — God's baptismal grace.

Gospel: Mark 1:9-15

Sermon Title: Wilderness Survival Training

Sermon Angle: If you are going to survive in the wilderness there are certain facts that you must know. You must know what you can eat and drink, where to find shelter, how to deal with enemies or dangers, and how to obtain help. Jesus must have had wilderness training. He knew how to survive in a hostile, enemy-held territory, deprived of normal comforts. His relationship with his Father gave him strength not only to survive but to become a stronger person.

Outline:
1. Tell a story of wilderness survival.
2. Explain that the real wilderness is not a geographical area but a spiritual state of being (loneliness, addiction ...).
3. Wilderness experiences make us more vulnerable to the devil.
4. Jesus survived his wilderness experience through training and the power of the Spirit. So can we.

*   *   *   *   *

An American fighter plane was shot down over Bosnia by hostile Serb forces. The pilot safely ejected, laid low in the forests during the day and traveled at night. This enterprising pilot put his survival training into practice, eating and drinking whatever nature provided. He wisely broadcast his distress signal only sparingly and under the cover of darkness. After six or seven days and nights he was rescued by a daring American commando raid, with no loss of life. During the numerous interviews after his rescue, he revealed that the power that kept him going was his faith in God. He gave the Lord primary credit for his wilderness survival and rescue. Like Jesus in his wilderness experience, he dwelt in the midst of wild beasts but God sent angels to minister to him.

Sermon Title: Begin Your Spiritual Fitness Program With This Exercise

Sermon Angle: Lent is a time of spiritual discipline and spiritual exercises. Athletes tone up and train their bodies through a regimen of special exercises which not only discipline the body but the mind as well. Lent is a good time to get serious about a regular program of spiritual exercises. Jesus announced the kingdom of God and then commanded his hearers to do two exercises in response to this new reality — repentance and faith (v. 15).

Outline:

1. Skilled athletes reach stardom because they know there is a reality they want to be a part of so badly that they engage in a life of discipline and exercise.

2. The kingdom of God, ushered in by Jesus, is a reality we can realize through spiritual discipline — repentance and faith.

   — Repentance means turning from our sinful life.

3. Practice these two exercises you can't live without — repentance and faith.

Lent 2

Revised Common	Genesis 17:1-7, 15-16	Romans 4:13-25	Mark 8:31-38
Roman Catholic	Genesis 22:1-2, 9-13, 15-18	Romans 8:31-34	Mark 9:2-10
Episcopal	Genesis 22:1-14	Romans 8:31-39	Mark 8:31-38

Theme For The Day: The road to God's kingdom is the way of obedience, suffering, and death, the way of the cross. Christ calls us to take up our cross and follow him.

BRIEF COMMENTARY ON THE LESSONS

Lesson 1: Genesis 17:1-7, 15-16 (C)

God establishes his covenant with Abraham and his descendants. Like the covenant with Noah, it is an eternal covenant. Unlike that covenant, the beneficiaries of this covenant are Abraham's descendants exclusively. God promises to multiply his progeny so that nations and kings come from his line. As a result of this new relationship, the names of Abram and his wife, Sarai, are changed to Abraham and Sarah. Abraham means "the divine father is exalted." Sarah translates as "princess." This demonstrates the power and authority of the name giver.

Lesson 1: Genesis 22:1-2, 9-13, 15-18 (RC); Genesis 22:1-14 (E)

God instructs Abraham to take his son Isaac and go to the land of Moriah and offer him up to Yahweh as a sacrifice. This was a test of the patriarch's faith because not only would this destroy his beloved son but also the means by which the Lord's covenant with Abraham was to be fulfilled. The angel of the Lord stays Abraham's hand just as he was ready to plunge the knife into his son's chest. Abraham passed the test. A ram caught in a thicket serves as a substitute sacrifice, provided by the Lord himself. Tradition identifies Moriah with Jerusalem and specifically the temple mount. The Samaritans claimed that Moriah was located on Mount Gerizim.

Lesson 2: Romans 4:13-25 (C)

The true descendants of Abraham are not those who seek to live by the law but those who live by faith. Abraham did not receive the promise of God because he adhered to the law but because he trusted the grace of God (v. 16). Abraham trusted God in spite of evidence to the contrary. After all, both Abraham and Sarah were far beyond the childbearing age.

Lesson 2: Romans 8:31-34 (RC); Romans 8:31-39 (E)

In Paul's day becoming a Christian was dangerous. One could be persecuted, even killed. Paul submits that human opposition does not ultimately matter. "If God is for us, who could be against us?" (v. 31). The God who gave us his Son will graciously give us everything we need in this life of the world to come. Through Christ believers will conquer astrological, spiritual, and angelic powers, let alone earthly powers. No power can separate us from God's love in Christ (v. 39).

Gospel: Mark 8:31-38 (C, E)

Right after Peter's great confession at Caesarean Philippi that Jesus was the Christ, the Lord teaches what his title and kingdom signify. He teaches that he must suffer, die, and be raised to newness of life. This message is contrary to what they had hoped and dreamed. The disciples were aiming for glory, not suffering. Peter expresses the protest of the disciples (v. 32). Jesus forcefully counters Peter's protest by accusing him of expressing attitudes that come from Satan (v. 33). Jesus further charges that if any person desired to be his disciple that he would have to deny himself, take up his cross and follow him (v. 34). The person who aims to save his life will lose it, and the person who loses his or her life for Christ's sake will find it.

Gospel: Mark 9:2-10 (RC)

See gospel lesson for The Transfiguration Of Our Lord.

Psalm Of The Day

Psalm 22:23-31 (C) — "All the ends of the earth will remember and turn to the Lord ..." (v. 27).

Psalm 16 (E)
Psalm 115 (RC)

Prayer Of The Day

Gracious God, your Son has called us to deny ourselves, take up our cross, and follow him. Yet, our blood curdles at the prospect of self-denial or any kind of suffering. Give us the fortitude and faith to follow you, wherever that may lead. In the name of the one who went all the way for us, Jesus, our Lord. Amen.

THEOLOGICAL REFLECTION ON THE LESSONS

Lesson 1: Genesis 17:1-7, 15-16

A covenant God. Last week we considered God's covenant with Noah. This week we deal with God's covenant with Abraham, the foundational covenant of our Jewish-Christian faith. Actually, the Bible is peppered with covenants. A covenant is an agreement between two parties to enter into a relationship and to fulfill certain duties. Another word for covenant is "testament," from which we derive the designations Old Testament and New Testament. Conquering kings would impose covenants on those they had subjected through force. God's covenant with Abraham is different. It is a covenant of grace. God promises to bless Abraham and make a great nation of him; God pledges that he will be the God of Abraham and his descendants, through whom all peoples will be blessed. In a day when people fear commitments, it's wonderful to realize that we have a covenant God who keeps his word.

A covenant of grace. The covenant between the Lord and his people was not hammered out through negotiation, nor is it an agreement between equals. Notice that God takes the initiative in making all the promises. "I will confirm my covenant ..." (v. 2). "I have made you father of many nations" (v. 5). "I will establish my covenant as an everlasting covenant" (v. 7). This is nothing less than a covenant of grace and favor. Our text doesn't mention it but the sign of the covenant with Abraham was circumcision (vv. 11-13). God has established a covenant of grace with us through Christ. Baptism confers to us all the wonderful promises of God — forgiveness, salvation, and eternal life.

Fruitfulness. God's promise to Abraham and Sarah can be defined by the word "fruitful." Sarah was barren and far beyond the childbearing age. Yet the Lord promises that they will be the father and mother of nations. God promises fruitfulness to them and their descendants (v. 4). Fruitfulness has traditionally been based on the ability to have children. Today we may want to define fruitfulness differently. Fruitfulness may be thought of as the ability to love others and bring out the best in them. It can also be thought of as the ability to take a few resources and multiply them. For Christians fruitfulness means utilizing our talents and time for God's glory; it surely means sharing Christ with our neighbors.

Lesson 1: Genesis 22:1-14

Final exam. God had tested Abraham's faith time and again. God asked him to leave his homeland and all that was familiar without telling him his exact destination. God promised that he would make a great nation of him but waited until he and his wife were old before he fulfilled that promise. Now it was time for the final exam. Would he be willing to give up his son, his only son, in obedience to the Lord? Such a demand seemed contradictory to God's promises. That three-day trip to Moriah must have seemed like an eternity. Yet, Abraham knew his subject and trusted that God would not ask him to do anything irrational or evil. Abraham passed his final exam with flying colors, much like Jesus did when we was led into the wilderness by the Spirit to be tested by Satan.

Lesson 2: Romans 4:13-25

Father of the faithful. "He is the father of us all" (v. 16). Abraham is known for his fatherly role. His name was changed from Abram (exalted father) to Abraham (father of many). He is father not only of the Jews but of all who have the kind of faith that he had.

Father of hope. "Against all hope, Abraham in hope believed ..." (v. 18). Hope is the future dimension of faith; hope centers on what God has promised to do. Hope, like an ivy vine, clings tenaciously to these promises. In our land there are many who have no father and they have no hope. They have no dreams, no goals; they live only for the present moment. Without hope life loses its value and leads to self-destruction and violence. We need to lift up the light of hope, centered not in some concept of human perfectibility but in God's promises.

Credited to our account. Paul maintains that Abraham's faith and hope were "credited to him as righteousness" (v. 22). The word translated "credited" has also been translated as "reckoned," "accounted," or "accepted." This is the language of financial accounting. Though Abraham was not necessarily righteous in a moral sense — he was still a sinner. The Lord credited his faith as righteousness. Abraham trusted the Lord and it was credited to his account as righteousness. The gospel offers Christian believers the promise of eternal life through Christ. When we truly trust in God's promise it is credited to our account as righteousness. Faith is a much better investment than money in the bank; it pays eternal dividends.

Gospel: Mark 8:31-38

Graduate school. Just prior to this lection, we have the great confession of Peter that Jesus was the Christ. Jesus was happy that his disciples knew who he was. They had passed their bachelor's degree in Christology. Now it was time for graduate school; Jesus needed to educate them as to the significance of the title *Christ.* Contrary to their thinking, Jesus' messiahship was not going to lead to immediate honor and glory; rather, it would entail suffering, shame, and death. Peter was so opposed to the idea of a suffering Messiah that he rebuked Jesus. The disciples would understand the deeper concepts of Christology only after the resurrection.

Plain talk. Prior to this point in Jesus' ministry, he had spoken primarily in parables. Now it was time for plain talk; after all, these were matters of life and death. It seems that when it comes to the subject of death, we try to escape the painful realities by talking in riddles and metaphors. We even prefer to evade the word "death." We say "she passed on" as if she were a drifter. Medical people are fond of employing the word "expired" for our final earthly state, as if the dead person were an overdue book. Jesus knew that death was difficult to deal with; that's why he spoke plainly to his disciples. To take some of death's sting away, he held out a great hope; three days after his death he would "rise again" (v. 31). Death can be dealt with redemptively if we are willing to talk plainly concerning it.

Secret agent. The Lord's sharp rebuke of Peter must have really stung: "Out of my sight, Satan!" he said. "You do not have in mind the things of God but of man" (v. 33). He was accusing Peter of being a secret agent. Ostensibly he was a disciple of Christ. Unwittingly, however, he was serving as an agent of Satan by opposing God's plan. How many times does even the most loyal Christian find himself serving as an agent of Satan by reflecting values opposed to those of the Lord?

SERMON APPROACHES WITH ILLUSTRATIONS

Lesson 1: Genesis 17:1-7, 15-16

Sermon Title: Keeping Covenant

Sermon Angle: In this passage God confirms his covenant with Abraham to bless him and make of his line a great nation. God initiates and confirms his covenant as an act of grace. Abraham is told that he and his descendants must also keep God's covenant (v. 9). The concept of covenant, a relationship involving promises, duties, and responsibilities, is the golden thread that ties together all of scripture. In our day the freedom of the individual is exalted above covenantal relationships. Is it any wonder that the fabric of society is becoming unraveled? We need to hold up high the importance of the covenant God made with us in baptism as the basis of all other covenants. The covenant of marriage, family, and friendship must also be exalted. Keeping our covenants with God and others opens the door to God's eternal blessings.

Outline:
1. The concept of covenant ties scripture together.
   — God bonded with the Hebrew people through the covenant with Abraham.
   — God bonds with all believers through Christian baptism.
2. Covenant also ties life together.
   — Marriage and family.
   — Community bonds.
   — Friendship bonds.
3. God will bless us as he did Abraham if we keep covenant.
4. Faithfulness to our covenants is more important than individual freedom.

* * * * *

The movie, *The Bridges Of Madison County*, confronts us with the importance of our covenants. The character, Francesca, is a middle-aged farmwife who decides to stay home while the rest of the family heads off to the state fair for a few days. A photographer for *National Geographic* stops by to seek directions to the famed covered bridges in the county. She invites him to dinner. He regales her with stimulating accounts of his world travels and she is irresistibly swept off her feet by this charming rolling stone of a man. They enjoy four unforgettable days of romance but then reality sets in. Francesca has to make a painful choice. Will she follow her heart and leave with her lover? Or will she stay true to her covenant with her husband and family? She finally decides that her leaving would only cause untold grief for her family and that the passion she felt for her lover would turn to resentment for having betrayed her family. She would remain in the fertile, but less than exotic, cornfields of Iowa, with her solid, but less than exciting, husband, who continued to love her. Francesca was temporarily unfaithful to her husband but, in the end, kept her covenant. It's about time, Hollywood!

*   *   *   *   *

Lesson 1: Genesis 22:1-14

Sermon Title: The Test

Sermon Angle: When God asked Abraham to sacrifice his son, it must have seemed grossly unfair and unreasonable. Remarkably, Abraham didn't try to second-guess the Lord or only proceed when he understood God's reasoning. Abraham trusted God implicitly with his life and that of his son. The patriarch understood that this life is something of an exam, a test. Abraham also knew the Lord to be just and good and so he was willing to follow his instructions to the letter.

Outline:
1. Abraham understood that life was a test of faith.
2. For him the goal of life was not self-expression but obedience to God.
3. God's order to offer his son as a sacrifice was the supreme test of faith.
4. God can only do great things through those who pass the absolute obedience test.

*   *   *   *   *

A young man recently took the bar exam in the state of Iowa. One section of the exam contained several questions. He had to answer a certain number of them (something like seven out of ten) but the instructions explicitly stated that a certain question must be answered in order to pass the test. A number of those who took the exam failed to properly obey the instructions. They didn't answer that specific question and so they failed the test. God has established the rules for that grand test we call life. If we heed his instructions we will pass the test.

*   *   *   *   *

Lesson 2: Romans 4:13-25

Sermon Title: Father Of Faith

Sermon Angle: "He is the father of us all" (v. 16). Paul argues that Abraham is not only father of the Jews but of the Gentiles as well. His fatherhood is not conferred genetically but spiritually. Abraham stands as the father of all the faithful. He wasn't the first person to trust God but his life stands as the basic textbook on faith. What Freud is to psychology, Abraham is to faith. Abraham is the exemplar of faith — faith that perceives, follows, obeys, and hopes. Abraham's faith is all the more remarkable because he lacked the revelation of God in Christ.

Outline:
1. Jews, Gentiles, and followers of Islam have a common father in Abraham. Abraham is the father of all who have faith in the living God.
2. Faith for us should be easier because we have come to know God through Christ.
3. To have the faith of Abraham today means to follow Christ wherever he would have us go.

Gospel: Mark 8:31-38

Sermon Title: Cross Bearing: The Essential Exercise For Christian Discipleship

Sermon Angle: Contrary to popular usage, every pain and sorrow we experience is not cross bearing. To bear our cross means to follow Christ wherever he leads. Such discipleship will certainly entail suffering for the sake of Christ. Our human nature seeks to eliminate pain and suffering, which is all right except for the fact that there are some things worth suffering for, even dying for. Proclaiming the gospel is certainly at the top of this list. To follow Christ means to help others carry their burdens, to share their pain and their death. Exercise your cross bearing daily to keep spiritually fit.

Outline:
1. The disciples sought only glory and honor. Jesus had to teach them the necessity of cross bearing for himself and his disciples.
2. Cross bearing involves two things — denying ourselves and following Christ (v. 34).
3. If we play it safe, we may gain the world but lose our souls (v. 36).

Sermon Title: What A Shame!

Sermon Angle: Cross bearing is a shameful thing in the eyes of the world. Jesus warns that if we are ashamed of Jesus or his gospel in this life, he will be ashamed to claim us as his own when he comes into his kingdom (v. 38). Christianity seems so square, so simple and naive in the eyes of the world. We have taken the easy way out and failed to name the name of Jesus when that name was being dragged through the mud. We have been fearful and ashamed to challenge the conventional wisdom of the world with God's wisdom. Jesus endured shame and scorn on the cross. What a shame it was! We have been ashamed to witness for Jesus. What a shame! What a godawful shame!

* * * * *

One summer, I worked with a crew of young men who were painting a gas storage tank. They weren't a particularly bad sort but kind of rough around the edges. Some would brag about their drinking and womanizing exploits. At that time, I knew that I was called to preach the gospel but I was afraid to reveal my faith to them. I didn't want to seem odd or different. Like most young people, I wanted to blend in with the crowd. There was another young man working there, headed for the ministry in the Methodist church. During break one day he confessed, "We're cowards. We're both afraid to share who we really are with the other guys." I hung my head in shame. I knew he was right.

Lent 3

Revised Common	Exodus 20:1-17	1 Corinthians 1:18-25	John 2:13-22
Roman Catholic	Exodus 20:1-17	1 Corinthians 1:22-25	John 2:13-25
Episcopal	Exodus 20:1-17	Romans 7:13-25	John 2:13-22

Theme For The Day: A call to spiritual renewal and cleansing. Since God has come to us as holy redeeming love, our response is to be cleansed of our sins and live holy lives. The Ten Commandments (first lesson) are guidelines for such lives. Jesus' cleansing of the temple (gospel) constitutes a call to moral and spiritual renewal, beginning with God's house and God's people.

BRIEF COMMENTARY ON THE LESSONS

Lesson 1: Exodus 20:1-17 (C, E, RC)

The decalogue, the Ten Commandments, is presented as Israel's response to God's act of redemption through the exodus (v. 2). In the Hebrew form, they were originally very brief, two words long, and called the "Ten Words." According to this account, God spoke first to all the people but they didn't want to hear God's voice directly (v. 19) and so God gave the commandments to Moses on Mount Sinai in written form. Both Jews and Christians regard them as the direct revelation of God's will. The Lutherans and Roman Catholics count the commandments differently than in Reformed tradition. In the former case, the command against graven images is viewed as an extension of the command not to have any other gods before the Lord. The command about coveting is divided into two commands — the ninth and tenth commandments. The Reformed tradition takes the opposite approach. The commandments are also divided into the so-called two tables of the law. The first three or four (depending how we count them) compose the first table of the law, having to do with duties toward God. The last six or seven focus on our relationship with other people.

Lesson 2: 1 Corinthians 1:18-25 (C); 1 Corinthians 1:22-25 (RC)

Paul receives reports of factions in the Corinthian church (v. 11). Different people claimed to possess the correct philosophy. The apostle informs them that a person cannot come to know God through human wisdom but through what the world considers foolishness, the gospel of Christ. We come to experience God not through the power of our intellect but through the power of the cross (v. 18). The Jews regard the cross as a stumbling block (scandal) and the Greeks viewed it as foolishness. For Christians the cross of Christ is both the wisdom and power of God (v. 24).

Lesson 2: Romans 7:13-25 (E)

The law of God remains good and pure, even though it exposes human sin. Paul discusses the inner spiritual conflict of his soul between his sinful human nature and God's will as revealed in the law. In this passage Paul seems to regard sin as an outside power that invades the human heart (v. 20). This would seem to relieve humans of responsibility for their actions. However, elsewhere in his epistles he maintains our accountability for our actions. These verses reveal our powerlessness to consistently do God's will, even if it is our fervent desire.

Gospel: John 2:13-22 (C, E); John 2:13-25 (RC)

In the synoptic gospels, this account of the cleansing of the temple comes toward the end of Jesus' life, conducted after he entered Jerusalem on Palm Sunday. This came as the immediate cause of his arrest. In John's gospel the cleansing of the temple takes place toward the onset of our Lord's ministry and leads to the Jews questioning his authority to commit such an act. The sign Jesus gave was the destruction of the temple and its rebuilding in three days, an allusion to his death and resurrection. In the synoptics, Jesus begins his ministry in Galilee but John has Jesus launching out in Jerusalem after an initial miracle at the wedding feast in Cana of Galilee. The act of overturning the money changers should not be viewed as an explosion of anger but of divine judgment against spiritual corruption, especially that of making the worship of God a big business.

Psalm Of The Day

Psalm 19 (C); Psalm 19:7-14 (E) — "The law of the Lord is perfect, reviving the soul" (v. 7).

Psalm 18 (RC)

Prayer Of The Day

Lord Christ, cleanse our hearts and minds of all impurity just as you cleansed the temple of the money changers and merchants. May our worship of you not stem from any base motive but only from a heart of gratitude for your gift of eternal life. In the pure and precious name of Jesus, our Lord. Amen.

THEOLOGICAL REFLECTION ON THE LESSONS

Lesson 1: Exodus 20:1-17

Indicative-imperative. The Ten Commandments begin with the indicative: "I am the Lord your God, who brought you out of the land of Egypt...." The commandments of God, which become the moral imperatives of human existence, are grounded in the divine being. In other words, they are grounded in that which is foundational for all existence. Some seek to base that which is good on custom, consensus, or human volition but none of these is universal or ultimate. The Ten Commandments are built on God's very being. From this locus of authority issue the imperatives of life. God first reveals himself redemptively to his people and then calls for a response of obedience.

We are not free agents (v. 2). The first two verses in this passage indicate that we belong to the Lord ("your God"), not the other way around. In the atomistic philosophy popular in our culture, millions of folks think of themselves as free agents, at liberty to contract with the highest bidder. Not so, by virtue of the Lord's acts of creation and redemption; we belong with the Lord's team eternally.

Coveting underlies all the commandments. The Ten Commandments end with the commandments to abstain from coveting the neighbor's house, spouse, servants, and so forth. But they also begin with the command not to covet the neighbor's gods (no other gods before him, no graven images). We are not to covet the authority that belongs to our parents or the time that belongs to God (sabbath day). We are not to kill, which stems from coveting the authority that belongs to God alone, or commit adultery, coveting your neighbor's spouse. We all know that stealing derives from covetous desires for that which belongs to the neighbor. Well, you get the picture. All sin derives from the inordinate desire to possess that which is not rightly ours.

Lesson 2: 1 Corinthians 1:18-25

Mind and miracles. Paul wrote that the Greeks sought wisdom, to apprehend God with the mind, while the Jews sought to experience God through powerful miracles (signs). The entire Christian church can still be found on a continuum between the polarities of mind and miracle. Those on the left flank seek to understand God and the mysteries of life rationally before they commit themselves to the Lord. Those on the right seek to experience God through the medium of powerful signs. However, contact with God cannot be established through mind or miracles until we first encounter him in the cross of Christ. For us the cross is both the power of God and the wisdom of God.

The weakness of God (v. 25). We normally attribute to God the trait of omnipotence. We derive comfort from the thought that God is all-powerful. Perhaps we need to rethink this concept. If God is all-powerful, why do we have wars? Why do so many innocents suffer? We might answer with the concept of human freedom. Sin and evil are negative outcomes of this freedom. God apparently is not strong enough to create us free and sinless all at once. The cross is the ultimate demonstration of God's weakness, which, through faith, becomes our strength and God's. God is able to make us into a new creation through a demonstration of weakness.

Gospel: John 2:13-22

Under the law (v. 13). Jesus went up to Jerusalem for the Passover, even though he lived far enough away that he wasn't required to. He put himself under the dictates of the Jewish law, even though he was God in the flesh, just as it was his custom to worship in the synagogue every sabbath.

Jesus overturns the tables (v. 15). Once Jesus invades our lives, it's never business as usual. Jesus overturns the tables on conventional religion. He becomes angry when he observes how some humans corrupt the faith, using God for material gain rather than being used by God for their spiritual gain.

Whose church is it? As Jesus overturned the tables of business in the temple courtyard, he identified the temple as "his Father's house" (v. 16). Some church members seem to feel that their congregation is their private domain, while some pastors feel the same way. Other folks don't feel that the church belongs to them and so they keep away. Let us remember that the church is God's house and offer hospitality to all who seek forgiveness and grace.

SERMON APPROACHES WITH ILLUSTRATIONS

Lesson 1: Exodus 20:1-17

Sermon Title: Love And The Law

Sermon Angle: When parents lay down the law for their children, the children feel that their parents are being mean. After they gain maturity they can see that the prohibitions are motivated by love. Likewise, God gave the law to his people because of his love for them. God's love does not have limits but his love does set limits. The law of God is not negative, as many detractors charge.

Sermon Title: Knowing Your Boundaries

Sermon Angle: The Ten Commandments are about boundaries. Humans seem to have trouble locating their boundaries. The boundaries that we constantly transgress are those between God and humans and the boundaries between my life and those of my brothers and sisters. Since God has made known our boundaries, we are accountable for our actions. If we abide by the boundaries that God has ordained we will experience joy and well-being.

Outline:
1. Most people feel more comfortable when they know their boundaries.
2. God sets our boundaries with the Ten Commandments.
3. We transgress those boundaries regularly and become alienated from God and each other.
4. The cross of Christ is God's way of restoring boundaries and relationships.

* * * * *

Hundreds of Christians gathered on the lawn of the county courthouse in Gladsen, Alabama, to demonstrate their support for Judge Roy Moore, who found himself embroiled in a dispute with the American Civil Liberties Union. Judge Moore had been accused of transgressing the boundaries of church and state. His accusers objected to a wood carving of the Ten Commandments, which hung on the Etowah County Courthouse wall. His detractors also disapproved of his practice of prayer on the day when the jury was organized. April 10, 1995, a crowd estimated to be about 500 gathered about the courthouse to lend their support to Judge Moore. The judge believed that he had done nothing wrong and that he was merely exercising his constitutional rights. He stated that the constitution was never intended to keep God out of the government but to prevent the government from interfering with the church.

* * * * *

Lesson 2: 1 Corinthians 1:18-25

Sermon Title: The Foolishness Of The Cross

Sermon Angle: The message of the cross is still regarded as foolishness today, even as it was in Paul's day. People prefer the so-called wisdom of our day and age, something more logical. The wisdom of God still comes through the foolishness of the cross.

Outline:
1. How does one come to know God?
2. The Jews thought they could know God through knowledge of his laws.
3. The Greeks thought they could know God through philosophy.
4. The gospel informs us that we can only know God through the foolishness of the cross.

* * * * *

At the notorious Re-Imagining conference, the cross of Christ was subjected to derision. One of the speakers, who attempted to empty the cross of its meaning and centrality for the Christian faith, was Beverly Williams, who declared: "I don't think we need a theory of atonement at all. I don't think we need folks hanging on crosses and blood dripping and weird stuff." According to an article in *Christianity Today*, Ingeline Nielsen, a Swiss missionary to Zimbabwe, attacked the hymn "Lift High The Cross" as presenting an oppressing view of God. A

146

professor of English, Virginia Ramey Mollenkott, claimed that the cross symbolizes an abusive parent. These women offer their supposedly enlightened wisdom in place of the foolishness of the cross. This attack on the central symbol of our faith was launched not by hostile outsiders but by those who claim the title of believer. Can anything be more destructive than attacks from those inside the family of faith?

*   *   *   *   *

Gospel: John 2:13-22

Sermon Title: Cleansing The Lord's House: An Exercise You Must Do At Church

Sermon Angle: Lent offers a time for spiritual and moral cleansing. We usually view this as an exercise for individuals but the church as an institution also needs to be washed clean of corruption. The history of Christianity bears eloquent witness to this truth. The Crusades, the Inquisition, the Reformation, the silence of the German church during the Nazi era are but a few outstanding examples of the corrupting of the church and the need for spiritual cleansing. The corruption in your congregation may not be nearly so dramatic. Perhaps it takes the form of lack of zeal for the Lord's house, apathy, or an unwillingness to serve those in need.

Outline:
1. The Lord attacked the merchants for corrupting the house of God.
2. Religion has a tendency to become corrupt, like all other institutions.
3. The church must ever be reforming and renewing.
4. What are the sinful institutional practices that need to be purged from your church?

*   *   *   *   *

Our local newspaper showed members of the Southern Baptist Convention with linked hands; they were people of different color. The denomination had officially repented of the sin of racism, which led them to support the practice of slavery during the Civil War era. A little late, you say? Better late than never. Pope John Paul, on behalf of the Roman Catholic church, has also sought forgiveness for the church's lack of action during the Nazi holocaust. Repentance is the first step in dealing with institutional corruption.

*   *   *   *   *

Sermon Title: We Are God's House

Sermon Angle: After Jesus cleansed the temple, irate merchants and temple officials demanded to know the source of his authority to do such a radical act. They demanded a sign, some credentials that authorized him to do this. Jesus responded: "Destroy the temple and in three days I will raise it up" (v. 19). As is often the case in the fourth gospel, there is a double meaning. The officials understood the temple to be the one in Jerusalem. Jesus was speaking of his body as a temple, which would be destroyed and raised again. Too often we identify the church with brick and mortar. Instead, we should think of it as a living organism, a body. God dwells not in buildings but in people, in particular, the people of God, the church. Our hearts are Christ's throne; the community of the faithful is the place where Christ has affixed his holy name. The hymn "Built On A Rock" says it well: "We are God's house of living stones, built for his own habitation."

147

Outline:
1. The Jews thought that the temple was the place to worship God.
2. Jesus refers to his body as the holy temple, which would be razed and then raised.
3. The church is the body of Christ, a holy place of worship.
   — The church is not so much a material structure but a community.
   — As Christ's body, we must die to sin and be raised to eternal life.

Lent 4

Revised Common	Numbers 21:4-9	Ephesians 2:1-10	John 3:14-21
Roman Catholic	2 Chronicles 36:14-17, 19-23	Ephesians 2:4-10	John 3:14-2₁
Episcopal	2 Chronicles 36:14-23	Ephesians 2:4-10	John 6:4-15

Theme For The Day: We are saved by grace through faith. God provided the bronze serpent for the Israelites bitten by the fiery serpents (Numbers 21), that those who gazed on it might live. So, too, the Father lifted up Jesus on the cross, that all who look to him in faith might have eternal life.

BRIEF COMMENTARY ON THE LESSONS

Lesson 1: Numbers 21:4-9 (C)

The Israelites grow impatient as they wander in the wilderness surrounding the country of Edom and complain about God's provision for their needs. The text states that God sent poisonous snakes among the people as punishment. The people confess their sin and seek Yahweh's mercy. The Lord commands Moses to fashion a bronze snake and put it on a pole in the midst of the camp. If anyone was bitten, he could look to the bronze serpent and have his life spared. God does not remove the problem but provides a means of dealing with it.

Lesson 1: 2 Chronicles 36:14-17, 19-23 (RC); 2 Chronicles 36:14-23 (E)

The tragic account of how the apostasy of the Israelites led to their capture by the Babylonians and the destruction of the temple in Jerusalem. God sent Cyrus, the king of Persia, to enable the Jews to rebuild Jerusalem and the temple.

Lesson 2: Ephesians 2:1-10 (C); Ephesians 2:4-10 (RC, E)

God loves us so much that he raised us to newness of life with Christ, even while we still are mired down in our sins. We are saved by grace (vv. 5, 8), which is taken hold of through faith. Salvation comes as a gift of God, never as the outcome of human achievement. Nevertheless, if we have been born anew, we will live new lives and realize the purpose for which we were created, good works (v. 10).

Gospel: John 3:14-21 (C, RC)

The passage constitutes a continuation of the account of Nicodemus' encounter with Jesus. The Lord relates the meaning of the new birth. Verse 14 connects to the story of the fiery serpents, contained in the first lesson. As the bronze serpent was lifted up as an antidote for the deadly bite of the poisonous serpents, so Jesus would be lifted up (on the cross) that all who look on him in faith might have eternal life. John 3:16 is often referred to as the little gospel or the gospel in a nutshell. It reveals that God is not a deity of retribution but of love and grace. To really see the Christ of the cross leads to repentance and new life. However, condemnation and judgment can be brought down on our heads when we turn our backs to Jesus.

Gospel: John 6:4-15 (E)

See gospel lesson for Proper 12.

Psalm Of The Day

Psalm 107:1-3, 17-22 (C) — "Bless the Lord ... who forgives all your sins, who heals all your diseases ..." (v. 3).

Psalm 122 (E)

Psalm 136 (RC)

Prayer Of The Day

God of mercy, you lifted up your Son, Jesus, on the cross, that all who believe in him might enjoy eternal life. By your Spirit, defang Satan's power to hurt and destroy; then, heal us body and soul. In Jesus' name. Amen.

THEOLOGICAL REFLECTION ON THE LESSONS

Lesson 1: Numbers 21:4-9

I don't deserve this! The Israelites, having just left behind a life of slavery in Egypt, grumbled and complained about the hardships of their journey to the promised land. Basically, they were saying, "I don't deserve this!" meaning that they deserved better than what God was delivering to them. Often, we mutter the same complaint: "I don't deserve this, God!" "I've been a pretty good person!" "Scoundrels enjoy greater fortune than I." Have you ever noticed, however, when things are going well for us, when the sun is shining and the flowers are blooming, we don't ever exclaim: "I don't deserve these blessings, Lord!"

Seeing our past through rose-colored glasses. I know a couple of people who look back on their childhood as an idyllic time of endless joy. However, I was there and I know that there were some less than wonderful things that transpired in their lives. They are viewing their childhood through rose-colored glasses. The Israelites were slaves in Egypt; they had to work hard but all their needs were taken care of. There were few decisions that they had to make. Freedom meant struggle and hardship, a more adult mode of existence. They began to view their time of slavery positively. They had had plenty of good food and drink, in contrast to the spartan fare they were now served, and so they complained (v. 5). They saw only the advantages of their former life, without its drawbacks. The sting of the serpents woke them out of their self-destructive nostalgia.

Take the serpents away (v. 7). The people viewed the sting of the serpents as a punishment for their grumbling against the Lord. They repented and requested Moses to pray to God for the removal of the snakes. Note that the Lord does not remove them. Instead, he orders Moses to fashion a bronze serpent, which would serve as an antidote for the snakebite. In the Genesis account of the fall, the serpent serves as the instrument of temptation to sin. God does not remove the power of evil or the source of temptation but offers us an antidote for its potentially deadly bite. For the Jews, it was the bronze serpent; for us Christians, it is the crucified Christ. Referring to this story, Jesus exalts: "And just as Moses lifted up the serpent in the wilderness, so must the Son of Man be lifted up" (John 3:14).

Lesson 2: Ephesians 2:4-10

Our God is rich (vv. 4, 7). Our God is rich in mercy, love, and grace. God not only holds the universe in the palm of his hands but is rich in the qualities that make life worth living. Through faith, we eternally draw on this treasure trove, willed to us through the death and resurrection of Christ.

150

A done deal. Twice Paul makes the statement: "by grace you have been saved" (vv. 6, 8). Note the past tense. Our salvation is a done deal, accomplished through the death and resurrection of Christ. The hand of faith merely reaches out to accept the gift of new life in Christ. "Nothing in my hand I bring, simply to thy cross I cling."

An analogy from the farm. To try and conceptualize the relationship of grace, faith, and good works, let's consider a farm tractor. We might say that grace is the engine, the source of power. However, that power has to be channeled. That's the work of the transmission, which takes the power of the engine and transmits it to the wheels. Faith is the transmission that makes God's power and love available to us. A tractor generally pulls something behind it, a planter or disc, to accomplish good works. A tractor is not designed for the purpose of driving around but for accomplishing good works. So too, God created us anew in Christ Jesus for good works (v. 10).

Gospel: John 3:14-21

The enthronement of Christ (v. 14). For the synoptic gospels, the enthronement of Christ as Lord and king occurs after the ascension. For John, the cross is Christ's throne, revealing his glory and power. Being lifted up on the cross is equivalent to being lifted up on a throne. John has a point. In the cross we view the surpassing greatness and majesty of our God.

Antitoxin. For the Jews in the wilderness, the cure for snakebite was to look at a representation of the very creature that had the potential to harm. The serpent symbolizes both death and healing. God took the form that death took and transformed it into life. The cure for snakebite is detoxified venom, transformed to serve life rather than death. So, too, the cross was the paramount instrument of death in Jesus' day, but God transformed it into the universal symbol of life. He drained death, symbolized by the cross, of its power to destroy. Jesus' death provides us with an antitoxin for sin.

God loves the whole world (v. 16). Radical groups like "The Aryan Nation" dare to assert that God loves only white people, preferably Nordic types. The Black Muslims assert that only black people are the apple of God's eye and the whites are Satan. Various Christian groups have had the audacity to claim that the Lord only listens to people in their group. For all of these groups and more, God is merely a projection of themselves. The God we know in Jesus Christ claims the whole world as his own. Broadcasting this good news provides the church's reason for being.

The test of true love (v. 16). "God so loved ... that he gave...." How does one know that he or she is really loved? What marks love as authentic? The giving of self. God gave himself to us in Jesus Christ; he held nothing back. Such giving is costly and so many people in our culture have substituted things material for self. It's easier to give your kid ten bucks than to spare your time.

It's difficult to condemn someone you love (vv. 16-17). Susan Smith, the mother in North Carolina who put her children into a car and then pushed it into a lake, was convicted by her neighbors of murder. However, they did not condemn her to death. It's hard to condemn someone you know and love, someone who is your neighbor. It's much easier to condemn a stranger, a fiend cloaked in anonymity. That's why executioners formerly wore hoods and why those condemned to death also were shrouded. The law of God pronounces the sentence of guilty upon us but God has also come to know us and love us in Jesus Christ. He offers us pardon and freedom from condemnation.

SERMON APPROACHES WITH ILLUSTRATIONS

Lesson 1: Numbers 21:4-9

Sermon Title: The Venom Of A Complaining Spirit

Sermon Angle: The wilderness wandering consumed forty years of painfully slow progress. The writer of Exodus states that it took so long because of the sin of the people; the Lord vowed that none of the generation that left Egypt would enter the promised land. Not even Moses was allowed to enter. Time and again the people complained and grumbled against the Lord. In our current text they complained about their spartan diet. The text states that the serpents were sent to punish the people for their complaining spirit. Actually, the negative spirit of the people was more venomous than the snakes. Their accusations against God were poisoning their souls and their society. The snakes were sent not to kill but to heal, by bringing the people to repentance.

Outline:
1. The complaining spirit among the Jews was poisoning their souls.
2. Cite examples of the toxic effect of such a complaining spirit in our day.
3. God sent the serpents as agents of judgment to bring repentance.
4. The bronze serpent that God ordered was a sign of his healing presence.
5. When afflicted, they could look to the bronze serpent and be saved.
6. When we look in faith to the crucified Christ, we are saved from our sins, not the least of which is a complaining spirit (John 3:14).

Sermon Title: The Gift Of Judgment And Grace

Sermon Angle: You may have trouble seeing God's judgment as a gift, but it is. Just think how horrible life would be if our actions were never judged wanting and if our sins were never punished. True judgment alerts us to the need for repentance and renewal, as it did in our text. However, judgment unmitigated by grace destroys rather than heals. The poisonous snakes were agents of God's judgment, while the bronze serpent was a visible demonstration of God's grace. Judgment and grace are not two separate realities but two sides of the same reality; both are gifts of God.

Outline:
1. In this text we see both God's judgment and grace.
2. Actually, judgment and grace are inoperable.
   — Judgment points to the need to repent.
   — Grace gives us the courage and strength to actually repent.
3. God's judgment may sting, but it is intended to lead us to life in the Lord.

* * * * *

Luther Murrow, a member of a snake-handling cult in the region of Grasshopper, Tennessee, was bitten by a rattler during one of their services. He went about his business, unfazed by the attack, but the snake died shortly thereafter.

* * * * *

Lesson 2: Ephesians 2:4-10

Sermon Title: Bad News For Legalists

Sermon Angle: The gospel spells bad news for legalists. Legalists like rules, rules that they and other legalists have constructed. By these rules they judge themselves innocent and all those who don't live by their rules as guilty. The gospel of Christ says that we are saved by grace, not by the keeping of the rules. Salvation is a gift of God (vv. 8-9). Yes, the gospel is bad news for all legalists because it will not permit them to take pride in their spiritual and moral achievements.

Outline:

1. The gospel is bad news for all legalists and hypocrites.
   — It will not permit them to take credit for their own salvation.
2. The gospel is wonderful news for all sinners who know their need of grace.
3. Grace is what saves us and faith is the conduit that delivers God's grace into our lives.
4. Accept, celebrate, and pass on God's gift of grace.

*   *   *   *   *

As I was driving to the hospital recently, I was listening to Chuck Swindoll preach about the legalism of the scribes and Pharisees. He cited some of the seemingly ridiculous rules, such as regulations concerning work on the sabbath. You couldn't lift anything in the ordinary way because that was work but whatever you could lift on the top of the hand, with the ears, elbows, or knees, was not considered work and was permitted. (By the way, how do you lift something with your ears?) Swindoll also shared how he encountered a woman who had heard him preach on legalism. She related that her husband had been the pastor of a very legalistic church and that she and her mate were the foremost of legalists. If you belonged to their church, you couldn't go to movies, you couldn't go dancing, women had to dress a certain way — you get the picture. One day, their children announced that they were dropping out of the church. They couldn't countenance the sham and hypocrisy of that kind of religion. This cut the parents to the heart but they listened. They came to confess that their children were right. The congregation didn't want to change its legalistic way and so the pastor resigned his call and went into another line of work. The couple joined a church that preached and practiced the gospel of grace, which has made all the difference in the world.

*   *   *   *   *

Gospel: John 3:14-21

Sermon Title: Lift High The Cross: An Exercise That Builds The Body Of Christ

Sermon Angle: God allowed Jesus to be lifted up on the cross that all the world might see the love and grace of God and be saved. Our calling as the church is to lift up the crucified and risen Savior, that the world might experience the love of God. We do not lift up the crucified one to save ourselves (we are saved by grace) but that others might see and accept the gift of the gospel.

Outline:

1. God's salvation is not hidden. God lifts up his salvation for all to see and be saved (the bronze serpent on the pole and Jesus on the cross) (v. 14).
2. For John the cross lifts up Jesus' glory and power.

3. The cross offers eternal life to all who accept Jesus as Lord and Savior.
4. We must lift up the cross that others might see and accept God's salvation.

Sermon Title: No Condemnation In Christ

Sermon Angle: God's purpose is to save the world, not condemn it (vv. 17-18). Why then was Christ pictured in ancient and medieval art as an implacable judge? Could it be that the church literally wanted to scare the hell out of people? It seems that for some time the church lost contact with the grace of God and reverted to legalism. The law condemns and kills but God's mercy in Jesus Christ gives us life. There is condemnation for those who refuse to come to God's light, but it is self-condemnation, not the will of God in Christ.

Outline:
1. The world is quick to judge and condemn us.
2. God sent his Son to save us, not condemn us (v. 17).
3. Since God shows us his grace, we should withhold our judgment of others.
4. When the venom of guilt and sin strikes, look up to the Christ of the cross.

*   *   *   *   *

Michelangelo's famed fresco on the ceiling of the Sistine Chapel in Rome has recently been restored to some semblance of its original apocalyptic glory. When the original was unveiled on October 31, 1531, Pope Paul III sank to his knees and implored his creator: "Lord, charge me not with my sins when thou shalt come on the day of Judgment." Apparently the writhing swirl of the damned plunging into the abyss had its intended effect. Even the expressions of those who are not plummeting into the fire convey uncertainty, with the possible exception of the Virgin Mary. This was not the message that the church of that time wanted to convey. Michelangelo's vision of the Last Judgment leaves everyone and everything hanging, including the artist. In his final confession, at the age of 89, the great artist repined: "I regret that I have not done more for the salvation of my soul."

Lent 5

Revised Common	Jeremiah 31:31-34	Hebrews 5:5-10	John 12:20-33
Roman Catholic	Jeremiah 31:31-34	Hebrews 5:7-9	John 12:20-30
Episcopal	Jeremiah 31:31-34	Hebrews 5:(1-4) 5-10	John 12:20-33

Theme For The Day: The heart of Jesus was broken in death so that he might create within us a new heart. In the first lesson, the new heart is promised. In the second lesson, Jesus poured out his heart of suffering to the Father. In the gospel, Jesus promises that he will unite our hearts through the cross [draw all people to himself] (v. 32).

BRIEF COMMENTARY ON THE LESSONS

Lesson 1: Jeremiah 31:31-34 (C, RC, E)

Written after the destruction of the nation by the Babylonians, the prophet promised that God will establish a new covenant with both Israel and Judah, not carved in stone but on the human heart. The covenant would be different from the one forged in the infancy of the nation, the wilderness wandering period during which God gave his laws to Moses. God had to take them by the hand (v. 32) and lead them out of Egypt. This portrays a relationship of childlike dependency. In the future God would imprint his will on their hearts, an image of maturity (v. 33).

Lesson 2: Hebrews 5:5-10 (C); Hebrews 5:7-9 (RC); Hebrews 5:(1-4) 5-10 (E)

This lection is part of a larger section concerning Jesus in the role of high priest (4:14—5:14). It refers to Jesus' passionate prayers in the Garden of Gethsemane, offered up to the Father with heart and soul. Jesus learned obedience (submission) by the sufferings of the cross. Christ's sacrifice made him perfect; that is, he completed his role as high priest. In so doing Christ becomes the source of salvation for all who have faith.

Gospel: John 12:20-33 (C, E); John 12:20-30 (RC)

Some Greeks, possibly just a term for Gentiles, come to Philip, asking to see Jesus. Perhaps they wanted to investigate the possibility of becoming disciples of Jesus. Philip goes to Andrew (who introduced Peter to Jesus) with the request. They both approach their master. Jesus responds that it was now time for his ministry to add the crowning touch. While the synoptic gospels identify the resurrection as the time of glorification, John sees the crucifixion and resurrection in the same frame. The cross lifts up Jesus in all his glory and power. These Greeks who wanted an audience with the Lord can see him in all his glory on the cross. Like a grain of wheat, Jesus would have to die so that his life might bear fruit (v. 24). Those who follow him must be willing to lose their lives for his sake. Though the thought of dying on the cross distresses Jesus, he accepts it as his appointed mission (v. 27). Since the cross cannot be avoided, he asks the Father to glorify his name. God responds with a thundering voice. Those who hear it realize that Jesus is God's Son. Jesus exults that he will draw all mankind to himself through the cross (v. 30).

Psalm Of The Day

Psalm 51:1-12 (C); Psalm 51 (E) — "Have mercy on me, O God, according to your unfailing love" (v. 1).

Psalm 50:12 (RC)

Prayer Of The Day

Merciful God, we have beheld your glory in the face of your crucified Son. As we are transfixed by the wonder of your love, purify our hearts of sin and unite them with all who confess your name. In Jesus' name. Amen.

THEOLOGICAL REFLECTION ON THE LESSONS

Lesson 1: Jeremiah 31:31-34

Promise fulfilled. God promises through Jeremiah that in the future he will establish a new covenant with his people. In Christ that covenant has been established and that promise has been fulfilled. However, it's better than what Jeremiah prophesied; we not only know God's laws but we have his love in our heart.

School dismissed (v. 34). The time will come when we will not need to teach God's will or ways. Everyone will know the Lord firsthand. School will be dismissed forever in God's kingdom, where we will enjoy God forever.

Selective memory (v. 34). Depending on our personality type, we choose to remember either the good things that happen to us or the bad things. Some people can recall in detail every affront to their dignity, while others retain only golden memories. God has made a conscious decision to forget the sins of his repentant children. He not only forgives our offenses, he treats them as if they never occurred.

Lesson 2: Hebrews 5:5-10

Passionate prayers. According to the writer of Hebrews, Jesus prayed passionately, with heart, mind, and strength. No perfunctory pray-er was he. There was good reason for his passion. Not only was his future on the line but that of the whole world. Only prayer that comes from the heart is really worthy of the name.

How God answers prayers. The passage states that the Father heard Jesus' prayer (v. 7) even though he didn't grant what Jesus begged for (escape from suffering and death). Hearing our requests and granting them are two different actions. Sometimes God answers by saying, "No" or "Later" or "I have something else in mind for you."

A perfect Christ, a perfect Christian (v. 9). Jesus learned obedience through what he suffered and was made perfect but how are we to understand the meaning of "perfection"? The word actually denotes a sense of completion. The suffering he experienced as a result of his obedience made Jesus complete in his high priestly role as Lord and Savior. A perfect Christ indicates a life of complete submission to the Father's will. Whatever we suffer for the cause of righteousness completes and perfects the follower of Christ. This, of course, does not mean that we are free from sin.

Gospel: John 12:20-33

We wish to see Jesus (v. 21). Jesus had a way of drawing people to himself. Some Greeks came to Jesus with the request, "Sir, we wish to see Jesus." There is a sign on the inside of the pulpit at my church with these very words. The problem is that most people don't feel free to approach Jesus directly. They want and need to be introduced. That's where we come in. We who have come to experience Jesus' love and grace are called to share him with others. Most people will not be so bold as were the Greeks who came to Philip with the request to meet the Lord. We will need to anticipate their need to see Jesus.

Glory in the cross (v. 23). Jesus speaks of the cross as his hour of glory, a different perspective than we find in the second lesson from Hebrews, where Jesus prays passionately that the Father might provide some other way than the cross. The Christ we see in John is viewing the cross from the vantage point of the resurrection. The glory of the cross is the glory of God's self-giving love that could not be destroyed.

You can't find your life until you lose it (vv. 24-25). Jesus compares human life to a grain of wheat, which must first die in order to give rise to new life. In the same way, Jesus teaches that we must first lose our lives before we can find them.

What to pray in time of trouble (v. 27). The prospect of the cross caused a very human response within the soul of Jesus. He was troubled. The first instinct when confronting trouble is to run, to escape. Jesus did not pray that God would spare him suffering or remove the cross. No, he prayed for the strength to carry through the Father's will. We would do well to pray in the same manner, asking not for escape but for strength to accomplish whatever the Lord has in store for us.

The magnetic Christ (v. 32). Jesus viewed his cross as the magnet that would draw all manner of people unto God. "And I, when I am lifted up ... will draw all people to myself." As we lift up the Christ who gave his life on the cross, human existence will come together, drawn by the irresistible force of God's great love.

SERMON APPROACHES WTH ILLUSTRATIONS

Lesson 1: Jeremiah 31:31-34

Sermon Title: Growing Up In God

Sermon Angle: The images of the relationship that God established with his people, as he brought them out of Egypt, are familial. Taking his people by the hand (v. 32) suggests a parent leading his child. In the same verse, Yahweh refers to himself as Israel's husband. Both images suggest dependency to the people of Jeremiah's day. The new covenant that Jeremiah predicts states that the source of Israel's morality would come from within rather than from without. The morality of a child comes from outside himself. "Momma told me not to do it." Or, "if you do this, you'll get spanked." When a person becomes mature, the intellectual, ethical, and spiritual center comes from within. Jeremiah suggests a future time when God's people will have grown in God.

Outline:
1. When we were children, our sense of right and wrong came from parents (moral and spiritual immaturity).
2. For the Jews of Jeremiah's time, morality was also external (the law).
3. Jeremiah envisions an internal source for morality (the new covenant of the heart).
4. The new covenant is fulfilled in Christ and marks the attainment of spiritual maturity.

157

Sermon Title: The New Deal

Sermon Angle: To lift the nation out of the depression, President Franklin Roosevelt came up with his "New Deal." The government was going to reach down and help all the citizens of the land. The "New Deal" marked a fundamental shift in the relationship between the government and the people. The Republicans' "Contract With America" promised yet another covenant between the government and the citizens, which led in an opposite direction from the "New Deal." The new covenant that Jeremiah holds up promises a new deal of a different sort. He holds up the prospect that God will relate to his people in an entirely new manner. He will put his laws and precepts within us and make himself personally known to his people. This new covenant has come through Christ and the gift of the Holy Spirit.

Outline:
1. Jeremiah realized the provisional nature of the Old Covenant and the need for a new covenant (a new deal).
2. The new deal (covenant) involved a new way for God to relate to his people.
   — God would change the hearts of his people.
   — God would communicate to his people heart to heart (personal relationship).
   — God would forgive his people's sins.

Lesson 2: Hebrews 5:5-10

Sermon Title: The Source Of Salvation

Sermon Angle: Jesus, the one who gave his life to God in perfect submission, becomes the source of salvation to all who have faith. The world offers other sources of salvation — success, sex, power, even good works. We need to ask our people to name the source of their hope for salvation. Jesus is the only true source of salvation. The Evangelism Explosion program by James Kennedy opens by getting the potential converts to state whether or not they are sure of going to heaven. If they do think they are going to heaven, they are then asked how they know this is true. The purpose here is to get them to disclose the source of their salvation. Is the source some concept of good works or God's grace?

Outline:
1. Are you going to heaven when you die? If so, what is the basis for your belief? Do you think you'll get there merely because of your church affiliation? Or do you expect to arrive there because you're a good person?
2. Christ is the only source of our salvation; through him, we experience God's grace (v. 9).
3. Return to the source of your salvation in whose name you were baptized.

Gospel: John 12:20-33

Sermon Title: An Eye Exercise That Creates Community: Seeing Jesus

Sermon Angle: Our text begins with a request to see Jesus. Later in the reading (v. 32), Jesus speaks of himself being lifted up from the earth (so that all could see his sacrificial love) and drawing all people unto himself. Focusing the eyes of your soul on the one who gave his life for the world brings us into a community of grace that has no end.

Outline:
1. Some people are born with weak eye muscles (lazy eye) that can be strengthened through exercise.
2. The eyes of our soul become fuzzy unless we focus on Jesus.

3. Christ was lifted up on the cross so that we might focus on his grace and love.
4. Exercise the eyes of your faith daily as you look up to the crucified Christ.

*   *   *   *   *

Joseph Sardler experienced a fortuitous accident in 1981 when he stumbled over his dog's dish, tumbling headlong down the basement stairs. Sardler had been blind for six years, due to optic nerve damage, but when he hit his head during the fall the miracle of sight was restored to him. He stayed up all night gazing at pictures and flowers and the stars in the heavens. Sardler can't thank and praise God enough for returning to him the ability to see. Sometimes it takes something like what happened to this man to open our eyes to the presence of Jesus in our lives. A hospitalization, the loss of a job, or a divorce, to name only a few, can stimulate the optic nerve in our spirit to see the one who was lifted up on a cross for us all.

*   *   *   *   *

Sermon Title: Doorkeepers

Sermon Angle: Secretaries and receptionists are doorkeepers, who grant or withhold access to the boss. They serve the vital function of bringing into their boss' presence those whom he would most like to see and screening out those who will only waste his time. The Greeks referred to in this text (vv. 20-21) came to Philip, requesting to see Jesus. Philip and Andrew were the doorkeepers, who sought to bring these people into the presence of Jesus. Our calling as the church is to refuse access to those who oppose the gospel and grant access to those who really want to meet the Lord.

Outline:
1. Secretaries are doorkeepers, granting or withholding access to the boss.
2. The disciples were doorkeepers for Jesus (vv. 20-22).
3. The church is the doorkeeper for the Lord.
   — What we do intentionally or unintentionally affects access to Jesus.
4. Are you introducing to Jesus those who want to see him and know him?

Sermon Title: The Appointed Time

Sermon Angle: When Philip and Andrew approached Jesus, the Lord announced: "The hour has come for the Son of man to be glorified" (v. 23). Jesus had a sense of destiny. The hour had come for him to commit the supreme act of God's self-giving love on the cross. Earlier in his ministry he sometimes withdrew from hot spots of trouble because his time (hour) had not yet come. The writer of Ecclesiastes (ch. 3) reflects that there is "a time and season for everything under heaven." There is a time to be born, a time to marry, a time to follow, and, finally, a time to die. That appointed time had come for Jesus. It would not only be a time of grief and sorrow (v. 27) but, more importantly, a time of glory and victory (v. 28). Will we be ready to embrace our "appointed time" and will it be a time when God is glorified?

Outline:
1. Everything has its proper time and season (an appointed time).
2. For Jesus the appointed time came for him to give his life on the cross.
   — This was a time of trouble. (His humanity recoiled at the prospect of death.)
   — This was also a time of glory. (His death would bring eternal life.)

159

3. The appointed time has come for us to take up our cross (vv. 25-26).
4. In Christ, we become ready for our appointment with death.

*   *   *   *   *

Baseball has become so identified with the American way of life that it has become a gauge of the nation's pulse. The baseball strike of 1994-95 caused people to reflect not only on the state of the game but on the spiritual health of the nation. Catholic theologian and ethicist, George Wiegel, felt that the only thing fans could do was "pray for the conversion of the human heart." He shared that we could only pray that the hubris of owner and player alike would be exorcized during the Lenten season of 1995. "Neither side shares a basic sense of what is right or wrong and so they can't communicate ... All they care about is power and money."

Jesus summed up the problem and the solution of what is wrong in the world this way: "... unless a grain of wheat falls into the earth and dies, it remains alone; but if it dies, it bears much fruit" (v. 24).

*   *   *   *   *

Sermon Title: Christ Is The Magnet, We Are The Steel

Sermon Angle: Jesus glories in the cross as he proclaims: "And I, when I am lifted up from the earth, will draw all people to myself" (v. 32). Jesus had a magnetic attraction when he walked on this earth but in death his magnetic pull increased dramatically. He has the power to draw all people to God through himself; all they have to do is place themselves within the force-field of his love and grace.

Outline:
1. Already in life, Jesus attracted those outside the Jewish people (vv. 20-23).
2. In his sacrificial death, he has the power to draw all people to God (v. 32).
3. Situate yourself within the circle of his sacrificial love.
4. Then let Christ's magnetic power work through you to draw others.

160

Passion/Palm Sunday
(Lent 6)

Revised Common	Isaiah 50:4-9a	Philippians 2:5-11	Mark 14:1—15:47 or Mark 15:1-39 (40-47)
Roman Catholic	Isaiah 50:4-7	Philippians 2:6-11	Mark 14:1—15:47
Episcopal	Isaiah 45:21-25 or Isaiah 52:13—53:12	Philippians 2:5-11	Mark (14:32-72) 15:1-39 (40-47)

Theme For The Day: The God of the universe takes on the form of a servant, suffering not only abuse and scorn, but giving his life for the redemption of the world.

BRIEF COMMENTARY ON THE LESSONS

Lesson 1: Isaiah 50:4-9a (C); Isaiah 50:4-7 (RC)

The third servant song. The Lord gives his servant the task of comforting his beaten people. His efforts meet with rejection and abuse but his faith in Yahweh remains unwavering.

Lesson 1: Isaiah 45:21-25 (E)

Lesson 2: Philippians 2:5-11 (C, E); Philippians 2:6-11 (RC)

Paul shares this lovely hymn of Christ's humility to restore to the Corinthian church a sense of unity. The hymn contrasts the divinity of the Lord with his humanity. Jesus was in the form of God pre-existent and divine, yet he emptied himself (v. 7), the ultimate in self-giving service. Consequently, God honored him for his self-abandonment by making him the sovereign of the universe, who would eventually receive the worship and praise of all that inhabit the universe.

Gospel: Mark 14:1—15:47 (C, RC); Mark (14:32-72) 15:1-39 (40-47) (E)

On Passion/Palm Sunday we have two options for the gospel, a long or abbreviated version of the sufferings and death of our Lord. Since so few Christians attend Good Friday services, a strong argument can be made for employing the long form. However, to keep the interest of the congregation, I would highly recommend doing so in the form of a readers' theater that involves the entire congregation. Those who have major parts should practice them beforehand. A sermon would not necessarily be needed in this case but adequate time should be allocated for meditation. A five-minute meditation would also be acceptable. If you employ the shorter text, a ten- to fifteen-minute sermon is possible.

The longer version of the passion text begins with the account of Jesus' anointing by a woman in preparation for his burial. The shorter version commences after Jesus' arrest, on the morning of the day of crucifixion, and ends with the burial of Jesus in Joseph of Arimathea's tomb. Mary Magdalene and the other women mark the site of his burial. In the extended version, compassionate service of Jesus by women serve as parentheses for the passion of our Lord.

Psalm Of The Day

Psalm 31:9-16 (C) — "Be gracious to me, O Lord, for I am in distress ..." (v. 9a). "But I trust in you, O Lord ..." (v. 14a).

Psalm 22:1-21 (E)

Psalm 21 (RC)

Prayer Of The Day

O gracious God, we sing your praise for sending your Son to take on our humanity in all its frailty and brokenness. Through the power of Christ's Spirit, lead us through our valley of the shadows and raise us to newness of life, in Jesus' name. Amen.

THEOLOGICAL REFLECTION ON THE LESSONS

Lesson 1: Isaiah 50:4-9a

Facing the enemy. The servant faces shame and ridicule by his enemies but does not turn away, hide his head, or flee. "I have not drawn back ..." (v. 5). "I did not hide my face from mocking or spitting ..." (v. 6). "Therefore, I have set my face like a flint ..." (v. 7). The servant, probably identified with the prophet himself, did not attempt to strike down his enemy but neither did he back away from his God-given mission. Jesus faced down his enemies in precisely the same way, not by attacking them but by withstanding the fury of their misguided hatred.

The best defense possible. Verses 8 and 9 imply legal language. The servant stands confident that Yahweh is his defense attorney and that he would ultimately win him an acquittal. With such an advocate, he stands ready to face his foes. "Who is my accuser? Let him confront me!" (v. 8). What better defense than the one who created the laws of the universe? Likewise, those who stand acquitted through the mediation of Christ need not fear any foe they face in the cause of right.

Lesson 2: Philippians 2:5-11

Having the right attitude and altitude. Attitude and altitude are two vital measures that a successful pilot must constantly assess. Attitude has to do with the pitch of the plane, whether the nose of the aircraft is up or down. Altitude measures how far the plane is above sea level. Having the correct attitude and altitude are essential aspects of successful flight. In fact, altitude is directly related to attitude. So too, having the right attitude toward God and one another is critical for maintaining the proper spiritual altitude. Our attitude should be that which was manifested by Christ Jesus who was in the form of God but lowered himself to become our human brother and servant.

Taking on a new identity. The poem that Paul quotes states that Jesus was in the very nature of God (v. 6) and took on our nature or humanity (v. 7). Those of us who are children of God find ourselves cloaked in a very human nature; yet in Christ we are empowered to take on the very nature of God, a new identity. However, the divine nature does not seek to dominate but serve. In a phrase, God took on our human nature that we might be clothed with his divine nature.

162

He made himself nothing (v. 7). I fear that some people might read a kind of false humility into this passage. God does not want us to feel that we are nothing, that we are garbage, just as Jesus did not feel that way about himself when he became our servant. The RSV states that Jesus "emptied himself"; that is, he poured himself out in service. In order to pour yourself out, you must first have something in your cup. We must first have a healthy sense of self before we can empty ourselves in service. Jesus didn't become "nothing" but acted as if he were nothing. This means that he didn't let who and what he was prevent him from pouring out his life, even unto death.

Gospel: Mark 14:1—15:47

The extravagance of love (14:3-9). As Jesus dined in the home of Simon the Leper, a woman came and anointed Jesus' feet with an extremely expensive perfume (nard), probably imported from India. Those present commenced to criticize her for such an extravagance. Jesus, always a gracious receiver, sticks up for her and accepts her ministry in the spirit which it was given. It was a great act of love, probably rendered in appreciation for what Jesus had done for her. Love does not count the cost.

Loyalty has its price (14:10-11). There seems to be a relationship between the extravagance of the anointing and the betrayal by Judas. Judas was the treasurer for Jesus' disciples, perhaps he was greedy or maybe he was merely practical. It could be that letting the kind of money that the nard represented slip through his hands was just too much for a worldly man. Judas decided to betray his Master for the price of a slave. His loyalty definitely had its price. Does ours?

Cowardice and the cross. The time of crisis brings out the good and evil in all of us. In the story of Jesus' suffering and death we see mostly cowardly responses. Judas betrayed his Master. The unnamed young man (14:51-52), probably John Mark, nakedly flees the danger. Peter, the Rock, professes stalwart loyalty but denies that he even knows Jesus in the courtyard of the high priest (14:66-72). Pilate was convinced of Jesus' innocence, yet Pilate wished to satisfy those whom he was attempting to govern. His political future hung by a thread and so he too played the coward. The soldiers heaped cowardly abuse on an apparently helpless and innocent victim (15:16-20). The crowd at the foot of the cross hurled cowardly jeers and jests in the face of the one who absorbed all of their craven abuse. When any innocent victims suffer cowardly abuse, Christ is crucified anew. Do we bravely stand with them or do we flee the fury of cowards?

Open access (15:38). The curtain in the temple divided the holy of holies from the holy place. This inner sanctuary could only be entered by the high priest once a year (the day of atonement). The curtain of the temple being torn indicates open access to God through the crucifixion of Christ.

Women of the passion. This pericope opens with a woman ministering to Jesus by anointing his head with ointment, a kind of pre-burial rite. With interest we note the story of our Lord's earthly life closes in the company of a host of nearby women disciples, most of whom are nameless (15:40-41). There were no women counted among the original twelve for a number of reasons, but there have always been women ministers among the followers of Jesus. Jesus never put women in their place and they were among his most loyal disciples.

163

SERMON APPROACHES WITH ILLUSTRATIONS

Lesson 1: Isaiah 50:4-9a

Sermon Title: The Power Of The Word

Sermon Angle: The prophets have long recognized the power of the word, not their own word but the word of the Lord. The servant of this passage acknowledges that the Lord has given him the power to sustain and strengthen through God's word (v. 4). God's word has the power to lift up and encourage, as the prophet had learned. He also discovered that the power to speak God's word was dependent on the ability to hear God's word (v. 5). God's word also enabled the servant to stand fast in holy purpose against the onslaughts of a cynical world.

Outline:
1. Give examples of the power of the word (Martin Luther King).
2. God gave his servant the power to encourage through God's word.
3. God's word made his servant a fortress of strength against the foe.
4. Give a contemporary witness of the power of God's word.

Sermon Title: High Noon

Sermon Angle: *High Noon* was one of the stellar movies of the 1950s. Like most westerns, the battle between the good guys and the bad guys composes the core of the plot. However, this western presents the reality of evil more convincingly than most. The plot has this small western community at the mercy of a band of bad guys. The leaders of the town decide to do something about it and so they hire a crack sheriff. The key confrontation was to come on a certain day at noon. The sheriff tries to get the community to stand together against the dark force but they refuse to put themselves at risk. The sheriff is left to face the outlaws by himself, though a few do get around to lending a hand at the last minute. The sheriff's wife tries to convince him to quit the conflict; the town isn't worth the effort. The sheriff does manage to destroy the band of desperados and he becomes a hero. However, the cowardice of the town's folk so disgusts him that he takes off his badge and rides into the sunset. To the casual observer of Isaiah's servant, it would appear that he was left alone to battle the enemy. However, the servant is able to act bravely because he knows that he is never alone. "Behold, the Lord God helps me ..." (v. 9).

Outline:
1. In the battle against evil, it might appear that God's people stand alone, like the legendary lawman of the movie *High Noon*.
2. The messianic figure in our text faced a myriad of foes but knew that he was not alone. God was on his side.
3. Jesus felt alone on the cross ("My God ... why have you forsaken me?"), yet God raised him from the dead.
4. Foes might outnumber us, but with the Lord we always have the edge.

Lesson 2: Philippians 2:5-11

Sermon Title: Knee Bends: An Exercise That Will Keep You Humble

Sermon Angle: Paul maintains that because Jesus so emptied himself, even to death, God has bestowed on him the name above every name, the name of Lord and king. This name has the power to cause all human or superhuman beings to bow the knee in worship.

Sermon Title: An Attitude That Gains Altitude

Sermon Angle: Jesus Christ provides our role model. He had a humble attitude, the demeanor of a servant. God rewarded him by exalting him to the highest place (vv. 9-11). A Christian ought not consciously to aim for humility, nor should we regard humility as the gateway to glory. Humility is not an attitude that we can set our sights on. We can only focus on the glory of God and doing his will; then humility will trail behind like a caboose. Nevertheless, the attitude of humility enables the child of God to gain altitude.

Outline:
1. Paul encourages believers to have the servant attitude of Jesus.
2. This attitude gained Jesus altitude.
3. Assume the servant role, which will give you an attitude of humility.
4. Those who follow Jesus' example will gain altitude into God's presence.

Gospel: Mark 15:1-47

Sermon Title: Be Loyal: Don't Give Up The Exercise Of Your Faith

Sermon Angle: Mark 15:40-41 lifts up the women disciples of Jesus from Galilee, who cared for Jesus' needs. They were women ministers who stood by him to the end and prepared his body for burial. They were among the most faithful followers of our Lord. Perhaps that's why one of their number (Mary Magdalene) was the first to behold the risen Christ. We who live in society of Teflon loyalties (non-stick) would do well to hold high these women who did not waver in their devotion to Christ.

Outline:
1. Do you have a friend who has stuck with you through thick and thin? Have you been such a friend to others?
2. Most of Jesus' disciples fled after his arrest, Judas betrayed him, but the women disciples from Galilee stayed by him to the end.
3. Though there might be lapses in our loyalty, the gift of eternal life is promised to those who are faithful unto death.

Sermon Title: Falling On Deaf Ears

Sermon Angle: When our Lord's accusers brought him to Pilate, Jesus was asked to give his self-defense. To the governor's amazement, Jesus refused to speak (15:3-5). Why? Did he want to die? No, Jesus knew that anything he said would fall on deaf ears. The religious leaders were stirring up the crowd to shout for his blood. The silence of Jesus stands in sharp contrast to the bloodcurdling shouts of the mob (15:9-14). Pilate's request for the mob to register a valid charge against Jesus also fell on deaf ears. The crowd didn't care about justice. Their blood was set to boil through an appeal to emotion. When someone pushes a person's emotional hot spot, rational considerations fly out the door and fall on deaf ears. We can thank the Lord that our pleas for forgiveness and help do not fall on deaf ears.

Outline:
1. Jesus was silent before Pilate — any defense would fall on deaf ears.
2. Pilate's request for a valid charge against Jesus also fell on deaf ears.
3. We can thank God that he has not turned a deaf ear to us.

Sermon Title: False, Authentic And Christian Worship

Sermon Angle: In the passion scene where the soldiers were mocking Jesus, the text says (15:19): "Falling on their knees, they worshiped him." False worship at its worst. We might contrast this scene to that found in our second lesson (Philippians 2:10), where it states that "every knee shall bow and every tongue confess that Jesus Christ is Lord...." This will be authentic worship in the sense that all flesh will know that Jesus Christ truly is Lord and worship him as such. The problem is that, for many, this worship is rendered only after the verdict on Jesus' lordship stands irrefutable. However, Christian worship consists of acknowledging the Lordship of Christ in this present age, when all the evidence is not in. Christian worship is fueled by faith.

Sermon Title: The Most Godforsaken Place

Sermon Angle: We sometimes refer to a barren landscape as "godforsaken." There are areas in the landscape of our lives that seem godforsaken: a loved one dies, we lose a job, a friend betrays us. Jesus also experienced a godforsaken place in his life — the cross. God did not save him. His enemies were right: He saved others but he could not save himself (15:31). Then, of course, there's the soul-piercing cry of abandonment: "My God, my God, why have you forsaken me?" Jesus experienced separation from God, the existential loneliness and hell caused by our sin. Jesus experienced that ultimate godforsaken place, the cross, that we might enjoy eternal fellowship with God and all the saints.

Outline:
1. Tell of a time when you felt godforsaken.
2. Ask your hearers to name their most godforsaken place.
3. Speak of the cross as Jesus' most godforsaken place (separation caused by our sin).
4. The point: God did not ultimately forsake Jesus but raised him from the dead. We will never be godforsaken if we trust in Jesus.

*   *   *   *   *

Our Lord experienced loneliness time and again. He struggled in spiritual isolation at Gethsemane to discern the Father's will. When he was arrested, the disciples all fled. On the cross, he felt totally abandoned. "My God, my God, why have you forsaken me?"

The other day I heard on the radio that the average male does not have a single close friend. He may have plenty of companions or acquaintances but there are few, if any, with whom he can share his fears or failings. Maybe it's because society seems to tell men they must always be in control, always on top. Many men don't feel they can afford the luxury of being vulnerable. That's a really lonely spot to be in.

Women are, on average, less lonely than men. They have not been given the message by society that they must dominate and always be in control. Women are traditionally the relationship keepers. In a family, who is it that does the lion's share of the communicating with other family members? Right, the women. A wife usually maintains ties not only with biological family but also with her husband's. Women spend much more time talking and sharing. That's probably why widows survive longer after their spouse dies than widowers do. They have a built-in network of relationships that they can plug into.

Maundy Thursday

Revised Common	Exodus 12:1-4 (5-10) 11-14	1 Corinthians 11:23-26	John 13:1-17, 31b-35
Roman Catholic	Exodus 12:1-8 (11-14)	1 Corinthians 11:23-26	John 13:1-15
Episcopal	Exodus 12:1-14a	1 Corinthians 11:23-26 (27-32)	John 13:1-15 or Luke 22:14-30

Theme For The Day: The institution of the covenant meal for both Jews and Christians.

BRIEF COMMENTARY ON THE LESSONS

Lesson 1: Exodus 12:1-4 (5-10) 11-14 (C); Exodus 12:1-8 (11-14) (RC); Exodus 12:1-14a (E)

This contains the priestly tradition concerning the institution of the Passover, the covenant feast of the Hebrew people. The Passover took over a more ancient springtime agricultural festival, infusing it with fresh content. The month of Nisan (March-April) in which the feast took place marked the beginning of the year for the post-exilic Jews. Formerly, the year commenced in the autumn. The various clans congregated in the evening for the feast. The blood was considered the proper portion for God, since it was identified with the life force. The blood on the doorpost and lintel was a reminder of Yahweh's saving power. They were ordered to eat the meal fully clothed, with walking staff in hand. This was a token of the haste with which they exited Egypt. The people of Israel are ordered to keep this feast as a memorial to Yahweh's wonderful redemptive actions, which made them a people.

Lesson 2: 1 Corinthians 11:23-26 (C, RC); 1 Corinthians 11:23-26 (27-32) (E)

The institution of the Lord's Supper appears within the context of the apostle Paul dressing down the Corinthians for abusing the Lord's Supper. In recalling this direct *ipsissima verba* from the Lord, the apostle wishes to impress upon the unruly Corinthians the sacredness of the Eucharist's origins. The church members are to remember the roots of the church's meal and observe it with reverence. The verse about profaning the Lord's Supper (v. 27) has been widely misunderstood. Discerning the Lord's body has to do with recognizing the Lord's presence in the more humble and lowly members of the church.

Gospel: John 13:1-17, 31b-35 (C); John 13:1-15 (RC, E)

John's version of the Last Supper. The words of institution are not cited by the fourth gospel. Rather, John uses it as a springboard for Jesus washing his disciple's feet. The footwashing becomes a living parable that teaches humility. It illustrates the hymn to Christ's humility found in Philippians 2, our second lesson for Passion Sunday. Jesus, the master and teacher, assumes the role of the servant. This action serves as a great teaching moment. The disciples of Jesus are not to lord it over others but stoop to serve others, as the Lord has served them.

Psalm Of The Day

Psalm 116:1-4, 12-19 (C) — "I love the Lord because he has heard my cry for mercy" (v. 1).

Psalm 115 (RC)
Psalm 78:14-20, 23-25 (E)

Prayer Of The Day

God of mercy, with tears we call to remembrance the night in which you were betrayed, when you gave yourself to your disciples under the forms of bread and wine and stooped to wash their feet. May our hearts be so transformed by your self-giving love that we allow ourselves to be broken for others. In Jesus' name. Amen.

THEOLOGICAL REFLECTION ON THE LESSONS

Lesson 1: Exodus 12:1-14

A new year (vv. 1-2). The Passover marked a new way of measuring time and looking at time. God's great act of redemption was the birthing point for the Hebrew nation. Older calendars followed the agricultural cycles. The Jews came to realize that the times of their lives did not revolve around nature but God's nurturing and saving action. An analogous event for Christians is Christ's resurrection. For us this event marks the beginning of a new way of looking at time and of eternity. Theologically speaking, our church year should probably begin with Easter rather than Advent.

The lamb is for sharing (v. 4). The lamb of the Passover meal was not to be wasted but no one was to be deprived of a portion, no matter what his economic circumstances. The Passover lamb was for sharing. For Christians, Jesus is the Lamb of God and we are to see to it that all our neighbors are invited to his feast. They too need to receive the Lamb, so that they might be a part of God's redemptive fellowship and be strengthened for their life's journey.

Blood brothers and sisters (v. 13). God told the Hebrews to put the blood on their doorposts and frames so that when he saw it, the angel of death would pass over. Those covered by the blood were blood brothers and sisters. Christians are also blood relatives, blood brothers and sisters, covered and protected by the blood of Christ.

Lesson 2: 1 Corinthians 11:23-26

Pass it on (v. 23). Paul claims that the tradition of the Lord's Supper is not something that he has concocted but that which he has himself received from the Lord. He feels that his calling is to pass on to others that which he has received. Knowledge of God's redemptive actions has been passed on to us as a gift. Our duty and privilege consists in passing it on to others.

Broken for you (v. 24). Jesus' body was broken like bread for you and for me. The great God whom we worship in Jesus Christ gives himself to us and for us. The Lord's Supper is the most personal of God's gifts.

Gospel: John 13:1-17, 31b-35

Lasting love (v. 1). The RSV translation has it that Jesus loved his disciples "to the end." This communicates the extent of his love better than the NRSV's "he now showed them the full extent of his love." The love of God in Jesus is endless love, a lasting love; further still, he loves us with an everlasting love. This is a love that goes with us all the way.

Circle of love (v. 3). John states that Jesus had "come from God and was returning to God." Jesus was going full circle. Jesus comes as an incarnation of the eternal life of God without beginning and ending. If you take the beginning and end of a line and connect them together, you have a circle. That's what God does for us in Christ. He connects the beginning and ending of our lives together and places our lives within the eternal circle of his love and grace.

Imitation of Christ (v. 15). Jesus told his disciples that they should love one another after the fashion that he has loved them. Children learn by imitation; we call it play. Play is not some frivolous waste of time, it is practice time in which the youngsters strive to put into practice that which they have observed in their elders. A good and godly example is needed now more than ever. The world contains enough precepts and philosophies; what we really need are worthy models to imitate.

Love is an imperative (v. 34). Jesus commands his disciples to love one another, a new command for a new covenant. Oh, yes, the old covenant commands God's people to love their neighbor (fellow Jew) but Jesus goes much further. He commands us to love one another in the manner in which he has shown his love for us. He holds up a love that goes all the way in pouring oneself out. In our society, to make love an imperative (command) seems strange. Common understanding has it that love flows from feelings. It just happens or it doesn't happen, we are told. No, love is an imperative, controlled by our will. Jesus didn't feel like dying on the cross, he was merely obeying the imperative of his Father to love the world.

SERMON APPROACHES WITH ILLUSTRATIONS

Lesson 1: Exodus 12:1-14
Sermon Title: An Evening Meal For A New Day
Sermon Angle: Moses ordered the people to slaughter their lambs at twilight. The Passover was an evening meal that marked the beginning of a new day, a new era. The night of judgment was at hand (v. 12). A new day was about to dawn, which would reveal God's great act of redemption. The Lord's Supper also marked the end of one day and the beginning of another. The old day of judgment had ended, a new day of grace and love had begun.
Outline:
1. The Passover was an evening meal that led to a new day of freedom.
2. The Lord's Supper was also an evening meal that led to
   — a new day of grace and forgiveness.
   — a new covenant.
   — a new people.

Sermon Title: Celebrate The Feast
Sermon Approach: The Passover was a great feast of celebration. God had won for the Israelites their freedom. Passover was like the Fourth of July for those of us who are Americans; it marked the defeat of their enemy and the birth of their nation. It celebrated the truth that they were one nation under God. The Lord's Supper is a greater feast yet. It marks our liberation from the minions of sin and a community of love and grace that knows no boundaries.

Lesson 2: 1 Corinthians 11:23-26

Sermon Title: The Sermon Of God's Saints

Sermon Angle: Not many Christians would feel comfortable preaching a sermon but that is what we do nonetheless. Our lives preach a sermon which either glorifies our self or our God. Paul claims that when we partake of the Lord's Supper, we preach a sermon; the Eucharist is a communal proclamation. What is the content of the message?

Outline:
1. We proclaim the Lord's real presence ("This is my body ... my blood").
2. We proclaim the forgiveness of sins.
3. We proclaim the Lord's death and resurrection (v. 26).
4. We proclaim Christ's coming again (v. 26).

Gospel: John 13:1-17, 31b-35

Sermon Title: When Parting Is Sweet Sorrow

Sermon Angle: Jesus realized that it was time to leave those whom he had loved on earth and return to the Father. Parting is never easy but it can indeed be sweet when we love people completely and fully. Jesus left his disciples in the knowledge that he had loved them to the end, to the fullest extent possible. None of us can ever say that we have accomplished that completely. It is the incompleteness of our loving and living that makes death a bitter pill to swallow. To know that we could have loved but didn't is what truly brings tears to our eyes. Jesus' parting sorrow was sweet because "he had shown them the full extent of his love" (v. 1).

Sermon Title: "How To" Christianity

Sermon Angle: "How to" books are the hottest items in bookstores. How to lose weight, how to cook, how to become successful, how to overcome guilt, and so forth. Shortly before the Passover, Jesus gave his disciples a crash "how to" course in being his disciples. He washed his disciples' feet and afterward told them that they should do to others as he had done for them. This is how you love, he was saying, this is how you serve. Do this and you will know how to be my disciple. It's interesting that when the sand had almost emptied out of the hourglass for Jesus, he didn't give a crash course on dogmatics. Just a simple yet profound "how to" demonstration on loving and serving.

Outline:
1. Establish the popularity of "how to" books.
2. We would rather have a personal guide rather than a road map.
3. Jesus gave a "how to" demonstration when he washed his disciples' feet.
   — How to love and serve.
   — How to truly be his disciples.
4. We must demonstrate to others how they might be Christ's disciples, too.

Sermon Title: Knowing And Doing

Sermon Angle: After Jesus had finished washing their feet he said: "Now that you know these things, you will be blessed if you do them" (v. 17). Knowing something and doing it are two different things. The truth that Jesus spoke, "You will know the truth and the truth will set you free," remains. However, having knowledge does not mean that one will benefit from the knowledge or use it. We can know a lot of useful things but unless we do them, we gain no benefit. Jesus told his disciples, "Now you know what to do but you will only gain a blessing if you actually do it."

Outline:
1. Jesus showed his followers how to function as his disciples.
2. The key was serving and loving.
3. The doing is more difficult than the knowing — it requires humility.
4. We will be blessed if we do what Jesus has taught us.

*   *   *   *   *

The church can get caught up in our world's success syndrome, where success is defined in terms of size and prominence. Jesus informs us that service rather than size more accurately defines what it means to be his disciples.

If you happen to visit the Chicago metropolitan area on a Sunday, you are likely to encounter school buses, some rather rickety looking, with the inscription on the side: First (Blank) Church, and then underneath the name, "The World's Largest Sunday School."

The claim is probably true. They have a fleet of buses, drivers, and mechanics larger than many school districts. They have established routes all over the metro area and beyond. Some parents probably like it because they have their Sundays to themselves, free babysitting. Children like it. They meet new friends and have something to do. First (Blank) Church may do a lot of good with their Sunday school busing program but their motto, "The World's Largest Sunday School," really bothers me. It causes me to ask, "Is the aim of this church to bring children to Christ or is this an ego trip?" It seems that they are saying: "We're the First (Blank) Church and we're number 1, the World's Largest Sunday School. Hooray for us!" My reaction could be overly judgmental but it appears to me that this motto better reflects the values of the world, which glories in size and preeminence rather than the values of the kingdom.

*   *   *   *   *

There's a doll produced in St. Louis without a face. In place of the face is a mirror. The child looks into the face of her doll and sees a reflection of herself. Some psychologists argue that this is a good teaching tool but is this not an example of the problem that plagues far too many people? Wherever they turn, whatever situation they happen to be in, they see a reflection of themselves. They constantly ask: What's in this relationship for me? How can involvement in this group give me the recognition I deserve? In other words, those who live in a house of mirrors ask themselves: "How can I get somebody to serve my needs?" rather than asking "How can I serve others in the name of Christ?"

Good Friday

Revised Common	Isaiah 52:13—53:12	Hebrews 10:16-25	John 18:1—19:42
Roman Catholic	Isaiah 52:13—53:12	Hebrews 4:14-16; 5:7-9	John 18:1—19:42
Episcopal	Isaiah 52:13—53:12 or Genesis 22:1-18	Hebrews 10:1-25	John (18:1-40) 19:1-37

Theme For The Day: Healing and eternal life through the sufferings and death of Jesus Christ, God's suffering servant and our Savior.

BRIEF COMMENTARY ON THE LESSONS

Lesson 1: Isaiah 52:13—53:12 (C, RC, E)

This is the fourth servant song. The usual scholarly interpretation identifies the servant with the nation of Israel. I must straight out confess that I have real problems with this interpretation. First of all, the images are intimately personal. "He was despised and rejected by men; a man of sorrows and acquainted with grief ..." (v. 3). A second problem, the author identifies himself with a collective ("our griefs, our sorrows"). In all probability, he is identifying himself with the nation of Judah. However, he refers to the servant separately: "Surely he has borne our griefs ... carried our sorrows." Thirdly, the author of this passage lifts up the servant as one who suffers innocently, unjustly, and vicariously. All the other prophets regard the destruction of Israel, Judah and Jerusalem as God's judgment on his sinful people. The sacrificial lamb for the Passover and other sacrifices was required to be perfect, unblemished. How could a sinful and rebellious nation be the sin bearer for the world (v. 6)? Fourthly, the author states that the servant was stricken for the transgressions of God's people (v. 8). If the servant is to be identified with the nation, then the nation is stricken for its own sins. This is clearly not the intent of the author of this portion of scripture, who plainly speaks of the servant's sufferings as innocent and vicarious. Why can't we admit that we have here an inspired portrait of Jesus Christ, even though the author may have had some other contemporary of his in mind?

Lesson 2: Hebrews 10:16-25 (C); Hebrews 10:1-25 (E)

In this epistle the author continues to demonstrate the superiority of Christianity to Judaism. He maintains that there is no longer need for bloody sin offerings. Rather, we can all enter into the inner sanctuary of God's presence, corresponding to the most holy place in the temple, through Christ's sacrificial death and priestly ministration. The anonymous writer encourages his Christian friends to draw near to God through Christ, cling tightly to their faith, and to come regularly together for mutual encouragement and corporate worship.

Lesson 2: Hebrews 4:14-16; 5:7-9 (RC)

See second lesson for Lent 5 and second lesson for Proper 23.

Gospel: John 18:1—19:42 (C, RC); John (18:1-40) 19:1-37 (E)

This is John's passion account, beginning with Jesus' arrest in the garden. John portrays Jesus as being very much in control, not a victim of circumstances. The sufferings and death of

Jesus show his glory and power. Following his arrest Jesus is conveyed to Annas, the former high priest, for an informal hearing. Then Jesus is bound over to Caiaphas and the Sanhedrin. Finally, since the Jews could not convict anyone of a capital offense, the Lord's enemies bring him to Pilate. They more or less blackmail Pilate into convicting Jesus. A subplot lifts up Peter's denial of Jesus in the courtyard of the high priest. Jesus carries his own cross to Calvary. The soldiers gamble for his seamless robe. A unique aspect of John's account has Jesus commending his mother to the care of his beloved disciple, John (vv. 26-27). The piercing of Jesus' side produces an outpouring of blood and water (v. 34), symbolic of baptism and holy communion. Not only does Joseph of Arimathea bury Jesus' body in his own tomb but Nicodemus brings ointments for the preparation of the Lord's body (v. 39).

Psalm Of The Day
Psalm 22 (C); Psalm 22:1-21 (E) — "My God, my God, why have you forsaken me?"
Psalm 30 (RC)

Prayer Of The Day
Great God, you have entered into the valley of human suffering and death in the person of your Son, our Savior, Jesus Christ. We give you endless thanks that by his death, you have destroyed the power of death for all believers. In Jesus' name. Amen.

THEOLOGICAL REFLECTION ON THE LESSONS

Lesson 1: Isaiah 52:13—53:12
Sin bearer (vv. 4-5). From the earliest times Christians have regarded Christ as the suffering servant of Isaiah. Christ took on the role of being the sin bearer of the world.

The problem of innocent suffering. This chapter speaks eloquently to the topic of innocent suffering. "By oppression and judgment, he was carried away ..." (v. 8). Who can deny that countless lives have been snuffed out, afflicted, or marred by the actions of others? This fact is the devil's greatest tool for promoting unbelief. However we identify the servant, the prophet maintains that he suffers for the sins of other people. We cannot deny that nations and individuals do suffer for the sins of other nations and other people. The prophet has no explanation for this injustice but asserts that the servant's innocent suffering must be viewed as a sin offering. It is not meaningless but has redemptive purpose. This brings to light the truth that God's people can let their suffering make them bitter or they can use it redemptively. The child of God continues to believe that all things do indeed work together for good (Romans 8).

Light at the end of the tunnel (v. 11). The suffering servant is given hope that the light of life will follow the dark tunnel of suffering. Those children of God who suffer, and who of us does not, can also be assured that our suffering and pain will lead to the light of a new day.

Lesson 2: Hebrews 10:16-25
Christ brings us into God's presence (vv. 19-20). The writer of Hebrews contends that Christ brings us into the presence of God (most holy place) through his sacrifice of himself (v. 19) and in his priestly role (v. 20). Through the offering up of himself we are sprinkled clean of our sins which separate us from God.

Hold on to your hope (v. 23). The writer of Hebrews addressed a group of Christians whose faith was waning. They were considering a return to their Jewish expression of faith. Perhaps since Christ had not yet returned, they began to question the veracity of their faith. They are reminded that God is faithful so they must hold tightly to their faith.

Keep assembling together (v. 25). The secret to keeping our faith and hope strong is in assembling together. An ember that is removed from the fire and placed by itself soon grows cold. So too, when a believer increasingly separates himself from the worship assembly of other believers, his heart will soon grow cold to the concerns of Christ.

Gospel: John 18:1—19:42

No sweat (v. 1). John's Jesus does not struggle with his lot in life, he does not seek to avoid suffering or death, he does not sweat great drops of blood as in Luke (Luke 22:44). John's Jesus does not pray for himself but for his disciples. Jesus is always in control. While John's depiction of Jesus clearly reveals his divinity, Jesus' humanity becomes less obvious. Notice how Jesus goes out to meet those who have come to arrest him and asks who they were seeking. When he replies that he is the one they were searching for, they fall to the ground (18:5), an action denoting fear and reverence. Jesus is calling the shots, not his foes.

Screwy scruples (18:28). After Jesus is taken to Annas, then to Caiaphas and the Sanhedrin, he is brought to the Roman governor. The scribes and Pharisees would not go into this pagan place because they did not want to become ceremonially unclean and not be able to keep the Passover. They had no scruples about killing a man and breaking one of the great moral laws of God, but they had scruples about breaking minor ceremonial laws. Such scruples are screwy, wouldn't you agree? It reminds me of the priest who was being held up by a robber. When he was handing over his billfold, he stuttered:

"I-I-I'm so-so-sorr-y but I d-d-don't have much mo-money. I'm-m-m a priest."

The robber replied: "Oh, I'm sorry, Father. I didn't know. Here's your billfold back."

The priest was enormously relieved and offered the robber a cigar. The thief retorted:

"Thanks, Father, but I've given up smoking for Lent."

Near the cross (19:25). In Mark's depiction of the crucifixion, the female disciples of Jesus are standing at a distance (Mark 15:40). John has these women near the cross, possibly because Jesus commends his mother to the care of John (vv. 26-27) and would be in need of talking range to do so. I prefer to think that these faithful women were indeed near the cross of the one they loved so dearly. Lent and Holy Week call on us to remain near the cross.

Mission accomplished (19:28). Jesus is in control of his life and his death. He has finished the mission the Father assigned him. He had completed his earthly responsibilities (commending his mother to John) and he had fulfilled the scripture passages concerning himself. His last words were: "It is finished!" Mission accomplished! Who of us does not pray that our mission will be accomplished when we are ready to give up our spirit?

SERMON APPROACHES WITH ILLUSTRATIONS

Lesson 1: Isaiah 52:13—53:12

Sermon Title: The Mission Of The Suffering Servant

Sermon Angle: This passage of scripture tells how our suffering servant, Jesus, ministered to our needs.

Outline:
1. He took up our infirmities (53:4).
2. He carried our sorrows (53:4).
3. He was punished for our sins (53:5-6).
4. He died in our place (53:8-9).
5. He made us righteous (53:11).

* * * * *

In the late '70s, a powerful movie was produced called *The Deer Hunter*. A group of American GI's is captured by the Viet Cong and subjected to cruel torture. One of the men, Nick, cannot free himself from the horror of having to play Russian roulette. After their release, Nick stays in Saigon and continues to play the same deadly game for the entertainment of a group of sadistic gamblers who meet in a smoke-filled bar. A short time later, Nick's friend, Michael, who had returned home, comes back to Saigon to find his friend. He eventually finds him ensconced in a drugged stupor, playing Russian roulette. Michael tries to convince Nick to quit the insane game but he can't get through to him. Finally in desperation, in an attempt to shock him into reality, Michael picks up the revolver and puts it to his head. He is willing to risk his life in order to save his friend. Most people would view such an action as foolish but it enthroned human love as nothing else could. The cross is also viewed as foolishness by many, yet it showed the love of God as nothing else could. The cross is no defeat, no humiliation, precisely because it is the supreme act of divine love. Jesus, the suffering servant, enters into our sickness, our sorrow, and our death to free us from our self-destructive bondage.

* * * * *

Lesson 2: Hebrews 10:16-25

Sermon Title: Blessed Assurance

Sermon Angle: The writer of Hebrews invites us to draw near to God in full and confident assurance. Through faith in Christ we can approach the almighty with confidence (v. 22). In baptism we are washed clean. Each time we confess our sins, every time we receive the Eucharist, the tarnish of our iniquities is scoured away. What a privilege it is to come to the Lord with blessed assurance! This confidence does not derive from the fact that Jesus is mine but that I, that we, belong to Jesus.

Outline:
1. Have you ever stayed away from worship or prayer because of a guilty conscience?
2. As Christians, we can come to God in full and blessed assurance because ...
   — we are baptized (v. 22) and belong to the Lord.
   — Christ offered himself for our sins and we are forgiven.
3. Come into God's presence not with fear, nor complacency, but assurance.

Sermon Title: Positive Reinforcement

Sermon Angle: The believers are encouraged to be encouragers. "Let us consider how we might spur one another on toward love and good works" (v. 24). The way to be an encourager is through positive reinforcement. You don't provoke others to better things by always telling them what they are doing wrong; rather, you encourage them to employ their gifts. Another kind of positive reinforcement takes place when we work as a team. When I attended high school, these principles were put into effect most every Friday when our football or basketball team played. The whole school would assemble in the gymnasium for a "Pep Rally." The team was given the message: "We support you, we're in this together; let's go out there and gain the victory."

Gospel: John 18:1—19:42

Sermon Title: What Would You Do With The King Of Truth?

Sermon Angle: In Pilate's questioning, he asks Jesus if he is the king of the Jews. If true, this charge would make him guilty of treason. Jesus responds affirmatively and then adds that he was born to testify to the truth. Pilate makes his cynical query: "What is truth?" (v. 38). In effect, Jesus claims to be the king of truth and Pilate has to decide what to do with him. What would you do with the king of truth? What have you done with him? These are the questions we need to get our congregation to deal with.

Outline:

1. Pilate asked Jesus if he were a king.
2. Jesus responded that he was a different sort of king — the king of truth (18:37).
3. Pilate had to decide what to do with this king of truth.
4. What have you done with the king of truth?
5. To know him is to know the truth about one's self and the goal of existence.

Sermon Title: Mistrial

Sermon Angle: Prolonged trials such as that of O. J. Simpson brought to focus the weaknesses of our legal system. Justice and truth seem to have gotten lost in this legal circus. At this point in time, most observers expect a mistrial. The trial of Jesus certainly qualifies for mistrial status, or should we say "mock trial"? As so often happens, expediency, not justice, wins the day. Both Pilate and the Jewish authorities were cynical creatures who came up with their own definitions of the truth. Fortunately for us all, the supreme source and court of all truth reversed the verdict and set Christ free to be Lord and Savior of the world.

Outline:

1. Relate to a case where a mistrial was declared because of a technicality.
2. Show how Jesus' trial should have been declared a mistrial but that God used it for our salvation.
3. Establish how God reversed this unjust sentence posthumously.
4. Jesus is our king of truth and guarantee that grace will conquer both justice and injustice.

Sermon Title: Coming Out Of The Closet

Sermon Angle: Homosexuals speak of their coming out of the closet when they publicly make known their sexual preference. Joseph of Arimathea and Nicodemus were closet Christians. They were afraid to reveal their religious preference for fear of the censure of their eminent peers. Jesus' death brought them out of the closet to some degree. They mustered the courage to go to Pilate and ask for Jesus' body. Then they paid their final respects by preparing his body for burial (19:38-42). Our world is full of closet Christians. Jesus wants them to come out of the closet. It's not enough to declare him our religious preference; Jesus calls us to enthrone him as Lord and king.

176

The Easter Season

The Development Of The Season

The resurrection of Jesus Christ forms the focal point for the Christian faith and calendar. In the primitive church there was no special day singled out to celebrate the Lord's resurrection. Every Sunday was a mini-celebration of the Lord's victory. Since the resurrection occurred around the same time as the Jewish Passover, early Christians referred to the church's chief festival as the *Pasca*, the Greek word for the Passover. Jesus became the Passover Lamb who frees us from the bondage to sin and death. The efficacy of his sacrifice is shown in the fact that God raised him from the dead. It seems ironic that the most sacred festival and season of the church calendar came to be called by the name of the Anglo-Saxon goddess of the dawn.

There is sparse written evidence for yearly liturgical celebration of the resurrection before 200 AD, but it is likely that it was well established in most churches by 100 AD. The earliest records inform us that the *Pasca* consisted of a vigil beginning on Saturday evening and ending on Sunday morning, incorporating a remembrance of the Lord's crucifixion together with the celebration of his resurrection. The vigil was crowned with the baptism of those who had been instructed in the mysteries of the faith. The liturgical celebration not only centered around the baptism of new converts but also the celebration of the Eucharist. Around 300 AD, most churches commemorated the passion and death of our Lord on Good Friday and devoted Easter Sunday to the resurrection. In some churches the celebration of the resurrection lasted for eight days. The newly baptized were required to attend the daily services until the Sunday following Easter. Since they were required to wear a white baptismal robe, the Sunday after Easter came to be known as "White Sunday."

In the first centuries of the Christian church there was a good deal of controversy concerning the proper date to observe the resurrection. Those with close affinities to the Jewish faith insisted that it occur on the fourteenth of Nisan in the Hebrew calendar; this was the date of the crucifixion according to the gospel of John. Most rejected this suggestion because this would mean that most years Easter would not fall on Sunday, the weekly mini-celebration of the resurrection. The Council of Nicea in 325 AD established the procedure for determining the date for the resurrection celebration. The formula is based on the lunar calendar. Easter falls on the first Sunday following the vernal equinox. To put it more simply, Easter is the first Sunday after the first full moon following the onset of spring. If the first full moon is Sunday, then Easter is the following Sunday. In the Orthodox tradition Easter falls ten days later than for the Western church because it is based on the Julian rather than the Gregorian calendar. In recent years there has been something of a movement to establish a permanent date for Easter; the second Sunday in April has been suggested.

The celebration of the resurrection is associated, in the minds of many, with the cycle of renewal in nature since it occurs in springtime. Symbols of fertility and renewal have been associated with Easter and, in some cases, have been baptized as tools for the telling of the story. As an example, the Easter egg has been employed as a symbol of Christ's resurrection. In fact, the name for the queen of all Christian feasts is derived from the name of the Anglo-Saxon goddess of springtime and of the dawn. Therefore, it is far better for Christians to refer to the central celebration of their faith as the Resurrection of our Lord rather than its pagan appellation.

The Importance Of The Season

The importance of Easter for the church can be discerned from two facts. First, the entire church year pivots around this event. The length of the Pentecost season is determined by the date of Easter. When Easter falls late, the length of the Pentecost season is shortened. The other fact that indicates the great importance of Easter has to do with what happens just before. The Resurrection of our Lord is so crucial that it is preceded by the forty days (not counting Sundays) of Lenten preparation. The problem for the Western church is that the time of preparation (Lent) has assumed a life of its own. Lent soon came to eclipse the season of Easter. For many, Easter is a glorious skyrocket that suddenly bursts over our head a shower of brilliance and joy but soon falls cold to the earth. The memory of its glory lingers for a while but soon fades with the resumption of normal activities. An argument could be made for giving less emphasis to Lent and more to the season of Easter. Yet we err even to try to define Easter as a season. No, Easter is not truly a season but an event that radically alters the way we view all the seasons of life. Through Christ's resurrection we transcend earth, time, and seasons.

A Preview Of The Easter Season

You will note that the lessons for the Easter season come overwhelmingly from three books of the Bible. For the Sundays of Easter, not counting the festival itself, the lections are taken from the following books of the Bible. The first lesson employs the book of Acts. The second lesson derives from the epistle of 1 John and presents a semi-continuous reading. The gospel lections hail primarily from the gospel of John, except for Easter 3, when it hails from Luke. If the preacher were to base the sermons for the Easter season on either the first lesson, second lesson, or the gospel, his or her listeners would see the resurrection from a particular perspective. This would enable the preacher to focus on the theological perspective of that particular biblical witness. If desired, a sermon series could easily be created.

Possible Thematic Series For The Easter Season

The Greek word for resurrection, *anastasis*, means literally "to stand again." The followers of our Lord were dejected, defeated, and fallen creatures after the Lord's crucifixion. The triumphal procession at the start of the last week of our Lord's life lifted their hearts and their hopes; maybe Jesus would finally usher in his kingdom. Jesus' talk of betrayal at the Passover seder sounded an ominous tone that caused their hearts to shake with anxiety. The arrest of their Lord, later that night, caused their hearts to implode with fear and dread. The brutal crucifixion of their master and Lord toppled their existence into a pile of rubble. As they gathered the shattered pieces of their lives into the Upper Room following the crucifixion, they must have felt that they would never rise again. Without the presence of their Lord, their faith and hope didn't have a leg to stand on. The risen Christ changed all that. When word of his resurrection got out there was anxiety, fear, skepticism. Then, as the word spread, hope caused their dried spiritual bones to come together. Finally, they witnessed the risen one for themselves and a miracle happened! Sinew and flesh attached to their parched bones; their hearts began beating, blood commenced flowing, and strength pulsed into every cell of their being. Before long, they were standing. Their spiritual legs were still a bit wobbly, but they took a few steps, tentatively at first, then stepped out more confidently. In no time they were running, skipping, dancing, and singing the praises of the one who raised them to new life; the one who lay moldering in the house of the dead had been raised up again to newness of life. Alleluia! By the power of his resurrection, they could stand again.

As frail children of dust, we fall time and time again. We fall into sin, our faith falters and we stumble to our knees, disease and death knock us to the mat with their one-two punch. We may find ourselves down but not out. We will rise, we will stand again through the power of Christ's resurrection. This seasonal thematic bridge might be developed as follows. Each chapter contains a sermon title, approach, and outline that develop the following themes.

Title: *How To Stand Up Through The Power Of The Resurrection*

Festival	Theme	Scripture
Easter 1	Stand Up — On Christ's Resurrection	Mark 16:6
Easter 2	Stand Up — On Our Faith	1 John 4:4-5
Easter 3	Stand Up — On The Promises Of God	Luke 24:44-49
Easter 4	Stand Up — With The Flock	1 John 3:1-2
Easter 5	Stand Up — Connected To Christ	John 15:1-8
Easter 6	Stay Standing Up — Through Christ's Love	John 15:9-17
Easter 7	Stand Up — Through The Spirit	1 John 4:13

Easter Day

Revised Common	Acts 10:34-43	1 Corinthians 15:1-11	John 20:1-18 or Mark 16:1-8
Roman Catholic	Acts 10:34-43	Colossians 3:1-4	John 20:1-9
Episcopal	Acts 10:34-43	Colossians 3:1-4	Mark 16:1-8

Theme For The Day: Through Christ's resurrection we are raised to newness of life.

BRIEF COMMENTARY ON THE LESSONS

Lesson 1: Acts 10:34-43 (C, RC, E)

Peter witnesses to the Roman officer, Cornelius, and his household concerning Jesus' earthly ministry, his crucifixion, and especially his resurrection. Luke, the author of Acts, points to the Holy Spirit as the source of Jesus' power. The disciples of Jesus, those who communed with Christ, are witnesses to the resurrection. They are to proclaim that Jesus is the judge of the living and the dead. Those who believe in the risen Christ receive forgiveness in Christ's name.

Lesson 2: 1 Corinthians 15:1-11 (C)

Against a background where some Christians were beginning to question the reality of the resurrection, Paul restates the essentials of the gospel, that which was of greatest importance, that is, Christ's sacrificial death, burial, and resurrection. Paul claims that Jesus first appeared to Peter, then to the twelve (actually eleven), then to some 500 believers. This differs from the gospel accounts, where Christ first appeared to some women (the Marys). Why the women are not mentioned we do not know. We do know that Paul's narrative is the first written account of the resurrection appearances. The last appearance of the risen Christ was to the apostle himself (a reference to Paul's conversion experience).

Lesson 2: Colossians 3:1-4 (RC, E)

Paul argues that since believers have died (through repentance, faith, and baptism) and have also been raised to newness of life in him, they should set their hearts and minds on the things above (spiritual things) and not the affairs of this earth.

Gospel: John 20:1-18 (C); John 20:1-9 (RC)

Mary Magdalene goes to Jesus' tomb early Sunday morning and notices that the stone at the entrance of the grave was pushed back. She runs to Peter with the news. Peter and John run to the tomb, go inside, and find it empty. They return home perplexed as to what has happened. Mary lingers behind outside the tomb, weeping. A man appears whom she believes to be the gardener. She asks if he has moved the body. Then the man speaks and Mary recognizes Jesus' voice. Apparently, Mary reaches out for Jesus but Jesus instructs her not to hold him back, for he is soon to ascend to his Father. The Lord sends her as witness to the other disciples.

Gospel: Mark 16:1-8 (E)

Mary Magdalene and Mary, the mother of James, and Salome bring spices to anoint the Lord's body for burial after the sabbath has past. On the way to the tomb they are trying to figure out whom they might get to roll the stone away from the entrance to the tomb. On arriving, they discover that the obstacle is removed. They enter the tomb where they encounter an angel. They are filled with fear and awe as the angel attempts to quiet their fears. He then announces that they won't find Jesus here. He is risen from the dead. He orders the women to tell the news to the apostles and to Peter. Peter is specifically mentioned not only because he was the chief leader among the disciples but as a sign of God's grace to the man who denied, in the courtyard of Caiaphas, that he even knew Jesus. The women flee the tomb in fear and astonishment.

Psalm Of The Day

Psalm 118:1-2, 14-24 (C); Psalm 118:14-24 (E) — "I will not die but live, and proclaim what the Lord has done" (v. 17).

Psalm 117 (RC)

Prayer Of The Day

Living Christ, don't permit our celebration of your resurrection to become commonplace. As you amazed the first witnesses of your resurrection, so too fill us with awe and wonder as we confront your living presence in our daily lives. In your name. Amen.

THEOLOGICAL REFLECTION ON THE LESSONS

Lesson 1: Acts 10:34-43

No favorites with God (v. 34). Peter's encounter with Cornelius showed Peter that God loves all people and listens to the prayers of all who seek to do his will. Formerly, he thought that Jesus was only for the Jews. The Holy Spirit revealed that the Lord wants all people to be in his family.

Good news of peace (v. 36). The gospel of Christ shows us how we might have peace with God and with one another. God's plan was to effect peace through the death of his chosen one. We hear daily of radical Islamic terrorists detonating bombs that kill innocent bystanders as well as themselves. The blast may injure many others. These terrorists bring increased division and hostility through death, the opposite of what God accomplished through the cross of Christ.

Lesson 2: 1 Corinthians 15:1-11

Here we stand (v. 1). Paul reveals that the good news of Christ's death and resurrection provides the foundation on which we stand. We must also take our stand on the gospel, as Martin Luther did almost 500 years ago. Otherwise, we are sure to fall down and away from the Lord.

Of first importance (v. 3). We sometimes get caught up in non-essential matters in the church (like the color of the narthex carpet) and we lose sight of that which is foundational to our faith, namely, Christ's sacrificial death and resurrection. If only we would get our priorities right and keep them before our face.

Pass it on (v. 3). Paul reminds the Corinthians that he merely passed on the facts of faith concerning Christ's death and resurrection, which he had first received from others. All of us have received the good news of Christ from others. We are all called to pass it on. Christianity remains one generation away from extinction if we do not pass it on.

Gospel: John 20:1-18

Jesus misplaced. Mary Magdalene came to the tomb to find the grave open and empty. She thought that someone had moved the body; perhaps the gardener knew where it was. When the angels asked why she was weeping, she responded: "They have taken my Lord away, and I don't know where they have laid him" (v. 13). I wonder how many of us have misplaced Jesus? Well, he was right here when I left him five years ago. I've been too busy to keep in contact. Can anybody inform me as to Jesus' whereabouts?

A living Christ in place of a corpse. Of course, Mary Magdalene didn't misplace Jesus, nor did anyone else. God raised Jesus from the grave. Our God is not in a grave; our God is on the move! Unless you stay close to the Lord, you lose track of him.

Why are you crying? (vv. 13, 15) The angels and Jesus inquire of Mary as to why she is crying. It should be obvious. Isn't crying a natural part of the grief process? Nevertheless, it's good to examine why we are weeping. Are we weeping because the life of one whom we loved was taken before his time? Or, are we weeping because we know that life will now be more difficult for us? Perhaps our tears are brought on by the realization of our own death. Whatever the cause, crying seems out of place in the presence of the risen Lord.

Gospel: Mark 16:1-8

Why does the tomb have such a heavy door? On the way to the tomb, the two Marys were discussing how they might open the heavy door to the grave (v. 3). But why did the tomb have such a heavy door? And why do we bury corpses under six feet of dirt and place a large stone thereon? Is it the fear that someone will go into the grave? No, the fear is that the dead will leave their burial site. The object is to keep the dead separated from the living. No tomb could closet the risen Christ! No door could keep him in the netherworld of dark shadows.

When we look up, things happen (v. 4). As the women slinked their way to the tomb with downcast demeanor, they pondered how they might remove a major obstacle in their path (the dense stone door to the tomb). But when they looked up, behold, the obstacle was no longer there. So it is for us. When we look up to the living Lord, we observe that the obstacle has vanished and our way stretches endlessly before us.

He is going ahead of us (v. 7). The angels announced that Jesus was going ahead of them to Galilee, where they would see him. They would see their Lord again in the old familiar places. Since Christ was the first to rise from the grave, he always goes ahead of us. The risen Lord is always a step or two ahead of us, as he should be.

SERMON APPROACHES WITH ILLUSTRATIONS

Lesson 1: Acts 10:34-43

Sermon Title: All In The Family

Sermon Angle: Peter's encounter with Cornelius, a Roman officer, transformed his thinking; he now realized that the Lord wanted all people to be saved (v. 34). God opens the family door to all who sincerely seek to know him and do his will. Human distinctions do not matter; we're one in Christ. We're all in the family.

Outline:
1. Peter and the twelve had thought that the kingdom was only for Hebrews.
2. The resurrection revealed that the kingdom was transnational — for all believers.
3. Our mission is to show all people how they might all be part of God's family.

*   *   *   *   *

Archie Bunker of *All In The Family* fame inhabited a very small world. Only people like himself were completely acceptable. Minorities were like aliens, women had to be kept in their place, and all whose political views varied from his own were communists. He treated his wife, daughter, and son-in-law (his family) with disdain. Edith, Archie's wife, on the other hand, unselfishly served the needs of her family and sought to reconcile their differences. They were all different, but they were all in her family and they were all loved.

*   *   *   *   *

Sermon Title: Dining With The Risen Lord

Sermon Angle: Peter states that he and the other disciples ate and drank with Jesus after he rose from the dead (v. 41). What a privilege that must have been! Yet, we, too, are his disciples and Christ has accorded us the same privilege of dining with him. We call it Eucharist, the Lord's Supper, holy communion. Whatever we call it, dining with Christ is the greatest of privileges, for the one who is appointed judge of all (v. 42) bestows his forgiveness and his presence. It is just a foretaste of the feast to come.

Outline:
1. The risen Christ revealed himself to his disciples in eating and drinking.
2. By his presence he forgave them, empowered them, and commissioned them to preach the good news (vv. 42-43).
3. We, too, are forgiven, empowered, and sent out to witness.
4. Our feast is but a foretaste of the feast to come.

Lesson 2: 1 Corinthians 15:1-11

Sermon Title: Hold Tight

Sermon Angle: Have you ever observed passengers on the back of motorcycles? They are holding tightly to the driver in front or to the seat. Should they lose their grip, they might fall off and never get where they are going. Something far worse could also happen; they could lose their life! Paul reminds the Corinthians of the gospel, which he has preached to them and they have received. Unless they hold firmly to it, they might fall from the faith and never reach their eternal destination.

Outline:
1. We are saved through the gospel into which we were baptized if we hold firmly to it in faith (v. 2).
2. If we stop believing in the risen Christ, our former faith will have been in vain.
3. As you travel with Jesus through life, hold tight to him and the gospel. (Suggest some ways of holding tight — worship, prayer, Bible study, and so forth.)

183

Sermon Title: Priority Preaching

Sermon Angle: We have priority mail, which means that it is supposed to receive special handling so that it reaches its destination before the other mail. Paul claims that the news of Christ's sacrificial death and resurrection is a priority in preaching (v. 3).

Gospel: John 20:1-18

Sermon Title: The Resurrection Run

Sermon Angle: When Mary observed the open tomb on the first Easter, she was so frightened that she ran to tell Peter. Hearing the report, both Peter and John ran as fast as they could to the Lord's grave. Most of us are also running, running for our lives. Only we're trying to run away from the grave, not to it. We're running as fast as we can to enjoy all that this world has to offer, to garner every trophy available to us. But like a nightmare, no matter how hard and fast we run, the mighty winds of mortality keep pushing us ever closer to the grave. Christ's resurrection has changed all that. We don't have to be afraid of death. We don't need to flee from the grave because it is merely an open door to eternal life.

Sermon Title: Don't Hold Back The Dawn

Sermon Angle: When Mary finally realized that Jesus was raised to life, standing beside her, she reached out to Jesus in joy as she cried "Rabboni!" Jesus told her to not hold him back (v. 17). Mary probably thought that things would be like they had been. Not so! God was doing something new! Instead of returning to the old days, Mary was to tell his disciples of the dawning of a new day. It was her mission to lead others into the light of that new day. That remains our mission as well.

Outline:
1. Mary came to the tomb just before the dawn of a new day.
2. She was still mourning the good old days.
3. Jesus appeared to her and she wanted to hold on to him.
   — Mary thought that resurrection meant returning to the old days.
   — Jesus informs her that a new day has dawned.
   — Her mission was to announce the dawning of the new day.
4. Our mission consists of proclaiming a new day, which God is ushering in through Christ's resurrection.

Gospel: Mark 16:1-8

Sermon Title: Left Standing On The Resurrection

Sermon Angle: Mark's resurrection account leaves us in a lurch. The risen Christ makes no appearance. Instead, the women come to the tomb and find the stone rolled back. Upon entering, the two Marys are scared out of their wits by the presence of an angel sitting where the body had lain. The angel attempts to soothe their fears, telling them that Jesus has risen. They are commanded to tell Peter and the other disciples that Jesus will meet them in Galilee. This account leaves us standing on the proclamation of Jesus' resurrection. As the women leave the tomb, they are filled with fear and terror. Like the women, we are left standing on news that Jesus has defeated death and that he will appear to us in the familiar places of our lives (v. 7).

Outline:
1. The other gospels recount appearances of the risen Christ.
2. Mark's gospel leaves us standing on nothing but the empty tomb and the proclamation that Jesus is risen.
3. The proclamation of the resurrection is the only place we have to stand.
4. The risen Christ promises to meet us where we live.

Sermon Title: The Resurrection Turns Our World Topsy-Turvy

Sermon Angle: The two women leave the tomb trembling and bewildered (v. 8). You would think that the good news of the Lord's resurrection would fill them with joy. But the empty tomb and the announcement of the resurrection changed everything, the way they looked at life and death. Change of any sort is upsetting to many people. Life means change and transformation and eternal life opens up a whole new dimension of being beyond the earthly. The resurrection of Christ turns our world topsy-turvy because now we have to render an accounting of our lives, now we have to become new creatures in Christ.

* * * * *

A young police officer pulls a van over on a routine traffic stop. He's a rookie; he has only been on the Omaha Police Force for a year, following in the footsteps of his father and grandfather. He's engaged to be married and for him life stretches to the distant horizon. He is young, strong, and committed to making his community a safer place. Before he can exit his car, several shots ring out and he slumps into a fatal swoon. Three life-hating thugs race away in a brown van. The officer is rushed to the emergency room but all they can do is preserve his organs for harvesting. This story presents us with another example of a person who gets up in the morning with every expectation of confronting life but instead is ambushed by death. Mark's tale of the resurrection of Christ describes the experiences of two women who go to a graveyard, expecting to encounter death, but instead are suddenly face-to-face with life. It was such a shock that their initial reaction was to run away in terror. Are we like them? Death we can deal with; we've encountered it before, but life, eternal life, scares us silly!

Easter 2

Revised Common	Acts 4:32-35	1 John 1:1—2:2	John 20:19-31
Roman Catholic	Acts 4:32-35	1 John 5:1-6	John 20:19-31
Episcopal	Acts 3:12a, 13-15, 17-26	1 John 5:1-6	John 20:19-31

Theme For The Day: The risen Christ confronts us in our doubts and fears with his living presence, fortifying our faith, so that we might withstand the doubt.

BRIEF COMMENTARY ON THE LESSONS

Lesson 1: Acts 4:32-35 (C, RC)

The church in Jerusalem witnessed to the power of the risen Christ through the quality of their communal life. They were united in faith and love, freely sharing their possessions. In fact, many of those with property sold it and made the funds available to the whole community.

Lesson 1: Acts 3:12a, 13-15, 17-26 (E)

See first lesson for Easter 3.

Lesson 2: 1 John 1:1—2:2 (C)

The epistle of 1 John begins in a similar fashion to the gospel of John with the eternal Word of God. John claims to have personally encountered the eternal life of God; this word he proclaims to all who will hear, that they might have fellowship with the Father, the Son, and the whole communion of faith. As in the prologue to the gospel of John, John equates light with God's grace and darkness with sin and death. If we live in unconfessed sin, we live in the darkness, but if we confess our sin, God is gracious and forgives our iniquities, cleansing us from all unrighteousness. Jesus stands as our advocate, one who represents us to God, and as the expiation for our sins.

Lesson 2: 1 John 5:1-6 (RC, E)

See Easter 6.

Gospel: John 20:19-31 (C, RC, E)

On the evening of resurrection day, fear caused the disciples to huddle together in the upper room for protection. The news of the empty tomb and of the Lord's resurrection had not yet transformed their spirits. The risen Jesus appeared among them, breathed into them his Holy Spirit, and commissioned the disciples to extend his reconciling grace. For John the resurrection, the ascension, and pentecost merge into a single event. Thomas was not present but was told that the Lord has made an appearance to them. Thomas would not believe without seeing the Lord and placing his hand in Christ's wounds. The Lord did answer Thomas' skepticism with the proof he sought but Christ utters a benediction on all who believe without seeing the evidence.

Psalm Of The Day
    Psalm 133 (C) — "How good and pleasant it is when brothers live in unity" (v. 1).
    Psalm 111 (E)
    Psalm 117 (RC)

Prayer Of The Day
    Living Lord, how grateful we are that you have not left us to our doubts and fears but have revealed yourself to us in the assembly of the faithful. In Jesus' name. Amen.

THEOLOGICAL REFLECTION ON THE LESSONS

Lesson 1: Acts 4:32-35

Welcome to paradise. If you've ever flown to Hawaii, you will recall the phrase: "Welcome to paradise!" Some people do indeed feel that way about our fiftieth state but then most of these people probably haven't lived there. Luke describes the Christian community in Jerusalem as a kind of spiritual paradise. "All the believers were of one heart and mind" (v. 32). Nobody was in need and everyone shared with his neighbor. If that isn't paradise, I don't know what is. Unfortunately, that particular community of faith didn't remain as it began. In almost every parish you will find negative, argumentative, and divisive people. If you've found the kind of congregation described in Acts, you've probably died and gone to heaven.

Grace and giving. Grace and giving go hand in hand. Luke describes a grace-full community, where people freely shared their goods. Their giving spirit was a sure indication of their new life through the power of Christ's resurrection.

Lesson 2: 1 John 1:1—2:2

Word of life (v. 1). For John, the Word of life is the person of Jesus, the Christ. John claims to have experienced this Word personally, through his bodily senses. He makes this point in some length to counter the gnostic heresies, which claimed that Jesus had not come in the flesh. The same point is made in the prologue of John's gospel: "The Word became flesh and dwelt among us ..." (John 1:14).

Fellowship (v. 3). Fellowship is a key concept in this passage. John contends that the end result of proclaiming the risen Christ is fellowship (community). In fact, the thread of community runs through all three pericopes this week. More will be said about this under "Sermon Approaches With Illustrations."

Walk in the light. John calls on the believers to match their words with their actions. If we say we have fellowship with the Lord and his people, while we walk in the darkness, we make ourselves liars. But if we walk in the light (walk our talk), we have fellowship with Jesus Christ and with one another (vv. 6-7).

Jesus for the defense (2:1). John holds up the ideal of a pure life for believers but concedes that we live in a sin-permeated world. Therefore, when we do sin we have an advocate (lawyer) to plead our case before the judgment seat of God. In fact, Jesus is the one whom the Father has chosen to judge the living and the dead. He who judges us is also the one who died and rose again for justification.

Gospel: John 20:19-31

He stands among us (v. 19). As the disciples huddled together for protection, Jesus came and stood among them. In our fears, our confusion, and our anxiety, the risen Lord stands with his own and among his own. The Lord stands among us with the peace of his presence.

Social security and insecurity. Many people are gravely anxious about our Social Security system, as it is predicted to go bankrupt if we do not act. Social insecurity also takes the form of the fear of being a victim of violent crime. The disciples ensconced themselves behind locked doors to protect themselves from becoming victims. The resurrected Christ freed them to open the door and witness boldly concerning that which they had seen and experienced. Community with the risen Christ creates real social security for this world and the next.

Hands-on faith. Thomas insisted on a hands-on faith. He not only wanted to see the wounds of his Lord, he wanted to touch them. He needed to make sure that it was really Jesus, not just some manifestation of mass hysteria. What others said wasn't good enough, he wanted to experience Christ himself. Yes, those who believe without seeing are truly blessed but sometimes they are also conned into a false or immature faith. We would do well if more people demanded a hands-on faith.

SERMON APPROACHES WITH ILLUSTRATIONS

Lesson 1: Acts 4:32-35

Sermon Title: One In The Spirit, One In The Lord

Sermon Angle: The Christian community is filled with all sorts of people from every walk of life. We have different political views, we come to some different social stands, and express ourselves uniquely. However, we have one magnet that draws us all together: the Spirit of our Lord and risen Savior. "We are one in the Spirit," as the song says, "we are one in the Lord; and we pray that all unity may one day be restored." This is the source of unity that Luke describes so glowingly in this passage.

Sermon Title: The Resurrection Frees Our Clenched Fists

Sermon Angle: You've probably heard the story of the chimp who reached through the narrow neck of a large jar to obtain the fruit inside. He clenched the luscious treat in his fist but the neck of the jar would not allow him to withdraw his fist with the fruit in it. He could have freed his hand by unclenching his fist but he refused to do that. He was imprisoned by his lust. The living Lord freed the believers in Jerusalem to release their grip on their possessions. They didn't regard any of their possessions as their own. They shared them freely. Not only did the apostle's preaching testify powerfully to the Lord's resurrection but also to the spirit of sharing in the Christian community.

Outline:
1. Tell the story of the chimp or a similar opener.
2. Greed keeps our fists clenched and attached to things.
3. The risen Christ opens our hearts and unlocks our grip on things.
4. The resurrection frees us to share with one another.

Lesson 2: 1 John 1:1—2:2

Sermon Title: Koinonia

Sermon Angle: All three lessons testify to the power of Christian community, the fellowship of believers. The New Testament word for the common life is *koinonia*. The root word here is *koin*, meaning "common" or "that which is held together." This lesson declares that the purpose for witnessing to the resurrection is that they might share in the fellowship with the Father, the Son, and other believers (v. 3). The first lesson, from Acts, describes the community in Jerusalem as a closely knit fellowship. In the gospel, the risen Lord appears to those sharing a kind of fellowship of suffering. They were all mourning the death of their Lord and master. The living Lord transformed that fellowship of suffering into a community of grace and life.

Outline:
1. The most prominent sign of the resurrected Christ is Christian fellowship.
2. All three lessons testify to its power. (Explain briefly.)
3. To be Easter people is to live in a Christ-centered community.

Sermon Title: Self-Deception

Sermon Angle: John boldly states that if we deny the reality of our sin, we are not only deceiving ourselves but living a lie (v. 8). We can fool others for a time, but God cannot be fooled; he sees the recesses of our heart. Self-deception proves dangerous; it leads to isolation, fragmentation of our personality, and separation from God. Self-deception is dangerous to your health and well-being. John urges us to come clean through confession of our sins. It opens the door to fellowship with God and one another.

Outline:
1. To deny our sin is to live a lie — it leads to sickness, broken relationships, and isolation.
2. To confess our sins is like walking in the light — nothing to hide.
3. If we confess, God will cleanse and forgive us.

* * * * *

The movie, *The Godfather*, graphically depicts how some people appear to be living in the light, while they are actually walking in the darkness of sin and death. Michael Corleone and his wife were having their baby baptized in the church while at the same time Michael's henchmen were carrying out a murderous assault on the rival mob family. The scenes from the baptism were interspersed with bloody murder scenes. The baptismal vows were a lie, a deception on Michael's part. How many of us compartmentalize our lives into outer rooms of light and inner rooms of darkness, thinking that few people will see beyond the foyer?

* * * * *

Gospel: John 20:19-31

Sermon Title: Jailbreak!

Sermon Angle: The disciples were still closeted behind locked doors that first Easter evening. Fear had driven them to lock themselves up, to fear for their lives. Suddenly, Jesus broke into their midst, giving them his peace. Before long they left their jail. They went out into the highways and byways with the good news of eternal life, forgiveness, and peace. From time to time some of them got thrown back in prison but they were always free. Christ had opened the jail door from the inside.

Outline:
1. Following the crucifixion, the upper room became a prison — fear kept them inside.
2. The risen Lord broke into their prison and freed them from fear of death.
3. They eventually broke out with the good news of freedom through the risen Christ.
   — Freedom from fear, sin, and death.

Sermon Title: To Stand Up Again Through The Power Of Faith

Sermon Angle: The crucifixion knocked the followers of Christ to the ground like a hand grenade. When the risen Lord invaded their space, their faith was flatter than a pancake. When Christ showed himself, they were soon ready to stand up again through the power of renewed faith. Thomas refused to be buoyed by their faith after Christ's first appearance. Yet even for him, the risen Lord lifted him out of the sinkhole of doubt on to the rock of a solid faith. We all have life experiences that sweep the legs of our faith out from under us. Thank God! We can stand again through the power of his resurrection!

Outline:
1. The crucifixion knocked the disciples to the pavement.
2. Fear of death kept them there for a time.
3. The Greek word for "resurrection" can be interpreted "to stand again" and that's what the risen Christ enabled them to do.
4. We might stumble and fall but the risen Christ will raise us up again.

Sermon Title: Believing Is Seeing

Sermon Angle: For Thomas, seeing was believing, as the saying goes. However, most of us must be content to see Christ through the eyes of faith. For us believing is seeing. Faith opens up a realm we never dreamed of. Jesus pronounces his blessing on those who have not seen and yet believe (v. 29).

*   *   *   *   *

Blaise Pascal, the great French scientist, mathematician, and philosopher, was working at his laboratory shortly after his beloved daughter had died. A friend dropped by and was amazed by Pascal's quiet serenity in the face of tragedy. The friend observed: "I wish I had your creed, then I would live your life." Pascal countered: "Live my life and you will soon have my creed."

The faith that frees us is practical and experiential.

Easter 3

Revised Common	Acts 3:12-19	1 John 3:1-7	Luke 24:36b-48
Roman Catholic	Acts 3:13-15, 17-19	1 John 2:1-5	Luke 24:35-48
Episcopal	Acts 4:5-12	1 John 1:1—2:2	Luke 24:36b-48

Theme For The Day: Jesus fulfills all of God's plans and promises. Repent and believe in him and God will give you a new life.

BRIEF COMMENTARY ON THE LESSONS

Lesson 1: Acts 3:12-19 (C); Acts 3:13-15, 17-19 (RC)

In the first part of the chapter, Peter heals a crippled beggar at Solomon's Colonnade in the temple. Great crowds are attracted to Peter and the other disciples and so Peter uses the opportunity to preach the gospel. Peter is brutally blunt in his preaching, accusing them of killing Jesus, even if it was in ignorance. The God of their fathers has glorified Jesus by raising him from the dead. The apostle then pleads with his hearers to repent so that their sins might be washed away and a time of spiritual refreshment might come.

Lesson 1: Acts 4:5-12 (E)

See first lesson for Easter 4.

Lesson 2: 1 John 3:1-7 (C)

The child of God is to live in holiness and obedience so that he does not sin. However, if anyone does sin, we have but to trust in Jesus, God's atoning sacrifice, and our sins will be washed away. A true child of God will not persist in unconfessed and intentional sinning because he has been transformed by the grace of God.

Lesson 2: 1 John 2:1-5 (RC)

Lesson 2: 1 John 1:1—2:2 (E)

See second lesson for Easter 2.

Gospel: Luke 24:36b-48 (C, E); Luke 24:35-48 (RC)

Two disciples encounter the risen Christ on the road to Emmaus and return to Jerusalem to share the good news with the other disciples. As they are still speaking, Jesus comes into their midst. They shirk back, thinking that he is a ghost. Jesus eats some fish to demonstrate that he is not a ghost, that he has a body. He then proceeds to explain how his death and resurrection fulfills scripture, just as he had done on the road to Emmaus. The risen Christ still takes on the role of teacher. Repentance and forgiveness is to be preached in his name to all nations. Jesus would soon send his Spirit to help them in their witnessing task.

Psalm Of The Day

Psalm 4 (C, RC) — "Know that the Lord has set apart the godly for himself" (v. 3a).

Psalm 98 (E)

Prayer Of The Day

Lord God, we thank you for the grace and forgiveness we receive through Jesus, who came to us according to your divine plan. Make our lives a glowing witness to his resurrection power. In the precious name of Jesus. Amen.

THEOLOGICAL REFLECTION ON THE LESSONS

Lesson 1: Acts 3:12-19

Give God the glory. After the healing of the crippled beggar, the crowds looked at Peter and John as if they were great. Peter informs the people that they are nothing special but that it was through the power of Jesus that he was healed (vv. 12-13). Peter did not hesitate to give Christ the glory.

They got the point. The worshipers at the temple who heard Peter preach got the point. It was like pounding a stake into their heart with a sledgehammer. "You handed him over to be killed!" BAM! "You disowned him before Pilate ..." BAM! "You disowned the Holy and Righteous One...!" BAM! "You killed the author of life!" BAM! BAM! BAM! They got the point all right and it hurt.

But! There wasn't any good news in the spiritual bludgeoning on Peter's audience. It was all law and guilt. However, once he got their attention he introduced the gospel with a *but*: "but God raised him from the dead" (v. 13). There was hope that the Lord could undo what they had done. He makes the further point that it was by the name of Jesus that the crippled man was healed. They had all sinned in condemning Jesus *but* God raised Jesus and offers new life to all who repent and believe in his name. When people tell you how bad things are, just interject the conjunction *but*; but remember, God raised Jesus and God can raise us all to newness of life. God's little three-letter word gives us hope.

Lesson 2: 1 John 3:1-7

Lavish love (v. 3). The NRSV makes a verb of the word "lavish" to describe the wondrous love with which God has favored us in Christ. The word "lavish" connotes extravagance, profusion, unstinting in giving. It comes from an old French word *laver*, meaning "to wash" or "downpour." In Christ, we are awash in God's great love and grace.

What we are and what we shall be (v. 2). John states boldly that we already are (present tense) God's children but what we shall be has not yet been revealed to us. We only know that when Jesus returns we will be like him because we will see him as he really is. Though we know Jesus, our image of him is clouded by sin and mortality. In glory we will see Jesus for real and what a transforming experience that will be!

Are we living in sin or living in the Son? Christ came to take away our sin. John clearly states that any person who intentionally persists in sin is not born of God. If we are living in and through God's Son, we cannot at the same time live in sin. None of us, of course, is free of sin, but we are in the process of being liberated from its control as we walk with Christ. This process is called sanctification.

Gospel: Luke 24:36b-48

He stands among us (v. 36). As the disciples were discussing the mysterious events surrounding the first Easter, the Lord himself came and stood among them. In their confusion and fear he came with his peace. He stands among us still, whenever we gather in his name.

How do we know he's real? When the believers saw the risen Jesus, they thought they had seen a ghost. Jesus showed them the marks of crucifixion and he ate some fish to demonstrate that he was real, body and all. There are many Jesus clones, various and sundry representations of the Christ. There's the glitzy Jesus in designer suits and ties, sitting on a couch of gold, selling his latest formula for success. There's the pinched nose Jesus, raising his eyebrows contemptuously to those who do not agree with his concept of God. There's the teddy bear Jesus; he just wants to be hugged and cuddled. He's always there for you and, this is the good part, he won't raise his hand, prophet-like, and intone "Thus, says the Lord!" or "Repent!" How do we know the real Jesus? Look at his hands and feet and observe if his wounds are there. They are the marks of love. Real love, like the real Jesus, is not afraid to get dirty or bloody or to give one's life for the world.

Look at his hands (v. 39). I bought a paperback book of sermons one time called *A Cross Study Of Hands*. Each week, he would lift up different hands communicating various messages. For instance, there were the accusing hands of the religious authorities, the angry hands of the crowd, and the praying hands of Jesus. You can tell a great deal about a person by examining his hands. Like how he earns his living or how meticulous he is. When you look at the hands of Jesus, they won't be silky white or satin smooth. They will bear the imprint of hard nails but they are strong, sensitive, and loving hands.

Surprised by joy (v. 41). The disciples were surprised by joy. There is no better way to explain it. They hadn't expected it. In fact, it was the furthest thing from their mind. The resurrection of Jesus reminds us that we must always be ready to be surprised by joy. God turns our dirge into a dance.

SERMON APPROACHES WITH ILLUSTRATIONS

Lesson 1: Acts 3:12-19

Sermon Title: Guilty

Sermon Angle: Peter came out of the corner swinging, as he leveled accusations against the Jews in the temple. "You handed him over to be killed ... You disowned the Holy and Righteous One ..." and much more. With no ambiguity, he charged, indicted, and convicted them as being guilty of killing the Christ. Most of us would not be comfortable in being that direct. Yet, the truth remains that unless we accept our guilt we cannot receive the gift of salvation. The problem with Peter's preaching for me lies in the fact that he does not lift up his own guilt. He himself, one of the inner circle of disciples, denied three times that he even knew Jesus. Who am I to advise the rock on homiletics? Yet wouldn't his message have had greater impact if he had included himself among those who crucified Christ? After all, it wasn't just the Jews who crucified Jesus. We all warrant the sentence: "Guilty!"

Outline:
1. Peter preached a sermon that made his hearers squirm — they were guilty!
2. Underlying truth — we must admit guilt to receive grace (law and gospel).
3. The good news — though they were guilty, God had forgiven them.
4. The resurrection of Christ is good news for us all — God forgives and renews all who repent and trust in Jesus (v. 19).

193

Sermon Title: There's Something About That Name

Sermon Angle: The 1994 national champions of college football, the Nebraska Cornhuskers, were once dubbed the "Bugeaters." I don't think that they would ever have attained their exalted status had they retained that handle. Names have power to shape us, shame us, inspire us, or even heal us. Peter makes clear that he did not heal the crippled man in his name but through the name of Jesus (v. 16). Believers and even some skeptics have discovered that there is definitely something about the name of Jesus, that name above every name.

Lesson 2: 1 John 3:1-7

Sermon Title: Adopted Into The Family Of God

Sermon Angle: The text does not mention adoption but that is what it describes. What else would you call it when someone considers you his child? John equates the lavishness of God's love with our being taken into God's family. "How great is the love the Father has lavished on us, that we should be called children of God!" We have a name, an identity. Not just any name. Not just any identity. We are children of God.

Outline:
1. Is anything more pathetic than to be nameless — without home or family?
2. We are children of God (v. 2).
3. This identity is a sign of God's favor.
4. To persist in a life of sin shows that we do not know God — we lose our identity (vv. 4-5).

*   *   *   *   *

The national news on August 25, 1995, showed a mass grave in the form of a long trench. The bodies rested in plain wooden boxes, with their name, if known, affixed to the top. The boxes were so close together that you couldn't put a matchbook in between. These were not the victims of genocide in Africa or Bosnia. They were victims of a severe heat wave in the city of Chicago, mostly the aged and the infirm. No one was there to grieve their loss. Nobody claimed their bodies; their families had either lost touch with them or they had no family. In this mass grave, these poor souls lost their identity and their humanity. They were nobody's child and no one's mother or father. They had apparently lost their identity and sense of worth some time prior to their miserable death or they wouldn't have died alone and forsaken. Yet as Christians, we have the hope that the Lord knew them and claimed them as his children.

On the same newscast they featured the mass wedding of 70,000 Moonies, who were united together in a stadium in Seoul, Korea. These couples did not know one another, they did not fall in love with one another, nor did they have any role in selecting their mates. These young people of different races had forfeited their individuality and their identity. It was not totally a free choice. Moon viewed himself as a messiah who brought to life a new and godly race of humans. How unfortunate that the church was not able to reach these young people with the good news that the king of creation desires to claim them as his own dear children.

*   *   *   *   *

Sermon Title: Family Likeness

Sermon Angle: People are always comparing us to other family members. "She looks just like her mother." "He has his father's eyes and his mother's bad temper." Well, you get the picture. John states that when Christ returns, we shall be like him (v. 2). Already the family resemblance should be apparent. When people view our words and deeds, wouldn't it be wonderful if they thought, "God must be like that."

Gospel: Luke 24:36b-48

Sermon Title: Stand Up On The Promises Of God

Sermon Angle: The risen Christ appeared to the disciples and after he established his identity, he explained to them how he was the fulfillment of the promises that God made through the prophets and the psalms. We see the same process in effect in the preaching of Peter, featured in the first lesson. This not only shows God's faithfulness in fulfilling his promises but helps us see that the life, death, and resurrection of Jesus are not disconnected events but central features of a much larger picture. God's people have always found him to be faithful. We can stand up on the promises of God.

Outline:
1. The history of God's people reveals a series of God's promises made and fulfilled.
2. Jesus told his disciples he would rise from the dead but they didn't understand.
3. The disciples of Jesus were knocked off their feet by the crucifixion.
4. Jesus appeared among them and raised them up — gave them hope.
5. Jesus explained how his death and resurrection was a fulfillment to God's promises.
6. They stood up on the promises of God and so can we.

Sermon Title: Connections

Sermon Angle: The Discovery Channel developed a series called *Connections* to help us understand the relationship between scientific discoveries and also to comprehend how various historical events formed the foundation for other events. The crucifixion was a particularly jarring and disconnecting event. The disciples thought that Jesus was going to establish an earthly kingdom but the crucifixion smashed that idea as if it were a flowerpot that had fallen from a ten-story building. The resurrected Jesus came into their company and proceeded to explain how what had happened to him was connected to what God had done and said before. Making connections is what any religion is about, helping people understand how they fit into the cosmos, how their lives connect with the past and the future and, most importantly of all, how we connect with God. The resurrection of Christ teaches us that our connection with God and others does not end when our mortal-cord is severed.

Outline:
1. The death of Jesus cut connections to the past and future for the disciples.
2. The risen Christ revealed to them how everything that happened was connected.
   — The crucifixion and resurrection were part of God's plan (vv. 44-46).
   — A fulfillment of the promises of God.
3. Christ also connected the church to the future — to be his witnesses (vv. 47-48).

Sermon Title: How To Recognize The Risen Christ

Sermon Angle: When Christ appeared to his disciples in the upper room, they didn't recognize him right away. They thought he was a ghost. John's account of the resurrection reveals that Mary Magdalene didn't recognize the risen Christ, either. It isn't any easier in our day because there are so many descriptions of the living Lord. (Refer to the "Theological Reflection On The Lessons" section.) Jesus pointed to his hands and feet to help his disciples recognize him, they bear the marks of God's endless love.

*   *   *   *   *

I read the story of an English girl whose parents died when she was a teenager. Being the oldest, she assumed the mother's role of caring for her siblings. After a couple of years of hard labor, she was taken ill to a hospital. The doctor discovered that she was dying. Hearing of her plight, a minister decided to visit her and prepare her for eternity. He seemed more interested in having her recite the proper doctrinal formulation than he was in sharing with her the love of Jesus. The right words weren't coming from her lips and he was becoming somewhat annoyed as he asked: "But what will you have to show the Lord when you stand before his judgment seat?" The girl quietly responded with wisdom that could only have been drawn from the well of suffering love: "I will show him my hands."

Easter 4

Revised Common	Acts 4:5-12	1 John 3:16-24	John 10:11-18
Roman Catholic	Acts 4:8-12	1 John 3:1-2	John 10:11-18
Episcopal	Acts 4:(23-31) 32-37	1 John 3:1-8	John 10:11-16

Theme For The Day: Jesus is the good shepherd who gathers us, saves us, and keeps his flock together.

BRIEF COMMENTARY ON THE LESSONS

Lesson 1: Acts 4:5-12 (C); Acts 4:8-12 (RC)

Peter and John are arrested by the temple guards for preaching the resurrection and healing the crippled man in the temple. The suspects are brought before the family of the high priest for questioning. The interrogators wanted to know by what power Peter effected the healing. Inspired by the Holy Spirit, Peter boldly proclaims that this man was healed through the name of Jesus. Jesus is the stone that the builders (the religious establishment) rejected, but God has made him the cornerstone.

Lesson 1: Acts 4:(23-31) 32-37 (E)

See first lesson for Easter 2.

Lesson 2: 1 John 3:16-24 (C)

God shows his love for us by calling us his children (vv. 1-2) and by laying down his life for us (v. 16). Therefore, we also should lay down our lives for one another and share our goods with those in need. John sums up God's commands in two phrases: to believe in Jesus Christ and to love one another (v. 23). These are the marks of obedience.

Lesson 2: 1 John 3:1-2 (RC); 1 John 3:1-8 (E)

See second lesson for Easter 3.

Gospel: John 10:11-18 (C, RC); John 10:11-16 (E)

Jesus is the good shepherd who truly cares for his sheep. Those who are hired to tend the sheep flee in the face of danger, but not the good shepherd, who stands ready to lay down his life for his sheep. The relationship between the good shepherd and his sheep is characterized by mutual knowing and self-revelation. There are other sheep, not of his fold; he must bring them into the flock so that there might be one flock and one shepherd. The image of shepherd is widely employed by the prophets to describe the leadership of God's anointed king. Jesus employs the shepherd style of leadership for those who follow him as the Christ.

Psalm Of The Day

Psalm 23 (C, E) — "The Lord is my shepherd...."
Psalm 117 (RC)

Prayer Of The Day

Shepherd and guardian of our souls, when we wander away from your tender care, gently lead us back into your fold, where we are known and loved. In your precious name. Amen.

THEOLOGICAL REFLECTION ON THE LESSONS

Lesson 1: Acts 4:5-12

The godfathers. After the arrest of Peter and John, there was a confab amongst the high priestly clan — Annas, Caiaphas, John, and Alexander. They were the godfathers of the temple; Jesus had disrupted the family business when he walked as a mortal, now he was causing even more trouble after his death. A follower of Jesus was healing in his name and hundreds of Jews were becoming disciples of Jesus. The priestly clique was intent on doing whatever was necessary to dispose of those who were meddling in the family business.

Prescription for good health (v. 10). The apostles carried on Jesus' healing ministry. Health, in all its dimensions, is associated with the coming of God's kingdom. Health begins with holiness, knowing one's self as God's child, and being centered in the Lord.

Stumbling stone or cornerstone? Peter preaches that Jesus is like a stone that the religious establishment (God's builders) has rejected. It becomes a stumbling stone of offense. Peter boldly asserts that God has made Jesus the cornerstone, the most important building block of all, for it ties the whole edifice together.

Lesson 2: 1 John 3:16-24

How do you know you're in love? This is the question that young people ask. Of course, they are thinking of love primarily as an emotional state rather than something we do. John would phrase the question differently. He would say: How do we know love? The answer would be: We know love in Christ, who loved us so much that he offered up his life for us (v. 16). We also know love when we share ourselves and our substance with those in need. We know love through actions and deeds (vv. 17-18).

Blessed assurance (vv. 18-22). The best antidote for a guilty conscience is to live in love and to live out our love. The acts of love will help reassure our hearts that we really are God's children. If love is an emotion, we are always in a quandary as to whether or not we have attained the proper love feeling. Even if our hearts or consciences condemn us, John reassures us with the knowledge that God is greater than our hearts. We have the blessed assurance, through Jesus, that God knows us and yet loves us, even when our hearts condemn us.

Prescription for a powerful prayer life (vv. 22-23). John suggests that a holy life leads to a clean conscience, which leads to a bold and powerful prayer life. This makes sense because sin separates us from God. When we know we're forgiven and are trying to live in obedience to God's will, this makes us bold to storm the gates of heaven. The alienation caused by sin has been overcome when we trust in Christ and embrace God's grace.

Gospel: John 10:11-18

Employee mentality. The passage contrasts the owner of the sheep from the hired hand. The shepherd cares for the sheep because they belong to him. Their lives are intertwined with his own. In contrast, the hired hand is only doing the job for money. He doesn't really care for the sheep; no personal bond exists. For the shepherd there is a "me and mine" relationship; for the hired hand it's "me and them." The shepherd will sacrifice for those who are precious to him but the hired hand refuses to give himself for those who are only a number.

The ground of being. The phrase, "I am," repeats itself with some regularity in chapter 10 of John. When Moses asked God who he was that was sending him to free the Hebrew people, the Lord told Moses to say that I Am has sent you. Paul Tillich refers to God as the ground of being. Such a title seems philosophical and impersonal. The gospel of John gives content to this title. "I am the way, the truth, and the life." "I am the vine and you are the branches." "I am the bread of life...." In this pericope, the object of the verb "to be" is the word shepherd. This title is the most beloved of all the I Am passages in the gospel of John, because it connotes a personal relationship of love and caring. How wonderful to know that within the ground of our being there beats a shepherd's heart.

One flock, one shepherd (v. 17). This passage, expressing missionary consciousness, suggests that the missionary spirit of the early church had its source in the Spirit of Jesus himself. Salvation was not limited to the Jews. Jesus had other sheep that were not, as yet, in his fold. When the kingdom had fully come, there would be only one flock and one shepherd. This word of Christ encourages us to manifest not only a missionary spirit to non-Christians, but an ecumenical attitude toward those who find themselves in other Christian folds.

SERMON APPROACHES WITH ILLUSTRATIONS

Lesson 1: Acts 4:5-12
Sermon Title: Credentials

Sermon Angle: During the interrogation, Peter and John were asked the source of their authority for the healing of the crippled man (v. 7). Peter boldly appeals to a higher authority, the name of Jesus, the one whom God raised from the dead. Peter states that it's in the name of Jesus, the one they had rejected and tried to destroy, that the crippled man stood whole and well. In Christ's name this man was healed. We are empowered with the same name in baptism. No other credentials are needed.

Outline:
1. The high priestly family called Peter to present his credentials for healing the crippled man.
2. They considered him to be practicing without papers (credentials).
3. Peter appealed to the authority of the risen Christ (Christ's name).
4. The one whom they disbarred and killed is Lord and judge of all.
5. Our baptism gives us the credentials (we bear Jesus' name) we need to make others whole.

Sermon Title: The Rock Preaches The Rock And Becomes A Rock

Sermon Angle: A student of scripture is struck by the difference in Peter's demeanor right before the crucifixion, when he denied his Lord, and after the resurrection, when he boldly proclaims Jesus as Lord. In the first instance he is the rock in name only. He behaved more like a quivering bowl of Jell-O. After the resurrection Peter is reborn and preaches Jesus as the main rock (cornerstone) in the edifice of God's kingdom. Christ, the rock discarded by the Jewish leaders, is the building block that gives the kingdom its shape and form. The difference between the former and the latter Peter derives from the power of Jesus' resurrection and the Holy Spirit.

Lesson 2: 1 John 3:16-24

Sermon Title: How To Find Your True Love

Sermon Angle: John informs us how we can find our true love. First of all, he tells about the one who truly loves us and gave his life for us, Jesus Christ. This informs us about how we can be the object of love. This is love as a noun. If he left us here, however, we would not yet know the fullness of love. No, John instructs us how we can find our true love as a verb, as something that we do to and for others. The second love flows from the first. "We love because he first loved us." To put it simply, true love consists not only in being loved but in loving others. If only people were as interested in giving love as they are in receiving love, there would be love overflowing.

Outline:
1. Most of the magazines and movies deal with finding one's true love.
2. Society defines love as something we receive from another.
3. Finding true love means finding the right person.
4. God defines love as the willingness to lay down one's life for another.
   — Christ gave his life for us (v. 16).
   — We are to give our lives to one another (vv. 17-18).
5. We find our true love in Christ (as the objects of love and as the subjects of love).

Sermon Title: The New Commandments

Sermon Angle: John reduces the Christian life into two imperatives. We are to believe (trust) in God's Son and love one another (v. 23). The Jewish religion had become entangled in a morass of rules and restrictions. John cuts to the core of true religion. Namely, to trust in God's forgiving grace and then to extend this freeing grace to others through acts of love.

Gospel: John 10:11-18

Sermon Title: The Shepherd's Psalm

Sermon Angle: The good shepherd theme is also featured in the Psalm Of The Day, Psalm 23. This psalm is attributed to King David, who was a shepherd himself. This shepherd/king realized that he needed an over-shepherd. A sermon on this most beloved and widely used of all scripture passages would certainly be appropriate.

Outline:
Introduction: What does it mean to say that "the Lord is my shepherd"?
1. God personally cares about us and supplies our needs (I shall not want).
   — God supplies our physical needs (green pastures, still waters).
   — God supplies our spiritual needs (restores our soul, leads along right pathways).
2. God will always walk with me, even when my life is threatened (valley of the shadow of death). Christ, the good shepherd, laid down his life for us (gospel).
3. God will honor me in the presence of those who are my enemies (a table in the presence of my enemies).
4. God's goodness and love will lead me from this life into eternity (surely goodness ...).

* * * * *

Pastors are shepherds, entrusted with the formidable task of helping people triumph over life and death. We have the privilege of shepherding our flocks through the "valley of the shadow of death." Our task is to enable those facing death to do so in a spirit of openness and faith. Our natural tendency is to shun that which causes us pain. Sometimes pastors also need shepherds to lead them through the valley of shadow. My mother was shepherd to her family while she was dying. She made it possible for herself and her loved ones to triumph over death by requesting that we write her notes and letters for her last birthday. These notes prompted us candidly to deal with life, with death, with the past, present, and future. One thing is sure. Nobody wants to die alone. When it comes to this business of dying, we all need a shepherd and pastors can't do the job by themselves. The family of God needs to be instructed in ways that they too can shepherd others through the valley of the shadow of death. An article I found in the *Leadership* magazine would be of great help in this task. "Asimakoupoulos: Shepherding in the Shadow of Death" by Greg Asimakoupoulos: 1994, Christianity Today, Inc./*Leadership* journal.

*   *   *   *   *

Some pastors are like the hired hand that Jesus speaks of in the good shepherd discourse; it's just a job for which they are paid, but inside the majority of pastors there beats a true shepherd's heart. In a survey conducted by the *Leadership* journal, only a little over 10% of the pastors polled would leave the ministry for a secular pursuit that paid more money. Over 70% of them reported that pay was not a key factor in determining whether of not they remained in the ministry. Some 86.5% of the pastors polled cited a strong sense of call as the reason they remained in the ministry. When asked if they would select a career in the ministry if they had it to do all over again, 83% responded affirmatively. (Statistics gleaned from "Pastor's Pulse" by Richard Doebler, a contributing editor for *Leadership*, 1995.)

*   *   *   *   *

Sermon Title: Stand Up Together With God's Flock
Sermon Angle: The risen Christ appeared primarily to his disciples as they assembled together. They were able to stand up again through their common experience of the risen Christ. In the real crisis of life and faith, we are not able to "pick ourselves up, dust ourselves off, and start all over again." We are empowered to stand through Christ's resurrection, but we are only able to stay erect if we stand together in faith with other members of his flock.

Sermon Title: What's Good About The Good Shepherd?
Sermon Angle: Jesus refers to himself as the good shepherd (leader). This implies that there must also be such a thing as a bad shepherd (leader). We'll start with the bad shepherd; what does he look like? He's merely an employee (v. 13). He doesn't care personally for the sheep (v. 13). There is no sense of relationship; he doesn't know the sheep. They are merely numbers to him. In contrast, what does the good shepherd look like? He cares for his sheep with his life (v. 11). He owns them and therefore they are precious to him. He knows them and loves them (v. 14). He yearns for those sheep who have strayed and seeks to bring them back into his fold (v. 16).

201

Outline:
1. The world longs for genuine leadership (real shepherds).
2. The world is filled with examples of bad shepherds. (Give examples.)
3. Give characteristics of the bad shepherds (noted in Sermon Angle).
4. Give characteristics of Christ, the good shepherd (Sermon Angle).
5. Use Jesus as a model for leadership.

*　*　*　*　*

A legend about John, known as the disciple whom Jesus loved, has the elderly man teaching some of his young disciples the principles of the kingdom. After he got their attention, John raised his hand for emphasis and uttered a word of wisdom: "Little children, love one another." One of the eager recruits retorted: "That's fine, John, but how do we heal as Jesus did?" The old gentlemen replied: "Little children, love one another." Another neophyte chimed in: "We get your point, John, but how can we be truly great and dynamic leaders?" A third time, the beloved disciple repeated: "Little children, love one another." Love remains the essence of Jesus' shepherding style of leadership.

Easter 5

Revised Common	Acts 8:26-40	1 John 4:7-21	John 15:1-8
Roman Catholic	Acts 9:26-31	1 John 3:18-24	John 15:1-8
Episcopal	Acts 8:26-40	1 John 3:(14-17) 18-24	John 14:15-21

Theme For The Day: The life of faith, begun in baptism, remains alive if we stay close to Christ. Christ is the vine and we are the branches.

BRIEF COMMENTARY ON THE LESSONS

Lesson 1: Acts 8:26-40 (C, E)

Philip is instructed by an angel to go to the road that leads from Jerusalem past Gaza down to Egypt. On the road he encounters an Ethiopian official, the steward of the queen's treasury. He is traveling along in a chariot and reading Isaiah 53 in the Old Testament. He was either a proselyte of the Jewish faith, one who was circumcised and accepted the whole of Jewish law, or he was a God-fearer, which means that he wasn't circumcised or baptized but he read the Hebrew scriptures and adhered to the moral principles of the Jewish religion. Philip runs up alongside the chariot and asks the official if he knows what he is reading. The official is puzzled by the identity of the suffering servant in Isaiah 53. Philip sits alongside him and explains how Christ fulfills the Hebrew scriptures. The official is won to Christ and asks to be baptized in a body of water near them. When the official comes up out of the water, Philip is spirited off to another place, Azotus. The new convert continues his journey, rejoicing. Many feel that he was the person who first missionized the Ethiopian people.

Lesson 1: Acts 9:26-31 (RC)

After his conversion, Paul gets himself in trouble by boldly preaching Christ. His enemies plot to kill him and so his disciples let him down in a basket from an opening in the city wall. Paul travels to Jerusalem, where the church greets him with suspicion. Barnabas vouches for Paul, which makes him accepted by the church. The apostle makes enemies amongst the Hellenistic Jews, who want to kill him. Fellow believers spirit him off to Tarsus, his birthplace. Meanwhile, the church continues to prosper and grow.

Lesson 2: 1 John 4:7-21 (C)

John urges the believers to love one another because God is the source of love. Whoever loves, knows God, but the reverse is true as well. God's love is shown in the sending of his Son, which ought to be the inspiration for our love. The invisible God becomes visible in us when we live in love.

Lesson 2: 1 John 3:18-24 (RC); 1 John 3:(14-17) 18-24 (E)

See second lesson for Easter 4.

Gospel: John 15:1-8 (C, RC)

The relationship of the believer to Christ is compared to the relationship of the branches to the trunk of the vine. Just as the branches derive their existence from the trunk of the vine, so believers receive their life from Christ. The object of the believer's existence is to bear fruit (the works of love). A note of judgment is also sounded; those who do not bear fruit are pruned from the vine and burned (v. 6). We can do nothing good or of eternal consequence if we do not remain close to Christ.

Gospel: John 14:15-21 (E)

If the believer loves God by keeping his commandments, Christ will ask the Father to send to them the counselor, the Holy Spirit.

Psalm Of The Day

Psalm 22:25-31 (C) — "All the ends of the earth shall remember and turn to the Lord ..." (v. 27).

Psalm 21 (RC)

Psalm 66:1-11 (E)

Prayer Of The Day

O God, form the minds of your faithful people into a single will. Make us love what you command and desire what you promise, that amid all the changes of this world our hearts may be fixed where true joy is found. Amen.

THEOLOGICAL REFLECTION ON THE LESSONS

Lesson 1: Acts 8:26-40

The treasurer finds true treasure. The eunuch was treasurer for Candace, the queen of Ethiopia (Candace is a title, not a name). Yet he was looking for something more in life and was attracted by the Jewish religion. Still he was searching for more. As he read Isaiah 53, God answered his prayers by sending Philip to explain the gospel to him. After being baptized he then possessed the true treasure, Jesus Christ, our Lord.

Spiritual guides (vv. 31-32). When Philip reached the Ethiopian official and he was reading the Bible, Philip asked if he understood what he read. He replied, "How can I unless someone guides me?" Philip proceeded to interpret scripture in light of the Christ event. Before long, everything fell into place for the official and he was ready to commit his life to Christ and be baptized. It never would have happened had God not sent the official a spiritual guide.

Christ is the key. The Ethiopian could not clearly understand the Bible without knowing about Christ. Philip was able to supply the key, Christ, that enabled the eunuch rightly to understand scripture and respond in faith. The word can only be understood when one personally encounters the Word incarnate.

On his way rejoicing (v. 39). After the official was baptized, Philip vanished and he went on his way rejoicing. And why shouldn't he? He had been reborn; as he came out of the waters he was a new person. As Christ's baptized disciples, are we going on our way rejoicing?

Lesson 2: 1 John 4:7-21

This is love. Many people spend their lives looking for love but they probably wouldn't know real love if it stared them in the face. John is telling us: You want to know what love is? This is love, "not that we loved God but that he loved us and sent his Son to be the atoning sacrifice for our sin" (v. 10).

Beloved. John employs this address time and again. The very form by which he addressed the church reminded them that they were the objects of God's love, that they were precious in God's sight.

The circle of love. John states that if we love one another, "God lives in us, and his love is perfected in us" (v. 12). The word "perfect" connotes a sense of completion. If God is the source of love, and Jesus is the conveyor of that love and we are the recipients of that love, then to complete the circle of God's love we must share God's love with one another. As the old Bible school song says, "The circle of love goes around, the circle of love goes around, reach out your hand, someone needs you. The circle of love goes around."

Gospel: John 15:1-8

Pruned but not cut off (v. 2). There's a difference between cutting and pruning. To cut is to remove and destroy. Pruning is to cut off certain unproductive parts of the vine so as to stimulate further growth. The word for pruning is the same as for cleansing. When we confess our sins and God prunes them, our soul becomes cleansed. God may have to prune us to produce greater fruitfulness.

Jesus is the vine. In Old Testament imagery the Jewish people are the vine. Isaiah says that the vineyard of the Lord is the house of Israel (Isaiah 5:1-7). Ezekiel also likened the nation to a vine (Ezekiel 15; 19:10). Other passages could be cited as well. Jesus is claiming here that he is the true or authentic vine, not Israel. The Jews believed that the way to stay alive spiritually was to keep in close contact with their ethnic and spiritual identity. "Not so," says Jesus, "I am the true vine." To stay alive spiritually you must adhere to Christ, you must be grafted into the true vine. To be a child of Abraham will not, by itself, save a person. To merely partake of the rituals will not give you life. Only in Christ will our lives prove fruitful.

Hang close. Jesus tells us in this passage that to be fruitfully alive we must hang close to Christ, the source and conduit of our spiritual existence. We hang close through an active prayer and worship life. Hanging close to Christ, the trunk of the vine, also means that we hang close to those other clusters of disciples. Hanging close means living in community with Christ and other Christians.

SERMON APPROACHES WITH ILLUSTRATIONS

Lesson 1: Acts 8:26-40

Sermon Title: A Company Of Angels

Sermon Angle: Philip ran down toward Gaza at the instigation of an angel. The Greek word for angel (*angelos*) also means "messenger." In the past five to ten years there has been a surge of interest in angels. Numerous folks claim to have had brushes with angels where the heavenly being saved them or delivered a message to them. In our story the angel was a messenger and so was Philip. Actually, all of God's people are messengers. We belong to a company of angels.

Outline:
1. There's been much interest of late in angels. (Share an angel story.)
2. We find an angel in our first lesson. (Explain his role.)
3. The word "angel" means messenger. Philip was also an angel (messenger).
4. Philip communicated to the Ethiopian the gospel of Christ.
5. The Ethiopian received the message of Christ and was baptized.
6. To whom are we going as angel messengers?

Sermon Title: Interpreters Of The Word

Sermon Angle: For many people the word of God is something of an enigma. The thought forms, the history and the manner of speech seems foreign to them. Until we are well versed on the scriptures, we need others to help us interpret and understand. The problem comes from the fact that many so-called interpreters of the word of truth represent some narrow or sectarian point of view. The world needs interpreters who will translate the gospel against the backdrop of God's entire word. Too many distortions derive from taking one or two passages out of context. Those who do this treat the word of God not as a text but as a pretext for their own brand of religious philosophy. Of course, the key to unlocking the riches of the scriptures is the Word made flesh, Jesus Christ. The role of the preacher is to help people understand the meaning of God's word for their own lives so that they might commit or recommit their lives to Christ.

Outline:
1. The Ethiopian needed an interpreter so that he might understand God's word.
2. Philip interpreted the meaning of scripture to him, using these principles:
   — He started with the man's present question (v. 34).
   — He interpreted that passage in light of the whole of scripture.
   — Christ was the key to unlocking the mystery of the word.
   — He led him to commitment.
3. The Ethiopian rejoiced that he understood and received the Word (v. 39).

Lesson 2: 1 John 4:7-21

Sermon Title: Love Child

Sermon Angle: Many young people turn to violence because they perceive that they are nobody's love child. They know that they were not conceived in love and that nobody really cares for them as their own dear child. When it comes to our second birth, we are all love children; we are God's love child. We are born not only because of love but for love. We are God's love child. John states that the sign that points to our identity as God's child is that we love (v. 7).

Outline:
1. It is a great sorrow to be born for any other reason than as an expression of love.
2. No matter the circumstances of our birth, we are God's love child.
3. God's Son was born out of God's love for the world (v. 10).
4. In Christ, we are God's love child.
5. Let us show that we are God's beloved child by loving others (vv. 11-12).

*   *   *   *   *

It seems that if we don't find ourselves in a family, a church, or a community that truly loves and values us, we will fall prey for whatever substitutes are available. Street gangs are a self-destructive form of belonging, yet many will choose this option to not belonging at all. These young men, largely devoid of faith, love, and spiritual values, see violence as a way of coping with what they regard as a loveless and godless universe. Listen to Maurice, a New York street gang member.

"I believe the universe came together with, like, one big bang, man. I don't believe in God, man ... I also believe that the human race are like pestilent aliens ... You know, I don't have words for it, man, but, like _____ (expletive deleted), man, it's like you, it's like me; we're individuals raised from evolution of the earth and time. That's all there is, man, time and span.

"So I'm like, into partying my life away into a higher existence, man. (laughs) 'Cause we all gonna die one day anyway, and there's no hell and no heaven, right. We all gonna die anyway." (Excerpt from *The Search For Meaning* by Philip L. Berman.)

*   *   *   *   *

Sermon Title: The Circle Of Love
Sermon Angle: God cannot love apart from us. It's true! Love, by its very definition, needs an object. If God is love, God must have someone to love. God's love began when he created us in his image. However, God's love is shown most powerfully in the sending of his Son. Love begins with God, who reaches out to us and makes his home in us. However, that love is not perfect (complete) until God's love is beamed back to him through actions of love toward others. His love is then perfected in us (v. 12), making the circle of God's love complete. (See also the Theological Reflection On The Lessons.)
Outline:
1. One cannot love in solitude — love requires an object, another person.
2. God cannot love without us — we are the objects of his love.
3. Love is a circle — begins with God, goes to us, through us to others, and then back to its source.
4. Keep the circle of love going round.

Gospel: John 15:1-8
Sermon Title: We Stand Connected
Sermon Angle: It's happened to us all. We make an erroneous statement and somebody else chimes in. "Sorry, but you're mistaken...." We respond: "Sorry, I stand corrected." Through Jesus' resurrection we rise (stand up) to newness of life. In communion with Christ and the community of the faithful, we stay standing if we stand connected, just as the grape branches stay standing and fruitful if they stand closely connected to the vine trunk. If we stay connected to Christ and the church, God promises that we will stand eternally in his presence.
Outline:
1. The vine branches stay standing alive and fruitful when connected to the trunk.
2. We can't stand vibrant and fruitful by ourselves but only if we stand close to Christ.
3. How do we stand close?
   — Receive and share God's love — prayer, worship, sacraments (v. 9).
   — Keep his commandments (v. 10).

Sermon Title: An Old-Fashioned Word For A New Day

Sermon Angle: The word "abide" seems as old-fashioned to our ears as thee or thou, though it is sometimes employed in legal affairs. Not only does this word sound old but its meaning seems old-fashioned to millions of moderns. Abide means to live, to stay, remain, continue, be faithful ... Well, you get the drift. We're not into abiding these days. We're into rising to the top, we're into going places. The concept of abiding seems boring to modern ears. Yet how many hearts could have remained unbroken, how many marriages could have been saved and how many people could have been kept from spiritual shipwreck if only there had been more abiding? Abiding in Christ is the necessary prerequisite for all other kinds of abiding. Abide: We need this old-fashioned word for this new day.

Outline:
1. Abide is an old-fashioned word.
2. Even the meaning of the word seems old-fashioned. (Explain.)
3. Yet countless lives have been injured by not abiding.
4. Abiding means to make Christ and his life our abode and to be faithful to our commitments.

Sermon Title: Understanding The Branch Church

Sermon Angle: Using the vine analogy, the church has three kinds of branches among its members. There are the branches that bear plentiful fruit of the Spirit (v. 8). These are ready for harvesting. There are the branches that bear a little fruit. They require severe pruning (v. 2). Finally, there are those branches that are dead; these produce no fruit at all because they have shriveled from the vine (v. 2). These need to be severed from the trunk and burned as useless (v. 6). However, it remains sometimes difficult to distinguish these last two types. It is best first to attempt to bring all branches to fruitfulness through pruning (cleansing) and cultivation. A fourth type of branch remains; these are supporting branches. They don't appear to possess much fruit themselves but they support those branches that are more productive in fruiting. These branches need to be nourished and appreciated for their vital function.

Outline:
1. List the four different kinds of branches.
2. Look at worship stats, giving, and involvement to see how many of your congregants fall into the respective categories.
   — What kind of branch church are you?
   — What kind of a branch are you in your church?
3. How can we move, as a congregation, to greater fruitfulness?

Easter 6

Revised Common	Acts 10:44-48	1 John 5:1-6	John 15:9-17
Roman Catholic	Acts 10:25-26, 34-35, 44-48	1 John 4:7-10	John 15:9-17
Episcopal	Acts 11:19-30	1 John 4:7-21	John 15:9-17

Theme For The Day: God calls his own and chooses those who are to live as his dear friends, regardless of our human categories and distinctions.

BRIEF COMMENTARY ON THE LESSONS

Lesson 1: Acts 10:44-48 (C); Acts 10:25-26, 34-35, 44-48 (RC)

The pericope for the Revised Common Lectionary features the outcome of Peter's encounter with Cornelius, the Roman centurion. As Peter was explaining the gospel, the Holy Spirit came down on all the believers, including, for the first time, Gentiles. Since God had favored the Gentiles with the Holy Spirit, Peter's party could not refuse them water baptism in the name of Jesus. This marks the beginning of the universalizing of the church, transforming it from a sectarian to a truly catholic religion. The Roman Catholic lectionary also includes the greeting of Peter and Cornelius (vv. 24-25) and the beginning of Peter's sermon (vv. 34-35), so as to tie the story together.

Lesson 1: Acts 11:19-30 (E)

Lesson 2: 1 John 5:1-6 (C)

Everyone who trusts in Jesus as the Christ is born of God, loves God, keeps his commandments, and conquers the world through faith.

Lesson 2: 1 John 4:7-10 (RC); 1 John 4:7-21 (E)

See second lesson for Easter 5.

Gospel: John 15:9-17 (C, RC, E)

This continues the vine and branches discourse from last week's gospel. Knowing that the end of his earthly life was approaching, Jesus instructs his disciples to abide in his love, to show forth the same kind of love as that shared between the Father and the Son. Our love is shown by keeping Christ's commandments; those who do so are not merely servants but friends. We are friends because Christ has revealed his heart to us through Christ (v. 15). Our salvation comes as a gift of God; it is not a simply a matter of our own choice (v. 16). Christ chose us to bear fruit that does not spoil.

Psalm Of The Day
Psalm 98 (C) — "Make a joyful noise to the Lord, all the earth" (v. 4).
Psalm 33 (E)
Psalm 97 (RC)

Prayer Of The Day

Merciful Lord and Savior, your beloved disciple has told us that we may regard you not only as our God but our friend. You have opened that relationship in the complete giving of yourself. Help us not to betray your love but share it with others. In Jesus' name. Amen.

THEOLOGICAL REFLECTION ON THE LESSONS

Lesson 1: Acts 10:44-48

Confirmation. While Peter was preaching, the Holy Spirit descended on all the congregation, both Jew and Gentile. The Holy Spirit accompanied and confirmed the word that Peter spoke. When the Word is truly proclaimed, the Spirit always is powerfully present. This remains true whether the Word comes as a sermon or in the form of a sacrament.

God broke loose. The Jewish believers were amazed that the Spirit had been bestowed on the Gentiles (v. 45). They thought they would keep God confined within their Jewish heritage. Well, God fooled them. He broke loose! God shows no partiality; he is Lord of all who fear him (vv. 34-35). God will never remain confined in our narrow concepts of ethnicity, sexuality, or theology. Just when you think you have him cornered, he breaks loose.

Baptism of water and the Spirit. Traditional Roman Catholic and mainline Protestant theology identifies baptism as the main entrance for the Holy Spirit into our lives. This account shows us that the Spirit comes powerfully present wherever the word is proclaimed. The Spirit can and does work in the lives of the unbaptized. On the other side of the coin, many times one can discern very little sense of the Spirit's presence in the lives of those who are baptized, because they have cut themselves off from the word. The Spirit remains free to go where he wills. My intent is not to disparage baptism (God forbid!) but to keep us open to the Spirit's visitation.

Lesson 2: 1 John 5:1-6

Who does God claim as his child? Sometimes we refer to all humans as children of God. This is true in a biological sense; God made us all. However, biology does not define the child of God, rather spirituality. John stipulates that only those who are born of God spiritually, who believe that Jesus is the Son of God (v. 1), are truly his children.

If you love the parent, love the child (v. 1). John maintains that if you love God (the Parent of us all), you must love his children (those who are born anew in Christ). You can't love God without loving every other Christian. I also believe that God calls us to love every human, Christian or not, but that goes beyond the scope of this passage. However, if all Christians really loved one another, everybody would want to become a Christian.

In this sign conquer (vv. 4-5). Constantine, before his decisive battle that made him supreme emperor of the Roman Empire, reportedly saw a cross in the sky and heard the words: "In this sign conquer." I don't know how accurate this story might be but I do know that millions have conquered sin and death in the name of the crucified and risen Savior. Faith in the Christ of the cross is the sign, according to John, by which we can and will conquer the world.

Gospel: John 15:9-17

What kind of love (v. 9). Jesus claims that his love for us is the same kind of love that the Father showered on him. Yet what kind of love was it? The Father's love didn't keep Jesus from suffering, from feeling abandoned, and from dying a shameful death on the cross. The love of God does not shelter us from pain, sorrow, or death. Rather God shows his love by sustaining us with his presence to the bitter end, when he raises us up to newness of life.

Just do it! (v. 12). Jesus said, "This is my commandment, that you love one another as I have loved you." Wow! What an order! How can we love others with the kind of sacrificial love with which Jesus loved the world? He was the "Man for others." We're still basically living for ourselves. Jesus is telling us through John's gospel to "just do it!" Don't wait around for a warm fuzzy feeling, don't tarry 'til your neighbor shapes up. Just do it! Love is not an emotion. Rather love is that which we do after we say yes to God. One might reason, I can't do it! I can't love that person or that group of people; I'm too weak! However, we find that when we attempt to "just do it" God gives us the strength to keep on doing it.

Friends of the king (v. 15). In the courts of the Roman emperors and the eastern kings there was a category of very special people called "the friends of the king." They came into the king's bedchamber at the beginning of the day and were generally favored with unhampered access to the royal presence. The king would share the affairs of state with them even before he did so with his governing officials. Jesus offers all who are his disciples that title of "friends of the king." What a privilege! No more viewing God through a telescope; for the friends of the king it's strictly up close and personal.

Chosen (v. 16). This word "chosen" speaks of God's greatness and God's grace. First of all, God's greatness and sovereignty. Jesus said, "You did not choose me but I chose you." God rules and chooses who does what; he bars or grants access with the whisk of his scepter. God initiates and we respond one way or another. The word "chosen" also speaks to God's grace. He has chosen what is lowly, weak, and sinful, namely us, to be his own. We do not deserve or earn God's favor, initially shown in baptism, we merely say yes or no. We obey his commands or go our own way. Yet how sweet it is to be chosen, to be loved and valued highly by the Lord of all!

SERMON APPROACHES WITH ILLUSTRATIONS

Lesson 1: Acts 10:44-48

Sermon Title: The Sacrament Of The Word

Sermon Angle: Protestants have been accused of making preaching a sacrament. Preaching the word of the Lord does not meet the usual criteria for a sacrament because there is no outward physical element or sign (water, bread, wine) that is connected with it. However, words are sort of sacramental in that they convey the sacred to us; words are carriers of the Spirit. The text says that "the Spirit fell on all those who heard the word" (v. 44).

Sermon Title: Jailbreak!

Sermon Angle: The Spirit of God keeps breaking loose from our man-made prisons. We try to imprison the Spirit in our limited understandings, our thoughts, and our traditions. The Jewish people tried to confine God to their experience and so they weren't open to the Word made flesh. The disciples of Jesus attempted to confine Jesus to their perception of what a Messiah should be. In this lection the Jews that accompanied Peter were "amazed" that the Spirit was bestowed "even on the Gentiles" (v. 45). They thought that their race had a lock on the gospel. The Spirit of God will never be confined by the bars we attempt to place about it.

Outline:
1. The scriptures tell the story of God's jailbreak. We attempt to imprison God's Spirit in our limited perceptions, ideas, or rituals.
2. The command against graven images was to prevent man from limiting God to one form.
3. God broke out of the Jewish understanding of being exclusively chosen as God's people. At first the gospel was preached only to Jews.
4. In our text the Spirit had broken loose of the notion that Gentiles could not be baptized or receive the Spirit (v. 45).
5. Let God break you loose from concepts that limit or hinder God's Spirit.

Lesson 2: 1 John 5:1-6

Sermon Title: How To Come Out On Top

Sermon Angle: Americans are into winning. We pay our star athletes fabulous amounts of money. We reward our top CEOs with six- or seven-figure salaries, plus a host of other perks. We try beating out the other guy at the office for the promotion. Unfortunately, we even play power games in our marriage and family life. Our lection tells us how to conquer the world. How do you come out on top? Have faith in the one who conquered sin and death (v. 5). This does not mean that we conquer as the world defines the term. No, we conquer by being born of God (v. 4) and obeying his commands (v. 3).

Outline:
1. Everybody loves a winner.
2. Define the difference in the concept of winning between the world and our faith.
3. You are a winner if you
   — are born of God.
   — have faith in Christ.
   — obey God and love others.

Sermon Title: Christ's Commands Are No Burden

Sermon Angle: John reports that Christ's commands are not burdensome (v. 3). These thoughts echo the words of Jesus in Matthew, "For my yoke is easy and my burden is light" (Matthew 11:30). It's never burdensome to do something from your heart, to do an act of kindness for those you love. Legalism makes God's commands a burden because they are performed out of guilt or fear. When we are born of God, divine love fills our hearts, causing us to want to do what we ought to do.

Outline:
1. Have you ever experienced life as a burden? (Give examples.)
2. Many people find religion as a burden — they are motivated by legalism and guilt.
3. Christ's commands are not burdensome for those who live in love (v. 3).
   — They naturally spring from a reborn heart.
   — They are motivated by grace and love (fruits of the Spirit).
4. Let the Spirit lift your burdens and make you a blessing.

Gospel: John 15:9-17

Sermon Title: The Gift Goes On

Sermon Angle: Jesus says: "As the Father has loved me, so I have loved you." The Father gifted the Son with his perfect love and the Son has gifted the world with his self-giving love. Those who are born of the Spirit pass this gift along to others and the gift goes on and on and on.

Outline:
1. Christ gifted us with the love he received from his Father (v. 9).
2. We learn to love from being loved.
3. The love we receive is a gift.
4. The gift cannot be hoarded — pass it on.

Sermon Title: A Friend For All Seasons

Sermon Angle: Alan Alda's movie, *The Four Seasons*, is a photo album of friendship through the seasons of life. Three couples are very close but then one of the marriages splits up, which severely changes the dynamic of friendship. The man marries a younger woman who is resented by the others. In the end, a crisis reconciles them. During the crisis, one of the friends makes a comment to the effect: "I know one thing. I need friends." We all need friends. Yet, I fear that most of us are enjoying fewer friendships. Our mobility, our style of life, our mistrust of others hinders close friendship ties. As Christians, no matter what happens to us in life, we all have at least one friend. Jesus makes the unbelievable statement: "I do not call you servants any longer ... but I have called you friends" (v. 15). Friends share what's on their heart. Jesus has opened his heart to us. "I have made known to you everything I have heard from my Father" (v. 15).

Outline:
1. Talk about loneliness and the need for friends.
2. Suggest that we make friends by being a friend.
3. What is a friend?
   — Someone who shares what's on his heart.
   — Someone who loves us unconditionally.
4. Assert that Jesus is our friend because has given his life for us (v. 13).
5. Trust him with your life.

* * * * *

Elie Wiesel reflected on his childhood in an article in *Parade* magazine (August 27, 1995). He recalled the friends who were swallowed by the Nazi monster, which led him to philosophize on friendship. The Talmud puts it tersely: "friendship or death." Without friends, life is sterile and meaningless. In a person's life friendship rates ever higher than love. Love may lead a person to kill, but friendship never. Cain killed his brother Abel because he was only his brother and not also his friend. We remember David as a great king not because of his conquests but because of his great friendship with Jonathan.

After the Wiesel family had been herded into a ghetto, their Christian housekeeper, Maria, a dear friend of the family, managed to get in so she might implore them to follow her to safety in her country cabin. They hadn't yet comprehended the gruesomeness of their fate and so they refused her gracious offer. The bonds of community kept them together with their neighbors. Elie reflects that if only more Christians had acted like Maria, there would have been fewer crowded trains straining to the death camps. If only priests and pastors had raised their voices; if only the Vatican had spoken out, the enemy's hands would not have been so free. Alas, their only concern was for themselves. Oh, how we have all failed the Christ who laid down his life for his friends!

*   *   *   *   *

Sermon Title: You Are Chosen

Sermon Angle: When I was a child playing sandlot baseball, we would pick two captains who would then take turns choosing players for their respective teams. You always prayed that you would not be one of the last ones picked. We all want to be chosen and valued. Early in my ministry I met a man who was smarting from never having been chosen for the church council. Our baptism into Christ tells us that we are chosen. Jesus asserts: "You did not choose me but I chose you" (v. 16).

Outline:
1. Recall a memory of when you were chosen for something great or a nightmare of when you were not chosen.
2. Christ tells us that we have been chosen. (Relate to baptism.)
3. We have been chosen not for privilege but for mission. (Bear fruit.)

Sermon Title: How To Stay Standing Through Christ's Love

Sermon Angle: The world tries to knock us for a loop, but if we abide in Christ's love (v. 10) we will be able to stand tall for time and eternity. Christ wants our lives to produce fruit that lasts (endures, stands) (v. 17). We can only stay standing in relationship to the community of grace and love.

Outline:
1. Everything dies that is not born in love. (Example: communism.)
2. We, too, will die, but what we have formed through Christ's love will remain.
3. When we are in danger of falling, Christ, through the community of love (the church) keeps us standing up (we are the branches, Christ the vine).

The Ascension Of Our Lord

Revised Common	Acts 1:1-11	Ephesians 1:15-23	Luke 24:44-53
Roman Catholic	Acts 1:1-11	Ephesians 1:17-23	Mark 16:15-20
Episcopal	Acts 1:1-11	Ephesians 1:15-23	Luke 24:49-53 or
			Mark 16:9-15, 19-20

Theme For The Day: The crucified and risen Jesus has ascended to the Father. His disciples are to wait for empowerment from the promised Holy Spirit.

BRIEF COMMENTARY ON THE LESSONS

Lesson 1: Acts 1:1-11 (C, RC, E)

The gospel of Luke and the book of Acts are the only two books in the Bible addressed to an individual (Theophilus). In this introduction, Luke informs Theophilus that he is taking up where his gospel ended. The gospel of Luke concludes with the witness to the resurrected Christ and Acts begins by putting to a close this forty-day string of appearances. The disciples are still anticipating a kind of earthly reign (v. 6) but Jesus tells them not to be concerned with God's chronology but to wait for the baptism of the Holy Spirit, which would empower them for witness to the world. Having said this, he rose out of their sight. The ascension, largely ignored by most Christians, provides a necessary transition from Jesus of Nazareth to Christ, the victorious Lord of all. Without the ascension, the risen Christ would be left earthbound.

Lesson 2: Ephesians 1:15-23 (C, E); Ephesians 1:17-23 (RC)

This poetical passage sings the praises of the "Father of glory" for the riches of his grace and power, which are made known to those of us who believe in his Son. Christ has received the scepter of divine authority and power over all the universe, because God has put all things under his feet. Christ assumes his rule, not just for his benefit, but for the sake of his body, the church (v. 22).

Gospel: Luke 24:44-53 (C); Luke 24:49-53 (E)

The risen Christ interprets to his disciples how his ministry, especially his death and resurrection, is a fulfillment of the scriptures. Christ proposes that forgiveness of sins be offered to all nations, beginning in Jerusalem. He reminds them that they are witnesses of all these things but that they should wait until they have received the promised Spirit from on high. Christ led his disciples to Bethany and while he lifted his hands in blessing, he ascended to the Father. The disciples responded to these events with unsurpassed joy and praise, as they worshiped continually in the temple.

Gospel: Mark 16:15-20 (RC)

The original gospel of Mark ends with verse 8, no resurrection appearances or ascension. Our text, therefore, is not part of the original ending to Mark but it is part of the traditional conclusion. In these verses, Jesus commissions his disciples to preach the gospel to the whole creation. Those who believed and were baptized would be saved. The preaching of the gospel would be accompanied with certain signs — casting out demons, speaking in other tongues, and so forth.

Psalm Of The Day
    Psalm 47 (C, E, RC) — "God has gone up with a shout ..." (v. 4).

Prayer Of The Day
    Exalted Lord, as we have celebrated your victory over sin and death, so we lift up our praises to you as the Lord of all, the sovereign of all time and eternity. Our hearts are at peace because the one who has been raised as ruler of all creation was once lifted up on a cross. In the name of Jesus we pray. Amen.

THEOLOGICAL REFLECTION ON THE LESSONS

Lesson 1: Acts 1:1-11
    Forty-day feast follows forty-day fast (v. 3). Luke states that Jesus appeared to his followers during a forty-day period, providing "many convincing proofs" that he was alive. Thus, we have a forty-day Easter season. A forty-day feast follows a forty-day fast, representing the forty days when Jesus was tempted by Satan. For the Christian, times of abstention and loss give way to feasting, fullness, and celebration.

    Let's not get ahead of God. Jesus told his disciples to wait in Jerusalem until they were empowered by the Holy Spirit (v. 4). Had they not been warned to wait, they might have shoved out of port on their mission without any wind for their sails. There remains a very real danger of getting ahead of God and doing more damage than good. The Spirit of God provides both the direction for ministry and the power. To act without the Spirit's presence provides a sure prescription for failure and frustration.

    Going international (v. 8). Even after the resurrection, the disciples were still thinking in terms of a Jewish state for the kingdom of God (v. 6). God had a better idea. God was transforming them from a Jewish sect to an international religion, moving from Jerusalem to Judea, the surrounding region, through Samaria, home of the partly Jewish Samaritans, and into the farthest reaches of the Gentile world. Why isn't Galilee mentioned? Some have suggested that Galilee was already Christian. The resurrected Christ was reforming the church from the particular to the universal, from the national to the international.

    They had a martyr complex (v. 8). The risen Christ informed his followers that they were going to be his "witnesses." The Greek behind this translation means both witness and martyr. So when I say that they had a martyr complex, I don't mean to say that they possessed some macabre desire to die for their faith but that they were highly motivated to witness to their living Lord. If that should mean death, they would gladly pay the price. Unfortunately, a large segment of the church has lost its martyr complex.

Lesson 2: Ephesians 1:15-23
    Power transmission (vv. 19-20). God's power, the energy of the Holy Spirit, was always there. That power was felt at various times, as the Old Testament reveals, but only a few select people were transmission lines for God's power. Also, most of the people did not know how to make God's power work for them. Luke asserts that God "put that power to work in Christ,"

when God raised him from the dead. The Lord finally put that power to work for all believers at Pentecost. The risen Christ and his living Spirit are the transmission lines to make God's power work for each of us. Through faith, we plug into that power.

Power for us (v. 19). This passage extols God's power and glory to the utmost but this is not purposeless power, aimed to make our knees buckle in dread. No, Paul characterizes this as "power for us who believe." God graciously employs his power for our benefit; God's power is *for us.*

Gospel: Luke 24:44-53

Spiritual power and worldly power. There are two basic types of power — spiritual power and earthly power. Spiritual power is what Jesus referred to when he told his disciples to wait in Jerusalem until they were clothed with power from on high (v. 49). Spiritual power comes as a gift of God; the closer we are to God, the more committed our lives, the more spiritual power God bestows. Worldly power, in contrast, comes to those who have the greatest strength and the strongest will to power. Such power is seized from others, imposed through violence, threats, and intimidation. Those who crave worldly power seek it to satisfy their own ends but the person who has spiritual power aims to serve the neighbor. Spiritual power does not seek to affect change by external force but by inspiring people to inward renewal. Worldly power addicts believe that there is only so much power to go around and so they seek to hoard it; those who possess spiritual power know that the more God's power is shared, the more it increases. We find both kinds of power being exercised in the church but when the Spirit of God gains full reign, spiritual power predominates.

Benediction (v. 50). As Jesus was blessing his loved ones, his disciples, he was lifted out of their sight. The last vision the disciples had of their Lord was of him blessing them. That image would linger indelibly in their mind. That's why we end our worship services with a blessing. The Christ ascended into heaven so that he might grant his blessing to all his people, of every nation, race, and tribe, down through the ages.

Blessed to be a blessing. Luke relates the reaction of the disciples after Jesus ascended to heaven. They worshiped him and were continually in the temple blessing God (vv. 52-53). When a person is blessed of God, that same person becomes a blessing to God and to others.

SERMON APPROACHES WITH ILLUSTRATIONS

Lesson 1: Acts 1:1-11

Sermon Title: A Time For Waiting And A Time For Working

Sermon Angle: Jesus commanded his disciples to wait in Jerusalem until they had received the promise of the Father (v. 4), the Holy Spirit. In life, there is a time of waiting and a time for working. This principle proves especially relevant for the spiritual life. We must have times of recreation through rest, prayer, worship, and meditation to permit our bodies to catch up with our soul and to give opportunity for the Spirit to invade our existence with power. Once we've waited for God's Spirit to fill us, we are ready to go to work with vision and energy.

Outline:
1. The disciples were told to wait for God's promised visitation (v. 4).
2. The Christian life alternates between times of waiting and times of working.
   — If we work without waiting for the Lord, we will work aimlessly and without power.
   — Waiting allows God's Spirit to catch up with our body.

Sermon Title: Where Is Jesus Going?

Sermon Angle: The disciples were obviously excited to see their Lord again after they thought they had lost him forever. Understandably, they wondered concerning the significance of his resurrection. Thus, they asked: "Lord, will you at this time restore the kingdom to Israel?" (v. 6). They were thinking that Christ's reappearance meant that things were going to be as they were. Jesus didn't answer them directly. Rather, he pointed them to the future, when God would do something new in their midst. Then, as Jesus rose up from the earth and receded into the clouds, two angels appeared and asked them why they were gazing into heaven, because Jesus was going to return to the earth some day (v. 11). Though this passage does point to the *parousia* at the end of history, it remains a fact of faith that Jesus did return on Pentecost. This suggests that Jesus cannot now be experienced in some otherworldly frame, but that he can be perceived in our midst here on earth. Consequently, Jesus directs us to not build our house of faith in the past, because God is moving ahead to a new destination. Secondly, the Lord does not want us to scan the heavens for his presence but look for him in the lowly and the earthly. Where is God going? He's going ahead but he has not left his people behind.

Outline:
1. Where does the risen Christ lead us?
2. He will not lead us back to where we were (restore the kingdom) (vv. 6-8).
3. He directs us away from the speculation about the otherworldly. (Why do you stand looking up to heaven?)
4. He leads us to encounter him through his Holy Spirit and the gospel.

Lesson 2: Ephesians 1:15-23

Sermon Title: The Seal Of The Son

Sermon Angle: Movies such as *The Omen* make much of the mark of the beast, designating the anti-Christ. This passage speaks of the seal of the Son, which is the Holy Spirit (v. 13). The Spirit is compared to earnest money, the pledge of our inheritance of the kingdom. We were marked with that seal in our baptism.

Sermon Title: Everything You Wanted To Know About God's Power

Sermon Angle: Verses 19-22 speak eloquently of God's power. While the title of this sermon is misleading, our text does inform us concerning God's power. In these verses, no less than four different Greek words are translated by the word "power." The chief word for power, which summarizes the meaning of the other three words, is *dynamis*, translated "I am able." This passage extols a God who is able and a God who enables his own to win the victory of life.

Outline:
1. Many sermons deal with the love of God but few consider the power of God.
2. I can't tell you everything you want to know about the subject but our text informs our thinking.
3. The power of God is power for us — guided by grace and love (v. 19).
4. The power of God is power in Christ (v. 20) who is risen, ascended, and possesses all authority.
5. The resurrection and ascension reveal a dynamite God. (He is able — explain the meaning of the word *dynamis*.)
   — God was able to raise Jesus from the dead and lift him to heaven.
   — God is able to raise us to newness of life.

218

Gospel: Luke 24:44-53

Sermon Title: Final Blessing

Sermon Angle: Luke relates a precious aspect of the ascension story lacking in his account in Acts 1; he states that Jesus was blessing his disciples as he was ascending into heaven. It was his final blessing. How important that was. Most of them had failed their Lord miserably. They had failed to understand his teachings. When the heat was turned up, they melted down. The blessing by Christ told them that they were loved and forgiven. That blessing they would carry with them through life; that blessing would empower them. Like those first disciples, we need Christ's blessing; we must know that, in spite of our spiritual cowardice and weakness, he still loves us. In a like manner, children desperately crave the blessing of their mother and father. Children need this final blessing before their parents make their final exit.

Outline:

1. The last image of Christ carried by his disciples was of his arms extended in blessing of them.
   — This blessing showed that he loved, forgave, and approved of them.
2. Christ's blessing empowered them to turn the world upside down.
3. Many of us lead a tortured existence because we have not received the blessing we have sought from an important person in our life. (Give example.)
4. Give your blessing to those who look up to you. (You never know when it might be your final blessing.)
5. We have been blessed by the Lord of all existence that we might bless God (v. 53) and others.

*   *   *   *   *

Jessica Savitch was the first woman to attain the status of a national news anchor. The story of her tortured life was revealed in the made-for-television movie, *Almost Golden*. Jessica was a gregarious little girl who adored her father, who had always affirmed her. She basked in the light of his blessing until kidney disease took her father from her. From this loss, she never fully recovered. A high school sweetheart introduced her to broadcasting and eventually she co-hosted a musical show for teens; this brought her into the spotlight, where she received the recognition she so desperately sought. She set her goal to become a national news anchorwoman by the age of thirty, a goal in which she eminently succeeded. Yet, the faster she ran, the more she achieved, the more tortured and insecure her life became. Jessica had several failed relationships with men. She was beaten by her lover and one of her husbands committed suicide. She got hooked on booze and cocaine. Her career collapsed suddenly, like a house made of playing cards, when she did her newscast stoned and was fired. Jessica finally surmounted her drug problem and seemed to be getting back on track when the car she was riding in overturned into a Pennsylvania canal on a dark and rainy night.

Jessica Savitch exemplifies the thousands who are driven by the profound need to receive a blessing from their father, mother, or other significant person in their life. No matter how high she soared, it was never high enough. How tragic and driven life can be when we fail to realize the blessing of our Father in heaven. That blessing calms our anxious hearts with the assurance that we are accepted just as we are.

*   *   *   *   *

Sermon Title: Clothing For The Upwardly Mobile

Sermon Angle: Newspaper columnists and advertisers seek to inform the upwardly mobile how they might dress-up, in order to rise above the ordinary into the rare atmosphere of the super-achievers. Appearances and clothing do seem to play a significant part in attaining success in this world. Clothing is important for spiritual upward mobility, too. Jesus told his followers to wait in Jerusalem until he had clothed them with power from on high (v. 49); such clothing would enable them to ascend to the highest heavens, as well as rising above things here on earth. Without the Spirit of God, we are naked and powerless. The Holy Spirit remains the only clothing needed by the spiritually upward mobile.

Outline:
1. We are told that clothing makes the man or the woman.
2. Our clothing does express who we are or would like to become.
3. Jesus told his disciples to wait until they were clothed with his Spirit of power.
4. This clothing empowers us to rise above the ordinary and ascend into the very presence of God.

* * * * *

You will recall that every time Clark Kent transformed himself into Superman, he would go into a telephone booth and strip off his ordinary business suit, revealing his official Superman costume. He could only stop locomotives and lift skyscrapers when he was properly clothed in the outfit that revealed his true identity. As Christians, we can do no mighty deed unless we are properly clothed with the Spirit of God, which discloses our true spiritual selves and supplies the power to do wondrous things.

Easter 7

Revised Common	Acts 1:15-17, 21-26	1 John 5:9-13	John 17:6-19
Roman Catholic	Acts 1:15-17, 20-26	1 John 4:11-16	John 17:11-19
Episcopal	Acts 1:15-26	1 John 5:9-15	John 17:11b-19

Theme For The Day: The church organizes for mission and Christ prays that the ways of the world will not subvert that mission but that the Father would keep them in his grace.

BRIEF COMMENTARY ON THE LESSONS

Lesson 1: Acts 1:15-17, 21-26 (C); Acts 1:15-17, 20-26 (RC); Acts 1:15-26 (E)

The post-resurrection church begins very small, some 120 souls. Once again, Peter takes the lead in filling the slot left by the bloody death of Judas. They selected two men who met the criteria. They had witnessed the resurrected Jesus and they were in the company of Jesus' disciples since the baptism of John. They cast lots, a common Jewish practice, especially as it relates to the service schedule for the priests. Stones with the individual's name were placed into a jar. The one that fell out was held to be the chosen of God. Matthias won the draw and is never again heard from. Is it possible that the church acted prematurely, rather than waiting for the guidance of the Holy Spirit? Some maintain that the apostle Paul was the one that God picked to fill the vacancy left by Judas. It is interesting to note that Judas, from the town near Hebron called Kerioth and the only disciple not to hail from Galilee, turned out to be the betrayer.

Lesson 2: 1 John 5:9-13 (C); 1 John 5:9-15 (E)

John reasons that if we receive the testimony of men about the veracity of something, the testimony of God should be all the more readily received. (Note the legal language here.) God testifies to his Son as the Savior of the world. The Father testified to Jesus through his mighty works, his teachings, at his baptism, at the transfiguration, and especially the resurrection. Those who believe God have this testimony in their heart and those who do not believe are, in reality, calling God a liar (v. 10). The way to God is very narrow. Only those who trust in God's Son have life eternal. John's purpose for writing is to elicit faith and the assurance that we belong to God (v. 13) and that God will hear our prayers (v. 14).

Lesson 2: 1 John 4:11-16 (RC)

See second lesson for Easter 5.

Gospel: John 17:6-19 (C); John 17:11-19 (RC); John 17:11b-19 (E)

In Jesus' high priestly prayer, he prays that the Father would guard his disciples and preserve them from Satan. Jesus thanks the Father that he has kept all his disciples, except Judas, the son of perdition. Perdition suggests eternal lostness, hopelessness, and an unrepentant spirit. Jesus contrasts his disciples, who have accepted the truth, to the world, which chooses to remain in spiritual darkness. John's theology does not view human existence in shades of color but in black and white. The disciples are not of the world but are in the world. The term world does not indicate geography but rather the sinful rebellion to which humans have fallen. Jesus sends his disciples into the world with the truth of the gospel.

Psalm Of The Day
Psalm 1 (C) — "The Lord watches over the way of the righteous..." (v. 6a).
Psalm 68:1-20 (E)
Psalm 102 (RC)

Prayer Of The Day

Lord of the church, you have set us in a sinful world with the light of your gospel. Keep us close to you so that our witness might give light and hope to those who are lost and groping for direction. In the powerful name of Jesus. Amen.

THEOLOGICAL REFLECTION ON THE LESSONS

Lesson 1: Acts 1:15-17, 21-26

The difference between sorrow and repentance. The gospels and the book of Acts agree that Judas was sorrowful after he saw the outcome of his treachery. He probably didn't intend that Jesus would die. He may have been trying, in his perverted way, to force the hand of Jesus. At any rate, he hated himself for what he had done and killed himself in a fit of despair. Judas had sorrow, but not godly sorrow that leads to repentance. Repentance looks to God in the hope that God will forgive and that the future can be different than the past. Godless sorrow sucks a person into the black hole of despair and death.

Special election. Judas violently vacated his office of apostle after he betrayed his Lord. When the church was born, after the resurrection, Peter decided that it was time for a special election. The qualifications were established; the candidate would have to be a witness of the resurrection and a long-time follower of the Master (vv. 21-22). After the nominating committee had secured qualified candidates, the church prayed earnestly for God to reveal his will. Then they cast their ballots (lots) and Matthias was chosen. That was the church's first special election. When we view the matter from another perspective, all of Christ's followers have won special election, although not through our own efforts. Listen to Peter describe our election: "But you are a chosen race, a royal priesthood, a holy nation, God's own people, in order that you may proclaim the mighty acts of him who called you out of darkness into his marvelous light" (1 Peter 2:9).

Looking for someone who knows Jesus. The qualifications for the candidate that would fill Judas' vacancy, described above, boil down to this: They were looking for someone who knew Jesus firsthand. The office of apostle required someone who had lived through Jesus' triumphs and tragedies, someone who knew the meaning of loyalty and faithfulness. They were looking for someone who had died and been raised to newness of life with Christ. These requirements are still the key ones today for those who would hold office in Christ's church.

Lesson 2: 1 John 5:9-13

God on the witness stand (vv. 9-11). The O. J. Simpson trial brought before the world the importance of having credible witnesses. The officer who investigated the crime scene, Mark Fuhrman, originally testified that he had not used the "N" word during a specific time period. Later, tapes of him using the word with other racist remarks cast a thick shadow on his credibility as a witness. John asserts that God's testimony remains steadfast and sure, much more reliable than that of humans. God testifies that he has given us eternal life through Jesus, his Son.

Assurance (v. 13). John writes to a church immersed in a culture that put forth many different claims to eternal truth. John writes to steady the hearts of the believers with the assurance that "you may know that you have eternal life." How can a person know he has eternal life? Very simply. "Whoever has the Son has life ..." (v. 12). To have indicates possession. To have the Son is more than intellectual assent to his identity as God's Son and Savior of the world. To have the Son means to take hold of him experientially through faith, to cling tenaciously to him in bad times and good, in times of testing and times of triumph.

Thank God for answering your prayers (vv. 14-15). John boldly declares that if we ask anything that accords with God's will, he has already heard us and granted our petition. We may not have received yet that which was asked for but we can have the confidence that it's in the bag. God is merely processing our request, waiting to send it at the proper time. Therefore, we should thank God for answering our prayers even before we take delivery of the item requested. There's only one condition — our prayers must be in sync with God's will.

Gospel: John 17:6-19

Name recognition. When a candidate seeks office, he or she aims to gain widespread name recognition. That's how great military leaders and movie actors have attained eminent office. Without name recognition you're dead in the water whether you seek an office or desire to sell a product. This pericope begins with Jesus' assertion that he has made God's name known (v. 6). The biblical concept of revealing God's name goes far beyond our modern-day concept of name recognition. To make God's name known equates to making God's real character, purpose, and person known. Jesus was not able to make God's name known to everybody but only to those who would accept the truth. In contrast, the modern-day business of gaining name recognition may actually seek to conceal the real character and intention of the person behind the name. Publicity experts seek to widely market an image rather than the real person behind the name.

Pass the word (v. 8). Jesus claims the he has passed on to his disciples the message that the Father first gave him. His good news of grace and forgiveness was not his idea, it came from the Father. We in turn are given the mission of passing on to others what we have received from the Father through the Son.

Out of this world (v. 16). Those whom God has called to be his own are really out of this world. They live in the world but the world does not live in them. The ethic of Christ and his kingdom are opposed to the predominant value system of the world. The world puts forth self-expression and self-aggrandizement as its highest values, while those who belong to Christ seek to be servants of God's will. Christians must never forget that we live as a minority within the predominant worldview. Our vision for life comes from beyond this world. A major factor in the malaise that grips most so-called mainline churches relates to their having become too identified with the secular worldview.

Heaven-sent (v. 18). As the Father sent Jesus into the world with the message of salvation, so God sends us into the world. God doesn't want us to live in a religious ghetto, sealed off from the rest of the world. Nor does the Lord send us, like tourists, to a foreign country where we see the sights but don't mingle with the natives. We are heaven-sent into the world, not only to know the world but to make God's word known in the world.

SERMON APPROACHES WITH ILLUSTRATIONS

Lesson 1: Acts 1:15-17, 21-26

Sermon Title: Special Election

Sermon Angle: The apostolic office of Judas became vacant after his betrayal of his Lord and his self-imposed punishment. Peter called a special election but asked God to make his will known in the choosing (v. 24). We are not all chosen to be elected officials in the church but we are all called, by our election in baptism, to fulfill some special role as Christ's disciples. (See "Theological Reflection On The Lessons.")

Outline:
1. Judas' betrayal left a leadership gap.
2. Peter called a special election of qualified candidates.
3. Our church has leadership gaps.
   — Ask God for guidance to find those whom God has elected to these posts.
   — Consider: Are we fulfilling our role as Christ's elect?

Sermon Title: When You're Not The Number One Pick

Sermon Angle: Many folks in our society set their sights to be number one, the first chosen, and the best. Recall the Jessica Savitch story in the previous chapter. We take a keen interest in the identity of the number one pick for the National Football League or National Basketball Association. Judas was not the first one selected by Jesus but he was picked to be on the first team, the starting lineup; sadly, his dishonorable conduct disqualified him. Two men were chosen as candidates to fill the slot but only one of these men was chosen. The winner was number two for Judas' position and the loser was kicked to the number three position, or lower. If these men had big egos, they might have taken offense that they were not the number one pick. Apparently, that was not the case because we don't know anything much about either of them. They weren't as ambitious as Judas but they were apparently willing to serve wherever they were needed. They had taken Jesus' lesson to heart; his disciples were not to distinguish themselves through status but service.

Outline:
1. Give some examples of the drive to be the number one pick.
2. Judas sought position (treasurer) and power (the reason of his betrayal).
3. Seeking status and power can lead to death (spiritual and physical).
4. Matthias was second string — he wasn't a star but he was apparently an effective team player.
5. Fill the position God calls you to, with honor.

*   *   *   *   *

Cal Ripken Jr., the former shortstop for the Baltimore Orioles, broke Lou Gehrig's record by having played in 2,131 consecutive games as of September 6, 1995. He continued this streak and continues to hold the record of 2,632 consecutive games. In 1995, when he first broke the record, he took off his jersey and cap and presented it to his wife and two small children and a torrent of emotion gushed precipitously. He returned to the dugout but the crowd would not abate the revelry. A few of his teammates pushed him out of the dugout to parade around the periphery of the field — bowing, waving, acknowledging, and shaking hands with fans and coaches. Finally, Cal's energy was spent. He trotted into the dugout and refused to reemerge. Finally, reluctantly, the applause came to a conclusion after 22 minutes. What was all the hoopla about? Was he a baseball star of the caliber of Babe Ruth or Mickey Mantle? No, that was not it. He was good! Really good! But not that great. What was it then? Ripken was called to do a job and he carried out that call with tenacity, faithfulness, and don't forget joy! He always gave his all. That's more than you can say about the majority of big league baseball players. Cal Ripken Jr. showed what can happen when a person doesn't concern himself with being number one but lives life with gusto, fervor, and tenacity, faithful to his call. People come to recognize eventually that there is something stellar about that kind of life. Baseball became badly tarnished during that time period, but Cal Ripken Jr. helped restore some of its luster.

*   *   *   *   *

Lesson 2: 1 John 5:9-13

Sermon Title: Witness Within

Sermon Angle: John employs legal language when he speaks of the testimony or witness of God. He writes: "Those who believe in the Son of God have the testimony in their hearts" (v. 10). That testimony comes through the Bible but is confirmed to us by the witness within our hearts, the Holy Spirit.

Outline:
1. Knowing the truth depends on having faithful witnesses.
2. Jesus witnesses to the saving love of God.
3. God witnesses to Jesus, his Son, through the external word and the Holy Spirit.
4. The witness of the Word is confirmed by the witness within.

Sermon Title: Stand Up, Stand Up With Jesus!

Sermon Angle: One of the most vivid signs that death was sucking the life from my father occurred when his legs buckled beneath him as he was mounting the stairs. Eventually, he lay prostrate, then silent. Lying down symbolizes both sleep and death; maybe that's why we confuse the two. Life and vitality has us standing erect, tall and strong. As we travel through this world, Christ can keep us standing when we are dealt a gut-wrenching blow. Christ keeps us standing after we die as well, through the power of his resurrection. "God gave us eternal life, and this life is in his Son" (v. 11).

Outline:
1. Have you experienced life when you couldn't stand up anymore?
2. The forces of death knock us down but his Spirit within sustains us (v. 10).
3. Death steals our physical life but the risen Lord gives us life (vv. 11-12).
4. We stand up strong through faith in Christ and the power of the Spirit.

Gospel: John 17:6-19

Sermon Title: Our Marriage To God

Sermon Angle: In Jesus' high priestly prayer he asserts that he has given his followers God's name and made that name known. As God's baptized children we are given the name of God — Father, Son, and Spirit. To carry God's name is more than a label, it means to enter into the deepest of all relationships, earthly or celestial. Jesus claims to have made God's character and person known to us. The Spirit of God permeates his name. The closest counterpart, in the earthly plain of relationships, is marriage. In marriage, not only does the bride usually take on the groom's name but comes to know and love that which the name signifies. The groom likewise first comes to know the name of his beloved and then the person behind the name. Revealing our name signifies a process of unveiling and of making our deepest selves known. Marriage, as it was intended to be, presents us with an apt illustration of the believer's relationship with God.

Outline:
1. Marriage is a relationship of intimacy beginning with our names.
2. In the biblical sense, to disclose one's name was more than sharing a label; it meant to reveal one's character and person.
3. Christ has given us God's name — we come to know him personally.
4. Let us honor that name in all that we do.

Sermon Title: Great Is The Power Of His Name

Sermon Angle: Jesus prays that the Father will protect his disciples through the power of his name (v. 11). There is also power in the name of Jesus, when we come to know and serve the one represented by that name. The name of Jesus is not magic, like in some vampire movie, when the fiend is stopped by the mere sight of the cross. No, there is power when we enter into a personal relationship with the God we come to know in Jesus' name. When we lift up the name of Jesus in genuine prayer, praise, and thanksgiving, we are empowered for life and ministry.

Outline:
1. God's children carry his name. This implies a familial relationship.
2. Jesus prays that the Father would protect and keep those who know his name.
   — Protection does not mean sheltering from all adversity.
   — Rather, Jesus prays that God will keep his children in the true faith.
3. There is power in the name of Jesus.

The Pentecost Season

The Meaning Of The Name

The name "Pentecost" comes from the Greek *pentecoste* meaning fifty. Pentecost comes fifty days after the Festival of the Resurrection.

The Festival Of Pentecost

The historical event that led to the Festival of Pentecost is reported in the Acts of the Apostles, chapter 2, which records the descent of the Holy Spirit on the church in Jerusalem. All of the gospels record Jesus' promise to send the Spirit to empower, strengthen, and guide the believers. The gospel of John differs from the Luke-Acts account, however, by merging the appearance of the resurrected Christ with the sending forth of the Holy Spirit. For John the relationship of the resurrected Christ and the Holy Spirit is more personal and direct. "When he had said this, he breathed on them and said to them, 'Receive the Holy Spirit' " (John 20:22). The church year follows the Lukan model, where Christ's resurrection, ascension, and Pentecost are related yet separate. The bestowal of the Holy Spirit makes Pentecost one of the church's major festivals, together with Easter and Christmas. Without Pentecost and the gift of the Holy Spirit the church would never have been born. In the practice of the church, however, Pentecost doesn't even come close to being recognized by most Christians as a major happening, worthy of pulling out all the stops. The reason for this neglect is probably tied to the fact that the Holy Spirit has become a rather intangible concept rather than a living reality. This was certainly not the case in the early church; the name "Holy Spirit" occurs 92 times in the Bible, mainly in the New Testament. However, the book of Acts, which records the growth of the early church, contains forty references to the Holy Spirit, not even counting the times when the adjective Holy is dropped from the word "Spirit." Often the Holy Spirit is spoken of by Acts as the "Spirit of Jesus." All of these references to God's Spirit speak eloquently of the awareness in the early church of the Spirit's guidance and empowerment. Pentecost has been called the birthday of the church, although some Christian thinkers would take exception to that statement. They prefer to push the birthday of the church back to the calling of the disciples or the confession that Jesus is the Christ or the appearance of Christ to the post-crucifixion assembled believers. Some congregations have linked Pentecost to confirmation, praying that the Holy Spirit would fill and empower those who are affirming their baptism. I would not recommend this practice because it detracts from the opportunity of lifting up the importance of the Holy Spirit for the life of the church.

The Season Of Pentecost

Pentecost is both a festival and a season. Prior to the unified lectionary in 1970, most Protestants celebrated Pentecost only as a festival. They counted the Sundays in the second half of the church year after The Holy Trinity. Trinity has been traditionally celebrated the Sunday after Pentecost. The Roman lectionary dubs the Sundays after Pentecost as "Ordinary Time." I prefer to call the second half of the church year the Pentecost season, because the Pentecost event was so crucial for the life of the church. Nevertheless, the chapters will follow the designation of the Revised Common Lectionary by referring to the Sundays after Pentecost as "Proper," followed by the number. The emphasis of this season is growth in Christ through the power of the Holy Spirit. The first half of the church calendar, Advent through Easter, celebrates the pivotal events in the life of Christ. The completing half of the church year draws out the meaning of the life, death, and resurrection of Christ for the life of the believer and of the church.

Relationship Of The Christian Pentecost To The Jewish Pentecost

A link exists between the Jewish and Christian Pentecosts. The Hebrews had the Feast of Weeks (Exodus 34:22) seven weeks after Passover. This feast was originally an agricultural festival, which took on historical significance. The Jewish Pentecost came to celebrate the giving of the law through Moses, which formed them into a nation. Likewise, Pentecost celebrates the giving of the Holy Spirit, which constitutes the church as we know it. Great crowds of faithful Jews would come to Jerusalem from all over the world to celebrate this festival. That explains how Peter could preach to such a great crowd of people after the descent of the Holy Spirit, as told in Acts 2.

Colors And Symbols Of Pentecost

The color of Pentecost is red, symbolic of the Holy Spirit alighting as tongues of flame on the assembled believers in Jerusalem. The flames remind us that the Spirit brings heat, light, and passion into the Christian community. Green is the color of the Pentecost season, since this is the season of spiritual growth for those who are in Christ. Sometimes the flames are divided into seven separate flames to represent the sevenfold gifts of the Holy Spirit.

The dove is a key symbol of the Holy Spirit, which descended like a dove on Jesus at the time of his baptism.

Preaching In Pentecost

At this juncture the preacher has about half-a-year of proclamation. It might be helpful for the preacher to preview which books of the Bible are featured during this season of the church year.

Lesson 1. The majority of the texts feature the united monarchy period under King David; Samuel, David, and Solomon are key figures. The pericopes come from 1 and 2 Samuel and 1 Kings and run from Proper 4 to Proper 16. The rest of the texts are taken mostly from the books of Wisdom literature — Proverbs, Job, and Ruth.

Lesson 2. The second lessons derive from four books: 2 Corinthians, Ephesians, James, and Hebrews.

Gospel. The gospel features Mark, in semi-continuous readings, except for eight readings that come from John's gospel. Five of the fourth gospel's readings derive from John 6.

The Day Of Pentecost

Revised Common	Acts 2:1-21 or	Romans 8:22-27 or	John 15:26-27;
	Ezekiel 37:1-14	Acts 2:1-21	16:4b-15
Roman Catholic	Acts 2:1-11	1 Corinthians 12:3-7, 12-13	John 20:19-23
Episcopal	Acts 2:1-11 or	1 Corinthians 12:4-13 or	John 20:19-23 or
	Isaiah 44:1-8	Acts 2:1-11	John 14:8-17

Theme For The Day: Through the gift of the Holy Spirit the church witnesses to the saving power of Jesus Christ. The Spirit gives life, testifies to Jesus, and distributes gifts on the church.

BRIEF COMMENTARY ON THE LESSONS

Lesson 1: Ezekiel 37:1-14 (C)

The vision of the valley of dry bones refers to the spiritual condition of the Jewish exiles. Their country and their national identity had been crushed beyond any hope of revivification. They felt that there was about as much chance of their fortunes being restored as there was for a skeleton suddenly to come back to life. Ezekiel's vision gives hope to the exiles that God would restore the nation to newness of life. Though the original context of this passage does not refer to personal resurrection, it does show that God's Spirit has the power and the will to raise his people from the clutches of death. Nothing is impossible with the God who gives life to all that exists.

Lesson 1: Acts 2:1-21 (C); Acts 2:1-11 (RC, E)

The promised Spirit comes upon the church in the midst of the throngs of pilgrims who were making their way to the temple to celebrate the Jewish festival of Pentecost. The believers in Christ received the Spirit in dramatic and visible form, as tongues of flame and the ability to speak in other languages. This is not *glossalalia* because the pilgrims heard the church speak in their own language. The people are perplexed and amazed and so Peter interprets the event as a fulfillment of Joel 2:28-29, that God would bestow his Spirit on all flesh, not just a select few. He urges the assembly to repent and be saved.

Lesson 2: Romans 8:22-27 (C)

Lesson 2: 1 Corinthians 12:3-7, 12-13 (RC); 1 Corinthians 12:4-13 (E)

Spiritual gifts proved to be divisive in the Corinthian church. Paul teaches that God supplies many different gifts and none of them makes the possessor of the particular gift superior to the believer who has been given another gift. All of the gifts are given by the same Spirit, not to enhance self-esteem, but are to be exercised in community for the common good (v. 7).

Gospel: John 15:26-27; 16:4b-15 (C)

Jesus teaches that he will send the counselor, the Holy Spirit, in his name. The Spirit will testify to the saving work of Jesus. The disciples are also called to witness to Christ. Jesus declares that it is to their advantage that he go away, so that the Spirit might come upon them. The Spirit will convict the world of sin. Some of those who crucified Jesus thought they were doing God's will. The Holy Spirit will convict them of their error. We cannot view the righteousness of God through Jesus without being convicted of sin. The Spirit will also convince the world of righteousness. This means that the world will see Christ as the preeminent example and source of righteousness. Finally, the Spirit will convict the world of judgment. The crucified and risen Christ proclaims that God takes sin seriously and that every person will have to answer to him. However, because of the grace and love of Jesus, we will be able to stand before the judgment seat of Christ and be acquitted. Jesus teaches that the Holy Spirit will complete his teaching task and guide his disciples to the truth.

Gospel: John 20:19-23 (RC, E)

See gospel lesson for Easter 2.

Psalm Of The Day

Psalm 104:24-34, 35b (C); Psalm 104 (RC); Psalm 104:25-37 (E) — "When you send forth your Spirit, they are created ... and you renew the face of the earth" (v. 30).

Prayer Of The Day

Holy Spirit of God, we thank you for coming to us amidst the clamor of competing claims for truth, to guide us unto the fullness of truth. By your Spirit empower us to witness to the reality of Christ, whose word alone remains true and abides forever. In Jesus' name. Amen.

THEOLOGICAL REFLECTION ON THE LESSONS

Lesson 1: Ezekiel 37:1-14

Preaching in a cemetery (v. 4). As Ezekiel is caught up in his vision, he enters a cemetery, but not a proper cemetery because the bones were scattered about rather than being buried. The Spirit of God asks Ezekiel if the bones could come to life. Ezekiel admits that only the Lord knows the answer. Then God orders the prophet to prophesy to the bones. In other words, he is told to preach to the dead, to proclaim God's word in a cemetery. To do so requires an act of faith, faith in the power of God and his word. We, too, are called to speak to the spiritually dead and those without hope. Do we have faith in God's life-giving word and the power of the Spirit?

Re-creation. This account reminds us of the creation account found in Genesis 2 where God created man out of the clay. The clay was merely a lifeless corpse; then, God breathed his Spirit into the inanimate clay and it became a living, breathing person. As Ezekiel prophesied, the bones came together, sinew and flesh and skin attached to the bones, but these were still corpses. Therefore, God ordered Ezekiel to prophesy to the four winds (v. 9), symbolic of God's omnipresent Spirit. As he did so the flesh and bones came fully alive. Both creation and re-creation are dependent on the Spirit of God.

Lesson 2: Acts 2:1-21

Together (v. 1). The church remained together in worship, fellowship, and service. The believers in Jerusalem were expecting the Spirit to descend as Jesus had promised. They were undoubtedly praying that this very thing would come to pass. The Spirit came upon the gathered church and filled them with power. The power of the Holy Spirit still comes when believers gather together expectantly, worshipfully, and prayerfully.

230

Gather and disperse (v. 5). Luke states that devout men from every nation were gathered together in Jerusalem. The Spirit's strategy is to fill us when we are gathered together so that he might disperse his people into the world for mission. That should be the pattern we follow every week; gathering for worship and scattering for mission and service.

The Spirit of prophecy (v. 4). The Spirit came upon every single member of the church and each of them began to prophesy in the name of the Lord, employing other languages. Not every believer has the ability to preach but all Christians have been given the capacity to tell others about the wondrous things God has wrought in their lives.

Translation of the Word (v. 11). The people who witnessed Pentecost heard the word of God in their own language, a reversal of the Tower of Babel. The Spirit gives us the ability to translate the good news of Christ into other languages and cultures. The church is constantly in the process of translating the gospel for a new age, a fresh generation, or a foreign people. Freshness of language is a sign of the Spirit's activity.

Gospel: John 15:26-27; 16:4b-15

A spirited defense (v. 26). The Lord relates to his disciples that though he was leaving them physically, he was not leaving them spiritually. The Father would send the counselor, the advocate, the spirit of truth, to speak on his behalf. There are many voices in our world that claim to be Spirit led, but if they don't testify to Jesus they are not of the Spirit of God. Jesus has a spirited defense, and so do all who belong to him.

Called to the witness stand (v. 27). Jesus reminded his disciples that they were his witnesses because they had been with him from the beginning. He frankly informs them that they can expect suffering and persecution because of their witness (16:1-4). That's the price a person might have to pay after being called to the witness stand for Jesus.

Coming under conviction (v. 8). Unless we are convicted, we cannot be pardoned. When a person opens her life to the Spirit, she comes under conviction concerning God's holiness and her own sinful state. Jesus states that the Spirit will convict us "concerning sin, righteousness, and judgment." This is not the same as a jury acquittal. What Jesus refers to is equivalent to a lawyer convincing a man who had committed a crime, but really felt that he was innocent of a crime, that he was actually guilty. The Spirit helps us take our sins and God's judgment seriously, so that we might take God's gracious offer of pardon seriously.

Learning by degree (vv. 12-13). The Lord shares that he has much more to teach them but they are not now ready for it. The day would come when they would be ready and receptive; then the Spirit would lead them into all the truth. Truth begins with the basic elements and then builds increasingly complex concepts. You can't teach algebra to the five-year-old who hasn't learned the basics of math. Spiritual truth must also be learned by degree. None of us is at exactly the same level on the spiritual learning curve and our education will not be completed in this life.

Gospel: John 20:19-23

The peace of his presence. Twice in this pericope Jesus pronounces peace to the crucifixion-battered disciples. Jesus gives his fearful followers the peace of his presence. That peace comes not only from the fact that Jesus is risen but that he forgave them for leaving him. Jesus then breathed into their souls the breath of his Spirit (v. 22) and commissioned them to share his peace and forgiveness with everyone.

231

SERMON APPROACHES WITH ILLUSTRATIONS

Lesson 1: Ezekiel 37:1-14

Sermon Title: Death Valley Reborn

Sermon Angle: Death Valley, California, can be one of the most desolate and godforsaken places on the planet. The valley is littered with the bones of man and beast, who eventually surrendered all hope. Their environment overwhelmed them. The Jews of sixth century BC also found themselves in a valley of death in Babylonia. As they looked about them it seemed like their environment had swallowed them up; as far as they could see, there was nothing but desolation and dryness. God sent Ezekiel with a word of hope for the desperate wayfarers. The Lord would breathe new life into them and they would flourish once more in their land.

Outline:
1. Death Valley is one of the most desolate places in the world.
2. The Jews were living in a spiritual death valley.
3. Ezekiel proclaims that God will transform their death valley into a verdant valley.
4. God's Spirit can lift us out of our death valleys.

Sermon Title: God Of Grace And The Grave

Sermon Angle: Ezekiel was not speaking of the resurrection of the body but what he uttered takes on new meaning in light of Jesus' resurrection. Ezekiel and the Jewish nation came to experience the Lord as a God of grace who raised the people from the grave of hopelessness and despair. Through Christ we now perceive a whole new vista of God's grace; the Lord literally raises up individuals from the grave, just as he raises up nations from the dustbin of history. "Behold, I will open your graves, and raise you from your graves, O my people" (v. 12).

Outline:
1. Ezekiel came to see that God was full of grace and that he would raise up the Jews.
2. God's word was fulfilled and the Jews went back home to a new life.
3. God's Spirit can raise us from our emotional and spiritual graves.
4. God's Spirit raises us from our physical graves, through Christ.

Lesson 2: Acts 2:1-21

Sermon Title: Baptized With The Spirit And Fire

Sermon Angle: John the Baptist predicted that Jesus would baptize with the Holy Spirit and with fire (Matthew 3:11; Luke 3:16). This prediction came to pass at Pentecost, when the Spirit descended in tongues of flame and inspired speech. Most Christians claim to have received the Spirit in baptism but many of those do not show any fire. Yet Spirit and fire belong together. The word for wind and spirit is the same and, as you know, fire is fed by the wind. So, too, the Spirit whips a little spark of faith into a blazing conflagration if we let the Spirit blow freely into our lives.

Outline:
1. John the Baptist predicted that Jesus would baptize with the Holy Spirit and fire.
2. The promise was fulfilled at Pentecost (vv. 3-4).
3. In baptism God bestowed his Spirit, but has that produced spiritual fire?
4. How can we recapture the fire of the early church?
   — Assemble together (v. 1).
   — Pray and worship with expectancy.

Sermon Title: Breakout!

Sermon Angle: Devout Jews had come to Jerusalem from all over the world (v. 5) to worship God for imparting his law and for calling the Jews into nationhood. They expected to encounter the Lord through the traditional liturgies, offerings, and sacrifices. However, they encountered God in a strange and unexpected manner. God had broken loose from the religious infrastructure. God's Spirit blows where he wills.

Gospel: John 15:26-27; 16:4b-15

Sermon Title: Spirit Unveiled

Sermon Angle: The Holy Spirit remains hidden in clouds of ignorance and mystery for many Christians. The story of Pentecost, as told by Acts 2, doesn't do much to clear up the picture. In the gospel of John, Jesus does much to unveil the shroud of mystery surrounding the Spirit.

Outline:
1. The Spirit is Christ's advocate and witness (v. 26).
2. The Spirit convicts us of sin (v. 8).
3. The Spirit convinces us concerning the righteousness of Christ (vv. 8, 10).
4. The Spirit judges Satan (v. 11).
5. The Spirit reveals the truth (v. 13).
6. The Spirit makes known what is to come (v. 13).

Sermon Title: Convicts For Christ

Sermon Angle: Many a person has been convicted of a crime and sent to prison. Yet many of those same people are not under any internal sense of conviction. That is, they do not feel guilty or remorseful. This kind of criminal is the most dangerous kind. Our society has sociologized sin by calling it anti-social behavior or psychologized sin by relegating it to a mental disease. Without a sense of conviction about sin, there can be no salvation for the individual or society. We need to admit that we are convicts for Christ, who has pardoned and freed us.

Outline:
1. We are convicts for Christ.
2. We stand convicted of sin (v. 8).
3. We see our guilt against the backdrop of Christ's righteousness (v. 8).
4. However, we are pardoned convicts through Christ.
5. Be proud to be a convict for Christ.

* * * * *

Many people, yours truly included, were suspicious of Charles Colson when this Watergate convict suddenly found Christ in prison. I do not endorse all of his views but have come to believe that he was truly convicted not only of his crime but of his sin and his need for a Savior. His life since then has borne this out. What other reason would account for his throwing himself into the Prison Fellowship Ministry, which he founded? How could he speak or write so forcefully for his faith if he had not experienced a conviction by the Holy Spirit that he was a sinner who needed Christ? Some convicts' hearts might be too hard to change. Only God knows. Looking at it from another perspective, it might prove easier for the Holy Spirit to convict their hearts of sin than those of us who lead upright and respectable lives.

* * * * *

Sermon Title: Spirit Guide

Sermon Angle: The New Age movement talks much about spirit guides, ghosts that can be accessed through séances, and the like. Or the spirit guides might be angels. Christians have only one true and authentic Spirit guide, the Holy Spirit. Jesus said, "When the Spirit of Truth comes, he will guide you into all the truth ..." (v. 13). We possess only partial truth now but the Spirit will guide us gradually into the fullness of truth.

Outline:

1. We all need guidance since we lack clarity of vision.
2. The Bible is a guide but the Spirit helps us interpret.
3. How can we know if a certain course is the truth? It witnesses to Christ (15:26).
4. Let the Spirit guide you into the fullness of truth (v. 13).

* * * * *

On our last vacation, my wife, Fran, and I traveled to Sedona, Arizona, with our son-in-law's parents. Some of you have been to this town in the beautiful red rock country and may or may not be aware that this is a center of the New Age religious movement. The night before, our host showed me a booklet he obtained the last time he was there. It was packed with advertisements from dozens of New Age spiritual guides and healers making available their wares to the gullible. Included were channelers, to put you in touch with the spirits of the dead; past life regressionists, to help you discover who you were in some previous life; hypnotists, to enable you to get in touch with your true self; and a host of so-called healers. New Age offers religion without Christ, blessings without any commitment. It holds out spirituality that is completely self-centered rather than God-centered. You are offered all these choices and none is of itself better than any other. According to the New Age, all that matters is what rings *your* bell.

Nevertheless, cradled against one of the red rock cliffs is the Shrine of the Holy Cross. It is a chapel constructed around a huge white cross, which commands a dominant view of the entire valley. All around are the covens of the gods of this present age, vying for your allegiance, but the cross lifts one's head to a higher righteousness, a higher good. The cross lifts one's head to the most high God, who was lifted high on a cross for our sins and our salvation. Jesus Christ is the *only* rock of our salvation, not one god among many. The Holy Spirit calls us to a higher good, a higher righteousness via the cross of Jesus.

The Holy Trinity

Revised Common	Isaiah 6:1-8	Romans 8:12-17	John 3:1-17
Roman Catholic	Deuteronomy 4:32-34, 39-40	Romans 8:14-17	Matthew 28:16-21
Episcopal	Exodus 3:1-6	Romans 8:12-17	John 3:1-16

Theme For The Day: The mystery of the divine presence. As Isaiah witnesses the heavenly scene, the God of holy terror shows his forgiving face. Jesus tells Nicodemus that he must be born from above to see and enter into the mysteries of the kingdom of God.

BRIEF COMMENTARY ON THE LESSONS

Lesson 1: Isaiah 6:1-8 (C)

The story of Isaiah's call by God in the temple, 742 BC, probably while he was officiating at worship. As Isaiah is viewing the Ark of the Covenant, enshrined in the most holy place, he sees the Lord in all of his majestic glory on his throne, attended by the heavenly creatures. The wings of the seraphim sat on top of the covenant box and was considered the throne of God. The cherubim call out to one another "Holy, holy, holy is the Lord of hosts ..." (v. 4), giving special emphasis to the holiness of God. Isaiah cringes in dread as he realizes that he does not deserve to be in the presence of the almighty. He cries out: "Woe is me! For I am lost...." The Lord sends a seraphim with a coal from the altar to touch and purify his lips. His sin is taken away. Then the Lord asks for a messenger. Isaiah volunteers, "Here am I, send me."

Lesson 1: Deuteronomy 4:32-34, 39-40 (RC)

Lesson 1: Exodus 3:1-6 (E)

Lesson 2: Romans 8:12-17 (C, E); Romans 8:14-17 (RC)

Paul contrasts the concepts of flesh and spirit. The flesh refers to the dominion of sin to which all humans are subject apart from the Spirit of God. Paul states that if we live according to the flesh we will die (spiritually), but if we permit the Spirit to put to death the sinful deeds of the flesh we will live. The children of God have been adopted into God's family and made co-heirs with Christ. Through the Spirit we are privileged to cry out to God as "Abba Father," Daddy Father, provided we are willing to endure suffering for his sake.

Gospel: John 3:1-17 (C); John 3:1-16 (E)

Nicodemus, a Pharisee and member of the Sanhedrin, comes to Jesus under the cloak of darkness to seek spiritual truth. He recognizes Jesus as a teacher from God. Jesus seems to anticipate his question even before he has a chance to utter it. "Very truly, I tell you, no one can see the kingdom of God unless he is born from above (again)" (v. 3). This teacher of his people does not understand; he takes Jesus' words literally. "How can a man be born when he is old?" (v. 4). Jesus responds that a person must be born of water (baptism) and the Holy Spirit to enter the kingdom of God. In the final part of this text (vv. 16-17) Jesus reveals that the way to be born of the Spirit is to believe in God's Son. He is the Father's love gift for the redemption of the world.

Gospel: Matthew 28:16-21 (RC)

Just prior to this lection, the risen Christ orders his disciples to meet him at a certain mountain in Galilee. They worship him but some have doubts. Christ announces that God has given him all authority. He commands them to go and make disciples of all nations, baptizing them in the name of the Father and of the Son and of the Holy Spirit. The task seems overpowering but Christ promises to be with them always.

Psalm Of The Day

   Psalm 29 (C) — "Worship the Lord in holy splendor ..." (v. 2b).
   Psalm 32 (RC)
   Psalm 93 (E)

Prayer Of The Day

Awesome God, you remain enthroned in mystery and majesty, yet you have stooped to show your face in the person of your Son, Jesus Christ, and you have brought us into your holy presence through the guidance of your gentle Spirit. Make us bold to witness to the triune truth of your redeeming presence, in the name of the Father and of the Son and of the Holy Spirit. Amen.

THEOLOGICAL REFLECTION ON THE LESSONS

Lesson 1: Isaiah 6:1-8

Our God is awesome. Isaiah encountered God during worship in all his awesome glory. In our era, when God is portrayed by George Burns and we attend church in jeans, we seldom experience God as awesome. God has become our buddy. Like Rodney Dangerfield, God might be saying: "I just don't get no respect." To really see God is to behold him high and lifted up. To really appreciate God's standing beside us in Jesus, we have to recognize that this God still lofts over us.

Thrice holy (v. 3). The one seraph called out to the other, "Holy, holy, holy is the Lord of hosts; the whole earth is full of his glory." My understanding has it that the Hebrew language repeats the word for added emphasis. However, we might take the expression to refer to a reality of which Isaiah was not aware, namely that God is thrice holy: holy Father-Creator; holy Son-Savior, and Holy Spirit-sanctifier. However we experience God, whatever we name him, he remains set apart and sovereign.

Sinking in sin (v. 5). After Isaiah was caught up in the heavenly scene, he felt himself sinking in sin, he felt doomed. "Woe is me! I am lost! I am a man of unclean lips and I dwell in the midst of a people of unclean lips...." Yet the confession had barely left his lips when the Lord ordered a seraph to touch Isaiah's lips with a hot coal as a symbol of God's purifying forgiveness. Just as Jesus lifted up a terrified Peter sinking in the waves of Lake Galilee, so God reached down to Isaiah to raise him up.

Rising to serve (v. 8). After the Lord purged Isaiah of his sin he was ready to rise from his knees that he might go out to serve the Lord. "Who shall we send?" "Here am I, send me!" Voluntary service is always a sign of one who has encountered the forgiving grace of God.

Lesson 2: Romans 8:12-17

Which spirit moves you? There are two spirits that can move us. The spirit of slavery to sin (v. 15) and the Spirit of God. God's Spirit empowers us to put to death our sinful human nature. This Spirit is the Spirit of adoption into God's family (v. 15), which frees us from fear.

The witness within (v. 16). God's Spirit witnesses to our spirit that we are children of God. If a voice within us convinces us that we are no good, it comes from Satan. The Christian's internal witness, the witness within, steadies our heart with the assurance that we are God's beloved children through Christ.

Who are God's children? (vv. 16-17). Paul states that we are children of God through adoption. Through faith in God's Son, we are accounted to be brothers in Christ. Our gospel lesson relates that we are God's children through being born again, a birth of water and the Spirit. Both passages affirm that we are not God's children merely through natural birth. Not every person is a child of God.

Gospel: John 3:1-17

From a distance. Nicodemus was attracted to Jesus. It's likely that he was a disciple of Jesus, but from a distance. You see, Nicodemus was an important man of eminent position. He was called to uphold the traditions of the past. He would lose face if his comrades knew of his affinity for this radical named Jesus. Nicodemus chose the cloak of darkness to talk to Jesus up close and personal, while at the same time keeping his distance. Nicodemus might be aptly termed an admirer of Jesus but he certainly wasn't a disciple, not yet anyway. One cannot be a disciple of Jesus from a distance.

The teacher flunked. As an elder, Nicodemus was a teacher of the Jewish religion. Yet he addressed Jesus as rabbi (teacher) and came to him to discover the secret of his miraculous powers (v. 2). The lesson that Jesus attempted to teach him did not penetrate his heart and mind. He did not see how a person could be born again. The eminent teacher could not comprehend the spiritual basics. He flunked out.

You cannot see until you are born (v. 3). Before we were born, the world certainly existed but we could not see it or enter it. Birth precedes sight. Jesus states that a person cannot see the kingdom of God unless he is born from above (again). Unless we come alive spiritually, we cannot see the kingdom of God. The kingdom is there but the spiritually unborn cannot perceive it. The twice-born can see the kingdom of God even before they die.

Look up and live (vv. 14-15). The Israelites grumbled against God as they wandered through the wilderness and were punished by lethal snakes. God provided an antidote, however: the bronze serpent on a pole. Whoever would look at the bronze serpent after being bitten would be saved. Jesus proclaims that whoever looks up in faith to the Son, lifted up on the cross, will not only be saved but be granted the gift of eternal life.

SERMON APPROACHES WITH ILLUSTRATIONS

Lesson 1: Isaiah 6:1-8

Sermon Title: Holy Smoke

Sermon Angle: Isaiah was in the area of the temple where he could view the altar of incense with its plumes of sweet smoke rising to the heavens, carrying the prayers of the people. Smoke, holy smoke, is one of the most vivid biblical symbols for God. Recall that the Israelites were led

237

by a pillar of cloud (smoke) by day and a pillar of fire by night. The smoke both conceals and reveals the God of mystery and might. Suddenly Isaiah is caught up in a vision where he sees beyond the holy smoke, where he catches sight of the great God himself. The prophet senses imminent doom because he knows that a sinful man does not deserve to stand in the presence of the almighty. Yet Isaiah is not swept away by God's wrath but rather his grace and forgiveness. Holy smoke represents the mystery of God. On this Trinity Sunday, we celebrate the truth that we are able to see beyond the holy smoke because Christ has brought us into the very presence of God. We see that God is Father, Son, and Holy Spirit.

Outline:
1. God revealed himself to Israel through cloud and smoke.
2. The cloud or smoke both represents and conceals God.
3. In Isaiah's worship God parted the holy smoke, enabling him to see God himself.
4. Jesus Christ reveals the God behind the smoke.
5. By being born again (gospel lesson) we can come into the presence of God.

Sermon Title: When God Invades Our Worship

Sermon Angle: Much that we call worship is routine. We recite our hymns, our prayers, our litanies but often feel little sense of transcendence. We offer our worship to God but don't really expect to encounter God personally. However, sometimes during a prayer, a song, a sermon, or a sacrament, the great God breaks into our worship with an awesome awareness of his presence and grace. We experience the reality behind the symbols of our faith. Isaiah had such an experience of God breaking through the tradition of worship and bringing the prophet into the very presence of the Lord. We cannot expect such dramatic encounters all the time, but we can expect God to break through worship as usual if we continue to assemble together. When God breaks through we will experience God's holiness and our sinfulness, but also God's gracious forgiveness. When God breaks through we will encounter a sense of God's call.

Outline:
1. How often does God break through the routine of your worship?
2. Often we go through the motions with little expectancy.
3. Suddenly God breaks through and brings us into his presence, as he did Isaiah.
4. When God invades our worship, we come to see ourselves, our God, and our mission.
5. When God invades our worship, it can never be church as usual.

Lesson 2: Romans 8:12-17

Sermon Title: Blessed Assurance

Sermon Angle: Most of us experience periods of doubt when we question our identity as God's children. After all, we walk by faith, not by sight. How do we know we are God's beloved children, that we are saved? Paul answers, "When we cry, Abba! Father! It is the Spirit of God bearing witness to our spirit that we are children of God" (v. 16). The very fact that we cry out to God as Father indicates that we have the Spirit and that we are coheirs with Christ. That Spirit inhabited our hearts when we were baptized into the name of the Father, and of the Son, and of the Holy Spirit.

Outline:
1. How do we know we are God's children?
2. Answer: through the Holy Spirit.
3. That Spirit was given to us in baptism and witnesses to our Spirit that we are indeed God's dear children.

Sermon Title: Not The Spirit Of Slavery But Of Sonship

Sermon Angle: Some of the Corinthian Christians were being sucked back into their own sinful ways (the flesh). Like the Israelites that Moses led through the wilderness, they were tempted to resubmit themselves to the yoke of slavery. Paul reasons: "You did not receive the spirit of slavery to fall back into sin, but the spirit of adoption (sonship)" (v. 15). No, I do not exclude half the human race by using the term "Son," because what I am referring to is the Spirit of God's Son, Jesus Christ. We have received the Spirit of the *Son*, which has nothing to do with sexuality and everything to do with love, grace, and assurance of our special relationship with God. Apart from God, we remain slaves of sin, self, and fear. God gives his own the Spirit of his Son, not of slavery. Praise the Lord!

Outline:
1. Some of the Corinthians, having been freed from sin's yoke, were ready to go back under bondage.
2. Those whose lives are led by the Spirit of God (obedience, love) are children of God (v. 14).
3. We have received the Spirit of the Son, not of slavery (v. 15).
4. Live according to the Spirit in which you were baptized.

Gospel: John 3:1-17

Sermon Title: Believing The Impossible

Sermon Angle: Nicodemus began his conversation with Jesus by commenting on how impressed he was with Jesus' miracles. Jesus counters that what's really important is that a person be born again. Nicodemus appears to misunderstand. "How can anyone be born again after having grown old?" A person might have the impression that this business of being born again or anew was foreign to Nicodemus. This is probably not so. Nicodemus was a learned religious leader and he knew that the prophets spoke of God giving his children a new heart (Jeremiah 31:31), similar to rebirth. Also, he must have been familiar with the mystery religions and their rituals of dying and rising with their gods so as to be reborn. What Nicodemus is questioning is the possibility of being born anew. He might have been saying that spiritual rebirth is about as possible as an old man entering into his mother's womb for a second time. The child of God dares to believe that it is possible to be born again, that a person can be so thoroughly transformed she is like a new person. The child of God dares to believe the seemingly impossible.

Outline:
1. Jesus states that being born again is absolutely necessary (v. 3).
2. Nicodemus questions whether being born again is possible (v. 4).
3. We are born again by water and the Spirit (v. 5).
4. We demonstrate that we are twice-born by lives of obedience (lesson 2).

Sermon Title: Going Beyond Understanding To Being

Sermon Angle: Nicodemus was on an intellectual trip. Religion was a matter of understanding and then doing God's will. Jesus is really telling Nicodemus that faith is not, at its source, understanding; rather, faith is a state of being that one enters through being born again. Jesus equates spiritual birth to the wind (v. 8), which is mysterious. You can feel it but you can't see it and you don't know its source or its end. Of course, the words wind and spirit derive from the same word (*pnuema*). So the words of Jesus have a double meaning. Salvation does not result from the degree of knowledge but the state of being. Christianity is not about understanding a theology as much as it is entering into a new life.

Outline:
1. Nicodemus approached religion intellectually.
2. He thought to engage Jesus in dialogue about the source of his authority (v. 1).
3. Jesus told him he could enter the kingdom only through becoming a new creature.
4. Christianity moves beyond understanding to being.

Sermon Title: There's No Ladder To Heaven

Sermon Angle: Jesus informs Nicodemus: "No one has ascended into heaven but the Son of Man who has descended from heaven" (v. 13). People have tried ascending into heaven for centuries. They have attempted it through leading ascetic lives and renouncing the world, as Martin Luther did. Many have attempted to ascend through the ladder of ritual. Still more have sought to rise up through attaining special knowledge. None of these ladders are effective. Only those who trust the one raised up on the cross will ascend. We rise up through God's grace and love (v. 16).

Outline:
1. The ancients had their towers to reach the deities (Tower of Babel).
2. We moderns continue to try to climb various ladders to heaven. (Describe.)
3. Jesus said that no one has ascended into heaven (v. 13).
4. God so loved the world that he gave his Son, so that all who believe would have eternal life (v. 16).

Corpus Christi

Roman Catholic   **Exodus 24:3-8**   **Hebrews 9:11-15**   **Mark 14:12-16, 22-26**

Theme For The Day: All three texts center around the idea that God has established his covenant with us, sealed in blood. The New Testament readings see Christ as both the lamb and the high priest.

BRIEF COMMENTARY ON THE LESSONS

Lesson 1: Exodus 24:3-8

After Moses and the elders commune with the Lord on the mountain, Moses builds an altar at the foot of the mountain with twelve pillars of stone, representing the twelve tribes. He assembles the people for a covenant ceremony. The people agreed to obey the Lord's commands as delivered by Moses. In witness to the covenant between God and the people, Moses ordered that many beasts be sacrificed. He took half the blood and dashed it against the altar, representing God's portion of the agreement. Then, he flung the other portion of the blood over the people, as a sign of the commitment of the people to their God. Afterward Moses announced: "See the blood of the covenant that the Lord made with you in accordance with all these words" (v. 8). The blood was a visible sign of their covenant with God.

Lesson 2: Hebrews 9:11-15

The new covenant is contrasted with the old as it relates to the function of the high priest. To get the context of this passage, you should read Hebrews 8-9. The high priest entered the holy place once a year to atone for his sins and those of his people but Christ entered the holy place of the cross once and for all. Christ's body is itself the tent or tabernacle through which he entered the holy of holies (the cross); there he offered a perfect and eternal sacrifice. The blood of sheep and goats could atone for sins for a time, but the blood of Christ brings us eternal redemption.

Gospel: Mark 14:12-16, 22-26

This is the story of the institution of the Eucharist, during our Lord's last Passover. Jesus sends two of his disciples to prepare for the Passover meal, instructing them to find a man carrying a water jar and to follow him. Such a man would stand out because men did not customarily carry water jars. That was the work of women. Mark heightens the drama of our Lord's impending crucifixion by stating that this took place on the day "when the Passover lamb is sacrificed." Thus, this phrase carries a double meaning. During the Passover meal, Jesus takes the bread, breaks it, and offers it to his disciples saying: "Take: this is my body." After they passed the cup, he announced: "This is my blood of the covenant." Some authorities add the word "new" before covenant, which makes better sense. Jesus offers a new covenant of grace that is written in blood. Unlike the old covenant, it is the blood of God's own Son.

Psalm Of The Day

Psalm 126 — "Those who go out weeping, bearing the seed for sowing, shall come home with shouts of joy, carrying the sheaves" (v. 6).

Prayer Of The Day

O Lord our God, king of the universe, we poor sinners throw ourselves on your mercy. With high praise, we gladly receive the sacrifice of your holy body and precious blood, the bread of heaven. In the name of Jesus, the Lamb of God and our great high priest. Amen.

THEOLOGICAL REFLECTION ON THE LESSONS

Lesson 1: Exodus 24:3-8

Get it in writing (v. 4). This text seems to suggest that Moses, first of all, gave the people a verbal rendition of what the Lord had told him, which they agreed to obey. Verse 4 states that Moses wrote down what the Lord communicated to him. There is something about writing that makes one's commitment and word more fixed, indelible, and real. For that reason, you should never write to another person angry and hurtful words. They can never be totally erased. In the same vein, an agreement between parties becomes more firmly established if it is recorded. Our recollection of what we said becomes hazy, but the written word does not change, unless amended.

Sealed in blood. The covenant that God established with his people he sealed with blood. First, he splashed the blood against the altar, symbolizing God's commitment to give himself to his people. The Lord took the lead in establishing the covenant. Then, after Moses read the covenant to the people, he scattered the blood over the people in token that they had pledged their lives to God and his covenant. The new covenant is also sealed in blood, the blood of Christ. Through faith in the God of our baptism, we are saved by Christ's blood.

Good intentions aren't enough (vv. 3b, 7b). "All that the Lord has spoken we will do." The people of Israel undoubtedly were sincere when they committed themselves unequivocally to the covenant. Maybe they were overwhelmed by the emotions of the moment, as they witnessed from a distance the awesome majesty of God. At any rate, they must have meant it, but their resolve was not strong enough to endure. That is why I don't make New Year's resolutions. I have little faith in the power of human resolve, least of all my own. That is where the old covenant is lacking. Though it tells us what to do, it provides no engine to keep us on the pathway of peace. The new covenant, through the power of the Holy Spirit, provides the horsepower to carry us to our destination.

Lesson 2: Hebrews 9:11-15

The already and the not yet (v. 11). "High priest of the good things that have come." Other ancient authorities put this in the future; Jesus is high priest of the good things that "are to come." Both translations fit theologically. Jesus entered into his high priestly function on the cross and this ministry presently benefits those who trust in him. However, Christ's atoning work will not be complete until the *parousia*. We live on the bridge between the already and the not yet.

Deep down clean (vv. 13-14). These verses bring to light an interesting analogy; the bloody sacrifices of the old covenant sanctify worshipers so that their "flesh" is cleansed, but the blood of Christ cleanses our conscience. The old covenant brought ceremonial cleansing, a type of superficial purging, but the blood of Christ cleans deep down to the center of our being, regenerating our conscience.

242

Gospel: Mark 14:12-16, 22-26

Preparations (v. 12). The Lord's disciples inquired about where he wanted them to prepare for the Passover. Jesus instructed them to follow a man with a water jar, who would lead them to the right place. Already, other preparations were taking place. Judas had gone to the temple officials and offered to hand Jesus over to them. Judas probably intended something other than Jesus' death, yet God uses even the failed schemes and deceits of sinful people to accomplish his purposes. Judas made his own preparations, which led to his doom, but the other disciples consulted the Lord and were partakers of his body and blood.

The blood of damnation or salvation. It seems that Judas got into trouble because he wanted to play God by forcing Jesus' hand. When his plot led to the Lord's crucifixion, Judas was overcome by his blood guilt. Judas was destroyed by the blood of Jesus, because he didn't repent, but the other disciples were saved by Jesus' blood, like the Hebrews who were covered by the lamb's blood during the first Passover in Egypt. Depending on our attitude toward Christ, his blood either acquits us or convicts us.

New covenant (v. 24). The word "new" is employed by some ancient manuscripts but deleted by others. If the word is left out, it implies that what Jesus is doing is in continuity with the Old Testament covenants. There is great truth here. However, the insertion of the word "new" shows that what Jesus is doing rises far above and beyond anything that God had previously done. This too, by faith, remains undeniable. God had previously offered remedies for sins but, in Christ, God was and is offering himself as that remedy. This was brand spanking new.

SERMON APPROACHES WITH ILLUSTRATIONS

Lesson 1: Exodus 24:3-8

Sermon Title: Signed In Blood

Sermon Angle: The gruesome murders at the Sharon Tate mansion by the followers of Charles Manson created a media sensation. Inscribed in blood on the wall was this cryptic message: "Pigs." We might say that the Manson family were blood brothers and sisters in the most horrific sense of the word. The people of Israel were also blood brothers and sisters in the family of God. Half of the blood from the sacrificed victims was thrown against the altar, symbolizing God's commitment to his covenant. The other half of the blood was collected in basins, and after Moses had finished reading the covenant to the people, it was flung over the multitude. The message was clear; they were offering their very lives to Yahweh. They were children of God and blood brothers and sisters. The New Testament develops this idea much further by asserting that God offered his blood on our behalf in order to establish a new covenant of grace. God has established a covenant with us signed in blood, his blood.

Outline:
1. In a destructive sense, those in the Charles Manson clan were blood brothers and sisters.
2. In a redemptive sense, God established his covenant with the Jews, signed in blood.
3. In Christ, God made a new covenant, signed with the blood of Jesus, his Son.

Lesson 2: Hebrews 9:11-15

Sermon Title: Dying Testate

Sermon Angle: "For where a will is involved, the death of the one who made it must be established" (v. 16). Before one can inherit money or property bequeathed in a last will and testament, a death certificate must be issued. It must be firmly established that the original owner of the property is really dead. Some have tried to fake death in order to collect insurance. The writer of Hebrews states that Jesus really did die. This is necessary so that what Jesus bequeathed to us might rightfully be conveyed to us. Not only did Jesus really die, but also he had established a will conveying his gifts to all who are members of his family. What did the Lord leave us? Not property or money. No, he conveyed to us forgiveness of sins, life, and salvation. The inheritance goes to all who are his family through baptism and faith. Because Jesus died testate, and his will is recognized by the supreme court of the universe, we can inherit an eternal estate.

Outline:

1. When someone dies, the death must legally be established and recorded. Once that is accomplished, it must be determined if there is a legally binding will.
2. The New Testament witnesses declare that Jesus really died (and rose) and that he left his last will and testament.
3. Christ wills to be our high priest and free us from our sins (v. 15).
4. Strive for Christ's eternal inheritance, not to amass an earthly estate.

*   *   *   *   *

In the movie, *Rain Man*, Charlie receives word that his father has died. He has been estranged from his father for years and only goes back to hear the reading of the will. Charlie discovers that his wealthy father has left him only a 1949 Buick Roadmaster convertible, the cause of their alienation, and some prize rose bushes. He is shocked to learn that the remainder of his father's estate went to an anonymous person. To cut to the quick, Charlie finds the identity of this mystery person to be his brother, Raymond, living in an institution for those with mental and emotional disabilities. Raymond's particular affliction is autism. Charlie decides to kidnap his brother and drive him back to California. His intent is to use his brother as a bargaining chip in a high stakes game to get half of his father's estate. When, at the end of the movie, the trustee for his father's estate offers Charlie a very large check in order to settle the dispute and get Raymond back, he refuses. Rather, he sends his brother back without strings attached. He has, to his great surprise, inherited a brother, whom he is learning to love. In a sense, he is also becoming reconciled with his father, by submitting to his will.

Through Christ's last will and testament, we gain both a Father and a family to love.

*   *   *   *   *

Gospel: Mark 14:12-16, 22-26

Sermon Title: Prepare For The Feast

Sermon Angle: Verses 12-16 speak of the need to prepare to meet God in worship. The disciples asked, "Where would you have us go and prepare for you to eat the Passover?" (v. 12b). Worship that transforms those who preside at the feast and those who celebrate the feast as participants requires careful preparation. Though the Lord sometimes surprises us, he most often comes when our hearts and minds are prepared to meet him. The ministers of the feast ought to give careful attention to detail, for they serve as the Lord's hosts. However, all ministers of the feast and participants in the feast must give the greatest concentration of effort to spiritual preparations. Fasting, prayer, and confession are some of the ways that we can make ready for the feast of Christ. However, the best preparation is a life of disciplined obedience.

Outline:

1. The disciples carefully prepared for the Passover, as Jesus meticulously prepared to sacrifice himself (vv. 12-16).
2. Worship and the Eucharist require careful preparation.
3. As you prepare for church, are you also preparing to personally and corporately encounter the Lord of the Feast?
4. If we truly prepare, we will leave communion with a joyful and full heart.

Sermon Title: The Taste Of New Wine

Sermon Angle: When Jesus consecrated the Passover wine and offered it to his disciples, he pronounced: "This is my blood of the (new) covenant poured out for many" (v. 24). It was the old Passover feast and same old wine, yet, Jesus was transforming it into something new. It was a taste of new wine. Christianity is meant to offer the world something new, fresh, and transforming. This wine was not the wine of mere remembrance. This wine was Jesus' blood, conveying his life and Spirit. Those who receive Jesus by word and sacrament will not be satisfied with an occasional sip of his new wine; they will want to drink deeply and daily. Yet, even this new wine will yield to something even more satisfying in the kingdom of heaven. Jesus remarked: "I tell you, I shall not drink again of the fruit of the vine until that day when I drink it new in the kingdom of God" (v. 25).

Outline:

1. Jesus' statement: "This is my blood of the (new) covenant" suggests that what he offers is really a taste of new wine.
2. Both the old and new wine (covenant) are signs of God's redemption, but only the new wine (new relationship) offered by Jesus has transforming power.
3. The Passover celebrated God's past acts of redemption and held the hope of a future salvation but could not give God's saving Spirit in the here and now.
4. As we receive Jesus' blood poured out for us all, may we also allow our lives to be poured out for others, that they might enjoy the taste of Jesus' new wine.

*   *   *   *   *

In certain dire circumstances, humans have had to resort to eating the flesh of their fellow human beings. The book, *Alive*, tells the fascinating and inspiring story of a planeload of Argentine passengers who became marooned high in the Andes Mountains after a plane crash. After several days, their meager rations of food were exhausted. Gnawing, persistent hunger forced them to break an ancient taboo against eating human flesh. After a discussion of the possibility of eating their dead comrades, four men got up and went outside. They removed the snow from one of the bodies. One of the men knelt down, exposed the buttocks of one of the victims, and with a jagged piece of glass began to strip thin pieces of human meat, each about the size of a matchstick. He put about twenty pieces on the roof of the plane to thaw in the sun, went inside the plane, and told his companions where they might find meat. No one came. This man, Canessa, took it upon himself to break the ice. He prayed that God might give him the strength to do what he knew to be right and necessary for the survival of those who were yet alive. He hesitated. Even with his strong resolve, the horror of the act he was about to commit paralyzed him. His hand would neither rise to his mouth nor fall to his side. Finally, his will won out over his revulsion, as he slowly lifted the thin strip of flesh over his mouth and dropped it in. A wave of triumph flashed across his face. He knew that they would survive. That night, several people went outside to eat.

We, too, live, not just survive, by eating Christ's body and drinking Christ's blood, given and shed for you, for me, and for all.

Proper 4/Pentecost 2/Ordinary Time 9

Revised Common	1 Samuel 3:1-20	2 Corinthians 4:5-12	Mark 2:23—3:6
Roman Catholic	Deuteronomy 5:12-15	2 Corinthians 4:6-11	Mark 2:23—3:6
Episcopal	Deuteronomy 5:6-21	2 Corinthians 4:5-12	Mark 2:23-28

Theme For The Day: The Lord sends his spokesmen to speak words of judgment against religious authorities. In the 1 Samuel text from the Revised Common Lectionary God speaks out against the corruption under Eli. In the gospel, Jesus challenges the common understanding of the sabbath, which leads to Jesus' condemnation of the powers that be.

BRIEF COMMENTARY ON THE LESSONS

Lesson 1: 1 Samuel 3:1-20 (C)

This pericope continues the story of Samuel from 2:26. The text begins with a statement about the spiritual poverty of Israelites under the priest, Eli, who is old and has lost control of his sons. "The word of the Lord was rare in those days; visions were not widespread" (v. 1). The word for "word" and "vision" is essentially the same. According to tradition, Samuel was twelve years of age. Similarities are apparent between this account and the story of our Lord in the temple at twelve years of age (Luke 2:40-52). Verse 3, "Eli's eyesight had begun to grow dim," speaks not only of his physical but also his spiritual state. The boy Samuel was sleeping in the sanctuary. "The lamp, near the Ark of the Covenant, was growing dim," indicates that it was near dawn. Samuel three times mistakes the call of Eli for the voice of the Lord. Finally, Eli perceives that God is calling Samuel and instructs the lad to reply: "Speak, Lord, for your servant hears." The word of the Lord that came to Samuel turned out to be a message of judgment against Eli and his sons.

Lesson 1: Deuteronomy 5:6-21 (E); Deuteronomy 5:12-15 (RC)

Lesson 2: 2 Corinthians 4:5-12 (C, E); 2 Corinthians 4:6-11 (RC)

Paul responds to some criticisms that his gospel is unclear. He responds that if it is veiled, it is hidden only to those who have had their eyes blinded by Satan. The treasure of the gospel is contained in earthen vessels (a symbol of our human mortality). The glory does not belong to the vessels but to the treasure they contain. The apostle refuses to be defeated by his afflictions and suffering and views them as a participation in the suffering and death of Christ. The carriers of the gospel take part in the death of Jesus but also the life of Jesus.

Gospel: Mark 2:23—3:6 (C, RC); Mark 2:23-28 (E)

The Pharisees attack the disciples of Jesus for plucking heads of grain on the sabbath, breaking their sabbath laws. Jesus defends their actions, citing the instance where King David and his men ate the holy bread, which was lawful only for the priests to eat (1 Samuel 21:1-6). The point that Jesus makes has it that human need takes precedence over ceremonial laws. Then Jesus enters a synagogue where there is a man with a withered hand. The Pharisees are watching Jesus to see if he heals the man, which he does, angered at their hardness of heart. The Pharisees immediately counsel with the Herodians, probably a secular political group.

247

Psalm Of The Day
   Psalm 139:1-6 (C) — "I praise you for I am fearfully and wonderfully made" (v. 14).
   Psalm 81:1-10 (E)
   Psalm 80 (RC)

Prayer Of The Day
   Lord Christ, free us from narrowness of mind and smallness of spirit, that we might see the needs all about us and respond with your great compassion and love. In the name of Jesus. Amen.

THEOLOGICAL REFLECTION ON THE LESSONS

Lesson 1: 1 Samuel 3:1-20
   Lack of vision (v. 1). The Bible relates how God spoke to his prophets through visions. Those visions were lacking during Eli's priesthood, because he did not reign in his rebellious sons for their sinful ways. God does not communicate to those who openly disregard his will. It seems that a lack of vision exists in our day as well, because we have turned our back to the Lord.
   God keeps the light on. The spokesman for Motel 6 ends his homey commercials with the phrase, "We'll keep the light on for you." This passage portrays a time when the light of faith was flickering but still burning. The dim-sighted Eli symbolizes the diminution of the light of faith (v. 2). The nearly burned-out sanctuary light conveys the same thought (v. 3). Nevertheless, God was going to reignite the lamp of God's presence through the young boy, Samuel, who grew to become one of the Lord's great prophets.
   Know the Lord, that you might hear his voice (v. 7). This verse states that Samuel did not, at this time, know the Lord. How could he recognize his voice? Samuel had lived and labored in the house of God, yet had never been personally introduced to the Lord. This tells us that we can be religious without knowing God or being able to recognize his voice.

Lesson 2: 2 Corinthians 4:5-12
   What we preach (v. 5). Paul defended himself against criticism by saying that what he preached was not himself but Jesus Christ as Lord. Some people are tempted to use the gospel and their Christian faith for their own ends, to draw attention to themselves. Whom does our life proclaim?
   Earthen vessels (v. 7). When the Dead Sea Scrolls were found, many of them were stored in clay pots. This great treasure, the oldest extant manuscripts of the Old Testament, was found in earthen vessels. We are earthen vessels, frail and feeble, yet God has placed in our hearts the treasure of the gospel; it is our treasure because it opens to us the door to eternal life. Why do we spend more time caring for the pot than we do the treasure?
   Down but not out (vv. 8-9). Paul was like a prizefighter. The foe might knock him down with a stinging blow, but he was not knocked out. Before the count was up, he was back on his feet. He could take all that the opponent had to offer because of the strength that Christ supplied. "We are afflicted in every way, but not rushed ... struck down but not destroyed." Few of us suffer for our faithfulness to Christ as Paul did, but life does deal us some terrible blows. Only Christ can give us the strength like that of a Timex watch, which "takes a licking but keeps on ticking."

Gospel: Mark 2:23—3:6

Sabbath sabotage. The sabbath was and is central to the exercise of the Jewish faith. It's easy to see why religious leaders got upset when Jesus appeared to disregard the sabbath laws. Therefore, they were watching him (v. 2). You might call this a sabbath sabotage. The religious leaders might even have planted the man with the withered hand for this express purpose. Keep in mind that Jesus did not break the commandment: "Remember the sabbath day to keep it holy." He merely disregarded the multitude of legalistic interpretations of that commandment.

Confusing the means with the end. Jesus maintained that we must consider the intent of God's commands rather than the letter of the law. The purpose of the sabbath is to restore and renew our bodies and our spirits. That's why Jesus cites the account of King David and his men eating the bread of the presence (v. 26). God gave his laws to preserve and protect humankind. Jesus is telling the Pharisees and scribes that they have it all turned around. "The sabbath was made for man, not man for the sabbath."

The reasons for the sabbath. The Bible states two reasons to keep the sabbath. The first reason is taken from creation. Exodus 28 states that God rested from his labors of creation on the sabbath. Therefore, humans should also rest from their labor. The second reason stems from redemption. God redeemed the Israelites from their bondage in Egypt. Therefore, according to Deuteronomy 5, God's people should worship God for his acts of redemption. Jesus maintains that God's intent for the sabbath is goodness (v. 4). The Genesis 1 creation account repeats the phrase: "And behold, it was very good." God's intent is that we restore goodness to creation. The second reason to observe the sabbath — God's redemptive activity — informs us that it is proper to restore God's creation on the sabbath day. That's why Jesus healed the man with the withered hand.

Christians do not observe the sabbath. Almost all Christians do not observe the commandment to keep the sabbath. As you know, the sabbath is the seventh day of the week, Saturday. Only a few groups, such as the Seventh Day Adventists, keep the sabbath day. The early Christians, who were Jews, observed the sabbath in the synagogue until they were thrown out, when Christianity ceased being a sect within Judaism. Christians do observe Sunday, the day of Christ's resurrection, as a time of worship and rest.

SERMON APPROACHES WITH ILLUSTRATIONS

Lesson 1: 1 Samuel 3:1-20

Sermon Title: Who's Calling?

Sermon Angle: There's a man that I know who calls me every three to six months. When I pick up the phone with my usual greeting, he never identifies himself, he just starts talking. For a few seconds I have to think to myself: "Who is this calling?" It doesn't take long for me to solve the mystery because I know his voice, even though I haven't heard it for some time. That's essentially what happened to the boy Samuel. God called and Samuel didn't know who it was because he had never conversed with the Lord before. Samuel thought that Eli had called him, as he probably had done many times before. The old man eventually suspected that the Lord was calling to the boy and informed him how to respond to the Lord's call. God doesn't always identify himself; he just starts talking, through other people, through events, and we need to learn how to recognize the Lord's voice.

Outline:
1. Wouldn't it be nice to receive a call from God when he clearly identifies himself and then gives us a message?
2. God doesn't normally identify himself when he speaks to us.
3. We need to learn to know the Lord's voice (scripture, worship, prayer, or silence).

Sermon Title: Dare To Discipline

Sermon Angle: The message that God eventually shared with Samuel was a word of judgment on Eli and his house. Eli was apparently a good man but weak. He had some sons that were real rebels, corrupt, immoral, and greedy. Yet, this father would not punish his sons for their sins, nor contain their lawlessness. He failed the primary responsibility of any parent, to discipline. His failure to reign in his sons led to the destruction of the house of Eli (vv. 12-14). Dr. James Dobson wrote a book titled *Dare To Discipline*. If we do not dare to discipline many people will reap the whirlwind.

Sermon Title: True Sons And Daughters

Sermon Angle: Eli's sons were his by heredity and birth but not in spirit. They rejected everything that their father stood for and in doing so they despised their father. Samuel was not Eli's birth son but his adopted son. He identified with Eli spiritually and was a respectful and obedient son. This text shows that Samuel was quick to answer to Eli's call, caring for the needs of the older man. Eli addressed him as "my son" (v. 6), which shows the love he felt for Samuel. Sons and daughters are spiritually conceived. So it is in our relationship with the Lord. We show that we are God's true sons and daughters by a life of obedience and love.

Lesson 2: 2 Corinthians 4:5-12

Sermon Title: Remember Your Mission

Sermon Angle: Paul defends his mission to the Corinthians by asserting that he and his party do not proclaim themselves but Jesus Christ (v. 5); they only make themselves known as their slaves, for Jesus' sake. We are like the warm-up group for a singing star; our job is to make Jesus look good and to get the crowd ready to receive him. Some Christians forget, thinking they are the stars, trying to get people to notice them and sing their praises. Remember that your mission is to proclaim Jesus as Lord; we are only Christ's servants.

Outline:
1. Paul was very clear about his mission — to proclaim Jesus as Lord, himself as servant (v. 5).
2. An organization will fall apart if it forgets its mission.
3. Is our church seeking to glorify Christ as Lord, or ourselves?
4. Remember that we are servants for the sake of Christ and his church.

Sermon Title: We're Cracked Pots

Sermon Angle: Paul reminds us of our human frailty, comparing us to earthen jars or pots (v. 7). Such jars were the main means for storage in Jesus' day. If there would be some flaw in the clay or if it weren't fired correctly, the jar would crack and the contents might spill out. As the years roll by we are more and more aware of our weaknesses and we observe a proliferation of cracks in our outward physical nature. What a wonder that God has chosen to house the treasure of the gospel in such fragile containers! That's a little bit like storing gold coins in ice cream cones. If we stay close to Christ he will use the fire of adversity to keep us from breaking and spilling the contents (vv. 8-11).

* * * * *

Ronald Hutchcraft, in *Peaceful Living In A Stressful World*, tells of taking his two sons to a restoration of an old American village, where they visited the potter's shop.

"Careful!" the craftsman exclaimed. "Please don't touch the pottery on that shelf. You'll ruin it." Then he surprised us when he said, "Why don't you touch the ones on the other shelf?" Needless to say, the Hutchcrafts were curious as to why some vases could be touched and not others.

Glancing at the "do not touch" shelf, the potter explained, "These haven't been fired yet." The potter explained that there was more to creating masterpieces than just making globs of clay into beautiful shapes. If he stopped at that point, the objects would quickly become marred and misshapen. Without the fire the objects would soon deteriorate and be of no use to anyone. Fire makes the objects firm and strong and enables the beauty to endure.

Suffering, pain, loss, failure, and the like, are like a fire — not a consuming fire but a refining fire — which not only increases the value of that which passes through her purifying flames but also makes it more durable, beautiful, and useful. The Lord allows us, his earthen vessels, to pass through the fire not because he is punishing us but because he loves us and wants to prepare us for time and eternity.

* * * * *

Gospel: Mark 2:23—3:6
Sermon Title: Sabbath Sabotage
Sermon Angle: The religious officials wanted to sabotage Jesus on the sabbath; they yearned to point the accusing finger at him for being a lawbreaker. What they didn't realize, and what Jesus was not able to put across, was God's intent for the sabbath. "The sabbath was made for man, not man for the sabbath" (v. 27). The sabbath was not a prison but a brief vacation from work and the cares of ordinary living, so that the people could focus on eternal things. Jesus' accusers, not Jesus, had sabotaged the sabbath with their narrow, judgmental viewpoints. Christians do not observe the sabbath but we do observe the Lord's day. Some Christian groups have been narrow in their understanding of our Sunday observance. However, the opposite danger seems to be prevalent in our day. Sunday is no longer the Lord's day, it is just another day for business, sports, or selfish pleasures. We have permitted the world to sabotage *our* sabbath!

Sermon Title: Losing Sight Of The End
Sermon Angle: Jesus' criticism of his critics in today's gospel makes it plain that he believed that they had lost sight of the end or object of the sabbath observance. The means became an end. The purpose of the sabbath and of our Sunday observance is that we might not lose sight of the end (object) of living and of that End above all ends, which we call God.

Sermon Title: Inter-mission

Sermon Angle: The Hebrew word *shabbat* means "sabbath." The first definition of the word on my computer concordance comes up "intermission." The first part of that word means "between." The last part of that word (mission) means "to send." The sabbath and Sunday observance is an interlude interspersed in our worldly mission, so that we might judge our course against the map of eternity. This makes it possible to correct our course if necessary.

*   *   *   *   *

We must be quick to point out that though Jesus criticized the attitudes that certain religious leaders displayed toward the sabbath, he was not condemning the proper observance of the sabbath. The proper observance of the day is meant to pull us out of the rapid stream of doing into the gentle pool of being, so that we might not be swept away by the torrents of life.

To celebrate our 25th anniversary, my wife and I flew to Hawaii. One afternoon we drove the notorious "Road to Hanna," a narrow, serpentine route overlooking the ocean. Toward the end of the road is the Garden of the Seven Pools. In this park a stream quickened down the hillside, transforming into a waterfall that emptied into a series of pools at various levels on its plunge to the ocean. In my haste to capture some scenes on my camera, I hurried ahead of my wife, Fran. When I finally circled back, I found her sitting soaking wet by the edge of one of the pools. It turns out that she had slipped on a wet rock and slid into the pool. She pictured herself going over the waterfall into the next pool and then the next, on down to the ocean. Fortunately, a man had the presence of mind to throw Fran the end of his beach towel, by which he pulled her to solid ground. Our lives are sometimes like that; we get swept away by the rapids of the stream of doing, so that our very life is at peril. If we observe Sunday as a day of rest, recreation, and worship, the Holy Spirit throws us a lifeline to lift us out of the rapids and into the garden of being in Christ.

Proper 5/Pentecost 3/Ordinary Time 10

Revised Common	1 Samuel 8:4-20 (11:14-15)	2 Corinthians 4:13—5:1	Mark 3:20-35
Roman Catholic	Genesis 3:9-15	2 Corinthians 4:13—5:1	Mark 3:20-35
Episcopal	Genesis 3:(1-7) 8-21	2 Corinthians 4:13-18	Mark 3:20-35

Theme For The Day: Facing the enemy. God and his servants can expect opposition. In the first lesson, Samuel and the Lord experience flack because the people want a king. In the second lesson, Paul continues to be pummeled by all sorts of enemies and by the weakness of his body. In the gospel, Jesus discovers that his opponents are not only the scribes but his own family, who regard him as crazy.

BRIEF COMMENTARY ON THE LESSONS

Lesson 1: 1 Samuel 8:4-20 (11:14-15) (C)

The people plead with Samuel to obtain a king for them so that they might be similar to all the other countries about them which had kings. The request displeases Samuel; he considers it a rejection of the Lord. Nevertheless, he prays to God about it. The Lord, too, feels the rebuff of the people but agrees to give them what they want. Only he charges Samuel to inform the people of all the abuse their king will heap upon them. He will heavily tax their possessions and their labor. Here we seem to have an instance of the Lord giving the people what they asked for, even though it would not prove best for them. In choosing a king the Israelites would lose some of the their uniqueness and the nation would become divided. Two viewpoints on kingship for Israel are contained in 1 Samuel, one favorable to kingship and one not favorable.

Lesson 1: Genesis 3:9-15 (RC); Genesis 3:(1-7) 8-21 (E)

Lesson 2: 2 Corinthians 4:13—5:1 (C, RC); 2 Corinthians 4:13-18 (E)

Paul remains confident that God will bring them all, missionary and missionized, into the eternal presence of God in spite of his hardships. Physical deterioration does not deter the untiring missionary. Though the believers' outer transient nature is fading away, their inner spiritual nature is being renewed daily. The temporary afflictions of this life are preparing God's saints for an incomparable glory. The apostle commends us to focus on the eternal rather than things transient.

Gospel: Mark 3:20-35 (C, RC, E)

Jesus' ministry builds momentum as great crowds flock around him, probably attracted by the healings and exorcisms. Jesus creates such a stir that the scribes send a deputation to check it out. They conclude that Jesus is possessed by Beelzebul (a pagan god identified with Satan). Jesus points out the absurdity of their charge; if this were true, Satan would be battling with himself, but a "house divided against itself cannot stand" (v. 24). It is in this context, where men are attributing the work of God to Satan, the warning against the so-called "unpardonable sin" occurs. Those who continue to maintain that the work of God springs from the evil one have cut themselves off from the light of God's presence. Jesus is not talking about a one-time sin but a continuing state of spiritual perversity and unbelief, such as was exhibited by the scribes. Not only do the scribes think that Jesus is possessed, but his own family comes to take him away, thinking that he has lost his mind. Jesus teaches the crowd that his real family is defined not by biology but by obedience to God's will.

Psalm Of The Day
    Psalm 138 (C) — "All the kings of the earth shall praise you, O Lord" (v. 4).
    Psalm 130 (E)
    Psalm 129 (RC)

Prayer Of The Day
    Great God, forbid that we ever be found to be opposing your good and gracious will. By your Spirit help us never to give ground to your foes and those enemies of our soul, but to stand in faithfulness with all your saints. In Jesus' name. Amen.

THEOLOGICAL REFLECTION ON THE LESSONS

Lesson 1: 1 Samuel 8:4-20 (11:14-15)
    Deja vu all over again (v. 5). The elders assemble together and decide that Samuel is getting too old to rule and his sons do not walk in his ways. It sounds like Eli and his sons all over again, though there is no mention of Samuel's sons being lawbreakers. There comes a time for us all to let someone else take our place.
    Listen to the people (v. 7). God orders Samuel to listen to the demands of the people, even though what they desire is not God's ideal will. God may be telling us, as leaders of the church, to listen to our people, even if what they want is less than ideal. Perhaps God gave in to his people's wishes to let them learn from experience. In the same way a wise parent might give in to the wish of her child, even though that course contains pitfalls.
    Who do you want to be king? The people wanted an earthly king; Samuel wanted God to be their only king. History shows that few of their kings were able and God-fearing rulers. In our day, most people want no king but themselves. Who do you want to be your king? Is Jesus your king?

Lesson 2: 2 Corinthians 4:13—5:1
    Expansive grace. "So that the grace of God extends to more and more people ..." (v. 15). God's grace, by its very nature, is expansive; like a gas, it seeks to distribute itself over the widest possible area. We distort God's grace when we try to keep it to ourselves, but when we give free reign to God's grace it multiplies praise and thanksgiving to God (v. 15).
    Brave heart. "So we do not lose heart" (v. 16). Paul confides that the Christian, when properly focused, does not lose heart, nor does he become discouraged about the deterioration of his physical body. Christians can maintain a brave heart because God is at work in our lives creating a new nature and will couple this nature with a new spiritual body in the resurrection of the righteous.
    Peering beyond time and space (v. 18). The child of God can maintain her composure when caught up in the entropy of earthly things; she focuses on that which is beyond time and space, the new creation in Christ. The glimpse of eternal glory makes the sting of mortality appear to be a mere momentary trifle.

Gospel: Mark 3:20-35

What's the buzz about Jesus? From the onset of his ministry, Jesus was and is a controversial figure. We see Jesus through the lens of our prejudice, our tradition, or our need. Jesus attracted great crowds of needy people (v. 20); they turned to him for hope and healing. Other folks considered him to be crazy, including his family, which came to restrain him. The scribes came to find some fault with him so they might discredit this troublemaker. Jesus caused quite a buzz in the highways and marketplaces of his time. Some claimed him as king and others cursed him as Satan. How do you interpret the buzz about Jesus?

Jesus in a straitjacket. Jesus' family set out to restrain Jesus; they tried to put him in a straitjacket (v. 21). Jesus was an embarrassment to his family. As you know, Jesus won't let himself be placed in a straitjacket. He may embarrass us in the presence of our friends; he may disturb our sensibilities, but if we try to tie him down, he has a way of coming back.

The unpardonable sin (vv. 28-30). Countless believers have feared that they have committed the unpardonable sin. What is the unpardonable sin? Mark answers this question forthrightly. It is the sin of attributing the work of Christ to Satan (v. 30). To do this a person turns evil into good and good into evil. In Luke's gospel this saying is in a different context (Luke 12:10). It occurs in the midst of a passage concerning the power and wisdom, which is made available to disciples when their faith is called into question by the world. In Luke's context the unpardonable sin is to refuse the Spirit's aid during times of trial, to commit apostasy and deny Jesus.

Family ties. This passage indicates that the family ties between Jesus and his earthly family had become frayed. Jesus offers a new definition of his family; his family consists of everyone who does God's will.

SERMON APPROACHES WITH ILLUSTRATIONS

Lesson 1: 1 Samuel 8:4-20 (11:14-15)

Sermon Title: Be Careful What You Pray For

Sermon Angle: The people of Israel wanted a king and so Samuel took their request to the Lord. Having a king was not the future that God envisioned for his people, but God decided to give the people what they asked for anyway. This constitutes a prime example of not prefacing our prayers with the petition "Nevertheless, not my (our) will but your will be done." It might prove dangerous simply to tell God what we want. He might give it to us, with consequences which we could never envision.

Outline:
1. The elders of Israel asked for a king (v. 5).
2. The request displeased Samuel and God.
3. God gave them what they wanted and it eventually led to disaster.
4. Be careful what you pray for — God might grant it.
5. Always seek God's will in your prayers.

Sermon Title: The Changing Face Of Leadership

Sermon Angle: The request of the elders for a king came out of a realization that different times call for a different style of leadership. The Israelites were no longer a nomadic people. They were getting settled in the land and they recognized that a different kind of leadership was needed for a new day. For instance, they may have seen that they needed a more centralized form of leadership in order to protect themselves from hostile countries surrounding them. Samuel was getting to be an old man and no new judges were in sight (v. 5). The problem was that they latched on to a solution to their leadership needs that was not the best for them. We need to be sensitive to the changing leadership needs in church, community, and country and shift as needed. At the same time we must never lose sight of the sovereignty of God.

Lesson 2: 2 Corinthians 4:13—5:1

Sermon Title: How To Grow Old Gracefully

Sermon Angle: Most Americans probably dread growing old. Old age is not highly touted in our society. We all want to look younger and feel younger. We will do almost anything to turn back the biological time clock. Paul also experienced the afflictions of age but knew the secret of growing old gracefully. He did not focus on the deterioration of his body but rather set his sights on the new nature that God was creating in him (v. 16) through his grace. Paul developed a sense of perspective, which is God's gift to us as we grow older. He viewed everything against the backdrop of eternity. The afflictions of the body were nothing when compared to the glory that awaits us. The secret of growing old gracefully is to become more keyed in to spiritual (unseen) realities and less concerned with our bodies and bank accounts.

Outline:
1. Our society denies death and the reality of aging.
2. Paul lifts up the secret of growing old gracefully.
   — Admit that the body is deteriorating but don't worry about it (v. 16).
   — Focus on our spiritual nature, which is being renewed daily (v. 16).
   — Set your sights not on past but future glory with God (v. 17).
   — Realize that unseen (spiritual) things are more real than things seen (v. 18).

*   *   *   *   *

Bessie Delaney and her sister, Sarah, authored a book in 1993 which became a best-seller. The book is called *Having Our Say: The Delaney Sisters' First 100 Years.* The sisters' award-winning memoir was on the *New York Times* best-seller list and has sold more than four million copies. The book has been translated into several foreign languages and made into a Broadway play and a television movie. They also authored a second book: *The Delaney Sisters' Book Of Everyday Wisdom*, which has sold nearly as many copies. You can be sure that they didn't focus on the increasing decrepitude of their bodies. They were caught up in the things of the mind and spirit. Bessie died in September 1995 and Sarah in January 1999, at the ages of 104 and 107 respectively.

*   *   *   *   *

President Reagan's Alzheimer's disease, a degenerative affliction of the nervous system, brought him closer to his family. Reagan disclosed that he had the disease in November of 1994. Nancy Reagan reported: "I think any illness ... brings things into focus and should re-shuffle your priorities." The former first lady said that she had reconciled with her daughter, Patti Davis, who had written books critical of her parents and posed nude for *Playboy*. Miss

Davis commented that the reconciliation started even before her father's disease was diagnosed. Reagan wrote notes to his daughter saying that he loved her, that he and Nancy loved her. Though the body and mind of our former president faded, his spirit became stronger as he became increasingly aware of the spiritual dimension of existence.

*   *   *   *   *

Sermon Title: Don't Worry About The Mosquito Bites

Sermon Angle: Paul describes the trials and difficulties of life as "a slight momentary affliction" (v. 17). In other words, they were mere mosquito bites compared to the glory of God's kingdom. You've experienced mosquitoes and mosquito bites; if you haven't, go to Minnesota or Michigan in the summertime. These creatures are pesky, and when they bite it may sting ever so slightly for a moment. The bite may even swell up and become red for several minutes, but before long you don't even know it was there, that is, if you don't scratch it. The afflictions of life are real but they are mere mosquito bites compared to the glory that shall be revealed to us.

Gospel: Mark 3:20-35

Sermon Title: About Trying To Place Jesus In A Straightjacket

Sermon Angle: All kinds of people have tried and continued to try to place Jesus in a straitjacket. His family came to Jesus with the intent of restraining him; people were saying that he was crazy (v. 21). The scribes attempted to rein him in by accusing him of casting out demons by Beelzebul, the prince of demons (v. 22). Through the ages folks have attempted to put Jesus in their peculiar straightjacket, whether it be a theological, philosophical, economic, or political straightjacket. Jesus may appear to be subdued for a time but, like Harry Houdini, he always finds a way to escape.

Sermon Title: A House Divided

Sermon Angle: The scribes accused Jesus of casting out demons by the power of the devil. Jesus responded: "If a kingdom is divided against itself, that house cannot stand. And if a house is divided against itself, that house cannot stand" (vv. 24-25). It was this rationale that prompted Abraham Lincoln to engage the northern states in a civil war with the south. It was this same principle that guided his reconstruction efforts; he refused to inflict humiliation on the vanquished. During World War ll, the US was galvanized by a common objective, to win the war. However, in recent decades our society seems to have become increasingly polarized. The church has witnessed the same phenomenon. Remember, Jesus came to gather the flock, not scatter it.

Outline:
1. Jesus said, "A house divided cannot stand" (v. 25).
2. Tyrants know the "divide and conquer" principle.
3. Society and church seem to have become increasingly polarized.
4. Knowing God and doing his will unites us with God's family (v. 35).

Sermon Title: Have You Committed An Unpardonable Sin?

Sermon Angle: The so-called unpardonable sin, the sin against the Holy Spirit (vv. 29-30), has troubled countless souls through the ages. They have given up all hope, thinking that they had done something so terrible as to be damned. What is this eternal sin? In Mark's gospel it is interpreted as attributing the work of God to Satan and the work of Satan to God. The unpardonable sin is to permit oneself to wander so far from God that spiritual darkness is complete and the proper distinction between good and evil has been lost. We aren't talking, I believe, about a one-time sin but about a continuous rejection of the very concepts of good and evil. It's safe to say that most people have not committed the eternal sin and the very fact that it concerns us shows that God's Spirit is still active in our lives.

Outline:
1. Is there any sin too great for God to forgive?
2. Jesus warns against committing the eternal sin (v. 29).
3. What is this sin? Murder? Rape? Robbery?
4. It is the sin of turning good and evil upside down.
5. If we are concerned about committing such a sin, we are in the clear.
6. Trust in the grace and mercy of God in Christ.

Proper 6/Pentecost 4/Ordinary Time 11

Revised Common	1 Samuel 15:34—16:13	2 Corinthians 5:6-10 (11-13) 14-17	Mark 4:26-34
Roman Catholic	Ezekiel 17:22-24	2 Corinthians 5:6-10	Mark 4:26-34
Episcopal	Ezekiel 31:1-6, 10-14	2 Corinthians 5:1-10	Mark 4:26-34

Theme For The Day: Life through death. In the first lesson, Samuel's hopes for God's kingdom die with God's rejection of Saul and are reborn in David. In the second lesson, Paul is looking forward to death, which would bring him into the presence of the Lord. The gospel contains the parable of the seeds, which also have to die to be reborn as living fruitful plants.

BRIEF COMMENTARY ON THE LESSONS

Lesson 1: 1 Samuel 15:34—16:13 (C)

God regrets having made Saul king and Samuel mourns Saul's fall from grace. The Lord instructs Samuel to quit mourning for Saul and go anoint his successor. Samuel goes to Bethlehem, ostensibly to conduct a feast before the Lord. The real reason is to anoint Saul's successor. The sons of Jesse are presented to him one by one. None of the seven eldest sons of Jesse are picked. Samuel asks Jesse if he has other sons. He responds that the youngest son is out in the field watching the sheep. David is brought before the prophet and anointed to be king of Israel.

Lesson 1: Ezekiel 17:22-24 (RC)

Lesson 1: Ezekiel 31:1-6, 10-14 (E)

Lesson 2: 2 Corinthians 5:6-10 (11-13) 14-17 (C); 2 Corinthians 5:6-10 (RC); 2 Corinthians 5:1-10 (E)

Paul does not let the weakness of the body and his earthly afflictions discourage him because he looks forward to putting off the cloak of mortality and being with Christ. No matter in what condition he finds himself, he aims to please the Lord. The love of Christ motivates him to proclaim the gospel; that Christ died for all people so that they might no longer live for themselves but for Christ.

Gospel: Mark 4:26-34 (C, RC, E)

This lection brings to conclusion Mark's section on Jesus' parables. The mystery of the kingdom is revealed to the disciples but remains obscure for outsiders. The first parable (vv. 26-29) lifts up the mystery of growth. The seed sprouts and grows of its own, not because of human efforts. The growth of the kingdom is a gift of God. The second parable (vv. 30-32) emphasizes the magnitude of the kingdom's growth and its small beginnings. The mustard seed begins as one of the smallest seeds and grows into one of the largest shrubs, habitat for countless creatures; so it is with the kingdom of God.

259

Psalm Of The Day
    Psalm 20 (C) — "Now I know that the Lord will help his anointed ..." (v. 6).
    Psalm 92 (E)
    Psalm 91 (RC)

Prayer Of The Day
    Spirit of God, you have planted the seed of faith in our hearts and rooted us in your kingdom. By your Spirit enable us to grow in faith, love, and obedience to your will, that we might reach the fullness of our potential in Christ. In Jesus' name we pray. Amen.

THEOLOGICAL REFLECTION ON THE LESSONS

Lesson 1: 1 Samuel 15:34—16:13
The beginning of the end. In the passage prior to this one, Samuel severely dresses down Saul for having disobeyed God in not utterly destroying the Amalekites. Samuel announces that the Lord will replace Saul with a more worthy king. Saul continues to reign for some time yet but his source of authority has been removed. It was the beginning of the end.

Grief work (v. 1). Samuel grieved over Saul. Apparently, there were close personal bonds. The Lord tells the prophet to snap out of his grief; it would do no good to mourn that which had happened and could not be changed. There must be a time of grief but that period of mourning must yield to the determination to tackle life anew. God wanted Samuel to focus on the new king, not the old one.

How God judges. When Samuel saw Eliab, Jesse's oldest son, he was impressed with his physical stature and demeanor. God said, "No! This isn't the man." Humans judge by outward appearance but God looks at the heart (v. 7).

Lesson 2: 2 Corinthians 5:1-17
Real estate (v. 1). It seems that most people like to possess a little real estate, at least a house and a little piece of ground. Paul compares earthly existence to living in a tent; a tent is quite fragile, temporary, and made for traveling. Yet, the apostle longs for some real estate, a dwelling not made with human hands, eternal in the heavens (v. 1). That's the only piece of real estate that really matters. There are no mortgage payments for this house, the debt has been removed through the death and resurrection of Christ.

A bearable burden (v. 4). Sometimes we strain and groan under the burdens of life. Two women called into the church office yesterday to share some of their burden; both had lost their jobs. One was told to clean out her desk and leave in thirty minutes. Both of them were groaning under the burden. Yes, life can be a real burden but it's still a bearable burden, as long as we have Christ to bear the burden with us. In Matthew 11, Christ bids all who are burdened to come to him for relief.

Home or away (vv. 6-9). Most people would consider the place where they live and love and work as home. Paul has a different perspective. He says that while we're at home in the body, we're away from the Lord. But when we leave our body we will go home to be with the Lord. Our real home is with the Lord, our real home is heaven.

In Christ, a new creation (v. 17). God doesn't just recycle us in Christ, he makes us completely new. The old selfish attitudes are gone. The old destructive habits and attitudes have been replaced by a fresh outlook.

Gospel: Mark 4:26-34

Growth is in God (vv. 26-29). Growth is a marvelous and mysterious force. While man can sometimes nurture growth, we cannot bring it about. "The earth produces of itself" (v. 28). Growth is of God and so is the growth of the kingdom of God.

The dynamics of growth. The parable says at least three things about growth. First, growth is independent of humans and mysterious; it's a gift of God. Second, growth is orderly; "first the blade, then the head...." Third, growth is fruitful; "full grain on the head." Fourth, there comes the harvest time.

Small beginnings (v. 31). Like the mustard seed that starts small and grows large, the kingdom ushered in by Jesus begins with just twelve men but will ultimately spread over all the earth. Most of us feel quite small at times and our efforts seem insignificant. The parable of the mustard seed gives us hope.

Special education (v. 34). Mark states that Jesus spoke only in parables, except that he explained everything to his disciples privately. You might say that the disciples received special education or tutoring. Being a disciple of Jesus affords us special opportunities to know the full counsel of God. Indeed, the full mystery of the kingdom can only become known by those who are in Christ. The Lord still gives his disciples special education through the Holy Spirit.

SERMON APPROACHES WITH ILLUSTRATIONS

Lesson 1: 1 Samuel 15:34—16:13

Sermon Title: Moving On

Sermon Angle: Samuel was an old man and had seen many changes in his lifetime. Now God had rejected Saul, the one who was to take from him the mantle of leadership. Samuel was depressed as he mourned for Saul, the lame-duck king. God came to him and told him to stop living in the past. It was time to move on. God was doing a new thing (v. 1). We learn from this story that it does no good to bewail the past. God told Samuel to fill his horn with oil, symbolic of God's Spirit, and pour it on the one ordained by the Lord. We too must go out with the anointing of God's Spirit.

Outline:
1. Samuel was caught in the past (like a grave).
2. He was told to quit mourning that which was ordained of God.
3. He was ordered out on a new mission, bearing God's Spirit.

Sermon Title: Seeing Through God's Eyes

Sermon Angle: Samuel was impressed with Eliab, the eldest son of Jesse, because he cut such an impressive figure (v. 6). The outward appearance of a person is usually the first thing we notice; it's only human. God sees what's on the inside, God sees the heart. Humans are impressed with statistics, who is the tallest, the fastest, the strongest, or the cleverest. God is concerned about spiritual qualities, such as a loving, caring, and serving spirit. Through God's Spirit we can learn to see through God's eyes.

Lesson 2: 2 Corinthians 5:1-17

Sermon Title: How To Take Possession Of Your Real Estate

Sermon Angle: When our children were little we did quite a bit of camping out in a tent. My wife enjoyed the experience for the most part but couldn't get used to sleeping in a tent. She felt

261

vulnerable and exposed. Actually, living in a tent is a metaphor for human existence. Paul tells us that if our tent is destroyed, God has prepared for his saints a new home, eternal in the heavens (v. 1). Through faith we take possession of our real estate.

Sermon Title: A Faith Walk

Sermon Angle: Have you ever participated in a faith walk? That's where two people take turns at leading and following. Typically, the person being led is blindfolded and the other person leads/guides the other person. The object is to develop trust. The apostle reminds us that life is a faith walk. "We walk by faith, not by sight" (v. 7).

Outline:
1. Begin your sermon with a demonstration faith walk. Ask the person how he felt as he was being guided about.
2. Life is a faith walk (v. 7).
3. The more we walk with Jesus, the more we learn to trust him.
4. In heaven faith will yield to sight.

Sermon Title: Your Point Of View

Sermon Angle: Paul points out that being a new creature in Christ causes us to abandon our typical human point of view. He observes that Christians no longer regard Christ from a human point of view (v. 16). Christ is not just a man or a teacher. He is our Savior and our Lord. Nor do we regard other people from a strictly human point of view. They are not objects but people for whom Christ died. We also see ourselves from a new point of view. "If anyone be in Christ, there is a new creation" (v. 17).

Gospel: Mark 4:26-34

Sermon Title: The Joy Of Scattering Seeds

Sermon Angle: Jesus says that the kingdom of God is like a person who scatters seeds (this was the method of sowing in Jesus' day) and then goes about his business in life. All the while, the seeds are growing toward maturity and the man doesn't know how. The farmer doesn't comprehend the dynamics of growth but he doesn't need to. All he has to do is scatter the seed and harvest the grain when it is ripe. I know this seems simplistic. Modern farmers understand much more of the dynamics of growth and are able to intervene in the process to increase the yield. Nevertheless, farmers are still highly dependent on forces outside themselves, which influence the mystery of growth. Nebraska farmers experienced an early freeze in September 1995, and suffered a 20-30% reduction in their soybean crop. For the children of God, our greatest joy is to scatter the seeds of the kingdom of God and watch them grow.

Outline:
1. Chances are, if you are here the seed of the kingdom has been planted in your hearts.
2. Others have received the joy of watching us grow.
3. We are called to scatter the kingdom seeds of faith, hope, and love.
4. We have the joy of watching God grant them growth.

* * * * *

Oh, God! is one of my favorite movies. God decides to communicate his love to the world through a grocery store manager. He appears to the manager while he is taking a shower. At first the manager tries to avoid being God's spokesman. Finally, he holds a news conference to deliver God's message, which precipitates embarrassment and chaos for himself and his family. Toward the end of the movie, the two are evaluating the success of their mission. The manager judges it to be a failure. "Oh, I don't think so," says God. "You never know; a seed here and a seed there, something will catch hold and grow."

*   *   *   *   *

Sermon Title: Seasons In The Son

Sermon Angle: The parable of the seeds speaks of three seasons for the crops; I call them seasons in the sun. There is the time of planting (v. 26), the time of growth (vv. 27-28), then the harvest season (v. 29). In the natural world these seasons come successively: planting, growth, and then harvest. The church has its seasons of the Son, Jesus Christ. The functions of planting, growth, and harvesting go on simultaneously. The time of planting can be equated with baptism and coming to faith. The period between baptism and death corresponds to the season of growth. The harvest season comes when the seeds of the gospel bear fruit and people are brought to faith or renewal of faith. Of course, death can be viewed as the ultimate harvest time when the seasons of the Son are brought to full fruit.

Outline:
1. The natural world has its seasons in the sun.
2. The church has its seasons of the Son.
   — Planting.
   — Growth.
   — Harvest.

Sermon Title: Small Beginnings

Sermon Angle: The parable of the mustard seed lifts up for us the miracle of growth. A mustard seed is ever so small and yet becomes a great shrub. Almost everything begins small. The human being begins when two microscopic cells come together and grow explosively both in size and complexity. The kingdom is part of this growth explosion, starting with a few people who transform into a multitude.

Outline:
1. The point of the parable is that small can become great.
2. We shouldn't worry about size but only about growing according to God's pattern.
3. The kingdom of God and the good we do in Christ's name will grow great.

*   *   *   *   *

The parable of the mustard seed makes much the same point, though the emphasis here is the smallness of the seed. God's kingdom starts out as a tiny, insignificant seed that grows astronomically. The power is in the seed. Speaking of small seeds growing large, an article about financier Warren Buffett, in *U.S. News*, states that if you would have been farsighted enough to have invested $10,000 in 1956 with Buffett's company, it would be worth an unbelievable $60,000,000 today. This, of course, has nothing to do God's kingdom except to demonstrate how some seeds have enormous potential for growth. If we scatter God's seed he promises that some will produce mightily.

263

Proper 7/Pentecost 5/Ordinary Time 12

Revised Common	1 Samuel 17:(1a, 4-11, 19-23) 32-49	2 Corinthians 6:1-13	Mark 4:35-41
Roman Catholic	Job 38:1, 8-11	2 Corinthians 5:14-17	Mark 4:35-41
Episcopal	Job 38:1-11, 16-18	2 Corinthians 5:14-21	Mark 4:35-41 (5:1-20)

Theme For The Day: Knowing God's presence and power in the midst of the storms of life.

BRIEF COMMENTARY ON THE LESSONS

Lesson 1: 1 Samuel 17:(1a, 4-11, 19-23) 32-49 (C)

The armies of King Saul are challenged by the champion of the Philistines, Goliath, a huge man who challenges the Israelites to select a man to fight against him. The victorious party would triumph not only over his opponent but his opponent's army. David comes down to the field of battle and goads Saul's army for their lack of courage. "Who is this uncircumcised Philistine that he should defy the armies of the living God?" (v. 26). David's words reach Saul and the shepherd boy is brought into the king's presence. David boasts that he has killed bear and lion in his duties as shepherd; he could do the same to Goliath. Saul agrees and has David don his armor but David feels awkward and clumsy. Taking his sling, he slays the giant with a deft shot to the temple and gains fame and recognition for his prowess.

Lesson 1: Job 38:1, 8-11 (RC); Job 38:1-11, 16-18 (E)

See first lesson for Proper 24.

Lesson 2: 2 Corinthians 6:1-13 (C)

Paul continues to defend his gospel and does so eloquently. The afflictions that he has endured for the sake of the gospel and the abundant gifts of the Spirit point to the genuineness of his gospel. Apparently, the Corinthians feel that Paul's teachings are too restrictive (vv. 11-12); Paul counters the charge with an appeal to open their hearts to him and to the gospel. He has not been restrictive in his dealing with them but they are restrictive in their affections (v. 12). He powerfully asserts that now (before Christ returns) is the time to accept Christ's reconciliation (v. 2) and share it.

Lesson 2: 2 Corinthians 5:14-17 (RC); 2 Corinthians 5:14-21 (E)

See second lesson for Proper 6.

Gospel: Mark 4:35-41 (C, RC); Mark 4:35-41 (5:1-20) (E)

The gospel continues where last week's left off. Jesus instructs the disciples to get in the boat and go to the other side of the lake, probably for rest. In the crossing a sudden storm, for which Lake Galilee is infamous, sweeps down upon them. The wind threatens to swamp the boat with water but Jesus is asleep. The disciples are possessed by panic and shake Jesus awake with the words: "Teacher, don't you care that we are about to perish?" This phrase captures the sentiment of millions down through the ages whose lives were also in peril. Note that they address Jesus as "teacher," not "Lord." Jesus rebukes the wind and the sea, as if they were demonic powers: "Peace, be still!" (v. 39) There is a great calm, not only externally but in the hearts of the disciples. They are amazed at his authority, that even the wind and sea obey him, and wonder at Jesus' true identity (v. 41). There's more to this man than meets the eye.

Psalm Of The Day
Psalm 9:9-20 (C) — "The Lord is a stronghold for the oppressed" (v. 9).
Psalm 107:1-32 (E)
Psalm 106 (RC)

Prayer Of The Day
Lord Jesus, when the storms of life rage about us, filling our hearts with fear, give us the confidence to trust in your presence. Then rebuke the forces that assail us with your eternal peace. In Jesus' name. Amen.

THEOLOGICAL REFLECTION ON THE LESSONS

Lesson 1: 1 Samuel 17:(1a, 4-11, 19-23) 32-49

Cure for heart failure (v. 32). David counseled King Saul: "Let no man's heart fail because of him" [Goliath]. Then he offered to go fight the giant. Heart failure for the army of Saul meant paralyzing fear. Those who were seized with fear had lost their trust in Yahweh. David had learned to depend on God's invisible presence during his shepherd watches, giving him confidence and strength to defeat his foes. Faith in the power of God cures heart failure.

God sends a boy to do a man's job. When David offered to fight the Philistine, Saul cautioned that Goliath was a seasoned warrior and that David was only a boy (v. 33). God sent a boy to do a man's job in order to reveal that God is the source of strength, not humans themselves.

Saving the lamb from the lion's jaw. David informed Saul that he had previously saved his lambs from the lion's jaw or that of the bear (vv. 34-35). At that point the nation of Israel was God's beloved lamb in the lion's jaw. David had the faith to know that God has a shepherd's heart and would pry open the lion's mouth.

Lesson 2: 2 Corinthians 6:1-13

Carpe diem. "Behold, now is the acceptable time; now is the day of salvation" (v. 2b). *Carpe diem* is Latin for "seize the day." Paul's point was that God had taken the lead in Christ to reconcile us to God. A window of grace is now open to all. Therefore, seize the day, grasp the gift of eternal life that is now being offered.

Offered for a limited time. We're all heard advertisers urging us to "Act now!" "This offer is only good for a limited time!" Such language seeks to move us to act *now*. Paul makes the same point. This gracious offer to be adopted into God's family, to receive his forgiveness, is available only for a limited time. The problem comes from the fact that we've heard this warning so many times that we don't take it seriously. We must not be lulled into complacency. This world is passing away and so are we. We have only a limited time to accept or extend this offer of grace. "Behold, now is the acceptable time; behold, now is the day of salvation!" (v. 2).

Weapons of righteousness (v. 7). The apostle defends his ministry with a catalogue of spiritual traits and experiences. In verse 7 he speaks of weapons of the right hand and weapons of the left hand. What are some of those weapons? They are numerous, some of which are sprinkled throughout this passage — endurance, purity, truthfulness, kindness, love, and the like. With the weapons of God we fight the wiles of the devil.

Bowel obstruction (v. 12). Paul had been accused of restricting the Corinthians. Perhaps his teaching on sexual purity was too narrow for their liking. The apostle counters the charge with the claim that their hearts (Paul's party) have been wide open, while the hearts of the Corinthians have suffered a narrowing of affections for them. The Greek word translated "affections" is *splangchnon*, which interprets as bowel or intestines. The word translated "restricted" indicates a narrowing or cramping. Thus the expression, "You are restricted in your own affections" means literally "a cramping, narrowing, or obstruction of the bowels." Bowel obstructions frequently are very painful. However, the obstruction of affections causes pain in others, not just ourselves.

Gospel: Mark 4:35-41

Going to the other side (v. 35). Jesus instructed the disciples to get into the boat and go to the other side of the lake. Jesus had been ministering to the crowds; he needed some rest. The "other side" symbolizes the place of renewing our strength and our spirits through rest and prayer.

Peace in the middle of the storm. If you fly into the eye of a hurricane you will experience a great calm, so peaceful that birds can be seen flying there. As you peer upward you do not see clouds but only blue sky. Jesus found himself in the eye of the storm; surrounding him was the tempest but his spirit was cradled in God's peace. The disciples were pounded by the tempest of fear because they had not yet learned to enter the eye of the storm through faith in God (v. 40).

Lord of the tempest (vv. 39-41). The disciples were awed that Jesus could still the wind and sea. Their picture of Jesus was enlarged; he was Lord of the tempest. The calm that Jesus brought showed his authority and power. In the midst of the storms of life, we need to remember that Jesus is the Lord of the tempest and the Lord of our lives.

SERMON APPROACHES WITH ILLUSTRATIONS

Lesson 1: 1 Samuel 17:(1a, 4-11, 19-23) 32-49

Sermon Title: The Power Of Positive Thinking

Sermon Angle: Norman Vincent Peale gained great fame and a large following with his positive thinking philosophy. I have problems with his philosophy when it is pushed too far because it seems to psychologize the gospel and place the emphasis on human response rather than God's grace. But let's not throw out the proverbial baby with the bath water. We all have experienced the destructive consequences of negative thinking and the power of positive thinking. The important point is that the source of the power for positive thinking is God. We can regard our obstacles and enemies with an open and hopeful attitude because we have experienced the power of God's grace in our lives. The army of Saul was paralyzed with fear because they felt that their foe was too mighty for them and their God. Their negative thinking was related to their lack of faith. David, on the other hand, had seen the power of God at work in his life, equipping him to defeat lions and bears. Certainly, God would free Israel from the fangs of their enemy, this young man argued with Saul.

266

Outline:
1. Many people are defeated not by life but by a negative attitude toward life.
2. Saul and his army were paralyzed by a defeatist attitude (v. 24).
3. David had a positive belief that God would give him victory (vv. 32, 37).
4. Christ has won the victory for us; therefore, we can think and act positively.

*   *   *   *   *

Almost everyone remembers the terrible accident that happened when Christopher Reeve, who starred as Superman, was thrown off his horse and suffered paralysis from the neck down. It seemed so ironic that the person who played the "man of steel," who could leap buildings at a single bound and stop locomotives, could have been reduced to a state of utter helplessness. Reeve was interviewed by Barbara Walters on the *20/20* television show some three months after the tragedy to find that Reeve was indeed a "man of steel," not physically but spiritually. Though he briefly contemplated the possibility of taking his life, the love and support he received from his devoted wife and family made him realize that they still needed him. Reeve told Walters that you can choose to look at life in two ways. You can regard it as the result of molecules coming together randomly, or you can look at the things that happen to you in life as having an underlying purpose and meaning. Reeve asserted that he chose to believe that there is a purpose for the accident that crippled him. Rather than see his accident as a *coup de grace*, he viewed it as a goad to accomplishing greater things. While Reeve stopped short of naming the name of Christ, he demonstrated the power that comes to one who believes positively that there is an underlying spiritual meaning or force in the universe.

*   *   *   *   *

Sermon Title: Choose Well Your Weapons
Sermon Angle: When Saul consented to let David face Goliath, he had him clad in the king's armor, carrying the king's sword. But Saul's weapons were too heavy and cumbersome for the shepherd boy. Besides, he wasn't accustomed to them. David discarded these weapons in favor of the one that he had mastered, the sling. Selecting five smooth stones from the brook, he stood before the foe. Goliath was deeply offended that Saul had sent such an unworthy opponent. "Am I a dog, that you come to me with sticks?" (v. 43). David had the courage to respond, "You come to me with sword and with a spear and with a javelin; but I come to you in the name of the Lord of hosts, the God of the armies of Israel ..." (v. 45). David's chief weapon was not his sling but his faith in the God of Israel.
Outline:
1. A soldier has his greatest opportunity for victory by using familiar weapons.
2. David chucked Saul's gear in favor of his trusted sling.
   — The principle: Victory comes from operating from our strengths.
3. David's chief weapon was his faith in Yahweh (v. 45).
4. God gives victory to those who choose to fight on the Lord's side and trust him for triumph (vv. 46-47).

Lesson 2: 2 Corinthians 6:1-13

Sermon Title: There's No Time But The Present

Sermon Angle: When encouraging someone to do something now, we might use the saying: "There's no time like the present." I propose changing that saying a bit to: "There's no time *but* the present." The past is but a memory and the future is so very uncertain. All the time we have is in the present. That's why Paul warns: "Now is the acceptable time; now is the day of salvation!" (v. 2).

Outline:
1. We are certain of no time but the present.
2. Therefore, use the present time to become reconciled to God and one another.
3. This is the day that the Lord has made — rejoice and be glad in it!

Sermon Title: Know Your True Greatness

Sermon Angle: In verses 8b through 10, Paul catalogues a series of contrasts between the way that the world sees the Christian and the way that God views the follower of Jesus. The apostle would have us view ourselves through God's eyes, not the eyes of the world. The world considers us imposters, God sees us as holding to the truth (v. 8b). To the world we are nobodies and unknown, but in the courts of the kingdom we are well known. The world views the faithful as sorrowful (killjoys), yet the child of God rejoices at the kingdom's banquet table (v. 10); the world sees us as impoverished (recall that most of the early Christians were from the working class), yet through the power of the Spirit, we make many rich in spiritual treasure. The secularist sees us as having nothing, yet we know that we possess everything we need, for time and eternity, through Christ (v. 11). Those held sway by the current worldview cannot see the true greatness of the kingdom or the child of God, but the sons and daughters of Christ know their true greatness; it is a greatness conferred through Christ.

Outline:
1. Are you aware of your true greatness as children of God?
2. Don't expect the world to recognize your greatness, because it is unaware of the spiritual domain.
3. Our lesson contrasts what the world thinks of us and who we really are in Christ (vv. 8b-11).
4. Know your true greatness and celebrate it as a gift of God.

Gospel: Mark 4:35-41

Sermon Title: Crisis Intervention

Sermon Angle: Sometimes the storms of life can suddenly swoop down upon us, threatening our very being. This was the situation in which the disciples found themselves. Life suddenly went out of control, their control, that is. They cried out to the Lord for crisis intervention. "Lord, don't you care that we are going to die?" Jesus did intervene to still the storm and calm their fears. Many of us find our lives going out of control at times. Some of us will call one of the crisis intervention telephone lines. Others will issue an SOS to a counselor, friend, or pastor. Many folks will plead with God for mercy. There is no shame in calling out for help when the storms of life threaten to flatten us. The Lord may not immediately still the external storm but God will give us the peace of his presence.

Outline:
1. The disciples found themselves embroiled in an unexpected crisis.
2. In the midst of the tempest they cried out for Jesus to intervene.
3. Jesus stilled the storm and imparted his peace.
4. In the crisis of our lives there is no shame in crying out for help.
5. God will either still the storm or impart the strength to ride it out.

Sermon Title: The Love Boat

Sermon Angle: You might recall the *Love Boat* television show, so popular back in the '70s. Every week some poor, lonely soul would find his love connection. Sometimes life feels more like a one-way cruise on the *Titanic*, when we cry out, "Lord, don't you care that we are about to die?" "If you're on board, help us!" When the disciples faced the vicious storm on Lake Galilee they must have felt that way. Fortunately, Jesus heard their desperate cries and stilled the tempest and their raging fear. Their boat, seemingly bound for oblivion, became the love boat because Jesus imparted the peace of his presence.

Sermon Title: Why Are You Afraid?

Sermon Angle: After Jesus calmed the storm he posed the question: "Why are you afraid? Don't you have any faith?" (v. 40). You would think that it was quite obvious why they were afraid. What bothered Jesus was the lack of trust that those closest to him showed when life loomed threatening. They could see that he was in the boat with them, yet they panicked. The question that Jesus put to his first disciples, he asks of us. "Why are *you* afraid?" Fears take many forms and we all have some fears. We need to look squarely at our fears to see what they disclose about our spiritual state. Jesus hits the nail squarely on the head when he indicates that fear shows a lack of faith. The more we focus on Jesus' loving presence in our boat and the less we zero in on the storms buffeting our boat, the less fear will possess us.

Outline:
1. Think of a time when you were gripped by the kind of fear that the disciples had.
2. What made you afraid? (Talk about various fears, including the fear of death.)
3. Fear and faith are inversely proportional.
4. In faith, picture Jesus in your boat, calming the tempest of your fears.
5. He wants you to experience the peace of his presence.

Proper 8/Pentecost 6/Ordinary Time 13

Revised Common	2 Samuel 1:1, 17-27	2 Corinthians 8:7-15	Mark 5:21-43
Roman Catholic	Wisdom 1:13-15; 2:23-24	2 Corinthians 8:7-9, 13-15	Mark 5:21-43
Episcopal	Deuteronomy 15:7-11	2 Corinthians 8:1-9, 13-15	Mark 5:22-24, 35b-43

Theme For The Day: The power of God in Christ to deliver us from sickness and death.

BRIEF COMMENTARY ON THE LESSONS

Lesson 1: 2 Samuel 1:1, 17-27 (C)

David's love for both Saul and Jonathan comes clearly through this elegy over the two men. David's unselfishness can be seen in the fact that David does not rejoice that those who stood in the way of his becoming king are slain. The love he had for Jonathan was greater that his love for any woman (v. 26).

Lesson 1: Wisdom 1:13-15; 2:23-24 (RC)

Lesson 1: Deuteronomy 15:7-11 (E)

Lesson 2: 2 Corinthians 8:7-15 (C); 2 Corinthians 8:7-9, 13-15 (RC); 2 Corinthians 8:1-9, 13-15 (E)

The rift between Paul and the Corinthian church has been healed. The apostle turns his attention to the physical needs of the church in Jerusalem. He encourages the Corinthians to complete their offering to the Jewish church, a project they began a year before. Prior to this passage (vv. 8:1 ff) Paul lifts up the example of the church in Macedonia. They were extremely poor but they gave sacrificially. The Macedonians provide an example of grace for their much richer Corinthian sisters and brothers. Paul also lifts up the example of Christ who, though he was rich (referring to his pre-existence), he became poor through his incarnation as a human, so that he might make the Corinthians rich in God's grace (v. 9). They are encouraged to give freely of what they have, not what they don't have, so that there might be equality. The Corinthians will then be enriched by the abundance of praise and thanksgiving to God that will overflow from their gifts. The phrase "the one who had much did not have too much and the one who had little did not have too little" comes from Exodus 16:18 and refers to the gathering of manna during the wilderness period.

Gospel: Mark 5:21-43 (C, RC); Mark 5:22-24, 35b-43 (E)

A portion of Mark between last week's and this week's gospel (5:1-20), the story of the casting out the demons of the man in the cemetery into the swine, has been skipped. After that event Jesus' party crosses the lake once again and is met by Jairus, a synagogue official, who literally begs Jesus to lay his hands on his little daughter and heal her (v. 23). Jesus agrees to go to his house and is accompanied by a large crowd. While en route, a woman who has suffered for years from a hemorrhage touches the fringe of his garment and is healed. Jesus stops, for he perceives that healing energy has flowed from him into another person and asks who has touched him. Jesus looks around and finally the woman comes forward in fear and trembling. It is important that she acknowledge the source of her healing. She must have expected a scolding but instead received a blessing. "Daughter, your faith has made you well; go in peace ..." (v. 34). As Jesus continues to the house of Jairus, word comes that the girl has died. Jesus assures the father, and continues on with Peter, James, and John. When they arrive, the crowd is in mourning. Jesus announces that she is not dead but sleeping. They laugh at him. Jesus dismisses them from the girl's presence and goes in to her with her family. Jesus takes her by the hand, saying, "Little girl, get up" (v. 41). He charges them not to broadcast the miracle, for fear that it would cause a tumult.

Psalm Of The Day
   Psalm 130 (C) — "There is forgiveness with you" (v. 4).
   Psalm 112 (E)
   Psalm 29 (RC)

Prayer Of The Day
   Lord Jesus, you have never turned away from those who truly seek you. Free us from fear, that we might cling to your promises even when the enemy of our souls seeks to pull us into the depths of despair. In the powerful name of Jesus. Amen.

THEOLOGICAL REFLECTION ON THE LESSONS

Lesson 1: 2 Samuel 1:1, 17-27
How the mighty have fallen (vv. 19, 27). David laments the death of his king and his dearest friend with the refrain above. The mighty of the earth do indeed perish and fall down as do the most lowly, but the mighty fall harder since they plummet from a greater height.

Jonathan, the faithful son and friend. Jonathan was not only David's dearest and most trusted friend but he was a loving son as well. This was not easy after Saul's jealousy of David caused him to seek to destroy Jonathan's best friend. Jonathan did not betray David, though a worldly person would have sought to do so, because David was likely to receive the throne rather than the rightful heir. Neither was Jonathan anything other than a loyal son, who fought and died at his father's side. Jonathan did not let personal ambition blunt his love for his father or his friend.

The wonder of being loved. In David's lament he extols Jonathan's love as being wonderful, surpassing the love of women. This is no little statement for a man who killed another man for the love of a woman. Being truly loved is indeed wonderful; nothing else in life can surpass it.

Lesson 2: 2 Corinthians 8:7-15
Another excellent way. In 1 Corinthians 12:31 Paul starts his love chapter by stating: "And I will show you a still more excellent way." Love is the greatest but generosity has to run a close second. Actually, generosity is an expression of love. Paul challenges the Corinthians: "Now as you excel in everything — in faith, in speech, in knowledge — so we want you to excel in this

generous undertaking" (v. 7). What undertaking? The offering for the needs of the saints in Jerusalem.

The test of love. Paul bluntly states that this business of being generous is a test of love (v. 8). He doesn't seem to mind challenging the Corinthians with the excellent generosity of another church (the Macedonians); nor does he shrink back from citing the example of the supreme generosity of our Lord in laying aside the glories of heaven for the trials of mortal existence (v. 9). Paul challenges the Corinthians to finish the test in a timely fashion (vv. 10-11).

Eager attitude (v. 12). Paul indicates that the attitude is what makes the gift acceptable or not. He urges an eager attitude in giving to the need of fellow Christians. I don't suppose the apostle to the Gentiles would agree with the saying: "The Lord loveth a cheerful giver but taketh from a grouch."

Fair balance (v. 14). The apostle's vision is not that some Christians should be givers and others receivers but that there be a fair balance between giving and receiving. It is not for us to determine the proper balance; God will see to it that those who give will also receive in return. Also, those who receive through the generosity of others will be empowered and encouraged to give.

Gospel: Mark 5:21-43

The power of persistent prayer. Jairus, a leader in the local synagogue, came to Jesus and begged him repeatedly to heal his daughter (v. 21). One might question why he had to beg repeatedly but whatever the reason, his begging reaped results. Jesus did come and heal the little girl. There is power in persistent prayer.

The healing touch (v. 23). Jairus specifically requested Jesus to come and lay his hands on his daughter in order to heal her. He had undoubtedly witnessed the Lord healing others in this manner. There is healing in Jesus' touch. We have been touched by Jesus and are called to share his healing touch with those who seek wholeness.

Give credit to your physician (vv. 26-34). The woman healed of her hemorrhages frequented many doctors but they were no help. As a last resort, she thought she would try Jesus. She reasoned that if only she touched Jesus' garment, she could be healed and Jesus wouldn't even know it. She touched the hem of the Lord's garment and felt immediately that she was healed. Her hope of anonymity was shattered when Jesus stopped and asked who had touched him. Finally she came forward to admit that it was she. Jesus is eager to heal those who reach out to him but he isn't interested in magic; that is, he doesn't want us to tap into his power without acknowledging and confessing him.

Faith healing. When the messengers came from the house of Jairus with the sad news that Jairus' daughter was dead, Jesus counseled the father not to fear, but to only believe (v. 36). Jesus needed and wanted the faith of the father and others to make the healing or resuscitating easier. When he got to the house he found the neighbors in mourning. He asked the reason for the uproar, since the child was not dead but only sleeping (v. 39). They reacted with derisive laughter. Jesus sent the unbelieving mob away and went in to the girl with her parents and his closest disciples. For him to do a miracle there needed to be a climate of faith. Almost all of the Lord's healings were faith healings.

SERMON APPROACHES WITH ILLUSTRATIONS

Lesson 1: 2 Samuel 1:1, 17-27

Sermon Title: The Cry Of Mortality

Sermon Angle: David lamented over and over again, "How the mighty have fallen!" He was, of course, mourning those of eminent standing, a king and a prince. David was in shock. It could be that for the first time he was struck with the stinging awareness of his mortality and the mortality of all living things. When someone of high estate dies, we reason with ourselves that if they can fall, how much more will we. In a sense, most of us think that we're mighty when we're young, that we're invincible; then someone close to us dies or we become sick or suffer the ravages of age. Our Lord too was mighty, in the very image of God, yet he also fell subject to the power of sin and death for our sake. Christ suffered our fallen condition, but he rose again from the dead. Like Saul and Jonathan, our mortal cord will be severed, but with Jesus we rise again.

Outline:
1. David was cut to the heart by the death of Saul and Jonathan. The lament "How the mighty have fallen!" expressed his grief.
2. David's lament might have also been a recognition of his own mortality.
3. We likewise lament our own mortality.
4. We have hope, which David did not, through the fallen and risen Jesus.

Sermon Title: Farewell To Arms

Sermon Angle: "How have the mighty fallen and the weapons of war perished!" (v. 27). One wonders if David didn't have a realization of the futility of brother killing brother with the weapons of war. How could he not realize the horrible waste of it all? Yet throughout his reign he continued to engage in battle and the sword continued to pierce his heart with sorrow, as his own sons took up arms against him or their brothers. The deaths of Saul and Jonathan point to the truth later spoken by Jesus: "Those who take up the sword will perish by the sword."

Lesson 2: 2 Corinthians 8:7-15

Sermon Title: How To Be A Truly Excellent Church

Sermon Angle: Different churches pride themselves on various things. Some take pride in their beautiful building; others point to their excellent choir or their gifted pastor. Some boast of their largess or the breadth of their programs. Paul urges the Corinthian church to be excellent in generosity, in giving (v. 7). Here are some indications of a church that is excellent in giving.

Outline:
1. It gives freely, not as a command (v. 8).
2. It focuses on the self-giving love of Jesus (v. 9).
3. It has follow-through (vv. 10-11).
4. It is eager to help (v. 12).

Sermon Title: Guidelines For Giving

Sermon Angle: Not long ago, I talked with a friend from another state who constantly has problems but won't commit himself to being part of a Christian community. When I questioned him on this issue, he said, "I already told you why I don't go to church. They are always talking about money." What an excuse! It's true that churches shouldn't be talking about money but they had better talk about giving because the Bible never tires of the subject. Our faith is founded on the self-giving love of God in Christ (v. 9). So let's talk about New Testament guidelines for giving. Many church leaders cite the tithe as one such guideline. I don't agree because the tithe is an Old Testament standard, based on legalism. Go ahead and tithe but not out of any sense of obligation. In the New Testament giving is always a free response to God's grace. Here are some guidelines from our text.

Outline:
1. Let love motivate your giving.
2. Let Jesus be the inspiration for your giving (v. 9).
3. Give eagerly (v. 12).
4. Give in accordance with your means (v. 12).

*   *   *   *   *

The relationship that Paul commended to the Corinthians might be called Christian symbiosis. Symbiosis can be defined as two creatures living together for a prolonged period of time in a relationship that may or may not be beneficial to both parties. Parasitism is a relationship where one creature lives off its host. The relationship is beneficial to the guest but destructive to the host. Tapeworms are an example of such a relationship. Commensalism is a relationship where one party in the relationship benefits but the other is unaffected. Certain ocean-dwelling fish attach to larger fish or sharks and hitch a free ride, as they gather the dinner scraps left by the host. Mutualism is a third form of symbiosis, which benefits both parties. Lichens are an apt example of mutualism. Lichens are a flowerless plant consisting of the cohabitation between algae and fungus. Algae provides the food, while the fungus stores the water. Lichens are found in many harsh and barren environments, clinging to rock, trees, and other objects, but neither could exist without the other.

The kind of symbiosis that Paul commends to the Corinthians is of this last type, mutualism. Rich and poor churches need one another. The rich churches can provide needed resources, funds, and training, while the poor churches can give back spiritual depth, an example of simplicity in living, and a chorus of praise and thanks to God. The aim of Christian symbiosis is not that one party be burdened and the other be relieved of responsibility but the free flow of mutuality.

*   *   *   *   *

Gospel: Mark 5:21-43

Sermon Title: No Hiding From Jesus

Sermon Angle: The woman with the hemorrhages approached Jesus in the midst of the crowd from the rear. She wanted something from Jesus (healing) but she didn't want Jesus himself (v. 27). She thought, if only I touch Jesus, I will be healed. Her plan was to sneak in, get what she wanted, and then get out of there. But Jesus was aware that someone had touched him in a special way (many people were pressing against him) and demanded that this person identify him or herself. We cannot steal Jesus' power and run. To receive Jesus' help and healing, we must also seek the Lord himself.

Outline:
1. The woman wanted to receive Jesus' help anonymously (v. 27).
2. Jesus demanded the person to identify herself (v. 30).
3. She came forward, confessing what she had done (v. 33).
4. Jesus announced that her faith made her well.
5. When we come out of hiding and approach Jesus face-to-face, we are made whole.

Sermon Title: Consumer Religion

Sermon Angle: We mustn't be too hard on the woman with the hemorrhages but her approach typifies an approach to religion that is popular in our day. We might dub it consumer religion. People seek to obtain a certain good or effect without a commitment to Christ or to his church. In addition to healing, they may seek knowledge on coping with life, entertainment, programs for their children, and much more. These things are all right but become pure consumerism if they are not wedded with commitment to follow Christ as Lord.

Sermon Title: An Unstoppable Faith

Sermon Angle: In this gospel we see three examples of an unstoppable faith. First there is Jairus. He pushes his way to Jesus in the midst of a large throng, falls to his knees, and implores Jesus repeatedly to heal his little daughter who is near death. On the way to Jairus' house, Jesus comes in contact with the woman who had the hemorrhages. This woman had seen all the doctors, tried all the cures, becoming destitute in the process. Yet she would not give up the quest for a cure. She heard about Jesus and believed that he could cure her. She found her way to Jesus even though he was being mobbed. The third person with an unstoppable faith was Jesus. He believed that he could indeed cure these sick ones. Even after it was reported that Jairus' daughter was dead, he never hesitated to believe that the Father would give him the strength to revive her. He counseled the girl's father "Do not fear, only believe" (v. 36). When he told the mourners that she was only sleeping, not dead, they laughed at him, but he persisted in belief (v. 40).

Outline:
Introduction: Three people demonstrated the power of an unstoppable faith.
1. Jairus continued to believe that Jesus could heal his daughter.
2. The woman with hemorrhages had faith Jesus could heal her.
3. Jesus believed he had the power to do all this and would not accept defeat.
4. God wants to give you an unstoppable faith through the power of his Spirit.

Proper 9/Pentecost 7/Ordinary Time 14

Revised Common	2 Samuel 5:1-5, 9-10	2 Corinthians 12:2-10	Mark 6:1-13
Roman Catholic	Ezekiel 2:2-5	2 Corinthians 12:7-10	Mark 6:1-6
Episcopal	Ezekiel 2:1-7	2 Corinthians 12:2-10	Mark 6:1-6

Theme For The Day: God gives us the authority to bring in his kingdom through our strengths and our weaknesses.

BRIEF COMMENTARY ON THE LESSONS

Lesson 1: 2 Samuel 5:1-5, 9-10 (C)

David first serves as king of Judah, with his capital at Hebron, for a period of seven years. The leaders of the northern tribes of Israel come to him at Hebron and they agree to make him king over the northern tribes. David's army captures the city of Jerusalem from its inhabitants and it becomes the capital of the united kingdom. David reigns as king of Israel and Judah for some 33 years.

Lesson 1: Ezekiel 2:2-5 (RC); Ezekiel 2:1-7 (E)

Lesson 2: 2 Corinthians 12:2-10 (C, E); 2 Corinthians 12:7-10 (RC)

Paul continues the defense of his gospel. Some time after 1 Corinthians was penned, the relationship between Paul and the Corinthians deteriorated. The apostle responded by sending a "severe letter" to them through Titus (2:4), in which he defends his apostleship. This pericope may have been part of Paul's severe letter, which gained the results that the apostle sought. In his own defense Paul refers to an abundance of revelations (v. 7) but in this passage lifts up only one of them. He refers obliquely to himself when he speaks of the man who was caught up in the third (highest) heaven. This man observed sacred and holy things that cannot be put into words. By speaking in this third person manner, Paul is seeking to convey the fact that he takes no personal credit for his revelations. He will boast on behalf of this man but of himself he will only boast of his weaknesses (v. 5). The apostle believes that God gave him a "thorn in the flesh" to keep him from being too proud of all the revelations he has received. There has been much speculation about the nature of this "thorn" but nothing can be proved. Paul accepts this affliction as a means of keeping his focus on God's grace rather than his own gifts (v. 9). Paul feels foolish in having to defend himself like this but blames the Corinthians for forcing him to do this.

Gospel: Mark 6:1-13 (C); Mark 6:1-6 (RC, E)

After a whirlwind teaching and healing tour, Jesus returns to his boyhood home. On the sabbath he taught in the synagogue. Many are impressed with his teaching and the signs associated with his ministry but tend to discredit Jesus because they know all about his family, his background, and so forth (v. 2). Jesus utters his famous line, "A prophet is not without honor, except in his own country...." He is hurt and disappointed because of their skepticism and could do no notable miracles there because of their unbelief (v. 5). Next Jesus pairs his twelve disciples and sends them out to proclaim the kingdom of God. Jesus gives them authority over evil spirits, charges them to depend on the hospitality of those that they encounter, to turn their backs to those who will not believe, and to preach repentance.

Psalm Of The Day
    Psalm 48 (C) — "Great is the Lord, and most worthy of praise ..." (v. 1).
    Psalm 123 (E)
    Psalm 122 (RC)

Prayer Of The Day
    Living Christ, because of the skepticism of your hometown people, you could not do any great work there. Free us from unbelief, that you might accomplish great and glorious things in places we inhabit. In Jesus' blessed and powerful name. Amen.

THEOLOGICAL REFLECTION ON THE LESSONS

Lesson 1: 2 Samuel 5:1-5, 9-10

Our own flesh and blood (v. 1). When the elders of Israel came to make David king they viewed David as one of their own, as their kin and fellow countryman. This was a positive factor for them. It is interesting to contrast this attitude to that displayed by our Lord's friends and neighbors. They discounted Jesus precisely because Jesus was the kid down the street; they had played with him. They knew his family. How could he be anything great? This could mean that we want our rulers to be one of us but we don't want them to get too close to us.

Military leaders (v. 2). Those who made David king were impressed with David's military leadership under Saul. Society hasn't changed that much; we are still attracted to military leaders. Military leaders can bring victories, protect our interests, and enhance our status. The objectives of war are clear; the enemy is apparent. You either win or lose. We jump to the conclusion that if a person can bring victory in war, he can also be a great civilian leader. Not necessarily so! More will be said about this under "Sermon Approaches."

Shepherd king (v. 2). David was a shepherd who became a king. The leaders of Israel were convinced that God called David, who was a shepherd of sheep, to become a shepherd of his people. Being a shepherd king means to know the people, to keep them together, to protect them and feed them. Unfortunately, too many kings and rulers have been more intent on fleecing their flock rather than caring for them.

Lesson 2: 2 Corinthians 12:2-10

Paradise (v. 4). The word comes from Persia and means literally "an enclosed wooded park or garden." Paradise came to be synonymous with heaven, though this word has a different derivation. The Hebrew word for heaven is *shamayim*, closely related to the Hebrew word for "waters," *mayim*. Thus, heaven was the partition separating the rain-producing heavenly waters from the waters on and beneath the earth. In this partition, stretched out like a tent (Isaiah 44:24), were windows like sluice gates, from which God watered the earth. The heavens were conceived as God's work place or treasure trove, from which God sends his blessings on earth. The heavens do not separate God from humans, since God can tear the heavens and come down (Isaiah 64:4). The heavens and the earth encompass the sum total of the universe. How fascinating it is that this vast expanse (the heavens) came to be identified with the enclosed garden (paradise).

Vision of paradise (v. 4). Paul speaks of his vision of paradise though he does not, and probably cannot, describe it. What is your vision of paradise? Lolling on a sandy beach? A lofty mountain retreat? For the child of God, our vision of paradise ought to be a world redeemed and reconciled to God.

Theology of thorns (v. 7). Paul was plagued with a thorn as he calls it, but we don't know what it was. It really doesn't matter. Paul prayed to have the thorn taken away but his petition was not granted. The apostle developed a theology of thorns to find meaning in his suffering. This theology states that God reveals his strength through our weakness. In such suffering we learn to depend on the Lord for strength (v. 9).

Gospel: Mark 6:1-13

That's amazing! The neighbors of Jesus were amazed at his wisdom, backed up by his mighty acts (v. 1). They were amazed but not convinced. Mark says that they took offense (v. 3). Jesus was also amazed at their lack of faith (v. 6). How people can hear God's word powerfully preached and taught and see abundant demonstrations of his power, and not believe, is both amazing and sad.

Hamstrung (v. 5). Jesus was clearly hamstrung by the lack of faith he found in Nazareth. God does not bully us into belief but works through our faith to accomplish great feats. Another way to explain it is that unbelief acts like a circuit breaker, disconnecting God's power from our habitations.

Leave home without them (vv. 8-11). The American Express commercials show some hapless travelers caught in some dire straits because they find themselves without funds. The punch line for the commercial goes: "American Express travelers' checks, don't leave home without them!" Jesus sent out his disciples two by two with these instructions: "Take nothing for the journey except a staff — no bread, no bag, no money in your belts" (v. 8). Furthermore, he instructed them not to pack extra clothes or shoes. Jesus wanted his disciples to leave home without these things so that they might learn to lean on God.

SERMON APPROACHES WITH ILLUSTRATIONS

Lesson 1: 2 Samuel 5:1-5, 9-10
Sermon Title: Like A Mighty Army
Sermon Angle: The people of Israel felt the need for strong leadership. They lacked unity and enemies threatened their existence. David had demonstrated his ability to lead men in battle. The people reasoned that David would also be able to lead the country like a mighty army. Their belief proved correct in this case. However, it is incorrect to assume that the same kind of leadership called for in war will also be effective in peace. It is very difficult for one person to provide the leadership needed in all circumstances, which is why democratic leadership is most effective.

Outline:
1. The Israelites wanted David as king because of his military leadership.
2. David proved to be a capable military and civilian leader.
3. The people wanted to be led like a mighty army — strong hierarchical leadership.
4. Military leadership is effective in crisis.
5. To wage the peace takes a different kind of leadership — cooperation rather than combat.

The United States has several times decided to enlist military heroes as presidents. Our first president, George Washington, gained fame first as a victorious general. He proved to be an effective leader. However, Ulysses S. Grant, a great general in the Civil War and a man of action, proved to be a terrible president. His term in office was noted for corruption and ineptitude. Dwight D. Eisenhower, the leader of the allied forces in World War II, is considered only a mediocre president. General Douglas MacArthur, though he never won the nomination for president, distinguished himself both as a great general during World War II and the Korean Conflict and as an outstanding administrator of the country of Japan in the post-war years. Like King David, he had the ability to win victory for his people on the field of combat and to shepherd and care for people during the periods of peace.

* * * * *

Sermon Title: The Lord Is My Shepherd
Sermon Angle: The man whom God called to lead his people was a simple shepherd; this was not the kind of leadership position that a person would think to put on his resume. In the Old Testament the king is often referred to as a shepherd of the people. David, who was called to shepherd his people, was well qualified because he first knew the Lord as his own shepherd. Psalm 23 is attributed to the shepherd-king. The point here is that to be a leader one must first submit to the leadership and authority of God.

Lesson 2: 2 Corinthians 12:2-10
Sermon Title: A Theology Of Thorns
Sermon Angle: The identity of Paul's thorn in the flesh has caused endless speculation. The guesses have gone all the way from malaria to epilepsy to stuttering. The identification of his thorn doesn't matter, but what does matter is his response to that thorn. What are our options in dealing with thorns? I've come up with three responses: 1) We can curse them, 2) we can try to remove them on our own, or 3) we can ask the Lord to help us to deal with the thorns.

* * * * *

Most of us have had thorns to deal with — a sickness, an accident, a sudden tragedy. Perhaps it is a chronic but equally painful condition that is our thorn, family problems, a less than loving marriage, or a nagging lack of self-esteem. OUCH!

Several years ago, when my extended family gathered for a Fourth of July picnic, almost everyone there had some kind of physical thorn to deal with. My youngest sister fell backward a month before and cracked her third vertebrae. My older sister twisted her ankle while playing with her grandson and fractured it; she was on crutches. One of my brothers-in-law was there, crippled with arthritis. He was scheduled for a total knee replacement. My mother was hampered with a heart condition and my father had cancer. My aunt was there and her ankles were swollen so badly they looked like those of an elephant.

I'm not trying to gain your sympathy; you have probably had far worse thorns to contend with. My point simply is to establish the universality of thorns. They are given to old people and young people, fat people and skinny people, rich people and poor people, but what is most difficult to understand, thorns embed their torturous barbs into bad people and good people alike.

* * * * *

Sermon Title: Strength Through Weakness

Sermon Angle: When Paul begged God to remove his thorn, the Lord replied: "My grace is sufficient for you, for my power is made perfect through weakness" (v. 9). Those weaknesses we cannot remove, let us offer up to God.

Outline:
1. Paul had many strengths that he offered up to God's service — teacher, writer, missionary, to name a few.
2. Paul also had weaknesses, such as the thorn in the flesh.
3. God showed him how to rely on God's grace in his weaknesses.
4. The cross is the prime example of offering to God our thorn for redemptive purposes.

Gospel: Mark 6:1-13

Sermon Title: Don't Leave Home Without It

Sermon Angle: Jesus instructed his disciples to take nothing with them except their rod or staff (v. 8). One could interpret this staff to mean a walking stick, which would provide something to lean on for their long journey. I choose to see a deeper meaning here. The Greek word is *rhabdos*, meaning "rod, scepter, or staff." The rod was a club used for protection, the scepter was a symbol of kingly authority, and the staff was used by shepherds tending their sheep. Jesus employs the shepherd analogy for his messianic role and it is likely that he carried a shepherd's staff with him. It is very possible that his disciples also did the same. At any rate, the staff could be interpreted as a symbol of our Lord's authority. It could also symbolize protection, kingly authority, and caring. In light of this, the Lord's specific instructions to take only the clothes on their back, the sandals on their feet, and their staff makes perfect sense.

Outline:
1. Jesus told his disciples to take only their staff on their mission.
2. Jesus was a shepherd of souls and most probably carried a staff.
3. The disciples apparently took staffs with them on their journeys.
4. The staff was a symbol of Christ's authority, power, and love (much like the rod of Aaron).
5. Don't leave home on your mission without the staff of Christ's authority.

Sermon Title: Christ's Ministry Is A Team Effort

Sermon Angle: Jesus sent out his disciples two by two (v. 7). Jesus didn't expect them to be supermen or superheroes but team players. The Hebrew scriptures teach that two witnesses are needed to corroborate a truth or bear witness in court. Jesus couldn't share the good news of the kingdom by himself; he needed and still requires multiple witnesses and a team effort.

Outline:
1. Jesus sent out his disciples in pairs to proclaim the kingdom by word and deed (vv. 12-13).
2. Christ is establishing a kingdom community.
3. The kingdom spreads as we share our gifts with one another and the world.

Sermon Title: Secret Weapon

Sermon Angle: World War II was brought to a swift conclusion by the detonation of the atomic bomb on two major cities in Japan. Until then this was a secret weapon. The disciples of Jesus were sent forth with a secret weapon, the authority of Jesus to cast out demons, heal diseases, and preach the word (v. 7). However, this authority was to be used only in cooperation with the people where they sojourned. They were not to use Jesus' power for destructive purposes but to move out from the places where the Word was not received (v. 11).

Outline:

1. The atomic bomb was a secret weapon used to bring Japan to its knees.
2. Jesus sent his disciples out with a secret weapon (v. 7).
3. Jesus wants to surprise with his gracious power, not destructive power.
4. We have been given the power of the Spirit to overthrow the power of Satan.

Proper 10/Pentecost 8/Ordinary Time 15

Revised Common	2 Samuel 6:1-5, 12b-19	Ephesians 1:3-14	Mark 6:14-29
Roman Catholic	Amos 7:12-15	Ephesians 1:3-14	Mark 6:7-13
Episcopal	Amos 7:7-15	Ephesians 1:1-14	Mark 6:7-13

Theme For The Day: Unity through the lordship and headship of Christ.

BRIEF COMMENTARY ON THE LESSONS

Lesson 1: 2 Samuel 6:1-5, 12b-19 (C)

David brings the Ark of the Covenant up from Kirjath-jearim to his new capital, Jerusalem. The Ark is set on a new cart and David and his men dance and sing in procession. On the way, the ox pulling the cart stumbles and Uzzah reaches out to steady the Ark and keep it from falling and is struck dead by the Lord for taking such liberties. David becomes angry with the Lord and also afraid. He leaves the Ark in the nearby house of Obed for the next three months. Obed's household experiences many blessings and the word of his good fortune reaches the ears of David. The king then brings the Ark up to Jerusalem with great celebration. David is caught up in the joy of the celebration and dances before the Ark with all his might. (It would be best to read verses 1-19 continuously and not leave out verses 6-12a.)

Lesson 1: Amos 7:12-15 (RC); Amos 7:7-15 (E)

Lesson 2: Ephesians 1:3-14 (C, RC); Ephesians 1:1-14 (E)

This is the first installment in a series of eight readings from Ephesians. The church constitutes the main theme of this epistle. Some scholars question Paul's authorship because the style and vocabulary differ and there are no personal references. I accept William Barclay's suggestion that the epistle differs because it was written under different circumstances than most of Paul's other letters; the apostle was in prison in Rome. Therefore, he had the time to reflect and carefully choose his words. Barclay maintains that this was a general letter, circulated to all the churches and not expressly written for the Ephesians, whom Paul held very dear. In this lection Paul marvels at the wonder of God electing us as his own dear children. Another major chord concerns how Christ unites heaven and earth through his blood. Later in the letter Paul shows how the church is charged with fulfilling Christ's reconciling ministry.

Gospel: Mark 6:14-29 (C)

King Herod hears about the ministry of Jesus and his miracles and jumps to the conclusion that Jesus is a reincarnation of John the Baptist, whom he has beheaded. The lection then tells the story of John's execution. Herodias, Herod's wife, had formerly been married to his brother, Philip. John had roundly accused them of adultery, which raised the ire of Herodias. She wanted to do away with him but Herod protected him. Salome, her daughter, danced before Herod at a banquet and so pleased the monarch that he promised her anything, up to half his kingdom. She consulted with her mother, who instructed her to demand the head of John the Baptist. Herod regretted his oath but to save face ordered the executioner to present John's head at the feast.

Gospel: Mark 6:7-13 (RC, E)
See gospel lesson for Proper 9.

Psalm Of The Day
   Psalm 24 (C) — "The earth is the Lord's and all that is in it" (v. 1).
   Psalm 85 (E)
   Psalm 122 (RC)

Prayer Of The Day
   O rock of ages, though the cause of evil seems to prosper, let us never lose faith that the cause of righteousness and justice will ultimately triumph. Give us the peace of your presence amidst a world of discord. In the powerful name of Jesus. Amen.

THEOLOGICAL REFLECTION ON THE LESSON

Lesson 1: 2 Samuel 6:1-5, 12b-19

Worship with all your being (vv. 5, 14). Whatever David was about, he did it with great gusto! His worship of God was no exception. David and those with him celebrated the Lord's presence (symbolized in the Ark) "with all his might." David's worship was not perfunctory but wholehearted. Like the charismatics of today, he wasn't afraid to get emotional about his relationship with God, nor was he embarrassed to worship the Lord with his body as he danced before the Ark. We could learn a thing or two from the shepherd king.

Getting angry with God (vv. 6-7). David got angry with God for striking Uzzah dead when he reached out to steady the Ark. He couldn't understand why the Lord would do such a thing to one of his faithful people. David then left the Ark with Obed-Edom. In his anger and fear he attempted to distance himself from God. Many people do the same in times of crisis. Many an accusing finger has been pointed at the Lord: "How could you do this to me, Lord?" Yet during this period, when the Ark rested in Obed's house, that household experienced innumerable blessings. In distancing ourselves from God, we also separate ourselves from the source of blessing. David realized his error and went down to bring the ark to Jerusalem. He once more danced before the Lord. Though he became angry with God, he could not stay angry.

The sin of Uzzah (vv. 6-7). The fate of Uzzah is as troubling to moderns as it was to David. Modern interpreters have suggested that, with slight variations in the text, a more rational explanation can be given than that which is supplied by the writer of this text (that Uzzah had transgressed the holiness of God). These interpreters suggest that the oxen, rather than stumbling, dropped dung, in which Uzzah slipped and hit his head on the Ark. I find such an interpretation facetious. Others have suggested that the Lord was angry that the Ark was not transported properly by the Levites, who would carry the Ark on poles strung through rings in the Ark. Instead the Ark was carried on a cart. Either David didn't know about these regulations or else he disregarded them. Thus, the sin consists of handling the Ark in a common or unholy manner. Some have suggested that it shows a lack of faith on Uzzah's part. He didn't think that the Lord could take care of his own Ark. This makes sense but we will never know for sure the true nature of Uzzah's transgression.

Lesson 2: Ephesians 1:3-14

God chose us (v. 4). Paul marvels at the fact of God's election of us in Christ. Here he lifts up the excellency of God's grace in choosing us sinful human beings. God's choice is not haphazard; he chose us before the world was created. Most Christians see in their baptism the locus of God's personal choice of them to be his own. Baptism is viewed as our adoption by God into his family (v. 5). This choice calls for a grateful response.

To be holy (v. 5). Why did God choose us? That we might live holy lives. *Hagios* means to be set apart or separate. God commanded Israel to come out from amidst the people and be separate and holy, worshiping only the Lord. Christians are likewise called to be different than the prevailing culture. How many of us are willing to take the risk?

Blameless (v. 5). Holiness is bad enough but blameless? The word for "blameless" refers to the animals offered up to God as a sacrifice. They were to be perfect, whole, and without blemish. This means that our whole lives are to be offered up as a perfect sacrifice to God. We are not perfect but, by the grace of God, we are called to permit the Holy Spirit to perfect us. We are talking about a process of becoming.

God's guarantee (v. 14). Paul alludes here to a legal contract. To this day, when a person wants to purchase a piece of property, he shows that he's in earnest, that he or she is serious about the offer to purchase. The money is a guarantee of the promise that is yet to be fulfilled. God has given us his Spirit as his earnest deposit, the guarantee of our adoption into the kingdom of light and love.

Gospel: Mark 6:14-29

What spin are you putting to Jesus? (vv. 14-16). In the media, we have the spin doctors who analyze public figures or events for significance and implications. Such was the case even in Jesus' day. The Lord's ministry caused quite a stir; everyone agreed that he was someone of great significance but the spin doctors couldn't agree. Some said he was a great prophet of long ago, others claimed that he was Elijah, and many thought that the spirit of John had come into Jesus. King Herod, who had John killed, was of this opinion (v. 16). Besides the tractional Christian interpretation of Jesus, there have been and continue to be many different spins. Keep focused on the gospel or you could spin out of orbit.

The danger of betraying yourself. Herod believed John to be a good and holy man; he liked to listen to him (v. 20). Yet, because Herod had married his brother's wife, John denounced the marriage as unlawful. This enraged Herodias, who wanted nothing more than to silence John. At his wife's instigation, Herod bound John over to the dungeon. This wasn't enough and so Herodias tricked her husband into giving her John's head on a platter. Herod is a despicable creature who betrayed his better self for the sake of domestic tranquility and the saving of face.

The voice of God cannot be permanently silenced. The voice of John was silenced by the executioner's sword but his message continued. Jesus sent his disciples out to proclaim the necessity of repentance (v. 12). To Herod it seemed that John had come back from the dead and was being heard through Jesus.

SERMON APPROACHES WITH ILLUSTRATIONS

Lesson 1: 2 Samuel 6:1-5, 12b-19

Sermon Title: Lord Of The Dance

Sermon Angle: My daughter just got married. Like many marriage celebrations, there was a feast and a dance. Dancing seems natural when you have someone or something great to rejoice in. David danced before the Lord (vv. 5, 14) as the Ark was brought up to the new capital, Jerusalem. Why not celebrate God's presence through dance? If our hearts are moved, so will our bodies, our lips, and our lives be moved. As the song says: "Dance then, wherever you might be, I am the Lord of the dance, said he."

Outline:
1. David danced before the Lord, rejoicing in God's favor and love.
2. His wife criticized him for making a spectacle of himself (v. 16).
3. God is in our midst in Christ; life is a joyous dance.
4. Dance then, wherever you might be, Christ is the Lord of the dance, said he.

Sermon Title: The Two Faces Of Authentic Worship

Sermon Angle: David was sort of a priest-king who understood the true nature of worship. Worship consists, first of all, in turning our faces to the Lord in praise and thanksgiving. The second phase of worship is to show God's face of mercy to other people through acts of love and sharing. David not only sacrificed to the Lord, but he gave gifts to his people (vv. 18-19).

Outline:
1. The first act of worship is to turn our faces to God in thanks, praise, and sacrifice.
2. The second act of worship is to show God's face of compassion to the world.

Lesson 2: Ephesians 1:3-14

Sermon Title: The Joy Of Being Chosen

Sermon Angle: Nothing is more devastating than not being chosen by those who matter to you. Also, nothing surpasses the joy of being chosen in love. Paul proclaims that all Christians are chosen by God to be his own dear children, redeemed and forgiven, heirs of eternity.

Outline:
We are chosen to be God's children (v. 4).
1. Chosen in Christ (v. 11).
2. Included through faith in the gospel (v. 13).
3. Sealed with the Holy Spirit (v. 13).

Sermon Title: State Of The Union Message

Sermon Angle: Paul foresees a time when all creation will find its unity in Christ; he will be the head (v. 10). This unifying process has already begun through the power of the gospel. Those who live the gospel are already included in Christ (v. 13). Unfortunately, the church is more divided than ever. Church leaders have tried to create a unified witness through organizations like the World Council of Churches, which sometimes has caused more division than unity, when their efforts were politically rather than spiritually based. The state of our union in Christ will improve only as we catch Paul's vision of unity under Christ's headship. This unity extends far beyond the church to encompass all creation. God intends to unify his creation through Christ.

Outline:
1. Many people are seeking unity through religious pluralism.
2. The only unity the gospel knows is in Christ.
   — In God's mind before the world was created (v. 4).
   — Revealed to us through our adoption in Christ (v. 5).
   — Consummated when the right time arrives (v. 10).

*   *   *   *   *

Many Christians are seeking unity in a gospel of pluralism and relativism. This philosophy goes something like this: "It doesn't matter what you believe, just as long as you believe something and are sincere. All religions are merely alternative routes to the same God and goal." Carl Braaten has an excellent article on the uniqueness of the gospel in *The Lutheran* magazine. The article is called "No Other Gospel." Braaten depicts this truth architecturally by describing the Bahai Temple in Wilmette, Illinois. The Bahais believe that all religions are equally valid pathways to the one God. This theology is expressed in the design of their temple. The temple has nine porticos, each dedicated to the prophet of one of the world's great religions. The nine spokes all lead to a single central altar, representing the one God to whom all of the religions point. No matter which path you take, you end up at the same destination. Braaten points out that this theology is accepted far beyond the pale of the Bahai faith but is making deep inroads into the Christian community. He also makes an important distinction between revelation and salvation. All religions may convey revelation, partial truth about God, but only Christianity confers salvation. Christianity must hold to the truth that there is no other name under heaven by which we must be saved (Acts 4:9-11).

*   *   *   *   *

Gospel: Mark 6:14-29
   Sermon Title: Murder She Wrote
   Sermon Angle: Herodias spelled out in her mind a devious and murderous plot to have John the Baptist destroyed. She wasn't at all uneasy about writing other people into the murder plot. She didn't mind using her daughter's beautiful body and her husband's vanity to spring the fatal trap. The ending was not a surprise for Herodias, as it was for her husband, because she was the author and the main villain, though in her mind John was the villain. Like most who plot murder, she wanted to rub out the witnesses to the truth.
   Outline:
1. Our society not only fears murderers but is fascinated by them.
2. Herodias was a premeditated murderer, who wrote out in her mind a simple plot.
3. Most murders start with a plot.
4. Why do people murder?
   — To silence the truth.
   — To create their own form of truth (to be God).
5. People like Herodias write murder plots, while God has written a pardon for all who believe in Christ.

Sermon Title: Decapitated Christians

Sermon Angle: This gospel tells the gory tale of John losing his head in prison. Not only was John decapitated but so were his followers. They didn't have a leader any longer and apparently John did not prepare any of his followers to succeed him in leadership. Unfortunately, many Christians are decapitated; Christ is not their head or they have no head whatsoever. The second lesson tells of Paul's vision for the unity of all things in heaven and earth under the headship of Jesus Christ. For the church, Christ is to be the head. Is he the head of your life or are you a decapitated Christian?

Outline:
1. John was decapitated because he witnessed to the truth.
2. This left his disciples without a head.
3. Jesus was also killed for his witness to the truth but still lives as head of the church.
4. Some Christians and congregations are decapitated — they don't honor Christ as their head.

Proper 11/Pentecost 9/Ordinary Time 16

Revised Common	2 Samuel 7:1-14a	Ephesians 2:11-22	Mark 6:30-34, 53-56
Roman Catholic	Jeremiah 23:1-6	Ephesians 2:13-18	Mark 6:30-34
Episcopal	Isaiah 57:14b-21	Ephesians 2:11-22	Mark 6:30-44

Theme For The Day: Building the kingdom of God.

BRIEF COMMENTARY ON THE LESSONS

Lesson 1: 2 Samuel 7:1-14a (C)

Some scholars judge chapter 7 to be an insertion from a later period. The purpose of this text is to explain why King David did not construct the temple. The setting for this pericope finds David victorious over his enemies; he has built himself an ornate palace and wants to build the Lord a worthy dwelling. At that time, the Ark of the Covenant was housed in a tent. David reveals his plan to Nathan, the prophet, who initially gives the go-ahead. Afterward, the Lord informs Nathan that David is not to build the temple. God submits that he never needed a temple, as he moved about with his people. In verse 11, we find a word play on the word translated "house." Instead of David building God a house, God is going to build a house (dynasty) for David and this house would be secure forever.

Lesson 1: Jeremiah 23:1-6 (RC)

Lesson 1: Isaiah 57:14b-21 (E)

Lesson 2: Ephesians 2:11-22 (C, E); Ephesians 2:13-18 (RC)

The Gentiles, once separated from God and alienated from the promises of God to Israel, are now brought into the community of faith. The wall of hostility has been removed by Christ, who has made peace through the cross. God also removes the law as the means of being accepted by God (v. 15). Through the cross we also have access to God by the same Spirit (v. 18). Paul compares the community of faith to a temple built upon the witness of apostles and prophets, Christ being both the cornerstone and the mortar, which keeps the whole structure together.

Gospel: Mark 6:30-34, 53-56 (C); Mark 6:30-34 (RC); Mark 6:30-44 (E)

The disciples return from their preaching, teaching, and healing mission exhausted from all their ministry. Jesus proposes that they get into the boat and go to a place of solitude, but wherever they go, the crowds follow them. Jesus heals all who are in contact with him. Between verses 30-34 and 53-56, we have the stories of the feeding of the multitudes and the account of Jesus walking on the water.

Psalm Of The Day

Psalm 89:20-37 (C) — "My faithfulness and steadfast love will be with him" (v. 24).
Psalm 22:22-30 (E, RC)

Prayer Of The Day

Shepherd of our souls, in our weakness and infirmity we seek your healing touch. Thank you, Lord Jesus, for stooping to help and heal us. Give us hearts of compassion, that we might reach out with your mercy and grace. In your precious name. Amen.

THEOLOGICAL REFLECTION ON THE LESSONS

Lesson 1: 2 Samuel 7:1-14a

Putting God in his place. David wanted to put God in his place. That is, he wanted to construct a permanent structure where God would live with his people. Yahweh reveals through Nathan that he is not going to be put in one place. Since Egypt he has traveled about with his people. We still try to put God in his place by relegating him to the realm of the sacred. That removes God from most of life. God's true home is in the hearts of his faithful ones.

God finds a place for us (v. 10). God doesn't need a place here on earth but God recognizes that we need our place, or space, where we can grow and flourish. We see something of this sentiment in the movie *Gone With The Wind* when Scarlett O'Hara's father passionately pleads with her to take care of the plantation, because a person is nothing without the land. God recognizes that his children of clay need their place in the sun, a piece of turf they can call home. "And I will appoint a place for my people Israel."

Forever sure (v. 16). God promises David: "And your house and your kingdom shall be made sure before me; your throne shall be established forever" (RSV). How do we interpret this, in light of the fact that David's kingdom was split asunder during the reign of his grandson, followed by further fragmentation and ultimately disintegration? The only interpretation that makes sense is to identify David's kingdom with the Son of David, Jesus Christ. Nothing remains long in this world; only Christ's eternal kingdom is forever sure.

Lesson 2: Ephesians 2:11-22

Then and now (vv. 12-13). Paul contrasts how the status of the Christian Gentiles has dramatically shifted; there's the then and now, before Christ and after Christ. "Remember that you were at that time separated from Christ ... but now in Christ Jesus you who once were far off have been brought near by the blood of Christ."

Pax Christi (v. 14). You have probably heard of the *Pax Romana*, a period of several hundred years when the Roman legions prevented the outbreak of most wars. This was a peace only in a relative and outward sense. The *Pax Christi*, the peace of Christ, breaks down the hostility between humans and God, between humans and other humans, and the enmity between groups. Paul lifts up the hostility between Jews and Gentiles, which Christ breaks down. "For he is our peace; in his flesh he has made both groups into one and has broken down the dividing wall, that is, the hostility between us."

Gospel: Mark 6:30-34, 53-56

Debriefing (vv. 30-34). When the apostles came back from their preaching, teaching, and healing mission, they had much to share with Jesus; they had all sorts of experiences that they needed to reflect upon. Jesus realized this and led them away to an uninhabited location. However, when they arrived there the crowds had preceded them. Sometimes our best plans need to be altered by the circumstances.

Interruptions. When I get involved in a project, I don't like to be interrupted because it interferes with my powers of concentration. However, interruptions in our plans may be God's way of capturing our attention for something he feels is more important. A pastor I serve with often quotes a saying that was told to him: "Pastors are in the business of being interrupted." Jesus' plans for a time of solitude with his Father and his disciples were interrupted by the overwhelming human need all about him.

Bringing others to Jesus (vv. 53-56). When Jesus and his disciples got to Gennesaret scores of people were scurrying about to round up the sick, many of whom were so ill that they had to be carried to Jesus on stretchers. There is a lesson here. We cannot come into Jesus' healing presence on our own. We come on the shoulders of the faith and commitment of those who have gone before us.

SERMON APPROACHES WITH ILLUSTRATIONS

Lesson 1: 2 Samuel 7:1-14a

Sermon Title: What Is God's Address?

Sermon Angle: Throughout the world there are innumerable buildings designated as God's house. Yet how can we presume to think that the Lord of heaven and earth lives in an earthly house? That's the question God raised through Nathan. "Would you build me a house to dwell in?" (v. 5). Imagine how presumptuous this was of David! If an architect is going to design a house that is to be built for someone, he or she needs to know the people who will be living there, their needs, interests, and so forth. Yet we humans, who have only minutely begun to comprehend the greatness of God, think that we can construct a structure that would fulfill God's needs. God has no address here on earth. Temples and churches are but post office boxes bearing God's name. We leave our letters there in hopes that they will be properly forwarded. We can be sure that these petitions will reach the throne of grace if they are addressed "in care of Jesus Christ." What is God's address? God lives in the hearts of the faithful.

Outline:
1. Where does God live?
2. David wanted to build a house for Yahweh but God refused.
3. How can we presume to build a house for the Lord to dwell in?
4. Churches are more like post office boxes or an email address.
5. God lives in the community of the faithful.

Sermon Title: God Builds Up Those Whom He Loves

Sermon Angle: David was grateful for God's blessings and wanted to respond by doing something for the Lord. That's why David wanted to build a temple for the Lord. But God was more interested in building up David and recites how he has done so. God transformed him from a shepherd to a king (v. 8); he accompanied David wherever he went and removed David's enemies (v. 9); God planted his people in a new land and promises to make a dynasty out of David's descendents (v. 16).

Lesson 2: Ephesians 2:11-22

Sermon Title: Before Christ And After Christ

Sermon Angle: Weight loss programs like to show before and after pictures to demonstrate visually what their program can do for people. This gives encouragement to overweight people that things can change for them. Paul contrasts the before and after picture for Jewish-Gentile relations, for those who belong to Christ. Before Christ the Gentiles were aliens and strangers to the promises of God, without God and without hope. After Christ they are brought into the family of faith. Formerly there was a wall of hostility, but after Christ, peace and unity. Only Christ can reconcile hostile groups.

Outline:
1. Weight loss groups and make-over artists like to contrast before and after pictures.
2. Our lives will look better after Christ.
3. Christ also can break down the walls of hostility between groups.
4. How might Christ lead us to break down walls between hostile groups?

Sermon Title: One New Humanity

Sermon Angle: Paul interprets the cross of Christ as God's effort to create a new humanity (vv. 15-16). This was also the intent of the flood, to destroy wicked humanity and create a new humanity from Noah and his family. That didn't work. This time God intends to construct a new humanity, not through the death of sinful people but through the death of God's own Son in atonement for the sins of the world. Through the cross God breaks down the walls of hostility between humans by giving us new hearts and the will to please God.

Sermon Title: How God Builds A House

Sermon Angle: In the first lesson, David wants to build God a house and God replies that he will build a house of David. In this lesson, Paul claims that God is building a house of those who believe. Here is how the house is constructed.

Outline:
1. God builds his house on the foundation of the apostles and prophets (v. 20).
2. Christ is the cornerstone (giving the house shape and form) (v. 20).
3. Christians are all building blocks (v. 22).
4. Christ is the mortar (v. 21).

Gospel: Mark 6:30-34, 53-56

Sermon Title: The Hiding Place

Sermon Angle: The late Corrie ten Boom wrote her well-known book, *The Hiding Place*, to describe her family's efforts to hide Jews from the Nazis. The attic in her house was a refuge from the cruelty of the world. We need another kind of hiding place, not so much from the cruelty of the world but from the busyness of the world — a place of solitude, of rest, where distractions are minimized, so we can fix our focus on the larger picture through rest, reflection, and prayer.

Outline:
1. Jesus and his disciples needed a hiding place to recreate and renew (v. 31).
2. Though they did not find it at that time, these periods were essential for Jesus' ministry.
3. We need to find our hiding place — a scene of solitude, where we can rest, reflect, and pray.

Sermon Title: Apostolic Assembly — Apostolic Action

Sermon Angle: Verse 30 is the only instance in the gospel of Mark where the word "apostle" appears. They are generally referred to in the first two gospels as "the twelve." At any rate, this verse informs us that the apostles gathered around Jesus — an apostolic assembly. In the strict sense of the word, an apostle was one who had witnessed our Lord's entire ministry, beginning with his baptism and concluding with his ascension. However, in a larger context of the word, all Christians are apostles, those who are sent by Christ on a mission. Every time Christians gather together for worship or learning, it is an apostolic assembly. However, we must always remember that our reason for coming together is that Christ might send us out anew on our apostolic mission. Apostolic action must alternate with apostolic assembly.

Outline:
1. We confess that we believe in the "Holy catholic and apostolic church."
2. What does it mean to be an apostle? (Define the word.)
3. Those sent must also assemble — the apostles returned from their mission and assembled around Jesus (v. 30).
4. Apostolic assembly is a time of reassessment, learning, prayer, and renewal.
5. As surely as exhalation follows inhalation, apostolic assembly must be followed by apostolic action (mission).

Sermon Title: A Sense Of Urgency

Sermon Angle: The crowds that witnessed the ministry of Jesus were seized with a sense of urgency. They hurried to bring their sick and infirm friends and neighbors into Jesus' healing presence. When Jesus got to the other side of the lake, people "at once recognized him and rushed about the whole region and began to bring people on mats to wherever they heard he was" (vv. 54-55). There was a sense of urgency because we had witnessed a wonderful window of divine opportunity in the ministry of Jesus. The church in many places today is languishing because we have lost this sense of urgency and opportunity. For many Christians, Jesus has passed through but a long time ago. They don't expect to encounter Jesus' healing presence in the marketplaces, highways, and byways of life. To recapture this sense of urgency we must also recapture a deep sense of Christ's living and life-giving presence.

Outline:
1. The crowds around Jesus were filled with a sense of urgency and opportunity.
2. They wanted to bring as many people into Jesus' presence as possible.
3. When's the last time you have brought a friend or neighbor into Jesus' presence?
4. Reach out to Jesus as a living presence in your life, then you will be filled with a sense or urgency to bring others into his presence.

* * * * *

Emmanuel Bronner is an 87-year-young man who refuses to get off his soapbox. Bronner is a soap maker of the most unique kind. He uses his soap not only to clean the body but the soul. His soap comes in a variety of natural fragrances — peppermint, almond, lavender — to name a few, and he claims that his soap can be used for a variety of functions, such as brushing your teeth. However, the attribute that sets Bronner's soap apart is recorded on the label. About 10% of the label is given to disclosing the ingredients in the soap, the other 90% is devoted to

Bronner's philosophy. Here is an example: "Absolute cleanliness is Godliness. Who else but God gave man love that can spark mere dust to life! Who else but God! Listen, children, eternal Father, eternal one!" Bronner's soap label is his soapbox, whereby he shares his faith. He is passionate and persistent about conveying his message of unity and love through the power of God. In his own way, Bronner is urgent about his task of bringing the souls of others into the presence of God. Wouldn't it be great if Christians were seized by such an urgency to bring their world into the presence of Jesus Christ?

Proper 12/Pentecost 10/Ordinary Time 17

Revised Common	2 Samuel 11:1-15	Ephesians 3:14-21	John 6:1-21
Roman Catholic	2 Kings 4:42-44	Ephesians 4:1-6	John 6:1-15
Episcopal	2 Kings 2:1-15	Ephesians 4:1-7, 11-16	Mark 6:45-52

Theme For The Day: God fills us with the bread of life for our bodies and our spirits.

BRIEF COMMMENTARY ON THE LESSONS

Lesson 1: 2 Samuel 11:1-15 (C)

King David has consolidated his power and no longer personally engages in the risky task of doing battle with his enemies. Getting up from his afternoon nap, he surveys his capital from his balcony, when he spies a beautiful woman taking her bath; it is Bathsheba, the wife of Uriah, one of David's valiant fighters. He has her brought to his palace and has sex with her. When she sends word that she is pregnant, David attempts to cover his sin by having Uriah take a leave from battle, that he might have intercourse with his wife. Uriah adheres to the laws of holy war and refuses to lie with his wife while others are doing battle. David sends a letter to Joab, his general, to put Uriah at the forefront of battle and then withdraw from him, so that he might be slain.

Lesson 1: 2 Kings 2:1-15 (E)

See first lesson for The Transfiguration Of Our Lord.

Lesson 1: 2 Kings 4:42-44 (RC)

Lesson 2: Ephesians 3:14-21 (C)

This lection repeats a phrase sounded in verse 1: "For this reason...." Just prior to verse 1, Paul celebrates the fact that Gentiles are incorporated into the family of God. In verse 1, he states that he is a prisoner for the gospel, to make it known to the Gentiles. In verse 14, Paul asserts that for the same reason, he praises the Lord. This passage is a poetic prayer and praise to God that the Christians, to whom Paul is writing, might be firmly rooted in the love of Christ and filled with the Spirit of God.

Lesson 2: Ephesians 4:1-6 (RC); Ephesians 4:1-7, 11-16 (E)

See second lesson for Proper 13.

Gospel: John 6:1-21 (C); John 6:1-15 (RC)

This is the first of a series of passages from John 6, which lift up Jesus as the bread of life. Jesus miraculously feeds a multitude of people, estimated as 5,000 people, using the barley loaves and fishes of a young boy's lunch. The crowd is so impressed by this sign that it wants to make Jesus their king. Jesus withdraws from them to a deserted place. Some interpreters see this story as John's version of the institution of the Eucharist, which was deleted from his passion account. This is the only miracle recorded in all four gospels. Verses 16-21 contain John's version of Jesus coming to his sea-tossed disciples via walking on the water.

Gospel: Mark 6:45-52 (E)

After feeding the 5,000, Jesus dismisses the people, puts his disciples into a boat, and retreats to a hilltop to pray. From this vantage point, he views his boatload of disciples struggling against the wind. He walks toward them on the waves. They react in horror, thinking it an apparition. Jesus immediately reassures them: "Take heart, it is I; have no fear" (v. 50). He boarded the boat and all was calm, but the disciples didn't know what to make of this (v. 52).

Psalm Of The Day

Psalm 14 (C) — "Have they no knowledge, all the evil doers who eat up my people as they eat bread ..." (v. 4).

Psalm 114 (E)

Psalm 144 (RC)

Prayer Of The Day

Merciful God, you desire that not only our physical needs be satisfied but that we be filled with the fullness of your love and grace through Christ Jesus our Lord. In the name of the compassionate Christ we pray. Amen.

THEOLOGICAL REFLECTION ON THE LESSONS

Lesson 1: 2 Samuel 11:1-15

It didn't just happen (v. 2). The story of David's sin with Bathsheba begins with the words "It happened late one afternoon...." Many times, when a person's adulterous affair comes to light, he responds, "It just happened," as if to suggest that he was not responsible for his actions, that he had no control. While sexual attraction is powerful, it never just happens; we permit it to happen. David could have prevented it from happening if he had turned the other way after seeing Bathsheba or if he wouldn't have sought out her identity or if he had not ordered her up to his palace. Few things just happen; there are causes and choices.

Fatal attraction. The movie, *Fatal Attraction*, tells the story of a man who is attracted to a woman who is not his wife and has an affair with her. When he breaks off the relationship, she will not let go. She attempts to destroy both her lover and his family. David's fixation with Bathsheba was a fatal attraction; no, David did not die, but Bathsheba's husband did. This sin would plague David and his household for years to come.

You can't hide from the naked truth. Sin has a way of coming out from underneath the covers, of becoming exposed. David attempted to cover up his sin but one failed attempt led to an even more desperate and heinous attempt to conceal his sin. Then, when he thought he had gotten away with his sin, God exposed the naked truth through Nathan the prophet. David eventually confessed his wrongdoing but it would continue to haunt him.

Lesson 2: Ephesians 3:14-21

The difference between paternity and fatherhood (vv. 14-15). In Paul's prayer for the church, he states that he bows his knees before the Father, "from whom every family in heaven and earth is named." God not only gives us life but he takes an interest in our lives; God invests himself personally in our sustenance and growth. There are many men who take pride in their ability to impregnate a woman but who take little interest in their offspring. Society needs men

295

who not only take pride in paternity but in fatherhood, who give themselves freely to the nurture of their children.

Nurturing your inner being (v. 16). Far too much attention is accorded outward appearance in our Western culture. The plethora of products to enhance and change one's outward nature testifies to this obsession. Paul prays that Christians might be strengthened in their inner being (man, *anthropos*). That which is interior is the wellspring of our being. Our inner being, shaped by our interaction with God's Spirit, is what really matters. Instead of beautifying our bodies, we should be opening ourselves to the strengthening presence of God's Spirit.

Love is the ground of our being (v. 17). God is love and love is the ground of our being. It is this spiritual soil that gives stability and strength to our lives. Many young people have grown wild, like a weed, because they have not been rooted and grounded in love during their formative years.

The infinity of love (vv. 18-19). Paul was so overwhelmed with the magnitude of God's love that he could hardly express it. In reality, he seems to be saying that the love of God in Christ is infinite (surpasses knowledge). He expresses his sense of the infinite using the words breadth, length, height, and depth. God's love is certainly beyond our measuring but not beyond our knowing (experiencing). When we love, we partake of the infinite.

A really large plate. The word translated "width" in verse 19 is *platos*. If you're a big eater and you're going through a really good buffet line, you know the importance of a wide plate. Such a plate can be heaped with good food. This passage attempts to express the exceeding magnitude of God's love, grace, and fullness, which he has heaped on our life's plate in Jesus Christ.

Gospel: John 6:1-21

The Lord's Supper (v. 4). John's understanding of the Lord's Supper is grounded in the account of the feeding of the 5,000. The mention of the Passover Feast shows an obvious attempt to cast this as a type of Eucharist. Jesus is the master of the feast. John does not emphasize the aspect of forgiveness but highlights Christ's compassionate and strengthening presence.

This is a test, this is only a test (v. 5). Jesus tested Philip by asking him how they were going to be able to buy enough bread to feed the multitude. Philip flunked the test, while Andrew did a little better. Every so often when you're listening to the radio, an announcer will inform the listening audience that there is going to be a test of the Emergency Broadcasting System. Then the airwaves go silent for several seconds, followed by another announcement. The concluding announcement states that this was just a test; had it been a real emergency, you would have been told what to do. The test that Jesus gave his disciples was not the real thing; Jesus knew what he would do. However, Jesus sought to prepare his disciples for the real thing by this test.

The problem of thinking small (v. 9). Andrew was aware of some resources to feed the multitude, the five loaves and two fish, but he minimized them. "But what are they among so many?" Andrew fell into the common trap of thinking small. Thinking small leads to minimizing not only our strengths and resources, but God's. Miracles do indeed happen when we lay our meager resources at Christ's feet.

The profligacy of God (vv. 11-13). The second lesson celebrates the extravagance of God's love. The gospel emphasizes the profligacy of God's grace. Every person at the feast had all he wanted to eat and yet there were twelve baskets left over (also symbolic of the twelve apostles and the twelve tribes of Israel). God doesn't parcel out his grace like a penny-pinching miser; he supplies our needs in abundance.

SERMON APPROACHES WITH ILLUSTRATIONS

Lesson 1: 2 Samuel 11:1-15

Sermon Title: Perils Of Prosperity

Sermon Angle: David was at the apex of prosperity and success; his enemies were in check, his capital was established, he had a fancy palace, and could now take his ease. As he arose from his nap, he was feeling somehow incomplete. He needed something more to reignite his internal fire. Strolling on his rooftop, he spied Bathsheba and thought that she might fill the empty spaces in his heart. David's heart became possessed with covetousness rather than the Spirit of the Lord. He thought that one more possession, an exquisite work of art, would satisfy his desire. Such are the perils of prosperity.

Outline:
1. David had succeeded beyond his dreams but it left him wondering: "Is that all there is?"
2. In looking for something to satisfy his emptiness, he spied Bathsheba.
3. Fulfilling his desire did not fulfill him but brought unhappiness.
4. The pursuit of material success leaves many Americans spiritually impoverished.
5. Fix your hearts on seeking God's will rather than your own desires.

Sermon Title: He Looked, Took, And Forsook

Sermon Angle: The above verbs aptly describe what David did when he committed adultery with Bathsheba. He was looking from the roof of his palace and saw Bathsheba in all her glory. Lust starts with the look. You can't help but see something at times, but you don't have to continue to look when something arouses your desires. Next, the text says that David sent his servants to Bathsheba and they took her (v. 4). He had no right to take her; she was the wife of one of his own soldiers. This led to adultery, deceit, and murder. In committing these sins he forsook the Lord. Fortunately, as we read later in this book, God did not forsake David.

Lesson 2: Ephesians 3:14-21

Sermon Title: How To Strengthen The Inner Man Or Inner Woman

Sermon Angle: The apostle passionately prays that God might strengthen the inner being of his disciples (v. 16). A few people are heavily involved in bodybuilding and many more are seriously engaged in physical fitness. They seek to strengthen the outer man or woman, to condition the physical body. Paul earnestly prays that his followers would permit God to strengthen their inner man or inner woman by the aegis of the Spirit of God and the power of faith (v. 17).

Outline:
1. Americans are obsessed with their outer appearance. (Give examples.)
2. Paul prays for his disciples' inner being (v. 16).
3. How do you strengthen the inner man or inner woman?
   — Open your life to God's Spirit (v. 17).
   — The Spirit will ground you in God's love and fill you with the fullness of God.

Sermon Title: The Joy Of Being Full

Sermon Angle: Is anything more satisfying after a hard day of labor than to push away from the supper table of your favorite food with a pleasantly full and satisfied feeling? This feeling is intensified in the presence of people whom you love and enjoy. Note, we are not talking about gorging oneself, which leaves you with a sick feeling. Imagine how a persistent, gnawing sensation of hunger must feel, whether it be a hunger of the body or the soul. Paul speaks of the pleasure of being filled with the fullness of God (v. 19), the fullness of his love and grace. Nothing can be more satisfying than that.

Outline:
1. Think of a time when your life was full, complete, and satisfying.
2. God wants you to experience that feeling and more (v. 19).
3. Some people gorge themselves with all sorts of things but it doesn't satisfy.
4. The pleasantly full feeling God gives lasts eternally, if we but let his Spirit fill us with his love and grace.

Gospel: John 6:1-21

Sermon Title: A Feast With An Attitude

Sermon Angle: The picnic which Jesus celebrated with the multitude was a simple meal, yet a feast, because everyone had plenty to eat and there was a feeling of wonder and community. This was a feast with an attitude: the attitude of gratitude. Jesus had the people sit down in groups, then he took the loaves and gave thanks to God (v. 11). It was truly a Eucharist. Whenever we assemble to give thanks to the Source of all life by breaking the bread of life, it is a Eucharist.

Outline:
1. Most feasts have an attitude — celebration, revelry.
2. Jesus was the host for a feast (feeding the 5,000).
3. The attitude of his feast was gratitude (v. 11) for the generosity of God's gifts.
4. This attitude dominates the Lord's Supper and is shown in the name Eucharist.
5. Life with Christ is a Eucharist.

Sermon Title: God Is A Conservationist

Sermon Angle: After the meal was served, Jesus ordered the leftover pieces to be gathered so that nothing would be lost (v. 12). While God is generous with the children of the earth, he does not waste that which he has created. "That nothing may be lost" conveys God's attitude toward his children; he sent his Son to gather in the broken fragments of his human family. God was the original conservationist and it is his will that the church conserve and save that which is the Lord's.

Sermon Title: There Is No Hunger Appeal

Sermon Angle: The Evangelical Lutheran Church in America has an ongoing emphasis on elimination of hunger, called the ELCA Hunger Appeal. The fact is that hunger has no appeal. Voluntary fasting may have an appeal as a spiritual discipline but imposed hunger has no appeal whatsoever. Those who are hungry can think of nothing else than their dire need for food. They cannot appreciate the higher things of the Spirit until their basic physical needs are met. Hunger organizations make their appeal to the relatively rich to share some of the scraps of bread that fall from their table. That task seems even more daunting to us than the prospect of feeding the 5,000 did to the disciples. We have only five loaves and two fishes. What good are they among so many? Have we lost faith that Christ can still miraculously multiply the loaves and the fish that we possess?

Outline:
1. Hunger organizations appeal for us to help the hungry.
2. Such a pitch is not appealing to many. Why?
   — The need is so great.
   — Resources are limited.
   — The need is not visible to many of us.
   — We rationalize the need away — it's somebody else's fault or responsibility.
3. Christ still asks us what we propose to do about the needs of the hungry (v. 5).
4. Possible responses.
   — Share what you have.
   — Get to know the hungry as people.
   — Rather than only giving them a fish, teach them to fish.

*   *   *   *   *

Discount airlines were sometimes referred to as a "peanut fare," because in order to offer the most reasonable fare possible, peanuts were the only food served. Peanuts have the connotation of being insignificant or of little value. Actually, the peanut is a wonderful little nugget. You may recall from your elementary education the story of George Washington Carver, the great scientist, who discovered at his laboratory at the Tuskegee Institute in Alabama over 300 marketable uses of the lowly peanut. The fact that you probably didn't learn at school was that Carver was not only a great scientist but a great Christian who spent two hours every morning communing with God through prayer. He credited his achievements not to his own genius but to his creator, who gave him the ability to multiply the uses of the peanut over 300-fold. He was dubbed a "Black Leonardo."

*   *   *   *   *

Be gentle when you touch bread. Let it not be uncared for, unwanted. So often bread is taken for granted. There is so much beauty in bread; beauty of the sun and soil, beauty of patient toil. Winds and rains have caressed it. Christ often blessed it. Be gentle when you touch bread.
— Author Unknown

Proper 13/Pentecost 11/Ordinary Time 18

Revised Common	2 Samuel 11:26—12:13a	Ephesians 4:1-16	John 6:24-35
Roman Catholic	Exodus 16:2-4, 12-15	Ephesians 4:17, 20-25	John 6:24-35
Episcopal	Exodus 16:2-4, 9-15	Ephesians 4:17-25	John 6:24-35

Theme For The Day: Receiving the true bread of life, Jesus Christ.

BRIEF COMMENTARY ON THE LESSONS

Lesson 1: 2 Samuel 11:26—12:13a (C)

This text continues the story of David's sin with Bathsheba and spells out the consequences. After Bathsheba's period of mourning, David brings her into his household and marries her. He might have thought that he had gotten away with his crime when Nathan the prophet tells him the story of the rich man who took the poor man's little ewe lamb to slaughter for a feast. David unknowingly pronounces judgment on himself when he declares to Nathan that such a man deserved to die. Then, dramatically, the prophet points to David: "You are the man!" The king then confesses his sin against God. Nathan responds that God has put away (forgiven) his sin but that, as a consequence of his sin, violence would never leave David's household and his little son would die.

Lesson 1: Exodus 16:2-4, 12-15 (RC); Exodus 16:2-4, 9-15 (E)

Lesson 2: Ephesians 4:1-16 (C)

The first three chapters of this epistle set out the doctrinal issues and 4:1 — 6:20 lay out the ethical implications. This pericope is an appeal for unity. Paul begs them to lead a life worthy of the gospel, to maintain the unity of the Spirit. He reminds them that there is only one Lord, one faith, one baptism, one God and Father of us all. We have all been assigned various gifts and roles — pastors, evangelists, teachers — for the building up of the body of Christ. God's aim for his church is unity.

Lesson 2: Ephesians 4:17, 20-25 (RC); Ephesians 4:17-25 (E)

Gospel: John 6:24-35 (C, RC, E)

The crowds search for Jesus and find him at Capernaum. They question how he got there. Jesus doesn't answer but confronts them with the fact that they are not seeking the bread of heaven but earthly bread. Jesus warns them to work for the bread that endures eternally, not the loaves that perish. They ask him what a person should do to be doing the work of God. Jesus declares that it is the will of God to believe in the one God has sent. They then ask for a sign, saying that God gave their ancestors bread from heaven. Jesus counters that he is the true bread from heaven, the gift of the Father, who gives life to the world. The people respond: "Lord, give us this bread always."

Psalm Of The Day
  Psalm 51:1-12 (C) — "Wash me thoroughly from my iniquity" (v. 2).
  Psalm 78:11-25 (E)
  Psalm 77 (RC)

Prayer Of The Day
  Bread of life, we sometimes consume that which does not truly satisfy and seek to fill the hunger of our soul with the bread of this earth. Satisfy us with the bread of heaven, Jesus Christ, our Lord, that we might never hunger again. In Jesus' name. Amen.

THEOLOGICAL REFLECTION ON THE LESSONS

Lesson 1: 2 Samuel 11:26—12:13a

The danger of devaluing life. In verse 25 a messenger reports to David from the battlefield that some of his men are dead and that Uriah was also dead. The king hadn't a care. He blithely announced: "Do not let this matter trouble you, the sword devours now one, and now another...." We all suffer when life becomes devalued and cheap. The hoodlums who roam our streets feel precisely the same way, not only about others but themselves. God values life so highly that he sent his Son.

Pronouncing judgment on yourself. Sometimes parents will say to their disobedient sons and daughters: "Now John, how do you think we should punish you for what you have done wrong?" David pronounced judgment on himself, albeit unwittingly (vv. 5-6). It's kind of a rule of life, the Lord judges us by the ruler we have used to judge others.

No fifth amendment rights before the Supreme Court. Often, those called into court to testify will answer a question by saying, "I assert my fifth amendment rights." The constitution says that we don't have to incriminate ourselves. David didn't assert any fifth amendment rights when he stood accused by God through his prophet, Nathan. He confessed, "I have sinned against the Lord" (v. 13). When we appear before the judgment seat of God, the supreme court of the universe, we cannot plead the fifth amendment but we can plead that we are covered by the blood of Jesus. We are guilty but stand acquitted.

Lesson 2: Ephesians 4:1-16

The peace bond (v. 3). During World War II, war bonds were promoted so that our nation might have the capital needed to fight our enemies. The war brought the people of our nation together in a common effort. The war bonds (saving bonds) were an expression of that effort and the unity of spirit that prevailed among us. Paul urges that Christians be eager to maintain the unity of the Spirit and "the bond of peace." This peace bond was purchased with the atoning blood of Christ. We don't have to buy it; all we need to do is maintain it.

Celebrate our unity (vv. 3-7). We hear a good deal about celebrating our diversity as a nation and a church. As the people of God, we would be better off celebrating our unity. "One Lord, one faith, one baptism, one God and Father of us all."

Growing up in God (v. 13). When it comes to our relationship to the Lord, we are all immature children. God has given each member of the church gifts to be exercised for the common good, so that we might all grow up in God. It is God's will that we strive to attain full spiritual maturity, measuring our lives by the pattern of Jesus.

301

Gospel: John 6:24-35

Food with a longer shelf life (v. 27). In this century, we have experienced a revolution in food technology — packaging, handling, and distribution. With this technology, we have been able to lengthen greatly the shelf life of food. Two or three generations ago most people had to buy perishable food just about every day. Even so, no food has an endless shelf life, and none of the things that we feel are so essential for our lives — cars, houses, televisions — will last very long. Jesus calls us to strive for the food that does not perish, the bread of life (v. 27).

Jesus, the original bread machine? (v. 26). Jesus accuses the masses of seeking him not because they sought spiritual truth but because they had their physical appetite satisfied. Perhaps they view Jesus as the original bread machine. They could obtain fresh bread with a minimum of effort.

Priorities. If you read this chapter literally, you come away with the idea that one must choose between earthly bread and heavenly bread, that it's an "either/or" proposition. Actually, Jesus is speaking of priorities. He's saying, "seek first the bread of heaven and then God will give you the earthly bread you need as well." Recall that our Lord teaches us to pray for earthly bread, "Give us this day our daily bread." However, Jesus instructs us to pray not for an endless hoard of bread but for that which we need at the present time.

SERMON APPROACHES WITH ILLUSTRATIONS

Lesson 1: 2 Samuel 11:26—12:13a

Sermon Title: Deserving Of Death

Sermon Angle: When Nathan told the story of the rich man stealing the pet ewe from the poor man, David pronounced: "This man deserves to die." How true! He did deserve death, so does every murderer, every criminal, every sinner. Oops! That includes us. We deserve to die but God is gracious. God was gracious in forgiving David and he is gracious to us as well. Though we must suffer the consequences of our sins, God saves our lives through the reconciliation offered to us in Christ.

Outline:
1. David judged rightly — the man in Nathan's parable deserved to die, but so did David.
2. Paul says: "The wages of sin is death" (Romans 6:23).
3. God offered forgiveness to David and pardon to all through Jesus Christ. "The free gift of God is eternal life through Jesus Christ, our Lord."

Sermon Title: Who Have You Sinned Against?

Sermon Angle: The television newscast the other day reported that the police had recovered a quantity of stolen goods in the car of a couple of young men. They admitted that they were stolen. The problem was, they had no victim. Nobody had reported any of these items missing. No crime can be charged without a victim. The fact of the matter is that when we sin, there are more victims than meet the eye. Some executive commits a white-collar crime, stealing from a large company, and he thinks that there are no victims but the company. Wrong! We all pay in terms of higher prices and a deteriorating sense of morality. What the sinner doesn't realize until too late is that he himself is victim of his own sins. Note the consequences that Nathan spelled out for David's sin. But it goes even further, the ultimate victim is God. David confessed: "I have sinned against the Lord."

Outline:
1. We like to think that our sins have no victims.
2. David thought that he had contained his sin against Uriah but came to see that he was victim of his own sin.
3. The ultimate victim is God (v. 13).
4. God can and does forgive but he can't undo the consequences of our sins.

*   *   *   *   *

In October of 1995, a Chicago priest who was accused of sexual misconduct against two boys was allowed to return to his parish. This misconduct occurred in 1976. Although the priest was warmly received by many members of the parish, others demonstrated in opposition to his reinstatement. The Survivors' Network of Those Abused By Priests picketed. The Catholic church has placed conditions on his return. He must have other adults present when he ministers to children and he must continue to undergo counseling. The story illustrates the principle of forgiveness. God forgives, many other people will forgive, but a cloud of suspicion remains because trust has been put into question. The sinner can never re-create the world as it was before his transgression.

*   *   *   *   *

Lesson 2: Ephesians 4:1-16
Sermon Title: War And Peace
Sermon Angle: Wars are either won or lost. Victory is usually defined by some decisive moment or crucial battle which assured an eventual victory. Peace, on the other hand, is not so much won as maintained. To keep the peace requires constant diligence and effort. Paul speaks of maintaining "the unity of the Spirit in the bond of peace" (v. 13). Christ has won the decisive victory against the forces of evil and gives us his peace through our baptism into Christ. However, the church is entrusted with the sacred mission of maintaining the peace. This comes about when we permit the Spirit to guide our actions so that we work together as one body. God's Spirit gives us humility, patience, and love, which maintains the peace bond.
Outline:
1. War requires a concerted effort but peace calls for a continued effort.
2. Christ has won the war, now the church must keep the peace.
3. How do we maintain the peace?
   — The Spirit (v. 3).
   — The Spirit grants patience, humility, and love (vv. 2-3).
   — Use our gifts for the building up of the church (vv. 11-12).

Sermon Title: Blest Be The Ties That Bind
Sermon Angle: Paul lifts up the essential ties that bind all Christians — "One hope ... one Lord, one faith, one baptism, one God and Father of us all...." In so doing, he raises the factors that define the essential catholicity of the church. Ties and being bound are not highly valued in our free-wheeling society that has deified individual rights. We Christians can provide a corrective for society by celebrating the blessed ties that bind us together in Christ.

303

Outline:
1. While society elevates individual freedoms, Christians are called to celebrate the spiritual ties that bind us.
2. What are the ties that bind us?
   — The one body and the one Spirit (v. 4).
   — The one hope (v. 4).
   — One Lord (Jesus), one faith, one baptism, one God and Father (vv. 5-6).
3. Offer the world what it needs — unity and community in Christ.

Gospel: John 6:24-35

Sermon Title: Why Are You Seeking Jesus?

Sermon Angle: Jesus had vanished. The crowds went looking for him and found him. The problem was that they were seeking him for the wrong reasons. Jesus observed: "Very truly I say to you, you are looking for me, not because you saw signs but because you ate your fill of the loaves" (v. 25). They wanted Jesus, not so they could get to heaven, but so that they might have their physical appetites satisfied. People seek Jesus for a host of reasons; not all of them are good. We need to ask ourselves, why are we seeking Jesus? Are you mostly interested in what you can gain from him to make this life a little easier? Or are you following Jesus because he is the bread of life and you want him, nothing less?

Outline:
1. The crowds were looking for Jesus for the wrong reason — for a handout.
2. They did not seek Jesus for salvation, nor see him as the Savior.
3. Why do you seek or follow Jesus?

Sermon Title: Locked In A Welfare Mentality

Sermon Angle: The crowds that were looking for Jesus were locked into a kind of welfare mentality. A welfare mentality is created in some people after they have been on the dole for some time. All they are interested in is a handout. What they need is a hand down. That is, they need help in changing their lives. They need to be told how they can become new people. They need to see a vision of how they can really live life, rather than merely exist. Many Christians are locked into a welfare mentality. They are merely seeking a handout rather than a hand down from heaven that will enable them to have life and have it abundantly.

Outline:
1. The crowds merely wanted help in living the same old life.
2. Jesus wanted to help them find new life in him.
3. Christians get caught up in a welfare mentality — make my life easier, Lord!
4. Christ wants to reinvent our lives, to make them great and to make them eternal.

Sermon Title: Real Food For Real People

Sermon Angle: One of the fast food chains had the motto: "Real food for real people." The crowd recalled the bread, which God gave their ancestors as they wandered though the wilderness. Jesus replied: "It was not Moses who gave you the bread from heaven, but it is my Father who gives you the true (real) bread from heaven" (v. 32). The law, for all its goodness, was not the real bread; it was not real food for real people. The real food (bread) is that which comes down from heaven and gives life to the world (v. 33). The gospel is real food for real people, to be received through faith (v. 29).

Outline:
1. Much of what we consume is garbage, not real food for real people.
2. The law was good, but was not real food because it could not change us inside.
3. Jesus is the bread of heaven — real food for real people.
4. Receive that bread by faith and live eternally.

* * * * *

The Great Harvest Bread Co., Geneva, Illinois, has this message on its front door, "No shirt, No shoes, No problem." The owners of this company have created a fun place where people can enjoy bread. They produce over a dozen varieties of specialty breads. Each loaf is made with freshly ground flour, abetted by such natural ingredients as apples, seeds, garlic, and blueberries. The thing that grabs the eye of visitors as they enter the store is a cutting board laden with fresh-baked bread, softened butter, and honey. Behind the board is a smiling baker urging them to sample a thick slice of fresh bread or the bread of their choice. "We love to watch our people enjoy bread, even if they don't intend to buy any," intoned one of the owners. Jesus also likes to see his children enjoy bread, but he most wants us to enjoy the bread of life, because it will satisfy the appetite of our souls.

Proper 14/Pentecost 12/Ordinary Time 19

Revised Common	2 Samuel 18:5-9, 15, 31-33	Ephesians 4:25—5:2	John 6:35, 41-51
Roman Catholic	1 Kings 19:4-8	Ephesians 4:30—5:2	John 6:41-51
Episcopal	Deuteronomy 8:1-10	Ephesians 4:(25-29) 30—5:2	John 6:37-51

Theme For The Day: Jesus is the bread from heaven that truly satisfies us.

BRIEF COMMENTARY ON THE LESSONS

Lesson 1: 2 Samuel 18:5-9, 15, 31-33 (C)

David's son, Absalom, rebels against his father to gain the crown for himself. David splits his army into three parts and surprises Absalom's troops near a wooded area. The rebellious army is put into panic and Absalom flees into the woods on his donkey where his hair is caught in the thicket of a tree. He is left hanging there but is still alive. David had charged his men prior to battle not to harm the young man, so when one of Joab's soldiers spies Absalom he reports it to his commanding officer. Joab asked him why he hadn't killed the young rebel and then proceeds to thrust the king's son through with three spears. The last portion of the pericope, verses 31-33, relates how David was told the news of the battle and of his son's death, but seems somewhat disjointed. I would suggest including verses 16-30, which narrate the story of the messengers who brought the news to David. Joab sent the Cushite with the message but Ahimaaz begged to go, also. Finally, Joab relents, and so two men are running to the king with the same message. Ahimaaz got there faster but he didn't know how to share with David the news of Absalom's death. The Cushite had just the right words: "May the enemies of my lord the king, and all who rise up to do you harm, be like that young man." David wept bitterly for his fallen son.

Lesson 1: Deuteronomy 8:1-10 (E)

Lesson 1: 1 Kings 19:4-8 (RC)

Lesson 2: Ephesians 4:25—5:2 (C); Ephesians 4:(25-29) 30—5:2 (E); Ephesians 4:30—5:2 (RC)

The theme for this lection is sounded in verse 17, where Paul says, "... you must no longer live as the Gentiles live...." Since Christians are members of the same body, we are to be truthful with one another, dissipate our anger, abandon stealing, and earn an honest living. We are not to grieve the Holy Spirit by engaging in angry and contentious behavior. Paul's admonitions are summed up by 5:1-2, "Therefore be imitators of God as beloved children, and live in love, as Christ loved us and gave himself for us...."

Gospel: John 6:35, 41-51 (C); John 6:37-51 (E); John 6:41-51 (RC)

Jesus declares that he is the bread of life, that anyone who comes to him will never hunger of thirst again (spiritually). Those who ate of the manna were hungry again but not so those who eat of the bread of heaven. Some of the people take offense at this claim; they see him only as the son of Mary and Joseph. Jesus makes the sublimest of claims for himself: that anyone who eats of him (receives in faith) will be given the gift of eternal life. However, no one can come to him unless he is drawn by the Father.

Psalm Of The Day
Psalm 130 (C) — "Out of the depths I cry to you, O Lord" (v. 1).
Psalm 34 (E)
Psalm 33 (RC)

Prayer Of The Day
Bread of life, we confess that we are spiritually malnourished; we have fed on that which cannot satisfy the deepest longings of our soul. Fill us with the fullness of your grace and love, that our souls might be sustained eternally. In Jesus' name. Amen.

THEOLOGICAL REFLECTION ON THE LESSONS

Lesson 1: 2 Samuel 18:5-9, 15, 31-33
The compassion of the king (v. 5). King David pleads with his commanders to deal gently with his rebellious son. Though his son tried to unseat him from the throne, David still loved him. We see in David a picture of God's love for us sinners. Though we rebel against him, Jesus, his Son, pleads for mercy on our behalf.

He was left hanging between heaven and earth (v. 9). Absalom was caught by his head, probably his hair, on a branch of a tree, and left hanging between heaven and earth. Absalom was completely vulnerable and helpless. Jesus Christ was also lifted up on a tree, left dangling between heaven and earth. He, too, was completely vulnerable, exposed, and helpless. He, too, had a spear thrust into him; the soldier pierced his side but the treachery of those who betrayed him and denied him also pierced his heart. It appeared that he, like Absalom, was defeated by the powers that be, but Jesus won the victory through the resurrection. Two men were hanging between heaven and earth but what led them there was radically different. Absalom was hanging as a result of his own treachery, while Jesus was left hanging as a consequence of *our* treachery. David mourned his son's death, while we celebrate life, because Jesus hung between heaven and earth for our sins and our salvation.

The art of bearing bad tidings (vv. 31-32). Two men brought tidings to the king. Ahimaaz was anxious to go and he was a swift runner but he did not know how to bear bad tidings. The Cushite arrived later but he possessed the right words to let the king down gently, as he conveyed the sad news of his son's death: "May the enemies of my lord the king ... be like that young man" (v. 32).

Lesson 2: Ephesians 4:25 — 5:2
Anger is no sin (v. 26). Paul says, "Be angry but do not sin," which indicates that he doesn't think anger is a sin. Anger is an emotion which certain events can spark in our heart. Anger only becomes a sin when we permit it to burn out of control or let it smolder over a long period of time. "Do not let the sun go down on your anger" is good advice. If our anger dissipates quickly, it will do little damage.

The virtue of honest labor (v. 28). Thieves are warned that they must give up stealing and engage in honest work. But for what reason are we to labor? If you would ask the average person, he or she would say that they want to make money and be able to afford the good things of life. This is not, however, a Christian rationale for work. Paul claims that we should do honest work in order to have something to share with the poor.

Let no garbage issue from your mouth (v. 29). The word translated "evil talk" is *sapros*, meaning something rotten (like garbage). Filthy, slanderous words are verbal garbage. Our airwaves are laden with all kinds of words, many of them verbal garbage. Elie Wiesel, noted Jewish writer and lecturer who lived through the holocaust, asserts that all acts of bigotry, prejudice, and genocide start with evil words.

Christian mimes (v. 1). Paul urges followers of Christ to be imitators of God. The word is *mimetes*, from which we get the word "mime." Christ is our model for imitation.

Gospel: John 6:35-51

A truly satisfying meal (v. 35). Is anything more gratifying than a satisfying meal? But what makes for such a repast? Filling our stomachs is not, in itself, satisfying. In fact, we may be left feeling bloated. Gourmet food is not necessarily more satisfying than common food. A satisfying meal will probably be a nourishing, balanced, and tasty meal. Moreover, such a meal will probably be enjoyed in the company of friends.

Broken bread. Jesus offers himself as bread and bread must be broken in order to give life. First of all, wheat is broken down into flour and becomes the main ingredient of bread. Once the loaf is baked, it must be broken to be eaten. The metaphor of bread suggests Jesus' humiliation, suffering, and death; Jesus was broken for our sake and offered to us as the bread of life.

Jesus does God's will (vv. 38-40). Jesus makes plain that he has come to earth not to accomplish his own will but the will of his Father in heaven. What is God's will? That all who believe in Jesus might have eternal life. Jesus promises to raise them up on the last day.

SERMON APPROACHES WITH ILLUSTRATIONS

Lesson 1: 2 Samuel 18:5-9, 15, 31-33

Sermon Title: Caught In The Web

Sermon Angle: Absalom got caught in his own treacherous web of deceit. He stirred up a rebellion against his father but he became the victim. As he was fleeing David's troops, he was caught by his hair in the limb of a tree. All who practice treachery will eventually fall victim of their own designs.

Sermon Title: Know Why You're Running

Sermon Angle: After David's forces defeated the rebels and Absalom was killed, Joab decided that David needed to be informed. Ahimaaz begged to be accorded the task of being herald. Joab knew that this man was not the right person for the task and so he sent a Cushite. Nevertheless, Ahimaaz continued to importune his commander, who eventually gave in. Though the Cushite got a head start, the other man took another route and overtook him, appearing first before the king. Yet, he was not able to relate the sad news of Absalom's death, pleading ignorance. The Cushite, slower of gait, knew why he was sent and was able to tell the king both the good news and the bad news in a gentle and compassionate fashion. A lot of people possess energy, drive, and swiftness in the race of life, but they have forgotten why they are running and have no message.

Outline:
1. The world is full of messengers who run fast but have no message.
2. Ahimaaz was eager to be messenger for the king but hadn't given sufficient thought to what he would say when he arrived.
3. The Cushite was slower but had a message to bear and the ability to relate it compassionately.
4. Don't be so concerned about getting there fastest. Rather, give priority to the content and sharing of your message.

Lesson 2: Ephesians 4:25—5:2

Sermon Title: Give The Devil No Room

Sermon Angle: When you are constructing your spiritual edifice, make no room for the devil (v. 27). Most of us give Satan opportunity to gain a foothold. We let our anger fester rather than dealing creatively with it. Rather than feast on God's Word, we let our minds be filled with trashy movies, books, and magazines. The idea is to crowd out the devil with that which is good and loving, so that the prince of darkness will have no room to settle in.

Outline:
1. The best way to combat Satan is to crowd him out of our lives.
2. Most of us build the devil a room in our lives with the tools of festering anger, gossip, an unforgiving spirit, and the like.
3. Let your words and deeds be seasoned with grace, peace, and love (v. 29).

Sermon Title: The Power Of Words

Sermon Angle: Almost all evil deeds are preceded with slanderous and hateful words. When assaulted with words, children sometimes say, "Sticks and stones may break my bones but names can never harm me." This is not true. Words can harm and kill but words can also free and give life when they are eternal words of truth. "So then, putting away all falsehood, let all of us speak the truth to our neighbors...." Words can be employed destructively or constructively. If Jesus, the Word made Flesh, lives in our hearts, we will use our tongues to build up our neighbors and never tear them down (v. 29).

Outline:
1. Besides God, the most powerful force in the world is words.
2. Slanderous and hateful words destroy.
3. We are called to speak the truth with our neighbors (v. 25).
4. Use God's truth to build up one another (v. 29).

* * * * *

Several years ago, the exchange student we had from Germany was summoned to court for the crime of shoplifting. As we waited in the courtroom, we witnessed the proceedings. Those who stood before the bench were mostly young people who were answering for infractions of the drug and alcohol laws, as they relate to minors. One teen was asked by the judge, "Where did you get the beer?" "I found it in the parking lot," he replied. "You mean it just dropped out of the sky?" the incredulous judge responded. It was obvious that he was telling a lie by concealing the truth. The others who appeared before the court basically followed the same course. When our student stood before the court, she was asked if she had stolen any other objects than the food she was charged with taking. She said that she hadn't. She too was lying through her teeth. If our society does not do better in living out the truth, our deceit will eventually do us in.

*   *   *   *   *

Sermon Title: The Proper Way To Play God

Sermon Angle: Paul admonishes the church to imitate God, as his beloved children. Children's play usually consists in playing out adult roles, imitating those who are closest to them. Paul invites us to play God, to imitate the almighty. Some people do this improperly. They really think they are God and take it upon themselves to create or destroy life. In other words, they seize power and prerogatives that are not rightfully theirs. Playing God the right way means imitating his grace, love, and forgiveness. We are called to emulate God's character.

Gospel: John 6:35, 41-51

Sermon Title: Eat To Live, Not Live To Eat

Sermon Angle: No, I'm not suggesting a sermon on gluttony, though such a sermon would not be irrelevant in our day. Rather, the point that needs to be made is that Jesus is the food we need to eat in order to live eternally, beginning now. Bread is the symbol of all that we need, as in the Lord's Prayer, and Jesus offers himself to us as bread: "I am the bread of life. Whoever comes to me will never be hungry ..." (v. 35). On the other side of the coin, there are many people who merely live to eat, to consume, or to satisfy their desires. We need to reissue our Lord's invitation to eat of him and live.

Outline:
1. Many people live to eat (not only food but other products).
2. Food is to sustain life.
3. Jesus offers himself to us as the bread of life.
4. Eat of Jesus by faith and live.

*   *   *   *   *

Last summer, I was invited to dine at a local all-you-can-eat restaurant. They had at least four serving stations — one for salads, one for hot dishes and meats, one for fresh baked breads, and one for desserts. The amount and variety of food was phenomenal! The place was packed! I couldn't help but notice the huge quantities of food that people were piling on their plates and quite a number of the people there were really enormous, 100 or more pounds overweight. One such lady had obvious disabilities because she was in a wheelchair. What came to mind was a feeding frenzy, like a school of piranhas devouring a pig. The scene presented a prime example of living to eat, rather than eating to live. You may wonder how much I ate. Too much! Far too much! I felt bloated and uncomfortable for a couple of hours afterward. It's easy to get caught up in the feeding frenzy of those who live to eat.

*   *   *   *   *

Sermon Title: Jesus Came Down To Raise Us Up

Sermon Angle: Jesus makes clear who he is and where he is from. He is the bread of life, who has come down to earth from heaven (v. 41). Why did he come? To raise us up, to give us the gift of eternal life (v. 44). We could say that Jesus came to free us from our earthboundness,

310

so that we might learn to soar with the angels. Faith in Jesus is the vehicle that frees us from the pull of earthly things.

Outline:
1. The fact that Jesus came down from heaven shows that he is God in the flesh.
2. Why would God stoop so low? To raise us up with him to eternal life.
3. How can we ascend with Jesus? Trust in him (v. 44).

Sermon Title: Eternal Life As A Present Possession

Sermon Angle: Jesus declares: "Very truly, I tell you, whoever believes has eternal life" (v. 47). Note the present tense. The person who believes *has* eternal life *now*. There is, of course, a future dimension to eternal life; Jesus talks about raising up those who believe on the last day (v. 44). However, that does not take away from the fact that eternal life is a present possession. Eternal life denotes a quality of life and not merely length of days. Eternal life is to experience the love, grace, and nurture of God, beginning now.

Outline:
1. We commonly think eternal life starts after we die.
2. Jesus asserts that whoever believes in him has eternal life right *now* (v. 47).
3. All who embrace the grace of God through faith in Jesus now have eternal life.

Proper 15/Pentecost 13/Ordinary Time 20

Revised Common	1 Kings 2:10-12; 3:3-14	Ephesians 5:15-20	John 6:51-58
Roman Catholic	Proverbs 9:1-6	Ephesians 5:15-20	John 6:51-58
Episcopal	Proverbs 9:1-6	Ephesians 5:15-20	John 6:53-59

Theme For The Day: Being filled with the wisdom and Spirit of God.

BRIEF COMMENTARY ON THE LESSONS

Lesson 1: 1 Kings 2:10-12; 3:3-14 (C)

The story of David comes to an end. He reigned as king a total of forty years. Solomon rules in his father's place, offering lavish sacrifices at the high places of worship. Early in his reign, God appears to him in a dream and tells him to request whatever he desires. Solomon confesses his inadequacy for the task of being king and asks the Lord for wisdom, that he might discharge his duties justly. God is pleased with this request and grants Solomon more than he requests; in addition to wisdom, he bestows wealth and fame.

Lesson 1: Proverbs 9:1-6 (RC, E)

Lesson 2: Ephesians 5:15-20 (C, RC, E)

Paul warns his children in the faith to watch carefully their manner of living. They are to live wisely and not be fools who are carried away with drunkenness and debauchery. The secret to wise living is to be possessed by God's Spirit, who puts an eternal hymn of praise in our heart.

Gospel: John 6:51-58 (C, RC); John 6:53-59 (E)

Jesus teaches that his followers must eat his body and drink his blood to enjoy eternal life. This passage presents modern preachers with a challenge because our people do not readily grasp the meaning of sacrifice. For the audience of Jesus' day and John's day, the understanding of sacrifice was taken for granted. Almost all of the religions had some form of sacrifice. In the sacrifice, only a part was burned or offered to the god. A portion was given to the priest and the rest was consumed by the giver of the sacrifice, together with his family and friends. They believed that the spirit of their god actually inhabited the sacrifice that was consumed by the worshipers. This conception may seem crude to modern ears, but it relays an important truth. True religion means receiving the Spirit of God within our being. Such receiving of Christ's Spirit is associated with but not limited to the Eucharist.

Psalm Of The Day

    Psalm 111 (C) — "The fear of the Lord is the beginning of wisdom" (v. 10).

    Psalm 147 (E)

    Psalm 33 (RC)

Prayer Of The Day

God of wisdom, fill us with your Spirit that we might understand the true meaning of our existence. Make your Christ the food that we eat, your Spirit the water that gives us life, that we might experience the true satisfaction of your fullness and grace. In Jesus' name. Amen.

THEOLOGICAL REFLECTION ON THE LESSONS

Lesson 1: 1 Kings 2:10-12; 3:3-14

Firmly established (v. 12). The writer of 1 Kings comments that at the beginning of Solomon's reign, the kingdom was "firmly established." His father had ruled wisely, fought hard, and feared the Lord, which led to a secure realm. Solomon inherited a good thing. But as you read on the story of Solomon's rule, you see things starting to unravel, so that shortly after his death the nation split. The lesson here is that we cannot take our blessings for granted. The price of prosperity and security is eternal vigilance.

Beyond his wildest dream (3:5 ff). Solomon had a dream in which God invited him to ask for whatever he desired. The king requested wisdom and understanding, to justly rule his people. God was so pleased with Solomon's request that he gave him far more. God is anxious to bless his children with gifts beyond our wildest dreams. All he asks is that we seek him first.

How to lengthen your life (v. 14). God offers Solomon the prospect of long life, if the king will honor him and walk in all his ways. Attached to the commandment on honoring our fathers and mothers also comes the promise of long life. If we honor the Lord and those whom God has placed in authority over us, God promises a long and fruitful life.

Lesson 2: Ephesians 5:15-20

Care-full (v. 15). Paul warns, "Be careful!" Not that the Lord wants us to filled with worries and concerns. The admonition "Be careful!" acknowledges dangers and opportunities. First, the dangers. Since moral and spiritual pitfalls and minefields abound, we need to negotiate our way with great care and precision. Second, we have opportunities to grasp. We must take care to make sure we don't flub the opportunities that God puts in our path.

You will know them by their music (v. 19). The lives of those who do not know God are characterized by dissonance and disharmony, so too the life of the fool. The child of Christ has a melody in his heart and a song of praise and thanksgiving to God on his lips.

Gospel: John 6:51-58

Christianity is conceiving. Christianity is more than a mind trip, it is more than understanding with our minds. Conceiving, giving life, starts with loving another person so much that you receive that person into your life. Christ conceives eternal life within us when we receive him into our life by faith. Jesus compares this receiving that leads to conceiving with eating and drinking. In eating and drinking, that which we consume becomes part of us. Jesus says that we must eat his body and drink his blood (v. 51). This is not to be taken as a crude literalism but as a way of stating that we must individually receive him into our hearts and thereby conceive eternal life within us.

A visceral faith. The language that John employs here is very visceral and earthy. This chapter speaks to the real humanity of Jesus; he was God in the flesh, not a phantom or a holy gust of the Spirit. You can't get much more earthy than talking about eating Christ's flesh or

313

drinking his blood. Martin Luther, a great man of God, was also very earthy in his understanding of the faith. He said that when the devil attacks us we should turn our backsides to him and let loose some wind in his face.

The language of sacrifice. This passage is shot through with the language of sacrifice. Christ offers himself to God as our sacrifice for sin. In the understanding of sacrifice when the one for whom the sacrifice is offered partakes in the sacrifice he receives the expiation of his sins by eating the sacrifice. We eat the sacrifice of Christ by placing our faith in him.

SERMON APPROACHES WITH ILLUSTRATIONS

Lesson 1: 1 Kings 2:10-12; 3:3-14

Sermon Title: The Right Request

Sermon Angle: This story conjures up in my mind the image of a genie coming out of a bottle to grant three requests. This is not the case here though. God did not say, "Ask for whatever you want and I will give it to you." No, he merely said, "Ask what I should give you" (v. 5). In other words, God was testing Solomon to see if he would be wise enough to ask for the right thing. God is saying, "Are you wise enough, Solomon, to know what I *should* give you?" God wanted to know if Solomon knew about what was really needed in his life, if he recognized that which is of highest value. The Lord granted him more than he asked for because he made the right request first.

Outline:
1. God is not a genie, granting us whatever we want.
2. God asked Solomon what he should give him (v. 5).
3. God is always ready to give us what we really need or what will benefit others.
4. What are you asking the Lord to give you? Is it wisdom? Love? Grace? Is it what you should have?

Sermon Title: Dreams Can Come True

Sermon Angle: Solomon had a dream in which God appeared and asked what he should give Solomon. Most people dream of riches or power or fame but Solomon dreamed of wisdom to be an effective ruler. Anything great and glorious begins with a dream. Dreams can come true but some dreams are not worthy. Solomon had a good dream. He dreamed of being a good and godly king and wanted the Lord to impart his wisdom more than anything. God is in the business of making worthy dreams come true.

Outline:
1. Solomon had a dream: He wanted to be a wise ruler.
2. God heard his dream and more than fulfilled it.
3. What is your dream? Is it worthy?
4. God is in the business of making good dreams come true.

Lesson 2: Ephesians 5:15-20

Sermon Title: Wise Up

Sermon Angle: Paul teaches the flock to "Be careful how you live; not as unwise people but as wise, making the most of the time." In other words, "Wise up!" Those who are wise do look up to the Lord and the things of God. The wise desire to know and do God's will and fill their day with good and uplifting activities. The wise are filled with God's Spirit. The unwise devote themselves to the unfruitful works of darkness (v. 10). One might say that the unwise wise-down, while the truly wise wise-up.

Outline:
1. Paul calls the Christians to live wisely — to wise up (v. 15).
2. To live wisely means to know and do God's will (v. 17).
3. To wise up means to look up to God in worship, praise, and thanksgiving.

Sermon Title: What Kind Of Spirit Moves You?

Sermon Angle: Paul warns against being filled with alcoholic spirits, which leads to debauchery and drunkenness. Being full of booze causes one to act in a foolish and destructive manner (v. 18). Instead, be filled with God's Spirit, which draws songs of thanksgiving from our hearts to our lips (v. 19).

Outline:
1. Many people are so immobilized by life, they look for some force to move them.
2. Often they turn to alcohol.
3. God's people are moved by the Spirit to thanksgiving and praise.

Gospel: John 6:51-58

Sermon Title: Christians Require Meat To Eat

Sermon Angle: When you think of eating heartily, most people think of meat. What can be more inviting than a nice juicy steak? Many churches are offering spiritually light food. It may temporarily satisfy the palate but leaves one spiritually malnourished. Christ invites us to eat real food, to eat his flesh and drink his blood. Earlier in the gospel of John (4:32), when his disciples asked him about whether he had eaten, he replied: "My food (meat) is to do the will of God who sent me...." To do God's will is not light food, it led Jesus to the cross, but it was what the Father required of him. Paul accused the Corinthians of being spiritual babes, living on milk, rather than solid food (meat) (1 Corinthians 3:2). To know God, to love God, and to do the will of God is the meat we need to eat.

Outline:
1. Many people still build their meal around the meat, because it's so satisfying.
2. Some Christians are living on spiritually light food.
3. To live eternally, we must eat (receive) Jesus as our meat and main course (v. 56).

*   *   *   *   *

Sermon Title: Holy Communion

Sermon Angle: The story of survival in the book, *Alive,* illustrates a type of holy communion. It was a sacred and communal act because it gave life. This sixth chapter is John's account of the institution of holy communion. Holy communion is:

Outline:
1. eating Christ (v. 55).
2. abiding with Christ (v. 56).
3. living forever in Christ (vv. 57-59).

Sermon Title: Unsolved Mystery

Sermon Angle: The Jews were scandalized by Jesus' talk of eating his flesh. They asked: "How can this man give us his flesh to eat?" (v. 52). We might scoff at their unbelief but this is a good question. How indeed does Christ give us his flesh to eat? They wanted to understand rationally one of the key mysteries of faith. Eucharist, holy communion, salvation itself, remains an unsolved mystery. We can't grasp it with intellectual constructs but we can experience the mystery and benefit from it. To experience the mystery fully we must quit trying to explain it away. We must enter into the mystery.

Outline:

1. The mystery of eating Jesus' body and blood scandalized the Jews.
2. We, too, can be scandalized by the mystery if we demand that it fit our thought categories. It remains an unsolved mystery.
3. Accept Jesus' invitation to experience the mystery through faith.

*   *   *   *   *

The mystery of eating our Lord's body and blood, of receiving Jesus into our lives, might be compared to a book on French cooking sitting on your kitchen shelf. The book is full of all kinds of luscious recipes but unless you take the book down from the shelf, open it, cook up one of the recipes, and eat it, you will never experience the wonder of French cooking. Let's say, further, that you bake your recipe and serve it to your neighbor, without revealing how you created it. Your neighbor eats it and finds it delightful. How it was made remains a mystery to her. She doesn't need to know how you created this gastronomical delight to enjoy it and experience it. So it is with the feast of Christ.

Proper 16/Pentecost 14/Ordinary Time 21

Revised Common	1 Kings 8:(1, 6, 10-11) 22-30, 41-43	Ephesians 6:10-20	John 6:56-69
Roman Catholic	Joshua 24:1-2, 15-18	Ephesians 5:21-32	John 6:60-69
Episcopal	Joshua 24:1-2a, 14-25	Ephesians 5:21-33	John 6:60-69

Theme For The Day: The difficulty of discipleship and of keeping God's covenant.

BRIEF COMMENTARY ON THE LESSONS

Lesson 1: 1 Kings 8:(1, 6, 10-11) 22-30, 41-43 (C)

After completing the temple, Solomon has the Ark of the Covenant brought into the temple, accompanied by a solemn assembly of the people. The holy presence of the Lord appears as a cloud of smoke in the inner sanctuary. Solomon prays to Yahweh that he might listen to the prayers of his people that are offered in the temple and that he might also heed the prayers which foreigners offer from that place.

Lesson 1: Joshua 24:1-2, 15-18 (RC); Joshua 24:1-2a, 14-25 (E)

Lesson 2: Ephesians 6:10-20 (C)

Paul concludes his letter to the Ephesians with words of admonition. He urges all Christians who read the letter to be strong in the Lord and to put on the whole armor of God. The image Paul employs is of the Roman foot soldier, comparing the parts of his gear to spiritual realities: helmet of salvation, breastplate of righteousness, belt of truth, sword of the Spirit, and so forth. The last mentioned weapon is the only one that could be interpreted as offensive. Though imprisoned by the Romans, Paul is well aware that the battle is not only against worldly powers but against the invisible spiritual powers of wickedness. Only the protection which God affords his children can ward off the vicious attacks of the hosts of wickedness.

Lesson 2: Ephesians 5:21-32 (RC); Ephesians 5:21-33 (E)

Gospel: John 6:56-69 (C); John 6:60-69 (RC, E)

Jesus' talk of eating his flesh and drinking his blood offends his followers, for they interpret it in crude literalism. When Jesus ascends to heaven, it will show that he is speaking of spiritual realities (v. 62). Some are also offended by his claim to have come down from heaven. The crux of the matter is unbelief; some people refuse to believe. Humankind can be separated into two groups, those who believe and those who do not. Some of those who had followed Jesus discontinued their discipleship. Jesus asks the twelve, "Do you also wish to go away?" Peter answers in a manner reminiscent of Caesarea Philippi: "Lord, to whom shall we go? You have the words of eternal life."

Psalm Of The Day
    Psalm 84 (C) — "How lovely is your dwelling place, O Lord of hosts!" (v. 1).
    Psalm 16 (E)
    Psalm 33 (RC)

Prayer Of The Day

Lord Christ, you have never promised that being your disciple is easy or popular. Forbid that we should ever be numbered among those who have fallen away from the gospel. By your Spirit, give us the grace to follow you all the way to the cross and beyond. In your precious name. Amen.

THEOLOGICAL REFLECTION ON THE LESSONS

Lesson 1: 1 Kings 8:(1, 6, 10-11) 22-30, 41-43

Octoberfest. When Solomon brought the Ark into the temple for the consecration of the house of God, it was in the September to October period, several months after the completion of the temple. Solomon wanted the dedication to coincide with the fall harvest and new year festival, the high point in the liturgical calendar. The Germans celebrate the completion of the harvest time with an orgy of drinking, the Octoberfest. The Jews of Solomon's day celebrated the harvest with an orgy of sacrifice to God.

Yahweh the incomparable (v. 23). There were many gods in Solomon's day but Yahweh stood out from the rest. Solomon does not lift up the Lord's power but rather his love toward his servants and his faithfulness; he was a God who kept his covenant.

Immediate obsolescence (v. 27). If you buy a computer, it becomes obsolete long before the warranty wears off. It soon becomes too small, too slow. Solomon was well aware of the smallness and inadequacy of the house that he had built for God. "Behold the heavens and the highest heaven cannot contain you; how much less this house I have built!" All of the structures we make for God are immediately obsolete and inadequate.

Lesson 2: Ephesians 6:10-20

The whole *armor of God* (v. 11). The word is "panoply," the complete set of armor as opposed to pieces of it. Some people might like to put on the helmet of salvation but not want to gird on the belt of truth or be shod with the gospel of peace. Putting on only part of God's armor leaves us vulnerable to the onslaught of the devil.

A spiritual warfare (v. 12). "For we are not contending against flesh and blood ... but against the spiritual hosts of wickedness...." Paul realized that the real enemy of Christianity was not Rome, by whom he was imprisoned, nor the Jews, who opposed the preaching of the gospel. Underlying human conflicts we find a war between good and evil. To defend ourselves, we must be able to identify our real foe, not the ostensible enemy. The spiritual foundation of human conflict can be seen in the dissolution of the communistic system. It imploded because its spiritual infrastructure was rotten.

Launch the offense. The only offensive weapon listed is the "sword of the Spirit" (v. 17). Paul identifies this weapon with the word of God. Jesus used this weapon against the temptations of Satan, just prior to launching his ministry. Martin Luther used the sword of the Spirit, the Word of God, to wage spiritual warfare in his day, declaring in his famous hymn "A Mighty Fortress," "one little word shall fell him" (Satan).

Gospel: John 6:56-69

Why are you living? Jesus said that he lives because of the Father and that we live because of Christ, the bread of life (v. 57). On the news tonight was a story of a young lady who received a liver transplant because a young man accidentally shot himself. This was not exceptionally unusual except that the parents of the boy who was shot had heard of the plight of the girl needing the liver and donated their son's liver specifically for her. Yes, the liver was compatible. This young woman gratefully acknowledges that she lives because of three other people — the boy and his parents. We live because of the grace of the Father who created us and the grace of the Son who redeemed us.

The non-politically correct Jesus. Jesus had many more disciples than the twelve. Most of them dropped away because Jesus offended their sensibilities with all this talk of being the bread of life, coming down from heaven, and the like. They complained: "This is a hard saying: who can listen to it?" (v. 60). If only Jesus would have known about the gospel of political correctness, he could have avoided all that nastiness of the cross and stayed at the top of the popularity polls. Thank God that he was more interested in being faithful than politically correct.

Logo-therapy. Jesus teaches that the Spirit gives life and that the flesh is of no avail (v. 63). Victor Frankl, the creator of Logo-therapy, came to the same conclusion when he observed those who barely existed with him in Nazi concentration camps. Those who found meaning in life in some purpose beyond their own survival fared much better in the hellish environment of the camps.

Dead end. Jesus asked the twelve, "Do you also want to go away?" Peter replied, "To whom shall we go? You have the words of eternal life" (v. 68). The others walked away but the paths that they chose were all dead-ends. Peter knew that Jesus is the only way to go, the only road that is the way of eternal life.

SERMON APPROACHES WITH ILLUSTRATIONS

Lesson 1: 1 Kings 8:(1, 6, 10-11) 22-30, 41-43
Sermon Title: Confirm The Covenant
Sermon Angle: In Solomon's dedicatory prayer he claimed the Lord's covenant promises. He prayed that Yahweh would confirm and carry out the promise made to his father that a descendent from his line would always remain on the throne. That promise was conditioned on David's descendents walking in the ways of the Lord (v. 25). The people of Israel also had to confirm the covenant. Because the people broke God's covenant, the line of Davidic kings ended in 586 BC with the Babylonian captivity. God has confirmed his covenant with us; we must also confirm that same covenant through a life of faith and obedience.

Sermon Title: God's Home Page
Sermon Angle: If you're into computers and have gotten on to the internet, the worldwide web, you will have discovered something called a "home page." Many churches and denominations have home pages, which provide information about themselves and informs folks as to how they might come in contact with the various services they provide. The home page is not the place where the church dwells but is a link to it. When Solomon prayed, he realized that his house could not house God; indeed, the whole earth cannot contain his presence (v. 27). However, it was the place where God chose to leave his name. It was a site where God's people and foreigners alike could, through their prayers, be brought into the presence of the almighty. It was a link between heaven and earth. So too, our churches cannot contain the Spirit of God but

are home pages that link us with the Lord. We are to point beyond ourselves to another site, the realm of the holy.

Outline:
1. Explain the nature of a home page.
2. The home page is not the organization but a link to it.
3. Our church structures cannot encapsulate God's Spirit but link us to that Spirit.
4. We, too, can be God's home page, who point beyond ourselves to Jesus.

Lesson 2: Ephesians 6:10-20

Sermon Title: A Permanent Shield

Sermon Angle: One of the key weapons against the forces of evil is the shield of faith. Paul urges us to pick up the shield of faith in order to put out the flaming darts and arrows of the evil one. The Roman soldier carried a large oblong shield composed of two layers of wood glued together. When the flaming arrows sunk into the shield, the fire would be extinguished. Paul likens faith to a permanent shield, which protects us from the assaults of Satan.

Outline:
1. The Roman legions gained tactical superiority by placing their large shields side by side, which formed an impregnable barrier to their enemy's projectiles.
2. Paul lists faith as the Christian's shield, to protect against Satan's attack (v. 16).
3. Faith is our permanent shield in this battle between good and evil.

*   *   *   *   *

President Reagan wanted to protect the United States from the missiles of the Soviet Union with his so-called Star Wars scenario. This high-tech missile defense system would supposedly destroy enemy missiles before they reached their target. This system would supposedly provide a permanent shield of defense from our enemies. History has shown that spiritual projectiles are far more dangerous and threatening than ICBMs. Greed, godlessness, and materialism have already inflicted serious damage into the fabric of society. Only the shield of faith will save us.

*   *   *   *   *

Hundreds of citizens in Detroit, Michigan, responded to a call to protect against the fires and destruction of Devil's Night. The night before Halloween has been known as Devil's Night for many years and is celebrated with a rash of fires in abandoned buildings, trash cans, and the like. The fires peaked in 1985 but since have declined after the then mayor of the city, Coleman Young, enlisted the support of citizens to patrol and protect against the wiles of the lawless ones. Devil's Night fires peaked in 1985 at 297, but in 1995 there were only 26 fires, far below the daily average of about fifty blazes, due to the shield of support supplied by 35,000 volunteers who helped put out the fiery darts of Devil's Night.

*   *   *   *   *

Sermon Title: Those Who Do Not Take Up The Sword Will Perish

Sermon Angle: Jesus told Peter to put away his sword when he was being arrested because "those who take up the sword will perish by the sword" (Matthew 26:52). In this lesson, Paul encourages us to take up the sword of the Spirit, which is the word of God. The sword of the word is the most potent offensive weapon against the spiritual hosts of wickedness. Those regimes that seek to tyrannize the people make every effort to sheathe the sword of the word. This sword can deal a mortal blow to corruption, as those inflamed with the truth wield the pen as a sword. The word of God was the supreme weapon in the struggle for truth known as the reformation. Many other examples could be raised to show that those who do not take up the sword (God's word and truth) will perish.

Gospel: John 6:56-69

Sermon Title: You Are What You Eat

Sermon Angle: Jesus proclaims that his flesh is food (v. 55) and that whoever eats his flesh and drinks his blood will abide in him and live eternally. As the saying goes, you are what you eat. Whatever we incorporate into our life, that which consumes our time, energy, and money, affects who we are. If we consume garbage into our mind, our soul will become polluted with garbage. If we drink in the Spirit of Christ, our soul will be strengthened and purified.

Outline:
1. We are what we eat.
   — The right foods can help prevent disease.
   — Organic foods are eaten because some people take this saying seriously.
2. We are what we eat spiritually.
   — If we consume garbage, our soul will become filled with refuse.
   — If we consume good things, our soul will be purified.
3. Jesus invites us to eat and drink of his Spirit. If we do ...
   — we will live in Christ and Christ will live in us (v. 56).
   — we will live eternally (v. 58).

Sermon Title: The Hard Sayings Of Jesus

Sermon Angle: F. F. Bruce writes a helpful book called *The Hard Sayings Of Jesus.* The saying of Jesus about eating his body and drinking his blood comprises the first chapter. What do we mean by hard sayings? In some cases, the sayings are hard in the sense that they are difficult to comprehend. In more instances, however, they are not hard to comprehend but difficult to carry out, such as when Jesus told the rich young man to sell everything that he had and come follow him. Jesus uttered many hard sayings which we've tried to explain away or soften their impact. We want to make Jesus in our image. He may be the Lamb of God but he is also the lion of Judah. In this pericope Jesus' sayings are hard for many of his disciples to understand and to accept, once they do fathom what he is saying (v. 60). He is telling his disciples (that's us) that it isn't enough to be in his company or to listen to his teaching. We must so consume the person and Spirit of Jesus that he becomes integral to who we are.

Outline:
1. The Lord's teachings about consuming him as food were offensive to many disciples.
2. They groaned that his teachings were hard (v. 60).
3. Do we reject Jesus quietly because his sayings are too hard for us?
4. Do we inoculate the church against the hardness of Jesus' teachings with an antidote of the gentle, all-accepting Jesus?
5. If we reject the real Jesus, who challenges us to authentic discipleship, where do we have left to go? (v. 68).

Sermon Title: Discipleship 401

Sermon Angle: Most university courses are prefaced with a numerical designation. The "100" level courses are the most elementary, required of freshmen. The "200" level courses build on the introductory courses and are designed for sophomores. The most advanced courses are denoted with a "400" designation. These courses in most universities are suitable for graduate studies. Jesus probably began the education of his disciples on the most basic level but then moved to much more difficult things, such as we find in today's gospel. Multitudes were dropping out of his course because it was just too hard for them (v. 66). Jesus asked the twelve if they, too, wanted to drop out (v. 67). Peter replied that they would stay; there was no other teacher who could lead them to eternal life. Too many Christians are satisfied to stick to the elementary things of Christ. To continue as his disciples we must move on to not only graduate studies but to daily field work in his kingdom.

Outline:
1. Explain how the difficulty of university courses is designated by numbers.
2. Jesus was leading his disciples beyond elementary courses in discipleship to graduate studies.
3. Many of them dropped out because it was too hard (v. 66).
4. Have we been satisfied with the elementary things of Christ and dropped out of graduate studies?
5. To go on with Jesus, we must consume (receive) him as bread (vv. 56-58).

Proper 17/Pentecost 15/Ordinary Time 22

Revised Common	Song of Solomon 2:8-13	James 1:17-27	Mark 7:1-8, 14-15, 21-23
Roman Catholic	Deuteronomy 4:1-2, 6-8	James 1:17-19, 21-22, 27	Mark 7:1-8, 14-15, 21-23
Episcopal	Deuteronomy 4:1-9	Ephesians 6:10-20	Mark 7:1-8, 14-15, 21-23

Theme For The Day: Purity is an inside job.

BRIEF COMMENTARY ON THE LESSONS

Lesson 1: Song of Solomon 2:8-13 (C)

The whole of the Song of Solomon is a love poem. In this passage the bride hears the voice of her lover as he approaches her house, then with desire sees him through the lattice. He joyously announces that the winter rainy season is past and that the earth is in full bloom. He beckons his lover to come and celebrate love and life around them and within them.

Lesson 1: Deuteronomy 4:1-2, 6-8 (RC); Deuteronomy 4:1-9 (E)

Lesson 2: James 1:17-27 (C); James 1:17-19, 21-22, 27 (RC)

James emphasizes the practical aspects of the Christian faith, especially ethical considerations. He identifies the Father of Jesus with the God of heavenly lights (stars) and asserts that he is the source of all blessings. James warns against moral impurity and counsels believers to be "quick to hear, slow to speak (in wrath), and slow to anger." Receiving the implanted word (Christ) will save our souls and produce an abundance of good deeds (v. 21).

Lesson 2: Ephesians 6:10-20 (E)

See second lesson for Proper 16.

Gospel: Mark 7:1-8, 14-15, 21-23 (C, RC, E)

Jesus becomes embroiled in conflict with the scribes and Pharisees. They ask him accusingly why his disciples do not wash their hands ceremonially and observe the other traditions of the elders. The Lord responds that it is not that which enters a person from the outside that makes him unclean but what emanates from within the unredeemed heart — murder, envy, covetousness, and the like. Jesus places little credence in the so-called "oral laws," which later were incorporated into the Talmud. In contrast to the moral laws of God, these laws were basically the invention of men and not binding. Jesus places the emphasis on the spiritual transformation and purification of the heart through the power of God.

Psalm Of The Day

Psalm 45:1-2, 6-9 (C) — "You are the most handsome of men" (v. 2).

Psalm 15 (E)

Psalm 14 (RC)

Prayer Of The Day

Lord Christ, cleanse our hearts and purify our minds, free us from futile faith and vain religion, that we might love you from our heart and serve you with all our mind and strength. In Jesus' name. Amen.

THEOLOGICAL REFLECTION ON THE LESSONS

Lesson 1: Song of Solomon 2:8-13

Love leaps (v. 8). The female lover observes her partner leaping to meet her. He can hardly wait to behold the face of his beloved. Love puts a spring in your step and your heart skips a beat as well. Even when passion cools down, love bounds and abounds.

Anticipation (v. 9). The lovers observe one another through the window, their hearts throbbing with anticipation at being united with the beloved.

The springtime of love (vv. 11-13). The author indicates that winter is over. Spring is the season when life renews and blossoms forth. The springtime of love is filled with anticipation but love has other seasons as well.

Lesson 2: James 1:17-27

Father of lights (v. 17). For James, God is the Father of the stars, creator of the heavenly luminaries. Every good gift comes from him. The Father of Jesus is also the Father of stars and galaxies.

From whom there is no variation or shadow due to change (v. 17). Does this mean that God does not change? James is trying to say that God is the architect of change, not the object of the process of change. Everything changes but God's love and grace remain immutable.

Heart transplant (v. 21). James would have us put away all moral impurity and permit God's word to be implanted into our hearts, which is capable of saving our souls.

Gospel: Mark 7:1-8, 14-15, 21-23

Defiled hands or hearts? (v. 7). How human it is to sweat the small stuff, to major on minors. The scribes and Pharisees got caught in this trap. Outward religious ritual assumed a place of paramount importance. They got all bent out of shape when some of the Lord's disciples were seen eating with defiled (unwashed) hands. Jesus' response to them can be paraphrased in this manner: "Don't get all upset about defiled hands; rather be concerned about defiled hearts, hearts that are blackened by sin." The defilement comes from inside the human heart.

Lives must follow where your lips lead (v. 6). Jesus quotes Isaiah: "This people honors me with their lips but their heart is far from me." We confess God with our lips; our lips lead the way but our lives must follow.

Anthropology as theology (v. 7). Jesus contended that the religious leaders were teaching anthropology as revealed theology. He said that they were teaching as doctrines the precepts of men (v. 7). This is something religious people do all the time.

The source of uncleanness (vv. 14-15). Jesus indicates that sin is the source of defilement, which comes from our heart, a heart turned in on itself. Preoccupation with ritual impurity diverts attention away from the real source of spiritual impurity.

SERMON APPROACHES WITH ILLUSTRATIONS

Lesson 1: Song of Solomon 2:8-13

Sermon Title: Love Leaps

Sermon Angle: Not only does love quicken the step but love leaps over obstacles that get in its way. But romantic love is not sufficient to leap over mountains and surmount great difficulties, it takes mature love to do that. This is the kind of love that accepts people for what they are; it is the type that hangs close even when the going gets rough. Yes, real love has resiliency and bounce.

Outline:
1. Young love leaps — it's the hormones.
2. Mature love also leaps — it's a gift of God, who is love.

Sermon Title: A Feast For The Senses

Sermon Angle: Romantic love is symbolized by the spring season; in this season of life, the senses are stimulated. The flowers stimulate the eyes (v. 12); the scents of new life are everywhere (v. 13); the birds delight us with their songs, for it is a time of singing (v. 12). Romantic love activates the senses, causing its captives to be tuned into realities they never noticed before. When we fall in love with God, our senses are also activated as we marvel at the wonder of God's love.

Outline:
1. If you've fallen in love, you might recall that the world looked different; you noticed things you never observed before.
2. Romantic love activates the senses of sight, smell, hearing, and so forth.
3. When we experience the love of God, we also see the world in a new way, our spiritual senses are activated.
4. Open yourself to the love of God each day.

* * * * *

It's no accident that springtime is the season when lovers do their leaping, flowers do their blooming, and birds do their singing. It's the light! In the winter it's rainy, cold, and overcast. In the winter, unless you're an avid skier, your shoulders droop and your spirits lag. But in the spring, the days get longer and the rays of the sun are brighter and warmer. The sunlight draws out all the colors of life and love; the sky is bluer, the grass greener, and our senses are in resonance with the light of life. What our hearts told us all along is now being confirmed by science. It is no secret that more people become depressed in the winter, if you live in a more northerly climate. However, researchers are now onto the source of this condition. It is a result of light deprivation. They call it SAD, Seasonal Affective Disorder; they tell us that these people respond positively to light therapy. If those depressed with this condition are exposed to a couple of hours of bright light in the morning, it helps set their body clock and they feel much happier. This is just another indication that God made us to live and love and leap in the light of his presence.

* * * * *

Lesson 2: James 1:17-27

Sermon Title: God Beams His Blessings

Sermon Angle: James does not accept the concept prevalent in the Old Testament that Yahweh is the Lord of weal and woe, good and evil. James states that God is the source of good and perfect gifts (v. 17). He is not the source of evil or of temptation (vv. 13-15). The God of light beams his blessings to all and especially to those who follow the light of the world.

Outline:
1. God is not the source of evil but of blessing.
2. As the Father of light, he beams his blessings to us through creation.
3. We are saved through the redeeming light of his Son.

*   *   *   *   *

I like James' description of God as the "Father of lights." All life and beauty are a consequence of light. James proclaims that "Every good endowment and every perfect gift come down from above, from the Father of lights" (v. 17). The primary gift of our luminous Creator is light and from this light come all manner of blessings. Only certain things emit light: the sun, other suns, light bulbs, and so forth. Almost all other objects do not emit light on their own, they merely reflect or re-emit part of the light that falls on them. To re-emit the light, objects must be in resonance with the light source. This is a scientific way of saying that the source of the light and the object that re-emits the light are on the same wavelength. To be in Christ is to be on the same wavelength as the Father of lights.

*   *   *   *   *

Sermon Title: Circuit Breaker

Sermon Angle: When an electrical circuit gets too much juice, a circuit breaker does what its name implies, it severs the circuit. This keeps the appliance and possibly the lives of those in the house from getting burned up. After the precipitous stock market crash of 1987, the Federal Trade Commission designed a circuit breaker to stop the program trading when the action got too hot. They feared a meltdown. James enjoins that Christians should be quick to hear, but slow to speak and slow to anger (v. 19). What we need is a spiritual circuit breaker that kicks in every time our passions or temper get overheated. Indeed, when we submit to God's Spirit, he supplies such a service.

Outline:
1. Many people have died in fires for lack of circuit breakers.
2. Many people have suffered injury and death for lack of emotional self-control.
3. James says, "Be quick to hear, slow to speak, and slow to anger" (v. 19).
4. Let God's word and Spirit provide a spiritual and emotional circuit breaker in you.

Gospel: Mark 7:1-8, 14-15, 21-23

Sermon Title: Clean Heart, Clean Hands

Sermon Angle: A clean heart leads to clean hands, not the other way around. That's the point that Jesus was trying to make with the scribes and Pharisees. They thought that they were ready to approach God if their hands were clean. For them, ritual had replaced righteousness. When we confess our sins to Christ and ask for his forgiveness, God washes us with cleaning agents that penetrate all the way to the wellspring of our spiritual existence.

Outline:
1. The religious leaders criticized Jesus because his disciples were not ritually clean.
2. They thought clean hands issued in a clean heart.

326

3. Jesus taught that the source of defilement was from within (vv. 14-15, 21-23).
4. Only God can cleanse the heart through confession and forgiveness.
5. A clean heart leads to clean hands that praise and serve God.

Sermon Title: Vain Worship

Sermon Angle: In responding to the narrow-mindedness of the scribes and Pharisees, Jesus quotes Isaiah: "In vain do they worship me, teaching as doctrines the precepts of men" (v. 7). Why was their worship vain and fruitless? It majored on externals rather than penetrating to the heart of the matter, for one thing. For another, it confused human philosophy with God's revelation. Thirdly, it neglected God's moral law in favor of ceremonial law and religious customs. To sum the matter up, their worship was vain because they were out of touch with the one who is the way, the truth, and the life. To this day, there is no shortage of vain and useless worship.

Outline:
1. Jesus accused the scribes and Pharisees of vain worship (v. 7). What made it so?
2. It was out of touch with God's revealed truth (v. 8).
3. It replaced righteousness with ritual (vv. 3-4).
4. It judged people by superficial criteria (v. 5).

Sermon Title: When Religion Becomes Obsessive-Compulsive

Sermon Angle: The religion of the scribes and Pharisees was obsessive-compulsive. Obsessive-compulsive disorders manifest themselves in ritualistic behavior. This behavior is destructive in that the person doesn't really know why he feels compelled to repeat this behavior. It is action devoid of conscious reason, which diverts the sufferer from the real tasks of living. The religion that Jesus pointed to was behavior that was non-productive and vain. All the rules and regulations were close to being obsessive-compulsive. They diverted attention away from the living Lord. Much that passes as Christian religion is compulsive rather than living faith.

Outline:
1. Explain obsessive-compulsive behavior.
2. Religion becomes obsessive-compulsive when religious activity is divorced from the living God.
3. The ritual of washing was an example of this tendency among the Jews.
4. How much of your Christian faith is obsessive-compulsive?
5. Turn to the living Lord and worship God from the heart.

*   *   *   *   *

Several years ago, the parish coordinator of the church where I served had attended a convention of the Evangelical Lutheran Church women. Upon returning, she reported that a speaker on the subject of worship renewal made a statement that stuck in her head. He stated: "The trouble with Lutherans is that they are afraid of the big C word. No, the big C word is not Christ or commitment, but *change*." This is not only true of Lutherans, it's true of most Christians and non-Christians alike. We fear change. The critics of Jesus, the scribes and Pharisees, didn't want to let go of the past. Instead of worshiping God, they honored the traditions of their fathers. Tradition is not necessarily a bad thing, unless it keeps us from encountering the Spirit of the living God. We need not fear the big "C" word because God is in control of the process of change.

Proper 18/Pentecost 16/Ordinary Time 23

Revised Common	Proverbs 22:1-2, 8-9, 22-23	James 2:1-10 (11-13) 14-17	Mark 7:24-37
Roman Catholic	Isaiah 35:4-7a	James 2:1-5	Mark 7:31-37
Episcopal	Isaiah 35:4-7a	James 1:17-27	Mark 7:31-37

Theme For The Day: Faith active in good works.

BRIEF COMMENTARY ON THE LESSONS

Lesson 1: Proverbs 22:1-2, 8-9, 22-23 (C)

Practical advice concerning values. A good name is better than riches. The person who shares his wealth will be blessed by God but the unjust will experience calamity. God will judge those who beat down the poor.

Lesson 1: Isaiah 35:4-7a (RC, E)

Lesson 2: James 2:1-10 (11-13) 14-17 (C); James 2:1-5 (RC)

The church is warned of the dangers of showing partiality to the wealthy and making the poor take a back seat. James warns that the rich of this world are the ones who cause oppression. He also admonishes that faith must be displayed in good works and that faith without works is dead.

Lesson 2: James 1:17-27 (E)

See second lesson for Proper 17.

Gospel: Mark 7:24-37 (C); Mark 7:31-37 (RC, E)

Jesus retreats to the region of Tyre and Sidon on the Mediterranean coast, a Gentile area. He went there not to minister but to retreat from the rigors of ministry for a while. He entered a home hoping not to be recognized, but a woman (a Syrophoenician) came, fell to her knees, and begged Jesus to deliver her daughter from a demon. Jesus responded that it wasn't fair to take the children's bread and give it to the dogs. Some have tried to attenuate the harshness of Jesus' response by translating "dogs" as "puppies." Some interpreters suggest that Jesus is testing the level of her faith. It certainly was true that his primary mission was to the Jews. The notable thing about this passage is that this woman gets the best of Jesus. Her love for her daughter was so strong that she would endure any humiliation if it would deliver her daughter from the demon. She responds to Jesus: "Yes, Lord, but even the dogs under the table eat the children's crumbs" (v. 28). What presence of mind, what humility we see demonstrated through her actions! For that saying, Jesus granted her petition.

After this, Jesus returned to Galilee to the region of the Decapolis (the ten cities). Some people brought to Jesus a man who was deaf and had an impediment in his speech. Jesus took him aside, put his fingers into his ears, then spat and touched his tongue with the saliva. Jesus looked up to heaven, sighed, and said an Aramaic word, *Ephphatha*, that is, "Be opened"

(v. 35). Jesus told them to keep this under covers but to no avail. They reported it throughout the region, commenting, "He does all things well; he even makes the deaf to hear and the dumb to speak" (v. 37).

Psalm Of The Day
Psalm 125 (C) — "Those who trust in the Lord ... which cannot be moved ..." (v. 1).
Psalm 146 (E)
Psalm 145 (RC)

Prayer Of The Day
Spirit of love, you know our human frailties and weaknesses, not from a distance, but up close and personal through your Son. When we turn to you in faith for help, with even a weak faith, hear from heaven and grant us deliverance. In Jesus' precious and powerful name. Amen.

THEOLOGICAL REFLECTION ON THE LESSONS

Lesson 1: Proverbs 22:1-2, 8-9, 22-23
Rich man, poor man (v. 2). The world is enthralled by the lifestyles of the rich and famous; the wealthy and famous are elevated to a place of prominence. With God, the rich man, the poor man, and everyone in between are all on the same plane. God is not impressed with wealth but character.

A bountiful eye (v. 9). This turn of speech in the Revised Standard Version of the Bible struck me. What is a bountiful eye? Probably the opposite of a covetous eye. A bountiful-eyed person enjoys sharing with those in need. "He shares his bread with the poor." The problem is that covetous eyes seem to outnumber bountiful eyes. A believer with a bountiful eye is surely focused on our bountiful creator, who provides for the needs of all in plenitude.

At the gate (v. 22). This verse warns against crushing the afflicted at the gate. What does this mean? The poor and destitute would assemble at the city gates or perhaps the gate of the temple to beg for help. They were at the gate, but outside the gate. Though our cities no longer have gates, the poor and needy still gather outside the gate, the place of commerce, the busy street corner. They are hoping that someone will open the gate for them and that they might be accepted as citizens and not aliens in the city. Today they wait at the gate; tomorrow they might try to knock the gate down.

Lesson 2: James 2:1-10 (11-13) 14-17
Love is blind. James warns the church against showing partiality to the wealthy and those who are richly attired. Don't let your attention be distracted by the glitter of their gold so that you discount the brother or sister who is poor. Like the statue of Lady Justice, eyes blindfolded, holding out the balance of justice, our love of Jesus should cause us to be blind to outward human differences.

Love and the law (v. 8). James refers to the precept to "love your neighbor as you love yourself" as the royal law. In effect, he is saying much the same thing that Paul says in 1 Corinthians 13:13, when he concludes "Faith, hope, love abide, but the greatest of these is love." But how can love be a law? Like John, James considers love to be subject to the will. Thus, it can be commanded, like a law. Love is not a matter of feeling but of obedience.

Mercy triumphs over judgment (v. 13). Oftentimes we become indignant when some law-breaker seems to get away with his crime. However, we are all dependent on God's mercy in Christ, since we all deserve the pronouncement of "guilty!" As James states in verse 10, "Whoever keeps the whole law but fails in part of it, has become guilty of all of it." Thank God that mercy triumphs over judgment.

Gospel: Mark 7:24-37

Jesus couldn't get away (v. 24). Apparently, Jesus was trying to get away from the incessant crowds for a time of respite when he went to the region of Tyre. Yet he couldn't get away; he couldn't remain incognito. A desperate woman came to him for help. Just today, I read an article in the paper that reports how our electronic tools — cellular phones, modems, faxes, and the like — leash us to our jobs. Increasingly, people find it difficult to get away from their work. One man reported in the article even quit his job because he couldn't take the constant pressure. For those who experience this problem, you can find solace in Jesus; he couldn't get away from his work, either. The New Testament reveals a Christ who is always available to those in need.

The power of persistent prayer (vv. 25-30). The Bible is filled with admonitions to persevere in prayer. Why do we have to keep bugging God? Maybe God wants to see if we're really serious about what we ask for. Perhaps persistence shows a depth of character that the Lord is looking for. Or maybe persistence enables us to refine and purify our petitions. The Syrophoenician woman is a showcase of persistent prayer that triumphs.

How to have a "Great Faith." The Syrophoenician woman had a great faith. In Matthew's version of this same story, Jesus says so (27:28). What does it take to have a great faith? Here are some ingredients we can discern from this account: to have an unshakable faith in the power of God; to be focused on the needs of others; a persistence that won't let go of God; the willingness to humble oneself; to beg, if necessary, for the sake of the oppressed. These are but a few ingredients of a great faith.

Hearing and speaking (vv. 31-37). There is an essential link between hearing and speaking. To speak well, we must hear well. The man brought to Jesus spoke haltingly because he could not hear. Jesus understood. He put his fingers in the deaf man's ears and touched the man's tongue with his spittle. Immediately he could speak plainly. Jesus told them to keep it under wraps so as not to create a sensation, but the tongues of those who witnessed this miracle could not be stopped. The majority of Christians have a speech impediment when it comes to declaring the wonderful works of God. The problem is that we are deaf to the word of God. Without listening we cannot clearly proclaim the good news of Christ.

The Jesus touch. You've heard of the Midas touch, based on the story of King Midas, who when he touched something turned it to gold. The New Testament speaks of the "Jesus touch." Some people brought the deaf man to Jesus, imploring that he would lay his hands on the man (v. 32). Instead Jesus touched his ears and tongue. The people of Jesus' earthly days, as well as the faithful down through the ages, have recognized that there is power to heal the body and spirit in the touch of Jesus.

The key (v. 34). Jesus prayed, fingers in the deaf man's ears, "Be opened!" The man was imprisoned in a body that could not freely enjoy or express the world around him. Jesus opened him up; he is the key. Jesus is the key that opens the door to life, freeing us from the prison of sin, guilt, and fear. God wants to open up our ears and unlock our tongue.

SERMON APPROACHES WITH ILLUSTRATIONS

Lesson 1: Proverbs 22:1-2, 8-9, 22-23

Sermon Title: The Choice

Sermon Angle: Life presents us with many choices. A restaurant that I sometimes dine at has a vast menu; to make a choice is difficult. Life presents us with much tougher choices than that, however. Our text presents one such choice, the choice between a good name and riches. The writer concludes: "A good name is to be chosen rather than great riches." A good name represents a godly life of integrity and righteousness. There are certainly many rich people of integrity and good name but oftentimes the choice is presented to us between a good name or great riches. In other words, the world tempts us to compromise our integrity, character, and good name for the sake of financial success. The devil, the world, and our own sinful nature tempt us to choose immediate gratification rather than an eternal treasure that will not be taken away from us.

Outline:
1. The world offers many choices. (Give examples.)
2. The choices are not just of commodities but of whom we will become.
3. The Bible urges us to seek a good name, a life of godly integrity (v. 1), over financial gain or immediate gratification.

Sermon Title: Bountiful Eyes Are Beautiful Eyes

Sermon Angle: The eyes are the window of our heart, mind, and soul. What we perceive with the eyes depends not only on what's in the outer world but also what's in our inner world. If we perceive with covetous eyes, it's because our hearts are covetous. If we see the world through bountiful (generous) eyes, it's because God has opened up our heart, mind, and spirit. May God give us bountiful eyes to behold the plenitude of his gifts and to share them. (Note: If you use this approach, be sure to refer to the Revised Standard Version of the Bible.)

Outline:
1. What our eyes see depends on what's in our hearts.
2. Many behold the world with covetous eyes because they are misers.
3. The believer sees the world with bountiful eyes that flow from a redeemed heart.
4. Those with bountiful eyes behold God's many gifts and share them freely (v. 1).

Lesson 2: James 2:1-10 (11-13) 14-17

Sermon Title: Don't Be A Cur

Sermon Angle: A cur is a little dog or pup, which characteristically yaps and jumps at the feet of its master in order to win attention and treats. James warns the church against such behavior when it comes to seeking favors from the wealthy. The church should not surround the rich with solicitous yelping, nor should we roll over on our backs so they can stroke our vanities. The world is quick to curry favor with the rich and powerful but the Bible warns against the dangers of such behavior. Rather, treat the poor with equal dignity; they, more often than the rich, inherit the true treasure of the kingdom. "Has not God chosen the poor of the world to be rich in faith and heirs of the kingdom" (v. 5). There is only one whose favor we should seek, the Lord who created and redeemed us rich and poor alike.

Outline:
1. James warns against making value judgments on people based on wealth.
2. The church should eschew all value judgments based on human distinctions.
3. Seek only to please God.

Sermon Title: Saving Faith

Sermon Angle: James maintains there are two kinds of faith — living faith and faith that is dead. Dead faith has been disconnected from both the Spirit of God and from the human family. It is faith in that which is not ultimate, such as one's theological understanding or ecclesiastical connections. Living faith, on the other hand, is saving faith, because the person who is possessed by it is connected to both the Lord and to others. Her faith has found expression in good works. James asks of the person who says he has faith but without works: "Can his faith save him?" (v. 14). The answer is obvious. That is the question you need to direct to your hearers. Do I have a living and saving faith? If the question is no, you will need to offer some suggestions for finding such a faith.

Outline:
1. There are two kinds of faith — theoretical (dead) faith and living faith.
2. Living faith is connected closely to both Christ and the world.
3. Real faith translates into love of neighbor.
4. Do you possess a saving faith?

* * * * *

Most Christians and Jews believe that they should apply their faith to their work but they need more help from the clergy, according to a study by the Chicago-based Center for Ethics and Corporate Policy. These results come from a study involving 1,529 participants who belong to a myriad of religious bodies. A sociology professor, Stephen Hart, claims that clergy would be smart to deal much more with work-related issues. Some participants complained that clergy don't understand very much about business and sometimes are scornful about the world of profit-making. This response turned up time and again in the interviews: Either clergy are biased against business or they do not understand the realities of the corporate world. One executive of the ministry branch of the Evangelical Lutheran Church in America submitted that "pastors are concerned about keeping the life of the congregation vital and do not see enabling the ministry of lay people through work as their primary pastoral activity." On the other side of the aisle, few workers discuss their faith at work. How can we help our people show forth their faith in good works if we don't give them on-the-job training and they, in turn, don't share their work lives with us, so that we pastors receive valuable vocational training? (gleaned from an article in the *Omaha World-Herald*)

* * * * *

Gospel: Mark 7:24-37

Sermon Title: How To Get God's Attention

Sermon Angle: Jesus has sort of gone into hiding in this Gentile region, perhaps seeking some rest and recreation. He entered a house where he hoped to remain unnoticed. A local woman somehow found out that Jesus was there and, entering the house, she fell to her knees, begging Jesus to free her daughter from a demon. There was nothing meek or laid-back about her approach. Uncharacteristically, Jesus does not seem ready to help. He even seems to insult her: "Let the children be fed, for it is not right to take the children's bread and throw it to the dogs" (v. 27). Now listen to what got Jesus' attention and his help: "Yes, Lord, yet even the dogs under the table eat the children's crumbs." How do you get the Lord's attention? First you have a legitimate need or request. Then you hang in there until you get an answer. Finally you must get your ego out of the way, as you humbly persist in seeking the Lord's favor.

Outline:
1. Sometimes it seems that God is far removed. How do we get God's attention?
2. Look at the story of the Syrophoenician woman (vv. 24-30) for pointers.
   — She found Jesus' address (we do so in prayer).
   — She had a worthy request.
   — She begged and pleaded for what she needed (persistent faith).
   — Her humility kept her from being put off by what appeared to be an uncharitable response.
3. Such faith, active in love, gets God's attention.

Sermon Title: Just The Right Touch

Sermon Angle: The people who brought the deaf man to Jesus (v. 32) had apparently heard about the wonder of Jesus' touch. They begged Jesus to lay his hands on the deaf man. Jesus had the healing touch. Even science is finding that there is healing in the touch, the touch of love, concern, and sympathy to name a few. Jesus touched the man's ears and his tongue, since those were the parts that were not whole, which opened his ears and freed his tongue. Unfortunately, there is also a wrong touch. Shoving a sister away, hitting a neighbor, inappropriate and destructive sexual contact are examples. Jesus had just the right touch, which people are still seeking, a loving touch, a healing touch, the divine touch.

Outline:
1. The deaf man was brought to Jesus because Jesus had the right touch.
2. Jesus' touch healed him and opened him to life (vv. 33-34).
3. Many are harmed from the wrong kind of touch. (Give examples.)
4. Ask Jesus to give you his healing touch, just the right touch.

Proper 19/Pentecost 17/Ordinary Time 24

Revised Common	Proverbs 1:20-33	James 3:1-12	Mark 8:27-38
Roman Catholic	Isaiah 50:5-9a	James 2:14-18	Mark 8:27-35
Episcopal	Isaiah 50:4-9	James 2:1-5, 8-10, 14-18	Mark 8:27-38 or
			Mark 9:14-29

Theme For The Day: Seek true wisdom; follow Christ.

BRIEF COMMENTARY ON THE LESSONS

Lesson 1: Proverbs 1:20-33 (C)

Wisdom personified warns the fool to heed its words of wisdom and instruction or face dire consequences. The foolish will be destroyed by their own devices; when they call for help on the day of trouble, it will not be granted to them. However, those who listen to the voice of wisdom will dwell secure.

Lesson 1: Isaiah 50:5-9a (RC); Isaiah 50:4-9 (E)

See first lesson for Passion/Palm Sunday.

Lesson 2: James 3:1-12 (C)

Chapter 3 revolves around the subject of true wisdom. James warns that not many should seek to become teachers, because they will be judged by a stricter standard than others. Perhaps as an act of self-confession James confesses that "we" all make mistakes. The person who makes no mistakes is like an exquisitely trained horse, completely under the control of its master. This leads the writer to warn against an unbridled tongue. He compares the unleashed tongue to a raging fire (v. 6). Undisciplined speech is one of the dangers of being a teacher. Again, the tongue is like a serpent, full of deadly venom (v. 8). Employing yet another image, the tongue is like a polluted well (v. 11). How can it spew forth both blessings and curses?

Lesson 2: James 2:14-18 (RC); James 2:1-5, 8-10, 14-18 (E)

See second lesson for Proper 18.

Gospel: Mark 8:27-38 (C, E); Mark 8:27-35 (RC)

Jesus and his disciples enter Caesarea Philippi, the source of the Jordan River and a center of pagan worship going back to the dawn of history. On the way, Jesus asks his disciples: "Who do people say that I am?" They reply John the Baptist or one of the prophets. Then the really big question! "But who do *you* say that I am?" Peter confesses Jesus to be the Messiah, the Christ. Again Jesus requests that they keep his messiahship a secret. Straight away the Lord instructs his disciples concerning the true meaning of his messiahship. He will suffer, die, and on the third day rise again. Peter rebukes him for interjecting the idea of suffering and death, which was contrary to common expectation. Jesus sees in Peter's protest the work of Satan and replies: "Get behind me, Satan!" Jesus then directs himself to other followers. "If anyone wants to come after me, let him deny himself, take up his cross and follow me."

Psalm Of The Day
Psalm 19 (C) — "The heavens are telling the glory of God" (v. 1).
Psalm 116 (E)
Psalm 114 (RC)

Prayer Of The Day
O Lord Jesus, open our hearts to receive you, unleash our tongue to confess you as Lord and Savior; then, by your Spirit, empower us to follow wherever you lead. In your name we pray. Amen.

THEOLOGICAL REFLECTION ON THE LESSONS

Lesson 1: Proverbs 1:20-33
The silly life and the simple life. Wisdom personified as a prophetess cries out in the streets for the citizens to turn away from the simple life. This is not the kind of simple life that the Shakers sought to live out, meaning plain or unadorned. Simpleness in this passage might better be interpreted as foolish or stupid. Wisdom was really calling its hearers to leave silliness rather than simpleness. In fact, the simple life might prove to be very wise.

The fool refuses to listen (v. 24). Why does the fool refuse to listen? He thinks that he knows better than anyone else what is good. The fool turns his back on the voice of experience and knowledge because it goes against his desires.

Eating spoiled fruit (v. 31). Wisdom teaches that the foolish will eat the fruit of their folly, rotten fruit that will poison the whole body. "Therefore, they shall eat the fruit of their way."

Lesson 2: James 3:1-12
We all make mistakes (v. 2). How true! Yet the meaning of that phrase often changes, depending on whether we are talking about ourselves or somebody else. We sometimes apply this aphorism to ourselves when we are attempting to excuse ourselves for carelessness and stupidity. Or it can be a healthy confession of our human weakness. "I made a mistake but I can't dwell on it. Let's go on." In reference to other people's mistakes, this saying can serve as a humble admission of our common humanity.

The power of little things (vv. 4-5). James compares the tongue to the rudder of a ship. The rudder is a small device but has the power to control the movement of the entire craft. The tongue is also small but has great power to move people and events. James keys in on the destructive power of the tongue but it also has great power to influence people for good. There is indeed great power in little things.

The taming of the tongue (vv. 7-8). James feels that no person can tame the human tongue. Yet God can and does tame the human tongue. He turns it from an instrument of hate and cursing to an implement that brings grace, truth, and love.

Gospel: Mark 8:27-38
Identity crisis (vv. 27-29). We hear a great deal about those caught in the clutch of an identity crisis. We see this especially in the confusion over the issues of gender in our society. During Jesus' earthly ministry there was something of an identity crisis pertaining to Jesus. Not that Jesus was having an identity crisis but those around him were certainly having trouble nailing down the Lord's identity. Most thought he was some prophet or another. Peter correctly

identifies Jesus as the Messiah but he didn't know what that meant. Those who call themselves Christians and those who don't are still having an identity crisis concerning Jesus. He is identified as a teacher, prophet, phony, idealist, superhuman, revolutionary, and guru. Those who really know him confess that Jesus is Son of God, Lord, and Savior.

The true meaning of confessing Christ. Peter correctly identified Jesus as the Messiah but he did not deeply know who he was or what this identity entailed. When Jesus told his disciples that he was going to suffer, die, and rise, Peter didn't understand what Jesus was saying and couldn't accept it. There is more to confessing Christ than merely knowing his name. We must also know his nature and follow him.

Where did you lose your life? (v. 35). We're all going to lose our lives; the question is: How and why will we lose our lives? I suspect that the question that Christ is going to raise at the judgment is: "Where did you lose your life?" Did you lose your life by default, through carelessness? Or did you lose your life intentionally? Jesus calls on all who follow him to lose their life for his sake and that of the kingdom. He promises that those who lose their life will find eternal life.

The bottom line (vv. 36-37). In the corporate world, all eyes are fixed on the bottom line. That is, all decisions seem to be based on whether a particular action will be profitable or not. Jesus has a different way of looking at profits, a divergent way of figuring the bottom line. He maintains that we win eternal profits if we lose our lives for the sake of the kingdom of God. Life, eternal life, is the ultimate profit, everything else is loss.

SERMON APPROACHES WITH ILLUSTRATIONS

Lesson 1: Proverbs 1:20-33
Sermon Title: Fatal Choice

Sermon Angle: The fool does not become a fool by default; he or she chooses to become one. Wisdom personified teaches: "Because they hated knowledge and did not choose the fear of the Lord ... therefore they shall eat the fruit of their labor." This passage counsels that the fool makes stupid, even fatal, choices that will have dire consequences (v. 32). Have you noticed how some people make the same foolish choices over and over again because they are not able to discern the true cause of their failure? For instance, they blame their mistakes on others rather than looking squarely at themselves. The wise person learns from the poor decisions he makes and corrects them; the fool never learns from experience. The wise person chooses to listen to the word of the Lord, which the fool has discounted.

Outline:
1. The wise person and the fool are separated by the quality of their choices.
2. The unwise decisions of the fool come back to slay him (v. 32).
3. The wise person is kept secure by listening to the wisdom of the Lord (v. 33).

Sermon Title: Knowledge Without Wisdom Is Foolish

Sermon Angle: We live in a society where the level of knowledge concerning our world has never been greater, and the pace at which further knowledge is added ever quickens. At the same time, we have spurned wisdom, which would allow us to employ this knowledge in a manner that would benefit all. We have tons of information at our fingertips, yet we're still in kindergarten when it comes to the issues of justice, love, and just getting along with our neighbors. With the torrent of new knowledge we have rejected the voice of wisdom, distilled in the hearts and minds of our elders through time and experience. We foolishly discard wisdom in favor of new knowledge but in so doing, we also cut ourselves off from the mind of God.

Outline:
1. We live in a world of exploding knowledge.
2. Wisdom (understanding the purpose of life) cries out to be heard in the marketplace (v. 20) but is spurned.
3. The world seeks knowledge and facts, so as to control the world.
   — God considers such people fools.
4. Those who heed wisdom will live securely and confidently (v. 33).

Lesson 2: James 3:1-12

Sermon Title: We All Make Mistakes

Sermon Angle: To say that "we all make mistakes" can drive us in two directions. On the one hand, we can seek to excuse ourselves with this somewhat trite expression and so we learn nothing and we do not grow. On the other hand, we can also use this phrase to mean "Yes, it is human to make mistakes and I've made plenty of them but I'm going to learn from them and grow." The child of God confesses his sins and his mistakes to the Lord, asking the Lord to perfect him.

Outline:
1. Yes, we all make mistakes.
2. Is this confession an excuse or a challenge?
3. God not only forgives our mistakes, he wants to perfect us.

Sermon Title: The Danger Of Speaking Out Of Both Sides Of The Mouth

Sermon Angle: One of the problems that plagued Bill Clinton's presidency was that he would say one thing and then, at a later time, take a position at odds with what he spoke earlier. His critics accused the president of speaking out of both sides of the mouth. James speaks to that danger. He laments that we bless God with our tongues but also curse our neighbor with that same tongue (vv. 9-10). We might say that he is accusing them of speaking out of both sides of their mouths. James reasons that it is not possible for pure and polluted water to come from the same well. The danger of speaking out of both sides of our mouth is that we lose all credibility as God's people.

Outline:
1. James accused some Christians of speaking out of both sides of their mouth (vv. 9-10).
2. Do we speak out of both sides of our mouths?
3. The danger of so speaking is that we lose credibility with God and our neighbors.
4. Let God control both sides of your mouth.

Gospel: Mark 8:27-38

Sermon Title: Your Opinion Counts

Sermon Angle: Jesus took something of an opinion poll with his disciples. "Who do people say that I am?" They reported what they had heard. Then he sought their personal opinion concerning his identity, to which Peter uttered his historic confession. "You are the Christ!" Your opinion counts with Christ Jesus. Who do you say that he is, with your lips and with your life?

Outline:
1. Jesus wanted to know what the public thought of him (v. 27).
2. More importantly, Jesus wanted people to truly know him.
3. Your opinion counts with Christ.
4. So make your decision concerning discipleship count for eternity.

Sermon Title: A Painful Lesson

Sermon Angle: Jesus endeavored to teach his disciples the true meaning of his messiahship. It meant rejection, suffering, and death (vv. 31-33). It was a hard and painful lesson for the disciples. Peter chastised Jesus for ever broaching the subject; the lesson was completely contrary to his expectations. Some of life's most valuable lessons are painful ones. Eternal life does not entail evading pain and suffering but facing them in the name of Jesus Christ. Those who rise must first die.

Outline:
1. Life teaches some hard lessons. (Give examples.)
2. When Jesus informed his disciples of his passion, Peter objected (v. 31).
3. He thought that following Jesus would be sweetness and glory.
4. Do we, like Peter, reject the cross?
5. Those who reject the cross are servants of Satan (v. 33).
6. Following Christ means taking up our cross (v. 34).

* * * * *

Jesus saw Peter's response to the cross as the embodiment of Satan (v. 33). Such attitudes are humanistic rather than theocentric. These attitudes are embodied in a Satanic movement in America, as the following quote reveals:

> *The most infamous public Satanist organization is Anton LaVey's Satanic Church in America, founded in 1966. The Satanic Church's creed is based upon a denial and reversal of orthodox Christianity. What LaVey terms the Christian Church's seven deadly sins: greed, pride, envy, anger, gluttony, lust, and sloth, are to be fully indulged, as they lead to physical, mental, or emotional gratification. LaVey's beliefs are a combination of Machiavellian social ethics, hedonism, and simple narcissism as the highest good. He states:*

> > *Hate your enemies with a whole heart, and if a man smite you on the cheek, SMASH him on the other! ... Life is the great indulgence — death, the great abstinence. Therefore, make the most of life — HERE AND NOW!*

> *Who or what does LaVey's brand of Satanism believe in or worship? The answer is Satan, but as defined by LaVey — the material world, man, and his carnal nature or appetites. Satanism for LaVey is the worship of man, just the way he is, with all of his fleshly desires and appetites. It is a religion of indulgence of man's carnal passions as symbolized by the term "Satan," codified and practiced by the inversion of Christian ethics. LaVey's "god" is himself, and the gods of his followers are themselves.*

> (Used by permission of the Christian Research Institute)

338

*   *   *   *   *

Sermon Title: Life Saving Tips

Sermon Angle: The media is full of articles on how you can save your own life. The topics range from how to eat healthfully, to learning to relax, to controlling anger, to defensive driving, and it doesn't end there. Jesus offers a much more important course titled: "How To Save Your Life By Losing It." We save our lives by losing them in the service of Christ, who teaches us to lose ourselves in serving and loving our neighbor. "For those who want to save their life will lose it, and those who lose their life for my sake, and for the sake of the gospel, will save it" (v. 35).

Outline:
1. The world offers advice on how to save (extend) and enrich your life.
2. Christ offers his life saving strategy involving: denying self, taking up our cross, following him, and losing our life (vv. 34-37).
3. In seeking to serve Christ and others, you save your own life.

*   *   *   *   *

The book, *One Flew Over The Cuckoo's Nest*, features a battle between men on a psychiatric ward and the evil nurse, Ratchet, who delights in punishing the men for infractions by administering electroshock treatments. McMurphy is a ringleader who refuses to comply with the rules. He seeks to liberate the patients from their bondage, even at the risk of his own life.

Throughout the book, electroshock therapy has been used as a symbol of Christ's crucifixion. One victim of the treatment stands unceasingly crucified against the ward's walls; the author's narration of the procedure mentioned its cross-shaped table and electric crown of thorns. As McMurphy approached this punishment, we hear of Pontius Pilate and a hymn: "It's my cross, thank you, Lord, it's all I got, thank you, Lord." Strapped to the table, McMurphy speaks biblically to the attendant, "Anointest my head with conductant. Do I get a crown of thorns?" Many have asked in what way he is supposed to resemble Christ. After all, McMurphy is a drinker, a brawler, a gambler, a womanizer — not a saint. Even so, he is affixed to a cross-shaped table, with an electric crown of thorns about his head. Like Christ, he has spread a gospel of light and life in a world of darkness and death, and is about to be sacrificed.

Proper 20/Pentecost 18/Ordinary Time 25

Revised Common	Proverbs 31:10-31	James 3:13—4:3, 7-8a	Mark 9:30-37
Roman Catholic	Wisdom 2:12, 17-20	James 3:16—4:3	Mark 9:30-37
Episcopal	Wisdom 1:16—2:1 (6-11) 12-22	James 3:16—4:6	Mark 9:30-37

Theme For The Day: A warning against selfish ambition, which fractures community. Rather, Jesus teaches us to receive the kingdom like a child and find our joy in Christ-like service.

BRIEF COMMENTARY ON THE LESSONS

Lesson 1: Proverbs 31:10-31 (C)

This description of a more than capable wife contrasts with the position of women in most of the societies of the Middle East. In many cultures women were almost considered property. In this description, she is able to purchase property on her own and she has her own business. Four traits seem to dominate this description of the capable wife — she is trustworthy, industrious, caring, and God-fearing.

Lesson 1: Wisdom 2:12, 17-20 (RC)

Lesson 1: Wisdom 1:16—2:1 (6-11) 12-22 (E)

Lesson 2: James 3:13—4:3, 7-8a (C); James 3:16—4:3 (RC); James 3:16—4:6 (E)

James calls upon the Christians to manifest goodness borne of wisdom and to divest themselves of envy and selfish ambition, which leads to disorder and wickedness. Divine wisdom is peaceable, gentle, and willing to yield in a spirit of love. James believes that all conflicts and disputes issue from internal craving and desire. The lust of things leads to violence. Rather than take what we want, Christians should ask God for the things we need. The reason we don't receive what we pray to God for is because we only desire to satisfy our own selfish cravings. James issues a call to take sides. If we are friends with the world, we are enemies of God (v. 4). In summation, his advice: resist the devil and submit to God (v. 7).

Gospel: Mark 9:30-37 (C, RC, E)

Jesus issues the second announcement of his passion but the disciples do not seem to understand. When they get back to Capernaum, Jesus asks them what they were arguing about along the way. At first, they remain silent. They were ashamed to admit that they had a dispute concerning who among them was the greatest. Jesus counsels that he who would be the first must be the servant of all. To illustrate his point he takes a child in his arms and pronounces: "Whoever welcomes one such child in my name welcomes me...." The Father extends his welcome not to those who are great but those who love his little ones.

Psalm Of The Day

Psalm 1 (C) — "Happy are those who do not follow the advice of the wicked" (v. 1).
Psalm 54 (E)
Psalm 53 (RC)

Prayer Of The Day

Humble Lord, free us from selfish ambition and the pride that seeks to dominate others. Make our source of pride the glorious truth that we are your dear children in Christ. As you have received us, so open our hearts that we might receive your other children, in your precious name. Amen.

THEOLOGICAL REFLECTION ON THE LESSONS

Lesson 1: Proverbs 31:10-31

The right kind of ambition. The woman described in this passage is very ambitious and industrious, which is not a virtue in and of itself. However, her ambition is indeed virtuous because she is not seeking wealth or power for herself; she is endeavoring to provide for her family. Her ambition is service-directed, rather than self-directed.

Busy hands, serving hands (vv. 19-20). The capable wife is not too busy providing for the needs of her family to open her hands and her heart to help the poor and needy. "She puts her hand to the distaff ... She opens her hand to the poor...."

She's a good scout. The Boy Scouts have the motto "Be prepared!" The woman of this passage anticipates future needs. She is a good scout in this regard. Her family has warm clothing for the winter (v. 21). "She laughs at the time to come" (v. 25).

Lesson 2: James 3:13—4:3, 7-8a

Who is wise? (v. 13). That's a matter of opinion. Some people would point to those who have become eminently successful in business as being wise — the Bill Gates and Warren Buffetts and Donald Trumps. According to James the wise and understanding person is the person of good and godly character. Such a person shows forth the wisdom from above (v. 17), which is essentially identical with those traits lifted up by Jesus in the Beatitudes.

A rich harvest (v. 17). Those who show forth the wisdom from above produce fruits. The apostle Paul would attribute these fruits to the Holy Spirit. The wisdom from above is a gift of God, which produces a rich harvest of goodness.

Choose your friends carefully (v. 4). Parents desire nothing more earnestly for their children but that they choose good friends. The wrong friends can lead us astray. James passionately teaches that we have two basic friendship choices — we can either be friends with the world or with God. We can't have it both ways.

Gospel: Mark 9:30-37

Tuning out the teacher (vv. 30-32). Jesus was trying to explain to his disciples his coming passion and death but they didn't understand. They were tuning out their teacher. We tend to tune out the teacher when the lesson is unpleasant or contrary to our cherished hopes and dreams.

Blind ambition (vv. 33-34). Ambition can be blind; those possessed of this malady don't see the people who love them and they don't correctly perceive the importance of things. All they see is that on which they have set their hearts. The disciples were so blinded by their pride that they did not see or hear the Lord as he shared his approaching death with them.

Silent shame (v. 34). When Jesus asked the disciples what they had been talking about along the way, they were silent because they were ashamed to admit they had been discussing who was the greatest among them. When people are willingly or unwillingly involved in shameful

341

activities, it tends to drive them into a stony well of silence. Jesus realized that the shame had to be brought into the open, into the light of God's grace.

Paying the piper. The disciples each wanted to be number one, but if you're going to be number one you have to pay the piper. The distinction of being number one comes only to those who are willing to pay the price. Jesus tells his disciples that if they want to be in the first position they must pay the price of being servant of all (v. 35).

SERMON APPROACHES WITH ILLUSTRATIONS

Lesson 1: Proverbs 31:10-31

Sermon Title: A Model Wife

Sermon Angle: The wife described in our pericope is a keeper, almost too good to be true. Yet my sense is that this narration is based on a real-life model rather than just a composite of the ideal wife. What does she look like? Well, physical beauty isn't that important, neither is charm (v. 30). The basic trait is that she's trustworthy (v. 11). Beyond that, she provides for her family (v. 15), she's a shrewd investor and businesswoman (vv. 16-19), she's strong (v. 17), compassionate (v. 20), wise (v. 26), kind (v. 26), and praiseworthy (vv. 28-30). The preacher needs to be careful in presenting this text, so as not to induce a sense of guilt or failure in those women who don't feel that they will ever be model wives.

Outline:
1. Talk about how our concept of the model wife has changed (Harriet Nelson, Jackie Kennedy, and so forth).
2. Talk about the characteristics of the model wife in our text.
3. Pull out of the model some timeless traits that will serve well the modern wife.
4. Point out that God loves us even when we aren't models of perfection.

Sermon Title: A Working Model

Sermon Angle: The model of womanhood presented in this text is literally a working model. This woman generates more power than Wonder Woman and Niagara Falls put together. But why does she work so hard? Is she trying to prove something? No, all her labors are directed toward the needs of her family and those of the poor. The source of her strength is her love for the Lord (v. 30).

Outline:
1. It is well known that a woman's work is never done.
2. As with the capable wife of Proverbs 31, she must balance the roles of mother, provider, wife, and career person.
3. Women need to ask themselves why they are working so hard.
   — To prove one's self?
   — Out of love for family?
   — Pride in doing the job well?
   — Love for the Lord?
4. Women and men both need to work wisely by not losing sight of their own needs, as well as those of their loved ones.

Lesson 2: James 3:13—4:3, 7-8a

Sermon Title: What Is The Aim Of Your Ambition?

Sermon Angle: James points to the dangers of envy and selfish ambition. One might receive the impression that ambition is itself suspect. This would be unfortunate; the writer only castigates *selfish* ambition. Without human ambition, the world would grind to a halt. A person can and should be ambitious for goodness, ambitious to provide for family, ambitious to serve the needs of brothers and sisters, to name only a few objects of worthwhile ambition. That which makes our ambition good or evil is its aim. What is the aim of your ambition?

Outline:

1. James points to the evil effect of selfish ambition (v. 16).
2. Lift up modern examples of selfish ambition.
3. Blind ambition seeks to possess and control (v. 2).
4. Godly ambition seeks to serve (v. 17).
5. What is the aim of your ambition?

Sermon Title: The Secret Of Unanswered Prayer

Sermon Angle: James states that Christians ask God for things and do not receive them because we ask wrongly (v. 3). Then he goes on to point out the secret of unanswered prayer. He says the reason God doesn't answer our prayers is that they are self-centered. We are not seeking God but the things that will gratify our pleasures and desires. Closely related to this, God does not answer us because we have unconfessed sin and continue to live in sin. Effective prayer always possesses the attitude that Jesus had when he prayed: "Nevertheless, not my will but thy will be done."

Outline:

Why doesn't God answer some of our prayers?

1. We ask wrongly (v. 3).
2. We ask selfishly.
3. We do not draw near to God (v. 8).

* * * * *

William J. O'Malley begins an article titled "Praying" in *U.S. Catholic* magazine with this analogy: "Praying is a bit like sex. If we engage in it, we're nervous talking about it, and parents wouldn't dream of telling their children what goes on when they do it." He goes on to explain that in other ways praying is not at all like sex. Not many of us submit alibis for not engaging in sex. "I'm really too busy; yes, I know it's important but ... Work is sex." What O'Malley says is true of the Catholic church is also true of most congregations. He believes that his church spends a great deal of time educating their youth *about* God, discussing the signs that point to God — sacraments, Bible, history, tradition — but it doesn't give much effort to helping its children get to know God himself. We need to spend more time teaching our people how to pray, not theoretical instruction but learning by doing. James teaches: "You do not have because you do not ask" (v. 2). And what is it that we need? We need to have God in our life and our life in God.

* * * * *

343

Gospel: Mark 9:30-37

Sermon Title: Death And Denial

Sermon Angle: When Jesus was explaining his upcoming sufferings and death, Mark says that the disciples didn't understand him and were afraid to ask (v. 32). It seems likely that the disciples did not understand because they did not want to deal with the subject matter. They didn't want to deal with death. Instead they chose to deny this ultimate reality in hope that it would go away. Their denial isolated them from Jesus. Jesus was not able to share the burden of the cross with them in a satisfying way. Death is the last great taboo; we would still rather deny it than openly deal with it. The cross and resurrection of Jesus give us the strength to deal with death openly.

Outline:

1. Jesus shared his upcoming death with his disciples but they would not receive it.
2. Like them, we seek to shun the reality of death and deny it.
3. Denial isolates us from others and increases our dread of death.
4. Jesus openly confronted death and won the victory and so can we.

* * * * *

An article I read in *Christianity Today* magazine struck home. The title: "Wise Christians Clip Obituaries" by Gary Thomas. It struck home because I have I lost my mother and father to death during the past two years. In addition, my youth group advisor when I was a teen, a woman of sixty well-lived years, died rather suddenly recently. The prayer service at the funeral home and the funeral itself were attended by large numbers of people. It seems that when a younger person dies, it hits us between the eyes. Death is a sudden, unwelcome reminder of our extreme vulnerability; it's an omen of our own fate. I do not yet clip the obituaries but I read them. Life can no longer be taken for granted.

Francois Fenelon, a seventeenth-century French mystic who wrote the classic *Christian Perfection*, spoke articulately of the denial of death: "We consider ourselves immortal, or at least as though (we are) going to live for centuries. Folly of the human spirit! Every day those who die soon follow those who are already dead. One about to leave on a journey ought not to think himself far from one who went only two days before. Life flows by like a flood."

When my father was nearing the terminus of his earthly life, he finally realized the gravity of his situation. "I got some bad news," he said. "What's that?" I responded. "I'm not going to make it," he retorted. Summoning my store of knowledge from my clinical pastoral education course and years of dealing with sickness and death, I asked, "How do you feel about that, Dad?" My father, who was always loathe to reveal too much of his feelings, shot back: "How do *you* feel about it?" (my death, not his own). I remained mute. My first thought was, "But, Dad, I'm not dying, you are." On a deeper level I knew that he was right, I too was dying. I needed to deal with my death as well as his own. Yet, I wanted to deny that the shadow of my own death was looming ever larger. In light of my reactions to the prospect of death, it's not hard to sympathize with the disciples of Christ, as Jesus shared with them that he was going to suffer and die. They could not, would not, deal with his death and their own. Denial had set in.

* * * * *

Sermon Title: How You Can Be Number One

Sermon Angle: Notice that Jesus doesn't outwardly chide his disciples for wanting to be number one in the kingdom. Instead he redefines the meaning of being number one. "Whoever wants to be first must be last of all and servant of all" (v. 35). An example of being number one in God's eyes is welcoming children, loving those with no position or power or any of the things that this world counts as treasure. For Christians, Jesus is number one, and we can be Jesus in the flesh when we are willing to give our lives as he gave his.

Outline:

1. It seems like everyone wants to be number one.
2. Things haven't changed; look at the disciples (vv. 33-34).
3. Jesus tells them and us how to be number one (be a servant).

Sermon Title: Children's Sermon

Sermon Angle: Many churches have children's sermons, usually an object lesson geared so that children might understand what the word of God is saying to them. Jesus gave the first and the best children's sermon. He took a child into his arms and said that those who receive such children receive him and that those who receive him receive the Father (vv. 36-37). Jesus also taught that we must receive the kingdom of God like a child, simply, sincerely, and without pretense.

Outline:

1. Many churches use children's sermons to make children welcome in worship.
2. Children's sermons must boil the gospel down to the essentials.
3. Jesus gave the first children's sermon, using a child as the object (v. 36).
4. Being his disciple has little to do with greatness and everything to do with being God's child and welcoming God's children (v. 37).

Proper 21/Pentecost 19/Ordinary Time 26

Revised Common	Esther 7:1-6, 9-10; 9:20-22	James 5:13-20	Mark 9:38-50
Roman Catholic	Numbers 11:25-29	James 5:1-6	Mark 9:38-43, 45, 47-48
Episcopal	Numbers 11:4-6, 10-16, 24-29	James 4:7-12 (13—5:6)	Mark 9:38-43, 45, 47-48

Theme For The Day: Providing a preserving and redemptive effect on the world.

BRIEF COMMENTARY ON THE LESSONS

Lesson 1: Esther 7:1-6, 9-10; 9:20-22 (C)

The book of Esther, written about 460 BC, makes no mention of God, worship, or prayer. It doubtless was included in the canon because it is sort of an Easter story concerning the Jewish people. The wicked Haman had laid plans for the genocide of the Jewish people. Mordecai catches wind of the plot and intercedes with his adopted daughter, Queen Esther, who intercedes with King Ahasuerus during a feast. Haman is hanged on the very gallows he had prepared for Mordicai, a kind of poetic justice. This text explains the institution of the Feast of Purim.

Lesson 1: Numbers 11:25-29 (RC); Numbers 11:4-6, 10-16, 24-29 (E)

Lesson 2: James 5:13-20 (C)

The concluding remarks of James continue the practical nature of the book. Those who suffer are instructed to pray, the joyous are to sing, and the sick are to contact the elders, so they could anoint the sick with oil and pray over them. Confessing one's sins is also commended as a part of the healing and redemptive process. Anyone who brings a sinner back to God's grace will save the soul of the sinner.

Lesson 2: James 5:1-6 (RC); James 4:7-12 (13—5:6) (E)

Gospel: Mark 9:38-50 (C); Mark 9:38-43, 45, 47-48 (RC, E)

In the first part of this lection (vv. 38-40), the disciples object that a man is casting out demons in Jesus' name but is not a part of their group. Jesus counsels them to leave him alone, because nobody who does a mighty work in his name will soon be able to speak evil of him. The Lord encourages tolerance. On the other hand, Jesus is not tolerant of those who cause others to fall into sin (literally "stumble"); it would be better for such a person if a millstone were tied around his neck and he were thrown into the sea. Jesus advises the sinner to remove the cause of sin to save his soul. "If your hand causes you to sin, cut it off; it is better for you to enter life maimed than for your whole body to be cast into hell" (v. 44). Such advice constitutes hyperbole, an exaggeration for the purpose of making a point. The word translated "hell" is the word *Gehenna*, Valley of Hinnom. This valley in the region of Jerusalem was the area where children were sacrificed, during the period when Ahaz encouraged the heathen fire-worship cult. It later became a city dump, an unclean place of refuse, where the fires continued to burn. The passage concludes with sayings that employ the metaphor of salt, which are not necessarily related in any other way.

Psalm Of The Day
Psalm 124 (C) — "Our help is in the name of the Lord" (v. 8).
Psalm 19; Psalm 135:1-7 (E)
Psalm 18 (RC)

Prayer Of The Day
Merciful Lord, give us the courage to remove any cause of temptation to sin and forbid that anything that we do would cause pain or scandal to one of your precious children. In Jesus' name. Amen.

THEOLOGICAL REFLECTION ON THE LESSONS

Lesson 1: Esther 7:1-6, 9-10; 9:20-22
Trapped. Haman had plotted to destroy Mordecai and the Jews by stealth and treachery but found himself snared in his own trap and executed on the gallows prepared for Mordecai. Those who practice evil eventually find themselves destroyed by their own plots, caught in their own trap.

King's favor (v. 2). Esther finds favor in the king's eyes and he offers her the desire of her heart, up to half his kingdom. It reminds me of the story of Salome, who danced before King Herod. She so pleased the king that he too offered her anything she wanted, up to half his kingdom. You will recall that her mother put her up to requesting the head of John the Baptist. Herodias and Salome sought revenge and the death of their enemy through the king's favor. Esther requested life and deliverance for her people. The Lord God grants his favor to those who seek life, not death.

Doomed by his deceit (v. 8-10). The text mentions that they covered Haman's face. This was a custom performed on the doomed. The sense of this punishment is similar to the millstone around the neck that Jesus mentions in the gospel lesson. Both images convey utter hopelessness and doom. What really doomed Haman was not the king but his own deceit.

Lesson 2: James 5:13-20
Reach out and touch (v. 13). James advises sufferers to share their misery with God and the church. "Are any among you suffering, let him pray." Share your misery with the Lord; he will hear, he will help. "Are any cheerful? Let them sing." Let others hear your praises. "Are any sick? They should call for the elders of the church and have them pray over them, anointing them with oil in the name of the Lord." God heals through the ministering touch of his people. Misery may enjoy company but sufferers need community.

The healing ministry of the church (v. 14). The healing ministry of the church has mostly become limited to hospitals and trained professionals, both clergy and lay. James indicates that the leaders of the early church exercised a healing ministry. They didn't just attend meetings and form budgets, they were physicians for the soul. The sick are encouraged to call on the elders for the laying on of hands and the anointing with oil. The healing ministry of the church is sacramental, involving earthly means, God's word, and promised blessings.

Sin and sickness (vv. 15-16). In the same breath that James speaks of healing, he also lifts up the forgiveness of sins. He is right in doing so; science has come to realize what people of faith have always known, that there is a link between sin and sickness. However, we must caution that the relationship is not necessarily a direct one. The presence of physical illness is not inevitably the product of sinful behavior. On the other side of the coin, there is no wellness or wholeness unless we know God and have received the forgiveness of sins. This remains true even if the doctors say that a person is free of illness.

Gospel: Mark 9:38-50

The ministry of the non-ordained (v. 38). The disciples came to Jesus with the complaint that a man outside their group was casting out demons in Jesus' name. We might say that he was an irregular, not a part of the ordained ministry of Jesus' followers. God often employs those outside of the normal channels to do his work.

Support staff (v. 41). "Whoever gives you a cup of cold water because you bear the name of Christ will by no means lose his reward." There are many people who do not call themselves Christians, yet may be sympathetic to the gospel and the mission of the church. They may support us or work together with us on areas of common interest. They are our support staff.

An ounce of prevention (vv. 42-47). Employing hyperbole, Jesus urges an ounce of prevention to obviate the pound of cure. Actually, Jesus warns that the time will come when a cure is not possible, as in hell. "If your hand causes you to sin, cut it off; it is better to enter life maimed than to have two hands and be thrown into hell." Remove the obstacle or cause of offense before you fall into the pit or break your neck.

The most damnable condition (v. 42). Jesus indicates that the worst sin that one can commit is to cause one of his disciples (little ones) who believe in him to fall away from grace. The Lord comments that it would be better for such a person to lose his life in the most inglorious fashion, such as a millstone around his neck as he is thrown into the sea, than to cause one of his own to fall away.

SERMON APPROACHES WITH ILLUSTRATIONS

Lesson 1: Esther 7:1-6, 9-10; 9:20-22

Sermon Title: The Importance Of Knowing Who You Are

Sermon Angle: Esther was an orphaned, alien Jew who became queen in Persia. Once she became queen, she might have forgotten her former lowly identity but she didn't. She chose to put her life on the line to save her people because she remembered who she was. In living out her Jewish identity, she became both powerful and authentic. As children of God, we too are called to know and remember who we are.

Outline:
1. Esther was queen of Persia and a Jewish woman.
2. In a conflict between those identities, she chose to side with her imperiled people (v. 3).
3. Like Moses, she chose to identify with her lowly roots, rather than her exalted position.
4. Authentic living comes from knowing and living out your true identity.
5. Our true identity rests in our baptism into Christ.

Sermon Title: The Joy Of Being Saved

Sermon Angle: Mordecai proclaimed throughout the empire a day of feasting and celebration for the Jewish people who had been saved from holocaust. In issuing the edict, he describes this feast as "the month that had been turned for them from sorrow into gladness and from mourning into a holiday ..." (v. 22). This feast combines some of the spirit of both Christmas and Easter. Christmas, because of the practice of gift giving, and Easter, because of the reversal of fortunes; those doomed were delivered. Though the book of Esther does not mention God, it speaks to the joy of being saved, a joy which cries out to be expressed in celebration and giving. This joy was only a brief foretaste of our salvation in Christ.

Outline:
1. Imagine the feelings of one condemned to death who is pardoned!
2. The Jews, set for slaughter, were saved — imagine their joy!
3. This deliverance was marked by celebration, exchange of food, and giving to the poor (vv. 22-23).
4. Every Sunday is a celebration of our deliverance in Christ. Show your joy by giving of yourself and your substance.

Lesson 2: James 5:13-20

Sermon Title: The Original HMO

Sermon Angle: In an effort to cut the cost of medical care in our country, Health Maintenance Organizations (HMOs) have assumed a much greater importance. The HMOs attempt to prevent many of the maladies that plague us and maintain a high level of health. The church was the first HMO, whose mission it was and is to bring wholeness to body, mind, and spirit. Confession is our fundamental diagnostic tool and prayer is our primary therapeutic appliance.

Outline:
1. Healing of illness has always been a central element of the church's mission.
2. The church was the first health maintenance organization.
3. The sick are instructed to contact the church leaders for healing ministry (v. 14).
4. We are all part of the health maintenance team.

Sermon Title: Confession Is Good For More Than The Soul

Sermon Angle: James indicates that the prayers of the righteous are effectual not only for the body but the soul (v. 15). He links forgiveness and healing. Then James urges the church to pray for one another and confess our sins to one another, so that we might be healed. Guilt, fear, and bitterness can destroy our bodies and/or souls, if we do not tend to them. Counseling may assist those who are so dis-eased but only God and prayer can heal both body and spirit.

Outline:
1. Our confession of sins at church is often perfunctory.
2. We think confession can help our souls but not our bodies.
3. James urges us to confess our sins to one another, that we might be healed in every way (v. 16).

*   *   *   *   *

Confession is productive of good health because it releases us from bitterness. Holding on to offenses eats away at our body and our spirit. Guy de Maupassant, in his short story "The Piece of String," writes about a man who found a piece of string on the pavement of a busy street one morning. Thinking that he might find a use for it, he bent down to pick it up. Later, he was accused of having found a wallet at the same spot. Though he protested his innocence, he was taken to the police station for interrogation. The wallet was found the next day, but the man felt that he had been wronged. He could not let this incident go and brooded daily over it. The string became a symbol of the injustice done him, affecting his work, his family, and his health. Every person that he met would hear about his injustice. He died a bitter and broken man, mumbling "a piece of string."

*   *   *   *   *

Gospel: Mark 9:38-50

Sermon Title: Brand Name Or Generic?

Sermon Angle: In the field of medications, there may be one brand name for a particular medicine, but after the patent has run out one may get the same medicine with a generic label at a fraction of the cost. What I am about to say is not a perfect analogy but might prove to be a helpful construct. The church of Christ is filled with brand-name Christians, with the name of Christ affixed upon their forehead in baptism. Some of them live out their faith well, others do not. At the same time, there are people out in the world that hold many of the values and beliefs of brand-name Christians but without the label. Their lives might be composed of basically the same ingredients. Didn't Jesus say, "Those who are not against us are with us"? Didn't Jesus rebuke the disciples for wanting to forbid the outsiders from ministering in Jesus' name? Though the generic Christian might be composed of pretty much the same stuff, keep in mind that he or she is a copy of brand name, a facsimile of the real McCoy.

Outline:
1. Discuss the differentiation between generic and brand name medicines.
2. Use this analogy for followers of Christ, inside and outside the institutional church.
3. We can work together with those who hold basically our same beliefs and values.
4. The generic believer is a copy of the brand-name Christian — without the brand name, there would be no generic.
5. Salvation still comes through Christ.

Sermon Title: Don't Cause A Wake

Sermon Angle: If you're a boater, you will eventually go through areas posted as "no wake" zones. That means that the boats are required to keep their speed down so as not to cause a wake, waves that follow the boat and are created by the speed and movement of the boat. Wakes can upset fishing boats, swamp swimmers, and gouge out the shoreline. Wakes are to the sea what stumbling blocks are on the land. When James counsels against putting stumbling blocks in the way of one of his little ones (disciples) (v. 42), it is the same as saying, "Don't swamp the lifeboat of one of my disciples." Those whose careless and reckless actions inundate those disciples who do not know how to swim well in the sea of life will be judged severely.

Outline:
1. If you've gone fishing, you probably have been adversely affected by some other boat's wake.
2. Wakes are the nautical equivalent of stumbling blocks.

3. Life is a "no wake" zone, so we don't upset someone else's lifeboat.
4. We must carefully consider our effect on those who find themselves in our wake.

*   *   *   *   *

Sermon Title: There Is No Salt Substitute

Sermon Angle: To control their blood pressure, some people have to lower their salt intake. To do this, some of them use a salt substitute. The problem is, they don't taste like salt and they don't season like salt (personal opinion). Salt was a very important commodity in the ancient world; it was so precious that in some cultures, it was a medium of exchange. At the conclusion of our gospel lesson, there are three sayings involving salt. We will consider the one in verse 50: "Salt is good but if it has lost its saltiness, how can you season it?" To explicate this saying, we must first understand the function of salt. First, salt was a purifier and preservative for food, absolutely essential before the days of refrigeration. Second, as we know, salt also enhances the taste of food. Third, even the ancients must have known that salt was essential to preserving health. Finally, salt is powerful; a little goes a long way. Christians are meant to be preserving and purifying agents in society. We are also to give life zest and flavor. Even though committed Christians may be a minority, our influence can penetrate every strata of society. We don't really lose our saltiness, except when our faith is mixed with a host of impurities.

*   *   *   *   *

Elie Wiesel, a Jewish author who survived the Holocaust, conveys the story about a faithful and just Jew who came to a wicked village in order to save it from destruction. Night and day he walked the streets preaching against vice and corruption. At first, the people listened to the stranger and smiled condescendingly. After a short time, they stopped listening; he no longer was able to even entertain them. The thieves went on stealing, the corrupt officials kept taking bribes, spouses kept on cheating on their spouses, and the children continued being disobedient to their parents. One day, a youth, puzzled by the stranger's behavior, asked, "Poor stranger, you shout and wear yourself out. Don't you see that it's useless?" "Yes, I see," answered the just man. "Then why do you go on?" "I'll tell you why. I'm not sure to what extent, if any, I can change this village. But if I still shout today and if I still scream, it is to prevent them from changing me."

Proper 22/Pentecost 20/Ordinary Time 27

Revised Common	Job 1:1; 2:1-10	Hebrews 1:1-4; 2:5-12	Mark 10:2-16
Roman Catholic	Genesis 2:18-24	Hebrews 2:9-11	Mark 10:2-16
Episcopal	Genesis 2:18-24	Hebrews 2:(1-8) 9-18	Mark 10:2-9

Theme For The Day: Remaining true to our covenants of faith. In the first lesson, Job remained true to God in his trials. In the second lesson, the writer of Hebrews calls the Jewish Christians to keep from falling away from Christ. In the gospel, Christ calls us to keep our marriage covenant.

BRIEF COMMENTARY ON THE LESSONS

Lesson 1: Job 1:1; 2:1-10 (C)

This lection comprises the first of four readings from the book of Job, one of the books of biblical wisdom literature. This reading is part of the introduction (1:1—2:13), which sets the stage for the plot of the book. God is holding an assembly of the heavenly creatures, at which Satan makes an appearance. God brags-up Job as being faithful and righteous. Satan, not yet the embodiment of the demonic, suggests that if Job's health is adversely affected, Job will curse God. The Lord permits Satan to test Job by afflicting his body with terrible sores. Job's wife calls on him to curse God and die. Job refuses: "Shall we receive good at the hand of the Lord and shall we not receive evil?" (v. 10). Job remains blameless.

Lesson 1: Genesis 2:18-24 (RC, E)

Lesson 2: Hebrews 1:1-4; 2:5-12 (C)

Hebrews was written for a Jewish audience, to keep them from abandoning their Christian faith in favor of returning to Judaism. The writer emphasizes that Christ is superior to the prophets (vv. 1-3). Christ holds the very nature of God and upholds the universe by his power. The writer also asserts Christ's superiority over angels (vv. 1:4-5; 2:5). Humanity, described by the psalmist (8:4-6) and quoted in this passage as being a little less than the angels, attains its glory through the sufferings of Jesus (v. 10). Jesus is the pioneer of our salvation and our elder brother (v. 11).

Lesson 2: Hebrews 2:(1-8) 9-18 (E); Hebrews 2:9-11 (RC)

Gospel: Mark 10:2-16 (C, RC); Mark 10:2-9 (E)

The Pharisees attempt to trip Jesus by asking a question about divorce. "Is it lawful for a man to divorce his wife?" Jesus admits that Moses allowed for divorce but he goes on to explain that this was not God's intention from the beginning. Jesus grounds his point of view in the creation account. Marriage is instituted of God and should not be devalued by humans (v. 9). In private, the Lord further instructs his disciples on the topic. Whoever divorces his wife or her husband has committed adultery. The second part of this lection has mothers bringing their children to Jesus for his blessing. The disciples are indignant about the practice and try to bar access to Jesus. Jesus becomes angry about this and orders the children to be brought to him. If a person does not enter the kingdom like a child, he shall not enter it at all. This lesson indicates that the kingdom is a gift to be received with childlike faith.

Psalm Of The Day
    Psalm 26 (C) — "O Lord, I love the house in which you dwell ..." (v. 8).
    Psalm 8 (E)
    Psalm 127 (RC)

Prayer Of The Day
    Gracious Lord, the devil, the world, and our own sinful inclinations lead us away from our basic commitments to you and to those we love. In a fickle world of self-exaltation, keep us true to our covenants, in Jesus' name. Amen.

THEOLOGICAL REFLECTION ON THE LESSONS

Lesson 1: Job 1:1; 2:1-10
Where have you come from? (v. 2). Satan pops in on the heavenly assembly and God asks him where he's come from. He responds that he has been roaming the earth. The question is one that millions have pondered; where has Satan come from? Though Satan did not derive from earth, he seems to be very much at home here, testing God's children.
    What will you give for your life? (v. 4). "All that people have they will give to save their lives." You may recall the joke that Jack Benny told about being robbed. The robber pointed a gun at him and demanded, "Your money or your life?" Benny did not respond and so the crook jabbed the fire iron into his ribs and shouted: "Didn't you hear me? Your money or your life?" Flustered, Jack responds, "I'm thinking, I'm thinking." Well, Satan may be right but it seems to me that there are many people who sacrifice their lives for things and a few that will sacrifice their lives for others.
    Job passed the test (v. 10). The writer concludes that Job did not sin with his lips. He preserved his integrity.

Lesson 2: Hebrews 1:1-4; 2:5-12
The superiority of the Son (vv. 1-4). The book of Hebrews was written to convince believers that Jesus was superior to other means of revelation. He is superior to the prophets of old, the spokesmen for God. He is also superior to angels, messengers from God. Hebrews asserts that Jesus is the very image of God; seeing him, we view God.
    The dawn of a new day (vv. 1-2). The Hebrews of the first century divided time into two ages — the present age, dominated by sin and death, and the new age, when the kingdom was to come in power and glory. Between these two ages was a period when the old was yielding way to the new. It is this in-between age, the dawning of a new day, that the writer of Hebrews refers to as "these last days."
    More than a message (v. 3). The prophets were called by God to deliver a message; angels, by the very definition of their name, are messengers. In Jesus, God delivered more than a message, he communicated the light and glory of his holy presence. "He is the reflection of God's glory...."

Brother Jesus (v. 11). We normally speak of Jesus as Savior and Lord. It's hard for us to conceive of him as our brother, because the term connotes equality. Yet, this passage claims that Jesus became our brother through taking on our suffering, sin, and death. We can call Christ brother because all those who are cleansed by the blood of Christ have one Father.

Gospel: Mark 10:2-16

The Great Satan. The leaders of Iran still hold that the United States is the Great Satan. In a sense, we are their Satan because we are an adversary; we oppose their very narrow worldview. Those Pharisees who came to Jesus with the intent of tripping him up were Satan for Jesus. They wanted to accuse, to prosecute, and to slander.

The intent, not the letter of the law. Jesus despised the legalism that permeated the religion of his day. God's moral laws are good, of course, but the scribes and Pharisees were preoccupied with framing and interpreting detailed legal rubrics. They had lost sight of the intent of the law. The same kind of legal malpractice occurs in our day, too. The Pharisees were focused on the specific interpretation of the law on divorce, while Jesus zeroed in on God's intent (v. 6) for lifelong fidelity between husband and wife.

No scarlet letter. The Scarlet Letter features a woman who comes to the Massachusetts colony ahead of her husband to set up house. Her husband later is shipwrecked and presumably lost. She has a sexual liaison with the town parson and becomes pregnant. She refuses to divulge the identity of her lover and so they imprison her and then, when she is released, force her to wear a scarlet letter on her dress, "A" for adulterer. The letter is to serve as a reminder of her shame. In our day, there is little shame associated with adultery, which is the most frequent cause of divorce. Some people think that this is an improvement. I am not one of them. Some actions deserve shame.

No such thing as no-fault divorce. Many states have made divorce easier by establishing no-fault divorce. The concept is ludicrous. If there wasn't fault or sin, no divorce would have occurred. In some cases, the fault may be approximately equal. However, in most of the divorces that I observe, one of the marriage partners has committed adultery and thus broken their marriage covenant. As far as I'm concerned, the onus of fault rests on that party, though there is no such thing as absolute innocence. If we accept the premise of no one being at fault, no one will learn from his or her mistake. We see the result of glossing over the fracture of divorce in the lives of those who experience multiple failed marriages. It's easier to blame their partners than to look honestly at themselves.

SERMON APPROACHES WITH ILLUSTRATIONS

Lesson 1: Job 1:1; 2:1-10

Sermon Title: The Fall Of Satan

Sermon Angle: The Bible provides glimpses of Satan's fall from grace. Originally, he was an angel of light. In Job, Satan still inhabits the court of the heavenly ones and serves as God's prime tester of humans. By the time Jesus comes on the scene, Satan stands as the diabolical one, who slanders God and deceives humans.

Sermon Title: Satan, Suffering, and Sin

Sermon Angle: In the dialogue between Satan and God, God allows Satan to inflict suffering on Job to see if he would forsake God and commit sin. Satan postulates that suffering will cause sin. In contrast, some people feel that affliction is a consequence of their sin or somebody else's. They ask, what did I do to deserve this? What is the relationship between Satan, sin, sickness, and suffering? It is plain that some suffering and sickness is a result of sin, and Satan certainly has a role in that: for instance, abusing our bodies through food, drink, and drugs. Some suffering and sickness have nothing to do with personal sin, such as the consequences of heredity and environment. And yes, it is likely that God allows Satan to afflict us in order to test and purify us. Cause and effect are not easily determined. What we can know for certain is that Satan's power to hurt is limited by God's power and that God is working in everything to reveal to us his love and grace.

Outline:
1. Why we all suffer is something of a mystery.
2. Some feel that suffering is a punishment for sin; it would be better to say that suffering is sometimes a consequence of sin.
3. In our text, Job was innocent and righteous and yet he suffered. This shows that suffering is not necessarily a consequence of sin.
4. Does God permit Satan to inflict suffering to test us? Sometimes!
5. One thing we know: all things work together for good to those who love the Lord.

Lesson 2: Hebrews 1:1-4; 2:5-12

Sermon Title: The Superiority Of Our Savior

Sermon Angle: The writer of Hebrews has been trying to establish the superiority of Christ over the old revelation, but what really is the source of his superiority?

Outline:
1. The writer argues that Christ is superior to the Jewish faith, but how?
2. He is superior in divinity (he bears the very nature of God) (vv. 2b-3).
3. He is a superior intermediary and priest. He made purification for our sins (v. 3).
4. He is superior in suffering (vv. 9-10).
5. He is superior in bringing salvation to completion (vv. 10-12).

Sermon Title: Christ Died To Restore Us To Glory

Sermon Angle: Hebrews 5b-8a refers to Psalm 8:4-6, which states that God has made humans a little lower than the angels. The writer of Hebrews adds that he left nothing outside our control. A very glorious state indeed. Yet, because of sin and weakness, we have not attained that glory. Christ came into the world, suffered, and died to restore our lost glory.

Outline:
1. God created humans to have mastery over the world.
2. We have fallen from that glory through sin.
3. Jesus came that, by his death and suffering, we might realize our original glory.

Gospel: Mark 10:2-16

Sermon Title: Passing The Test

Sermon Angle: The Pharisees put Jesus to the test once again (v. 2) on one of the hot topics of his day and of our day, too — divorce. Jesus flunked, according to their standards, and that's what they wanted him to do. Once again, Jesus takes his stand not according to the opinion polls but according to divine truth. Once more, he takes a stand on the side of the weak and defenseless, women, in this case. In Jewish society, women were never the initiators of divorce, they were victims of the capricious whims of their husbands. Many interpretations of the grounds for divorce were very liberal. Our Lord's teaching on divorce remains unpopular and largely ignored. Of course, it doesn't really matter if he passes our test, only that we pass his.

Outline:
1. The Pharisees tested Jesus on the subject of divorce (v. 2).
2. He found that many people were failing to live up to God's standards.
3. Divorce is not God's will, but his concession to the reality of sin (v. 5).
4. In marriage, two people become one.
5. Divorce murders a living thing, marriage.
6. Christ calls us all to preserve the unity of marriage.

Sermon Title: What Has God Joined Together?

Sermon Angle: Jesus concludes his teaching on divorce. "Therefore, what God has joined together, let no one separate" (v. 9). Yet it is beyond belief that all who marry are following God's will. Some marriages are not made in heaven. This is likely the basis for the Roman Catholic practice of annulment. It differs from divorce in that annulment postulates that a valid marriage never took place. Christians should pray earnestly when seeking a husband or wife that the potential spouse is the one God intends. The distinction between annulment and divorce is open to abuse; even though God may not have brought two people together, he can even turn our mistakes into something good. Despite all that has been said about the oneness of marriage, some relationships are so destructive that divorce is the lesser of evils. Some relationships fail because God never joined them together.

Outline:
1. Christ says that marriage is a unity of one man, one woman, and God (one flesh).
2. Christian marriage is according to God's will (what God has joined together).
3. Some marriages are the result of human willfulness and hubris — God never joined them together.
4. In some such marriages, divorce may be the lesser evil.

* * * * *

If anyone had grounds for divorce, it was Tony Toto of Allentown, Pennsylvania. The story of Tony and his wife, Fran, was made into a movie titled *I Love You To Death.* Several times Fran attempted to dispatch her spouse to husband heaven. The first try came in 1982. A fourteen-year-old friend of one of Tony's sons tried to kill him with a baseball bat. A couple of months later, his daughter's boyfriend ran a wire from the distributor to the gas tank of Tony's car. It didn't work. In 1983, the daughter's new boyfriend agreed to do the job. He shot Tony in the head but when the bullet lodged in his skull, he panicked and ran away. He recommended his two cousins to finish the job and Fran agreed to pay them $500 each. They shot Tony in the heart but he didn't die. You might think that Fran would give up the murder racket and seek a simple divorce at this point. Right? Not Fran, she fed Tony soup laced with barbiturates. The police finally rescued Tony from this coterie of bumbling assassins, finding him in a semi-conscious state.

Fran served two years at the state prison for women in Muncy, Pennsylvania, and another two years at a minimum-security prison. Tony waited for her. The first night she was home, they went out for pizza. "We never mention the words 'divorce' or 'separation,' " Tony said in an interview with the *Philadelphia Inquirer*. "I don't understand it, why people break up over silly things. I think people need to sit down and talk."

* * * * *

Sermon Title: Let Jesus Bless You

Sermon Angle: It was the custom of Jewish mothers to bring their children to a noted rabbi for a blessing, especially on their first birthday. The disciples viewed these mothers as a distraction rather than an opportunity for ministry. Children and women had relatively little status or importance. Jesus became angry and ordered that the children be allowed to come to him. He took them in his arms and blessed them. This scene is depicted in thousands of Sunday schools. The Lord teaches that if we want to be one of God's blessed ones, we must become as a little child — powerless, humble, open, trusting. Jesus wants to bless all his children.

Outline:

1. The disciples thought Jesus had more important things to do than blessing children.
2. Jesus scolded his disciples and ordered the children to come to him for a blessing.
3. Jesus teaches that each of us must come to him as a little child — in weakness, openness, trust (vv. 14-16).
4. Don't let your sin or pride keep you from coming to Jesus. He wants to bless you!

Proper 23/Pentecost 21/Ordinary Time 28

Revised Common	Job 23:1-9, 16-17	Hebrews 4:12-16	Mark 10:17-31
Roman Catholic	Wisdom 7:7-11	Hebrews 4:12-13	Mark 10:17-30
Episcopal	Amos 5:6-7, 10-15	Hebrews 3:1-6	Mark 10:17-27 (28-31)

Theme For The Day: The difficulty of entering the kingdom of heaven when material things have a hold on you.

BRIEF COMMENTARY ON THE LESSONS

Lesson 1: Job 23:1-9, 16-17 (C)

Job responds to Eliaphaz, one of Job's friends and supposed comforters. Job wants to talk with God face-to-face, to make his case and hear God's response. But Job experiences only God's absence and it upsets him. Job's arguments sound like what humanistic philosophers of the twentieth century have said about the so-called death of God. Yet the absence of God is a feeling that even the most pious individual has felt at times in life.

Lesson 1: Wisdom 7:7-11 (RC)

Lesson 1: Amos 5:6-7, 10-15 (E)

Lesson 2: Hebrews 4:12-16 (C); Hebrews 4:12-13 (RC)

The lection begins with an exhortation to diligence, girded by the reminder that the word of God is mighty, able to discern thoughts and the intention of the heart. A second resource to strengthen our faith in Jesus is the thought that Jesus is our great high priest who, on the one hand, offers himself as our sacrifice for sin and, on the other hand, understands and sympathizes with our weakness, because he too was tempted to sin. Jesus offers mercy for past sins and grace to cope with temptation in the present and the future.

Lesson 2: Hebrews 3:1-6 (E)

Gospel: Mark 10:17-31 (C); Mark 10:17-30 (RC); Mark 10:17-27 (28-31) (E)

As Jesus was setting out on his journey to Jerusalem, a man ran up to Jesus, fell at his feet and asked: "Good Teacher what must I do to inherit eternal life?" Note the passion of his inquiry, which Jesus quickly pours water on by asking, "Why do you call me good?" Jesus wants him to think soberly about what he is doing. Jesus points to the commandments of God, but notice that all of the commandments he mentions are from the second table of the law, having to do with our relationships with other people. The man claims to have kept them all. Jesus looks intently at the man and loves him but spies a terrible fracture in his soul, because of his attachment to his wealth. "You lack one thing," said Jesus. "Sell all you have, give it to the poor and come and follow me." The man's face drops like a brick. He stomps away like a groom jilted on his wedding day. The Lord then teaches his disciples concerning the dangers of having great possessions. The "camel through the eye of a needle" proverb means that it's either impossible or very difficult for a rich man to enter the kingdom of God, humanly speaking. Of course, all things are possible with God. The Lord's lesson shocked the disciples because it was the opposite of the accepted theology of the day, which said that material prosperity was a sign of piety and of God's blessing. The disciples then claim that they have left everything for Jesus. The Lord assures them that they would receive interest on all that they left, many times over in this life, and eternal life in the world to come.

Psalm Of The Day
> **Psalm 22:1-15 (C)** — "O my God, I cry by day, but you do not answer" (v. 2).
> **Psalm 90 (E)**
> **Psalm 89 (RC)**

Prayer Of The Day
Gracious God, we accept your bountiful blessings with gratitude but we pray that no attachment to the things of this world would keep us from the true treasure, Jesus Christ our Lord. Amen.

THEOLOGICAL REFLECTION ON THE LESSONS

Lesson 1: Job 23:1-9, 16-17
Finding God (v. 3). Job felt that he had lost contact with God. If he could find God, he would lay his case before him to establish his innocence. In every generation, there are those who have lost sight of God; he is no longer real to them. Where do we find God? In his word (second lesson) and particularly in Christ (gospel).

The danger of defending yourself. Job is possessed with the urge to defend himself before God, to storm the very gates of heaven, so convinced is he of his innocence (v. 7). A man who killed several people in the subway of New York insisted on being his own lawyer, which was a big mistake on his part. He only succeeded in showing how wacky he really was. When we think we can defend ourselves before God, we stand on shifting sands. We cannot see things as God does.

Fear of God (vv. 16-17). Job confesses that he is terrified of God, feeling that God has been cruel and unfair. Luther also was possessed of great angst concerning his relationship with the Lord, until he submitted to the grace of God in Christ. Few people fear God in twenty-first-century America.

Lesson 2: Hebrews 4:12-16
Cut to the quick (v. 12). Hebrews describes God's word as sharp, able to cut to the heart of things. But cutting can be very painful, like when a person cuts into the quick of the fingernail. God's word can be very painful, like surgery without anesthesia, because it exposes us for what we are, our thoughts, feelings, and failures. The intent of God's word is not to hurt but to heal.

Naked as the day we were born (v. 13). When we were born into this world, we were completely exposed. As we get older, we learn to conceal, to hide from ourselves and from others. God's word lays bare our identity as sinner and saint.

Approach God with boldness (v. 16). In Job's diatribe, he thinks that he wants to storm God's abode, that he might defend himself. The writer of Hebrews claims that we can approach God's throne of grace with boldness because of Jesus Christ, our great high priest. He has given his life to defend and save us.

359

Gospel: Mark 10:17-31

To have one's cake and eat it, too. The wealthy man in this story had all that the world could offer — wealth, position, respect — but he wanted more. He had probably inherited his wealth but he also wanted to inherit eternal life. Jesus told him that he would have to choose. This left him sad and dejected because he wanted to possess this world's treasure and the treasure of the kingdom as well. He desired to have his cake and eat it too, one might say.

No one but God is good (v. 18). The rich man fell at Jesus' feet in a gush of emotion and exclaimed: "Good Teacher, what must I do to inherit eternal life?" Jesus poured cold water on the man's enthusiasm by saying: "No one is good but God alone." Why didn't Jesus accept this tribute? He was good, wasn't he? No, Jesus didn't come into the world to draw attention to himself but to point beyond himself to the Father and the kingdom of God.

Righteousness is not a negative. All of the commandments that Jesus recited, with the exception of the last one, were framed negatively; you shall not murder, you shall not commit adultery, and so forth. The Ten Commandments can give one the impression that righteousness is a matter of not doing certain things. Jesus didn't dispute the rich man's claim to have kept these commandments since his youth. When Jesus told him to sell his goods and come follow him, he was trying to tell him that righteousness is defined by what you do, not merely what you don't do.

Respectability is not enough. The rich man was very good by human standards, exceedingly respectable, but that isn't enough. We can achieve respectability by leading a relatively good life, supporting our community, and being a good neighbor. Respectability is granted by humans. God demands righteousness, the willingness to abandon all at God's beckoning. Righteousness is a gift of God.

SERMON APPROACHES WITH ILLUSTRATIONS

Lesson 1: Job 23:1-9, 16-17

Sermon Title: Where To Find God

Sermon Angle: Job wants to find God but doesn't know where he is (vv. 2, 8-9). Suffering sometimes has a way of making us feel God-forsaken when we don't understand that God stands with us in the midst of our suffering. Job, of course, didn't have the benefit of learning that at the foot of Christ's cross. Job thought, together with most others in the Old Testament, that prosperity was the sign of God's favor and that suffering indicated his disfavor. The book of Job moves beyond this idea to the notion that suffering is a time of testing allowed by God. God does not abandon us in suffering but merely deals with us in another manner, to the end that we are strengthened spiritually.

Outline:
1. Job felt abandoned by God. When have you felt that way? Was it a time of suffering and pain?
2. Jesus also felt abandoned on the cross. "My God ... why have you forsaken me?"
3. Where does one find God? In the cross of Christ.

Sermon Title: How To Fear God

Sermon Angle: Job confesses that he is terrified of God (v. 16). He feels that God is vindictive and hurtful. That's the wrong way to fear God. Job mistakenly held that Yahweh was cruel and unfair. There is a right way to fear the Lord; to hold him in respect and honor. If we want only to disobey God, we should fear his chastening presence, but if we honor him we have no reason to be in dread of God's presence.

Lesson 2: Hebrews 4:12-16

Sermon Title: Logo-Surgery

Sermon Angle: The text compares the word of God to a two-edged sword, which is sharp enough to lay the inner parts bare. As the writer proclaims, "It divides soul from spirit, joints from marrow; it is able to judge the thoughts and intentions of the heart" (v. 12). Science has provided laser surgery but the word of the Lord has been conducting logo (word) surgery for hundreds of years. The word exposes our thoughts, our fears, and our sins. It also cuts away that which is diseased in us. Relating to the gospel lesson, Jesus, the Word made flesh, could see into the heart of the rich man; he attempted to cut away that which was causing his spiritual malady. The man walked away because he hadn't the courage to go under the knife.

Outline:
1. The word of God is sharp, like a sword, says the text.
2. The word of God lays bare our hearts, like a surgical scalpel (v. 13).
3. Jesus cut to the soul of the rich man and saw his heart but this man wouldn't let him cut out his disease (gospel).
4. Jesus sees your disease, let him cut it away.

Sermon Title: We Have A Friend In High Places

Sermon Angle: The writer of Hebrews writes to those whose faith was being tested. He encourages them with the thought that Christians have a friend in high places. Jesus is our high priest, who experienced our weaknesses, our suffering, and our death. This Jesus, our friend and high priest, has passed through the heavens (ascension). Because of his self-sacrifice, we can approach the throne of God with confidence.

Outline:
1. The text gives courage to us when we are being tested by life, because we have a friend in high places.
2. Jesus experienced our tribulations but without sin (v. 15).
3. Since Jesus is our heavenly Lord, we can hold fast to our faith (v. 14).

Gospel: Mark 10:17-31

Sermon Title: Estate Planning

Sermon Angle: My wife and I are in the process of doing some estate planning. We want to make sure that our goods and/or values carry on after we are gone. Inheritance was much simpler in Jesus' day but I wonder if the rich man was not engaging in some estate planning, not for this world but for the next. He wanted to know how he could inherit eternal life. Jesus was the lawyer/teacher, whom he hoped would tell him how to set up his life in such a way that he would be the beneficiary. Jesus told him how to ensure eternal life, but the fee was too great. It would cost his life as he knew it.

Outline:
1. The rich man had inherited earthly treasure and now wanted to make sure he received the treasure of the kingdom. "What must I do to inherit eternal life?"
2. Estate planning is wise and good. We need to give thought not only to what we leave behind but to what we will inherit when we die.

3. The rich man would not take Jesus' counsel — too attached to this world.
4. We can inherit eternal life if we give up our attachment to this world's treasure and follow Jesus.

Sermon Title: How To Win The Prize

Sermon Angle: It seems that most everybody wants to win the prize, to strike it rich. The problem is that they want to do so with little sacrifice or sweat. Thousands buy Powerball lottery tickets in hopes of pulling the winning combination of numbers, which would make them wealthy for life. The rich man in the gospel lesson also wanted to win the prize but the stakes are infinitely greater in the game of eternal life. What advice did Jesus give the rich man?

Outline:
1. Divest — "Sell all that you have."
2. Invest — "and give to the poor."
3. Confess — "Come and follow me."

Sermon Title: Investing For The Long Haul

Sermon Angle: Warren Buffett of Berkshire Hathaway fame has made billions for himself and his investors by picking good, solid companies and holding on to them. Investing for the long term is good investment advice. Jesus tells us to sell off our short-term holdings, from which we hope to gain a quick profit, and invest our lives in God's eternal kingdom. Listen to Jesus' investment advice. "Go and sell ... give to the poor ... come and follow." Jesus knows that as long as we are heavily invested in this world, we will not be prepared to invest for the long haul, for eternity.

Outline:
1. The rich man wasn't bad, just shortsighted.
2. He wanted to inherit the treasure of eternal life but wasn't willing to invest for the long haul.
3. We see charity as giving away but Jesus would have us view it as an investment that never stops paying benefits.
4. Investing our lives in Jesus is the most secure long-term investment imaginable.

Sermon Title: Beyond Respectability And Security

Sermon Angle: The rich man had what most of us are seeking — respectability and financial security. It wasn't enough. He knew it and Jesus certainly knew it. Jesus recognized that the man's source of security was inadequate. Jesus challenges him to risk it all for the sake of the kingdom of God. He was certainly a respectable man but that doesn't cut it with the Lord, either. Christ calls us to leave our attachments to the treasures of this world and to come follow him. When a person becomes a Christian, Christ calls us beyond respectability to righteousness and beyond security to service.

Outline:
1. The rich man had respectability and security but Jesus said he was still lacking (v. 21).
2. He was morally respectable but this wasn't enough.
3. He was financially and socially secure but that wasn't enough.
4. Christ called him to abandon his source of security in favor of Christian service.
5. Christ also called him to move beyond passive respectability to active righteousness.
6. Christ calls us to find our security and righteousness in him.

* * * * *

Ed Casteen is a 55-year-old sociology professor at William Jewell College in Liberty, Missouri. His passion is to combat hate and prejudice. The weapon he crafted to combat these foes is an organization called "Hate Busters." This organization throws three-day "Human Family Reunions" comprised of hundreds of people from myriad cultures. He also sponsors 100-mile "Hate Buster" bike hikes. Since Ed was afflicted with multiple sclerosis in 1981, he has also given himself to the cause of assisting others who have this disease. One day, while riding his bike, he conceived of an audacious idea. He would bike across the country and raise the consciousness of people concerning this sometimes devastating disease. Casteen's wife was worried that this promotion would devastate their family finances. "No, it won't," Ed responded. "I won't spend a penny. I'll ask people to help." He traveled 5,126 miles in 105 days and relied exclusively on the kindness of strangers. Over 500 Good Samaritans responded by providing food, lodging, and other necessities. Only five people turned him down. Casteen also raised over $10,000 for multiple sclerosis research. This trip taught him the concept of audacious asking, the main component in his philosophy of social change. This was also a mainstay of Jesus' approach to ministry.

Ed made a statement that I think underlaid the spiritual sickness evidenced by the rich man in today's gospel: "A lot of people take it as is sign of weakness if they ask for help, but I feel most powerful when I depend totally on others." The rich man in our gospel couldn't conceive of parting with his wealth because he thought it would make him weak. He didn't realize how strong he could be by relying on Jesus. (gleaned from article in *Parade* magazine, October 20, 1991)

Proper 24/Pentecost 22/Ordinary Time 29

Revised Common	Job 38:1-7 (34-41)	Hebrews 5:1-10	Mark 10:35-45
Roman Catholic	Isaiah 53:10-11	Hebrews 4:14-16	Mark 10:35-45
Episcopal	Isaiah 53:4-12	Hebrews 4:12-16	Mark 10:35-45

Theme For The Day: Our human pride gets in the way of our worshiping and serving the Lord.

BRIEF COMMENTARY ON THE LESSONS

Lesson 1: Job 38:1-7 (34-41) (C)

The arguments of Job's four friends come to a conclusion and God himself answers from a whirlwind, a frequent setting for theophanies. God chides Job for his lack of wisdom and addresses him with a series of rhetorical questions. The entire chapter presents an argument from creation. Job was not present at the creation of the world; how can he dare to question the sovereign God?

Lesson 1: Isaiah 53:10-11 (RC); Isaiah 53:4-12 (E)

Lesson 2: Hebrews 5:1-10 (C)

The writer continues to demonstrate how the Christian religion is superior to the Jewish faith from which it sprang. In this lection, he presents Christ as our great high priest but one who is superior to the regularly appointed high priests. Jesus is appointed directly by God. Christ differs from the Jewish high priest who had to offer up sacrifice for his own sins, as well as the sins of others. Jesus was sinless, yet human in all respects, so he is able to empathize fully with us in our weaknesses and struggles. Many interpreters believe that verse 7, which states that Jesus offered up prayers "with loud cries and tears," is a reference to the Garden of Gethsemane experience. The prayers of Jesus were heard but he had to learn obedience through suffering. His obedience unto death made him perfect (*telios*-complete), so that he could be the source of eternal salvation for all who obey him.

Lesson 2: Hebrews 4:14-16 (RC); Hebrews 4:12-16 (E)

See second lesson for Proper 23.

Gospel: Mark 10:35-45 (C, RC, E)

James and John, who with Peter formed a sort of inner circle of disciples, ask Jesus for a favor. They request that, after Jesus wins his victory and is established in his kingdom, they might sit in the places of honor, one at his right hand and one at his left. The concept of a suffering Messiah was still foreign to them; what Jesus was trying to communicate about his suffering and death had not sunk in. Though they may have possessed their share of pride, they still had great confidence in Jesus' ultimate victory; this in spite of the fact that the Lord had many enemies in high places. Jesus tells them that they are asking the wrong question. He asks them whether they think they can drink his cup and be baptized with his baptism. Drinking the cup is an expression that indicates the willingness to accept God's will. Being baptized with

Jesus' baptism means to be submerged in Jesus' suffering and death. Jesus concludes that it is not his prerogative to grant this honor but that it goes to those for whom it has been prepared.

Psalm Of The Day
   Psalm 104:1-9, 24, 35c (C) — "O Lord, how manifold are all your works!" (v. 24).
   Psalm 91 (E)
   Psalm 32 (RC)

Prayer Of The Day
   Humble Lord Jesus, we so often let our pride get in the way of following you. Like James and John, we strive to put ourselves first and seek the best positions for ourselves. Give us a spirit that strives only to follow you and to serve our neighbor. In your precious name. Amen.

THEOLOGICAL REFLECTION ON THE LESSONS

Lesson 1: Job 38:1-7 (34-41)
   God answers Job's arrogance. Job claimed that he wanted to contend with God and put forth arguments against the almighty. The Lord challenges Job to explain his creative power. He is but an arrogant and foolish man who cannot plumb the depths of God's Spirit.
   God the architect and builder. This passage presents creation as God's plan, which was carefully planned and carried out by the architect and builder of the universe. Contrary to some in modern science, this world didn't just happen by chance. There is a grand design.

Lesson 2: Hebrews 5:1-10
   Earthly and heavenly high priest. The writer contrasts the role of earthly high priest to that of Christ as the heavenly high priest. He points out that the high priest is not self-appointed. The earthly high priest was appointed by others. Christ was appointed high priest by the election of his Father. The earthly high priest offered sacrifices for his own sin and that of his countrymen. Christ offered up not only fervent prayers (loud cries and tears, v. 7) but his whole life as a sacrifice to God. The earthly high priest conducted his sacrifices on earth. Jesus serves out his high priestly role in heaven (v. 10).
   A priestly people (v. 5). This verse indirectly links Jesus' high priestly role with his baptism. The writer quotes Psalm 2:7, a coronation psalm for a Hebrew king. This equates quite closely with the voice of God that was heard at Jesus' baptism. In baptism, Jesus was ordained into his high priestly role. In our baptism, we also are ordained as a priestly people, to offer prayers and supplications on behalf of the world.
   Boot camp (v. 8). "Although he was a Son, he learned obedience through what he suffered." When a person enters the military, he must first go to boot camp. The method of teaching the new recruits to obey orders is to inflict on them pain and suffering. If even the Son had to learn obedience to God through such humiliation, why should we expect anything different for ourselves?
   Source of salvation (v. 9). Through his suffering and sacrificial death, Jesus became the source of salvation for all time and for all people. His suffering, which he willingly accepted, made him perfect (complete) in his high priestly role.

Gospel: Mark 10:35-45

Political patronage (vv. 35-37). Political patronage has been around for a long time. Certain people help those seeking power and, in return, expect to receive favors. The former mayor of Chicago, Richard Daley Sr., was extremely deft at the art of political patronage. In our gospel, James and John seek special favors of the Lord; they want to sit in the places of honor and power when Jesus comes into his kingdom glory. Some might marvel at their gall but when you look at it from their perspective, they were merely seeking payment for having left everything to follow Jesus. They hadn't learned that the kingdom was not a reward for faithful service or support but rather a gift of God.

Wisdom: knowing which questions to ask (v. 38). Jesus answered James and John that they didn't know what they were asking. My wife and I were talking to another pastor, whose son was studying for his doctorate in some aspect of history. My wife said something to the effect that he must have to learn a lot of names and dates. "No," replied the father, "they don't do that anymore; they basically learn to raise the proper questions." Wisdom resides in knowing the right questions to ask, whether it's relating to God or to others. Jesus revealed to James and John that it wasn't proper to ask God for ego-enhancing favors.

Servant leadership (vv. 42-45). Jesus laid out for his disciples a new paradigm for leadership. They were not to follow the model imposed by the world, where leaders delighted to subject others to their authority in order to inflate their own ego. Jesus laid out a prototype of leadership in the kingdom that emphasized service rather than position and power. "Whoever would be great among you must be your servant" (v. 43).

SERMON APPROACHES WITH ILLUSTRATIONS

Lesson 1: Job 38:1-7 (34-41)

Sermon Title: Who's Calling The Plays?

Sermon Angle: Before Job's troubles, it seemed that he was calling the plays in the game of life and every play went for big yards. Then the tide suddenly turned and the opposite side ran all over him. He blamed God for his losing ways. The problem was that he didn't understand the game plan and had lost confidence in his coach. In today's lesson, God responds to Job's complaints by challenging Job to explain how the game of life should be played. "I will question you and you shall declare to me" (v. 3). In other words, when he could understand how to create the world, then he could question God.

Outline:
1. Many armchair quarterbacks like to call the coach into question.
2. When life is going well, we don't question God, because it seems like we are in control.
3. When the game of life is going poorly, we blame our losses on God, the coach. That's basically what Job did.
4. When you are doing things right and life still seems to be running over you, keep faith that it is only one part of God's game plan for victory.

Lesson 2: Hebrews 5:1-10

Sermon Title: God's Mercy For The Ignorant And The Weak

Sermon Angle: The sins for which sacrifices were offered were basically sins of ignorance and weakness (v. 2). The sacrifices did not claim to cover those who sinned wantonly or arrogantly, without remorse and repentance. On the cross, Jesus carried out his high priestly role by offering a prayer for mercy on behalf of those who were ignorant. On the other hand, Jesus was hard on those who knew God's law but wantonly disregarded it, such as the scribes and Pharisees. If God has mercy on us in our ignorance and weakness, so too we must have mercy on other ignorant and feeble sinners.

Outline:
1. The high priest only offered sacrifices for sins of ignorance and weakness, not open and flagrant rebellion (v. 2).
2. The rebel cannot receive God's forgiveness until he repents but the fool is already covered by the ministry of our high priest.
3. Christ's life was offered up to God as our source of salvation for all sins (v. 9).
4. As Christ forgives us for our foolish and flagrant sins, so must we forgive others.

Sermon Title: Spare The Rod, Spoil The Child

Sermon Angle: The saying encapsulated in the sermon title was popular many years ago, when children were expected to obey their elders. I am certainly not recommending physical beating but there's a truth here. Pain, symbolized by the rod, is one of the best teachers. If a child puts his hand in an open flame one time, it isn't likely that he will repeat it. Without suffering we would not learn our limits and other crucial lessons in life. Even Jesus learned obedience through his suffering (v. 8). Were God to spare us the rod of affliction, we would be the most weak and spoiled creatures imaginable.

Outline:
1. Pain, both physical and mental, is a tool to learn the important lessons in life.
2. Pain is part of the discipline (learning) process.
3. Jesus learned discipline through suffering (v. 8), like a soldier.
4. We must consider undeserved suffering a means of God's perfecting us.

Gospel: Mark 10:35-45

Sermon Title: How To Secure Your Future

Sermon Angle: Last week, the gospel featured the rich man who fell at Jesus' feet, begging to know how to inherit eternal life. His earthly future was well feathered but he wanted to nail down eternity. "What must I do to inherit eternal life?" was the right question but the answer was unacceptable. He was unwilling to follow Jesus. In today's gospel, James and John were looking out for their future. They asked that Jesus would accord them the chief places of honor. They were asking the wrong question but they were willing to follow Jesus. All three men should be commended for trying to plan ahead. We, too, need to give serious thought to our future. The decisions we make now will determine what that future will be.

Outline:
1. Many Americans do estate and retirement planning to secure their future.
2. Securing our future has more to do with spiritual investments than financial ones.
3. The rich man in last week's gospel and James and John all wanted to secure their future. The latter two recognized that Jesus was their future.
4. We, too, need to plan for our future in God's kingdom by being a servant of Christ.

Sermon Title: What Do You Want Jesus To Do For You?

Sermon Angle: James and John asked that Jesus grant their request. "What do you want me to do for you?" he asked. Well, you know what they wanted. What do you want from Jesus? That's the question we need to put to ourselves and to our congregation. Do we want Jesus to make us rich and powerful? Do we want him to humiliate our foes? If so, we're asking the wrong things of Jesus. If, however, we want Jesus to make us more loving and forgiving and if we want him to grant us the strength to surmount our weaknesses, we are indeed making the right requests of Jesus.

Outline:
1. James and John petitioned for Jesus' favor (vv. 35-37).
2. They asked Jesus to do the wrong thing for them.
3. What are you seeking from Jesus? Is your desire purified of selfishness?
4. A sign of spiritual maturity is to make the right request of Jesus.

Sermon Title: How To Keep A Full Cup

Sermon Angle: I'm a coffee drinker; when I go to a restaurant I like a waitress who keeps my cup full. After James and John asked for their favor, Jesus asked them, "Are you able to drink the cup that I drink?" (v. 38). This meant, are you willing to take whatever God gives you and drink the contents fully? Are you willing to pour your life out for the world, as I am about to do? They answered affirmatively, even though they didn't really know what they were saying. Our lives are like cups. God promises that if we pour them out, God will keep on filling them up. He calls it servant leadership. *(This sermon could be illustrated with a large cup as a visual aid. Have a pitcher and a pan, also. Pour water into the cup as you explain that we like to have our lives full to overflowing. Then take a baster [siphon] and show how various demands seem to siphon off the contents of our cup [life]. Then show how, if we follow Jesus' concept of being a servant, as fast as we pour it out God pours it in. Tip the cup so that it flows into the pan but pour water into the cup from the pitcher at the same time.)*

Outline:
1. We all want our lives to be full. (Demonstrate with the cup and pitcher.)
2. Life seems to siphon off the content of our cup. (Demonstrate.)
3. We attempt to keep our cup full by taking it from someone else's cup.
4. Jesus teaches that the more we pour out our lives as servants, the more God pours back in. (Demonstrate by pouring it into a pan containing other cups.)

*   *   *   *   *

Brother Lawrence provides a treasured example of humble service, or servant leadership. He was a champion not of the grand way to God but the "little way"! For the last thirty years of his life, with his hands immersed in dishwater, he learned the discipline of prayer. Prayer itself is the link between all of life and the one who is life. And the "little way" is the path of those whose career is but an occupation and whose calling is knowing God.

God disappears when we insist on the limelight. No one is sent away empty from Christ except those who come to him full of themselves.

*   *   *   *   *

The arrogant person sees himself better than others while the person with a humble heart sees others as better than herself. James and John were yet to learn the lesson on humility; that exercise Jesus would teach them through his death and resurrection. Humility is often inflicted through defeat but is exceptional when a great triumph follows.

In 1994, Thurman Thomas, head bowed with his hands covering his face, sat on the Buffalo bench following his team's fourth straight Super Bowl loss. His three fumbles had helped seal the awful fate of his Buffalo Bills.

Suddenly, standing before him was the Dallas Cowboys' star running back, Emmitt Smith. Just named MVP for Super Bowl XXVIII, Smith was carrying his small goddaughter. Smith looked down at her and said, "I want you to meet the greatest running back in the NFL, Mr. Thurman Thomas."

Proper 25/Pentecost 23/Ordinary Time 30

Revised Common	Job 42:1-6, 10-17	Hebrews 7:23-28	Mark 10:46-52
Roman Catholic	Jeremiah 31:7-9	Hebrews 5:1-6	Mark 10:46-52
Episcopal	Isaiah 59:(1-4) 9-19	Hebrews 5:12—6:1, 9-12	Mark 10:46-52

Theme For The Day: God in Christ is ever available to hear and heed our cries for mercy.

BRIEF COMMENTARY ON THE LESSONS

Lesson 1: Job 42:1-6, 10-17 (C)

The story of Job comes to completion as the sufferer comes to acknowledge his own finitude and God's power. Job does not receive a direct answer to his questions but receives something better, the very presence of God. "I had heard of you by the hearing of the ear, but now my eye sees you" (v. 6). This verse contrasts knowledge of God from tradition with a more direct relationship of God, such as the prophets experienced. God instructs Job's friends to repent because of the bad counsel they rendered Job and to go to Job, that he might pray for them. After that, the fortunes of Job are restored and he has twice as much as before.

Lesson 1: Jeremiah 31:7-9 (RC)

See first lesson for Christmas 2.

Lesson 1: Isaiah 59:(1-4) 9-19 (E)

Lesson 2: Hebrews 7:23-28 (C)

This text compares the levitical priesthood to the priesthood of Christ. The first distinction is that the levitical priests ministered only during their lifetime while Christ's priesthood is eternal. Christ is then able to intercede for people of every generation. Another distinction is that earthly priests are sinners and their sacrifices have to atone for their own sins as well as the sins of their people. Christ was not infected with the blight of human sinfulness. The Son is made perfect forever, not only the perfect high priest but the perfect sacrifice for sin.

Lesson 2: Hebrews 5:1-6 (RC)

See second lesson for Proper 24.

Lesson 2: 5:12—6:1, 9-12 (E)

Gospel: Mark 10:46-52 (C, RC, E)

The healing of blind Bartimaeus presents a transition from Jesus' general ministry to the ministry of offering up his life in Jerusalem. Jesus is leaving Jericho when Bartimaeus started making a commotion because he heard that Jesus was passing by. He addresses Jesus by the messianic title "Son of David." The crowd tried to silence him but Jesus called the blind man to himself, asking what he desired. "Master, let me receive my sight," he requested. Jesus told him to go his way because his faith had made him well but Bartimaeus followed Jesus.

Psalm Of The Day
    Psalm 34:1-8 (19-22) — "I sought the Lord, and he answered me" (v. 4).
    Psalm 13 (E)
    Psalm 125 (RC)

Prayer Of The Day
    Gracious God, you sent your Son into the world to show us your mercy and to open our eyes to the light of your love. As you opened the eyes of the blind beggar, open our eyes through the power of faith, that we might see Jesus. In Jesus' name. Amen.

THEOLOGICAL REFLECTION ON THE LESSONS

Lesson 1: Job 42:1-6, 10-17
"I" trouble. The pronoun "I" comes up five times in this lection. This does not indicate egocentrism on Job's part but rather an intense awareness of his weaknesses and sinfulness. "I despise myself and repent in dust and ashes" (v. 6). In a sense, Job is confessing that he has "I" trouble. He was so focused on himself and his own suffering that he viewed God in a distorted light.

In over his head (v. 3). Job realizes that his desire to engage in philosophical discourse over his misfortunes put him in very deep water, far from shore. He was in over his head. "Therefore, I have uttered what I did not understand." Too many people permit their mouths to get ahead of their minds as they speak on subjects they know little about. The wise person knows the limits of his knowledge.

Firsthand experience (v. 5). Like most people, Job's experience of God was secondhand, but then Job encountered the Lord personally. "I had heard of you by the hearing of the ear but now my eye sees you." Job had wanted to lay everything on the table and have it out with the almighty but the actual experience of God's presence turned the tables on everything. The questions that were so pressing no longer were relevant because encountering God changed everything — his view of God, of life, and of himself.

Lesson 2: Hebrews 7:23-28
He gets the job done. The writer of Hebrews likes to contrast the incompleteness of the Judaic faith apart from Christ. The earthly priests were many because they were forced to lay aside their office through sin and death. In contrast, "He (Jesus) holds his priesthood permanently because he continues forever. He is able for all time to save those who approach God...." The sacrifices of the priests were imperfect because they had to be repeated but Jesus offered up himself for us as the one all-sufficient sacrifice (v. 27). All other religions are attempts to connect us with God but they are all incomplete. Jesus completes the work of salvation. He gets the job done.

Once for all (v. 27). Jesus offered himself for us once for all. The word "once" tells us that there is nothing we can add to the work of salvation that God offers us in Christ. Our sacrifices and good deeds cannot add to what God has already done for us; in fact, they detract from Christ's sacrifice if we think that we can earn his grace. This gives us a sense of assurance. There's nothing we have to do to be saved but to accept Christ. The word "all" is also instructive. Christ's sacrifice is not for only a few or for the enlightened, he offers himself and his salvation for all people. It's all wrapped up. Just open the package.

Gospel: Mark 10:46-52

Life was passing him by (v. 46). Bartimaeus was sitting by the side of the road, he was blind and a beggar, since he had to depend on the charity of others. Life was literally and figuratively passing him by. One day, an excited crowd was surging past him and he asked what was happening. Jesus of Nazareth is passing through, he was told. Bartimaeus had heard about this Jesus. He had restored sight to the blind and hearing to the deaf. Maybe he would do the same for him, if only he could let Jesus know of his need. Instinctively, he shouted at the top of his lungs "Jesus, Son of David, have mercy on me." Those around him found his shouts annoying and so they told him to shutup. But life was passing him by, Jesus was passing him by. He might never come this way again. Bartimaeus shouted all the more passionately. Jesus heard his plaintive plea and stopped the procession so that, for this man, life might no longer pass him by.

The cry above the crowd. It often happens that the individual gets swept away by the crowd. This story presents a refreshing reversal on that theme. The crowd is stopped by the insistent plea of the solitary individual, a poor man, a blind man, a beggar. The crowd was halted because Jesus heard the cry of Bartimaeus over the tumult of the multitude. This is particularly notable because Jesus was going to Jerusalem, where he would suffer and die for the sins of the world. One might expect that his mind would have been on his own troubles looming on the horizon. Ah, but Jesus' ears are finely tuned to hear the cries for mercy from even the lowliest of his little ones.

How to catch God's attention. Some people cry to God for mercy and it seems that he isn't listening. How does a person cry out to the Lord in such a manner that she will be heard? Do like Bartimaeus. Cry out as if your life depended on it. Don't let anything or anyone deter you by saying that God doesn't have time for your problems. You keep on praying, begging, or whatever it is that you have to do, until you arrest the attention of the almighty. The power of faith is an absolutely necessary prerequisite for catching and holding God's attention.

Extending Christ's invitation (v. 49). After Jesus heard the cries of Bartimaeus, he stopped in his tracks but he didn't go to the blind man. He ordered others to tell the blind man to come to him. Christ generally uses the invitations of others to draw men and women to himself. We in the church are called to extend Christ's gracious invitation to all who need Jesus' healing touch.

Second sight (v. 51). When Jesus asked Bartimaeus what he wanted, he begged to see *again*. This man was not blind his whole life. His eyes had once soaked in the beauty of God's creation. What he was asking for was the gift of second sight. I see this as a type of metaphor of our life with God. As a child, God created us to behold the beauty he has placed in us and around us. Sin and selfishness gradually blind us to the light of God's beauty and truth if we do not open our hearts to God's redeeming grace. Salvation opens the eyes of our mind and heart to behold wonders vaguely remembered.

SERMON APPROACHES WITH ILLUSTRATIONS

Lesson 1: Job 42:1-6, 10-17

Sermon Title: Getting More Than You Bargained For

Sermon Angle: When he was suffering, Job wanted an audience with the almighty to justify himself before God. Job was brought into the presence of God all right but it was not as he imagined. In the presence of God's holiness, he saw his own sinful condition. How foolish he was to think that he could go head to head with God. But God is gracious and gave Job much more than he bargained for; God gave him his grace through his very presence. In Jesus Christ, God grants us much more than we bargained for — his Son and salvation.

Outline:
1. Job wanted to justify himself to God and to get some answers.
2. God came to him and he realized how foolish he was (vv. 3-4).
3. Job got something better than he asked for — God himself (v. 5).
4. When we earnestly pray, God gives us more than we ask.

Sermon Title: All Is Well That Ends Well

Sermon Angle: Our text says that "The Lord blessed the latter days of Job more than his beginning ..." (v. 12). The writer goes on to catalogue all of the livestock that Job received. However, ending well has less to do with material prosperity than with spiritual maturity and wisdom. Through Job's trials, he moved from knowing *about* God (secondhand knowledge) to knowing God (firsthand knowledge). He also gained insight into his own being. It is wonderful to begin well but how much more important it is to end well. The latter days of those who remain faithful to the Lord are bound to be more blessed than the former days. Those who love the Lord for a lifetime will receive a rich harvest of blessings.

Lesson 2: Hebrews 7:23-28

Sermon Title: Always Accessible

Sermon Angle: Recently, I had trouble making contact with two different lawyers that I've dealt with. One has not returned my calls and the other didn't bother to show up for an appointment. Good legal counsel is not always available, not by a long shot. Unfortunately, the same can be said for many others in positions of responsibility and authority. Out text states that "... he always lives to make intercession for them" [us] (v. 25b). Christ is our eternally available high priest.

Outline:
1. Modern business caters to making things easily available and convenient.
2. Yet, the help we need is not always there when we need it.
3. Jesus is eternally available, so that we might reach him with our needs.

Sermon Title: It Is Finished!

Sermon Angle: "It is finished," Jesus cried as he completed his work of salvation on the cross. The author of Hebrews is fond of using the word *telios*, meaning perfect or complete. Jesus completed the work of redemption once for all, when he offered himself on the cross (v. 28). There's nothing we can add to it. It is indeed finished! All we need to do is accept the sacrifice of our heavenly high priest.

Gospel: Mark 10:46-52

Sermon Title: Beggars For Life

Sermon Angle: Bartimaeus had probably begged in public places for years. He begged for scraps and was only able to eke out a bare existence. He knew that he had almost no other options but to beg for the rest of his miserable life. Then Jesus passed his way and he was quick to recognize the wonderful opportunity afforded him. Perhaps Jesus could do for him what he is reputed to have done for others, restore his sight. He knew what he had to do, be a beggar for life; that is, he had to go for broke and not merely beg for a few coins or a few scraps. He was inwardly constrained to beg for his life. We are beggars, helpless to join eternity's procession, until Jesus calls us. We are blind until Jesus restores our inward sight. We must never settle for a few coins in our hands when we can possess heaven in our hearts. We truly are beggars for life.

Outline:
1. Bartimaeus begged for scraps, like many other poor people.
2. He knew that he would probably be a beggar all his life.
3. When Jesus came by, he was a beggar for his life (a new life).
4. Jesus healed him and he joined the procession of life, led by Jesus (v. 52).
5. We, too, are beggars for our lives and the lives of others. Don't let Jesus pass you by without receiving this gift of new life.

* * * * *

One of the Hebrew words for mercy, *racham*, is related to the word for womb. It has the connotation of the mother's affection for a child or a sibling's affection for his brothers and sisters. When Bartimaeus asked Jesus to have mercy on him, he was requesting the Lord to take him into his family and accept him as his dear child.

* * * * *

Sermon Title: The Poor Are People, Too

Sermon Angle: In many of our Lord's healing miracles, the person who is delivered is not named. The recipient of his sight had a name and his father had a name, Bartimaeus and Timaeus. Names give us identity, significance. Our names make us human, related to, but distinct from, every other individual. Oftentimes, the poor and unfortunates of this world appear as faces without names. Frequently they aren't even faces, because they are invisible. When we stop, as Jesus did, we find that the poor and disabled of this world are people, too.

Outline:
1. The poor and needy are often nameless and invisible.
2. Bartimaeus would have remained a nameless cipher if Jesus had not heard his cry.
3. Jesus heard Bartimaeus' cry, stopped, inquired into his need, and healed him.
4. Jesus recognized that the poor and disabled are people, too. Do we?

* * * * *

Zoe was supposed to join the Lutheran church on a certain November morning. Actually, she was supposed to have united with the congregation the week before but was prevented by a lingering case of pneumonia. I tried calling her toward the end of the week but couldn't reach her. Saturday, November 18, she called me about 11 p.m. She had just received my message. After apologizing for not responding sooner, she went on to explain what had happened. A friend had called from Utah earlier in the week. He was terminal with AIDS and didn't want to die in solitude. Because of his homosexuality, his Mormon family had rejected him; they would have nothing to do with him. "Would you please fly out?" he pleaded. At first, Zoe didn't see how she could get off work. After all, she had been absent from work two weeks or so due to the pneumonia. Her boss wouldn't let her go, she reasoned. As it turned out, her boss overheard the

374

conversation. Being gay himself, he identified with the man dying of AIDS. He told Zoe that she should go and not worry about her job. "If I were dying, I would surely want someone to be with me," he reasoned. Zoe flew to her friend, who asked if she could secure someone from the Mormon church to give him a final blessing. That church turned its back on the dying man. The friend also wanted to be baptized and so Zoe called the local Lutheran pastor, since that was her religious affiliation. This pastor put aside all judgment, came to the dying man, and baptized him. Zoe's friend relinquished his life a couple of days later and Zoe arranged a memorial service.

"What was I to do?" she exclaimed. "I don't really approve of the gay lifestyle but this man is my friend. How can you turn your back on a friend?"

"You did the right thing, the Christlike thing," I assured. The Bartimaeuses remain hidden along the busy thoroughfares of life, crying out for grace, love, and light. Christ heard the plaintive plea of the pariahs. Do we?

* * * * *

Sermon Title: The Danger Of Answered Prayer

Sermon Angle: Bartimaeus had no idea where his plea for mercy or his request to regain his sight would lead. Sometimes life might be more simple, if one were blind or had some disability that prevents a person from entering into the thick of life. There is a danger in having your prayer answered because it changes not just that one thing but everything. Jesus told Bartimaeus that he could go his way because his faith had healed him but the newly sighted Bartimaeus followed Jesus. Where was Jesus going? He was going to Jerusalem. What would happen in Jerusalem? He would be betrayed, arrested, convicted, and crucified. I believe that Bartimaeus became a follower of Jesus and witnessed all these things. How could he imagine what pain and sorrow he would see? Was he ever sorry that he had asked to receive his sight? When Jesus calls us to himself (v. 49) and when he opens the eyes of our soul (v. 52), we are never the same and life is never the same. Then, we see sin in all its horror and we enter into the pain and suffering of our Lord and of his people. Be careful what you earnestly seek from the Lord. It will change your life.

Outline:
1. The outcome of Jesus answering Bartimaeus' petition must have been far different than what he imagined.
2. Bartimaeus followed Jesus to Jerusalem and probably witnessed the horror of his crucifixion.
3. Seeing all those things transformed his life.
4. Fervent prayers are powerfully dangerous. They will change your life.

Reformation Day

Lutheran   **Jeremiah 31:31-34**   **Romans 3:19-28**   **John 8:31-36**

Theme For The Day: The church is renewed as it opens itself to the transforming power of the gospel of grace, through faith in Jesus Christ.

BRIEF COMMENTARY ON THE LESSONS

Lesson 1: Jeremiah 31:31-34

In Jeremiah 17:1, the prophet speaks of the sin of Judah being etched in stone with a diamond-tipped pen of iron. In this lection, the prophet asserts that God will cut a new covenant with his people, not written on parchment or etched in stone, but written on the human heart. God will bestow not only the desire but the power to do his will. This new covenant will be intrinsic rather than external. It will not be a covenant of judgment but of grace (v. 34).

Lesson 2: Romans 3:19-28

Paul lifts out the purpose of the law: to make us cognizant of our sins and our need for grace. No person will be accounted righteous by keeping the law of God. Nobody can earn salvation from keeping the law, since no one can observe it completely. The person who breaks part of it, is deemed guilty of it all. The good news proclaims that the righteousness of God is available to all people as a gift of grace. This righteousness becomes possible through Christ's atoning sacrifice. Through faith, we are deemed righteous and acceptable to God. Paul is anxious to establish not only our righteousness through the gospel but God's righteousness. The sacrifice of Christ shows that God takes sin seriously and dealt with it decisively through the cross (vv. 25-26).

Gospel: John 8:31-36

Jesus tells the Jews that they shall know the truth, which will make them free. They misunderstand and reply that they have never been in bondage to anyone. Their reply reveals a denial of their history. Jesus retorts that anyone who sins is in bondage to sin. Jesus, the Son, is the only one who can make people truly free from the bondage to sin and selfishness.

Psalm Of The Day

Psalm 46 — "God is our refuge and strength ..." (v. 1).

Prayer Of The Day

Renewing Spirit, we have let the power of sin capture us and hold us in bondage but your Son came into the world to set us free. Liberate us from a religion of mere formality and set our souls ablaze with a living faith that sheds light and warmth in our world. In Jesus' powerful name. Amen.

THEOLOGICAL REFLECTION ON THE LESSONS

Lesson 1: Jeremiah 31:31-34

Cut a covenant (v. 31). The English translation has it that Yahweh will make a new covenant. The Hebrew means literally "to cut." The image here is the cutting asunder of the sacrifice, so that the worshipers could walk between the parts. The new covenant also involved cutting; the flesh of Jesus, God's own Son, was pierced.

New covenant. Jeremiah, the prophet of doom and gloom, the weeping prophet, declares that the Lord will do a new thing. It will not be an act of destruction but a creative act. God will establish a new covenant with his people, not like the old one that they were unable to fulfill. This time, God will inscribe it on the human heart. The old covenant had served its purpose, to make the people aware of the holiness of God and of their own sinfulness. Now they were ready for something new.

Hope. The concept of new covenant is a profound example of hope at a time of national despair. The source of Jeremiah's hope is the graciousness of God. Note the theocentric character of this hope. "I will make ... I will put ... I will write...." Though God was roundly punishing his people, he was not abandoning them.

Regeneration. Jeremiah was not placing his hopes in the possibility of human reformation but in regeneration. Reformation can be seen as something basically extrinsic. You take the same old elements and put them together in a new fashion. Jeremiah put his hope in the Lord's regeneration of his people from the inside out.

Lesson 2: Romans 3:19-28

Accountable (v. 19). Paul maintains that the law of God makes the world accountable for their actions by publishing his law. We cannot claim ignorance, which would let us off the hook. We attempt to avoid being made accountable by giving excuses, putting the blame on somebody else.

A house of mirrors (v. 20). "... through the law comes knowledge of sin." Living with the law is like living in a house of mirrors; wherever we turn we see ourselves, warts and all. The law makes us cognizant of our sins.

No distinction (vv. 22-23). The law makes distinctions — this crime is a felony, this crime is a misdemeanor. The distinctions are sometimes meted out in years of punishment. However, as far as God is concerned, there are no distinctions. All have sinned. Sin is the great leveler. Some people may judge themselves better than other sinners but God doesn't see it that way.

The gift of grace (v. 25). Salvation comes through the atoning sacrifice of Christ, not by keeping the law. This is a key concept of Pauline theology, which Luther makes the centerpiece of his theology. Unfortunately, the notion of works righteousness dies hard because it's difficult on our ego to accept a free gift.

Gospel: John 8:31-36

To be continued (v. 31). Some of Jesus' disciples were ready to turn their backs to Christ and go back to their old ways. Jesus challenges them: "If you continue in my word, you are truly my disciples, and you will know the truth and the truth will make you free." Only those who continue with Jesus to the end of the journey establish that they are truly his disciples.

The quest for truth. The truth of which Jesus speaks is not all truth or truth in general but divine truth. However, no matter what kind of truth we are speaking of, it never comes easily.

The truth about life comes to those who struggle to find it. Scientific truth often comes through experimentation and observation. The truth of God comes through experience in relating the wisdom of the word to the world. Experience takes time; that's why Jesus points to the necessity of continuing with him.

Truth frees. Sin, corruption, and all forms of tyranny exist in an environment of lies and deceit. Psychological health, spiritual well-being, and sometimes physical health are dependent on discovering the truth. Jesus said, "I am the way, the *truth*, and the life, no one comes to the father but by me" (John 14:6).

SERMON APPROACHES WITH ILLUSTRATIONS

Lesson 1: Jeremiah 31:31-34

Sermon Title: Eden II

Sermon Angle: Jeremiah did not envision a new religion evolving from the old humanity and the old covenant. No, he was envisioning nothing short of the re-creation of humankind. He pictures something of a second Garden of Eden. Jeremiah saw that his people could not be saved through cosmetic surgery; they needed nothing less than a new heart, soul, and mind. While sinful humans can never re-create themselves, God can and does in Christ.

Outline:
1. Jeremiah could see that his prophetic ministry of bringing his people back to the Lord had failed. They had not changed and their unwillingness to repent had brought judgment upon themselves.
2. God informed Jeremiah that he was going to re-create his people — a second Eden. He would inscribe his law upon their hearts.
3. Our hope is in God.

* * * * *

On the television show *20/20*, they featured a woman who had set out to refashion herself in her own image. Or, maybe I should say, in the image of Barbie. Yes, that's right, she decided to reform her body into the likeness of a Barbie doll. After more than twenty plastic surgery operations, she is near her goal. She made the decision to re-create herself after her father died and left her some money. She decided that rather than blow the money on clothes or travel, she would use it to cut a new image. She wasn't born ugly. In fact, she had a very pleasant appearance. However, she observed that plain people didn't get any respect, while the beautiful people got all the perks. This real-life Barbie doll lives in London, where she has a business advising other people on the ins and outs of plastic surgery. She is now forty and fabulously beautiful, claiming to enjoy being admired and being the center of attention. She has a new body, a new face, but the same old heart. Only God can remake her heart.

* * * * *

Sermon Title: Prophets, One And All

Sermon Angle: Jeremiah places great importance on knowing the Lord personally. He predicts: "They shall all know me ..." (v. 34). In the prophetic era, God usually only spoke personally and intimately to his prophets. The great mass of the people only knew the Lord through his

378

laws and ordinances, passed on down through the generations. Jeremiah's revelation is that one day *all* of God's people would know the Lord personally, like the prophets. In a sense, all of the people would be prophets.

Outline:
1. The prophets were the only ones in Jeremiah's day who knew God directly. Other people knew of God through oral and written traditions.
2. Jeremiah envisions the time when all of God's people will know him like the prophets (v. 34).
3. In Christ, we have the new hearts Jeremiah foresaw. With these new hearts we know and love God intimately.

Lesson 2: Romans 3:19-28

Sermon Title: Not Guilty Is Not The Same As Being Righteous

Sermon Angle: After the Michael Jackson verdict, some people stated: "He is judged 'not guilty' but that doesn't make him innocent." "Not guilty" may mean that the jurors did not feel that the evidence was sufficient to establish guilt. According to the law, Jackson is not guilty but that doesn't mean that he was righteous. The justification that God offers in Christ means more than being acquitted, though guilty. His justification actually works to make us righteous by giving us the will and the strength to do that which God requires, through faith (v. 28).

Outline:
1. The verdict of "not guilty" does not ensure innocence or righteousness.
2. God declares us "not guilty" through faith in Christ, though we are not innocent.
3. God's righteousness can more than acquit us, it can transform us.

Sermon Title: There Are No Braggarts In Heaven

Sermon Angle: In verse 27, Paul returns to the subject of boasting. He submits that boasting is excluded, not on the basis of works but on the principle of faith. If heaven were awarded to all those who surpassed a certain baseline of righteousness, we might have good reason to boast. Some make it, others do not. Some would far exceed the minimum requirements, while others might barely squeak by. When we compare levels of human achievement, boasting, though never gracious, might be somewhat justified. When it comes to salvation, no one can boast because redemption comes as a gift of God. How can we boast about that which we have not achieved? That's why there won't be any braggarts in heaven.

Outline:
1. Works righteousness leads to pride and pride leads to boasting.
2. Paul maintains that Christians have no right to boast because our salvation is a gift.
3. If we must boast, boast of God's great love and grace.
4. There will be no boasting in heaven, because heaven will be populated only by those who are humble enough to accept God's gift of salvation, by faith.

*   *   *   *   *

Thomas Carlyle once referred to Martin Luther as "great, not as a hewn obelisk, but as an Alpine mountain, so simple, honest, spontaneous, not setting up to be great at all; there for another purpose than being great at all!" That "purpose" was, in Luther's mind, to preserve and proclaim God-given doctrine. The thought never rooted in Luther's mind that the doctrine for which he gave himself was his own creation. "It is not my doctrine, not my creation, but God's gift," he declared in a 1531 sermon. "Dear Lord God, it was not spun out of my head, nor grown in my garden. Nor did it flow out of my spring, nor was it born of me. It is God's gift, not a human discovery."

* * * * *

Gospel: John 8:31-36

Sermon Title: The Danger Of Turning Your Back On The Truth

Sermon Angle: Apparently, Jesus has more disciples at the height of his career than he did at the end. Some of them stopped believing. John refers to the Jews who *had* believed in him (v. 31). Jesus pleads with these disciples to continue in his word: "If you continue in my word, you are truly my disciples." Jesus pleads with them because their spiritual existence was in jeopardy. The danger, which Jesus wanted them to avert, was of losing their way in the darkness. They were about to turn their backs to the truth. Already they were living in an illusory world. They claimed that the Jews had never been in bondage. Jesus is talking about being in bondage to sin but their statement is a blatant denial of history. The danger of turning your back to the truth is that one is doomed to the land of shadows and illusions.

Outline:
1. Jesus pleaded with those who were about to leave him. Their souls were in grave danger.
2. The danger of turning away from the truth is that one is doomed to an illusory existence.
3. Martin Luther was grasped by the truth and then challenged a church riddled with illusory hopes for salvation (good works).
4. Let us cling to the truth of the gospel.

Sermon Title: I'm An Addict, You're An Addict

Sermon Angle: Jesus said: "Everyone who commits sin is the slave of sin." It sounds like an addiction to me. An addiction is a monster that has you by the throat and won't let go. The only way to gain the upper hand over an addiction is to, first of all, admit your weakness and your need for saving help. Sin is our addiction. We are all junkies. We want to be free from our addiction. Some of the time we're doing quite well and we think we have the monster on the run; then, he grabs us again with renewed vengeance. Our faith in Jesus probably won't free us from all desire to sin but it will give us the power to bind the dragon.

Outline:
1. Addiction is a huge problem.
2. We all know an addict — ourself! Our addiction is sin.
3. Talk about the "12-Step" program.
4. Have you admitted to Jesus your inability to be free of your addiction?

Sermon Title: Truth Isn't Free

Sermon Angle: Truth makes us free, as Jesus stated, but truth is never free. The price is dear. It costs us our prejudices, our illusions, our secret sins, some of our traditions, and our view of history, to name a few. Not only that, the truth will lead us to actions and stands that may not be popular. Look what it cost the Lord! Because of the high cost of truth, many folks prefer to live in a world of shadows. In order for Luther to encounter the truth, he had to be willing to challenge cherished traditions.

Outline:
1. Jesus challenges us to know the truth, saying that the truth will make us free.
2. Though the truth makes us free, it is not itself free.
3. Those who stood for the truth, like Luther, had to pay a price.
4. Certain disciples of Jesus were not willing to pay the price. Are you?

*   *   *   *   *

Faith is not what some people think it is. Their human dream is a delusion. Because they observe that faith is not followed by good works or a better life, they fall into error, even though they speak and hear much about faith. "Faith is not enough," they say. "You must do good works, you must be pious to be saved." They think that, when you hear the gospel, you start working, creating by your own strength a thankful heart that says, "I believe." That is what they think true faith is. But, because this is a human idea, a dream, the heart never learns anything from it, so it does nothing and reform doesn't come from this "faith," either.

Instead, faith is God's work in us that changes us and gives new birth from God (John 1:13). It kills the Old Adam and makes us completely different people. It changes our hearts, our spirits, our thoughts, and all our powers. It brings the Holy Spirit with it. Yes, it is a living, creative, active, and powerful thing, this faith. Faith cannot help doing good works constantly. It doesn't stop to ask if good works ought to be done, but before anyone asks, it already has done them and continues to do them without ceasing. Anyone who does not do good works in this manner is an unbeliever. He stumbles around and looks for faith and good works, even though he does not know what faith or good works are. Yet he gossips and chatters about faith and good works with many words. (Martin Luther: "An Introduction To Saint Paul's Letter To The Romans")

All Saints

Revised Common	Isaiah 25:6-9	Revelation 21:1-6a	John 11:32-44
Roman Catholic	Revelation 7:2-4, 9-12	1 John 3:1-3	Matthew 5:1-12
Episcopal	Sirach 44:1-10, 13-14	Revelation 7:2-4, 9-17	Matthew 5:1-12

Theme For The Day: Who are saints? Those who rely on God for comfort and salvation.

BRIEF COMMENTARY ON THE LESSONS

Lesson 1: Isaiah 25:6-9 (C)
Through his prophet, the Lord promises to make a joyous feast for his people on Mount Zion, replete with rich food and wine. God will remove the pall of gloom and sorrow by destroying death and personally wiping away the tears from the eyes of his people.

Lesson 1: Revelation 7:2-4, 9-17 (RC)
See second lesson, Episcopal.

Lesson 1: Sirach 44:1-10, 13-14 (E)

Lesson 2: Revelation 21:1-6a (C)
John's vision of the new heaven and new earth, predicted by Isaiah (65:17; 66:22): The sea, symbolic of unrest and turbulence, is no more. The new Jerusalem descends from heaven, with all the beauty of a bride. The voice of God himself is heard: "The home of God is among mortals. He will dwell with them and be their God; and they will be his people." As in Isaiah's vision, God will wipe the tears from their eyes; death, mourning, and crying will be done away.

Lesson 2: 1 John 3:1-3 (RC)

Lesson 2: Revelation 7:2-4, 9-17 (E)
John sees a heavenly vision. Hosts arrayed in white robes stand before the throne of God, singing praises. The seer is asked to identify the throne. He defers to the elder who asked him. He responds that these are the ones who have come out of the great tribulation and have been purified by the sacrifice of Christ. As in the previous two passages, God's living presence comforts and shelters the elect: They will hunger and thirst no more (v. 16).

Gospel: John 11:32-44 (C)
Jesus arrives at the home of Mary and Martha, four days after his friend, Lazarus, died. Mary greets Jesus with the words: "Lord, if you had been here, my brother would not have died." The words carry some sense of disappointment that Jesus' visit had not been more timely but they also convey her strong faith. Some of the crowd are also critical of Jesus. The Lord is moved to tears by the sorrow and weeping that he sees all around him. They go to the tomb and Jesus orders the stone removed. Mary cautions concerning the stench. Jesus challenges them to believe. He calls Lazarus forth from the tomb and when he appears, orders that the grave wrappings

be removed. Many people believe in Jesus but John also cites this incident as the direct cause for Jesus' arrest.

Gospel: Matthew 5:1-12 (RC, E)

The Beatitudes from the Sermon on the Mount. Those who humble themselves before God are the "blessed ones," the saints of God.

Psalm Of The Day

Psalm 24 (C) — "Who shall ascend the hill of the Lord? ... Those who have clean hands and pure hearts" (vv. 3a, 4a).
Psalm 149 (E)
Psalm 23 (RC)

Prayer Of The Day

In our baptism, you have set us apart for your service and made us your saints. By your Spirit, empower us to realize our calling and to follow the blessed example of those who have already inherited the crown of eternal glory. In the name of Jesus, whose blood makes us his and makes us holy. Amen.

THEOLOGICAL REFLECTION ON THE LESSONS

Lesson 1: Isaiah 25:6-9

Don't cut the fat from the feast (v. 6). As I write this, Christmas is a few weeks away. In yesterday's paper, an article about holiday feasting stated that the average American puts on two to five pounds over the holidays. The author contended that it isn't good to abstain from all rich holiday fare; that would make us grumpy and lead to binge eating. Instead, pick the rich foods you really like and compensate by abstaining from some other fattening delectables. The kingdom feast that God has prepared for all his people centers around rich food and fine drink. "A feast of rich food, a feast of well-aged wines...." Our celebration of life and love will know no constraint.

The shroud (v. 7). The Shroud of Turin has raised a great deal of controversy. Some people make a very convincing case for this being the burial cloth of Jesus. Shrouds or other forms of covering have traditionally clothed the dead. The purpose is to keep the contamination of death away from the living. The gospel text from John 11, the raising of Lazarus, vividly describes how the grave wrappings still clung to the resurrected disciple. Death casts a pall of fear over the face of the earth. In Christ, that pall is removed; death is swallowed up by the victorious Christ.

Death is a bitter pill to swallow (v. 7). Isaiah exalts that God will swallow up death forever. We are able to taste the feast of victory because Christ first tasted the poison of death for all people. It was a bitter pill indeed! Because Jesus freely swallowed death for our salvation, we can feast forever.

Lesson 2: Revelation 21:1-6a

It's a new ball game. The vision of Isaiah is of a new heaven and a new earth. In the new heavenly Jerusalem, the old rules won't apply anymore — no pain, sorrow, weeping, or death. Instead, God will dwell in the midst of his people, always visible, always accessible.

City of God (v. 2). The new life with God is described as a city. Sin separates us from one another but Christ redeems us to function as citizens of the city of God. Heaven is a community of grace, love, and forgiveness.

Lesson 2: Revelation 7:2-4, 9-17

Singing saints (v. 12). The saints in heaven are pictured singing praises to God. Saints on earth also have been known for their love of singing God's praises.

Songs of victory (v. 14). Who are these singing saints? "These are they who have come out of the great ordeal ..." (v. 14). No wonder they have a song in their hearts. With Christ, they have won the victory over sin and death.

Made in the shade (v. 16). "The sun shall not strike them, nor any scorching heat." Life can be experienced as a smoldering Death Valley-type experience. With Christ as our shepherd, leading us to cool waters, we have it made in the shade.

Gospel: John 11:32-44

What makes Jesus cry? When Jesus observed the grief and sorrow all around him, he was moved to tears. He wasn't crying that Lazarus was dead; death would not have the last word. He was weeping because of the pain that death caused the living. Jesus is touched by our sorrow.

Anger at God's absence. When Mary greeted Jesus, she knelt and stated: "Lord, if you had been here, my brother would not have died" (v. 32). Her confession of faith is laced with anger and disappointment. The unuttered question was: "Lord, why weren't you here? Where were you?" When God does not prevent life's tragedies, we have a tendency to be angry, to feel that God is detached from our lives.

The upward look (v. 41). After the tomb was opened, Jesus stood there, looked upward, and prayed. In the midst of betrayal, pain, sorrow, and death, he kept looking up. His upward look was conveyed not only by the position of his head or his eyes but his spirit. His prayer showed a spirit of thanksgiving and faith. He knew that the Father had already heard, had already reached out his hand to save. Nothing can destroy us if we keep the upward look.

Death binds us, Jesus frees us (v. 44). When Lazarus emerged from the tomb he was still bound by the grave clothes. Jesus ordered that he be unbound, that he be freed. Fear of death binds many of us. Only Jesus, through his resurrection, can free us and does free us.

Gospel: Matthew 5:1-12

Things aren't always what they seem. Those whom Jesus pronounces as the blessed ones are almost precisely the ones the world judges worthless. The world blesses strength, happiness, self-assertion, but Jesus considers those who are weak, who rely on God for strength, to be the truly blessed ones.

SERMON AP PROACHES WITH ILLUSTRATIONS

Lesson 1: Isaiah 25:6-9

Sermon Title: A Feast For All

Sermon Angle: Isaiah proclaims that the feast of God's kingdom is for *all* people. The rich and famous feast regularly but many people are excluded from the feast of life because of race, class, income, or other reasons. God's eschatological feast is to include all sorts of people. The

Eucharist is a foretaste of that heavenly feast for all who have been washed clean and made ready by the blood of Christ (Revelation 7:14). The community that gathers around Christ's table can never be satisfied to let some hapless souls eat the crumbs that fall from our table.

Outline:
1. Isaiah proclaims a feast for all people (v. 6).
2. The fulfillment of that prophecy is in Christ.
3. If we feast on salvation around God's eucharistic table, how can we be content for others to eat scraps from the dinner table of life?

Sermon Title: Handkerchiefs From Heaven

Sermon Angle: You've seen the movies where the hero hands his dewy-eyed woman companion his handkerchief. Isaiah holds up a moving image of God wiping away tears from all eyes (v. 8). Scripture testifies that the Lord is moved by our sorrows. He reaches out to tenderly daub our tear-stained cheeks.

Outline:
1. This is the day we give special effort in remembering our departed saints and loved ones.
2. Three of the lessons picture God as being moved by our sorrows.
3. In this text, God wipes away the tears from all sorrowing ones (v. 8).
4. We could say God is our handkerchief from heaven.
5. We too are handkerchiefs from heaven — sent to comfort those who mourn.

Lesson 2: Revelation 21:1-6a

Sermon Title: The One Funeral For Which There Will Be No Weeping

Sermon Angle: All of the lessons for All Saints lift up the prospect of the time when death will itself die. At the funeral of death, there will be no weeping, only rejoicing. The first order of business, when God gathers his people into the kingdom, is to lay death to eternal rest. This and other lections for today could celebrate the death of death. A fitting topic for celebrating the lives of departed saints.

Outline:
1. Death will be no more; God will wipe away every tear (v. 4).
2. God will swallow up death (Isaiah 25:7).
3. Jesus raises Lazarus from the grave (John 11:32-44).
4. We celebrate the death of death when we celebrate the saints.

Lesson 2: Revelation 7:2-4, 9-17

Sermon Title: A Passing Mark

Sermon Angle: The heavenly scene reminds me somewhat of a great commencement exercise that celebrates the successful conclusion to years of hard labor, sweat, and tears. Those assembled there have received a passing mark. The four destroying angels are told not to harm the earth until the servants of God have received God's mark on their forehead. This mark would enable them to pass into the kingdom of God (v. 3). Those at a commencement wear robes; so, too, the elect wear white robes, cleansed by the blood of Christ. Those at a commencement might sing a school song and those in the heavenly commencement sing a song of salvation and praise.

Outline:
1. The heavenly scene features all those who have received a passing mark (v. 3). The mark was awarded not because of their goodness but because they clung to God's grace.
2. The privilege of wearing the white robe, like studying for a degree, goes to those who endure. Life is an ordeal which tries our faith (v. 14). Heaven is the prize for those who hang in there.
3. In the heavenly commencement we will sing songs of victory and praise (v. 12).

Gospel: John 11:32-44

Sermon Title: Death In Christ: The Ultimate Healing

Sermon Angle: It's plain that Mary and many others who were at Mary and Martha's home felt that Jesus should have come while Lazarus was still alive, to heal him. "Could not he who opened the eyes of the blind man have kept this man from dying?" (v. 37). For them, it was too late. There was nothing Jesus could do now. They were clearly wrong. Death is the ultimate healing for those who are disciples of Christ. We awake from the sleep of death into the realm where there is no pain or sorrow or death.

Outline:
1. Many of the Jews felt that Jesus should have come to heal Lazarus (v. 37).
2. Jesus purposely waited for Lazarus to die, so he could demonstrate his power to raise the dead and give glory to God (v. 40).
3. We may have prayed for God to heal a loved one and he didn't.
4. Death in Christ is the ultimate healing — it leads to a life free of pain and sorrow.

Sermon Title: The Stench Of Death

Sermon Angle: Those who lived near the Nazi death camps constantly had the stench of death in their nostrils, though most of them didn't realize what it was. Death does have a stench to it. Death stinks! The very idea of death makes our blood curdle and our flesh recoil. When Jesus ordered the stone to be removed from the entrance to the tomb, Mary warned that there would be a stench of death and deterioration. Jesus did not let the stench of death keep him from confronting that ugly spook. The stench of death yielded to the sweet smell of life as Lazarus emerged from the tomb.

Outline:
1. Mary warned Jesus about the stench of death (v. 39). Most of us would agree that death stinks.
2. Jesus challenges her to believe even in the face of death (v. 40).
3. Jesus confronts death with faith and prayer (vv. 40-44).
4. Lazarus still had to die one day but the stench of death had been replaced with the sweet scent of eternal life and love.
5. Faith in Jesus transforms the stench of death.

*   *   *   *   *

The Hapsburgs ruled in Europe for centuries, but the funeral of Emperor Franz-Josef I of Austria, who died in 1916, marked the last of the lavish imperial funerals. A processional of the rulers of this world and other dignitaries escorted the coffin, draped in the black and gold imperial colors. The cortege was accompanied by military bands intoning somber dirges. By the light of torches, they descended the stairs of the Capuchin Monastery in Vienna. At the bottom was a great iron door leading to the Hapsburg family crypt. Behind the door was the Cardinal-Archbishop of Vienna.

The officer in charge enacted the prescribed ceremony, formed centuries before. "Open!" he cried.

"Who goes there?" replied the Cardinal. "We bear the remains of his Imperial and Apostolic Majesty, Franz-Josef I, by the grace of God Emperor of Austria, King of Hungary, Defender of the Faith, Prince of Bohemia-Moravia, Grand Duke of Lombardy, Venezia, Styrgia...." The officer continued to list the Emperor's 37 titles.

"We know him not," rejoined the Cardinal. "Who goes there?" The officer spoke again, this time using a much abbreviated and less pretentious title.

"We know him not," the Cardinal said again. "Who goes there?" The officer made a third attempt, depriving the emperor of all but the humblest of titles: "We bear the body of Franz-Josef, our brother, a sinner like us all!"

At that, the doors swung open, and Franz-Josef was admitted.

In death, we are all equal. Wealth and accomplishment cannot open the way of salvation. The door of death opens only by God's grace, to those who know and love Jesus. Jesus calls forth from the tomb those who humbly confess their need.

* * * * *

Gospel: Matthew 5:1-12
Sermon Title: The Blessings Of Godly Grief
Sermon Angle: Jesus pronounces those who mourn to be blessed (v. 4). These will receive God's comfort. But is that really true? A sermon devoted to the topic of good and godly grief could prove very beneficial to your congregation, since nobody is spared the pangs of grief and loss. What are these blessings?
Outline:
1. Godly grief helps us to draw closer to God and to identify with Jesus' suffering and death.
2. Godly grief makes us more humble (destroys the Superman complex).
3. Godly grief draws us closer to one another.
4. Godly grief helps us cut loose from this world and prepares us for heaven.

* * * * *

Philip Yancey, a writer for *Christianity Today*, tells of a group of friends in Minnesota who gathered every New Year's Eve with seven other couples to celebrate the gift of life. They would discuss how the year had gone and attempt to ascertain where God had been in their lives. One man suggested that each couple would try to live out one of the Beatitudes during the coming year. They agreed and so each Beatitude was inscribed on a piece of paper and put into a hat. Each couple drew one out but did not divulge which one they pulled. When they gathered on New Year's Eve, they made a game of guessing which Beatitude the others had received. Without exception, they were able to discern which Beatitude the others had taken by the manner of their lives. It goes to show that Jesus' standards of saintliness are within the realm of possibility. None of us will ever perfectly embody these characteristics completely but if we are obedient to God's Spirit, we can be transformed not only in thought but in character.

Proper 26/Pentecost 24/Ordinary Time 31

Revised Common	Ruth 1:1-18	Hebrews 9:11-14	Mark 12:28-34
Roman Catholic	Deuteronomy 6:2-6	Hebrews 7:23-28	Mark 12:28-34
Episcopal	Deuteronomy 6:1-9	Hebrews 7:23-28	Mark 12:28-34

Theme For The Day: Getting back to the basics, to love God with one's entire being and to love the neighbor as oneself.

BRIEF COMMENTARY ON THE LESSONS

Lesson 1: Ruth 1:1-18 (C)

This story, known by even the biblically illiterate, finds its setting during the time of the judges. Elimelech and his wife, Naomi, migrate to Moab, probably for economic reasons, where they settle. Their two sons marry Moabite wives. During the course of time, all of the men in Naomi's family die. She hears that there is food in the land of her origin and decides to return to her roots. Ruth and her two daughters-in-law start trekking back to Judah but Naomi has second thoughts about her daughters-in-law returning with her. Thinking that they would be better off in their own country, she instructs them to go back to the homes of their origin. Orpah tearfully parts from Naomi but Ruth refuses to leave and vows to accompany her until death. This text provides a classic story of friendship and loyalty.

Lesson 1: Deuteronomy 6:2-6 (RC); Deuteronomy 6:1-9 (E)

Lesson 2: Hebrews 9:11-14 (C)

The author of Hebrews continues his comparison of the ministry of Christ with that of the Jewish religion. This lection compares the earthly religious sanctuary, where priests offered repeated sacrifices, to the heavenly sanctuary, where Christ offered his own blood, in atonement for the sins of humanity. The purpose of sacrifice was to purify but the sacrifices of the Jewish religion were not intended to remove the contagion of willful sin but to cleanse a person from an unintentional sin or from breaking a taboo, such as touching a dead body. The sacrifice of Christ removes more than a ceremonial impurity, it removes the moral adulteration of our soul; "... how much more will the blood of Christ purify our conscience from dead works ..." (v. 14). Cleansed by Christ's blood, we can worship God freely.

Lesson 2: Hebrews 7:23-28 (RC, E)

See second lesson for Proper 25.

Gospel: Mark 12:28-34 (C, RC, E)

Jesus finds himself in a lively dispute with the scribes, who interpreted the oral law. A particular scribe steps from the fringes of the debating party and asks Jesus which commandment is the "first of all." Jesus answers with the Shema (Deuteronomy 6:4-9), "Hear, O Israel: the Lord our God, the Lord is one; you shall love the Lord ..." but links to it the commandment to love one's neighbor as yourself. The scribe agreed with Jesus' response, which showed that he wasn't there just to justify his own position but to find the truth; he adds to what Jesus has brought forth the prophetic observation that such love is better than sacrifice. Jesus respected the man's integrity and told him that he was not far from the kingdom of God. The opposition fell silent.

Psalm Of The Day
>   **Psalm 146 (C)** — "I will praise the Lord as long as I live" (v. 2).
>   **Psalm 119:1-16 (E)**
>   **Psalm 17 (RC)**

Prayer Of The Day
God of grace, remove from our lives all that distracts us from that which is ultimate and foundational; that is, to love you body and soul and to love our neighbor as we love ourselves. In the great name of Jesus we pray. Amen.

THEOLOGICAL REFLECTION ON THE LESSONS

Lesson 1: Ruth 1:1-18

Widow's might. The story of Ruth is a saga of a widow's strength and determination. Not that Naomi envisioned going off on her own; after all, she had decided to reconnect with her family and her homeland. Nevertheless, she didn't want to encumber her daughters-in-law, urging them to return to their families. She had the confidence to take what life gave her and move on. Ruth also was a widow who showed great strength of character, refusing to part with Naomi.

Finding security (v. 9). Naomi ordered Orpah and Ruth to return to their ancestral homes in order to find security. Being connected with a family was a person's only security, especially for women. Orpah realized this and opted for security rather than a life of uncertainty with Naomi. Ruth, on the other hand, made security secondary to the loyalty and love she felt for Naomi. Love empowers a person to take risks.

Love that sticks (v. 14). "Orpah kissed her mother-in-law but Ruth clung to her." Both women truly loved Naomi; the thought of severing the relationship pulled at their heartstrings. Ruth's love was superior because it transcended emotion, it was a total commitment of herself to the older woman. It was truly a love that stuck.

Lesson 2: Hebrews 9:11-14

Priest of the past and present (v. 11). This verse is translated by some authorities: "Christ came as the high priest of the good things that have come" but other interpreters translate it "are to come." I like to think that Christ is the mediator and priest of the good things in both the past and the future. He is our eternal high priest.

The new and improved high priest (vv. 13-14). Manufacturers are always touting their products as being new and improved. The writer of Hebrews makes the same claim for Christ. The old priestly system could cleanse a person ceremonially, so that he could join in the community worship, but the sacrifice of Christ cleanses us in every way, so that we can stand eternally in God's presence.

Gospel: Mark 12:28-34

A pair of imperatives. Jesus summarized what God expected out of his people with a pair of imperatives. To love God and to love our neighbor is a command. The principles upon which the moral universe runs are not negotiable. They are commands! To love the Lord and the neighbor have little to do with feelings and everything to do with obedience.

Theological consensus. The scribe and Jesus reached theological consensus and Jesus informed the man that he was not far from the kingdom of God. Theological consensus is good because theology is a road map that tells us which streets are dead ends and which streets lead us to eternal life. However, we do not inherit eternal life merely by knowing the truth but only by living the truth. Too many theologically astute scholars equate knowledge of God with the experience of God.

Close only counts in horseshoes. Jesus told the scribe that he was not far from the kingdom of God (v. 34) but he didn't say that close was good enough. Let's say that a person is caught in a blizzard and he thinks he knows where home is but isn't sure. After wandering a long time, he lies down to rest and never wakes up. His family finds him the next day; he was only 100 feet from home, within a stone's throw of safety. His family wouldn't take comfort in the fact that he was so close to home; this fact would only increase their anguish. Being just outside heaven's gates is still outside.

The unitive principle (v. 29). In answer to the scribe's inquiry, Jesus repeats the prime article of Jewish faith, the *Shema*, which states that the Lord is ONE, the essence of God is not to be divided or separated. "You shall love the Lord your God with all your heart, with all your soul, with all your mind and with all your strength" (v. 30). Our love of God must remain whole and focused. Not only is God "one" but our love for God and our neighbor are also connected. You can't love one without the other. Our love of God and of mankind flow from the same river.

SERMON APPROACHES WITH ILLUSTRATIONS

Lesson 1: Ruth 1:1-18

Sermon Title: Three Strikes And She's Not Out

Sermon Angle: Naomi had three tremendous strikes against her during the decade she sojourned in the land of Moab. One by one, she was bereft of her husband and her two sons. Did she go back to the bench and cry about the unfairness of the game of life? No, she kept on swinging. She was not a quitter and neither was Ruth.

Outline:
1. In baseball, three strikes and you're out. Many states have adapted the same rule for those who commit serious crimes.
2. Naomi had three strikes against her but kept on swinging.
3. Faith in God keeps us swinging when life throws us strikes.

Sermon Title: Linked For Life

Sermon Angle: The philosophy of our time suggests that strength is demonstrated when the solitary individual asserts himself against the world. The Bible teaches that strength comes through relationships. Ruth might have figured that she would have been better off not to be saddled with an old woman in a strange land. Ruth was determined to link her life to her mother-in-law's for life. Love links us to other people, it links us to life. The bond of love is the source of our strength.

Lesson 2: Hebrews 9:11-14

Sermon Title: Once And For All

Sermon Angle: This passage speaks of the tent (tabernacle) and the Holy Place, which was contained in the tabernacle. The tent referred to is the body of Christ, the holy place is the cross, where Christ shed his blood and offered his life for the sins of the world. Christ entered once and for all into this holy place (v. 12). The work of salvation is complete, except that we must appropriate Christ's sacrifice for ourselves. We don't ever have to doubt our salvation; it's been accomplished once and for all.

Outline:

1. The sacrifices of the Jewish religion did not completely purge sin and had to be repeated.
2. The high priest would go into the Holy Place in the temple once a year to offer sacrifices for his sins and those of the people.
3. Jesus went to the Holy Place (the cross) once and for all (v. 12).
   — His sacrifice is good for all time and for all people.
4. Let us worship and live confidently because we are covered by Christ's sacrifice.

Sermon Title: Christianity Is A Bloody Religion

Sermon Angle: The cross and sacrifice are at the heart of the Christian faith. Ours is a bloody religion. Christianity is not the first to stress the importance of blood sacrifice but is the only religion that claims that, in some mysterious way, God offered himself as a sacrifice for our sins. The writer of Hebrews stresses the superiority of Christ's sacrifice over those of the Jewish faith but there are those who would like to have us throw out this whole bloody business. They would have us sanitize the Christian faith and present Jesus as only a prophet or teacher. The arguments made in Hebrews may seem strange and archaic to modern ears.

Gospel: Mark 12:28-34

Sermon Title: He Asked The Right Question

Sermon Angle: A lot of problems and misunderstandings stem from the fact that often we don't ask the right question, the question that hones in on the target. Jesus found himself in a theological dispute with a bunch of scribes, which apparently was going nowhere until a wise scribe put forth the right question. He inquired as to the identity of the principle of truth from which all others derive. "Which commandment is the first of all?" (v. 28). Jesus answered that question, the scribe agreed and there was no more discussion (v. 34). Today, many people are asking the wrong questions, such as "How can I find happiness?" Only when we ask the right question will we receive the right answers. The rest is up to us.

Outline:

1. In the theological debate, the scribes were not asking the key question.
2. The scribe who asked Jesus to define the "first commandment" brought the discussion to a resolution.
3. What is the question that guides your life?
4. Is your life guided by your desires or God's imperatives?

* * * * *

For fourteen centuries, astronomers were all asking the wrong question: "How do the sun and the planets revolve around the earth?" No one thought that the question itself might be wrong until a man by the name of Copernicus came along. Without any proof, he posited that it was likely that the earth and the other planets revolved around the sun. For raising this novel question, he was condemned as a heretic by the church.

For two decades, a professor of law put this equation on the chalkboard:

$$\frac{3}{2}$$

He would inquire: "What's the solution?" A hand would raise. "One." A voice would then chime in, "Five." The professor would not acknowledge these responses. Finally, someone would call out the final possibility. "Six." The teacher would shake his head disapprovingly and state: "None of you have raised the key question: What is the problem?" Without posing the right question, a person cannot expect to come up with the correct answer.

* * * * *

The fable is told of the lion who thought very highly of himself but seemed to need his ego massaged by the other beasts in the jungle. The lion came upon a little mouse and roared, "Who's the king of the jungle?" "You are!" he squeaked. Next the lion crossed paths with a baboon. "Who's the king of the jungle?" he bellowed. "You are!" hooted the baboon. Finally, he came across an elephant. "Who's the king of the jungle?" The words were scarcely out of his mouth when the elephant picked him up, twirled him around his head, and set him flying like a Frisbee. The lion landed with a terrible thud, fifty feet away. The lion, dazed and shaken, rose slowly to his feet. "You didn't have to blow your top just because you didn't know the answer to the question."

* * * * *

Sermon Title: Give Your Whole Offering

Sermon Angle: The commandment that Jesus described as of first importance uses the Greek word *holos* (whole, complete) repeatedly. "You shall love the Lord your God with your whole heart, your whole soul, your whole mind, and your whole strength," states Jesus. The scribe repeats these words in his reiteration of the commands but adds that to love God wholly is better than whole burnt offerings. This means that to offer up our lives completely as a sacrifice of worship is superior to giving to God a costly object through liturgical worship. Giving to God your whole offering doesn't mean to give your tithe but your whole being to God. That's what's of first importance.

Outline:

1. Are you holding back on your offering to the Lord? No, I don't mean your tithe, I mean your body, your life.
2. Jesus indicates that our first duty is to love God with our whole heart, whole soul, whole mind, and whole strength.
3. The scribe added that loving God wholly is better than generous liturgical offering (v. 33).
4. Have you given God your whole life?

Sermon Title: Keep It Simple, Stupid!

Sermon Angle: There were two contradictory tendencies among the ancient Jewish rabbis. On the one hand, they would add a host of interpreting rules and precepts to the major laws. On the other hand, there was a tendency to distill the commands down to their essence. Jesus felt most comfortable with the latter tendency. He felt that many of the laws of the Pharisees and the scribes were burdensome. Because of this, he issued his gracious invitation found in Matthew 11:28-30. A cardinal rule for journalism is "Keep it simple, stupid!" When we communicate that faith, we must abide by the same admonition. The precept to love God with everything we are and our neighbor as ourselves is eminently simple to comprehend, yet profoundly difficult to carry out. Only those who are possessed by the Spirit of Christ can accomplish it.

Outline:

1. Many of the scribes and Pharisees tried to complicate religion and take it out of the reach of simple people.
2. The scribe who asked the question (v. 28) wanted to get back to the basics.
3. Jesus simplifies what God requires into one word, "Love."
   — Love the Lord.
   — Love your neighbor.
4. Such love is possible when Christ lives in us.

Proper 27/Pentecost 25/Ordinary Time 32

Revised Common	Ruth 3:1-5; 4:13-17	Hebrews 9:24-28	Mark 12:38-44
Roman Catholic	1 Kings 17:10-16	Hebrews 9:24-28	Mark 12:38-44
Episcopal	1 Kings 17:8-16	Hebrews 9:24-28	Mark 12:38-44

Theme For The Day: Security. Naomi provided security for herself and Ruth through family connections. In the gospel, the widow gave away all she had because she discovered her security in trusting God.

BRIEF COMMENTARY ON THE LESSONS

Lesson 1: Ruth 3:1-5; 4:13-17 (C)

Recognizing the need for security, Naomi instructs Ruth in the proper customs of obtaining a suitable husband. She is told to bathe, anoint herself, and put on her best clothes. Then she is to go and lie at the feet of Boaz, one of the near kin of her husband. Marriages were arranged by parents and Naomi is serving in this role. When Boaz awoke, he accepted the obligation of marrying Ruth, after purchasing Naomi's lot. Marriage was not a matter of romance but a business transaction. After Boaz and Ruth marry, Ruth bears a son. Some interpret verses 14-17 as a ceremony whereby Naomi adopts Ruth's child as her own, who replaces her dead sons. The book of Ruth assumes importance in the Old Testament canon because Ruth's son, Obed, is the grandfather of King David.

Lesson 1: 1 Kings 17:10-16 (RC); 1 Kings 17:8-16 (E)

Lesson 2: Hebrews 9:24-28 (C, RC, E)

Christ's sacrifice is the real thing (v. 24). The ceremonies conducted in the Jewish religion were mere prototypes or shadows of the heavenly reality. This text claims that Christ's offering of himself was not a copy but the real thing, that Christ interceded on our behalf not in a man-made temple, but heaven itself.

God offers himself for our sin (v. 26). Sin is serious business. It leads to death. In order to save us from the consequence of sin, God offered up his own life in the person of his Son.

The second coming of Christ (v. 28). Christ came to deal with sin through offering up his life as a sacrifice. When he returns, it will be to receive those who those who have accepted his salvation and to usher them into his eternal kingdom.

Gospel: Mark 12:38-44 (C, RC, E)

This gospel continues to portray the conflict between Jesus and the scribes. He warns against the prideful hypocrisy so characteristic of their behavior. They love to go about in long robes, pray pretentious prayers, and be seen in the places of honor. They act piously but their behavior doesn't square with their image. "They devour widow's houses" (v. 40). For such spiritual sinning, they will receive a greater judgment than others. In contrast to their behavior, Jesus observes a destitute widow put all the money she had into the temple coffers. Though she gave practically nothing, it was more than the large sums of the wealthy. The two copper coins represented the giving of her whole self to God.

Psalm Of The Day
   Psalm 127 (C) — "Unless the Lord builds the house, those who build it labor in vain" (v. 1).
   Psalm 146 (E)
   Psalm 145 (RC)

Prayer Of The Day
   Merciful Lord Jesus, we thank you for your compassion, which reaches out to the poor and those without any visible means of support. Make us also instruments for lifting up those laid low by the misfortunes of life. In Jesus' merciful name. Amen.

THEOLOGICAL REFLECTION ON THE LESSONS

Lesson 1: Ruth 3:1-5; 4:13-17
   Homemaker (v. 1). Naomi was a homemaker. She realized that Ruth needed a home and family and she regarded it as her responsibility to help her obtain it.
   No generation gap (v. 5). Ruth explicitly and freely obeyed her mother-in-law. There was no generation gap then, because elders were respected as repositories of knowledge and wisdom. In our day, when young people are generally more knowledgeable concerning technology, those who set the tone for society seem to feel that other kinds of knowledge are insignificant. Unfortunately, they tend to discount the wisdom and knowledge that comes through experience.
   Love child (v. 15). So many children today are not conceived in love. Obed was a love child, more the product of the love of two women than of a man and woman. Obed was particularly precious to Naomi because he was borne by a daughter she loved better than life itself. The love of these two women led to life, for them and generations to come.
   God of the gaps (v. 15). When the men in the lives of Naomi and Ruth died, it left a large gap in their existence. The word for "widow" means literally to be bereft, to be without, to have a large gaping empty space in one's life. Yet, these women trusted God to fill this gap, which he did in the fullness of time.

Lesson 2: Hebrews 9:24-28
   He removes our sins, not our lives (v. 26). Jesus offered his life to God for us, so as to remove our sins, not our lives.
   An appointment you won't forget (v. 27). A couple of weeks ago, my wife and I had an appointment with our attorney to do some estate planning. He didn't show up. Few things bug me more than a missed appointment. The writer of Hebrews reminds us of a fact we would just as soon forget: We have an appointment with death. "It's appointed a person once to die...."
   Final evaluation (v. 27). "... and afterward the judgment." Most anywhere you work or go these days, someone is either evaluating you or asking you to evaluate him. Good feedback is a prerequisite of constructive change. Evaluation is nothing more or less than critical judgment. The Bible speaks of the final judgment, which sends shivers up the spine for many people. It's true that those without faith will not be judged acceptable, but I think that we should view our final judgment as an evaluation to help us grow eternally.

Gospel: Mark 12:38-44

Playing for the house (vv. 38-40). Jesus accused the scribes of being actors, playing a part, not living the life of faith. Everything they did was calculated to impress the audience, to bring down the house with applause. They wore garish garments to gain notice and loved long prayers. Wherever they went, they searched for the most visible and honorable places. God despises phoniness!

Nothing but the best (v. 39). Movie magazines and television shows like *Lifestyles Of The Rich and Famous* on television showcase the sumptuous lifestyles of celebrities. Nothing but the top of the line is good enough for them. Millions of people of common means drool over their goodies, imagining what it would be like to have what they have, to live as they live. For the scribes that Jesus referred to, nothing but the best was good enough for them either. The best clothes, the choicest seats, and the ultimate in respect and admiration. It's fine to want nothing but the best. The question is: Who defines what the best is? Is it God's word or is it the world?

Beyond the best (vv. 42-44). The widow didn't give merely her best to the Lord, she gave her all. She offered herself as a living sacrifice to God. What she had to give may not have been that much but it was beautiful to the Lord.

Jesus is watching what we give (v. 41). Church members often say that what they give is between God and them. I have a feeling that if a study were conducted comparing their offerings to that of the church population as a whole, the former group would contribute substantially less. Jesus apparently didn't feel that what God's people offer up to his work is a matter of indifference. Jesus situated himself opposite the temple treasury and observed what people placed in the chest. It's a rather discomfiting thought that Jesus is watching us as we put our offerings in the plate, especially if our gift is a mere token.

Sacrifice catches Christ's notice, not pretense (vv. 43-44). It's ironic that those who wanted to catch God's notice, and the attention of everyone else (the scribes), only earned Jesus' condemnation. But the widow, who quietly did her thing and gave all she had, found herself in the limelight. Jesus called attention to her giving because it was from the heart, the sacrifice of her very being. People may or may not notice such selfless giving but God does.

SERMON APPROACHES WITH ILLUSTRATIONS

Lesson 1: Ruth 3:1-5; 4:13-17

Sermon Title: Future Builders

Sermon Angle: Naomi was a builder of the future. She didn't live life just for herself but realized that it was her obligation to get the next generation established. That's why she came up with the scheme to unite Ruth with her kinsman, Boaz. Any society that does not give prime consideration to building the future for the next generations is derelict and will eventually self-destruct.

Outline:
1. Naomi felt bound to secure a home and a future for Ruth (v. 1).
2. God calls us to be future builders.
3. Because of her compassion and wisdom, their future was reborn (vv. 13-17).
4. What are we doing, individually and corporately, to build a future for the next generation?

Sermon Title: Winnowing Widow

Sermon Angle: The story takes place at the time of the barley harvest. Boaz and his helpers winnowed the grain in the evening, when the breezes blew from the Mediterranean Sea. When the winnowers would throw the grain into the air, the wind would blow away the lighter chaff from the more dense heads of grain. Separating that which is valuable and nourishing from that which is not goes on in all avenues of life. Naomi had done some winnowing for herself and had determined that Boaz was a worthy husband for Ruth. When Boaz found Ruth at his feet and determined that she wanted him to marry her, he also recognized that Ruth was no piece of chaff (3:11). A sermon on choosing your mate could be preached from this text. Many marriages fail because some people are willing to settle for chaff.

Lesson 2: Hebrews 9:24-28

Sermon Title: What Christ Accomplished For Us

Sermon Angle: Hebrews is big on Christology, relating what Christ has accomplished for us through his death and resurrection. Here are three things that Christ promises to accomplish for us.

Outline:
1. Christ intercedes on our behalf before God's throne (v. 24).
2. He offers himself as the final sacrifice for our sin (v. 26).
3. He will come to receive us to himself (v. 28).

Sermon Title: It Is Finished For Good!

Sermon Angle: The text contends that the sacrificial work of Christ does not need to be repeated (v. 25). One of the words Jesus uttered from the cross is "It is finished!" Even before the resurrection, Jesus was confident that everything that needed to be done for our salvation had already been accomplished. We cannot add anything or take anything away. All we can do is appropriate what Christ has already completed.

Outline:
1. When Jesus died on the cross, he cried, "It is finished!"
2. Jesus did not need to offer himself repeatedly (v. 25).
3. Sin has been dealt a fatal blow by his sacrifice (v. 26).
4. Do not think to add to Christ's sacrifice through your good deeds but accept by faith the finished work of Christ.

Gospel: Mark 12:38-44

Sermon Title: Beware Of Submerged Objectives

Sermon Angle: When you are boating, particularly in a river or close to the shoreline or adjacent to a coral reef, you have to be alert to submerged obstacles. It's not the things that you see which pose the greatest dangers but those you can't see. The same applies to religion. The lives of some religious folks glisten on the outside, but the inside is anything but pretty. Below the surface lies jealousy, lust, and covetousness. Jesus warned the people of his day to "beware of the scribes" (v. 38); underneath the placid surface lurked a spiritual minefield.

Outline:
1. When boating, never lose sight of the dangers beneath the water.
2. Jesus warned, "Beware of the scribes...." Beneath the righteous surface lurked the monster of pride.

3. The scribes concealed their true self, even from themselves, but the monsters would surface (they devoured widow's houses) (v. 40).
4. Beware of submerged objectives in your life and remove them by God's grace.

Sermon Title: Living Without Social Security

Sermon Angle: With all the talk about containing the national debt and scaling back Social Security and welfare benefits, many people are troubled by the prospect of possibly living with little or no Social Security. In the first lesson, the story of Ruth, Naomi secured social security by helping her daughter-in-law obtain a husband. The widow featured in the gospel had no social security whatsoever. She was left to rely on the charity of others, her own hard work and, especially, the goodness of God. Jesus marveled at her faith.

Outline:
1. Most of us are counting on Social Security for retirement.
2. Before the government stepped in, families provided social security.
3. Ruth and Naomi found Social Security in linking up with family.
4. The widow of the gospel had no security except through her faith in the Lord.
5. Living without Social Security would be very hard but living without spiritual security would be tragic.

Sermon Title: A Case Study On Loving God

Sermon Angle: The gospel for last Sunday featured the first and greatest commandment, to love God with all our heart, soul, mind, and strength. This week's gospel is a case study on what it means to love God in this way. The poor widow loved the Lord completely by entrusting to him everything that she possessed. Generally, if we trust God with our pocketbooks, we trust him with all the other arenas of our lives as well.

Outline:
1. In last week's gospel, Jesus taught that loving God was the greatest commandment.
2. The story of the poor widow illustrates the principle of loving God with all our heart, soul, mind, and strength.
3. Letting loose of our money is generally an indication that we truly love God and are willing to let God have the rest of our lives as well.

* * * * *

Being around the time of Thanksgiving, a member of the church I serve told me this story about a turkey, actually two turkeys. You may have heard that the Butterball Turkey Company has a website online and a hotline you can call to receive advice on preparing your turkey or ideas on what to do with the leftovers. One man called to ask if it would be all right to roast a turkey that had been in his freezer for three years. The representative explained that if the turkey had never been defrosted it would probably be safe to eat but that the meat was not likely to taste the freshest. After thinking a little while, the man came up with a solution as to what to do with the turkey that was in keeping with his character. "I know what I'll do; I'll give it to the church." Now you know why I said that this is a story about *two* turkeys.

* * * * *

Let me relate a widow story that contrasts with the widow featured as the heroine of our text. Agnes was a widow for many years. She lived on her farm in Iowa and had one son. Agnes was one of those people whom you find at least one of in every community; she was mentally astute, yet, she came across as being kind of strange. She wore dowdy clothes which dated to the 1920s or '30s; though she was clean, she appeared rather unkempt. Agnes was something of a miser. To save on food, she attended every funeral in town so that she might enjoy the lunch afterward. She usually skipped worship but showed up for coffee time, shoveling the leftover cookies into her purse before she left. Whenever you would meet her on the street, she would launch into a tirade about the poor farmers and seek sympathy for her impoverished condition. At first, her pastor felt sorry for her, thinking that she was a poor widow. He even considered seeking financial help for her and so he talked with her son. He revealed that his mother was actually very wealthy, with an impressive portfolio of stocks and bonds. Yet, when the pastor suggested that her poor widow act was something of a charade, she became incensed. Actually, Agnes was a poor widow, not poor economically, but in the spirit of charity.

Proper 28/Pentecost 26/Ordinary Time 33

Revised Common	1 Samuel 1:4-20	Hebrews 10:11-14 (15-18) 19-25	Mark 13:1-8
Roman Catholic	Daniel 12:1-3	Hebrews 10:11-14, 18	Mark 13:24-32
Episcopal	Daniel 12:1-4a (5-13)	Hebrews 10:31-39	Mark 13:14-23

Theme For The Day: Knowing the signs of the Lord's return.

BRIEF COMMENTARY ON THE LESSONS

Lesson 1: 1 Samuel 1:4-20 (C)

Elkanah and his wives went up to Shiloh annually to offer sacrifice to the Lord. He would give each one a portion of the offering based on the number of children each had. Hannah was barren and the other wife would rub this fact into her face, particularly at the time of their pilgrimage. Being barren was considered a great curse. Hannah became depressed, refusing even to eat. Elkanah was an understanding husband who gently consoled his wife. She decided to take her troubles to the Lord in prayer. As she prayed in the temple, her mouth was moving but no words came forth. Eli, the priest, accused her of being drunk. She relayed her concern and he prayed that her request would be answered. Her spirit lifted and she went home. In due time, she became pregnant. After she weaned her child (Samuel), she brought him to Levi, together with the appropriate sacrifices. Samuel stayed with Levi and became the last of the judges and a great prophet.

Lesson 1: Daniel 12:1-3 (RC); Daniel 12:1-4a (5-13) (E)

Lesson 2: Hebrews 10:11-14 (15-18) 19-25 (C); Hebrews 10:11-14, 18 (RC)

The text continues to hammer home the same point that we have dealt with the past several weeks. Christ's priestly ministry is superior to that of the Jewish faith. The sacrifices in the temple needed to be repeated daily but Christ's priestly ministry was accomplished once and for all, by his all-sufficient sacrificial death. Because of his sacrifice, we are bold to approach the throne of God. The author reminds the church of three ways God offers us to draw near to him: first, faith and worship (v. 22, 25); second, witness to Jesus (v. 22); and third, service of one another (v. 24). The awareness of the nearness of Christ's return serves as our source of motivation.

Lesson 2: Hebrews 10:31-39 (E)

Gospel: Mark 13:1-8 (C); Mark 13:24-32 (RC); Mark 13:14-23 (E)

The chapter is called the "Little Apocalypse" and deals with the signs of the end time. The teaching on the subject results from an observation by the disciples about the beauty and grandeur of the temple. Jesus replies that it will become a pile of rubble, even though it was not yet completed at that time. The disciples then ask what the signs of the end will be. The Lord then suggests a number of things that will occur before the end. Many will pretend to be the Messiah; there will be wars, earthquakes, and the like. The gospel selections for the Episcopal and Roman Catholic lectionary set forth the same theme presented in the first eight verses.

The Episcopal lectionary lifts up the desolation sacrilege (v. 14). To understand this reference one must be knowledgeable of the book of Daniel, which was composed during a period when Gentile practices were imposed in the Jewish temple. This intrusion was a shock to the spiritual soul of the nation. A similar intrusion was forced on the Jews with the sack of Jerusalem in 70 AD.

The Roman Catholic lectionary further speaks of the time just before the end as a cosmic upheaval, when constellations are forced from their orbits. Then, the Son of Man will appear from the heavens and gather the elect. The lection concludes with the statement that no one knows the exact day or hour of the apocalypse, only the Father (v. 32).

Psalm Of The Day
> **Psalm 16 (C, E)** — "I bless the Lord who gives me counsel" (v. 7).
> **Psalm 15 (RC)**

Prayer Of The Day
God of glory, make us deeply sensitive to the brevity of our existence here on earth and to the fact that we must render an account before you. May this truth not fill our hearts with fear, but with a resolve to employ all our strength in service of you. In the merciful name of Jesus. Amen.

THEOLOGICAL REFLECTION ON THE LESSONS

Lesson 1: 1 Samuel 1:4-20
Faith and fertility. The theme of bareness appears frequently in the Bible; in addition to the story of Hannah in this text, there are the stories of Sarah (Genesis 17:16-19), Rebekah (Genesis 25:21-26), Rachel (Genesis 29), the mother of Samson (Judges 13:2-5), and Elizabeth (Luke 1:5-17). All of them became mothers as a result of God's grace, through faith in God's promise.

God and fertility (v. 6). God was believed to be the source of fertility or the lack thereof. He was accused of closing up Hannah's womb. We now know that there are some genetic factors and that every birth is not a direct manifestation of God's will. Nevertheless, it's still safe to say that God is the giver of all life. When God brings a new life into this world it is both a gift and a blessing.

Love without strings (vv. 5, 8). For much of the history of humankind, women have been judged according to how well they fulfilled their role as mothers. A childless woman was like a parched spring or a fruitless vine. In spite of this, Elkanah loved Hannah for who she was, not what she could produce. His love was without strings. He consoled his wife by saying: "Am I not more to you than ten sons?" (v. 8). Their love was precious in and of itself.

She moved from sulking to supplication (vv. 8-11). Peninnah, Hannah's rival, really got under Hannah's skin, so much so that she went into a major sulk. Her husband's loving response brought her out of her sulk. From that point, Hannah rightly determined that supplication in the house of the Lord would be the more creative route to take. Her sincere supplication led to life for her and many other people as well.

Lesson 2: Hebrews 10:11-14 (15-18) 19-25

The single sacrifice for sins (v. 12). The text maintains that Christ offered in his body the single sacrifice that atones for the sins of all who have faith. What does that imply? That we don't have to spend our energies on useless efforts to justify ourselves in God's sight. Thus, we are free to serve and love him in our neighbor.

Offering for salvation, not for sin (v. 18). "Where there is forgiveness ... there is no longer any offering for sin." God does not call us to offer up our lives in atonement for sins but to offer up our lives in grateful service for the gift of salvation.

Confidence (v. 19). "... since we have confidence ... by the blood of Christ...." Millions of people have taken the Dale Carnegie course, which essentially aims at building confidence in people so that they might be successful in social relationships and in business. The writer of Hebrews wants those who read his letter to have confidence, not deriving from self but from God. The Christian way of building confidence is through the cross.

Gospel: Mark 13:1-32

Sign language (v. 4). Some of Jesus' disciples asked for the signs of the destruction of the temple (vv. 1-2). Some people hold that all these signs apply to the end of time and the world. If so, how does one reconcile Jesus' words: "Truly, I say to you, this generation will not pass away before all these things take place" (v. 30)? The destruction of the temple and the city of Jerusalem by the Romans is the original apocalypse that Jesus predicted. However, added to this is material concerning the end of the age and the last judgment. Reading God's sign language is not easy, especially for those who have not studied.

Sacrilege (v. 14). The reference to the desolating sacrilege has roots in the Jewish experience in the post-Alexandrian period, when Antiochus Epiphanies instituted heathen sacrifices in the temple. This led eventually to the Maccabean revolt. This sacrilege left a deep wound on the Jewish psyche. The destruction of the temple by the Romans was the sacrilege that Jesus referred to. It seems that we live in a sacrilegious age but the sacrileges seem to offend only a few. Sacrilege no longer offends because we have lost our sense of the holy.

Christ and crisis. This entire lection lists a host of crises that are to presage Christ's rule in power and glory. To name a few: religious breakdown (v. 2), nationalistic antagonisms (v. 8), and breakdown of the family (v. 12).

Day and date (v. 32). Countless believers have gotten themselves and other people in trouble by claiming to have access to God's appointment calendar. Jesus warned that nobody knows the day or the hour of God's visitation, not even the Son. This means that instead of looking for some calendar or the clock in the Bible, we should live and love in a constant state of expectancy.

SERMON APPROACHES WITH ILLUSTRATIONS

Lesson 1: 1 Samuel 1:4-20

Sermon Title: Dealing With Disappointment

Sermon Angle: Hannah faced one of the gravest disappointments for a woman in her day. She was not able to bear a child. Her rival would rub her face in it, which led to depression and withdrawal from life. For a time she wept and would not eat. Her husband wisely reassured her that she still had great worth, even if she was childless. That helped Hannah to deal constructively with her disappointment by taking it to the Lord in prayer and worship.

Outline:
1. Hannah's great disappointment was in not having a child.
2. This led to withdrawal from life and a sense of helplessness (v. 7).
3. Her husband reminded her of her worth (v. 8).
4. She then prayed in the temple and was assured that God heard her (v. 17).
5. After worship the next day, she went happily back home (v. 18).

Sermon Title: Pathway To Peace

Sermon Angle: The house of Elkanah was rocked by conflict between his two wives. Peninnah was able to have children and that pleased her husband but Hannah was the wife that he especially loved. Peninnah was able to really agitate her rival. It's hard to imagine how domestic tranquility could exist here. When the conflict came to a head, Hannah poured out the vexation of her spirit in prayer to the Lord. Honestly confessing our problems is the first step to tranquility. In her prayer, she didn't just ask the Lord for favors but also promised to give back to the Lord. When she was finished praying and worshiping, she had the faith to believe that God had indeed heard her. Since she was assured of her worth and of God's love for her, Peninnah would not be able to irritate her anymore. The prayer of submission is the pathway to peace.

Lesson 2: Hebrews 10:11-14 (15-18) 19-25

Sermon Title: Free Access To The Almighty

Sermon Angle: Christ has opened a new and wonderful way to approach God, through the sacrifice of the cross. The fact that Christ, our great high priest, has opened the curtain (symbolic of blocked access to the most holy place in the temple) (v. 20) calls us to exercise our freedom as outlined below:

Outline:
1. to confidently draw near to God in faith (v. 22).
2. to continue public witness to our faith (v. 23).
3. to encourage one another through service and love (v. 24).

Sermon Title: The Right Way To Stir Up The Church

Sermon Angle: Too many congregations have been adversely stirred through negativism, criticism, and gossip. However, there is a right way to stir up the church. To employ an analogy from cooking, if you don't stir up the pot on the stove, the ingredients will settle to the bottom, stick to the pot, and eventually transform into a mass of charred gunk. Therefore, stirring not only keeps the goodness from settling to the bottom but also serves to blend a dish that is savory, delicious, and nourishing. Through love, we are to stir up one another and encourage one another to do good works (v. 24).

Outline:
1. Give an example of a congregation that was stirred to conflict.
2. Assert that stirring can be done in a positive way (the cooking analogy).
3. Ask if their involvement in the church might be described as a settling to the bottom of the pot.
4. Charge them to stir one another up to love and good works (v. 24).
5. Remind them that to keep the pot cooking, we need to be regular in worship (v. 25).

Gospel: Mark 13:1-32

Sermon Title: Birth pangs!

Sermon Angle: A baby does not normally make her appearance into the world unless the mother passes through periods of sickness, even retching and vomiting. At the very end, the labor starts; the pain gradually crescendos to a point that can be described as excruciating. There is no birth without birth pangs. Jesus states that wars, earthquakes, and various other unpleasant experiences are but the beginning of the birth pangs for the world as we know it (vv. 6-8). Yet, these words contain hope. The more intense the pain, the nearer the birth of Christ's kingdom. Just when we think that we can take it no longer, the Christ will come with his glorious kingdom (vv. 26-27).

Outline:

1. Try to get a mother's description of a mother giving birth — the pain and the joy.
2. Explain that the pain and sorrow of this world are birth pangs.
3. Jesus describes the translation from this world to the kingdom as birth pangs (vv. 6-8).
4. Keep faith and the birth pangs will give way to new life in Christ's kingdom (v. 13).

Sermon Title: Christ In Conflict With Culture

Sermon Angle: All of the signs that point to the end/beginning have to do with conflict. The power of God is in conflict with the powers that hold sway on this earth. Christians will be brought into court to answer to the appointed officials (v. 11). Family members will deal with their believing brothers and sisters with treachery and violence (v. 12). Worship of the true God will be profaned (v. 14). Charles Colson speaks passionately about the culture wars in our country. While I don't quite agree with some of his stands, I do believe that he has a valid point. Christ and culture are in conflict. Christendom is dead but not Christianity.

Outline:

1. This passage states that increasing conflict between Christ and culture will signal the end of the age. (Give examples.)
2. Some churches avoid the battle, while others relish the fight (most are the former).
3. Christ calls us to take stands, based on the gospel. Being a Christian entails conflict with falsehood and the gods of the age.

Sermon Title: The Great Gathering

Sermon Angle: When Christ comes again and the world as we know passes away, Christ will gather his chosen ones (the elect). Then, Christ will send his angels to gather in the elect from the corners of the earth (vv. 26-27). Those who belong to Christ do not come from one race or one location, but are scattered throughout the world. Christ will not forsake his own. His word and promise are secure. "Heaven and earth will pass away but my word will not pass away."

Outline:

1. The persecutions described in verses 9-13 scatter the elect of God.
2. At the end of this world and the beginning of the next, God will gather his own (vv. 26-27).
3. Live in anticipation of the great gathering into the community of God's grace.

* * * * *

As I was completing this chapter, the mail woman deposited our mail. One of the letters was from Bill Bright, of Campus Crusade For Christ. He was soliciting funds for the teams going throughout the world showing the *Jesus* film. The purpose of the film is to present Jesus in such a compelling way that those seeing it will want to confess Jesus as Savior and Lord. He was particularly lifting up their work in some predominantly Moslem countries. The story he told seemed to coincide with the passage I was currently trying to shed light on. Here's the story:

> *In a closed Muslim nation, which is far more antagonistic to the gospel than communism, a Campus Crusade couple invited a Muslim husband and wife to their home to watch a video of Jesus. Even though they were fervently committed to Islam, they agreed. During the film, everything in the room began to shake. Yet, they were so gripped by the video they just kept watching!*
>
> *Before Jesus ended, unknown to the other, each prayed and received Christ. Fearful of the other's reaction, they returned home, not saying a word about their decisions. The next morning, they couldn't stand it any longer. At great risk, they each told the other what they had done. They wept as they discovered they had both received Christ as their Savior and Lord.*
>
> *When they revisited the Campus Crusade couple, they shared how they had both "felt the room shaking with great power." Even though they were the only ones who felt this "divine earthquake," they agreed that at the moment the shaking began, each knew it was a sign from God — his affirming to them the truth contained in the film. Today, these once-fervent Muslims are helping to translate training materials for Campus Crusade.*

Our Lord's teaching about earthquakes (v. 8) and concerning the fact that the gospel must first be preached to all nations (v. 10) came to my mind. I am of a somewhat skeptical bent; yet, I believe in miracles. Was this a sign for me? I was about to get out my checkbook when I read on the pledge card: "I understand that, on average, for every $100 I send, 100 more people will likely indicate decisions for Christ." Now there was a price on souls, a cheap price at that. Red flags started waving all over the place. My Lutheran history came to my rescue. A vision of Tetzel preaching to the peasants: "As soon as your coin in the coffer rings, a soul from purgatory springs." Whew, that was close! (Note: I'm not suggesting dishonest motives on Bright's part or putting him on par with Tetzel.)

Christ The King/Proper 29

Revised Common	2 Samuel 23:1-7	Revelation 1:4b-8	John 18:33-37
Roman Catholic	Daniel 7:13-14	Revelation 1:5-8	John 18:33-37
Episcopal	Daniel 7:9-14	Revelation 1:1-8	John 18:33-37

Theme For The Day: At this end of the church year we pay homage to Christ as our king through his cross.

BRIEF COMMENTARY ON THE LESSONS

Lesson 1: 2 Samuel 23:1-7 (C)

These words are purported to be the last words of King David, though some scholars think that it comes from a much later era. The introduction identifies him as: "King David, the son of Jesse ... a man raised on high." Like Jesus, he had a lowly beginning and exalted end. The passage is actually a song that raises the point that God blesses the people ruled by a righteous sovereign but the godless will be disposed of.

Lesson 1: Daniel 7:13-14 (RC); Daniel 7:9-14 (E)

Lesson 2: Revelation 1:4b-8 (C); Revelation 1:5-8 (RC); Revelation 1:1-8 (E)

This is the introductory salutation to the seven churches (not the sum total of all the churches but the number that conveys completeness). It was believed that each church had a representative spirit (angel), who interceded before the throne of God. Both the beginning and ending of this passage stress the eternal nature of God: "the one who is, who was and who is to come" (v. 4b); then, "I am Alpha and Omega...." The Christ is referred to as the One who loves us and freed us from our sins, making us a kingdom of priests. This Jesus is coming in glory and all those who have rejected him will lament when they see his kingly power.

Gospel: John 18:33-37 (C, RC, E)

Jesus is brought before Pontius Pilate's judgment seat. He has been charged with treason because his enemies report that he claims to be king of the Jews. Pilate asks Jesus if he really believes himself to be a king. The response of Jesus is ambiguous. "You say that I am." This can mean: You say that I am and it is true or that's just a charge that my enemies have made to you. I believe that Jesus is accepting the title of king but at the same time redefining it. He is not a worldly king but the king of truth.

Psalm Of The Day

Psalm 132:1-12 (C) — "Let thy priest be clothed with righteousness" (v. 9).
Psalm 93 (E)
Psalm 92 (RC)

Prayer Of The Day

Almighty and everlasting God, whose will it is to unite all creation under the glorious and gentle rule of your dear Son, Jesus, the Christ. Free us from all false allegiances, so that we might fall to our knees and confess that Jesus is our Lord, to the glory of God. In the precious and powerful name of Jesus, our crucified and risen king. Amen.

THEOLOGICAL REFLECTION ON THE LESSONS

Lesson 1: 2 Samuel 23:1-7

God exalts his chosen ones (v. 1). This verse identifies David as the son of Jesse but also as "the anointed of God." David had humble roots but God exalted him into a mighty oak. Some people seize power for themselves for a time, but only God grants true greatness.

Personal and corporate covenant (v. 5). David states that God has made with him an everlasting covenant. The covenant is not just with him personally but with his people. The Davidic covenant was both personal and corporate. So, too, God's covenant with us in baptism is both personal and corporate. Faith comes through the community but needs to be ratified by each individual and each succeeding generation.

Lesson 2: Revelation 1:1-8

The blessing of public worship (v. 3). John pronounces a blessing on the person who reads aloud these words of prophecy. Most people were not educated and so the person who could read the word at the assembly received a blessing from touching the lives of others with God's word. Next, he says that those who hear are blessed. God's word has the power to change lives. Third, he states that those who keep God's word are blessed. The real blessing that comes from God's word occurs when we obey it.

King of love (v. 5). In the salutation, Jesus is described as "him who loves us." The emphasis is on the present tense. His love is shown by freeing us from our sins. Thus, the present experience of God's love comes from the cross "by his blood." On this Christ The King day, we celebrate the king of love.

The coming king (v. 7). Though Jesus came to earth in humility, he will come again, cloaked in power and glory. Many people refuse to see or serve the king of love, who reigns from the cross. However, someday *all* eyes will see our king as he comes in power and glory. This will be a glorious sight for those who believe but a fearsome sight for those who have rejected his reign (pierced him).

Gospel: John 18:33-37

Who's on the stand? (v. 33). Jesus is brought before Pilate for judgment but who is really in the hot seat? The defendant (Jesus) answers Pilate's question with a question. "Do you say this of your own accord?" Jesus was the free man but Pilate was a pawn of the Jewish leaders.

Not of this world (v. 36). Jesus answered Pilate that his kingship was not of this world. We need to carefully interpret this saying. Some could interpret it to mean that Jesus' kingship exists in some other realm of time and space but not in this world. Such an explanation would have Jesus abdicating power in this world. A much better interpretation is this: Jesus is drawing a distinction between the manner in which the kings of this world rule and the way that he rules.

The kings of this world employ force, armies, threats, and the like to impose their will on others. The strength of Jesus' rule stems from being grounded in divine truth, which transcends this world.

What is truth? (v. 38). Pilate was no idealist. He was into politics, a civil servant of Rome. His reply reveals his cynicism concerning the reality of absolute truth. For Pilate and for millions of contemporary folks, the idea of objective truth is laughable. They believe that truth is invented by those who have the power to do so. There's very much of a contemporary flavor to Pilate's remark: "What is truth?" According to gurus of our age, truth is defined by our own thoughts and feelings. What is truth for you is not necessarily truth for me and vice versa. Jesus' claim that he was born to bear witness to the truth was incomprehensible to Pilate. We are called by Christ to witness to the truth as he did (v. 37), the truth of human sin and God's salvation.

SERMON APPROACHES WITH ILLUSTRATIONS

Lesson 1: 2 Samuel 23:1-7
Sermon Title: The Song Of Salvation

Sermon Angle: Verse 1 introduces David as the "sweet psalmist of Israel." David was a man of many talents — warrior, ruler, judge, poet, musician, and songwriter. One could say that verses 2-7 are a song of salvation, as are many of the psalms. David sings of God's gracious and everlasting covenant with him and his descendents. Not only did David weep before the Lord, he would also sing and dance. Why have so many pious souls made religion so boring, dull, and lifeless? The redeemed of God should have a song on their lips.

Outline:
1. David is noted as the sweet psalmist of Israel — his relationship with God put a song in his heart.
2. Why have we made our Christian religion so boring and devoid of song?
3. David could sing because he was close to God — "his word is upon my tongue."
4. Let us draw near to God and sing of his salvation.

Sermon Title: Are You Anointed?

Sermon Angle: David is also referred to as the "anointed of God," a term generally applied to the prophets, priests, and kings of Israel. When those holding these positions were set apart for their service, they were anointed with holy oil, which conferred God's Spirit. Also, when people would prepare for a banquet or special occasion, they would anoint their faces with oil, much like we use make-up and other cosmetics. The oil would make their face shine and cast a healthy glow. As I look at the lives of many Christians, they don't appear very anointed. We are the anointed ones of God, if we believe our baptismal theology. Like David, does the Spirit speak through us (v. 2)? Is there a glow on our face and a song in our hearts?

Outline:
1. David was God's anointed (v. 1) — set apart as king and endowed with God's Spirit.
2. Anointing was also symbolic of gladness and celebration.
3. We have been anointed in baptism.
4. Does our anointing show?

Lesson 2: Revelation 1:1-8

Sermon Title: The End Is Near, Never Fear, Christ Is Here

Sermon Angle: The book of Revelation was written during a time of persecution. Many Christians looked at what was happening with a great deal of fear and foreboding. Some renounced their newfound faith, under pressure. The word from John is a message of hope. The first part of the message is that "the end is near" (v. 3). Just hang in there a while longer, Christ was coming soon. The end of their earthly suffering would mark the beginning of Christ's reign. The second part of John's message: "Never fear, Christ is here." He doesn't say this in so many words but speaks of how much Christ loves us (present tense) by freeing us from our sins through his blood (v. 6). It was this living Christ who was speaking through John to encourage his people. A third point could be: "Christ is soon coming here" (v. 7). We don't know when Christ will establish the kingdom but we believe that he's coming here.

Outline:

1. The message for the end of the church year — the end is near.
2. This should not evoke fear — Christ is here to sustain and strengthen us.
3. Jesus is soon coming here.

Sermon Title: Why Christ Deserves To Be Our King

Sermon Angle: After hearing about some of the scandalous and self-destructive behavior in the House of Windsor, one might assume that most of them don't deserve their royal titles. Christ, our king, is far different. Here are some reasons he deserves to be our king. He shows his love for us by freeing us from our sins through the cross (v. 5b). He witnessed to God's grace faithfully, which was authenticated by his rising from the dead (v. 5a). He has made us a kingdom of priests (v. 6).

Outline:

1. Many people in our country have little faith in our rulers.
2. Some of these officials don't deserve their titles or the honors that go with it.
3. Jesus deserves to be our king forever and ever because:
   — he loves us.
   — he died and rose again for us.
   — he made us priests, who share in his reign.

Gospel: John 18:33-37

Sermon Title: Who Is The Real Traitor?

Sermon Angle: Jesus was accused by the Jewish leaders of treason, a capital offense. They said that he wanted to usurp the power of Rome and rule the Jews as their king. But who was the real traitor? The chief priests and the scribes had betrayed their faith by making religion a host of rules and regulations. They were the ones playing footsy with the Romans for their own political advantage. Then there's Pilate. He was called to uphold the most advanced justice system the world had ever known. Yet, he bowed to expediency rather than uphold the truth. He too betrayed that which was entrusted to him.

Outline:

1. Jesus was accused of treason — being a king.
2. Actually, Jesus' accusers were the real traitors — they betrayed their God and their conscience.

3. Pilate also betrayed his duty, to fairly administer Roman justice.
4. If you were charged with being a Christian, would there be enough evidence to convict you? Would you be guilty of treason against Christ?

Sermon Title: Who Do You Worship As The King Of Truth?

Sermon Angle: In answer to Pilate's query as to whether Jesus was a king, Jesus states that he was born to bear witness to the truth (v. 37). In other words, he is the king of truth. Most people have some power, which they serve as *their* king of truth. The bottom line of their business might be their king of truth. Perhaps it's their own pleasure. Maybe they look to some other person as their king of truth, much like children look to their parents. For some scientists, their senses are their king of truth. Pilate's sovereign of truth was political expediency. Your sermon might profitably pose the question to each worshiper: "Who is your king of truth?"

Outline:

Introduction: Pilate scoffed at the idea of absolute truth. That's true of many people today. Yet, we all have some power that rules in our life, our king of truth.
1. For Pilate it was political expediency.
2. For the chief priests and scribes it was preserving the status quo.
3. Truth is embodied in Jesus. He lived and died for the truth (second lesson).
4. His resurrection proves that he is the king of truth.
5. Who do you worship as the king of truth?

Sermon Title: Born To Bear Witness

Sermon Angle: "For this I was born and for this I have come into the world, to bear witness to the truth" (v. 37). Jesus certainly did not deny that he was a king but he was not interested in asserting his kingship because he knew that what he said would be misconstrued. Jesus was not interested in claiming titles. He was consumed by a passion to accomplish the mission God gave him to do, to bear witness to the truth. The word for "witness" is the Greek word from which we also derive the word "martyr." Jesus was so committed to the task of proclaiming divine truth that he was willing to sacrifice himself. To be a follower of the king of truth means that we are willing to bear witness to the truth with our very lives.

Outline:
1. Kings were born to rule. Jesus was born to rule as the king of truth, "to bear witness to the truth" (v. 37).
2. In our baptism, we are called to bear witness to the truth.
3. As Jesus bore witness with his life, so too must we. Does your life bear witness to the king of truth?

* * * * *

When somebody is well-off financially, we say that he is living like a king. My wife and I recently got a chance to see just how lavishly kings, queens, and their families really lived. No, we weren't invited to Buckingham Palace by Queen Elizabeth for high tea. Together with another couple, we traveled to the "Treasures Of The Czar" exhibit in Topeka, Kansas. I have never seen such an array of jewels in my life, thousands of rubies, diamonds, emeralds, sapphires, and other precious stones, which bedecked not only the jewelry but their clothing, the liturgical apparel of their priests, even the saddles of their horses. In the room containing the

410

coronation clothing, observers paused in reflective silence, imagining what it must have been like to be so splendidly arrayed. A regally suited herald stood in one display case, with his special leather bag containing notices of the coronation festivities. The life-sized picture of the last Czar of Russia, Nicholas II, commanded our attention with its majestic pose and handsome visage.

Against this background, Jesus' assertion that his kingdom is not of this world makes a good deal of sense. When Pilate said: "So you are a king" (v. 37), I can imagine a snicker in his tone. The charge seemed absurd! This Jesus, charged as claiming to be the king of the Jews, possessed none of the trappings of kingly power.

*   *   *   *   *

Sermon Title: King Of Truth vs. Cult Leaders

Sermon Angle: When religious leaders assert absolute power over the lives of their adherents, you can be sure that they are not servants of Christ, the king. Such leaders rule through deception, guilt, and intimidation. Take Jim Jones, the founder of the People's Temple in Guyana. Loyalty to him meant renouncing family, selling all possessions, and obeying his dictates without question. He ultimately demanded the lives of his followers, and over 900 died through murder or suicide. What are some of the differences between the way Christ rules as king of truth and the manner in which cult leaders operate?

Outline:
1. The cult leaders enslave through deception, Christ frees us through the truth.
2. Cult leaders have their devotees leave the world but Christ instructs us to serve the world.
3. Cults leaders employ guilt to manipulate their followers, Christ frees us from guilt through the cross.
4. Cult leaders want their people to put their minds on hold but Christ calls us to serve him with all our heart, soul, and mind.
5. Finally, cult leaders call people to render absolute obedience to a human, while Christ calls us to render obedience to God.

Thanksgiving Day

| Revised Common | Joel 2:21-27 | 1 Timothy 2:1-7 | Matthew 6:25-33 |

Theme For The Day: Rejoice in God's goodness and render thanks for all his blessings.

BRIEF COMMENTARY ON THE LESSONS

Lesson 1: Joel 2:21-27

The first part of this chapter (vv. 1-17) is the traditional text for Ash Wednesday. These verses call the people to a solemn assembly so that they might repent of their sins and plead for Yahweh's mercy. This action is ordered because of a devastating invasion of locusts. Our lection for Thanksgiving follows the call to repentance with a message of hope and restoration. God will restore the land to fertility; the earth will yield its increase and the people of God will give thanks for all his blessings. "You shall eat in plenty and be satisfied, and praise the name of the Lord your God, who has dealt so wondrously with you" (v. 26).

Lesson 2: 1 Timothy 2:1-7

Paul urges that prayers and supplications be offered for all people and especially for those who are in positions of political authority, so that the believers might live peaceful lives. Such intercessions are pleasing to God, who desires all people to embrace the truth of the gospel. His hope for universal salvation is solidly based on embracing the particularity of the Christ event. "For there is one God and one mediator between God and humankind, Christ Jesus, himself human, who gave himself as a ransom for all" (vv. 5-6a). Paul adds that this is his express function and calling as an apostle.

Gospel: Matthew 6:25-33

In Jesus' teaching from the Beatitudes Jesus warns against trusting in worldly wealth and not worrying about food, clothing, and shelter. There are more important realities than material needs. If God takes care of his creatures in the natural world, will he not take much more care of those who are created in his image? If we make God's will our first priority, God will give us everything else we need to live.

Psalm Of The Day

Psalm 126 — "May those who sow in tears reap with shouts of joy" (v. 5).

Prayer Of The Day

God of grace, may we so trust in your bounteous goodness that we are freed from worldly anxiety and the clutch of things material. We render joyous thanks for all your wonderful and loving gifts, especially Jesus Christ our Lord. Amen.

THEOLOGICAL REFLECTION ON THE LESSONS

Lesson 1: Joel 2:21-27

Do not fear (vv. 21-22). The soil and the animals are told not to fear because the Lord was going to bless them with fertility. This resonates with the gospel when Jesus warns us not to worry about physical needs but to trust in the Lord. Trust in God's providence "and rejoice in the Lord your God" (v. 23).

I will repay you (v. 25). God promises to repay his people for that which was taken away by the locust plague and drought. Joel seems to suggest that though the Lord might withhold from his people for a time in order to wake them up, his ultimate will is to do good to his own. God will more than compensate for that which he permits to be taken away.

You shall be satisfied (v. 26). This passage refers to the satisfaction of our physical hunger, but I think that it implies more. There is more to being truly satisfied than having our stomachs full. Being satisfied has a strong spiritual component to it. Being satisfied goes beyond the idea that God wills to prosper his people with an increasing abundance of material things. Being satisfied may mean getting by with less, simplifying our tastes, and lowering the level of our needs. More importantly, being satisfied has more to do with the source of our satisfaction than anything else. The spiritually mature find satisfaction in the Lord rather than in the gifts that fall from his hands.

Lesson 2: 1 Timothy 2:1-7

First things. "First of all, then, I urge that supplications, prayers, intercessions, and thanksgivings be made for everyone ..." (v. 1). The first business of the church is to engage in a serious ministry of prayer, not only for the sake of the church but for the world. In the congregation that I serve, we lift up many people by name every Sunday during worship. The prayers of the church may run three or four minutes, for which we are regularly criticized by some people. "The prayers are too long!" they complain. It seems that they have lost sight of the first things of the faith.

Thanksgiving. Have we forgotten that thanksgiving is prayer, too? In fact, it could be considered the purest form of prayer, because the person uttering thanksgivings seeks not to get but to give. Indeed, thanksgiving expresses the spirit in which all other forms of prayer are to be offered. In our congregation, we also pray for all the members of the church on a rotational basis. Two or three days before they are scheduled to be prayed for, we call and ask what particular prayers they would like us to raise on their behalf. In only a small percentage of the cases does the person ask us to thank God on his behalf for blessings received.

Prayer for the salvation of the world. "This is right and acceptable in the sight of God our Savior, who desires everyone to be saved and come to the knowledge of the truth" (vv. 3-4). God desires that everyone be saved, but that doesn't mean that everyone will be saved. Many churches pray for the sick, the grieving, and the like, but few find time to pray specifically for the salvation of other people, that they might come to personally know and experience the truth that is Jesus.

Gospel: Matthew 6:25-33

Don't worry, be holy. Several years ago, there was a song on the airwaves called: "Don't Worry, Be Happy!" Jesus has better advice; he tells us, "Don't worry; be holy." Jesus teaches that we shouldn't worry about food, shelter, or clothing, but to "seek first the kingdom of God

413

..." (v. 34), and the Lord will supply what is lacking. Worshiping the Lord (being holy) will enable us to live life fully in all its dimensions.

Strive for the prize. Jesus teaches that we shouldn't major on minors — food, clothing, shelter, and the like. Rather, we should go for the prize — the kingdom of God (v. 33).

The futility of worry. "Can any of you by worrying add a single hour to your span of life?" (v. 27). Worry is an exercise in futility; nothing is accomplished thereby. Not only does worry not add to the span of our lives, but it also takes away. First of all, worry may physically shorten our lives. Secondly, worry deprives us of living fully in the present because it distracts us from more creative expressions. Jesus urges us to turn from the futility of worry to faith in the goodness of God.

SERMON APPROACHES WITH ILLUSTRATIONS

Lesson 1: Joel 2:21-27
Sermon Title: Praise The God Of Fruitfulness

Sermon Angle: Earlier in this chapter, Joel calls the people to national repentance to avert or lessen the destructive locust armies. In this lection, the prophet calls his people to thank and praise the Lord for restoring the fertility of the land and for abundantly feeding his people. It was time to rejoice in God's blessings. "O children of Zion, be glad and rejoice in the Lord your God ..." (v. 21). The Lord comes both in judgment and in blessing. Both ways that the Lord comes to us call for an appropriate response. Judgment should lead to repentance, and blessings rendered should result in praise and thanksgiving to the God of all fruitfulness.

Outline:
1. God comes to his people in both judgment and bounty.
2. God's ultimate will is to bless his people with good things (v. 25). He is the God of fruitfulness.
3. Rejoice in God's goodness and praise his name (v. 26).

Lesson 2: 1 Timothy 2:1-7
Sermon Title: The Church's First Order Of Business

Sermon Angle: Much of the Christian church languishes because we have lost sight of that which is of prime importance. We have fallen prey to various interest groups, on both the left and the right, that seek to place their pet causes at the forefront. Some would have social justice be the first order, while others would put forward the proclamation of the gospel. Both of the above are critical elements of our mission, but something else comes first. Paul puts it this way: "First of all, then, I urge that supplications, prayers and intercessions, and thanksgivings be made for all people ..." (v. 1). Before we do anything, we are called to engage in the priestly ministry of prayer. Paul asserts that we must pray for all people and especially those in leadership positions. Unless we are filled with God's Spirit and with the knowledge of his will, we will not realize our mission.

Outline:
1. This letter was addressed to a church that was splitting into factions, much like today.
2. The apostle lifts up that which is foundational for the church — prayer (vv. 1-4).
3. Prayer unites us as we reach out to the one God and mediator (v. 5).
4. Are we making prayer the first order of our personal and communal life?

Sermon Title: Eucharist

Sermon Angle: Four different words are utilized in lifting up the importance of prayer. The first of these is *deesis*, translated "supplication" in the NRSV, but it literally means "request." The second word is *proseuche*, translated "prayers," which is a literal rending of the word. *Deesis* can be employed in reference to requests of humans as well as God but *proseuche* has only a divine object. The third word is *enteuxis*, translated as "intercessions," but it literally means "petition." The fourth word for prayer is *eucharistia*, which literally rendered means "thanksgiving." When we speak of prayer, the first association is that of asking God for something. The heart and soul of prayer is thanksgiving because instead of seeking something from God, it returns something of great value, a grateful heart, to God. During this season of national thanksgiving, we most commonly render thanks for the gifts of creation — food, family, friends, and so forth. This text directs us to give thanks also for the greatest gift of all — salvation through Christ. We need to render thanks that we have a gracious God, who desires all people to come to the knowledge of his love and grace. The best way that we can show our thanks to God is by sharing the gift of his Son.

Outline:
1. The church has been given a ministry of prayer.
2. We are a eucharistic community — our worship and our lives are to be a sacrifice of thanksgiving and praise.
3. Let us remember to give thanks not only for the gifts of creation but also for the gift of salvation.
4. Thank the Lord by sharing Jesus with a neighbor.

Gospel: Matthew 6:25-33

Sermon Title: Put God In The Driver's Seat

Sermon Angle: One of the national bus companies had this advertising motto: "Leave the driving to us." The inference is that when you travel with them, you can relax and let go of your worries because someone trustworthy inhabits the driver's seat. Jesus is endeavoring to teach us this same truth. Don't worry about what you are going to eat or drink or wear. God knows what you need; the Lord is in the driver's seat. Just trust him!

Outline:
1. Is your life filled with anxiety about your job? Do you worry that you might lose the ability to provide for your needs and those of your family? Do you worry about running off the road of life?
2. Jesus enjoins us to put God in the driver's seat. "Seek first the kingdom of God...."
3. If God provides for the birds and the fields, will he not provide for all your needs?
4. Life is more than material needs; it is a journey of faith that leads to eternal life.

Sermon Title: Spandex For The Spirit

Sermon Angle: Jesus asks: "And can any of you by worrying add a single hour to your span of life?" (v. 27b). Worry not only does not expand the length of our lives, it can actually decrease the breadth of our existence. Worry and anxiety block all creative and life-enhancing responses. Worry makes us brittle, subject to breaking. On the other hand, the faith in God that Jesus commends expands both the breadth and depth of our existence. Faith is like the fabric spandex, so popular in sporting circles because it clothes while offering flexibility for movement and expansion. Faith allows us to extend the span of our existence by enveloping us in the eternal. We have room both to exercise and to grow. We cannot extend the span of our lives through worrying, but we can through faith in God. Faith is the spandex for the spirit; it clothes us and gives us shape, while providing flexibility for growth and movement.

Outline:
1. Many people are anxious about death and try to extend the length of their lives (such as the exercise and health food crazes).
2. Many people wear spandex as they exercise because it adjusts to the movement and activity of the body.
3. Jesus warns against worry because it makes us weak and brittle (we cannot increase the span of our lives through worry) (v. 27).
4. Jesus commends us to trust in God, to exercise our faith in God first of all (v. 33).
5. Faith is the spandex for the soul (it clothes us as we develop in righteousness).

* * * * *

We call our national day of gratitude "Thanksgiving." Unfortunately, we have transformed thanks-giving into thanks-feeling. We think that if we feel grateful in our hearts, we have done all that is necessary. This is not so. Returning thanks must be expressed through giving. An example of thanks-giving is incarnated through the efforts of the Mennonites of York, Nebraska. A crew of about sixty volunteers labors at canning meat and broth from dawn to dusk during the week after Thanksgiving. In 1995, two-pound cans of Nebraska beef and broth were shipped to Bosnia, Serbia, Cuba, Haiti, and other countries. Volunteers have donated $54,000 in cash, in addition to meat and hard labor. The effort resulted in 15,000 to 16,000 two-pound cans of beef chunks and two-pound cans of broth. These Mennonites have discovered that gratitude is not just what you feel but tangible thanks that you give to God through others.

* * * * *

A *Money* magazine article told of the life of a woman who saved 80% of everything that she earned, investing it all in the stock market, and turned it into a $22 million fortune fifty years later. The article is titled "How She Turned $5,000 into $22 Million" with the subtitle, "And how you might, too...." As one reads the article, however, it raises real questions about how this woman, Anne Scheiber, made her fortune and whether the cost was worth it. She was alienated from her family and was without friends. She eked out a life of penury, even as her fortune swelled. She would walk to work in the rain rather than spend the bus fare. She limited herself to a few dollars a week on groceries and wore the same old coat and hat season after season. Her clothing became tattered and threadbare but none of that mattered; the bottom line on her brokerage account was what she gave her life for.

The author of this article on how to invest your money even concluded that there must be more to life than the bottom line of your net worth statement. "As intelligent as Anne Scheiber was, she failed miserably on this one. She died without one real friend; she didn't get even one phone call during her last five years of life." Her broker concludes: "A big day for her was walking down to the Merrill Lynch vault near Wall Street to visit her stock certificates. She did that a lot."

The life of this poor woman is not the success story it might appear to be on the surface, even by the world's materialistic standards. Rather, it is a tragic illustration of a life driven by a misguided set of priorities. That is why Jesus taught that we shouldn't be worried about what we eat, drink, or wear. If we do as the Lord says and "seek first the kingdom of God and his righteousness," we will inherit the true treasure and possess everything else that we require as well. If we possess God's kingdom, we have everything. That is the first and foremost reason to give thanks to God.

US/Canadian Lectionary Comparison

The following index shows the correlation between the Sundays and special days of the church year as they are titled or labeled in the Revised Common Lectionary published by the Consultation On Common Texts and used in the United States (the reference used for this book) and the Sundays and special days of the church year as they are titled or labeled in the Revised Common Lectionary used in Canada.

Revised Common Lectionary	Canadian Revised Common Lectionary
Advent 1	Advent 1
Advent 2	Advent 2
Advent 3	Advent 3
Advent 4	Advent 4
Christmas Eve	Christmas Eve
The Nativity Of Our Lord/Christmas Day	The Nativity Of Our Lord
Christmas 1	Christmas 1
January 1/Holy Name Of Jesus	January 1/The Name Of Jesus
Christmas 2	Christmas 2
The Epiphany Of Our Lord	The Epiphany Of Our Lord
The Baptism Of Our Lord/Epiphany 1	The Baptism Of Our Lord/Proper 1
Epiphany 2/Ordinary Time 2	Epiphany 2/Proper 2
Epiphany 3/Ordinary Time 3	Epiphany 3/Proper 3
Epiphany 4/Ordinary Time 4	Epiphany 4/Proper 4
Epiphany 5/Ordinary Time 5	Epiphany 5/Proper 5
Epiphany 6/Ordinary Time 6	Epiphany 6/Proper 6
Epiphany 7/Ordinary Time 7	Epiphany 7/Proper 7
Epiphany 8/Ordinary Time 8	Epiphany 8/Proper 8

The Transfiguration Of Our Lord/
   Last Sunday After The Epiphany
	The Transfiguration Of Our Lord/
	   Last Sunday After Epiphany

Ash Wednesday	Ash Wednesday
Lent 1	Lent 1
Lent 2	Lent 2
Lent 3	Lent 3
Lent 4	Lent 4
Lent 5	Lent 5
Sunday Of The Passion/Palm Sunday	Passion/Palm Sunday
Maundy Thursday	Holy/Maundy Thursday
Good Friday	Good Friday
The Resurrection Of Our Lord/Easter Day	The Resurrection Of Our Lord
Easter 2	Easter 2
Easter 3	Easter 3
Easter 4	Easter 4
Easter 5	Easter 5
Easter 6	Easter 6
The Ascension Of Our Lord	The Ascension Of Our Lord
Easter 7	Easter 7
The Day Of Pentecost	The Day Of Pentecost
The Holy Trinity	The Holy Trinity
Proper 4/Pentecost 2/O T 9*	Proper 9
Proper 5/Pent 3/O T 10	Proper 10
Proper 6/Pent 4/O T 11	Proper 11
Proper 7/Pent 5/O T 12	Proper 12
Proper 8/Pent 6/O T 13	Proper 13
Proper 9/Pent 7/O T 14	Proper 14

Proper 10/Pent 8/O T 15	Proper 15
Proper 11/Pent 9/O T 16	Proper 16
Proper 12/Pent 10/O T 17	Proper 17
Proper 13/Pent 11/O T 18	Proper 18
Proper 14/Pent 12/O T 19	Proper 19
Proper 15/Pent 13/O T 20	Proper 20
Proper 16/Pent 14/O T 21	Proper 21
Proper 17/Pent 15/O T 22	Proper 22
Proper 18/Pent 16/O T 23	Proper 23
Proper 19/Pent 17/O T 24	Proper 24
Proper 20/Pent 18/O T 25	Proper 25
Proper 21/Pent 19/O T 26	Proper 26
Proper 22/Pent 20/O T 27	Proper 27
Proper 23/Pent 21/O T 28	Proper 28
Proper 24/Pent 22/O T 29	Proper 29
Proper 25/Pent 23/O T 30	Proper 30
Proper 26/Pent 24/O T 31	Proper 31
Proper 27/Pent 25/O T 32	Proper 32
Proper 28/Pent 26/O T 33	Proper 33
Christ The King (Proper 29/O T 34)	Proper 34/Christ The King/ Reign Of Christ

Reformation Day (October 31)	Reformation Day (October 31)
All Saints (November 1 or 1st Sunday in November)	All Saints' Day (November 1)
Thanksgiving Day (4th Thursday of November)	Thanksgiving Day (2nd Monday of October)

*O T = Ordinary Time